THE EMPIRE
OF THE STEPPES

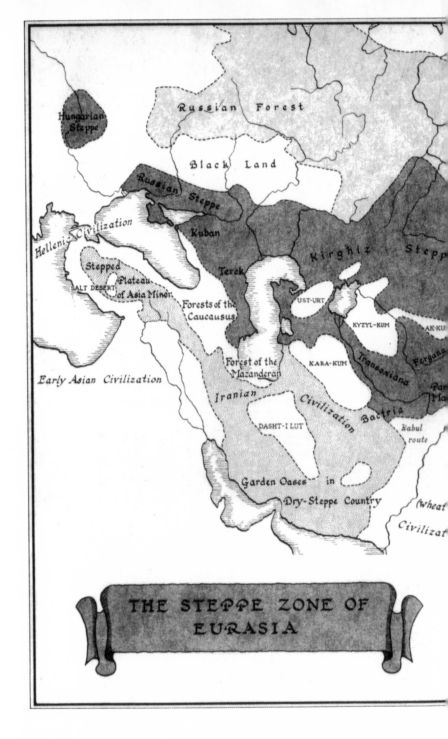

THE STEPPE ZONE OF EURASIA

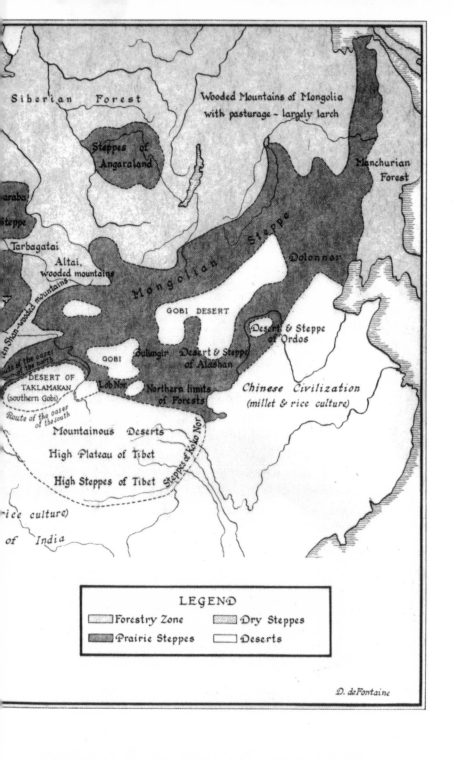

THE EMPIRE
OF THE STEPPES

A History of Central Asia

RENÉ GROUSSET

Translated from the French by Naomi Walford

RUTGERS UNIVERSITY PRESS
New Brunswick, New Jersey, and London

Sixth paperback printing, 1999

Library of Congress Catalogue Card Number 77-108-759
ISBN 0-8135-0627-1   0-8135-1304-9 (pbk)

Foreword

Attila and the Huns, Jenghiz Khan and the Mongols, Tamerlane and the Golden Horde—these almost legendary names are familiar to the educated layman. Unquestionably, he has also read of the Hungarians, and the Bulgars, and the Ottoman Turks. If he has an interest in ancient history, he may have an acquaintance with the Cimmerians, the Scythians, even the Sarmatians. He may have heard also of the Avars and the Khazars. But it is improbable that he will know of the Onogurs, Kutrigurs, and Utrigurs—Bulgar tribes to be encountered in the steppes of southern Russia—or the Pechenegs, Cumans, and Uzes, the last-named related to the Seljuk and Ottoman Turks.

These were all nomads, peoples of the vast steppes of Asia and Russia, and a major force in history. Their historical significance lies not so much in the empires they established, empires which in most instances and certainly in the steppes proved ephemeral. Rather, it was the pressures of their movements eastward and westward, brought to bear on China, Persia, India, and Europe, which substantially affected the historical development of these lands. The early history of the steppe nomads is shrouded in obscurity, an obscurity which lifts somewhat only after their contact with cultures possessing written histories. But even when information about them becomes relatively more plentiful, linguistic complexities make its interpretation extremely difficult. Thus, while the number of specialized monographs and technical studies devoted to them is impressive, general works embracing the many disciplines involved, or syntheses on a grand scale encompassing the sprawling history of these peoples, are exceedingly scarce. Among these very few, René Grousset's monumental *L'Empire des Steppes* is uniquely great.

Grousset's classic work was first published in 1939, and has since

appeared in a number of reimpressions, with no significant re-
visions. An appendix discussing publications between 1939 and
1951 on the art of the steppes was added to the 1952 edition, just
before the author's death. Nevertheless, the main body of the text
has retained its validity, and remains to this day the most engross-
ing and vital general account of this immense subject.

The present volume, the first edition in English, was translated by Naomi Walford from the French edition of 1952. Traian
Stoianovich, Professor of History at Rutgers University, checked
the translation and helped to establish uniformity in nomenclature
and transliteration. The late James F. McRee, Jr., completed the
final typographic editing of the text. The outdated appendix on
the art of the steppes was dropped, and the copious annotation
was brought into conformity with present-day academic usage.
A large and comprehensive index was compiled and added, and
nineteen maps were prepared expressly for this edition. Our aim
throughout has been to make available an English-language edition useful to the general reader as well as to the specialist,
but above all an edition which retains the majestic sweep and
grandeur, as well as the overriding intellectual grasp, of Grousset's
original masterwork.

PETER CHARANIS
Voorhees Professor of History
Rutgers University

Preface

Attila, Jenghiz Khan, Tamerlane: their names are in everyone's memory. Accounts of them written by western chroniclers and by Chinese or Persian annalists have served to spread their repute. The great barbarians irrupt into areas of developed historical civilizations and suddenly, within a few years, reduce the Roman, Iranian, or Chinese world to a heap of ruins. Their arrival, motives, and disappearance seem inexplicable, so much so that historians today come near to adopting the verdict of the writers of old, who saw in them the scourge of the Lord, sent for the chastisement of ancient civilizations.

Yet never were men more sons of the earth than these, more the natural product of their environment; but their motivations and patterns of behavior acquire clarity as we come to understand their way of life. These stunted, stocky bodies—invincible, since they could survive such rigorous conditions—were formed by the steppes. The bitter winds of the high plateaus, the intense cold and torrid heat, carved those faces with their wrinkled eyes, high cheekbones, and sparse hair, and hardened those sinewy frames. The demands of a pastoral life, governed by seasonal migrations in search of pasture, defined their specific nomadism, and the exigencies of their nomadic economy determined their relations with sedentary peoples: relations consisting by turns of timid borrowings and bloodthirsty raids.

The three or four great Asiatic nomads who burst upon us to rip up the web of history seem to us exceptional solely because of our own ignorance. For three who achieved the astounding feat of becoming conquerors of the world, how many Attilas and Jenghiz Khans have failed? Failed, that is, to do more than found limited empires comprising a quarter of Asia, from Siberia to the Yellow

River, from the Altai to Persia—an achievement which one must nevertheless acknowledge to have been of some magnitude. I would like to bring before your minds this great barbarian people, dominated by three mighty figures—Attila, Jenghiz Khan, Tamerlane—as they march through ten centuries of history, from the borders of China to the frontiers of the West.

The problem of the barbarians must be stated precisely. The classical world encountered many kinds of barbarians, that is, people so designated by their neighbors. The Celts were barbarians to the Romans for a long time, as were the Germans to Gaul, and the Slav world to Germania. Similarly, the land afterward known as southern China long remained a barbarian country to the original Chinese of the Yellow River. But because geographical conditions in all these regions imposed an agricultural way of life upon their inhabitants, they emerged from their backwardness to become increasingly identified with that life, so that by the second half of the Middle Ages almost the whole of Europe, Western Asia, Iran, the Indies, and China had attained the same stage of material civilization.

Yet one important area escaped this process—the wide belt stretching across the northern part of Central Eurasia from the borders of Manchuria to Budapest. This is the steppe zone, penetrated along its northern edges by the Siberian forest. Geographical conditions here allowed only a few patches of cultivation, so that the inhabitants were forced to follow a pastoral, nomadic way of life, such as the rest of humanity had known thousands of years earlier at the end of the Neolithic age. Indeed, some of these tribes—those of the forest zone—remained at the cultural stage of the Magdalenian hunters. Thus the steppe and forest region remained a preserve of barbarism—not, be it understood, in the sense that the people living there were inferior as human beings to the rest of mankind, but because local conditions perpetuated a way of life which elsewhere had long since passed away.

The survival of these pastoral peoples into an era when the rest of Asia had arrived at an advanced agricultural stage was a very important factor in the drama of history. It involved a sort of time shift between neighboring peoples. Men of the second millennium B.C. coexisted with those of the twelfth century A.D. To pass from one group to the other, one had only to come down from Upper Mongolia to Peking, or to climb from the Kirghiz steppe to

Ispahan. The break was abrupt and fraught with perils. To the sedentary peoples of China, Iran, and Europe, the Hun, the Turkoman, and the Mongol were savages indeed, to be intimidated by a display of arms, amused by glass beads and by titles, and kept at a respectful distance from cultivated land. The attitude of the nomads may be easily imagined. The poor Turko-Mongol herdsmen who in years of drought ventured across the meager grazing of the steppe from one dried-up waterhole to another, to the very fringe of cultivation, at the gates of Pechili (Hopei) or Transoxiana, gazed thunderstruck at the miracle of sedentary civilization: luxuriant crops, villages crammed with grain, and the luxury of the towns. This miracle, or rather its secret—the patient toil required to maintain these human hives—was beyond the comprehension of the Hun. If he was fascinated, it was like the wolf—his totem—when in snowy weather it draws near to the farms and spies its prey within the wattled fence. He too had the age-old impulse to break in, plunder, and escape with his booty.

The survival of a herding and hunting community beside a farming one—or, put differently, the development of increasingly prosperous agricultural communities within sight and contact of peoples still at the pastoral stage, and suffering the appalling famines inherent in steppe life in time of drought—presented not only a glaring economic contrast but a social contrast that was even crueler. To repeat, the problem of human geography became a social one. The attitudes of the sedentary man and the nomad toward each other recall the feelings of a capitalist society and a proletariat enclosed within a modern city. The farming communities that cultivated the good yellow soil of northern China, the gardens of Iran, or the rich black earth of Kiev were encircled by a belt of poor grazing land where terrible climatic conditions often prevailed, and where one year in every ten the watering places dried up, grass withered, and livestock perished, and with them the nomad himself.

In these circumstances, the periodic thrusts of the nomads into the cultivated areas were a law of nature. It should be added that whether Turks or Mongols, they belonged to an intelligent, level-headed, practical people which, drilled by the harsh realities of its environment, was ever ready for the word of command. When the sedentary and often decadent communities yielded under his onslaught, the nomad entered the city and, when the first few hours of massacre were over, without any great difficulty took the place of the rulers whom he had defeated. Unabashed, he seated himself upon the most time-honored and exalted thrones, as grand khan of China, king of Persia, emperor of India, or sultan of Rum, and adapted himself accordingly. In Peking he became half Chinese, in Ispahan or Rai half Persian.

Was that the final outcome—a permanent reconciliation between the steppe and the town? By no means. The inexorable laws of human geography continued to operate. If the Sinicized or Iranized khan was not removed by some native reaction, whether slow or sudden, from the depths of the steppes new hordes, and hungry ones, would appear at his frontiers, and seeing in their upstart cousin merely another Tadzhik or Tabgatch—Persian or Chinese—repeat the adventure, to his disadvantage.

How is it that the adventure was nearly always successful, and that the same rhythm recurred throughout thirteen centuries— that period between the Huns' entry into Loyang and the Manchus' into Peking? The answer is that the nomad, retarded though he was in material culture, always possessed a tremendous military ascendancy. He was the mounted archer. The technical arm, which gave him almost as great an advantage over sedentary man as artillery gave modern Europe over the rest of the world, was an incredibly mobile cavalry of expert bowmen. It is true that neither Chinese nor Iranians neglected this arm. From the third century B.C. on, the Chinese adapted their dress for riding. And Persia, from the times of the Parthians, knew the value of a shower of arrows delivered by a whirl of retreating horsemen. But Chinese, Iranian, Russian, Pole, or Hungarian could never equal the Mongol in this field. Trained from childhood to drive deer at a gallop over the vast expanses of the steppe, accustomed to patient stalking and to all the ruses of the hunter on which his food—that is, his life—depended, he was unbeatable. Not that he often confronted his enemy; on the contrary, having launched a surprise attack upon him, he would vanish, reappear, pursue him ardently without letting himself be caught, harry him, weary him, and at last bring him down exhausted, like driven game. The deceptive mobility and ubiquity of this cavalry, when handled by a Jebe or a Sübötäi—Jenghiz Khan's two great generals—endowed this arm with a sort of corporate intelligence. Piano Carpini and Rubruck, who watched it in action, were much struck by this decisive technical superiority. The phalanx and the legion passed away because they had been born of the political constitutions of Macedonia and Rome; they were the planned creation of organized states which, like all states, arose, lived, and disappeared. The mounted archer of the steppe reigned over Eurasia for thirteen centuries because he was the spontaneous creation of the soil itself: the offspring of hunger and want, the nomads' only means of survival during years of famine. When Jenghiz Khan succeeded in conquering the world, he was able to do so because, as an orphan abandoned on the plain of Kerulen, he had already succeeded, with his young brother Jöchi the Tiger, in bringing down enough game daily to escape death by starvation.

The arrow of the mounted archer who dashed in, let fly, and fled was for antiquity and the Middle Ages a form of indirect fire, almost as effective and demoralizing in its time as that of the gunners of today.

What put an end to this superiority? How is it that starting in the sixteenth century the nomad no longer had the sedentary peoples at his mercy? The reason was that the latter now met him with artillery, and thus overnight acquired an artificial ascendancy over him. An agelong position was reversed. The cannonades with which Ivan the Terrible scattered the last heirs of the Golden Horde, and with which the K'ang-hsi emperor of China frightened the Kalmucks, marked the end of a period of world history. For the first time, and for ever, military technique had changed camps and civilization became stronger than barbarism. Within a few hours the traditional superiority of the nomad faded into a seemingly unreal past, and the Kalmuck archers whom the romantic Czar Alexander I marshaled against Napoleon on the battlefields of 1807 were to appear as out of date as Magdalenian hunters.

Yet only three centuries had passed since those archers ceased to be conquerors of the world.

Contents

II. THE JENGHIZ-KHANITE MONGOLS

III. THE LAST MONGOLS

List of Maps

Drawn by Dorothy de Fontaine

Introduction:
The Steppe and History

In their physical manifestation, the high plateaus of Asia bear witness to the most tremendous geological drama in the history of this planet. The upheaval and isolation of this huge continental mass were due to the converging assaults of two great chains of folded mountains formed in two different periods: the Hercynian folds of the T'ien Shan and Altai ranges—the first of these being bordered by the Serindian mass and the second by the ancient Siberian plateau of Angaraland—and the Himalayan alpine folds, which in the Miocene period replaced the ancient "Mediterranean" Sea of Eurasia. The arc of the T'ien Shan and Altai to the north-west, and the opposing curve of the Himalayas in the south, together encircle and isolate Turkestan and Mongolia, leaving them, as it were, suspended above the surrounding plains. Because of their altitude and their great distance from the sea, these regions experience a continental climate of great extremes, with excessive heat in summer and bitter cold in winter. At Urga (Ulan Bator), in Mongolia, the temperature varies from $+38°$ to $-42°$ Centigrade. With the exception of the Tibetan massif, the great altitude of which produces almost polar vegetation, and also of the semicircular ranges of the Altai and T'ien Shan, which, for similar reasons, have an alpine climate characteristically graded from the forests of the foothills to the sparse vegetation on the peaks, almost the whole of continental Asia is covered by a longitudinal belt of grassy steppes, dormant in winter and dried up in summer. The prairie steppes—fertile in their irrigated areas, but shriveling and turning into desert in the central wastes—run from Manchuria to the Crimea, from Urga in Outer Mongolia to the regions of Merv and Balkh, where the North Eurasian prairie steppe gives place to the dry, subtropical steppe, more Mediterranean in character, of Iran and Afghanistan.

To the north, the longitudinal belt of the Eurasian steppes merges with the boreal forest region of central Russia and Siberia, and with the northern fringe of Mongolia and Manchuria. In three areas in the middle of the belt, the steppe imperceptibly yields to the desert: the deserts of Kyzyl-Kum in Transoxiana and Kara-Kum south of the Amu Darya; the desert of Taklamakan in the enclosed Tarim basin; and lastly the Gobi Desert, a vast area stretching from southwest to northeast, from the Lob Nor, where the Gobi joins the Taklamakan, to the Khingan Mountains on the borders of Manchuria. They are like cancerous patches devouring the grassy belt, on which they have been continually encroaching since protohistoric times. The situation of the Gobi Desert, lying as it does between northern Mongolia, the forests of Baikal, and the steppes of the Orkhon and Kerulen to the north and southern Mongolia and the steppes of Alashan, Ordos, Chahar, and Jehol to the south, is one of the enduring factors preventing the survival of Turko-Mongol empires, whether of the Hsiung-nu of antiquity or of the T'u-chüeh of the Middle Ages.

This rout of the steppe by the desert gave a particularly decisive turn to the history of the Tarim basin, in what is now Chinese Turkestan. Having escaped the nomadic life of the plains (though always threatened or dominated by the northern hordes), this area acquired the urban, commercial character of the oases of the caravan routes and, by the chain of these oases, formed a line of communication between the great sedentary civilizations of the West—those of the Mediterranean world, of Iran, and of India—and that of the Far East, namely, China. A double trail was laid in a double curve north and south of the dying Tarim River: the northern route ran through Tunhwang, Hami, Turfan, Kara Shahr, Kucha, Kashgar, the Fergana basin, and Transoxiana; the southern, by way of Tunhwang, Khotan, Yarkand, the Pamir valleys, and Bactria. This slender dual thread that crosses deserts and peaks by turns, frail as a winding, long-drawn-out line of ants moving cross-country, was strong enough nevertheless to ensure that our planet should consist of a single world and not of two separate ones, and to maintain a minimum degree of contact between the anthill of China and the Indo-European anthills. It was the Silk Road and the road of pilgrimage, along which traveled trade and religion, the Greek art of Alexander's successors and Buddhist missionaries from Afghanistan. By this route the Greco-Roman merchants mentioned by Ptolemy struggled to obtain access to the bales of silk from "Serica," and Chinese generals of the second Han dynasty sought to establish communication with the Iranian world and the Roman Orient. The maintenance of this great route of world commerce was, from the Han to Kublai Khan, an age-long principle of Chinese policy.

North of this narrow trail of civilization, however, the steppes provided the nomads with a route of a very different order: a boundless route of numberless tracks, the route of barbarism. Nothing halted the thundering barbarian squadrons between the banks of the Orkhon or the Kerulen and Lake Balkhash; for, although toward the latter point the Altai Mountains and the northern spurs of the T'ien Shan ranges seem to meet, the gap is still wide at the Imil River in Tarbagatai, in the direction of Chuguchak, as also between the Yulduz, the Ili, and the Issyk Kul basin to the northwest, where the horsemen from Mongolia beheld the further boundless expanses of the Kirghiz and Russian steppes. The passes of Tarbagatai, Ala-Tau, and Muzart were continually crossed by hordes from the eastern steppe on their way to the steppes of the west. In the protohistoric period, the movement must have been more often in the opposite direction; one gains the impression that nomads of Iranian—that is, Indo-European—stock, called Scythians and Sarmatians by Greek historians and identified as Saka by Iranian inscriptions, must have penetrated a long way to the northeast, to the region of Pazyryk and Minusinsk, while other Indo-Europeans populated the Tarim oases, from Kashgar to Kucha, Kara Shahr, and Turfan, perhaps even as far as Kansu. It is certain, however, that from the beginning of the Christian era the flow was from east to west. It was no longer the Indo-European dialects that prevailed—"East Iranian," Kuchean, or Tokharian—in the oases of the future Chinese Turkestan; it was rather the Hsiung-nu who, under the name of Huns, came to establish a proto-Turkic empire in southern Russia and in Hungary. (The Hungarian steppe is a continuation of the Russian steppe, as the Russian steppe is of the Asian.) After the Huns came the Avars, a Mongol horde which had fled from Central Asia under pressure from the T'u-chüeh in the sixth century, and which was to dominate the same regions, first Russia and later Hungary. In the seventh century came the Khazar Turks, in the eleventh the Petcheneg Turks, and in the twelfth the Cuman Turks, all following the same trail. Lastly, in the thirteenth century, the Mongols of Jenghiz Khan integrated the steppe, so to speak, and became the steppe incarnate, from Peking to Kiev.[1] [*]

The interior history of the steppe is that of Turko-Mongol hordes jostling one another for the best grazing grounds, and of their endless migrations from pasture to pasture, driven mainly by the needs of their herds. In some instances these alternating movements took centuries to complete owing to the vast distances involved, to which everything about these people—their physical build and their way of life—had become adapted. Of these unceasing wanderings between the Yellow River and Budapest, history, written by men of sedentary nations, has retained but little, and then only such events as affected themselves. They noted the onslaught of the waves that broke at the foot of the Great Wall or of their Danubian fortresses, Tatung or Silistra. But what do they tell of the inner turbulence of the Turko-Mongol peoples? In what may be termed the imperial district of Karabalgasun and Karakorum in northern Mongolia, at the source of the Orkhon, we find all the nomad clans which aimed at the domination of other hordes: there are the Hsiung-nu, of Turkic stock, before our own era; the Mongol Hsien-pi in the third century A.D.; the Juan-juan, also Mongol, in the fifth century; T'u-chüeh Turks in the sixth; Uigur Turks in the eighth; Kirghiz in the ninth; the Khitan of Mongol stock in the tenth; the Kerayit or Naiman, presumably Turkic, in the twelfth; and lastly, in the thirteenth century, the Mongols of Jenghiz Khan. Yet although we may be able to identify these alternately Turkic and Mongol clans which imposed their hegemony on others, we do not know how the great parent groups, Turkic, Mongol, and Tungus, were originally distributed. No doubt at the present time the Tungus occupy not only northern Manchuria but a great part of eastern Siberia, as well as the east bank of the middle Yenisei in central Siberia; while the Mongols are grouped in historic Mongolia and the Turks in western Siberia and the two Turkestans. It should be remembered, however, that in this latter region the Turks are latecomers and that their influence in the Altai may not have made

[*] Notes will be found in a group, beginning on p. 543.

itself felt until the first century of our era, in Kashgaria certainly not before the ninth century, and in Transoxiana not before the eleventh. The urban population both in Samarkand and Kashgar remains fundamentally of Turkicized Iranian stock. Nevertheless, history tells that in Mongolia itself the Jenghiz-Khanites Mongolized many apparently Turkic tribes: the Naiman of the Altai, the Kerayit of the Gobi, and the Öngüt of Chahar. Before the unification under Jenghiz Khan which brought all these tribes under the banner of the Blue Mongols, part of present-day Mongolia was Turkic; indeed, even now a Turkic people, the Yakut, occupy northeastern Siberia, north of the Tungus, in the Lena, Indigirka, and Kolyma basins. The presence of this Turkic group so near Bering Strait, north of the Mongols and even of the Tungus on the Arctic Ocean, necessitates caution in attempts to determine the relative positions of the "first" Turks, Mongols, and Tungus.[2] What it does indicate is that the Turko-Mongol and Tungus mass must originally have been established fairly far to the northeast; for not only present-day Kashgaria but also the northern slopes of the Sayan Mountains (Minusinsk) and the Great Altai (Pazyryk) were at that time peopled by Indo-Europeans from the "common Indo-European" cradle of southern Russia. Such a hypothesis is consistent with the views of such linguists as Pelliot and Guillaume de Hévésy, who, until further evidence is forthcoming, refuse to entertain any original connection between the Altaic languages (Turkic, Mongol, and Tungus) and those of the Finno-Ugrian group, centered in the Urals.[3] Moreover, the fairly wide divergence existing today, despite their original kinship, between Turkic, Mongol, and Tungus leads us to think that the three groups which during the historic period were united under common rule (hence frequent reciprocal borrowings of terms of civilization) may for a time have existed at some distance from each other, across the vastness of the Asian northeast.[4]

Were the history of the Turko-Mongol hordes confined to their expeditions and obscure skirmishes in the search for new pastures, it would amount to very little, at least as far as present interest is concerned. The paramount fact in human history is the pressure exerted by these nomads on the civilized empires of the south, a pressure constantly repeated until conquest was achieved. The descent of the nomads amounted almost to a physical law, dictated by the conditions prevailing in their native steppes.

Certainly, those Turko-Mongols who remained in the forest region of Lake Baikal and the Amur continued to be savages, and lived by hunting and fishing, as did the Jurchid down to the twelfth century and the "Forest Mongols" until the time of Jenghiz Khan; they were too closely barricaded by their wooded solitudes to conceive of other covetable territories. It was otherwise with the Turko-Mongols of the steppes, who lived by their herds and who were therefore nomads by necessity: the herd sought grass and they followed the herd.

Added to this, the steppe is the land of the horse.[5] The man of the steppe is a horseman born. Whether an Iranian of the west or a Turko-Mongol of the east, it was he who invented the riding dress, such as we see worn by the Scythians portrayed on Greek vases of the Cimmerian Bosporus, and hear of from the Chinese, who, in 300 B.C., to fight cavalry with cavalry, imitated the Huns in substituting trousers for robes. The horseman of the lightning raids was a mounted archer who brought down his adversary from a distance, shot while retreating—the Parthian shaft is in fact that of the Scythian and the Hun—and waged war as he pursued game or mares: with arrow and lasso.

On the threshold of these forays, where the steppes ended and cultivation began, he glimpsed a way of life very different from his own, one which was bound to arouse his greed. Winter on his native steppe is arctic; the steppe at that season is an extension of the Siberian taiga. Summer is scorching, for then the steppe is a continuation of the Gobi Desert, and to find pasture for his herds the nomad must climb the slopes of the Khingan, Altai, or Tarbagatai ranges. Spring alone, which transforms the steppe into a lush plain, strewn with flowers of every color, was a festival season for his beasts and for himself. Throughout the rest of the year, and especially in winter, his eyes were turned toward the temperate lands of the south, to Issyk Kul, "the hot lake" in the southwest, to the good yellow lands of the Yellow River in the southeast. Not that he had any taste for cultivated land as such; when he took possession of it, he instinctively allowed it to relapse into a fallow, unproductive state, and fields reverted to steppe, to yield grass for his sheep and horses.

Such was the attitude of Jenghiz Khan in the thirteenth century. Having conquered the Peking region, his genuine desire was to raise the millet fields of the fair plain of Hopei to the dignity of grazing land. Yet, although the man from the north understood nothing of husbandry (until the fourteenth century the Jenghiz-Khanites of Turkestan and Russia remained pure nomads, foolishly sacking their own towns and—at the least refusal to pay up on the part of the farmers—diverting irrigation canals to starve the land), he appreciated urban civilizations for their manufactured goods and their many amenities, as objects of sack and plunder. He was attracted by the mildness of the climate, a very relative mildness, certainly, for to Jenghiz Khan the harsh climate of Peking seemed too relaxing, and after each campaign he returned north to spend the summer near Lake Baikal. Similarly, after his victory over Jalal ad-Din, he deliberately shunned India, then at his feet, because, to this man from the Altai, India seemed the very caldron of hell. He was in any case right to mistrust the ease of civilized life, for when his great-grandsons settled into the palaces of Peking and Tabriz, they began at once to degenerate. But as long as the nomad kept the soul of a nomad, he regarded the sedentary man merely as his farmer, and town and tilled land as his farm, both farm and farmer being open to extortion. He roved on horseback along the fringes of ancient empires, exacting regular tribute from those who complied with a relatively good grace or, when the victim was ill-advised enough to refuse payment, plundering open cities in sudden raids. These men were like packs of wolves—and is not the wolf the old Turkic totem?—prowling round herds of deer, to fly at their throats or merely to pick up stragglers and injured beasts.[6] Whirlwind pillage alternating with the exaction of regular tribute—the latter euphemized so far as the Sons of Heaven were concerned by the name of "good-will gift"—was in general a regular feature of the relations between Turko-Mongols and Chinese from the second century B.C. to the seventeenth of this era.

From time to time, however, from among the nomads a man of strong personality would arise, well informed of the ruinous state of the sedentary empires (and these wily barbarians, like the Germanic ones of the fourth century, were wonderfully *au courant* with the Byzantine intrigues of the Chinese imperial court). He would make a pact with one Chinese faction or kingdom against another, or with a banished pretender. He would proclaim himself and his horde confederates of the empire and, under pretext of defending it, move into the border marches. In a generation or two, his grandsons would have acquired enough of the Chinese veneer to take the great step and, all unabashed, ascend the throne of the Sons of Heaven. The exploit of Kublai Khan in the thirteenth century is in this respect merely a repetition of those of Liu Ts'ung and the Toba in the fourth and fifth centuries respectively. In another two or three generations (unless chased over the Great Wall by some national revolt), these Sinicized barbarians, who had acquired nothing from civilization but its softness and its vices without conserving the sternness of the barbarian temperament, became in their turn objects of contempt and their territories the coveted prize of other barbarians who had remained, famished nomads, in the depths of their native steppes. And so the process was repeated. In the fifth century, the Toba arose on the shoulders of the Hsiung-nu and the Hsien-pi to destroy them and take their place. In the twelfth century, to the north of the Khitai, the over-Sinicized Mongols who had been peaceable lords of Peking since the tenth century, there arose the Jurchid; these were Tungus, little more than savages, who within a few months seized the great city, only to submit to Chinese influence in their turn and slumber until, just a century later, they were destroyed by Jenghiz Khan.

The same was as true in the West as in the East. In the Russian steppes of Europe, which are a continuation of those of Asia, there was a similar succession: Attila's Huns were followed by Bulgars (Bolgars), Avars, Hungarians (these were Finno-Ugrians, with a stiffening of Hunnic aristocracy), Khazars, Petchenegs, Cumans, and Jenghiz-Khanites. Similarly, in the lands of Islam, the process of Islamization and Iranization among the Turkish conquerors of Iran and Anatolia forms an exact counterpart to the Sinicizing noted among the Turkic, Mongol, or Tungus conquerors of the Celestial Empire. Here the khan became sultan or padishah, just as there he became a Son of Heaven; and as in China, he had soon to yield to other, rougher khans from the steppes. In Iran a similar sequence of conquest, succession, and destruction can be seen, the Ghaznavid Turks being followed by Seljuk and Khwarizmian Turks, Jenghiz-Khanite Mongols, Timurid Turks, and Shaybanid Mongols, to say nothing of the Ottoman Turks who, speeding like arrows to the outer rims of the Muslim lands, replaced the dying remnants of the Seljuks in Asia Minor and thence dashed on to their unprecedented triumph, the conquest of Byzantium.

To a higher degree than the Scandinavia of Jordanes, therefore, Continental Asia may be regarded as the matrix of nations, *vagina gentium,* and as the Germania of Asia, destined in its *Völkerwanderungen* to present ancient civilized empires with sultans and Sons of Heaven. These periodic descents by the hordes of the steppe, whose khans ascended the thrones of Changan, Loyang, Kaifeng or Peking, Samarkand, Ispahan or Tabriz (Tauris), Konya or Constantinople, became one of the geographic laws of history. But there was another, opposing law, which brought about the slow absorption of the nomad invaders by ancient civilized lands. This phenomenon was twofold in character. First, there was the demographic aspect. Established as a widely dispersed aristocracy, the barbarian horsemen became submerged in these dense populations, these immemorial anthills. Second, there was the cultural aspect. The civilizations of China and Persia, though conquered, in turn vanquished their wild and savage victors, intoxicating them, lulling them to sleep, and annihilating them. Often, only fifty years after a conquest, life went on as if nothing had happened. The Sinicized or Iranized barbarian was the first to stand guard over civilization against fresh onslaughts from barbarian lands.

In the fifth century, the Toba lord of Loyang constituted himself the defender of Chinese soil and culture against all Mongols, Hsien-pi, or Juan-juan who aspired to repeat the exploit. In the twelfth century, it was Sanjar the Seljuk who kept his "Watch on the Rhine" on the Oxus and the Jaxartes against all the Oghuz or Kara-Khitai of the Aral or the Ili. The story of Clovis and Charlemagne is repeated on every page of Asiatic history. Just as the Roman civilization in its efforts to resist Saxon and Norman Germanism found reserves of strength in the Frankish energy which it had assimilated, so the civilization of China found its best supporters in these fifth-century Toba, while Arabo-Persian Islam knew no more loyal champion than the valiant Sinjar mentioned above. An even better example is given by those Sinicized or Iranized Turko-Mongols who completed the work of the ancient Kings of Kings or Sons of Heaven. What no Chosroes, no caliph had been able to achieve—possession of the throne of the *basileis* and the ceremonial entrance into Saint Sophia—was accomplished by their unlooked-for successor, the Ottoman padishah of the fifteenth century, amid the acclamation of the Muslim world. In the same way, the dream of Pan-Asiatic dominion cherished by the Han and T'ang was fulfilled by the Yüan emperors of the thirteenth and fourteenth centuries, Kublai Khan and Temür Oljaitu, for the benefit of old China, by making Peking the suzerain capital of Russia, Turkestan, Persia and Asia Minor, Korea, Tibet, and Indochina. Thus the Turko-Mongol conquered the ancient civilizations only to wield his sword in their service. Born to rule, like the Roman of the poet of antiquity, he governed these ancient civilized peoples in keeping with their traditions and their age-long ambitions. From Kublai Khan to K'ang-hsi and Ch'ien-lung, these rulers in their administration of China carried out the program of Chinese imperialism in Asia and, in the Irano-Persian world, brought to fruition the Sassanid and Abbasid thrust toward the golden domes of Constantinople.

Governing races, imperial nations, are few. The Turko-Mongols, like the Romans, are of their number.

I

The High Plateaus of Asia
Until the Thirteenth Century

1

Early History of the Steppes: Scythians and Huns

The first known Eurasian route is that of the northern steppes. By this trail, in paleolithic times, the Aurignacian culture spread through Siberia—an "Aurignacian Venus" has been found at Malta, not far from Irkutsk, on the upper Angara River—and thence into northern China, where Teilhard de Chardin notes the presence of Aurignacian-type hearths buried in the loess at Kwei-tung, near Ningsia in Kansu, and at Siara-osso-gol, southwest of Yülin in the northern region of Shensi. Similarly, the Magdalenian culture seems to be represented in Siberia (on the upper Yenisei), in Manchuria (at Dolonnor [Tolun], Manchouli, and Khailar), and in Hopei. Here, in the upper cave of Chowkowtien, near Peking, a skeleton and personal ornaments were found, also bone needles, perforated canine teeth of animals, bones fashioned into pendants, pierced shells, pieces of mother-of-pearl, and stores of ocher.[1]

In the neolithic period, and more precisely toward its close, the Siberian steppe route was also the route by which comb ware found its way into Asia: that is to say, pottery decorated by "combed" lines, developed in central Russia during the first half of the third millennium. From here it spread into part of Siberia and so gradually influenced the proto-Chinese ceramics of Ch'i-chia-p'ing in Kansu. Similarly, in the ensuing period, at the beginning of the second millennium, it was probably through Siberia that the fine pottery decorated with painted spiral bands—a style originating in the Tripolye region near Kiev, at Schipenitz in Bukovina, Petreny in Bessarabia, and Cucuteni in Moldavia—spread from the Ukraine to China, where it flourished afresh at Yang-shao-ts'un in Honan about 1700 B.C., then at Panshan in Kansu. Finally, according to Tallgren, the bronze age began in western Siberia about 1500 B.C. and was linked with the great Danubian bronze civilization of the same period (the Aunjetitz civilization), while in central Siberia, at Minusinsk, the bronze age did not begin for another three hundred years (about 1200 B.C.). The axes and lance heads of western Siberia, imitated in China, led Max Loehr to suppose that the bronze technique was borrowed from Siberia by China at about this time (ca. 1400 B.C.).[2]

An outstanding feature of the ancient history of the steppes is the development of an increasingly stylized animal art, which was markedly original and was designed to adorn bronze, silver, or gold plates on harness and equipment: the nomad's one form of luxury. This art is represented in Kuban, in the Maikop burial, by a vase of electrum and by solid-gold or solid-silver figurines of animals (bulls, lions, etc.) which are clearly inspired by the Assyro-Babylonian style. Contemporary with the art of the Middle Minoan period, these art objects date, according to Tallgren, from about 1600–1500 B.C.[3] This original Assyro-Babylonian influence continues well into historic times—the sixth century B.C.—as can be seen in the famous ax of Kelermes.

Tallgren is inclined to think that from perhaps 1200 B.C. an Indo-European people, the Cimmerians, began to inhabit the Russian steppe north of the Black Sea. Believed to have been of Thraco-Phrygian origin,[4] the Cimmerians either "came" from Hungary and Rumania or, less hypothetically, "inhabited" those countries as well.[5] The eminent Finnish archaeologist attributes to the Cimmerians, at least in part, the fairly numerous finds of this period recently made in the Dnieper and Kuban region. Of these, the most important are the Borodino treasure (1300?–1100), the Shtetkovo treasure with its bronze sickles (1400?–1100), the bronze foundry of Nikolayev (1100?), and the bronze sickles of Abramovka (1200), all these discovered between the lower Danube and the lower Dnieper. At Kuban, moreover, there are the gold plaques and the solid-silver oxen of Staromishastovskaya (1300?). Finally, on the Terek River, there are the kurgans of Piatigorsk (ca. 1200?) and of the beginning of Koban (the age of pure bronze, ca. 1200?–1000). All this Cimmerian art of south Russia is linked with the Transcaucasian culture of Gandzha-Karabakh, where some fine bronze buckles ornamented with geometrical figures of animals were found. (This culture began between 1400 and 1250 and ended at latest in the eighth century.) It is also related to the Talysh culture, where bronze art flourished about 1200.[6]

The wooden-timbered tomb of Pokrovsk (now Engels), dating back to 1300–1200 B.C., indicates the spread of pre-Cimmerian or bronze Cimmerian civilization from the Volga to the Urals and toward Turkestan. At Seima, near Nizhni Novgorod (now Gorki), a "treasure" gives us a glimpse of an inferior culture of copper and bronze, including first and foremost socketed battle-axes (1300–800). In Kazakhstan a similar culture, known as that of Andronovo, reached Minusinsk and, around 1000 B.C., was prolonged by that of Karasuk. This was the first Siberian bronze age, with its socketed axes—which may have inspired those of Anyang in the China of the Shang—its flat dagger and javelin blades of the Seima type, and its purely geometrical ornamentation. Caucasian animal art seems not to have penetrated as far as this. Farther north, at Krasnoyarsk on the Yenisei, at a fairly late stage is found an aëneolithic type of art, which produced some remarkable stone carvings of elk and horses.

From 1150 to 950 the Cimmerian civilization continued to develop north of the Black Sea. This appears to be the period of the Novogrigorievsk treasure (bronze socketed axes) and of the Nikolayev bronze foundry on the River Bug (ca. 1100). On the Terek steppes, the pure bronze age of Koban shows interesting affinities with what is known as the Lelvar civilization in Georgia, which was in advance of that of the steppe—since iron is found there—and which (from about 1000 to 900) yields curious bronze belts adorned with human and animal figures, geometric in style, in scenes of hunting and husbandry. Furthermore, the local bronze culture glimpsed at Pokrovsk (Engels), between Samara and Saratov, continues in this region, as demonstrated by the tombs at Khvalinsk, which Tallgren estimates as dating between 1200 and 700 B.C. Tallgren further assigns this culture to the Scythians, the northern Iranian people who then appeared in

Russia for the first time and were to succeed the Cimmerians in dominating the steppes north of the Black Sea.

The last phase of Cimmerian culture occurred between 900 and 750. This is the period of the Mikhailovka treasure in Galicia, with its famous golden crown, which shows affinity with both the Caucasus and the Hallstatt culture of Austria (?800–700). It is also the period of the Podgortsa treasure south of Kiev, with its Caucasian influence; of the bronze socketed axes of Koblevo, east of Odessa; and, generally speaking, of the lances with two notches in the blade, then so plentiful in southern Russia (ca. 900–700). The Cimmerian bronze culture overflowed also into Rumania, taking the form of the Bordei-Herastrau and Mures cultures in Moldavia and of the Vartopu culture in Wallachia. The Cimmerian bronze culture then continued into Hungary. There is reason to observe, as does Tallgren, that the Cimmerians and Thracians still lingered in the bronze age when the southwest Caucasus and Hallstatt in Austria had entered upon that of iron (Hallstatt I, ca. 900–700). Elsewhere, the Khavalynsk group of cultures between the Volga and the Urals, attributed to the vanguard of the Scythians—the group which around 900 B.C. produced the bronze foundries of Sosnovaya Maza—is similarly retarded. During this time, at Minusinsk in Siberia, the second phase of the bronze age developed—this, according to Tallgren, was between 1000 and 500 B.C.—with socketed axes having two eyelets; the ornamentation is still mainly geometric, although there are a few rare animal figures which no doubt adorned the end of a hilt.[7]

It must be remembered that the Cimmerian bronze age of the Russian steppe was in communication during its last phase with two iron civilizations: that of Hallstatt in Austria and that of the Caucasus. Iron knives from Hallstatt have been found in the upper layers of Cimmerian culture, as in the early Scythian period.[8]

THE SCYTHIANS

Between 750 and 700 B.C., according to the evidence of Greek historians supplemented by Assyrian chronology, the Cimmerians were dispossessed of the steppes of southern Russia by the Scythians, who came from Turkestan and western Siberia. The peoples known to the Greeks by the name of Scyths (Skythai) are those whom the Assyrians called *Ashkuz* and to whom Persians and Indians gave the name of *Saka*.[9] As may be deduced from the nomenclature, the Scythians belonged to the Iranian race.[10] They were Iranians of the north who had remained nomads in "the original Iranian country" in the steppes of present-day Russian Turkestan, and who had thus to a large extent escaped the influence of the material civilization of Assur and Babylon: the civilization which so strongly affected their sedentary brothers the Medes and Persians, who had settled farther south on the plateau of Iran. The Scythians, like their kindred the Sarmatians, were to remain strangers also to historical Mazdaism and to the Zoroastrian reforms which shortly afterward would progressively transform the Medo-Persian beliefs.

Vivid portraits of these Scythians have been left on the Greco-Scythian vases of Kul Oba and Voronezh. They were bearded, and wore, like their Saka brothers in the bas-reliefs of Persepolis, the pointed cap that protected the ears against the bitter winds of the plains, and the roomy garments—tunic and wide trousers—common to the Saka and to their Median and Persian cousins. The horse—the splendid horse of the steppe, reproduced on the silver amphora of the Chertomlyk tumulus—was their inseperable companion, and their favorite weapon was the bow.[11] These mounted archers "had no city" save what one may call "traveling cities": that is to say, the wagon trains that accompanied them on their seasonal migrations, as was still the custom nineteen hundred years later, in the thirteenth century—the days of Piano Carpini and William of Rubruck—when similar convoys followed the Jenghiz-Khanite Mongols across these same Russian steppes. On these wagons they piled their women and their wealth: gold ornaments, plaques for harness and equipment, and no doubt carpets too—all wares for which the demand was to bring Scythian art to birth and determine its form and general orientation. Such as they then were, they remained lords of the Russian steppe from the seventh to the third century B.C.

Modern linguists believe that the Scythians should be classified as an Iranian people—an Indo-European family, of the Indo-Iranian or Aryan group. As was just noted, however, their way of life was very similar to that of the Hunnic tribes of Turko-Mongol stock which, at about the same time, became active at the other end of the steppe, on the borders of China. Indeed, nomadic living conditions on the steppe, whether north of the Black and Caspian seas or in Mongolia, were much alike, although in the latter region they were markedly more severe. No wonder then if—physical type and language apart—the Scythians described by Greek historians and portrayed on Greco-Scythian vases are reminiscent, so far as culture and general way of life are concerned, of the Hsiung-nu, T'u-chüeh, and Mongols described or painted by Chinese annalists and artists. A certain number of customs common to both groups is found, either because their similar ways of life compelled them to arrive at solutions (as, for example, the use by both Scythian and Hun mounted archers of trousers and boots instead of the robe of the Mediterranean peoples or of the early Chinese, and the use also of the stirrup,[12] or because actual geographical contact between Scythian and Hunnic peoples at the same cultural stage gave rise to the same practices. (An example of this is shown by the funerary immolations which continued to a very late period among both Scythians and Turko-Mongols, whereas in Western Asia and China they had long since disappeared, ever since the burials of Ur and Anyang.) [13]

Thus between 750 and 700, the Scythians (or rather a part of the Scytho-Saka peoples, for the majority of the Sakas remained round the vicinity of T'ien Shan, near Fergana and in Kashgaria) moved from the Turgai region and the Ural River into southern Russia, whence they drove out the Cimmerians.[14] Some of the Cimmerians, it seems, had to take refuge in Hungary, which was probably already inhabited by other peoples of Thracian affinities; and it is these fugitives who are believed to have buried the "treasures" of Mihaeni near Szilagyi and of Fokuru near Heves, and also that of Mikhailovka in Galicia. The rest of the Cimmerians fled via Thrace, says Strabo—or, according to Herodotus, via Colchis—into Asia Minor, where they wandered in Phrygia (ca. 720), then in Cappadocia and Cilicia (ca. 650), and finally in Pontis (ca. 630). Some of the Scythians set off in pursuit (720–700), but Herodotus says they took the wrong route, crossed the Caucasus through the Derbent Gateway, and came into contact with the Assyrian Empire, which their king Ishkapai attacked, though without success (ca. 678). Bartatua, another petty Scythian king, was more astute; he made friendly advances to the Assyrians, with whom he had a common enemy: the Cimmerians, who were threatening the Assyrian frontier in the region of Cilicia and Cappadocia. A Scythian army, acting in conformity with Assyrian policy, entered Pontis to crush the last of the Cimmerians (ca. 638). About ten years later, Bartatua's son, referred to by Herodotus as Madyes, came at the request of Assyria, which had been overrun by the Medes, and himself invaded and subjugated Media (ca. 628). The Medes soon rebelled, however; their king Cyaxares massacred the Scythian leaders, and the remainder of the Scythians turned back via the Caucasus to southern Russia. These are just a few—the most noteworthy—of the episodes of the Scythian invasions, which frightened Western Asia for nearly seventy years. Throughout this period, the great Indo-European barbarians were the terror of the Old World. Their cavalry galloped in search of plunder from Cappadocia to Media, from the Caucasus to Syria. This great stirring of peoples, of which an echo can be detected even among the prophets of Israel, represents the first irruption in historical times of the nomads of the northern steppe into the old civilizations of the south: a movement that will be repeated through some twenty centuries.

When the Persians replaced the Assyrians, Babylonians, and Medes as masters of Western Asia, they set to work to render sedentary Iran secure from fresh invasions from Outer Iran. According to Herodotus, it was against the Massagetae that Cyrus led his last campaign—that is to say, against the Scythians of the region east of Khiva (ca. 529). Darius launched his first great expedition against the Scythians of Europe (ca. 514–512). By way of Thrace and present-day Bessarabia he penetrated the steppe, where, following the usual nomad tactics, the Scythians instead of accepting battle retreated before him, luring him ever farther into the wilderness. He was wise enough to withdraw in time. Herodotus is inclined to regard this "Russian campaign" as the folly of a despot; yet in fact, the Achaemenid monarch intended by this to implement a quite natural policy: the Persianization of Outer Iran, or Pan-Iranian union. The enterprise having failed, the Scythians escaped Persian influence and remained in peaceful possession of southern Russia for another three centuries. Darius' expedition did at least result in securing permanent protection for Western Asia against the incursions of the nomads.[15]

Discoveries of Scythian art enable a glimpse, with Tallgren, of the progress of Scythian occupation in Russia.[16] At first, from approximately 700 to 550 B.C., the center of Scythian culture remained in the southeast, in the Kuban region and the Taman Peninsula. The Scythians were doubtless already dominant in the south of the Ukraine at this time, between the lower Dnieper and the lower Bug, as is proved by the finds at Martonocha and Melgunov, though apparently in a more sporadic manner. It was not until between approximately 550 and 450, according to Tall gren, that Scythian culture sprang vigorously into being in the Ukraine of today, to reach its peak from about 350 to 250, as may be seen from the great royal kurgans of the lower Dnieper, at Chertomlyk, Alexandropol, Solokha, Denev, and others. The most northerly area in the west to be reached by the Scythian expansion ran along the northern border of the forest steppes, a little to the south of Kiev and in the Voronezh region. Northeastward, the expansion moved up the Volga to Saratov, where important discoveries have been made and where Tallgren places the Scythian or quasi-Scythian people—Iranian in either case—the Sarmatians.

It is possible that the Scythians of southern Russia were never more than an aristocracy superimposed on a Cimmerian—that is, a Thraco-Phrygian—substratum. Benveniste points out that in Herodotus (IV, 5–10) information alleged to be of Scythian origin reveals a purely Iranian nomenclature, whereas other information about these same Scythians, stated to originate in Greece, reveals a nomenclature still Thraco-Phrygian.[17] Linguistic survivals have been corroborated by archaeological remains. "The Hallstatt culture of the Cimmerian bronze period," says Tallgren, "lived on in the Ukraine as a peasant culture even while Scythism and Hellenism were becoming established." [18]

Finally, north of the Scythian zone, with its more or less Cimmerian substratum, dwelt non-Scythian barbarians whom Herodotus calls Androphagi, Melankhlenes, and Issedones, and who may have been of Finno-Ugrian stock. Tallgren suggests that the Androphagi should be placed north of Chernigov and the Melankhlenes north of Voronezh. It is known that these two peoples joined with the Scythians to repel Darius' invasion. As for the Issedones, Benveniste seeks them in the Ural region, near Ekaterin-burg. Also, Tallgren attributes to the Androphagi and the Me-lankhlenes—that is to say, the Finno-Ugrian neighbors of the Scythians—the so-called Mordvian culture, of which traces have been found in the excavations of the Desna and the Oka, and which is characterized by a rather inferior geometric ornamenta-tion entirely lacking in the animal style of the Scythians.[19]

SCYTHIAN ART

The consequences of the great Scythian invasions of the Caucasus, Asia Minor, Armenia, Media, and the Assyrian Empire in the seventh century extend beyond the field of political history. The initial contact of the Scythians with the Assyrian world, of which they were allies and confederates—that close contact which lasted for nearly a century—is a fact of paramount importance to any student of steppe art. First, it is very probable that it was during their wanderings across Western Asia in the seventh cen-tury that the Scythians completed their transition from the bronze to the iron age.

The beginnings of Scythian art were not uninfluenced by the Hallstatt iron technique, in the Celto-Danubian region (Hallstatt between 1000 or 900 and 500 or 450, Scythian between 700 and 200).[20] But it was above all the Caucasus and the Median coun-try—in this case Luristan—which the tumult of peoples in the seventh century brought into such close relations with the Scythians. Franz Hančar, in agreement with his colleague of Vienna, F. W. König, holds that it is indeed to the seventh cen-tury that must be attributed a large proportion of the Koban bronzes in the Caucasus, as well as some of those of Luristan, on the southwest side of old Media. In Hančar's view, the Koban bronzes and even those of Luristan were partly due to the Cim-merians.[21] What is evident is the connection between both of these and the beginnings of Scythian art at this time, when squadrons of Scythian and Cimmerian invaders were eddying over the same regions.

There is irrefutable evidence of the direct influence exerted by Assyro-Babylonian Mesopotamia on the first Scythian works of art: the iron and gold ax of Kelermes in Kuban (dating from about the sixth century). This ax displays the old Assyro-Baby-

Ionian—and Luristanian—theme of two ibexes standing about the tree of life, together with some fine deer. The animals are depicted in a realistic manner, and the art form is clearly inspired by Assyrian animal art. However, it is specifically Scythian in the decorative use to which it is put.

From this starting point we behold the rise of all Scythian animal art, which may be defined as turning Assyrian (or Greek) naturalism to a decorative purpose. This art appears in its definitive form with the golden deer of the Kostromskaya tomb, whose antlers are stylized in spirals. Almost certainly in the sixth century, it also appears in Kuban.

In this manner the aesthetics of the steppe took up their centuries-long abode in southern Russia, with those clearly defined tendencies of which we shall follow the eastward development as far as Mongolia and China. From the beginning a dual stream is noted: the naturalist current, doubtless periodically renewed from Assyro-Achaemenid sources, on the one hand, and from Hellenic ones, on the other, and the decorative stream which, as has been stated, bends, twists, and diverts that current to purely ornamental purposes.[22] In the end, the realism of the animal style, never lost sight of by these horsebreakers and hunters, became merely the peg and the pretext for stylized decorations.

Such a tendency is explained by the nomadic way of life, whether of the Scytho-Sarmatians in the west or of the Huns in the east. Possessing neither stable settlements nor landed property, they remained strangers to statuary, bas-relief and painting, which alone require realism. Their luxuries were confined to richness of dress and personal adornment, and to ornamentation of equipment, harness, and so on. Objects of this sort—hooks and plaques for belts, harness plates, sword-belt buckles, wagon panels, all sorts of handles and hilts, to say nothing of carpets, as at Noin Ula—seemed designed for stylized, even heraldic, treatment.

As has been said, the northern nomads—whether of Iranian stock like the Scythian or of Turko-Mongol like the Huns—lived their steppe life on horseback, engaged in chasing herds of deer or wild asses and watching wolves hunt antelope over the boundless plains. Both their way of life and the peculiar character of their wealth made it natural that, of the Assyro-Babylonian influences they had received, they should have retained only heraldic themes and stylized representations of fighting animals. Lastly, as Andersson points out, it appears that these animal portrayals had a specifically magical purpose, like the frescoes and bone carvings of the Magdalenians.[23]

Except for Greco-Scythian examples of goldsmiths' work—Scythian only in subject, and executed by Greek artists working either for the Hellenic colonies of the Crimea or directly for the kings of the steppe—in almost all Scythian art the figures of animals are fashioned in a formal, geometrical style with a view solely to ornamental effect. There are examples at Kostromskaya, dating, according to Schefold, from the fifth century B.C.; at Elizavetovskaya, from the same period; at Kul Oba in the Crimea, between 450 and 350; in the treasure of Peter the Great, originating in western Siberia in the Sarmatian period (the first century of this era); and at Verkhneudinsk in Transbaikalia, in Hunnic art dating from approximately the beginning of this era. In all these are found deer antlers, horses' manes, and even the claws of felines proliferating in curls and spirals which at times double the height of the animal. The upper lip of the horse is coiled like a snail shell. In the Scytho-Sarmatian art of western Siberia, as also in the identically inspired art elaborated by the Hsiung-nu of the Ordos, the stylization of animal forms is at times so complete—they entwine and interlace with one another in such complexity, and branch in such unexpected profusion—that despite the sustained realism in the treatment of deer's and horses' heads, or in those of bears and tigers, it is only with difficulty that beast can be distinguished from ornamentation. Horns and tails of animals terminate in foliage or blossom out in the shape of birds. Animal realism ends by submerging and losing itself in the ornamentation that sprang from it.[24]

Steppe art is thus in direct contrast to that of neighboring sedentary peoples—Scythian versus Assyro-Achaemenid, Hunnic versus Chinese—and in the very field where they have most in common: scenes of hunting and of fighting animals. Nothing could be more different from the animal classicism—all swiftness and spare delineation—of the Assyrians or the Achaemenids on the one hand, the Han on the other, than the contortions, convolutions, and obscurities of steppe art. Assyrians and Achaemenids, like the China of the Han, show prowling beasts, pursuing or defying each other within a simple, airy setting. Steppe artists, whether Scythians or Huns, show scuffles—often as entangled as a thicket of lianas—between animals locked in a death struggle. Theirs is a dramatic art of crushed limbs, of horses or deer seized by leopards, bears, birds of prey, or griffins, the bodies of the victims being often wrenched completely round. No swiftness here, no flight; instead, a patient and methodical tearing of throats in which, as has been said, the victim appears to drag the slayer to his death. Yet there is an inner dynamic which, despite this "slowness," might have attained to tragic heights were it not for the luxuriant stylization by which the forms are interwoven and elaborated, and which usually removes all realism from the killings.

The varied elements and tendencies of steppe art are unevenly distributed over the huge area extending from Odessa to Manchuria and the Yellow River. The Scythian art of the steppe, spreading toward the forest region of the upper Volga, influenced the Ananino culture near Kazan (ca. 600–200 B.C.), which was doubtless a Finno-Ugrian civilization. A rich burial ground discovered there has yielded, in addition to the usual bronze spiked axes and daggers, some animal motifs in which the animals' bodies are curled up; these have Scythian affinities, though executed here in a somewhat meager and simplified form. Nevertheless, according to Tallgren's observations, the Scythian animal style was only partially adopted at Ananino, and the decoration continued to be based on geometric patterns.[25]

At Minusinsk, in central Siberia, the situation was not entirely the same. During the most flourishing period of the bronze age (sixth to third centuries), this important metalworking center of the Altai went on producing socketed axes decorated with purely geometric designs (e.g., the "angled" decoration of Krasnoyarsk). Yet from the same period the site yields animal bronzes of a sober, simplified stylization, in contrast to the intricate elaboration of other provinces. It is here, therefore, that Borovka is inclined to seek the origin, both topographical and chronological, of steppe art.

The importance of the question is evident. Was it at Minusinsk, the geographical center of this art, situated halfway between the Black Sea and the Gulf of Chihli, that the ancient smiths of the Altai hammered out the first animal designs? And were these designs, still elementary and weak, to become enriched both by the

Assyro-Achaemenid contributions of the Scythians in the southwest and the Chinese borrowings of the Hsiung-nu in the southeast? Or is the poverty of the Minusinsk animal designs explained, as Rostovtzeff believes, by the decline of Scythian art as it spread to the Siberian forests, as happened at Ananino to the art which was to spread to the forest region of Perm? If this is true, Ananino and Minusinsk represent no more than a faint echo of the Russian steppe.

It should be noted also that in southern Russia itself, at the beginning—that is, from the seventh and sixth centuries B.C.—only somewhat austere examples of animal stylization are found, as in the bronzes of the Seven Brothers tumuli, of Kelermes, Ulski, and Kostromskaya in the Kuban, of Chigirin near Kiev, of Kerch and Kul Oba (these being dated as early as the fifth and fourth centuries) in the Crimea, for example. In the fifth and fourth centuries, the stylization apparently became more complex, as at Solokha near Melitopol on the Sea of Azov. There, alongside a fine piece of Greek goldsmith's work based on Scythian themes, are contorted animal figures with characteristic branchings and elaboration. The same holds true at Elizavetovskaya near Azov, where floral and ramifying motifs pierced in bronze are wrought for their own sake.

THE SARMATIANS AND WESTERN SIBERIA

At Prokhorovka in the Orenburg region, near the Urals, a local culture has been found dating from the fourth century B.C., with important collections of lances. Since the lance was the characteristic arm of the Sarmatians, the Prokhorovka tombs, according to Rostovtzeff, would represent the first appearance of these people in European Russia.[26] However this may be, in the second half of the third century B.C. the Sarmatians—of the same lineage as the Scythians, belonging like them to the northern nomadic Iranian group, and until then established north of the Aral Sea—crossed the Volga and invaded the Russian steppe, driving the Scythians back toward the Crimea.[27] Polybius (XXV, 1) mentions them for the first time as a force to be reckoned with in 179 B.C.

The two peoples were ethnically related and both were nomads.[28] The newcomers differed markedly, nevertheless, from their predecessors. The Scythians, it has been noted, were mounted archers, wearing the cap of the Sakas and roomy garments; they were barbarians with a smattering of Greek culture, and had developed an animal art which through its stylization yet retained the memory of a more plastic, naturalistic form. The Sarmatians were essentially lancers, with conical caps, and coats of mail. Still basically of the animal style, their art displays a far more exclusive taste than that of the Scythians for stylization and geometrical ornament, and they delight in incrustations of colored enamels set in metal. In short, their art shows a very marked "oriental" reaction of stylized floral decoration based on Greco-Roman plasticism. This is the first appearance in Europe of premedieval art, an art which the Sarmatians were to hand on to the Goths and the Goths to all the Germanic tribes of the *Völkerwanderung*, or great migration of peoples.

The transition from Scythian to Sarmatian art occurred at the beginning of the third century B.C., as may be concluded from the great discoveries made at Alexandropol near Ekaterinoslav. Sarmatian art became established in southern Russia during the third and second centuries, as shown by the jewelry of Buerova Mogila, Akhtanizovka, Anapa, Stavropol, Kasinskoye, and Kurdzhips in the Kuban. It is also revealed by the Sarmatian layer at Elizavetovskaya near Azov, and may be seen in the celebrated silver and enamel belt of Maikop. Bearing a design of a griffin devouring a horse, the Maikop belt is said to be an example of Sarmatian art dating from the second century B.C. The same style continues in the Sarmatian plaques of the succeeding period and is found at Taganrog and Fedulovo near the mouth of the Don, at Siverskaya near the mouth of the Kuban (second–first century B.C.), and, as of the first century of this era, at Novocherkask, near Azov, at Ust-Labinskaya, at the Zubov farm, and at Armavir in the Kuban.[29]

With this group, and in particular with the plaque of the Maikop belt, are associated the gold and silver plaques of western Siberia, today part of the treasure of Peter the Great, which are ornamented with fights between griffins and horses, tigers and horses, griffins and yaks, eagles and tigers, and so on, treated in a very stylized and arborescent manner. All these Siberian plaques, attributed by Borovka to what is certainly too early a period (third–second centuries B.C.), are dated by Merhart from the first century B.C. and by Rostovtzeff—more credibly—from the first century A.D.[30]

One is the more inclined to attribute the gold and silver plaques of western Siberia to peoples of Sarmatian affinities in that, according to recent Soviet finds, human skulls of the period discovered at Oglakty, near Minusinsk—that is to say, much farther east, in central Siberia—seem unlikely to be of Turko-Mongol origin. On the other hand, they may well have belonged to Indo-European peoples living in contact with Scythians, Sarmatians, and Sakas.[31]

PRE-TURKIC CULTURES OF THE ALTAI

The metalworking center of Minusinsk, on the upper Yenisei, was from approximately the beginning of the fifth century the scene of a new activity.[32] It is then, according to Tallgren, that the pit graves in rectangular stone enclosures appear, coinciding with the period known as "Bronze III," the "full bronze" of Merhart (ca. 500–300 or 200 B.C.). This period is characterized by a profusion of animal motifs, especially those of recumbent or standing deer, of deer looking backward, and of the curled-up animal which, according to Tallgren, originated in southern Russia.

It is between 500 and 300, too, that the first manufacture of Siberian bronze daggers and knives occurs, and also that of the "cup cauldrons" which were to spread from Minusinsk both to the Ordos of the Hsiung-nu period and to the Hungary of the great invasions.[33] The knives of Minusinsk and Tagarskoye, thin and slightly curved, with a hilt terminating in a delicate deer's head, were evenly distributed throughout Mongolia as far as the Ordos of Hsiung-nu times.

About 330–200 B.C. the iron age triumphed at Minusinsk, producing spiked axes, partly bronze and partly iron, and a group of large collective burial places. Apart from this, Minusinsk has provided ornamental bronze plaques which doubtless date back, according to Merhart, to the second and first centuries. Showing bulls head-on in defiance, or fighting horses, the plaques reveal creatures with ears, hoofs, tails, muscles, and hair treated in the "hollow trefoil" manner. This technique is clearly related to the Sarmatian art of southern Russia and western Siberia, which many archaeologists think was handed on by Minusinsk to the Hunnic art of the Ordos.

Minusinsk is situated on the northern face of the Sayan Mountains. Farther to the southwest, at Pazyryk, on the north side of the great Altai, near the headwaters of the Ob and the Khatun, the Griaznov mission of 1929 uncovered burial places dating from 100 B.C. or a little earlier, containing the bodies of horses "masked as reindeer." (This, by the way, seems to prove that the people of the region had replaced the reindeer by the horse.) [34] These horse masks, and their harnesses of leather, wood, and gold, are ornamented with stylized animal motifs: ibexes and stags at full gallop, a winged griffin killing an ibex, panthers leaping upon deer and ibexes, a bird of prey attacking a deer on the ground, and cocks confronting one another. All these themes are still fairly close to Scythian and even Greco-Scythian animal realism, without its later ornamental complexities. The stylization, orderly and restrained, produces a splendid decorative effect.

At Pazyryk too are found bearded mascarons (masks) of well-defined Greco-Roman origin, which were doubtless inspired by the Hellenistic kingdom of the Cimmerian Bosporus. Similar Greco-Roman masks, dating from approximately the same period —second and first centuries B.C.—are found in the Minusinsk group: at Trifonova, Bateni, Beya, Kali, Znamenka, etc.[35] The Altai group comprises, besides Pazyryk, the kurgans of Shibe, Karakol, and Oirotin, dating mainly from the first century B.C. and having Sarmatian affinities. The objects of the Shibe group display the same animal art, with restrained stylization still not far removed from realism. A Chinese lacquer at Shibe, dating from 86–48 B.C., aids in fixing the chronology of this center.[36]

In the first century A.D., the Altai culture is represented by the kurgan of Katanda, where there are wood carvings of fights between bears and deer, the deer having antlers burgeoning into birds' heads; also bronze plaques and fragments of fabric adorned with stylized animal patterns, of which the fights of griffins and deer are reminiscent of the Hunnic motifs of the same period (2 A.D.) at Noin Ula in Mongolia. And just as Noin Ula yields a Greek fabric certainly originating in the Cimmerian Bosporus, so the kurgan of Tes, near Minusinsk, provides evidence, up to the time of the great invasions, of Greco-Roman influences from the same quarter, especially in earrings of Pontic inspiration.

During the first two centuries of this era, animal patterns in a transitional culture continued to flourish in the Minusinsk area. Teplukhov calls this the Tashtyk culture. To it belong in particular the finds at the village of Oglakty, about thirty-seven miles north of Minusinsk, below the confluence of the Tuba River with the Yenisei. These finds are dated by a piece of Chinese silk of the second Han period, and include some fine rock drawings of animals.

Shortly afterward, these centers of culture with Scytho-Sarmatian affinities found in the Altai and at Minusinsk appear to die out or, more precisely, to change. At the beginning of the seventh century A.D., the Minusinsk region is still producing bronze ornaments, of which the date is established by Chinese coins of the early T'ang dynasty. But in the interval the country apparently had been conquered by Turkic tribes, forebears of the Kirghiz, mentioned by Chinese historians in the fifth century.[37] According to Teplukhov, the Indo-European aristocracy with its Sarmatian connections was succeeded at Minusinsk by the Kirghiz after the third century A.D.[38] But, before disappearing, the cultural centers of Minusinsk, Pazyryk, and Katanda had played a considerable part in handing down stylized animal art—the art of the steppes—to the Hunnic nations of Mongolia and the Ordos.

ORIGINS OF THE HSIUNG-NU

While the nomads of Iranian stock—Scythians and Sarmatians—occupied the western part of the steppe zone, in southern Russia and no doubt also in Turgai and western Siberia, the eastern part was under the sway of Turko-Mongol peoples. Of these, the dominant nation in antiquity was known to the Chinese by the name of Hsiung-nu, a name cognate with that of Huns (Hunni) and *Huna*, by which Romans and Indians later designated these same barbarians.[39] Probably these Hsiung-nu (the name does not appear clearly in Chinese annals until the Ch'in dynasty in the third century B.C.) had been called *Hsien-yün* by the Chinese of the eighth and ninth centuries. Earlier still, they may have been known as *Hsiun-yü* or, more vaguely, *Hu*. The Hu known to the Chinese at the dawn of history were those dwelling on the borders of the China of those days, in the Ordos, in northern Shansi and northern Hopei. Maspero supposes that the "Jung of the

North," the Pei-Jung, established to the west and northwest of present-day Peking, were a Hu tribe. Other clans were sub-jugated in the fourth century B.C. by the Chinese of the kingdom of Chao. King Wu-ling of Chao (ca. 325–298) even captured from them the extreme north of Shansi (the Tatung region) and indeed the northern part of the Ordos of today (ca. 300 B.C.). It was to secure effective defense against the attacks of these no-mads that the Chinese of the kingdoms of Ch'in (Shensi) and Chao (Shansi) transformed their heavy wheeled forces into mo-bile cavalry. This was a military innovation which brought with it a complete alteration in Chinese dress, the robe of archaic times being replaced by cavalry trousers copied from the nomads, from whom Chinese warriors borrowed also the plumed cap, the "three tails," and the belt buckles that were to play so great a part in the art known as "Warring States" or "Fighting States." [40] It was also to defend themselves against the Hsiung-nu that the Chinese of Chao and the neighboring states began to build along their northern frontier elementary fortifications which, later unified and completed by Ch'in Shih Huang-ti, were to become the Great Wall.

According to the Chinese historian Ssu-ma Ch'ien, it was in the second half of the third century B.C. that the Hsiung-nu seem to have become a united, strong nation. They were led by a chief called the *shan-yü*, whose full title transcribed into Chinese is *Ch'eng-li Ku-t'u Shan-yü*, words which the Chinese translate as "Majesty Son of Heaven." In these words may be detected Turko-Mongol roots: *ch'eng-li* in particular is the transcription of the Tur-kic and Mongol word *Tängri*, Heaven.[41] Under the *shan-yü* served "two great dignitaries, the kings *t'u-ch'i*: that is to say, the wise kings of right and left, the Chinese transcription *t'u-ch'i* being related to the Turkish word *doghri*, straight, faithful. In so far as one can speak of fixed dwellings for essentially nomadic people, the *shan-yü* resided on the upper Orkhon, in the mountainous region where later Karakorum, the capital of the Jenghiz-Khanite Mongols, was to be established. The worthy king of the left—in principle, the heir presumptive—lived in the east, probably on the high Kerulen. The worthy king of the right lived in the west, perhaps, as Albert Herrmann thinks, near present-day Uliassutai in the Khangai Mountains.[42] Next, moving down the scale of the Hunnic hierarchy, came the *ku-li* "kings" of left and right, the army commanders of left and right, the great governors, the *tang-hu*, the *ku-tu*—all of left and right; then the chiefs of a thousand men, of a hundred, and of ten men.[43] This nation of nomads, a people on the march, was organized like an army. The general orientation was southward, as was customary among Turko-Mongol peoples; the same phenomenon is to be seen among the descendants of the Hsiung-nu, the Turks of the sixth century A.D., as well as in the case of the Mongols of Jenghiz Khan.

The Hsiung-nu are portrayed by the Chinese with the characteristic traits which we find among their Turkic and Mongol successors. "They are short," Wieger summarizes, "with a stocky body and a very large round head, broad face, prominent cheekbones, wide nostrils, a fairly bushy mustache and no beard except for a tuft of stiff hair on the chin; their long ears are pierced and adorned with a ring. The head is usually shaved, except for a tuft on top.[44] The eyebrows are thick, the eyes almond-shaped with a very fiery pupil. They wear a loose robe to the calf, split at the sides and gathered in by a girdle whose ends hang down in front. Because of the cold the sleeves are gathered in tightly at the wrists. A short fur cape covers their shoulders, and their head is protected by a fur cap. Their shoes are of leather, and they have wide trousers strapped in at the ankle. The sheath of the bow hangs from the belt in front of the left thigh. The quiver, also suspended from the belt, hangs across the small of the back, the barbs of the arrows to the right."

Several details of this dress, particularly the trousers strapped in at the ankle, are common to Huns and Scythians. The same is true of many customs, as for example the funerary immolations. Both Hsiung-nu and Scythians thus slit the throats of the chief's wives and servants on his tomb, to the number of a hundred or a thousand in the case of the Hsiung-nu. Herodotus (IV, 65) tells that the Scythians sawed through their enemy's skull at eyebrow level, covered it with a leather sheath, inlaid the inside of it with gold, and used it as a drinking-cup. The *Ch'ien Han Shu* testifies to the same custom among the Hsiung-nu, as may be seen exemplified in particular by the *shan-yü* Lao-shang drinking from the skull of the king of the Yüeh-chih.[45] Indeed, both Hsiung-nu and Scythians were head-hunters. Herodotus (IV, 64) saw Scythians for whom it was a point of honor to display among their battle trophies the heads which they had cut from their

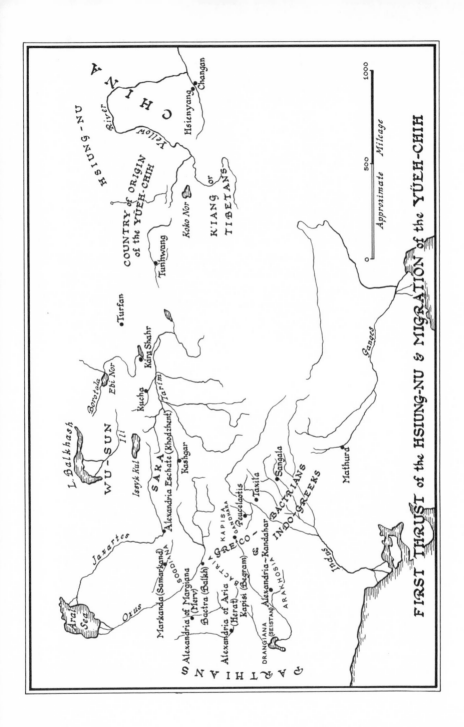

FIRST THRUST of the HSIUNG-NU & MIGRATION of the YÜEH-CHIH

victims, and the scalps of which dangled from their bridles.

Among the descendants of the Hsiung-nu, the T'u-chüeh of the sixth century A.D., the number of stones distinguishing a warrior's burial mound was proportionate to the number of men he had slain during his lifetime.[46] The same bloodthirstiness prevails among Indo-European and Turko-Mongol nomads. The Scythian sprinkles with the blood of his enemy the sacred scimitar driven into a mound of earth, and drinks a cupful of blood from the first foe he kills.[47] To consecrate a treaty, the Hsiung-nu drinks blood from a human skull.[48] To mourn the dead, both Scythian and Hsiung-nu gash their faces with knives, "so that blood flows with their tears."

Like the Scythians, the Hsiung-nu were essentially nomadic, and the rhythm of their existence was regulated by their flocks of sheep, their herds of horses, cattle, and camels. They moved with their livestock in search of water and pasture. They ate only meat (a custom which deeply impressed the far more vege-tarian Chinese), dressed in skins, slept on furs,[49] and camped in felt tents. Their religion was a vague shamanism based on the cult of Tängri or Heaven and on the worship of certain sacred mountains. Their *shan-yü* or supreme monarch summoned all of them together in the autumn ("the season when horses are fat") for the counting of men and beasts. All the Chinese writers pre-sent these barbarians as inveterate plunderers who would ap-pear unexpectedly on the fringes of cultivated land; attack men, flocks, and wealth; and flee again with their booty before any counterattack could be launched.[50] When pursued, their tactics consisted in luring the Chinese columns into the wilderness of the Gobi Desert or the steppe, scourging them there with showers of arrows without allowing themselves to be trapped, and never moving in for the kill until the foe had been exhausted and de-moralized by hunger and thirst. These methods, rendered effective by the mobility of their cavalry and their skill with bow and arrow, were to vary little if at all among the natives of the steppe from the first Hsiung-nu until the time of Jenghiz Khan. They were common to all these tribes of mounted archers, whether Huns in the east or Scythians in the west. As Herodotus relates, the same tactics were used by the Scythians against Darius. Darius appreciated the danger in time and withdrew before this "retreat from Russia" could end in disaster. How many Chinese generals were to lack this prudence and be slaughtered in the wilds of the Gobi, to which they had been lured by the deliberate flight of the Huns?

As regards the linguistic position of the Hsiung-nu among the Turko-Mongol group of peoples, certain writers, like Kurakichi Shiratori, are inclined to class them with the Mongols.[51] Pelliot, on the contrary, from the few opportunities of cross-checking afforded by Chinese transcriptions, believes that on the whole these people were Turkic, especially their political leadership.

HUNNIC ART

The Hsiung-nu possessed a very characteristic art, represented chiefly by belt plaques or plaques of other kinds, mounts, hooks, and studs for harness or equipment, made of bronze and bearing stylized animal motifs, or by the butts of staves terminating in the figures of hinds. This art is often known as Ordos art, from the name of the Mongol Ordos tribe which since the sixteenth century A.D. has occupied the loop of the Yellow River to the north of Shensi, a region where finds have been particularly plentiful. It is a branch of the stylized animal art of the steppes, tinged in southern Russia by Assyro-Iranian and Greek influences. At Minusinsk, whether original or impoverished, it is fairly simplified. In the Ordos it comes in contact with Chinese aesthetics, and steppe and Chinese art interact and exert their influence one upon the other. Ordos art is particularly reminiscent of that of Minusinsk, though richer and more imaginative, in its plaques ornamented with fighting horses, horses or deer in combat with tigers, bears, and fantastic beasts, and also in the ends of shafts decorated with stags or hinds on a round boss.

Hsiung-nu art of Mongolia and the Ordos country, according to archaeological research, appears to be as ancient as that of the Scythians. In 1933 the Swedish archaeologist T. J. Arne dated the Ordos bronzes of Lwanping and Süanhwa from the early part of the third century B.C. and even from the second half of the fourth.[52] In 1935, the Japanese archaeologist Sueju Umehara, believing that Ordos art had deeply influenced the Chinese style known as that of the Warring States, which had flourished from the fifth century B.C. at least, dated the first Ordos bronzes from that period.[53] More recently, the Swedish Sinologist Karlgren put the style of the Warring States even farther back in time, to 650 B.C., thereby proving that steppe art in the shape of Ordos art also existed then, since it had brought about a modification in the Chinese style of decoration known as the Middle Chou.[54] All are agreed that the influence of Ordos art is one of the factors which, together with the laws of internal evolution and apparently working in the same direction as these, caused the transition of archaic Chinese bronzes from the Middle Chou style to that of the Warring States.[55]

The principal sites of Hsiung-nu finds range from Lake Baikal to the borders of Hopei, Shansi, and Shensi, as follows. (1) In the north, the Chita tombs in Transbaikalia, dated by Merhart from the second and third centuries B.C., and those of Derestuisk near Troitskosavsk north of Kyakhta in High Mongolia, where Siberian plaques and Chinese Han coins have been discovered, issued after 118 B.C.[56] (2) In Outer Mongolia, Noin Ula near Urga, where the Kozlov mission discovered the tomb of a Hsiung-nu prince. This tomb contained bronzes of steppe art, splendid woolen fabrics adorned in the same manner (griffin fighting an elk, a member of the cat tribe attacking a yak), every subject being treated in the finest Sarmato-Altaian manner, and also a Greek fabric representing a man with a mustache, three-quarter length, no doubt the work of some artist of the Cimmerian Bosporus. Fixing the date of all of these was a Chinese lacquer of the year 2 A.D.[57] Belonging perhaps to the same group are the frescoes discovered not far from there, at Durbelji and Ilkhe-Alyk on the Orkhon; these cannot be dated, though some fine figures of deer seem again to reveal Sarmato-Altaian influence.[58] (3) In the Ordos, the remainder of the present-day provinces of Suiyuan, Chahar, and Jehol, where numerous sites have disclosed Ordos bronzes, in particular, Lwanping near Jehol; Hattin-sum and Hallong-osso, west of the Dolonnor and north of Kalgan; Süanhwa, south of Kalgan on the Peking road; Kweihwacheng near Suiyuan; and Yülin, on the borders of the Ordos and northern Shensi. Note that some of the Süanhwa finds are dated by the presence of a Chinese "knife-coin" bearing the character *t'u* and belonging to a type in use in China during the Warring States period, from 480 to 250 B.C.[59]

Although on the whole a fair proportion of the Ordos bronzes, that is to say, the Hunnic bronzes of Inner Mongolia, are contemporary with the Chinese Warring States period (fifth–third centuries B.C.), the same art continued to flourish both there and in Outer Mongolia throughout the Chinese Han period (from the beginning of the second century B.C. to the beginning of the third century A.D.), as is proved by part of the dated finds at Noin Ula, by the existence in the Ordos of a number of bronze plaques bearing designs of many-headed creatures which may be attributed with some accuracy to this period, and lastly by the presence among collections (the Cernuschi Museum, the Coiffard Collection, and the Loo Collection) of Chinese bronze hooks with Hunnic themes evidently copied from Ordos originals by Han artists.[60] In the succeeding period, known in China as that of the Six Dynasties (fourth and fifth centuries A.D.), the influence of Ordos art is no less apparent in certain Chinese bronze hooks ornamented with increasingly massive animal themes, all contortions and interwinings. During this same period the same steppe art is discernible in the clasps, plaques, and mounts of the West of the Great Invasions. Moreover, Arne has noted bronzes of western Siberia which preserved up to the ninth century the characteristics of the old animal style of the steppes.[61] The same art continues, perhaps until the Öngüt of the Jenghiz-Khanite period, in the little Nestorian bronzes—crosses, doves, and Paracletes—which are yielded in such numbers by the soil of the Ordos and adjacent regions.[62] Plaques of purely Ordos type, moreover, were manufactured in the middle of the Hsi-Hsia period (eleventh–twelfth centuries), unless the Hsi-Hsia characters which drew the attention of Salmony were reinscribed at that time, or unless these objects are Hsi-Hsia copies not in common use.[63]

THE FIRST THRUST OF THE HSIUNG-NU AND THE
MIGRATION OF THE YÜEH-CHIH

The Hsiung-nu appear for the first time in history as a power to be feared at the end of the third century B.C., just at the moment when China had achieved unity under the Ch'in dynasty (221–206).[64] Foreseeing the danger, the emperor Ch'in Shih Huang-ti (221–210), the founder of the dynasty, and his general Meng T'ien completed the Great Wall. This had served since 215 to protect Chinese territory from the Hsiung-nu, and around 214 Meng

T'ien drove these enemies from what is now the Ordos country, or the region enclosed by the great loop of the Yellow River. Meanwhile, however, the Hsiung-nu under their *shan-yü* T'u-man (d. about 210–209) began their expansion by attacking the Yüeh-chih, a people who until then had been established in western Kansu. In the east, Mao-tun, son of and successor to T'u-man (ca. 209–174), defeated the Tung-nu, other barbarians of the Manchurian borders. Taking advantage of the civil wars that had weakened China between the fall of the Ch'in dynasty (206) and the advent of the Han (202), he invaded the Chinese province of Shansi in 201 and laid siege to the capital, Taiyüan. The founder of the Han dynasty, the emperor Kao-ti, hastened to the scene, drove back the Hsiung-nu, but was then blockaded by them on the Paiteng plateau near Pingcheng, in the present-day district of Tatung, on the frontiers of Shansi. He extracted himself from this trap only by negotiation, in which he gained advantage over the barbarians. A Chinese princess or lady-in-waiting was given in marriage to the *shan-yü:* poor "partridge" delivered over to the "wild bird of Mongolia," as Chinese poets were later to sing.

About 177 or 176, Mao-tun brought disaster for the first time on the Yüeh-chih of western Kansu, which he boasts of having subjugated. His son and successor Lao-shang (ca. 174–161) was to put an end to the danger of the Yüeh-chih, make their king's skull into a drinking cup, chase them from Kansu, and force them emigrate westward, thus giving rise to the first historically recorded movement of peoples originating in the high plateaus of Asia.[65]

The name Yüeh-chih comes down—at any rate in this form—only from its Chinese transcription.[66] Many Orientalists, however, have long been inclined to identify this people with the Tokhari (a people well known to Greek historians from their having emigrated in the second century B.C. from Turkestan to Bactria) and with the Indo-Scythians of the same historians. According to this system, Tokhari and Indo-Scythians were names applied to a single people at two periods of their existence, this people being regarded as having Scythian affinities, or of Indo-European stock. This identification is based chiefly on the fact that in the Chinese region of present-day western Kansu—which according to Chinese historians had been in the early part of the second century B.C.

the country of the Yüeh-chih—the geographer Ptolemy noted as late as the second century A.D. a *Thagouri* people, a mount *Thagouron,* and a town *Thogara.*[67] Elsewhere Strabo mentions Tokharoi among the peoples who took Bactria from the Greeks exactly at the time when Chinese historians show the Yüeh-chih arriving at the end of their migration at the frontiers of Ta-hsia, that is, Bactria.[68] So consistent a parallel seems to form a strong argument in support of those who still see in the Yüeh-chih of the Chinese annals the Tokharoi of the Greek historians, the Tukhara of the Sanscrit texts, and the future Indo-Scythians of the Roman period.[69] Moreover, as late as the fifth and eighth centuries A.D., Indo-European languages were still spoken in the oases north of the Tarim, a region which must still have been a part, if not of the earlier domain of the Yüeh-chih (since these are shown to be natives of Kansu), then at least that of more or less kindred tribes at Turfan, Kara Shahr, and Kucha. These Indo-European languages were known to linguists until quite recently as Tokharian languages, though today they are content to designate them as Kuchean, Karashahri, and so on. It seems likely, then, that at the dawn of history, Indo-European tribes advanced a long way toward the Far East. The hypothesis is the more acceptable since western Siberia and perhaps even the Minusinsk region seem to have been inhabited before our era by peoples of Scytho-Sarmatian affinities, and since both faces of the T'ien Shan near Fergana and Kashgar were inhabited in the Achaemenid period by the Saka, a people of eastern Iranian speech. Thus a large part of the Turkestan of today would have been peopled by Indo-Europeans, those near Kashgar being of eastern Iranian stock, those of Kucha in Kiuchüan of Tokharian. The Yüeh-chih correspond to this latter branch.

The earliest information given by Chinese historiography, however, concerns the first reverses suffered by "Indo-Europeanism" at these outposts. As was seen, the Hsiung-nu under their *shan-yü* Mao-tun (ca. 209–174) had seriously defeated the Yüeh-chih. The succeeding *shan-yü,* Lao-shang (ca. 174–161), killed the king of the Yüeh-chih and had his skull made into a cup.[70] He forced these people to leave Kansu and flee to the west across the northern Gobi.[71] A small proportion of them, known by the Chinese as Little Yüeh-chih (Hsia Yüeh-chih), settled south of the Nanshan among the K'iang or Tibetans, whose language they adopted, as the *Ch'ien Han Shu* relates two and a half centuries later.[72] The other Yüeh-chih clans, called Great Yüeh-chih (Ta Yüeh-chih) by the Chinese, attempted to settle in the Ili valley and the Issyk Kul basin, but were at once driven out by the Wu-sun (pronounced Oo-soon).[73] Chinese historians describe these Wu-sun as blue-eyed, red-bearded people. Charpentier, relating this name Oo-soon to that of the Asianoi or Asioi—another name for the Sarmatian people known as Alans—sees in the Wu-sun the ancestors or kinsfolk of the Alans.[74] If this hypothesis is correct, it must be these Wu-sun who in part flocked in the direction of southern Russia under pressure similar to that of the Yüeh-chih and the Hsiung-nu; and here indeed, albeit somewhat earlier than the period in question, the Scythians were being progressively replaced by Sarmatian peoples.

However this may be, the Yüeh-chih were driven from Kansu by the Hsiung-nu, and in their westward surge hurled themselves upon the Wu-sun near the Ili. The Wu-sun were temporarily vanquished by the newcomers, but soon rebelled with the help of the Hsiung-nu. The Yüeh-chih then resumed their westward march and reached the upper Syr Darya (the Jaxartes of Greek geographers) in the province of Fergana (the Ta-yüan of the Chinese), where the *Ch'ien Han Shu* notes their arrival in about 160 B.C. There they were on the borders of the Greek kingdom of Bactria, where the Greco-Bactrian king Eukratides must have been coming to the end of his reign.

REPERCUSSIONS OF THE FIRST VICTORIES OF THE HUNS;
COLLAPSE OF GREEK DOMINATION IN AFGHANISTAN

The regions of Tashkent, Fergana, and Kashgar were inhabited by the people known to the Chinese under the name of *Sse* (ancient pronunciation, *Ssek*), to the Persians and Indians as Saka, or Shaka, and to the Greeks as Sakai: our Sakas. They were in fact the "Scythians of Asia." They formed a branch of the great Scytho-Sarmatian family; that is, they were nomadic Iranians from the northwestern steppes. The language which, since the works of Lüders, it seems reasonable to attribute to them—the Saka language, of which a number of manuscripts dating from the early Middle Ages were found at Khotan by the Aurel Stein mission—is an "East Iranian" dialect. The rebound of the Yüeh-chih upon the Saka populations had a general repercussion among them and resulted in their invasion of the realm founded in Bactria by Greek kings, Alexander's successors. According to the theory generally accepted up to the time of W. W. Tarn, the Saka, under pressure from the Yüeh-chih, overran Sogdiana and then Bactria, there taking the place of the Greeks. Between 140 and 130, Bactria was in fact captured from the Greek king Heliocles by nomad tribes, of whom the best known, according to Strabo, were the *Asioi, Pasianoi, Tokharoi,* and *Sakaraulai,* all from lands north of the Jaxartes (Syr Darya). It is in any case difficult to identify these tribes exactly. As has been said, Jarl Charpentier saw in the *Asioi,* whom Pompeius Trogus calls *Asianoi,* the Wu-sun of the Ili, mentioned by Chinese historians.[75] The *Sakaraulai* or *Saraucae* (*Saka Rawaka*) seem to suggest an ancient Saka tribe. As for the Tokharoi, according to the hypothesis maintained by H. W. Bailey, they were the very nucleus of the Yüeh-chih people.[76]

In 128 B.C., when the Chinese ambassador Chang Ch'ien came to visit the Yüeh-chih, the Chinese historian Ssu-ma Ch'ien mentions them as having conquered and occupied Sogdiana ("the country north of the river Wei," that is, north of the Oxus), where, the *Ch'ien Han Shu* tells, they had for their capital the town of Kienshih. Toru Haneda identifies this name phonetically with Kanda, an abbreviation of Markanda or Samarkand.[77] The two Chinese accounts add that the Yüeh-chih had subjugated "Ta-hsia"—that is, Bactria—though they seem not to have occupied it, at least at that time.[78] Tarn wonders (erroneously) whether the lords of Bactria thus conquered by the Yüeh-chih may still have been Greeks—in which case the Saka could not have driven them from the country—rather than the Saka themselves. Many Orientalists believe at any rate that very shortly afterward, say, about 126, the Yüeh-chih, being no longer satisfied with their suzerainty over Bactria, crossed the Oxus and actually occupied that province. They base this view on the passage in the *Hou Han Shu* which states explicitly that the Yüeh-chih emigrated to Ta-hsia and divided the country among five chiefs, or *She-hu* (*yabghu*). It is true that the *Ch'ien Han Shu,* a history written nearer to the time of these events, seems less clear on the point. It says merely that "the Ta-hsia [that is, the people of Bactria] had no great chiefs but only petty chieftains of towns and hamlets; they were a weak people who feared war [these then cannot have been rough Greek adventurers, but barbarians of some sort], so that at the sight of the Yüeh-chih, they all made submission." [79] This is an obscure and ambiguous text which allows of no conclusion either way. But there is another, unequivocal text— that of the *Hou Han Shu*—which states that in A.D. 84 the Chinese general Pan Ch'ao asked the king of the Yüeh-chih to remonstrate with the king of Sogdiana (K'ang-kiu). [80] This means that Sogdiana and the Yüeh-chih country were quite distinct at this date; therefore, the Yüeh-chih people must be sought elsewhere, probably farther south toward Bactria. After a sojourn north of the Oxus, they had crossed the river and then replaced the Saka in Bactria. According to Tarn (whose opinion we cannot accept), they had captured Bactria almost directly from the Greeks. [81] In any event, their migration was the signal for a general tumult of the peoples and a surge of nomads across eastern Iran. Thrust back in the south by the Yüeh-chih, the Saka occupied Drangiana (Seistan) and Arakhosia (Kandahar). The occupation was permanent, for from that time those countries became in Iranian nomenclature "the Saka country," Sakastana, whence the modern Persian Seistan.

From there all these nomads fell upon the Parthian Empire and came near to destroying it. The Parthian king Phraates II, threatened in Media by Antiochos VII, king of Syria, and his attempted Seleucid reconquest (129 B.C.), had been rash enough to invoke the aid of some of the barbarians. They came but soon turned against Phraates himself, who was defeated and killed (128 or 127 B.C.). A new king of Parthia, Artebanus II, was mortally wounded, Pompeius Trogus tells, during a counterattack against the Tokhari in 124 or 123. This would seem to prove that the Yüeh-chih of Chinese history—if they correspond, as supposed, to the Tokharoi of Greek history—were from that time established in Bactria, a country of which they later made a "Tokharistan." The Parthian king Mithridates II (123–88) succeeded, it is true, in stopping the nomad invasions and even in imposing his suzerainty over the Saka of Seistan. Nevertheless in 77 the Sakaraulai were strong enough in Iran to place on the Parthian throne an Arsacid of their own choice: their protégé Sinatrukes or Sanatroikes, who later sought to oppose them and perished under their blows (ca. 70 B.C.)

The subsequent destinies of the Saka and the Yüeh-chih of these regions form part of the history of Iran and India. It is enough to recall here that from Seistan and Kandahar the Saka expanded to Kabul and the Punjab; then, when these countries were occupied by the Yüeh-chih, to Malvan and Gujarat, where Saka satraps remained until the fourth century A.D. As for the Yüeh-chih of Bactria, Chinese history shows them as founding in the first century of this era the great dynasty of the Kushans (in Chinese, Kuei-shuang).[82] These Kushans, so the *Ch'ien Han Shu* tells us, were one of the five clans which about 128 B.C. divided Bactria between them.

The *Hou Han Shu* relates how the chief of the Kushans, Ch'iu-chiu-ch'ueh [83] (the Kujula Kadphises of coins), founded by means of the submission of the other Yüeh-chih clans the Kushan Empire, known to the Greeks and Romans under the name of Empire of the Indo-Scythians. The Kushan emperors Kujula or Kujolo Kadphises or Kadphises I (between 30 and 91 or 92), Vima Kadphises or Kadphises II (between 92 and about 132), Kanishka (between about 144 and 172), Huvishka (ca. 172–217), and Vasudeva (ca. 217–244) extended their sway from Kabul over part of northern India (the Punjab and Mathura).[84] It is also known how great a part Kanishka played in the dissemination of Buddhism into Central Asia. The aim here is to show the colossal impact of the first Hunnic thrust on the destinies of Asia. In driving the Yüeh-chih from Kansu, the Hsiung-nu had started a sequence of repercussions which were felt as far away as Western Asia and India. Afghanistan was lost to Hellenism; the last vestiges of Alexander's conquest in these regions had been wiped out; Parthian Iran had been temporarily shaken and the tribes thrust back from Kansu had found an unlooked-for empire in Kabul and northwest India. The same process continues throughout the history which is our present study. The slightest impulse at one end of the steppe inevitably sets in motion a chain of quite unexpected consequences in all four corners of this immense zone of migrations.

CONFLICTS BETWEEN THE HSIUNG-NU AND THE EARLY HAN;
SPLIT WITH THE WESTERN HSIUNG-NU

The removal of the Yüeh-chih increased the importance of the Hsiung-nu. From that time forward they dominated both sides

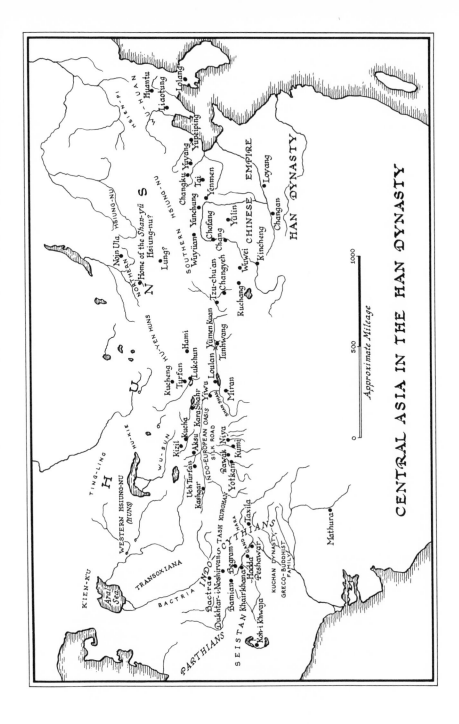

CENTRAL ASIA IN THE HAN DYNASTY

of the eastern Gobi: Upper Mongolia, where their *shan-yü* had one of his residences near what was to be Karakorum in the Orkhon region, and Inner Mongolia, at the foot of the Wall of China.[85] Their squadrons now executed daring raids into Chinese territory. In 167 they penetrated Shensi as far as Hweichung (west of the Chinese capital, Changan), where they burned an imperial palace. In 158 B.C. they returned north of the Wei, directly threatening Changan. In 142 they attacked the Great Wall toward Yenmen, near Tatung, north of Shansi. The Chinese frontier was being threatened at every point when a great emperor, Wu-ti (140–87), ascended the throne of the Han.[86]

The empire of continental Asia then belonged to the Hsiung-nu. The chief residence of their *shan-yü*—in so far as these nomads had a residence—or at least one of his summer quarters, was, as noted, on the headwaters of the Orkhon. Another of their centers, known to the Chinese by the name of Lung, is thought to have been farther south in the Gobi, toward the lower reaches of the Ongkin. Wu-ti formed a plan to drive them back to these haunts. But before giving battle, he tried to take them in the rear by allying himself with the Yüeh-chih, now settled in Sogdiana. With this aim, he sent the Yüeh-chih his ambassador, Chang Ch'ien. Having left China in 138, Chang Ch'ien was captured almost at once by the Hsiung-nu, who sent him to their *shan-yü* Kiun-ch'en.[87] There he was forcibly detained for ten years. At last he was able to escape, and reached the king of Fergana (Ta-yüan), whence he arrived in Sogdiana (K'ang-kiu). But the Yüeh-chih, pleased with their new domain, took no further interest in Gobi affairs. Chang Ch'ien set off upon his homeward journey. After being taken prisoner once more by the Hsiung-nu, who kept him for over a year, he at last returned to China in 126.[88] (In 115 a similar embassy was sent to the Wu-sun, in the Ili region, with as little success, as these people dared not engage in war against the Hsiung-nu.)

As the Yüeh-chih refused to provide the hoped-for diversion, the emperor Wu-ti started his war against the Hsiung-nu unaided. The latter had just made one of their customary raids in the direction of modern Peking (129). The Chinese general Wei Ts'ing, setting out from the region of northern Shansi, crossed the Gobi as far as Lung, on the Ongkin, and put them to flight. In 127, China established a military colony at Chofang on the Yellow

River, between the Ordos and the Alashan, to cover the great loop of the river. In 124, the Hsiung-nu invaded the Chofang marches and Wei Ts'ing drove them out. In 121, Wei Ts'ing's nephew, the young hero Ho K'iu-ping, at the head of ten thousand horsemen, also chased the Hsiung-nu from the part of Kansu formerly occupied by the Yüeh-chih and the Wu-sun, not far from the present-day towns of Liangchow, Kanchow, and Kwachow. The two minor hordes of Hsiung-nu who were in possession of this territory—the Huen-shih horde round Kanchow and the Hieuch'u round Liangchow—left the service of their *shan-yü*, offered themselves to the empire, and were established as confederates north of the Nanshan.[89] In 120, a compact Chinese colony was formed in the Ordos. In 119, Wei Ts'ing and Ho K'iu-ping—the first starting from the Kuku Hoto region in northern Shansi, the second from Shangkiu, near the modern Süanhwa, northwest of Peking—crossed the Gobi and reached what is now Outer Mongolia, the center of the Hunnic empire. Wei Ts'ing, as Albert Herrmann suggests, seems to have gone as far as the lower Ongkin. He took the *shan-yü* Yi-che-shih by surprise and put him to flight in the midst of a southerly gale which blew the sand in the faces of the Hsiung-nu. He killed or captured 19,000 barbarians. Ho K'iu-ping, by an even bolder expedition, penetrated 600 miles into Outer Mongolia as far as the approaches to the upper Tula and the upper Orkhon. He captured more than eighty Hun chiefs and made solemn sacrifices on the mountains of their country. Ho K'iu-ping died in 117, soon after his return. On this great horseman's tomb at Sienyang (Shensi) a powerful sculpture in high relief was erected, representing a horse crushing a barbarian.[90]

Once the Hsiung-nu had been thrown back into Upper Mongolia, the emperor Wu-ti created in Kansu between the years 127 and 111 a series of commanderies and military prefectures, with the object of preventing their return. The commanderies of Wuwei (near Liangchow), Changyeh (near Kanchow), Tzu-ch'uan (near Suchow), and Tunhwang, stretching from Lanchow to the Yümen pass, marked out the old Yüeh-chih country and guarded the Silk Road.[91] In 108, the Chinese general Chao P'o-nu pressed even further to the northwest, as far as the kingdoms of Loulan in Lob Nor, and of Kiu-shih, the Turfan of today. He took the king of Loulan prisoner and defeated the king of Kiu-shih.[92] For some years China had had commercial relations with Fergana (Ta-yüan in Chinese), a country inhabited no doubt by eastern Iranians or Sakas who supplied China with horses of the fine Transoxianian breed. About 105, weary of this requisitioning, the Ferganese assassinated the Chinese ambassador. In 102, the Chinese general Li Kuang-li, in a march of unexampled daring, advanced with more than sixty thousand men from Tunhwang all the way to Fergana. When he arrived, he had only thirty thousand men left. He reduced the capital of the country—perhaps Usrushna, the modern Ura Tyube—by diverting the waterways, and did not withdraw until he had received three thousand horses in tribute.[93]

Meanwhile, in the north, the Hsiung-nu had not disarmed, and the end of Wu-ti's reign was marked by a disaster similar to that of Varus, though far less serious. A young Chinese captain named Li Ling planned to lead an expedition into Upper Mongolia. Taking with him 5,000 foot soldiers he left China by Kiu-yen, on the northern reaches of the Etsin Gol, and for thirty days marched due north, in the direction of the Ongkin. Having arrived at Mount Siun-ki—no doubt somewhere near the mountain known as Tupshi—he found himself surrounded by 80,000 Hsiung-nu, whose mounted archers began harrying the little troop. He retreated toward the Chinese frontier, still pursued by nomad cavalry. "In one day the Chinese army shot 500,000 arrows and had none left. The chariots were abandoned and the march was resumed on foot. The soldiers had taken the chariot poles, and they brandished them. The officers carried knives no more than a foot long." Nevertheless, the retreating column came within thirty miles of the Chinese frontier, to the scene of the catastrophe. "They had entered a gorge. The *shan-yü* blocked the ends of it and, climbing to the top of the mountain, he caused boulders to be rolled down. Officers and men perished in great numbers. It was impossible to go forward." [94] Night was falling. Under cover of darkness, Li Ling attempted to steal into the midst of the Hsiung-nu to kill the *shan-yü*. He failed. It was each man for himself. Only four hundred Chinese succeeded in escaping and reaching the frontier; all the rest were taken prisoner, including Li Ling himself. At this news, the emperor Wu-ti flew into a rage, and the historian Ssu-ma Ch'ien, who sought to defend the reputation of the gallant Li Ling, was subjected to a cruel punishment. The "disaster of Li Ling" induced China to give up for a time this system of counterraids in Outer Mongolia. However, this moral defeat (for it involved no more than a minor detachment) did not imperil the boundaries of Kansu.[95]

Hunnic antiquities from this period come from Transbaikalia. There are, as mentioned, the recent discoveries of the tombs of Derestuisk, near Troitskosavsk, where Siberian bronze plaques are dated by Chinese coins issued since 118 B.C., and those of the tombs of Chita, which, according to Merhart, date from the second and first centuries B.C. Transbaikalia forms the Hunnic hinterland, from which the hordes who in autumn came to attack the Ordos loop drew their reserves.

During the ensuing period, the Hsiung-nu and China, without engaging in open conflict at the Great Wall or in Mongolia, struggled with one another for possession of the northern Tarim oases: that is, for control of the Silk Road. In 77, the king of Loulan in Lob Nor—which, allied with the Hsiung-nu, had revolted against Chinese suzerainty—was beheaded and a Chinese colony was established in that country, at Yi-sun. Under the Han emperor Siuan-ti (73–49), Chinese expansion in the Tarim basin made a decisive advance. "The Han," the emperor declared, "have their own code, which is a code of conquerors!" In 71, the Chinese general Ch'ang Huei went to the aid of the Wu-sun of the Ili valley against the Hsiung-nu. In 67, the kingdom of Turfan (Kiu-shih), which had joined the adherents of the Hsiung-nu, was reduced by the Chinese general Cheng Ki. In 65, another Chinese commander, Fung Fung-shih, overthrew the king of Yarkand and brought the oasis into subservience. Next year, it is true, the kingdom of Turfan was evacuated by its Chinese garrison and reverted at once to the Hsiung-nu, but it was reoccupied in 60 by Cheng Ki. After establishing an important military camp at K'iu-li, south of Kara Shahr, Cheng Ki installed himself as protector of the Tarim at Wu-lei, situated between Kara Shahr and Kucha, whence he could keep the whole region under surveillance.

Thus China snatched control of the Silk Road from the Hsiung-nu. That these should have put up so ineffectual a resistance was due to the fact that from 60 onward they were weakened by a series of civil wars. Two pretenders, Hu-han-ye and Che-che, claimed the title of *shan-yü*. In 51, Hu-han-ye went in person to the court of Changan to make an act of homage and seek the support of the Emperor Hsüan-ti. From 49, thanks to Chinese protection, he triumphed over his rival, and in 43 settled down as victor in the familiar encampments of the Orkhon. In 33, this tamed Hun went to pay court to the Son of Heaven at Changan, and received the supreme reward, coveted by all barbarians: the hand of a Chinese princess in marriage.

The vanquished Che-che, leaving old Mongolia to the vassal of China, went to seek his fortune in the west, in what is now Russian Turkestan (44 B.C.). On his way he defeated the Wu-sun of the Ili, brought under his sway the Hu-kie of the Imil and the K'ien-k'u of the Aral steppes, and made them his confederates; he even encroached upon the people of Sogdiana (K'ang-kiu) who had been so rash as to help him, and set up his camps in the steppes of the Chu and Talas rivers. This was the germ of a great Hsiung-nu empire in the west. But the Chinese left him no time to consolidate his position, for in 36 their general Ch'eng T'ang, in a raid of exceptional daring, penetrated as far as the Chu, took Che-che by surprise, and beheaded him (36–35). After this sudden drama, the Hunnic elements that had followed Che-che on his march to the Aral drop from sight. These Hsiung-nu of the west have no history, for lack of contact with any great civilized nation which might have preserved some information about them, as China did for the eastern Hsiung-nu. Not until the end of the fourth century A.D., about 370–375, when their descendants crossed the Volga and the Don to invade Europe, will these Huns be found again in classical history with Balamir and Attila.

CONFLICTS BETWEEN CHINA AND THE HSIUNG-NU DURING THE PERIOD OF THE LATER HAN DYNASTY; SPLIT WITH THE SOUTHERN HSIUNG-NU

The exodus of the western Hsiung-nu and the removal of those of the east from the affairs of the Tarim basin secured to the Chinese the hegemony of Central Asia. This situation, however, was imperiled by the civil wars in China which marked the fall of the early Han dynasty (A.D. 8 to 25). The *shan-yü* of the Hsiung-nu took advantage of these to seize the protectorate of the kingdom of Turfan (A.D. 10) and to raid the marches. The tomb of a Hsiung-nu chief of that period, discovered at Noin Ula near Urga by the Kozlov mission,[96] permits a glimpse of Hunnic culture, with fabrics displaying stylized animal motifs characteristic of Sibero-Sarmatian steppe art and the art of the Altai, as well as borrowings both from China and the Greco-Roman Crimea: namely, a Chinese lacquer dating from the year 2 of this era and a Hellenistic fabric originating in the Cimmerian Bosporus.[97]

When the second Han dynasty, known as that of the late Han, ascended the throne of China (A.D. 25), the Chinese protectorate of the Tarim had still to be restored. Very fortunately for China, the Hsiung-nu were at this time divided among themselves. In 48, the eight Hsiung-nu hordes of the south under their chief Pi rebelled against the *shan-yü* P'u-nu and made submission to China. Emperor Kuang Wu-ti bestowed upon them the status of confederates in Inner Mongolia, on the southern borders of the Gobi and the marches of Kansu and Shansi. Thus was founded the kingdom of the southern Hsiung-nu; and these, so long as China remained strong, continued as faithful dependents of the empire until, in the days of its decline in the fourth century, they became its destroyers. The story is paralleled among many federated Germanic peoples along the outskirts of the Roman Empire.

For the moment, China's only foes were the northern Hsiung-nu of the ancient Hunnic kingdom of the Orkhon in Outer Mongolia. Around A.D. 49, with the object of launching a flank attack against them, Tsi Yung, the Chinese governor of Liaotung, incited two neighboring hordes against them: the Wu-huan of the upper Liao River basin in Manchuria, and the Hsien-pi, who were most probably of Mongol stock and who led a nomadic life farther north, near the great Khingan and the River Nonni. Weakened by the secession of the southern Hsiung-nu and by the flank attack of the Hsien-pi and Wu-huan, the northern Hsiung-nu ceased to present any serious threat.

THE SILK ROAD

China profited by this success to recover the protectorate of the Tarim oases. These, as we have seen, formed a double arc running north and south of the Tarim basin. Those of the north were Turfan (then known to the Chinese as *Kiu-shih*), Kara Shahr (*Yenki*), Kucha (*Kuche*), Aksu (*Kumo*), Uch Turfan (*Wensu*), and Kashgar (*Shufu*). In the south were Loulan by the Lob Nor, Khotan (*Hotien*), and Yarkand (*Soche*).[98] That in the seventh century A.D. Indo-European dialects were still being spoken at Kara Shahr, Kucha, and no doubt also at Kashgar leads to the surmise that the inhabitants of the Tarim basin must have belonged at least in part to the Indo-European family. The Kuchean language, in its seventh-century form, shows affinity with Indo-Iranian, Hittite, Armenian, and Slavic. Though it may not be certain (as is contended by the German school of Sieg and Siegling) that the name Tokharian is applicable to the Kuchean and Karashahri dialects, their Indo-European nature is beyond dispute.[99] There is no reason to suppose that any Indo-European invasion of the Tarim took place at the beginning of our Middle Ages. It therefore seems logical to assume the existence there of an ancient Indo-European population, no doubt contemporary with the expansion of the Scytho-Sarmatians through western Siberia as far as the upper Yenisei, and with that of the Saka to both slopes of the T'ien Shan between Fergana and Kashgar. In addition to the linguistic evidence furnished by "East Iranian" in western Kashgaria and by Kuchean in the north, ethnographers adduce the testimony of Chinese historians concerning the blue eyes and red hair of the Wu-sun of the Ili, northwest of Kucha.

These petty kingdoms of the Tarim were of great economic importance, because the great caravan route between China and the Indo-Iranian and Greek worlds—the Silk Road—passed through these oases.[100] The existence of this road is confirmed by the geographer Ptolemy. Citing his predecessor Marinus of Tyre, Ptolemy states that in the first century A.D.—the period at which we have now arrived—a "Macedonian" trader named Maes Titianos sent agents to reconnoiter the route and its principal landmarks. The Silk Road started from Antioch, the capital of Roman Syria, crossed the Euphrates at Hierapolis (Menbij), entered the Parthian Empire, passed through Ecbatana (Hamadan), Rhagae or Rai near modern Teheran, Hecatompylos (Shahrud?) and Merv, and went on to Bactra (Balkh), a city which at this period belonged to the Indo-Scythians: that is to say, most probably the Yüeh-chih of the Chinese, or Tukhara of the Indians. From here the Silk Road ran on to the Pamirs. In a valley of those mountains, at the foot of the "hills of Komedai," Ptolemy relates, there was a stone tower (*lithinos pyrgos*) near which merchandise was exchanged between Levantine and "seric" (silk-carrying) caravans. Albert Herrmann places this spot between the longitudinal ranges of the Alai and the Trans-Alai, in the Pamir valley of the Kyzyl-Su, which leads from the basin of the upper Oxus to the valley of Kashgar. Hackin, who traveled in those parts, believes that the stone tower should be sought, as had been suggested earlier, near present-day Tash-Kurghan, between the Wakhan (Little Pamirs) and the headwaters of the Yarkand, north of the Minteke pass.

At Kashgar the Silk Road forked. The northern route led to Kucha, which according to Albert Herrmann was the Issedon Scythica of Alexandrian geographers; to Kara Shahr, their Damna; to Loulan on the Lob Nor, their Issedon Serica; and to the gate of Yümen Kuan (west of Tunhwang), their Daxata. We have already noted the course of the southern route from Kashgar—via Yarkand, Khotan, Niya, and Miran, the last town in the kingdom of Loulan—to the Lob Nor. The two roads reunited at Tunhwang, believed to be the Throana of Greco-Roman geographers. The Silk Road then entered China proper by way of Tzu-ch'uan (the Drosakhe of Greek geographers?) and Changyeh (Thogara?) and at last reached Changan (Sian), usually regarded as Ptolemy's Sera metropolis, and Loyang (Honan), the Saraga or Thinae of the same authority.

PAN CH'AO'S CONQUEST OF THE TARIM BASIN

Whatever the validity of the Greco-Chinese identifications, it is certain that, from the opening of the transcontinental Silk Road between the Roman and Parthian empires on the one hand and the Han Empire on the other, the petty Indo-European kingdoms strung out along the northern and southern oases of the Tarim basin came to be of considerable commercial importance. Indeed, Hsiung-nu and Chinese struggled with one another to gain control of them, the former keeping watch over the Tarim from the heights of the Altai to the north, the latter holding the points of egress in the frontier province of Tunhwang to the east.

The conquest—or reconquest—of the Tarim basin by the late

Han was a task methodically carried out during the reigns of the emperors Ming-ti (58–75), Chang-ti (76–88), and Ho-ti (89–105). The credit for it is due to a few great soldiers. In A.D. 73 the Chinese generals Keng Ping ("commander of the swift horses") and Teu Ku led a preliminary expedition against the northern Hsiung-nu, who fled before the Han legions.[101] The *ssu-ma* or cavalry general Pan Ch'ao, Teu Ku's second-in-command and one of the greatest leaders ever produced by China, was detached to attack the Hu-yen, a Hsiung-nu horde of Barkol and, having defeated them, "beheaded a great number of barbarians." [102] In the same year, 73, a Chinese military colony was founded at Yiwu, identified by Chavannes as Hami but located by Albert Herrmann between Loulan and the modern post of Yingpan, north of the Lob Nor.[103] In 74, Keng Ping and Teu Ku set forth to attack the country of Turfan, which at that time was divided into twin kingdoms, governed by members of the same dynasty: southern Kiu-shih round Turfan itself, and northern Kiu-shih toward Kucheng, on the other side of the T'ien Shan range. By a bold march, Keng Ping first attacked the more distant of the two, Kiu-shih of Kucheng, whose King Ngan-tö yielded before the onslaught: "He came out of the town, removed his cap and, embracing the hooves of Keng Ping's horse, made his submission." [104] Influenced by this capitulation, the king of Turfan, Ngan-tö's son, also surrendered. Two Chinese garrisons were left there, one in northern Kiu-shih (Kucheng), the other at Lukchun in Turfan proper.[105] Meanwhile, Pan Ch'ao was of the view that "he who does not enter the tiger's lair will never catch its cubs." Sent with a reconnaissance detachment into the kingdom of Shanshan, southwest of Loulan and the Lob Nor, he learned by a ruse that the king of that country was plotting with a Hun envoy against China. At nightfall he summoned his officers to a conference. He ought properly to have sought the advice of the Chinese civil commissioner who had been sent with him, but this he took care not to do: "He is a common civilian officer. If we tell him of our plans, he will let them leak out. At this very hour our fate is being decided. To die without glory is not the act of valiant men!" At dead of night, Pan Ch'ao and his little troop set fire to the huts in which the Hun envoys were lodged, and still further terrified the inmates by their cries and the beating of drums; they then either burned or beheaded all the barbarians. Next Pan Ch'ao summoned the king of Shanshan and showed him the severed head of the Hsiung-nu ambassador. The king, who had been on the brink of treason, reverted trembling to China's vassalage.[106] Pan Ch'ao then turned his attention to the affairs of Kashgaria proper.

In periods when neither Hsiung-nu nor Chinese intervened in their affairs, the petty Indo-European kingdoms of the Tarim quarreled among themselves. A king of Yarkand, known to the Chinese by the name of Hien (33–61), had for a time acquired hegemony over that region by subjugating Kucha (in 46), Fergana, and Khotan, but succumbed to a general rebellion.[107] Kucha then accepted the protection of the Hsiung-nu, while the king of Khotan overthrew Hien (in 61). South of the Tarim, hegemony passed to that same king of Khotan whom the Chinese called Kuang-tö and who became master of Yarkand. In the north, control went to the king of Kucha whom the Chinese called Kien. With the help of his protectors the Hsiung-nu, Kien captured Kashgar in 73.[108] At this juncture Pan Ch'ao, commissioned by the emperor Ming-ti to settle the affairs of the region, arrived in Kashgaria. He went first to Khotan, where the king, Kuang-tö,[109] who was elated by his recent successes and inclined to listen to the advice of the Hsiung-nu envoys, treated him with insolence. Pan Ch'ao summarily beheaded with his own hand the sorcerer who was the king's chief adviser. The king, in alarm, renewed his allegiance to China and, to prove his sincerity, massacred the Hun envoys. Pan Ch'ao then marched on Kashgar. Kien, the king of Kashgar, a dependent of the Hsiung-nu, had already subjugated Kashgar and placed upon its throne one of his own men, of Kuchean stock. Pan Ch'ao, taking the bull by the horns (he had very few men), arrested this foreign prince, deposed him, and restored the ancient Kashgarian dynasty in the person of a king known in Chinese transcription as Chung (A.D. 74).[110]

In 75, shortly before the death of the emperor Ming-ti, a general revolt against the Chinese protectorate broke out in the Tarim, supported by the Hsiung-nu. The king of Kara Shahr assassinated the Chinese resident, the "protector general" Ch'en Mu. The men of Kucha and Aksu came to besiege Pan Ch'ao in Kashgar, and for more than a year that hero held out against his assailants. Meanwhile, the Hsiung-nu overran the kingdom of northern Kiu-shih (Kucheng), slew the vassal king Ngan-tö, and laid siege to a local fortress of the Chinese general Keng Kung. Like his colleague Pan Ch'ao, Keng Kung put up a heroic resistance. Without provisions, and reduced to boiling and eating the leather of their equipment, he and the handful of men remaining to him held out to the last.[111] The government of the new emperor Chang-ti, however, ordered Pan Ch'ao and Keng Kung to evacuate the Tarim, for it was dismayed by these incessant rebellions and the sacrifices demanded by the Central Asian protectorate. But Pan Ch'ao realized that such a retreat would deliver the country into the hands of the Hsiung-nu. Hardly had he reached Khotan on his way home than he changed his mind and, in defiance of the orders he had received, returned to Kashgar. During his brief absence, the town had naturally fallen into the hands of the Kucheans, that is to say, the Hunnic faction. After beheading the leaders of the Kuchean party, he resumed his residence in Kashgar, determined now never to leave it. Better still, in 78, with auxiliaries raised in Kashgar and Khotan or recruited from as far away as Sogdiana, he captured Aksu and Turfan "and cut off 700 heads." [112] Meanwhile the Chinese legions of Kansu reconquered the Kiu-shih kingdom of Turfan from the Hsiung-nu. They cut off 3,800 heads and captured 37,000 head of livestock. The barbarians of the north fled in terror." [113] In adversaries such as Pan Ch'ao and Keng Kung, the Hsiung-nu had met their masters.

In a memorandum addressed to the emperor, Pan Ch'ao strove to convince the intimidated court by recounting his own experiences in the Great West. He showed that these remote campaigns, condemned by the literati as useless, were in fact realistic defensive measures, calculated to protect Chinese soil from periodic aggression by the Huns: "To capture the thirty-six kingdoms [of Central Asia] is to cut off the right arm of the Hsiung-nu." As to his method, it could be summarized in the famous formula: "Use barbarians to attack barbarians." Indeed, he had achieved the conquest of the Tarim, thanks to the contingents with which each newly conquered oasis was required to supply him for use against oases which were still in rebellion. The truly Chinese element was represented by no more than a handful of adventurers or exiles who had come to win new honor in the eventful life of the marches. All lived off the country, which they defended against the return of the Hunnic hordes. "At Yarkand and Kashgar," Pan Ch'ao explained, "cultivated land is fertile and extensive, and soldiers quartered there will cost the empire nothing." [114] This contemporary of Trajan—the conqueror of Dacia—shared that conqueror's views on military matters.

The main objective was to drive the Hsiung-nu back into Outer Mongolia, away from the Silk Road from which they derived food and wealth. With this great design in mind, Pan Ch'ao crushed fresh rebellions in Kashgar (80, 87) and Yarkand (88), and made the Wu-sun of the Ili his allies. In every instance Pan Ch'ao, who was kept informed by his spies and who had an excellent understanding of barbarian psychology, attacked his foes boldly and by surprise. At Kashgar, King Chung, his protégé and puppet, revolted in 84, together with the people of Yarkand, the Sogdians, and the Yüeh-chih or Indo-Scythians. In 87, having been driven from Kashgar by Pan Ch'ao, Chung feigned willingness to make his submission and requested an audience, at which he arrived with a strong body of cavalry, meaning to attempt a surprise attack. Pan Ch'ao pretended to be deceived and to believe in his visitor's good faith, and entertained him at a banquet. Then, "when the wine had gone round," he seized the prince and beheaded him. At the same moment the Chinese troops revealed themselves and, falling upon the enemy, massacred them. [115] In 88, before Yarkand, Pan Ch'ao had only a small army (numbering as many Khotan auxiliaries as Chinese) to pit against the inhabitants, to whose aid had come 50,000 men from Kucha and neighboring towns. During the night he pretended to withdraw; then, returning by a forced march, he fell upon the town, cut off five thousand heads, and forced the people to surrender. [116]

Only Kucha and Kara Shahr now remained in a state of rebellion, and these places were seeking allies against China from every quarter, from the Hsiung-nu of Mongolia to the Yüeh-chih or Indo-Scythians. In 90, the king of the Indo-Scythians —that is, the powerful emperor of the Kushan dynasty which ruled Afghanistan and northwest India, probably represented by Kadphises I—displeased at his failure to gain the hand of a Chinese princess in marriage, sent an expedition northeast of the Pamirs to help Kucha against Pan Ch'ao. Pan Ch'ao intercepted all the dispatches between this army and the people of Kucha, who might have victualed it, and then disappeared. The Indo-Scythians, having ventured among the limitless tracks of Kashgaria without provisions, were glad enough to withdraw unscathed. The court of the Kucha, wiser for an experience which had almost turned into disaster, reverted in the year 90 to the policy—traditional among the Yüeh-chih—of friendship with China.[117]

To the north, in Mongolia, generals Teu Hien and Keng Ping won a great victory over the northern Hsiung-nu (89–90). The two kings of northern and southern Kiu-shih (Kucheng and Turfan) at once renewed their bonds with the empire. In 91, the Chinese general Keng K'uei again inflicted a crushing defeat on the Hsiung-nu. He advanced as far as Outer Mongolia, most probably to the Orkhon, captured the mother and the whole household of the *shan-yü*, and nominated his brother Yu-ch'u-kien as his successor. When in 93 this new king revolted, China sent against him the Hsien-pi, a Mongol horde from the Manchurian borders, who defeated and killed him—a disaster from which the northern Hsiung-nu were never entirely to recover.

Thus deprived of the help both of the Hsiung-nu and of the Indo-Scythians, three of the four rebel towns north of the Tarim —Kucha, Aksu, and Turfan—surrenderd to Pan Ch'ao (91). The Chinese victor received from the imperial court the title of "protector general," in effect the viceroy of Central Asia. He took up his residence at Tokien, a small town near Kucha, while another Chinese general settled in Kashgar. Kara Shahr alone remained unsubdued. In 94, with auxiliaries from Kucha and Shanshan (Lob Nor), Pan Ch'ao marched on the rebel town. In vain had the people of Kara Shahr destroyed the bridges across the Yulduz. Pan Ch'ao forded the river waist-deep and entered the swamps before Kara Shahr. Some inhabitants were able to make their escape across Lake Bagrach, but the king had to give himself up. Pan Ch'ao, in revenge for old injuries, beheaded him at the very spot where, nineteen years before, the Chinese governor Ch'en Mu had been murdered. "Pan Ch'ao released his men to sack the town. They cut off more than 5,000 heads, took 15,000 people alive, and captured more than 300,000 head of livestock: horses, cattle, and sheep."[118]

The whole of the Tarim basin was now subdued. In 97, Pan Ch'ao ordered his second-in-command Kan Ying to set forth across Ansi—that is, across the Arsacid Parthian Empire—to Ta-ts'in, the Chinese name for the Roman Empire. But Kan Ying, alarmed by the Parthians' tales, never went beyond their territories, and turned about without reaching the Roman frontier.[119]

Pan Ch'ao retired and in 102 returned to China, where he died the same year. His successors could not emulate his native policy, which had been both flexible and realistic, and in 106 and 107 a general revolt broke out in the Tarim. The Chinese general Liang K'in was besieged in Kucha by the local inhabitants.[120] He extricated himself by a great victory, but in 107 the court of China, discouraged by these continual rebellions, recalled all the Tarim garrisons, even those of Lukchun and Yiwu. The following year the K'iang or Tibetans, who were then entirely savage and lived a nomadic life west and south of the Koko Nor, attacked the Chinese posts of Kansu, threatening to cut the Tunhwang road. Liang K'in, at the price of some fierce fighting, held them off (108). At last, in 109, the southern Hsiung-nu in Inner Mongolia launched an assault on the Chinese border. The Chinese governor of Liaotung, Keng K'uei, stirred up some Hsien-pi hordes against them. Nevertheless, the southern Hsiung-nu harried northern Shansi until in 110 Liang K'in compelled them to make peace.

On the whole, China was finding much difficulty in defending her own frontiers when in 119 the work of reconstruction began. The military colony of Yiwu (Hami or Lob Nor?) was re-established, Shanshan and the king of Turfan once more made submission; yet shortly afterward, the *shan-yü* of the northern Hsiung-nu and Kucheng Kiu-shih surprised and massacred the Chinese garrison of Yiwu. Pan Ch'ao's son Pan Yung at last restored all that his father had achieved. In 123, he re-established a military colony at Lukchun, near Turfan; in 124, he bolstered up the loyalty of the king of Shanshan, intimidated the kings of Kucha and Aksu, who came to make their submission, and, with the forces which they put at his disposal, drove the Hsiung-nu bands from Turfan. In 126, he temporarily subdued even the Hu-yen—a group of northern Hsiung-nu inhabiting the country northeast of Lake Bar Kol—and put to flight the main body of northerners who had aspired to intervene.[121] In 127, the Chinese completed the reconquest of the Tarim by entering Kara Shahr. In 130, the son of the king of Kashgar and also an embassy from the king of Fergana arrived at the Chinese capital in Loyang to pay court to the emperor Shuen-ti.

In the course of the succeeding years—except for a brief revolt from 140 to 144 of a chief of the southern Hsiung-nu of the left or eastern branch [122]—China's difficulties originated mainly with the Hu-yen Hsiung-nu of Barkol. In 131, they attacked northern Kiu-shih (Kucheng) and ill-treated its population; in 151, they almost destroyed the Chinese military colony of Yiwu, which was saved only by enormous effort. Nevertheless, in 153 northern Kiu-shih was still China's vassal. In 151, the inexpedient brutality of a Chinese commissioner provoked the revolt of the people of Khotan, who murdered him, though afterward the town made an *amende honorable*.[123] In 170, Chinese generals made use of contingents from Turfan, Kara Shahr, and Kucha in an admonitory expedition all the way to Kashgar as arbiters of local disputes; in 168–169, the Chinese general Tuan Kung repelled the incursions of the K'iang or Tibetans along the borders of Kansu.

CIVILIZATION OF THE TARIM OASES AT THE END OF ANTIQUITY
AND THE BEGINNING OF THE MIDDLE AGES

China's control of the Silk Road at the time of the later Han, by ensuring freedom of transcontinental trade along the double chain of oases north and south of the Tarim, favored the dissemination of Buddhism in the river basin, and with it Indian literature and Hellenistic art. Or, to put it more precisely, along the Silk Road, which was also the route taken by Indian missionaries who came to preach Buddhism in Kashgaria and China, trade and religion carried Greco-Roman art with them. The activities of Maes Titianos' agents were aimed much in the same direction as those of the apostles of Buddha.

The busiest route at this time seems to have been the southern one: the one passing through Yarkand and Khotan. At Yotkan, the ancient Khotan, the Aurel Stein expedition discovered Roman coins of the reign of Emperor Valens (364–378); at Rawak, east of Khotan, it came upon a series of Greco-Buddhic bas-reliefs, with fine Hellenistic drapery, of the purest Gandharan style. A little farther east, at Niya (Niyang), a site abandoned at the end of the third century, Roman seals and intaglios and Indo-Scythian coins were found. At Miran, southwest of Lob Nor, in old Shanshan, the same expedition uncovered some beautiful Greco-Buddhic frescoes, portraying chiefly the Buddha, his monks, and winged genies of a markedly Romano-Asian appearance. These frescoes were signed "Tita" in Indian characters—a name which has been identified with Titus—and all of them apparently date from the third and fourth centuries A.D.[124]

It was by this same Silk Road, at the period of the Chinese Peace, that the great Buddhist missionaries came to China. An Shih-kao, a Parthian, arrived there in 148 and died in 170; Chu Sho-fu, an Indian, and Che Ch'an, a Yüeh-chih—that is, an Indo-Scythian—both came about 170 and founded a religious community in Loyang, the capital. Between 223 and 253, Che K'ien, the son of a Yüeh-chih ambassador, was to translate several Buddhist writings into Chinese. Mention of these Yüeh-chih is interesting, for it shows that it was the Kushan Empire, then extending across Afghanistan, Gandhara, and the Punjab, which by means of the Silk Road so largely contributed to the propagation of Buddhism in the Tarim basin and in China. It is no less valuable to know that, besides these Kushan or Indian missionaries, there were so many Parthian converts to carry on the work of proselytism in High Asia and the Far East. The Chinese *Tripitaka* gives us a list of missionaries and translators who came via the Tarim to work in China. In the Tarim itself, other groups of monks, from eastern Iran and northwest India, engaged in translating their sacred Sanskrit texts into the local tongues, ranging from "East Iranian" to Kuchean. The example of the famous Kumarajiva (344–413) is characteristic, and deserves to be recalled here.

Kumarajiva belonged to a family of Indian origin, settled in Kucha. Ancestors of his had held exalted positions in the country. His father, a devout Buddhist, desired to renounce his worldly honors and embrace the monastic life, but the king of Kucha compelled him to continue in his secular occupations, and gave him his sister in marriage. Of this union Kumarajiva was born. As a boy he was taken to Kashmir by his mother, to be instructed in Indian literature and in Buddhism. On his return, Kumarajiva visited Kashgar, where he remained for a year and continued to study the *Abhidharma*. The text of his biography [125] shows that Kashgar, like Kucha, was at this time a rich center of Indian thought—so much so that the rulers of these two cities contended for the honor of lodging at their courts so learned a monk as young Kumarajiva. When Kumarajiva returned to Kucha, the ruler of the country, named in Chinese transcription Po Shuen, came to greet him, and two of the grandsons of the king of Yarkand became his disciples. He lived in Kucha with his Indian master Vimalaksha (who was originally from Kashmir) until 382–383, when, as we shall see, the Chinese general Lu Kuang, having invaded Kucha, carried Kumarajiva with him back to China. The story of Lu Kuang provides evidence of the splendor of the Kuchean palaces, which astounded the Chinese conqueror. His amazement leads one to suppose that the buildings and works of art which he beheld there were in the Indian and Iranian tradition rather than the Chinese, and that it is to approximately this period, as Hackin affirms, that the oldest paintings of Kizil must be attributed.

Civilization in Continental Asia, as such examples show, was sharply divided into two longitudinal belts. In the north, from Pontic Russia to Manchuria and the Ordos, is the art of the steppe: nomad art *par excellence*, characterized by bronze sconces and hilt terminals, a stylized animal art of a distinctly ornamental character. In the south, along the Silk Road from Afghanistan to Tunhwang through the double chain of oases surrounding the Tarim basin, and among the sedentary peoples of those caravan oases, there are paintings and sculptures inspired directly by Greek, Iranian, and Indian art, all three diffused along the Silk Road and blended together by the Buddhist religion, in terms of Buddhist demand.

The origin of this art of the Tarim at the end of antiquity and beginning of the Middle Ages must be sought in Afghanistan. There, in the Kabul valley in the fourth century, the last Kushan kings had been strongly influenced by Sassanian Persia, into whose orbit they were drawn, as may be seen by the Kushano-Sassanian coinage studied by Herzfeld and Hackin.[126] A Sassano-Buddhic civilization and a Sassano-Buddhic art were born on these Indo-Iranian borders, as is illustrated by the great frescoes of Bamian and Kakrak, produced at the end of the third century and during the fourth. In these—in the types and costumes portrayed and in the treatment of the figures—the Sassanian influence is striking. Further examples are provided by the Sassano-Brahman statuary recently discovered by Hackin at Khairkhana near Kabul (end of the fourth century), and the purely Sassanian frescoes of Dukhtar-i-Noshirvan, near Rui on the Kabul-Bactra road, where a royal Sassanid prince, governor of Bactria (fifth century), is represented. All these were discovered by the Hackin-Godard and Hackin-Carl expeditions. In them the Afghanistan of that time is seen as a land where Indian religions and Indian literary culture were closely associated with the material civilization of Persia in the days of the Shapur and Chosroes kings.[127]

This was the Sassano-Buddhic blend which Buddhist missionaries, emulators of Kumarajiva, implanted in all the Tarim oases and at the various stops along the Silk Road, which, thanks to them, had become the road of religious teaching. It was to the Bamian frescoes that the early style of the frescoes of Kizil—somewhat west of Kucha—was related: a style characterized by precise modeling and very gentle and discreet colors: gray, bister, red-brown, dark brown, and light green. Hackin, to whom is owed the chronology of these different periods, dates this style between approximately 450 and 650.[128] Indian influence predominates here with the dance of Queen Chandraprabha, reminiscent of the fine Indian nudes of Ajanta. Sassanian influence is also evident, notably in the Peacock Cave and the Cave of the Painter—the painter who portrayed himself in the guise of a young Iranian lord, wearing an elegant light-colored jerkin, fitting closely at the waist, with the large Kuchean turned-over collar (noted at Bamian in the frescoes reproduced by Madame Godard), trousers, and high boots, all garments borrowed from Iran. Then the wonderful stuccos discovered in 1937 at Fundukistan, west of Kabul, by Hackin and Jean Carl, and dated by coins minted by the Sassanid king Chosroes II (590–628), confirm us in the centainty that, up to the eve of the Arab conquest, Irano-Buddhic Afghanistan continued to inspire masculine fashion and dress in Kuchean society.[129]

The second style of the Kizil frescoes is placed by Hackin between 650 and 750; according to him, it was characterized by less definite modeling and brighter colors (lapis lazuli and vivid green), and by a predominance of the Sassanian style of dress. The Buddhic frescoes of Kizil and Kumtura, now in Berlin, thus show processions of the donors, male and female, who bring to life the court of the kings of Kucha from the fifth to the eighth century. This glittering aristocracy—clearly of Indo-European stock—was as pronouncedly Iranian in dress and other aspects of material civilization as it was Indian in its faith and its literature. Besides this court dress, the military scenes at Kizil —as, for example, in that of "The Sharing of the Relics"—show a Kuchean "chivalry" in plate armor, conical helmets, and coats of mail, carrying long lances and reminiscent both of Sassanian cavalry and the Sarmatian horsemen of Kerch (Panticapaeum) in the Crimea.[180]

This Irano-Buddhic complex is to be found also in the area south of the Tarim, particularly in the paintings on wooden panels of Dandan-Uilik, an oasis situated northeast of Khotan (end of the seventh century). Here are, side by side, a *nagi* of purely Indian type, akin to the most graceful nudes of Ajanta; a horseman and a camel driver, both Iranian in character; and a bearded bodhisattva wearing the tiara, long green coat, trousers, and boots of a Sassanian lord. Lastly, the same Iranian influences may be observed in the frescoes and miniatures of the Turfan region, at Bezeklik and Murtuk, for example. At Bezeklik, the divine personages wearing the cuirass remind one of the Kuchean horsemen in Sassanian armor of Kizil and Kumtura, while a certain Avalokiteshvara, notes Hackin, preserves a purely Indian grace. At Murtuk too, alongside bodhisattvas of an entirely Indian appearance, are donors arrayed in the same armor as is seen at Kizil, and wearing helmets adorned with spread wings, these again having clearly defined Sassanian affinities.[181] In sculpture, there are the delicate little stucco figurines of Kara Shahr, found by Sir Aurel Stein, which so curiously resemble a gallery of representative ethnic types. They bear a strong resemblance to the Greco-Buddhic figurines of Hadda in Afghanistan, now in the Guimet Museum.

Thus before the conquest of the country by Turkic nations in the second half of the eighth century, the Indo-European oases in the north and south of the Tarim, from Yarkand and Khotan to the Lob Nor, and from Kashgar, Kucha, and Kara Shahr to Turfan, derived their culture not from the Altai and the steppe civilization but from the great civilizations of India and Iran. They formed an Outer India and an Outer Iran extending to the Chinese frontier. In addition, it was owing to them that both India and Iran penetrated China itself, as is shown by Buddhic frescoes and banners discovered by the Pelliot and Aurel Stein expeditions near Tunhwang, the point at which the Silk Road entered what is today the Chinese province of Kansu.[132]

SUPPLANTING OF THE NORTHERN HSIUNG-NU BY THE HSIEN-PI IN THE EMPIRE OF MONGOLIA

While the Greco-Buddhic and Irano-Buddhic civilization throve undisturbed among the sedentary inhabitants of the Tarim oases, Turko-Mongol hordes were slaughtering one another in the northern steppe. Around 155, the northern Hsiung-nu, who were most probably of Turkic stock and were established in the Orkhon region of upper Mongolia, were crushed and subjugated by other hordes: those of the Hsien-pi, who originated in the Khingan region, on the Mongol-Manchurian borders. These Hsien-pi, long thought to be Tungus, seem, according to the research of Pelliot and Torii, more likely to have been Mongols.[133] Thus Mongol domination succeeded Turkic. The Hsien-pi chief, called by the Chinese Tan-shih-huai, having conquered the northern Hsiung-nu, advanced on western Mongolia as far as the Wu-sun people of the Ili, whom he defeated. Chinese chroniclers note that in 166 he held sway from Manchuria to the Wu-sun country, as far as Balkhash. No doubt this is something of an exaggeration; Hsien-pi dominion would scarcely have extended beyond the present-day territories of Bogdo-khan (Tushetu-khan) and Setserlik-mandal (Sain Noyan).

Having attained to this amount of power, the Hsien-pi chief began to pursue the same covetous aims against China as his Hsiung-nu predecessors. In 156 Tan-she-huai attacked what is now the province of Liaotung, but was driven back. He then turned upon the southern Hsiung-nu of Inner Mongolia, who owed allegiance to China, and later, having come to an understanding with them, induced them to join him in an attack upon the Chinese marches of Shensi and Kansu; but the combined hordes were forced to retreat before the Chinese army (158). A fresh attack by the Hsien-pi upon Liaosi—that is, upon the

Chinese province west of the lower Liao River in the southwest of Manchuria—was also repulsed in 177 by the Chinese general Chao Pao. At last the Wu-huan, nomad hordes of the Dalai Nor (Hulun Nor) and Shara Muren (Liao River) region south of the great Khingan range, were cut to pieces in 207, in what is now Jehol, by the Chinese general Ts'ao Ts'ao. In 215–216, having settled the remnants of the southern Hsiung-nu in the depopulated marches north of the present-day provinces of Shensi, Shansi, and Hopei, Ts'ao Ts'ao divided them into five hordes, placing at the head of each a native chief under the surveillance of a Chinese resident. The official *shan-yü* of the southern Hsiung-nu was held in semicaptivity at the imperial court.[134]

When in 220 the Han dynasty disappeared amid civil wars, the hordes of the northern steppe, who had been soundly beaten during the preceding period by Chinese legions, were still either too greatly intimidated or weakened to take advantage of the situation. The Indo-European Tarim oases also, despite the civil wars raging between the "Three Kingdoms" of China, successors to the Han, continued to owe allegiance to the chief of these kingdoms, that of Wei, master of northern China (220–265). Thus it was that in 224 Shanshan (Lob Nor), Kucha, and Khotan paid homage to Ts'ao Pei, the king of Wei. When Wei and the two other Chinese kingdoms were superseded by the Chin dynasty (Ssu-ma family) which reunited China, the king of Kucha sent his son to serve at the imperial court (285). The Hsien-pi, emboldened to attack the borders of Kansu near Liangchow (Wuwei), had been repulsed by the Chinese general Ma Lung in 279.

The great Hsiung-nu Empire had vanished, and the Hsien-pi who had taken its place showed themselves incapable of resuming their assault on the Chinese frontier. It was at this moment, when no perils from the steppe seemed to threaten China, that the great barbarian invasions of the fourth century began, those invasions so similar to the *Völkerwanderung* of our fifth century. However, unlike those of Europe, these invasions seem not to have been touched off by the turbulence of the barbarian hinterland or set in motion by any Attila, but to have been caused merely by the decline of Chinese might, which sucked in as by a vacuum the federated barbarians who until then had remained encamped along the frontiers.

THE GREAT INVASIONS OF THE FOURTH CENTURY; NORTH CHINA
CONQUERED BY THE HSIUNG-NU AND THE HSIEN-PI

We have noted the successive rifts which weakened the
Hsiung-nu. Since the third century B.C. they had dominated Outer
and Inner Mongolia under the rule of a *shan-yü* resident by preference on the Orkhon. The first breach occurred when, in 44 B.C.,
a chief named Che-che was driven by a rival from the lands of
his fathers in Mongolia and emigrated to the Balkhash region, in
what is now the Kazakh S.S.R. A separation was thus effected between the eastern Hsiung-nu in Mongolia, who were to remain
China's enemies, and the Hsiung-nu of the west, in the steppes of
Balkhash and the Aral, who under the name of Huns (the forebears of Attila) were to be the adversaries of the Roman world.

In 48 A.D., the empire of the eastern Hsiung-nu was itself di-
vided; the "eight hordes" of southern or Inner Mongolia split
away from those which remained loyal to the *shan-yü* of the
Orkhon. Thus two distinct new groups were formed: the northern
Hsiung-nu on the Orkhon in Outer Mongolia, and the southern
Hsiung-nu of Inner Mongolia, north of the Great Wall. As we
have just seen, the northern Hsiung-nu had been subjugated
around 155 A.D. by the Hsien-pi: Mongol hordes originating in the
Khingan region in eastern Mongolia on the Manchurian borders.
The Hsien-pi, as has also been noted, then dominated Mongolia
from the Manchurian frontier to the approaches of Hami and
Barkol.

Toward the end of the Han dynasty, the Hsiung-nu of the
south, with whom from now on we shall be exclusively concerned, having been thrust ever farther southward under pressure
from the Hsien-pi, took flight, as noted into the great loop of the
Yellow River, into the Ordos steppe, and into the adjoining portion of the Alashan, where they established themselves at the
period of the Three Kingdoms (220–265). Here they acted as
confederates of the Chinese empire, a role somewhat similar to
that of the numerous Germanic tribes on the outskirts of the
Roman Empire in the fourth century. The relations between the
leaders of these federated Hsiung-nu of the Ordos and the
Chinese emperors of the Wei and northern Chin dynasties (220–
265 and 265–316 respectively) were much like those prevailing

between the Gothic, Frankish, and Burgundian leaders of the fourth century and the Roman emperors of the line of Constantine or Theodosius. In both instances the barbarian chiefs frequented the imperial capital—Changan or Loyang, Milan or Constantinople—were admitted to these decaying courts as intimates, and, having profited by what they had seen, returned to their hordes.

As confederates, then—as troops in the emperor's service—the southern Hsiung-nu, pressing ever farther south, established themselves on the Chinese side of the Great Wall.[135] Their *shan-yü* Hu-ch'u-ch'uan (195–216) took up his residence at Pingyang in the heart of Shansi. It was the eve of the fall of the Han dynasty in China, and civil war was at its height. Hu-ch'u-ch'uan, recalling opportunely that one of his remoter ancestors had been a Han princess, assumed the patronymic of that great imperial dynasty: Liu. Thus legitimacy, extinguished in China by a series of usurpers, was reborn in the tents of the Hsiung-nu. In 304, one of these Hsiung-nu chiefs with the Han name Liu Yüan, now firmly established at Taiyüan in Shansi, obtained from the Chinese court of the Chin the title of *shan-yü* of the Five Hordes. In 308, at the head of an army of 50,000 Hsiung-nu, he proclaimed himself emperor at Taiyüan on the pretext of being the legitimate heir to the Han. The dynasty founded by this Hun ruler is indeed known by the name of the northern Han—Pei-Han—or of the early Chao—Ts'ien-Chao.

The son and successor of Liu Yüan, Liu Ts'ung (310–318), was China's Attila. In 311, his troops took possession of Loyang, the Chinese capital, burned the imperial palace, and took the emperor Chin Huai-ti prisoner; then pressed on to Changan, where they massacred half the population (312). The imperial captive was sent to Pingyang, the residence of Liu Ts'ung, who forced him to serve as his cupbearer until his execution in 313. After the departure of the Hsiung-nu, the new emperor of China, Chin Min-ti (312–316), had taken up residence at Changan, but in 316 the Hsiung-nu returned, blockaded the city, and compelled the feeble ruler to capitulate. Once more, at Pingyang, the enthroned Hun king received a captive emperor of China, forced him to "rinse the cups at banquets," and at last, in 318, had him too executed. Giving up all hope of defending northern China against the barbarians, a member of the Chin imperial family escaped and took refuge in Nanking (then known as Kienkang), where, sheltered by the line of the Yangtze, he founded a second Chin dynasty called the southern or eastern Chin (317). In the same way the last Romans of the fifth century were to abandon their western provinces to the Germanic invaders and take refuge in the empire of the East. For nearly three centuries (317–589), Nanking would take the place of Changan and Loyang, as Constantinople was to replace Rome.

Liu Ts'ung, the victorious Hun of northern China, was for a time a looming figure. Master of the old imperial capitals of Loyang and Changan, he kept court at Pingyang in Shansi and ruled over central and southern Shansi, over Shensi (except for the Han basin), northern Honan (except for Kaifeng), southern Hopei, and northern Shantung. But to the north of this Hunnic realm, whose chief, despite his barbarian way of life, retained some veneer of Chinese culture (he had been brought up at the imperial court), surged other hordes of purely barbarian character. The horde of the Tabgatch, or in Chinese Toba,[136] probably of Turkic origin, had set camp around 260 in the extreme north of Shansi, north of the Great Wall. During the succeeding years the Toba moved south of the Wall into the old Chinese commanderies of Yenmen (Shoping) north of Shansi, and Tai (near Yuyü), that is, in the Tatung district, where in 310 they were firmly settled.[137] Finally the Mu-jung clan of the Mongol Hsien-pi horde founded a new kingdom in Liaotung and Liaosi, in the southwest of present-day Manchuria.

Most of these Turko-Mongol states which arose in northern China during the fourth century were as unstable as the first Germanic ones of the fifth century in the Roman West, and for the same reason: the hordes fought to the death among themselves. After the death in 318 of Liu Ts'ung, the Hsiung-nu conqueror of northern China, his heirs were able to retain no more than the northwestern part of his territories, with Changan as their center. Full of zeal for conquest, however, one of his commanders—Shih Lei—carved out a principality for himself round Siangkuo (now Shuentö) in southern Hopei. In 329, Shih Lei deposed the royal house of Liu Ts'ung (the Ts'ien-Chao or Pei-Han dynasty) and founded a new Hsiung-nu dynasty known as the late Chao (Hou-Chao), which was to endure from about 330 to 350. Shih Lei installed himself somewhat south of Siangkuo, at

Ye, the Changteh of today, and chose as his second capital Lo-yang. This quite illiterate Hun, the annalists tell us, enjoyed having the Chinese classics expounded to him. His interest in grammar and theology bring to mind a Theodoric or Chilperic, the grammarian and theologian.

But the nomad mentality was no less effective for that, especially in his Hunnic descendants. The second successor to Shih Lei (d. 333) was Shih Hu (334–349), a debauched brute whom his son tried to assassinate and who executed his son. The son, one should note, was a thoroughgoing monster—a Tatar Bluebeard who had the prettiest of his concubines roasted and served up at table.[138] By an anomaly common among barbarians who fell under the spell of their first contact with civilization, Shih Hu was one of the most zealous defenders of Buddhism. His dominions, of which Changteh in northern Honan continued to be the capital, extended over Shensi (except for Hanchung, part of the southern Chinese Empire), Shansi (except for Tatung of the Toba), Hopei, Shantung, Honan, and even the northern part of Kiangsu and Anhwei, through which flows the Hwai River.

This vast Hunnic realm collapsed as rapidly as it had arisen. After the death of Shih Hu in 349, his heirs and generals fell out among themselves and slaughtered each other. The Mu-jung, who were of Hsien-pi stock—most probably Mongol, as has been noted —and who had founded a kingdom in Liaotung, took advantage of this state of anarchy to snatch the whole of Hopei (350, 352), Shansi, and Shantung. Their victorious chief Mu-jung Tsiun (349–360) chose as his capital Yen (or Chi), our Peking (350), and later Ye (Changteh, 357). His dynasty is known by the Chinese name of Ts'ien-Yen, early Yen (349–370). In 364, his successor occupied Loyang (after a brief recapture of that city by the imperial forces), and then the north bank of the Hwai (366). But this domination by the Mu-jung was to last for an even shorter time than that of the Huns who preceded them.

In the service of the Hsiung-nu ruler Shih Hu there was an officer named P'u Hung. He was probably a Mongol, although a Tangut (that is, a Tibetan) origin has often been ascribed to him. In 350, he set up an independent rule in Shensi, with Changan as his capital. His dynasty—for all these petty Turko-Mongol chiefs claimed to have founded authentic Chinese royal lines—is known by the name of early Ch'in, Ts'ien-Ch'in (350–394). P'u

Hung's grandson Fu Chien (357–385) was one of the most remarkable of these Turko-Mongol rulers. He was genuinely in sympathy with Chinese civilization and showed himself to be a humane administrator and a stanch defender of Buddhism. From the Mu-jung or Ts'ien Yen he captured first Loyang (369), then Taiyüan and lastly Ye (Changteh), the Mu-jung capital itself, whose king he took prisoner (370). Thus all the Mu-jung domains—Hopei, Shansi, Shantung, and Honan—passed to Fu Chien (370). As Fu Chien was already in possession of Shensi, he now found himself master of the whole of north China. In 376 he annexed another petty barbarian state, that of Liang in Kansu. In 382 he sent his subordinate Lu Kuang to subdue the Tarim. Lu Kuang received the homage of the rulers of Shanshan (Lob Nor), Turfan (southern Kiu-shih), and Kara Shahr (Yenki). The king of Kucha, called Po Shuen by the Chinese, having tried to resist, was defeated and driven out in 383. Lu Kuang occupied Kucha and on his return took with him, as already noted, the famous Buddhist monk Kumarajiva, whose achievement as a translator of Sanskrit texts into Chinese was to be so great.

Fu Chien, having subjugated all the barbarian states of north China, seemed on the point of conquering the Chinese national empire of the south and so unifying the country under his sole rule, as eight centuries later another Mongol conqueror, Kublai, was to do. In 383 he did indeed attack "the Empire" along the line of the Hwai, but on the upper reaches of the river he suffered a disaster from which his might was never to recover. A certain Mu-jung Ch'uei in his service, a descendant of the old Hsien-pi clan of the Mu-jung, rebelled and carried with him the provinces of Hopei and Shantung. Thus was founded the kingdom of the late Yen (Hou-Yen), which was to endure from 384 to 407, with its capital at Chungshan, present-day Tingchow south of Paoting in Hopei. At the same time (384) another member of the Mu-jung clan founded a western Yen (Hsi-Yen) kingdom in Shansi, but in 394 this was annexed by Mu-jung Ch'uei to Hou-Yen. Finally, Shensi and part of Honan were abstracted from Fu Kien by a one-time subordinate of his, Yao Ch'ang, who was most probably of Tibetan stock. In the conquered territories Yao Ch'ang founded the dynasty of late Ch'in (Hou-Ch'in), which had its capital at Changan, then known as Kingchaofu, and lasted from 384 to 417. Two other either Mongol or Turkic generals founded two other principalities in Kansu: that of the western Ch'in (Hsi-Ch'in, 385–400 and 409–431), with Lanchow (Yüan-ch'uan) as its capital, and that of the late Liangs (Hou-Liang, 386–403), the latter being founded by Lu Kuang.

THE KINGDOM OF THE TABGATCH TURKS, OR TOBA, AND THE MONGOL KHANATE OF THE JUAN-JUAN

Alongside these ephemeral hordes, whose realms of a day crumbled one upon another, there was one—the Tabgatch or, in Chinese, Toba—which increased in might and, by absorbing the rest, succeeded in establishing lasting dominion in northern China. In this it resembled the Franks who, surviving Burgundians, Visigoths, and Lombards, founded the Carolingian Empire upon their ruins, which was destined to link the Germanic present with the Roman past. The Toba achievement was similar; for, having united the other Turko-Mongol states of northern China, they so Sinicized them as to merge both people and dynasty with the Chinese mass. Moreover, their zeal in the cause of Buddhism is reminiscent of the fervor of the Merovingians and Carolingians for Christianity. Lastly, just as the Franks appointed themselves defenders of the Roman tradition against fresh waves of Germanic invaders, so the Toba mounted their "Watch on the Rhine" on the Yellow River against the Mongol hordes who had remained as savages in the depths of their native steppe. At the end of the third century A.D., as has been noted, the presumably Turkic Toba had established themselves in the extreme north of Shansi, in the Tatung region. Toba Kuei, an enterprising chief (386–409), brought good fortune to this horde by capturing from the Mu-jung of Hou-Yen first Tsinyang, our Taiyüan (396); then Chungshan, our Tingchow, south of Paoting (397); and lastly Ye, our Changteh (Anyang, 398).[139] He then adopted for his family the Chinese dynastic name of Wei and assigned to his horde a fixed capital, Pingcheng (Tai), east of Tatung. Thus constituted, the Toba kingdom of Wei included Shansi and Hopei as far as the Yellow River.

The Turkic China of the Toba was threatened by a fresh wave of barbarian invasion, that of the Ju-juan or, as the Chinese transcribed the name in a disparaging pun, Juan-juan, meaning "the unpleasantly wriggling insects." These, according to linguists, were a truly Mongol horde like the old Hsien-pi, to whom some believe them to have been related. Around 402, Shö-luen, one of their chiefs, founded the fortune of his race by subjugating a rival horde—that of the Kao-kiu—believed to have been situated near Kobdo and the Urungu and supposedly representing the forebears of the Töläch and Uigur Turks. At that time, the Juan-juan dominated the whole of the northern Gobi from the Liao in the east, on the Korean frontier, to the upper Irtysh and the Kara Shahr approaches in the west. It is among these Juan-juan rulers that we first find the titles "khan" and "khagan"; these must therefore be Mongol titles, taking the place of the old Hsiung-nu term *shan-yü*, which may accordingly be assumed to be Turkic.[140]

Faced by the menace of this new nomad empire, the Toba or Wei rulers of northern China distinguished themselves by their resolution in taking the offensive and launching a series of counterraids across the Gobi. Toba Kuei (386–409) set the example by a successful campaign in which the Juan-juan khagan Shö-luen was driven well back from the great loop of the Yellow River (402). Toba Ssu (409–423), while continuing to defend the approaches to the Great Wall in the north, increased his power in the south by taking the great city of Loyang, with all that part of Honan dependent upon it, from the national Chinese empire of the south (423). Toba Tao (423–452) succeeded his father Toba Ssu, and was at once threatened in his turn by the Juan-juan, whom he repulsed (424). In 425 he led a counterraid against them, in the course of which he crossed the Gobi from south to north with his cavalry (for no doubt the khagan of the Juan-juan had his headquarters near the Orkhon). He then turned upon another barbarian kingdom, that of the Hsia, founded in Shensi by the Ho-lien clan of the Hsiung-nu, and launched a surprise attack on the capital or royal camp (Tungwan near Paoan [Chihtan] in northern Shensi, 427), while his commanders harried Changan (426). By 431, the Ho-lien were destroyed and Shensi was added to the Toba domains. In 436, the armies of Toba Tao made a similar incursion into the kingdom of Pei-Yen (modern Jehol), last remnant of the Mu-jung territories, and took possession of that too. In 439, Toba Tao went on to conquer the state of Pei-Liang in Kansu (captured from Kutsang or Kanchow). The royal house of Pei-Liang—a Hunnic family settled there since 397 and bearing the patronymic Tsu-k'iu—fled to Turfan, took possession of it, and reigned there from 442 to 460.

With the annexation of the Pei-Liang territory, the Toba completed the conquest of all the Turko-Mongol kingdoms in northern China.[141] These now all formed part of the great (Turkic) Toba realm, the kingdom of Wei, as it was called in the Chinese manner, the only realm now remaining, apart from the Chinese national empire of the south, with Nanking as its Byzantium. In effect, the Roman world of the eighth century was similarly divided between the Franks, who subdued the West by destroying the other barbarian states, and the Byzantine Empire, which remained lord of Europe's Orient.

The impact of these conquests on the peoples of Central Asia was such that thenceforward northern China was known among them as the Toba country. Even the Byzantines themselves had the same name for it: *Tabgatch* in Turkic, *Tamghaj* in Arabic, *Taugast* in medieval Greek.[142]

Having unified northern China, Toba Tao led a great mounted expedition into the Gobi against the Juan-juan, whom he slaughtered in great numbers (429). In 443 he repeated this operation with equal success. In 445 a Toba army took reprisals against Shanshan (Lob Nor) for having blockaded the roads coming from the west, and in 448 the Toba general Wan Tu-kuei exacted tribute from Kara Shahr and Kucha. Toba Tao made a third expedition into the Gobi in 449 to give chase to the Juan-juan.

The history of the Toba or Tabgatch Turks who dominated northern China in the fifth century is particularly interesting because it presents a perfect example of a half-Sinicized Turko-Mongol horde—a horde, that is, which retained all its original military superiority over the Chinese and at the same time acquired from them the organizing ability that gave them the ascendancy over the still savage hordes of the north. When in 429 the "Tabgatch" king Toba Tao decided to lead some counterraids in the eastern Gobi against the Mongol Juan-juan horde, several of his advisers pointed out that the Chinese of the southern Nanking empire might take advantage of this to make some diversionary move. To this the gist of his reply was: "The Chinese are foot soldiers and we are horsemen. What can a herd of colts and heifers do against tigers or a pack of wolves? As for the Juan-juan, they graze in the north during the summer; in autumn, they come south and in winter raid our frontiers. We have only to attack them in summer in their pasture lands. At that time their horses are useless: the stallions are busy with the fillies, and the mares with their foals. If we but come upon them there and cut them off from their grazing and their water, within a few days they will be either taken or destroyed."

This double superiority later enabled Kublai the Jenghiz-Khanite to deal successfully with both Sung China and Qaidu's Mongols, and the first Manchus with the last Chinese rebellions and the hostility of the last Mongols. But this double advantage was never more than temporary; the moment always arrived when Toba Kublaids, or Manchus became completely Sinicized. They were then defeated by the hordes of the north and either eliminated or absorbed by the Chinese. This is the basic rhythm of Sino-Mongol history.

Toba Tao was the most forceful personality of this energetic Turkic family which so valiantly defended the ancient Chinese civilization against their still nomadic kinsmen. He was a man of outstanding courage, and he struck terror to the hearts of the Juan-juan, who, had they been opposed by effete Chinese dynasties, would not have hesitated to attack the frontiers. Thus he put an end to the great invasions, somewhat as Clovis was to do at Tolbiacum on behalf of Gaul. He had absorbed a fair amount of Chinese culture, but refused to become so far Sinicized as to bring about any slackening of the Turkic fiber in his horde. He declined therefore to exchange his old Pingcheng encampments near Tatung, in the extreme north of Shansi on the fringe of the steppe, for the historic capitals of old China, Loyang and Changan, which he had conquered by force of arms. He retained also the barbarous if prudent Turko-Mongol custom which required that, before the accession of a Toba king, the mother of the new ruler should be put to death so as to obviate the conquences of any ambition, covetousness, or grudge on the part of the future dowager. It need hardly be said that with this mentality he had a profound dislike of Buddhism, and here the sentiments of a barbarian warrior were reinforced by the Taoist hatreds of his entourage. In 438 he ordered the secularization of Buddhist monks and in 446 issued a regular edict authorizing persecution.

This persecution ceased, however, with the accession of his grandson Toba Siun, who succeeded him after a palace revolution (452–465). In the Buddhic caves of Yunkang, near Tatung, where artists were at work from 414 to 520, the finest sculptures and the ones which won enduring fame for Wei art date from this reign.[143] The religious fervor of these people inspired them to produce works of such profound mysticism from the traditional Greco-Buddhic forms—which had reached them from Gandhara along the Tarim routes—that they seem almost a prefiguration of Romanesque and Gothic sculpture. Indeed, it is more than likely that the purely Chinese dynasties would have been too greatly hampered by national prejudice and Confucian classicism to abandon themselves unreservedly to the mystic teachings of India. The Buddhic sculpture of the contemporary imperial dynasties of Nanking—even that of the Liang—is devoid of any such fervor. It was largely to their barbarian origin that the Toba, those Franks of the Far East, owed their ability to create at Yunkang and later at Lungmen the equivalent of Chartres and Rheims, and this is perhaps one of the most surprising results of the conquest of ancient China by the nomads of the steppe. In addition, the great invasions of the West in the fifth century, when barbarian society had come sufficiently under Christian influence, were to bring to birth after the Dark Ages the centuries of medieval splendor. The great invasions of the East in the fourth century produced a similar result, though much more quickly; for after no more than a hundred years, the China of the Wei absorbed enough of the Buddhist religion to create the great sculptures of Yunkang and Lungmen.

Some time was to elapse before the Turkic energy of the Toba became impaired by Chinese influence and by their conversion to Buddhism. During the reign of Toba Siun (452–465), the Toba occupied the Hami oasis (456) and launched a counterraid against the Juan-juan in the Gobi (458). The Juan-juan on their part occupied Turfan, deposed the Tsu-k'iu dynasty, and replaced it by a vassal family (460). Under Toba Hung (465–471), the Toba triumphs were resumed at the expense of the Chinese national empire of the south: Pengcheng (Sinhsien of Kiangsu) was taken in 466, in 467 came the conquest of the Hwai basin, and in 469 that of Shantung. In 470 the Toba castigated the T'u-yü-huen, a horde of Hsien-pi—that is, Mongol—origin, who had been established in the Koko Nor since the beginning of the century.

Toba Hung was so devout a Buddhist that in 471 he abdicated in favor of his young son in order to become a monk. This son, Toba Hung II [144] (471–499), showed himself on attaining his majority to be equally in sympathy with Buddism, and under its influence he introduced a more humane legislation. In 494 he completed the Sinicizing of the Toba by moving his capital from Pingcheng in Jehol to Loyang,[145] and it was exactly at this time that, at his instigation, work began on the celebrated Buddhic crypts of Lungmen, south of Loyang. The sculptures of these crypts were executed at various times during the period 494–759. But in unreservedly adopting Chinese culture and the Buddhist faith, the Toba had lost the tough, soldierly qualities of their Turkic ancestors. Their attempts to complete the unification of China under their rule by subduing the national empire of the south ended in failure. The king Toba K'iao (499–515) made one last effort, but his generals could not force the line of the Hwai, which marked the frontier of the two empires, and behind which the imperial fortress of Chungli (Fengyang in Anhwei) resisted all assaults (507).

After Toba K'iao's death in 515 his widow, Queen Hu, reigned over the Toba territories until 528. This descendant of the old Tabgatch was the last member of the dynasty to display the ancient Turkic strength. She was a woman of exceptional energy, bloodthirsty when occasion arose, and with a passion for power; nevertheless, she favored Buddhism. She added to the adornment of the Lungmen sanctuaries and sent the Buddhist pilgrim Sung Yün on a mission to northwestern India; he has left an interesting account of the state of Central Asia at this period. Sung Yün went by way of Shanshan (Lob Nor), Khotan, the Pamirs, and, as will be seen, visited the khan of the Ephthalite Huns in Badakhshan. He then entered Udiyana and Gandhara (lower Kabul), whence he brought back for his sovereign the Buddhist documents that interested her (518–521).[146]

The Toba were by now too Chinese not to have their own palace revolutions, family rifts, and civil wars. In 534 they split into two branches: the eastern Wei (Tung-Wei), who possessed Hopei, Shansi, Shantung, and Honan, with what is now Changteh as capital (534–550); and the western Wei (Hsi-Wei), who had

Shensi and Kansu, with their capital at Changan (534–557). Both were to be overthrown by their ministers, and it was thus that the Pei-Ch'i dynasty (550–577) was founded at Changteh in place of the eastern Wei, while the western Wei were superseded by the Pei-Chou dynasty (557–581) at Changan. But these royal houses, having become Chinese, no longer form a part of steppe history. What does affect that history, however, is the gradual slackening of the Turkic vigor—so marked among the first Tabgatch rulers—and its dilution and submergence in the Chinese masses. It is a pattern to be repeated over and over again through the centuries, with the Khitan, the Jurchids, the Jenghiz-Khanites, and the Manchus. It was the influence of Buddhism that played so large a part in the softening process among the Toba, as it did later among the Jenghiz-Khanites and later still among the Khalkhas. These ferocious warriors, once touched by the grace of the bodhisattva, became so susceptible to the humanitarian precepts of the sramanas as to forget not only their native belligerence but even neglect their self-defense.

THE LAST MINUSINSK CULTURE

Leaving these completely Sinicized Turks to their destiny, we return to the still-nomad hordes on the Asian steppes. In connection with the Toba, we spoke of the presumably Mongol horde of the Juan-juan, who, throughout the fifth century and the first half of the sixth, dominated Outer Mongolia. What we know of their political history is derived solely from the Chinese annals of the Wei and Sui dynasties, and before we can profitably discuss their civilization we must wait for systematic excavations in their ancient domains. Meanwhile, let us merely note that beyond and to the northwest of their territory a new culture was flourishing at about this period on the Yenisei in Siberia, round Minusinsk. This culture, known as that of the "Nomad Horsemen," has left behind ornaments, belt plaques, buckles, and mounts of bronze, also stirrups, bits, knives, daggers, sabers, lances, saddles, and so on, all fairly plentifully represented in the Minusinsk museum and also in Helsinki (Tovostin Collection).[147] This culture appears to be contemporaneous with the Juan-juan; it must have survived them by some time, since at the village of Tyutshta it is associated with Chinese coins of the beginning of the T'ang period (seventh century), and it seems not to have ended until the ninth century. It is of particular interest at this stage because, as Nandor Fettich points out, it presents striking similarities to the Avar culture of Hungary in the sixth to the eighth centuries, as also with the proto-Hungarian or Levedian culture of the ninth century.[148] Though this may not be a valid argument for regarding the Juan-juan as the direct ancestors of the Avars of Europe, it is at least proof that both had gravitated around the same cultural center.

After the Juan-juan, it is appropriate to consider a kindred horde, that of the Ephthalites, who, during the same period, were masters of western Turkestan.

THE EPHTHALITE HUNS

The Ephthalite Huns were a Turko-Mongol horde; in this case, it seems, more Mongol than Turk [149] and originating, according to Sung Yün, in the Kinshan hills—that is to say, in the Altai—whence they had come down to the steppes of present-day Russian Turkestan. Their name, given as Ephthalites by Byzantine historians, Hayathelites by the Persian historian Mirkhond, and Ye-tai by the historians of China, seems to derive from the name of the royal clan Ephtha or Ye-ta.[150] Byzantine historians knew them also by the designation—here somewhat erroneous—of White Huns.

At the beginning of the fifth century A.D., the Ephthalites were no more than a secondary horde, vassal of the greater one—Mongol, likewise—of the Juan-juan, which dominated Mongolia. In the second quarter of the fifth century, these same Ephthalites acquired considerable importance by the expansion of their dominion westward. Their rule extended from the upper Yulduz in the east (northwest of Kara Shahr) across the Ili basin to Balkhash, over the Chu and Talas steppes and the Syr Darya region as far as the Aral Sea. According to some sources, one of their khan's residences was near the town of Talas. By about 440 they had also occupied Sogdiana or Transoxiana (Samarkand) and, it seems, the country of Balkh, Bactria, or Tokharistan.

Several Orientalists, Noeldeke in particular, believe that it was during the reign of King Bahram Gor of Persia (420–438) that the Ephthalites settled in Bactria. They are thought even to have invaded the Sassanian province of Khurasan, whence Bahram Gor drove them back at the battle of Kusmehan near Merv. Marquart, on the other hand, believes that Bahram Gor and later his successor Yezdegerd II (438–457) had to defend themselves not against Ephthalite aggression but against that of the Khionites, another Hunnic tribe who led a nomadic existence north of Merv.[151] However this may be, it was certainly the Ephthalites who during the reign of the Sassanid king Peroz (459–484) attacked Khurasan and finally defeated and killed that monarch. The Ephthalite chief who won this victory was known by Arabo-Persian historians under the name of Akhshunwar or Akhshunwaz, apparently a corruption of the Sogdian title *khshevan* or king.[152]

After their victory over King Peroz, the Ephthalite Huns occupied not only the frontier district of Talekan (western Talekan, between Balkh and Merv), which until then had been the frontier town of the Sassanid Empire in the northwest, but also Merv and Herat.[153] Furthermore, they intervened in the palace quarrels of the Persian Sassanid dynasty. It was in this way that the Sassanid Kavadh, driven from the throne of Ctesiphon, took refuge with them, married the niece of their khan, and received from him an army, with whose aid he regained his crown (498 or 499). By then the Ephthalites had become a power to be reckoned with in Middle Asia. The *Liang Shu* notes the embassy sent in 516 to the Chinese court of Nanking by their king "Ye-tai-i-li-t'o."

Despite King Peroz' defeat, Sassanid Persia was too well defended for the Ephthalites to contemplate its conquest. They returned southeastward, in the direction of Kabul. There the first reaction to their approach seems to have been the replacement of the Kushan dynasty about the middle of the fifth century by another line of the same Yüeh-chih or Tukhara extraction from Bactria. Iranian sources tell of a "Kidarite" dynasty—established apparently south of the Oxus, between Balkh and Merv [154]—which was at war with the Sassanids. According to these same sources, the Sassanid Peroz (459–484)—the same who was to perish under the blows of the Ephthalites—fought the Kidarite chiefs, first the eponymous hero Kidara and then his son Kungas (Kungkas). It was after his defeat by Peroz that Kungas is believed to have left Bactria, which the Ephthalites promptly occupied, crossed the Hindu Kush, and entered Kabul, where he took the place of the last Kushan rulers.[155] These events are confirmed by the Chinese, though ascribed to an earlier date and consequently to somewhat different causes. Chinese sources, in which information seems to date from as far back as the years 436–451, record that "a king of the Yüeh-chih" from "Po-lo"—which here no doubt denotes the Tukhara of Balkh—had just left Bactria under Ephthalite pressure and moved to Gandhara, where he settled at Peshawar, bringing under his sway his cousins the Yüeh-chih of Kabul: that is, the last of the Kushans. The Chinese call this king Ki-to-lo, which corresponds exactly to our Kidara.[156] Thus it must have been the Ephthalites rather than the Sassanians who forced the Kidarites to leave Bactria and take refuge in Kabul. The Kidarites, however, were soon followed by the Ephthalites, who lost no time in crossing the Hindu Kush by the same route. Thus the whole of the old Yüeh-Chih territory—Bactria, Kabul, and Kandahar—passed into Ephthalite hands. In addition, from the heights of the Kabul valley the Ephthalite vanguard sprang forth—as the Kushans had done before them—to the conquest of India.

The greater part of India—the whole Ganges basin, the Malwa, Gujarat, and the northern Deccan—formed at that time a huge empire under the national dynasty of the Gupta emperors, a dynasty which reached its peak in the reign of Kumaragupta (ca. 414–455), who was succeeded by his son Skandagupta (ca. 455–470). It was either during Kumaragupta's last years or at the beginning of Skandagupta's reign that the Ephthalite Huns—known to the Indians by the Sanskrit transcription *Huna*—having conquered Kabul, came down into the Punjab and were brought up short against the frontiers of the Gupta realm, near Doab or the Malwa. On that occasion they were repulsed by Skandagupta, either soon after his accession or just before.[157] If before, the beginning of his reign may have coincided with a second Hun invasion, which was likewise beaten off. After this, as an inscription of 460 tells, the country was once more at peace.

Meanwhile the Ephthalites had entrenched themselves firmly on both sides of the Hindu Kush, in Bactria and Kabul. In 520, at the time of Sung Yün's pilgrimage, their khan lived north of the Hindu Kush, migrating seasonally from Bactria, where he spent the winter, to Badakhshan, his summer residence. At Kabul, in the old Greco-Buddhic provinces of Kapisa and Gandhara, a secondary Ephthalite chief had settled: a *tegin* who there founded a dynasty of which the second sovereign was reigning in 520. Here, amid the lofty culture of Gandhara, of which Hellenism jointly with Buddhism had made a new Hellas and Buddhic Holy Land combined, the Ephthalites behaved like barbarians, massacring the inhabitants and persecuting especially the Buddhist communities, sacking monasteries and works of art, and ruining the fine Greco-Buddhic civilization which by then was five centuries old. Persian [158] and Chinese texts agree in their descriptions of the tyranny and vandalism of this horde.

In the *Pei-Shih* and the story related by Sung Yün—who in 520, it will be remembered, visited first their khan at his summer residence of Badakhshan, and later the *tegin* of Gandhara—all these Huns are described as pure nomads: "They do not live in towns; their seat of government is a moving camp. Their dwellings are of felt. They move in search of water and pasture, journeying in summer to cool places and in winter to warmer ones. A large felt tent is erected for their king, measuring forty feet a side; on the inside, the walls are made of woolen rugs. The king's clothes are of ornamented silk, and he sits on a golden bed of which the feet are in the shape of four golden phoenixes. His chief wife also wears an ornamented silk robe which trails three feet along the ground. On her head she wears a horn eight feet long, decorated with precious stones in five colors." [159] Sung Yün also notes the Ephthalite custom of fraternal polyandry and their hostility to Buddhism. "They have no belief in the Buddhic law and they serve a great number of divinities. They kill living creatures and are eaters of bloody meat." On the testimony of Hsüan-tsang, the Ephthalites cut the throats of two-thirds of the Gandharan population, reduced the rest to slavery, and destroyed most of the Buddhist monasteries and stupas. [160]

From Kabul the Ephthalites eyed the riches of India. Driven back by the Indian emperor Skandagupta, they bided their time. Their opportunity occurred when, after the death of that ruler (ca. 470), the Indian Empire fell into decay. This may have been the result of the partition of the country between two branches of the Gupta dynasty, one reigning over the Malwa in the persons of Buddhagupta (ca. 476–494) and Bhanugupta (ca. 499–543), the other over Bihar and Bengal, where Puragupta and Narasimhagupta successively held power. Profiting from this decline of Gupta power, the Huns resumed their invasions of India. The

Hun chief who led them, and who is known in Indian literature by the name of Toramana (d. 502), was not the khan of the Ephthalites, as is sometimes contended. The khan, as we saw, lived north of the Hindu Kush, in Bactria and Badakhshan. This man was a secondary prince or *tegin;* no doubt the *tegin* of Kabul. Three inscriptions of his, found at Khewra in the Salt Range (northwest of the Punjab), at Gwalior, and at Eran, prove that he conquered not only the Indus basin but the Malwa as well. His coinage is an imitation of that of the Indian emperor Budd-hagupta, his contemporary.[161]

Mihirakula, Toramana's son and successor (known only by his laudatory Indian name "Race of the Sun" in classical Sanskrit), who seems to have ruled his horde from about 502 to 530, was indeed the Attila of India. He had taken up his residence at Sialkot in the eastern Punjab, and must have been that *tegin* of Gandhara whom the Chinese pilgrim Sung Yün met in 520. After conquering Kashmir, Mihirakula returned to Gandhara, where he perpetrated frightful massacres. Buddhist writers describe him as a terrible persecutor of their religion. Hsüan-tsang tells that the Gupta ruler of Magadha or Bihar, called Baladitya (perhaps identical with Narasimhagupta mentioned above), was the only one who dared to oppose him. Mihirakula advanced into the Ganges region in search of his opponent. At first, Baladitya is reported to have retreated before him; then, in a surprise attack, he seems to have defeated and even captured him. The narrative ends as a moral tale. Apart from this, the inscription of Eran, in the Malwa, dated 510, which recounts the victories of Bhanagupta—another Gupta prince—has given rise to the belief that these triumphs too were won over Ephthalite invaders. Lastly, in 533 a third Indian prince, Yasodharman, assumed to be a member of the dynasty of the rajas of Mandasur in the Malwa, boasts in his incriptions of having conquered the Huns and forced Mihirakula to pay him homage.[162] After these defeats, Mihirakula appears to have withdrawn to Kashmir, where for some unknown reason he took an appalling vengeance on his Gandhara subjects, as is reported by Chinese pilgrims. Buddhist texts assert that by way of punishment for his atrocities, he met with a ghastly death.

We do not know what became of the Hun clans camped in the Punjab after Mihirakula's decease. They must have continued to be troublesome if not dangerous neighbors, for in the second half of the sixth century the maharaja of Thanesar,[163] Prabhakara (d. 605), won honor and power by fighting them. In 605 his eldest son Rajyavardhana was still waging war on them, and later the successor to these two, the great Indian emperor Harsha (606–647), was acclaimed by the poets for his victories over these same Huns. Yet from the second half of the seventh century the Huns of India vanish from history, no doubt either exterminated or absorbed by the Punjabis. Some of their clans most likely succeeded in gaining admission to the Hindu aristocracy, in the manner of the "Rajput" clan of the Gurjara, which may possibly have the same origin.

THE HUNS IN EUROPE: ATTILA

From the year 35 B.C., we lose track of the western Hsiung-nu. It was then that Che-che, the dissident *shan-yü*, having carried with him some of the Hunnic tribes of Upper Mongolia to the steppes north of the Aral Sea and Lake Balkhash, was overtaken and killed by a Chinese expeditionary force. The descendants of the tribes which he led into this region were to remain there for centuries; but, as they lacked civilized neighbors to record their deeds and adventures, nothing is known of their history. Not until the fourth century A.D. do we hear of them again, when their entry into Europe brought them into contact with the Roman world.[164]

The Russian steppe north of the Black Sea had been occupied since the third century B.C. by the Sarmatians, who superseded the Scythians and who, like them, belonged to the northern branch of the Iranian race. The bulk of them were nomads, moving between the lower Volga and the Dniester. Certain Sarmatian tribes had developed an autonomous way of life. Among them were the nomadic Alans of the Terek, who traveled as far as the Kuban; the Roxolani, who since A.D. 62 had been established west of the lower Don; and the Jazyges, who from A.D. 50 occupied the plain between the Tisza and the Danube, that is, between the Dacians and the Roman province of Pannonia in the heart of modern Hungary.[165] The Sarmatians were separated from the Roman Empire—even after Trajan's annexation of Dacia (106)—by the Bastarnae, an eastern Germanic people who from 200 onward had come down the Dniester by way of the northern slopes of the Carpathians as far as the river mouth: a movement which represents the first known Germanic *Drang nach Osten*. About A.D. 200, a fresh Germanic thrust from the lower Vistula—that of the Goths, who originated in Sweden —threatened the Sarmatians' claim to the plains of southern Russia. In 230 the Goths had reached the limit of their migration and attacked the Roman town of Olbia on the Black Sea.

Southern Russia was divided at this time between the Goths to the west of the lower Dnieper and the Sarmatian peoples (Alans and others) east of that river. The Crimea, on the other hand, was still a Greco-Roman realm in vassalage to the Caesars. The Goths themselves were divided into Ostrogoths (between the lower Don and the lower Dniester) and Visigoths (from the lower Dniester to the Danube). A third Gothic tribe, the Gepidae, had occupied Dacia after its evacuation by Emperor Aurelian in 270. This is the period of the Gothic burials of Chernyakhov south of Kiev, and of Nikolayevka near Kherson on the lower Dnieper (third century). It is also the period, on the Sarmatian side, of the Kuban tumuli (Tbilisskaya, Vozdviz-henskoye, Armavir, and Yaroslavskaya), with plaques and clasps characteristic of Sarmatian art. To the north, in the forests of eastern and central Russia—at that time inhabited no doubt by Finno-Ugrian peoples—the Sarmatian influence was still evident in the culture of Pianobor near Kazan (ca. 100–300 or 400), the local inheritor of the Ananino culture. Farther west, the Kaluga group reveals fibulae of Germano-Roman inspiration (third and fourth centuries). Such was the ethnic and cultural situation in South Russia when the Huns arrived.

For what reason did the historic Huns—the descendants of the western Hsiung-nu—leave the steppes north of the Aral Sea and enter Europe? We do not know. About 374, having crossed the lower Volga, they pressed on under the leadership of a chief whom Jordanes calls Balamir, or Balamber, across the Don; defeated and subjugated the Alans of the Terek and Kuban; and attacked, west of the Dnieper, the Ostrogoths, whose aged king Ermanarich they defeated and who in his despair committed suicide. Vithimir, Ermanarich's successor, was defeated and killed in his turn. Most of the Ostrogoths submitted to Hun domination, while the Visigoths, fleeing from invasion, crossed the Danube and entered the Roman Empire (376). The majority of the Alans of the Kuban and Terek were compelled to submit temporarily to the Huns and remain in the land, where in about the tenth century they were converted to Byzantine Christianity. These were the forebears of the modern Ossetians. Other Alans set off for the West and joined with the western Germans in the great invasions. Some of their tribes were to settle in Gaul on the lower Loire,[166] others entered Spain, mixed with the Suevi in Spanish Galicia or, with the Visigoths, formed a composite ethnic element which may conceivably have given Catalonia ("Goth-Alan") its name.

The terror inspired by the Huns' irruption into the Roman and Germanic world has been well conveyed by Ammianus Marcellinus and Jordanes. "The Huns," writes Ammianus, "exceed anything that can be imagined in ferocity and barbarism. They gash their children's cheeks to prevent their beards growing. Their stocky body, huge arms, and disproportionately large head give them a monstrous appearance. They live like beasts. They neither cook nor season their food; they live on wild roots and on meat pounded tender under the saddle. They are ignorant of the use of the plow and of fixed habitations, whether houses or huts. Being perpetually nomadic, they are inured from childhood to cold, hunger, and thirst. Their herds follow them on their migrations, with some of the animals being used to draw the covered wagons in which their families live. Here it is that their women spin and make clothes, bear children, and rear them until puberty. If you inquire of these men whence they come and where they were born, they cannot tell you. Their dress consists of a linen tunic and a coat of ratskins sewn together. The tunic, which is of a dark color, is worn until it rots away on their bodies. They never change it until it drops off. A helmet or cap pushed back on their heads and goatskins rolled about their hairy legs complete their attire. Their shoes, cut without shape or measure, do not allow them to walk in ease: thus they are quite unsuited to fight as infantry. Yet mounted they seem riveted to their ugly little horses, which are tireless and swift as lightning. They spend their lives on horseback, sometimes astride, sometimes sideways, like women. They hold their meetings thus; they buy and sell, drink and eat—even sleep, lying on the neck of their mounts. In battle they swoop upon the enemy, uttering frightful yells. When opposed they disperse, only to return with the same speed, smashing and overturning everything in their path. They have no notion of how to take a fortified position or an entrenched camp. Yet there is nothing to equal the skill with which—from prodigious distances—they discharge their arrows, which are tipped with sharpened bone as hard and murderous as iron." [167]

Sidonius Apollinaris, who attributes the Huns' physical type to deliberate malformation in childhood, speaks with no less horror of these brachycephalic men with their flattened noses ("a shapeless, flat excrescence"), high cheekbones, and eyes sunk in their sockets as in a cavern ("yet their piercing gaze commands the farthest expanses"), the eagle eyes of the nomad, accustomed to scanning vast areas and discerning herds of deer or wild horses on the very horizon of the steppe. From the same author there is a fine verse depicting the eternal horseman of the steppes: "Below average height when afoot, the Hun is great when mounted on his steed!"

It is interesting to compare this portrait with the one left by Chinese annalists of the Hsiung-nu, who in type and way of life were identical, and also with a similar portrait of the thirteenth-century Mongols which has come down from both China and Christendom. The brachycephalic man of the steppe, whether Hun, Turk, or Mongol—the man with the big head, powerful body, and short legs, the ever-mounted nomad, the "archer on horseback" from High Asia prowling along the fringes of cultivation—has scarcely changed over fifteen centuries of raids against sedentary civilizations.

The submission of the Alans and Ostrogoths and the exodus of the Visigoths left the Huns masters of the entire plains area between the Urals and the Carpathians. By the Carpathian passes or the Wallachian plains, they next occupied the plain of Hungary, where the Gepidae became their subjects and whence they expanded even as far as the right bank of the Danube (405–406). At this time they appear to have been divided into three hordes under three chiefs, the brothers Ruas (Rugas or Rugila), Mundzuk (or Mundiukh), and Oktar, who about 425 were simultaneously in power. In 434, these hordes were being governed by Mundzuk's two sons, Bleda and Attila, the former being very soon removed by the latter.

It was then that Attila began his conquests. In 441 he declared war on the Eastern Empire. He crossed the Danube, moved up the now Serbian River Morava, took Naissus (Nis), plundered Philippopolis (Plovdiv), and ravaged Thrace as far as Arcadiopolis (Luleburgaz), which he sacked. At the peace of 448, the Empire had to cede to him a belt south of the Danube, extending in length from modern Belgrade to modern Svishtov, and in width as far as Nis.

In January and February of 451, having concentrated his army in the plain of Hungary, Attila made for Gaul, rallying to his side the Germanic peoples on the right bank on the Rhine. After crossing the Rhine, he attacked that part of Gaul which was still Roman, governed by the Roman patrician Aetius. On April 7 he burned Metz and went on to besiege Orléans. On June 14 the latter town was relieved by the arrival of the Roman army under Aetius' command and the Visigothic army under King Theodoric. Attila retreated toward Troyes. It was to the west of Troyes, on the Campus Mauriacus, that he was halted by Romans and Visigoths in a hard-fought and barely decisive battle which nevertheless saved the West (end of June, 451).

After this check, Attila retired to the Danube, where he spent the winter. In the spring of 452, he invaded Italy, but lingered too long over the siege of Aquileia, which in the end he reduced and destroyed. He also took Milan and Pavia, and announced his intention to march on Rome, whence Emperor Valentinian III had just fled. However, instead of pressing on to the capital of the world, he allowed himself to be dissuaded by the bishop of Rome, Saint Leo the Great (July 6, 452), who promised him tribute and the hand of Honoria, a daughter of the Caesars. Once more he returned to Pannonia, where he died in 453.

The Gothic historian Jordanes has left us a striking portrait of Attila. He was a typical Hun: short, broad-chested, with a big head, small deep-set eyes, and flat nose. He was swarthy, almost black-skinned, and wore a sparse beard. Terrible in his rages, he used the fear he inspired as a political weapon. Indeed, there was in him about the same coefficient of calculation and cunning as in the Hsiung-nu conquerors of the Six Dynasties, as described by Chinese historians. His utterances, with their deliberate emphasis and obscure threats, were strategic preliminaries; his systematic destruction (Aquileia, razed to the ground, never

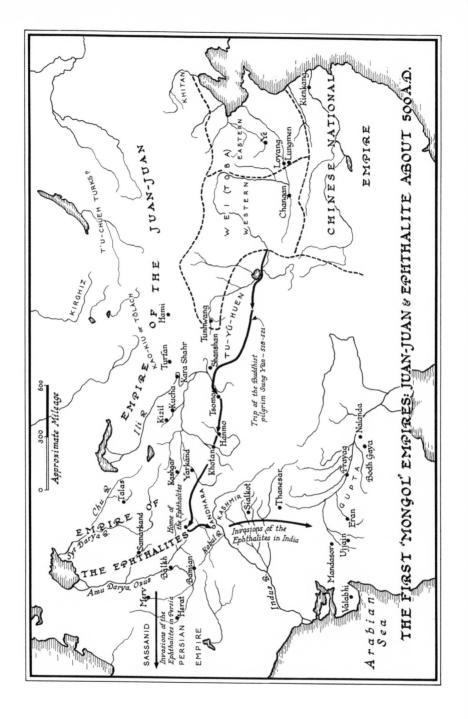

THE FIRST 'MONGOL' EMPIRES: JUAN-JUAN & EPHTHALITE ABOUT 500 A.D.

recovered after his passage) and his wholesale throat-cutting were intended primarily as a lesson to his adversaries. Jordanes and Priscus show him to have been in other ways a fair and incorruptible judge among his own people, generous to his servants, mild toward those who made genuine submission to him, and content to live a simple life amid the barbarian luxury of his fellows, using wooden platters where the rest ate from dishes of gold. To these traits may be added others to which the same sources allude: he was deeply superstitious, with a savage's credulity in his shamans, and his taste for alcohol caused ceremonies to end in drunken orgies. Yet he was careful to surround himself with Greek ministers and scribes such as Onegesis, Roman ones such as Orestes, and Germans like Edeco. Above all, curiously enough, characteristic of this leader of hordes was his frequent use of cunning and political tactics in preference to war. In war itself, he is prominent less as a captain than as a leader of men. With all this was combined an odd legalistic streak, which led him to seek diplomatic pretexts for his actions, in accordance with formal practice, so that he might at any rate appear to have right on his side. These traits remind one irresistibly of another founder of a nomad empire, another son of the steppe: Jenghiz Khan.[168]

As the empire of Jenghiz Khan, albeit symbolically Mongol, was to draw under its banners not Mongol nomads alone but also Turks and Tungus from High Asia, so Attila's empire with its Hunnic—that is presumably Turkic—nucleus absorbed and carried with it Sarmatians, Alans, Ostrogoths, Gepidae, and others, scattered between the Urals and the Rhine. Herein lay its weakness. After Attila's premature death in 453, his heterogeneous empire disintegrated. Ostrogoths and Gepidae immediately revolted and crushed the Huns in a great battle in Pannonia in the course of which Ellac, the conqueror's eldest son, was killed (454).

The Huns then withdrew toward the Russian steppe, led by a son of Attila named Dengizich or Dinzigikh. Other sons of his demanded lands from the Romans, who quartered one of them, Ernac, in Dobrogea (or Dobruja) and the two others, Emnedzar and Uzindur, in Mesia. Dengizich again led the Huns in an attack on the Eastern Empire near the Lower Danube, but was defeated and killed. His head—the head of Attila's son—was exhibited in 468 at Constantinople, amid the circus.

Other Hun clans survived north of the Black Sea in two hordes: the Kutrigur Huns, who led a nomadic life northwest of the Sea of Azov, and the Uturgur or Utrigur Huns, whose haunts were by the mouth of the Don. These two hordes quickly became enemies, their quarrels being secretly fomented by Byzantine diplomacy. About 545, Emperor Justinian incited Sandilkh, ruler of the Uturgurs, to march against the rival horde. The Kutrigurs were decimated by Sandilkh (548), but later rose again under their king Zabergan (or Zamergan) and tried to take revenge for the support given by Justinian to their foes. During the winter of 558–559 Zabergan and his horde crossed the frozen Danube and appeared suddenly under the very walls of Constantinople. But Belisarius saved the capital and Zabergan returned to the Don steppe, where he resumed hostilities against Sandilkh. Fraticidal war between the two Hunnic hordes started afresh, remorselessly, and was still going on when a third horde, that of the Avars come from Asia, crushed the two others and took possession of the Russian steppes. This new invasion was a repercussion of revolutions in Continental Asia, brought about by the appearance of the T'u-chüeh, or historical Turks.

2

The Early Middle Ages: T'u-chüeh, Uigur, and Khitan

In the year 540, the empire of the steppes existed as three vast Turko-Mongol dominions. The Juan-juan, who were apparently of Mongol stock, reigned in Mongolia from the Manchurian border to Turfan (even no doubt to the eastern extremity of Lake Balkhash) and from the Orkhon to the Great Wall. The Ephthalites, presumably a Mongol race also, dominated what is now Semirechye, Russian Turkestan, Sogdiana, eastern Iran, and Kabul, from the upper Yulduz (north of Kara Shahr) to Merv, from Lake Balkhash and the Aral Sea to the heart of Afghanistan and the Punjab. The two clans ruling the Juan-juan and the Ephthalites were allies. Around 520 the Ephthalite khan had married the aunts of the Juan-juan khagan A-na-kuei. The Juan-juan, lords of their native Mongolia, seem even to have maintained a certain ascendancy over the Ephthalites, who controlled the southwestern marches. Lastly, as was just seen, the Huns of Europe, who were no doubt of Turkic stock, held sway over the Russian steppe in the region adjoining the Sea of Azov and the mouths of the Don, although the rivalry of their two hordes—Kutrigurs in the west, Uturgurs in the east—undermined their power.

Among the vassals of the Juan-juan, say the Chinese, were the T'u-chüeh, a Turkic tribe which has given its name to a whole group of nations sharing a common language. Pelliot says that "the Chinese name T'u-chüeh must represent a Mongol (Juan-juan) plural form *Türküt*, from the singular *Türk*. Literally, it means "strong." [1] According to Chinese annalists, the T'u-chüeh totem was the wolf.[2] They were descendants of the old Hsiung-nu, a fact borne out by the proto-Turkic character attributed to the Huns by Pelliot. At the beginning of the sixth century, the T'u-chüeh appear to have inhabited the Altai region, where they practiced metalworking: "the trade of the smith." The power of the Juan-juan had recently been impaired by the civil war which in 520 brought about a clash between their khagan A-na-kuei and his uncle P'o-lo-men, rulers of eastern and western hordes respectively.

It was left to A-na-kuei (522–552), as sole surviving lord of the khanate, to quell the insubordination of the vassal Turkic tribes. In 508 one of these tribes, the Kao-kiu—now identified with the Tölös or Töläch, nomads pasturing south of the Altai near the Urungu, and seemingly forebears of the Uigurs—defeated the Juan-juan. In 516, however, the Juan-juan killed the king of the Kao-kiu and forced the tribe into subjection. In 521 the Kao-kiu once more vainly attempted to take advantage of the civil strife among the Juan-juan in order to regain their freedom. Shortly before 546, while planning a fresh revolt, they were balked by the T'u-chüeh, who, though of the same race, loyally warned the common suzerain, the Juan-juan khagan A-na-kuei, of the plot. As a reward for this service, the T'u-chüeh chief—who is known both by his Turkic name Bumin and its Chinese transcription T'u-men—requested the hand of a Juan-juan princess in marriage. A-na-kuei refused.[3] Bumin then allied himself with the Hsi-Wei dynasty of Toba stock—that is to say, most probably Turkic—then reigning at Changan in northwest China. Although entirely Sinicized, the Toba may have retained a sense of kinship with the Turkic community. In any event, they must have been glad of an alliance which enabled them to retaliate against their ancient foes, the Juan-juan Mongols, and they bestowed upon Bumin the hand of one of their own princesses (551). Having thus encircled the Juan-juan Mongols, Bumin crushed them utterly and drove A-na-kuei, their khagan, to suicide (552). The remnants of the Juan-juan abandoned Mongolia to the T'u-chüeh and took refuge on the Chinese frontier, where the court of the

Pei-Ch'i, successors to the Tung-Wei, established them as guardians of the marches.[4]

Thus the old imperial territory of Mongolia passed from Juanjuan to T'u-chüeh, or from Mongols to Turks. Bumin assumed the imperial title of khagan.[5] The seat of the new empire remained on the upper Orkhon, in that mountainous region which, from the days of the old Hsiung-nu to those of the Jenghiz-Khanites, was so often chosen by the hordes as their command post.[6]

Bumin-khagan, the Turkic hero, barely survived his triumph (552), and at his death his possessions were divided. His son Mu-han received Mongolia and the imperial title (553–572). Thus was founded the khanate of the eastern T'u-chüeh. Bumin's younger brother Istämi (in Turkic) or Shih-tie-mi (in Chinese transcription) inherited the princely title of *yabghu,* together with Dzungaria, the country of the Black Irtysh and of the Imil, and the basins of the Yulduz, Ili, Chu, and Talas. Thus was founded the khanate of the western T'u-chüeh.[7]

The chief of the western group, Istämi, clashed in the Talas region with the Ephthalites. In order to take them in the rear, he made a treaty with their hereditary enemies, the Persians, at that time governed by Chosroes I Anoshirvan, the greatest sovereign of the Sassanid dynasty. Istämi sealed the pact by marrying one of his daughters to Chosroes. Assailed in the north by the T'u-chüeh and in the southwest by the Sassanians, the Ephthalites were overwhelmed, and disappeared (ca. 565). A portion of them—the nomads pasturing in the Aral region in the northwest—had to flee to the West; and it may be these, rather than the remnants of the Juan-juan, who under the name of Uarkhonites and Avars founded a new Mongol khanate in Hungary.[8] In the succeeding period, indeed, a horde expelled from Asia and known to Greek and Latin writers by this name of Avar terrorized the Byzantine Empire and the Germanic West until the day of their destruction by Charlemagne.

The Ephthalite possessions were divided between the western T'u-chüeh and the Sassanians. The T'u-chüeh chief Istämi took Sogdiana, while Chosroes I Anoshirvan seized Bactria, a *terra irredenta* of Iranianism. Between 565 and 568, Bactria was thus restored to the Sassanid Empire. The reclamation was brief, however, for the T'u-chüeh were soon to take Balkh and Kunduz

—that is to say, this same Bactria—from the Sassanians, their erstwhile allies.

In this manner the two Turkic realms of the early Middle Ages assumed their definitive shape: the khanate of the eastern T'u-chüeh, founded by the khagan Mu-han in Mongolia and centered near the future Karakorum on the upper Orkhon, and the khanate of the western T'u-chüeh on the Ili and in western Turkestan, with its summer camp on the upper Yulduz north of Kara Shahr and Kucha, its winter quarters on the shores of the Issyk Kul or in the Talas valley. So far as essentially nomadic empires can be said to have frontiers, the boundaries of the two khanates were marked by the great Altai and by the mountains east of Hami.

From the beginning of Mu-han's reign (553–572), the eastern T'u-chüeh had few adversaries. In 560 or thereabout, he defeated the Khitan, a Mongol horde which had occupied the western bank of the Liao River near modern Jehol from apparently the middle of the fifth century. In northern China, the Pei-Chou king of Changan humbly requested Mu-han's daughter in marriage. Mu-han at this time was clearly playing the role of arbiter between the two successor kingdoms of the Toba Empire (ca. 565).[9]

Istämi, the *yabghu* or khan of the western T'u-chüeh, who reigned from 552 to 575, is known to Tabari as Sinjibu and to the Byzantine historian Menander as Silzibul, a corruption of this same title of *yabghu*.[10] He was sought as an ally by the Byzantines. Indeed, now that on the Oxus the T'u-chüeh had become the immediate neighbors of Sassanid Persia, it was in Byzantium's interest to act jointly with the T'u-chüeh. On his part, Istämi, who appears to have been a highly intelligent man, thought of taking advantage of his position at the crossroads of Asia to obtain the freedom of the silk trade through Persia, from the borders of China to those of Byzantium. To this end a Sogdian named Maniakh (in Central Asia the Sogdians were the greatest caravan guides of the day) visited Chosroes I Anoshirvan on Istämi's behalf. Intent on keeping its monopoly of the sale of silk in the Byzantine Empire, Persia rejected his overtures. Istämi then resolved to deal directly with the Byzantines against Persia. In 567 he therefore sent the same Maniakh to the court of Constantinople by way of the lower Volga and the Caucasus. Emperor Justin II must have been much interested in the proposals of the Turkic ambassador, for when the latter left for home in 568, he was accompanied by a Byzantine envoy, Zemarchos. Istämi received Zemarchos at his summer residence north of the Aqtagh hills—that is, the T'ien Shan—in the deep valley of the upper Yulduz northwest of Kara Shahr. A firm alliance was concluded against the common enemy, Sassanid Persia. A Sassanian envoy who appeared at this juncture and met Istämi near Talas was roughly escorted away and the Turkic king declared war on Persia. In 572 the Byzantines themselves embarked on a war against Persia which was to last for twenty years (572–591). Meanwhile, the western T'u-chüeh and the Byzantines maintained close relations. While Zemarchos was on his way homeward by way of the lower Volga, the Caucasus, and Lazica, Istämi dispatched a second ambassador, Anankast, to Constantinople. In return, Byzantium successively sent him as envoys Eutychios, Valentinos, Herodian, and Paul of Cilicia.

These various ambassadors enabled the Byzantines to acquire a fairly accurate idea of the customs and beliefs of the T'u-chüeh. "The Turks," Theophylactus Simocattes tells us, "hold fire in very extraordinary honor." Indeed, the influence of Iranian Mazdaism had caused them even to adopt the god Ormazd or Ahura-Mazda. "They venerate air and water also," and in effect among the Jenghiz-Khanites reverence for running water was carried to such lengths that Muslim ablutions and the washing of clothes were forbidden except under certain conditions. "But it is the author of heaven and earth alone that they worship and call god, sacrificing to him horses, oxen, and sheep." Such indeed is the cult of Tängri, the heavens in their divine aspect, common to all the ancient Turko-Mongol peoples. Finally, what Theophylactus says of "their priests who seem to them to foretell the future" applies to the Turko-Mongol shamans, who continued to exert great influence in the days of Jenghiz Khan.[11]

In 576, the Byzantine emperor Tiberius II once more sent Valentinos on an embassy to the western T'u-chüeh. But by the time the envoy arrived at the royal residence on the upper Yulduz, Istämi had died. His son and successor Tardu (575–603) —the Ta-t'ou of the Chinese historians—was greatly displeased because the court of Constantinople had concluded a treaty with the Avars, that is to say, with the remnants of the Juan-juan or, more probably, with the Ephthalites who had taken refuge in southern Russia. Tardu therefore received Valentinos very coldly. Moreover, as a reprisal for what he considered Byzantium's breach of the alliance, he sent a detachment of T'u-chüeh cavalry under the command of a certain Bokhan against the Byzantine settlements in the Crimea. With the aid of Anagai, the last chief of the Uturgur Huns, Bokhan laid siege to the Byzantine city of Bosporus or Panticapaeum, near Kerch (576). Likewise, in 581 the T'u-chüeh were under the walls of Chersonesus, and it was not until 590 that they were to evacuate the country permanently.[12]

This quarrel between the western T'u-chüeh and the Byzantines did not prevent the former from continuing their war against Persia. In 588–589, they invaded Bactria or Tokharistan and advanced as far as Herat. If they were repulsed by the Persian hero Bahram Chobin, as Persian tradition insists, they must certainly have taken advantage of the civil war which broke out in 590 between Bahram and Chosroes II Parviz. Indeed, having had the worst of it, Bahram finally took refuge among them, and it was no doubt at this time that they completed the conquest of Tokharistan north of the Hindu Kush. In any event, in 597–598 this country, with its capitals of Balkh and Kunduz, no longer belonged to Persia but was a dependency of the western T'u-chüeh.[13] In 630, when the Chinese pilgrim Hsüan-tsang made his journey, Tokharistan was the fief of a *tegin* or Turkic prince living at Kunduz; he was a son of the khan of the western T'u-chüeh.

Thus at the moment when in the Far East the purely Chinese dynasty of the Sui would finally reunite China (in 589) after three centuries of partition, Central Asia found itself divided into two vast Turkic empires: the empire of the eastern T'u-chüeh, extending from the Manchurian border to the Great Wall and to the Hami oasis, and that of the western T'u-chüeh, which stretched from Hami to Lake Aral and to Persia, from which it was separated by a frontier running south of the Oxus and between the Oxus and Merv rivers. All Tokharistan north of the Hindu Kush was thus enclosed within politically Turkic territory.

Kul-tegin's inscription at Kosho-Tsaidam, composed a century later, celebrates in epic terms this Turkic greatness at its height:

When the blue sky above and the dark earth beneath were created, between them were created the sons of men. Above the sons of men arose my ancestors, Bumin khagan and Istämi khagan. When they had become masters, they governed and established the empire and the institutions of the Turkic people. At the four corners of the world they had many enemies, but, making expeditions with armies, they subjugated and pacified many peoples at the four corners of the world. They made them bow their heads and bend their knees. They made us move eastward as far as the forest of Qadirkhan [the Khingan Mountains] and backward [or westward] to the Iron Gates [of Transoxiana]. Over all the land between these uttermost points the Blue Turks held sway as sovereigns. They were wise khagans, valiant khagans; all their officers were wise and brave; all their nobles and the whole people were righteous.[14]

The moral concepts implied by this famous passage are borrowed from the old cosmogony which formed the basis of Turko-Mongol shamanism. The principles of this cosmogony were very simple, according to the résumé by Thomsen.[15] The universe consisted of a series of levels, one above the other. The seventeen upper levels formed the heavens, or realm of Light, and the seven or nine lower ones constituted the underworld, or place of Darkness. Between the two lay the surface of the earth, where men dwelt. Heaven and earth obeyed a supreme being who inhabited the highest level of the sky and who was known by the name of Divine Heaven, or Tängri.[16] Heaven was also the habitation of virtuous souls, as the subterranean world was the hell of the wicked. Turkic mythology numbered many other deities, one of which was the goddess Umai, the caretaker of children.[17] In addition, countless genies inhabited "the earth and the waters" (these were the *yer-sub,* or in modern Turkish *yär-su*). Notable among the latter were the sprites dwelling in hills and springs, which were considered sacred places and whose cult would be perpetuated in the practices and laws of the Jenghiz-Khanites.

Chinese historians have given a physical portrait of the T'u-chüeh. An author writing in 581 depicts them thus:

They let their hair flow loose and they dwell in tents of felt. They move from one camp to another, according to the water and grazing to be found at each place. Their main occupations are the breeding of livestock and hunting. They show little consideration for their old people,[18] while men in the prime of life they hold in high esteem.

They are ignorant of ritual and of justice, and in this respect resemble the ancient Hsiung-nu. Their high officers are the ye-pu [*yabghu*], the she [*shad*], the te-k'in [*tekin* or *tegin*], the su-li-pat and the to-tun-pat [*tudun*], and other minor functionaries. These public officials form twenty-nine distinct classes, all appointments being hereditary. Their arms consist of bow, arrows, whistling arrows, breastplate, lance, saber, and sword. On their belts they wear ornaments hollowed or carved in relief. Their flagstaffs are topped by the image of a she-wolf's head in gold. The king's men-at-arms are called *fu-li*, a word meaning wolf [like *böri*]. When a man dies, each of his kinsmen kills a sheep or a horse and lays it before his tent as if offering him sacrifice. They ride seven times round the tent on horseback, uttering mournful cries, and when they come before the tent door they gash their faces with their knives, so that the blood is seen to flow with their tears. . . . On the day of the funeral, kinsmen and others close to him make sacrifice, gallop their horses, and gash their faces as on the day of death. After the burial, stones are placed by the grave in a number proportionate to the number of men slain by the deceased. On the death of a father, an elder brother, or an uncle, the son, the younger brother, and the nephews marry the widows and sisters. The khan's tent opens toward the east, out of respect for that part of the sky in which the sun rises. They revere demons and spirits and believe in magicians [shamans]. It is their glory to die in battle, and they would think shame to perish from sickness.[19]

PARTITION OF THE T'U-CHÜEH EMPIRES

The dual empire of the T'u-chüeh did not long endure at this peak of power. The great khagans celebrated in the Kosho-Tsaidam inscription were succeeded by others who lacked their genius. "Their younger brothers and the sons of these became khagans," the same text tells, "but the brothers were not created like their seniors, nor the sons like their fathers. Khagans without wisdom or valor ascended the throne and so brought about the dissolution of the Turkic Empire." [20]

What really destroyed the might of the T'u-chüeh was the rivalry between the two khanates, the eastern one on the Orkhon and that of the west on the Issyk Kul and the Talas. The twin Turkic empires, which dominated half of Asia from Manchuria to Khurasan, would have been invincible had they been able to preserve their union on the basis of 552, whereby the chief of the eastern T'u-chüeh took precedence, with the imperial title of khagan, while the western ruler was content with second place and the title of *yabghu*. But the khagan of the east, T'o-po, brother and successor to Mu-han, was the last of his line to receive the homage of the west.[21] Between 582 and 584, Tardu, the *yabghu* of the west, who, as is attested by Valentinos' account, was a very violent character, broke with the new sovereign of the east and himself took the title of khagan. China, where the forceful Sui dynasty had resumed the grand politics of the Han in regard to Central Asia, encouraged Tardu in this rebellion, which broke the Turkic power in two. Thereafter, the eastern and western T'u-chüeh were never again to be reunited, and indeed remained for the most part on hostile terms.[22]

Thus, at a time when China was reuniting, the Turks were disintegrating. This reversal rendered possible the triumph of Chinese imperialism in Central Asia under the Sui and T'ang dynasties (seventh to ninth centuries).

The T'u-chüeh of the east not only were confronted by the westerners' revolt but were torn by internal strife as well. Their new khagan, Sha-po-lo (581–587),[23] found his power disputed in Mongolia itself by his cousins Yen-lo and Ta-lo-pien. At the same time he was attacked in the west by Tardu, the new "khagan" of the western T'u-chüeh, and in the east by the Khitan of Liaosi. This development, however, was disquieting to the Chinese, for such a coalition, by crushing the Turks of Mongolia, threatened to render Tardu too powerful. Tardu must not be allowed to restore Turkic unity to his own advantage. Accordingly, the Chinese sovereign Yang Chien, founder of the Sui dynasty, abruptly reversed his alliances and supported the eastern khagan Sha-po-lo against Tardu (585). The easterners, preoccupied with their internal squabbles, were in any case no longer to be feared. Sha-po-lo's brother and successor Mu-ho most probably slew the anti-khan Ta-lo-pien (587), but died soon after; and the khagan who followed, Tu-lan (587–600), found himself opposed by another anti-khan, T'u-li, who was supported by the Chinese. It is true that Tu-lan drove out this rival in 599, but the emperor Yang Chien hastened to welcome T'u-li and his partisans, and established them as confederates in the Ordos. The eastern T'u-chüeh remained hopelessly divided.

On Tu-lan's death, Tardu, the khagan of the west, tried once more to take advantage of the demoralization of the easterners, so as to subjugate them, establish his rule over Mongolia and Turkestan, and effect the reunion of the Turks.[24] In order to forestall Chinese intervention, he resorted to intimidation. In 601 he threatened Changan, the imperial capital, and in 602 attacked T'u-li, the protégé of the Chinese, in his Ordos encampments. But Chinese policy was unobtrusively at work. Suddenly, in 603, one of the chief western tribes—the Tölös or Töläch, forebears of the Uigurs—who seem to have led a nomadic life in the regions of Tarbagatai, Urungu, and Dzungaria, rebelled against Tardu. Since his power had been undermined even in his own dominions, Tardu had taken refuge in Koko Nor, where he disappeared (603). His kingdom—that mighty khanate of the western T'u-chüeh, which had caused Persia and Byzantium to tremble and which some years earlier had threatened the Chinese capital—was immediately partitioned. Tardu's grandson Shih-kuei secured only the most westerly part of his inheritance, together with Tashkent, while a certain anti-khan Ch'u-lo made himself lord of the Ili. Ch'u-lo indeed was planning to continue the work of Tardu, but the Chinese were able to stop him in time. P'ei Kiu, the imperial commissioner, secretly abetted his rival Shih-kuei.[25] Ch'u-lo, having had the worst of it, took service at the court of China (611). Shih-kuei, who owed his success to Chinese policy, seems never to have taken any action against that country. Meanwhile, among the eastern T'u-chüeh, power remained in the hands of China's protégé, the khagan T'u-li (d. 609), and afterward in those of his son Shih-pi (609–619). In Mongolia, as in western Turkestan, the China of the Sui dynasty thus succeeded, by the pursuit of no more than the customary intrigues and without a major war, in splitting Turkic power, eliminating refractory khans, and bringing to power those khans who had resigned themselves to Chinese suzerainty.

The same thing was happening in Koko Nor. There the Hsien-pi (presumably a Mongol horde) of the T'u-yü-huen, whose presence had troubled the Chinese outposts in Kansu for three centuries, were crushed in 608 by Chinese legions and had to flee into Tibet.[26] In that same year China reoccupied the Hami oasis, and in 609 the king of Turfan, K'iu Pai-ya, came to pay homage to the emperor Yang-ti.

This whole structure crumbled when Yang-ti's luckless campaigns in Korea (612–614) undermined the prestige of the Sui dynasty. Shih-pi, the khagan of the eastern T'u-chüeh, revolted and almost captured Yang-ti himself in the fortress of Yenmen in northwest Shansi (615). The civil wars which then broke out in China (616–621), leading in 618 to the collapse of the Sui dynasty, fully revived the T'u-chüeh's old daring. When after the defeat of rival pretenders the new T'ang dynasty ascended the throne of China, the work of the Sui had all to be done again. The steppe hurled its hordes at the very heart of Shansi. In 624 the new khagan of the eastern T'u-chüeh, Hie-li, or El (620–630), took advantage of the chaos brought about by civil war and rode in at the head of his squadrons to threaten Changan, the imperial capital.

Fortunately, the T'ang dynasty possessed a remarkable warrior, the prince imperial Li Shih-min, who, for all this youth, was the true founder of his house. Boldly Li Shih-min advanced as far as Pinchow on the King River to meet the barbarians, and intimidated them by his resolute conduct. For a while the leaders of the horde conferred together, and then rode away without striking a blow. A few hours later a deluge of rain swept all that region. At once Li Shih-min summoned his captains. "Comrades!" the *T'ang Shu* reports him as saying, "the whole steppe is now a sea. Night will soon fall, and it will be of the darkest. Now is the time to march. The T'u-chüeh are to be feared only when they can see to shoot their arrows. Let us go to them, saber and pike in hand, and we shall rout them before they can prepare to defend themselves!" This was done. At dawn the Turkic camp was taken and the Chinese cavalry cut its way through to the tent of khagan Hie-li himself. Hie-li asked for terms and withdrew into Mongolia (624).[27] Soon after this spectacular action Li Shih-min, then aged twenty-seven, ascended the throne of China, thenceforth to be known to history by his imperial name of T'ai-tsung (626).

DESTRUCTION OF THE KHANATE OF THE EASTERN T'U-CHÜEH BY EMPEROR T'AI-TSUNG

The emperor T'ai-tsung (627–649) was the true founder of Chinese greatness in Central Asia. He destroyed the khanate of the

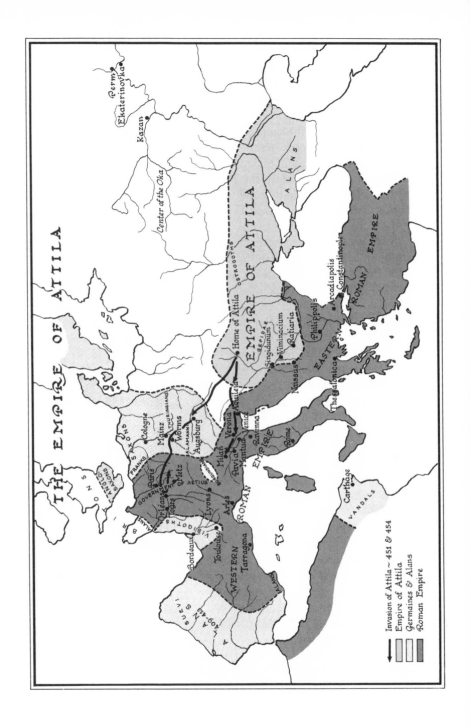

THE EMPIRE OF ATTILA

Invasion of Attila ~ 451 & 454
Empire of Attila
Germaines & Alans
Roman Empire

eastern T'u-chüeh, contributed to the dismemberment of the western T'u-chüeh—of whom his son was later to complete the conquest—and extended his protectorate to the Indo-European kingdoms of the Tarim.

In the year of T'ai-tsung's accession, the khagan of the eastern T'u-chüeh, Hie-li, once more led a mounted expedition to the very walls of Changan. On September 23, 626, his hundred thousand men appeared before the Penkiao bridge, at the north gate of the city. Here Hie-li made an insolent demand for tribute, backed with a threat to sack the capital. T'ai-tsung, who seems to have had only a few troops with him, acted boldly. Calling out all available men, he stationed them in front of the gates, while he himself with a handful of horsemen advanced along the Wei River toward the hostile army. Impressed by his bravery, the T'u-chüeh chiefs dismounted and saluted him. Meanwhile, the Chinese were deploying on the plain behind him, "causing their arms and standards to glitter in the sun." T'ai-tsung rode forward to within earshot of the Turkic camp and harangued the khagan and his lieutenants, reproaching them for the breach of truce. Hie-li, abashed, made peace next day after the traditional sacrifice of a white horse.[28]

To curtail Hie-li's power, T'ai-tsung gave his support to a rebellion of two dissident Turkic tribes: the Tölös or Töläch and the Syr Tardush. The former (the Uigur of later days) were established in Tarbagatai, the latter near Kobdo (627–628).[29] At the same time, in eastern Mongolia itself, T'ai-tsung favored the secession of an anti-khan named T'u-li, who had risen against Hie-li (628). Having thus helped to throw a hostile ring round Hie-li, in 630 the great emperor hurled the Chinese army against him under the command of Li Tsing and Li Shih-tsi. Encountering Hie-li in Inner Mongolia, north of Shansi, the Chinese commanders launched a surprise attack upon his camp and scattered his hordes. Hie-li himself was taken prisoner. For some fifty years (630–682) the khanate of the eastern T'u-chüeh was subject to China. "The sons of the Turkic nobles," runs the Turkic inscription of Kosho-Tsaidam, "became slaves to the Chinese people, and their innocent daughters were reduced to serfdom. The nobles, discarding their Turkic titles, accepted those of China and made submission to the Chinese khagan, devoting their labor and their strength to his service for fifty years. For him, both toward the rising sun and westward to the Iron Gates, they launched their expeditions. But to the Chinese khagan they surrendered their empire and their institutions." [30]

With such auxiliaries as these, T'ai-tsung, having crushed the Turks of Mongolia, would in the course of the next twenty years bring under his sway the Turks of Turkestan and the Indo-European oases of the Gobi. In him an astonished Asia beheld an unknown, epic China. Far from conciliating the barbarians and purchasing their withdrawal with gold, T'ai-tsung turned the tables upon them and made them tremble. Throughout three centuries of Turko-Mongol invasions, the Chinese people had assimilated the victorious hordes. Fortified by the injection of this fresh blood, they now turned upon the men of the steppe from whom they had derived their strength, adding to that strength the incalculable superiority of an age-old civilization.

DISSOLUTION OF THE KHANATE OF THE WESTERN T'U-CHÜEH

Having reorganized the territories of the Ordos and Inner Mongolia as border marches in 630, T'ai-tsung turned his attention to the western T'u-chüeh. These, as we have seen, had reunited in favor of the khan Shih-kuei. After the submission of the Syr Tardush of the Altai, Shih-kuei, who lived near the Tekes and the upper Yulduz, reigned between 611 and 618 from the Altai to the Caspian and the Hindu Kush. His brother and successor, T'ung Shih-hu—that is to say, T'ung the *yabghu* (between 618 and 630)—further extended this power. Already conqueror of the Töläch in the northeast, he reaffirmed his rule over Tokharistan or Bactria in the southwest and achieved hegemony in part of the Tarim basin.

At the time of the journey of the Chinese pilgrim Hsüan-tsang, who met him near Tokmak at the beginning of 630, T'ung Shih-hu was at the height of his power. He led a nomadic life governed by the seasons, between the valleys of the upper Yulduz, where, like his predecessor, he spent the summer, and the shores of the Issyk Kul, "the hot lake," near which were his winter quarters. He liked also to camp farther to the west, by the "thousand springs" near Talas, the Dzhambul of the present day. The king of Turfan was one of his client-rulers, and his own son Tardu-shad was king of Tokharistan, with his residence at Kunduz. The *T'ang*

Shu states that "he held hegemony over the western lands. Never had the barbarians of the west been so powerful." [31] The emperor T'ai-tsung, who for the moment was concentrating on the destruction of the eastern T'u-chüeh, thought he should "join with those who are far against those who are near"; consequently, he treated T'ung Shih-hu as an ally.

The description of T'ung Shih-hu left by Hsüan-tsang is that of an Attila or a Jenghiz Khan. "The horses of these barbarians were exceedingly numerous. The khan wore a coat of green satin and allowed all his hair to be seen, his brow alone being bound by several turns of a silken fillet ten feet long, of which the ends hung down at the back. He was attended by some two hundred officers wearing brocade coats, all with their hair braided. The rest of the troops consisted of riders mounted on camels or horses; they were clad in furs and fine woolen cloth, and carried long lances, banners, and straight bows. Such was their multitude that the eye could discern no limit to it." [32]

T'ung Shih-hu gave a warm welcome to the Chinese pilgrim. Indeed, he had always proved to be quite open to Buddhism. Some years earlier he had had as a guest an Indian missionary named Prabhakaramitra, who had set himself the task of converting the T'u-chüeh before going on in 626 to preach in China. [33] T'ung Shih-hu gave Hsüan-tsang a similar reception at his Tokmak headquarters, of which the pilgrim has left a colorful account: "The khan dwelt in a large tent ornamented with golden flowers that dazzled the eyes. His officers had spread long mats over the entrance and sat there in two lines, all wearing splendid garments of silk brocade. Behind them stood the king's bodyguard. Although this was a barbarian ruler sheltered by a felt tent, one could not behold him without esteem." It is strange to recall, in reading these lines, the almost identical impressions produced upon travelers from the West by Jenghiz-Khanite chiefs. Another scene, to be found also in Rubruck's description of the thirteenth-century Mongols, is that of the carousals held at the reception of foreign ambassadors. While Hsüan-tsang was staying with him, T'ung Shih-hu received envoys from China and from the king of Turfan. "He invited these envoys to be seated and offered them wine to the accompaniment of musical instruments. The khan drank with them. Then all were seen to drink one with another, with ever-increasing liveliness, clinking their cups together and filling and emptying them by turns. Meanwhile the music of eastern and western barbarians sounded its noisy chords. Half-savage though these airs were, they charmed the ear and rejoiced the heart. Shortly afterward, fresh dishes were brought in, quarters of boiled mutton and veal, which were piled in abundance before the revelers."

Some months after Hsüan-tsang's visit, this mighty empire of the western T'u-chüeh collapsed. In that same year, 630, one of the western tribes, the nomad Qarluqs, who seem to have made their seasonal moves between the eastern point of Lake Balkhash and the Chuguchak region of Tarbagatai, rebelled against T'ung Shih-hu and put him to death.[34] The khanate of the western T'u-chüeh was split into two groups, of which the names are known only in Chinese transcription: the Nu-shih-pi tribes to the west and southwest of the Issyk Kul, and the Tu-lu tribes northeast of that lake. Nu-shih-pi and Tu-lu wore themselves out in obscure battles. A Tu-lu khan, himself named Tu-lu (638–651), attempted at one stage to reunite the two groups, after which he made bold to attack the Chinese military colonies in the Hami area. But the Chinese general Kuo Hiao-k'o defeated him near the Bogdo Ola Mountains, between Kucheng and modern Urumtsi (ca. 642). Moreover, the emperor T'ai-tsung supported the Nu-shih-pi hordes against Tu-lu and the harassed khan had to take flight to Bactria, where he disappeared (651).[35]

THE INDO-EUROPEAN OASES OF THE TARIM AT THE
ACCESSION OF THE T'ANG DYNASTY

Having annihilated the T'u-chüeh, Emperor T'ai-tsung was able to re-establish Chinese hegemony in the Tarim oases, which were at least partly Indo-European, notably at Turfan, Kara Shahr, Kucha, and Kashgar in the north, and Shanshan, Khotan, and Yarkand in the south.

These ancient caravan cities, important as relay stations on the Silk Road between China, Iran, and the Byzantine world, were no less so as stages on the route of Buddhist pilgrimage from China to Afghanistan and the Indies. This aspect of them has been well described by the Chinese pilgrim Hsüan-tsang, who, leaving Kansu in 629, on his outward journey (629–630) took the northern route via Turfan, Kara Shahr, Kucha, and Aksu, traveling thence to Tokmak, Tashkent, and Samarkand. On his return in 644, he journeyed by the southern route, through the Pamirs, Kashgar, Yarkand, Khotan, Shanshan, and Tunhwang. His record shows that these petty kingdoms of the Tarim had been entirely won over to Buddhism, which brought with it so much of Indian culture that Sanskrit had become the religious language of the region, alongside the local Indo-European tongues: that is to say, Turfanese, Karashahri, and Kuchean (the old "Tokharian" A and B) and "East Iranian," the latter having apparently been spoken in the Khotan area.[36]

The manuscripts discovered by the Pelliot, Aurel Stein, and Le Coq expeditions also prove that Buddhic texts were translated from Sanskrit into these various local Indo-European dialects (the two kinds of Tokharian, or what were known as such, in the north; "East Iranian" in the southwest), while another Indo-European language, Sogdian, introduced by caravans from Bukhara and Samarkand, was spoken at the overnight camps from the T'ien Shan to the Lob Nor, where Pelliot discovered seventh-century traces of one of these Sogdian colonies.[37] As has been seen, caravaneers and merchants of the Silk Road as well as Buddhist missionaries, arriving from the Indo-Iranian borders, combined to introduce the arts of Iran and India to the Tarim oases, where they were to be fused into a curious synthesis by the workings of the Buddhist faith. In this connection has been noted the various borrowings—Greco-Buddhic, Indo-Gangetic, or Irano-Buddhic—which may be discerned in the Kizil frescoes near Kucha, and belong either to what Hackin calls the first Kizil style (ca. 450–650) or to the second (ca. 650–750).[38] There is also the peculiarly Sassanian character of the Buddhic paintings on wooden panels at Dandan-Uilik, east of Khotan (ca. 650). Lastly, the second Sassano-Buddhic style of Kizil, parallel with Indian influences reminiscent of Ajanta, extended even to the frescoes of the Turfan group: at Bezeklik, Murtuk, and Sängim. In addition to these Indian, Hellenistic and Iranian influences, that of China, as Hackin observes, was making itself felt at Kumtura near Kucha, and above all of course at Bezeklik and the other fresco sites of the Turfan group, the group nearest to the Chinese frontier.[39]

At the time of Hsüan-tsang's journey (630), the culture of this crossroads of civilization was at its height, especially in Kucha. Of all the Indo-European oases of the Gobi, Kucha is undoubtedly one of those in which Indo-Europeanism is most clearly demonstrated, through the plentiful Buddhic literature in the Kuchean tongue uncovered by the Pelliot, Stein, and Le Coq expeditions. The very transcriptions of the name Kucha in Sanskrit (Kuchi) and in Chinese (Kuche) seem very closely allied to the pronunciation Kütsi, which is supposed to have been that of the native—or, as it was until recently called, the Tokharian—tongue.⁴⁰ Under Buddhic influence, the Kucha dialect—that is to say, the particular Indo-European dialect designated for a time by Orientalists as Tokharian B, today known simply as Kuchean—had become a literary language, into which, from the fifth to the seventh century, part of the Sanskrit canon had been translated. Benefiting thus from its contact with Buddhist civilization—the intellectual heritage of India—and also by the wealth accruing from its caravan link with Iran, whose material civilization it copied, Kuchean society as revealed in the texts and frescoes of Kizil and Kumtura appears a phenomenal achievement, almost a paradox in time and space. It is like a reverie when one reflects that this elegant and polished society, the fine flower of Aryanism in Central Asia, blossomed but a few rides away from all the Turko-Mongol hordes, at the very frontiers of barbarian worlds, on the eve of its extinction by the least enlightened communities of primitive man. It seems a miracle that on the edge of the steppes, protected by desert alone and threatened daily by the fiercest onslaughts of the nomads, this society was able to survive so long.

The glittering Kuchean chivalry revived in the Kizil frescoes seems to have come, in defiance of chronology, from some Persian page of miniatures. The pure ovals of those delicate faces, meticulously shaven except for the slightest of mustaches, with their long, straight noses and well-arched eyebrows, those trim waists and long, slender bodies which appear to have escaped from some Timurid *Shah Namah*—all combine to display a markedly Iranian physical type. The same is true of the costume. First, court dress: the long, straight frock coats, drawn in at the waist by a metal belt and rolled open at the breast by the large lapels already noted in Afghanistan in the Sassanian-like Bamian frescoes, and the trimmings of braid, beads, and flowers borrowed from the immemorial Iranian style of adornment. Then the military dress:

Sassanid Persia and an elegance already "Persian" that evoke the proud lancers of the Kizil frescoes, with their conical helmets, coats of mail, long lances, and great cut-and-thrust swords. Lastly, the fair ladies and benefactresses of Kizil and Kumtura in their tight-waisted bodices and voluminous skirts recall—notwithstanding the Buddhic theme—that at all the halting places along the Silk Road, in all the rich caravan towns of the Tarim, Kucha was renowned as a city of pleasures, and that as far as China men talked of its musicians, its dancing girls, and its courtesans.

THE ESTABLISHMENT OF THE T'ANG PROTECTORATE IN THE TARIM BASIN

Although under the unifying influence of the Buddhist religion the material civilization of Kucha remained chiefly Iranian, Turfan (Kaochang) showed itself more strongly affected in this respect by China.[41] A comparison of the frescoes of the Kucha region (Kizil) with those of Turfan (Murtuk, Sängim, and Bezeklik) is convincing in this respect. Here the Indo-Iranian characteristics, passed on via Kucha, merge gradually into the T'ang aesthetic. China's proximity, as well as local history, explains this cultural slide. The country of Turfan was governed after 507 by the K'iu, a dynasty of Chinese origin. In 609, K'iu Pai-ya went to pay homage to the emperor Yang-ti of China. His successor K'iu Wen-t'ai (ca. 620–640) welcomed the Chinese pilgrim Hsüan-tsang with enthusiasm—so excessive an enthusiasm indeed that he almost refused to let his guest depart (end of 629 to the beginning of 630). This well-known episode does at least show the monarch's taste for Chinese culture and Buddhist fervor. In the same year (630), K'iu Wen-t'ai went to pay homage to the emperor T'ai-tsung, but toward the end of his reign he rebelled against T'ang suzerainty (640). T'ai-tsung sent general Heu Kiun-tsi against him. At the approach of the Chinese army, K'iu Wen-t'ai died of shock. Turfan was occupied and annexed, and became the seat of a Chinese prefecture and later of the Chinese government of the "Pacified West," Ansi (640).

The kingdom of Kara Shahr (Agni in Sanskrit transcription, Yenki in Chinese) seems to have been almost as lustrous an Indo-European center as Kucha.[42] As in Kucha, the religious culture—thanks to Buddhism—was borrowed from India, the material civilization was derived partly from Iran, and a large proportion of the art recalled that of Greco-Buddhic Afghanistan. The Kara Shahr stuccoes in Berlin are thus amazingly similar to those of Hadda in the Guimet Museum. But there too the China of the T'ang exerted its military might. In 632, Kara Shahr recognized the suzerainty of the emperor T'ai-tsung, but in 640 the reigning sovereign (known in Chinese as Tu-k'i-che), no doubt upset by the annexation of Turfan, allied himself with the western T'u-chüeh and raised the flag of rebellion. T'ai-tsung sent against him General Kuo Hiao-k'o, who, by a clever march, approached Kara Shahr from the direction of the Yulduz, under cover of night, and at dawn attacked and captured the surprised city. There he enthroned a brother of the deposed king, a pro-Chinese prince named Li-p'o-chuen (640). Some years later Li-p'o-chuen was deposed by his cousin Sie-p'o A-na-che, who had the support of the Kucheans and the T'u-chüeh. The imperial general A-shih-na Shö-eul (a T'u-chüeh prince in T'ang service) was commissioned by T'ai-tsung to subdue the rebel city for good. He marched on Kara Shahr, beheaded the usurper, and gave the throne to another member of the royal family (648).

After Kara Shahr, it was Kucha's turn.[43] Kucha (Kuche) was ruled by a dynasty called in Kuchean the Swarna family (in Sanskrit, Suvarna; in Chinese transcription, Su-fa), that is to say, the Golden Family. In 618, the king, known in Chinese as Su-fa Pu-shih (in Sanskrit, Suvarna Pushpa: Golden Flower), had paid homage to Yang-ti the emperor of China. His son, the Su-fa Tie of Chinese annals (Swarnatep in Kuchean, and in Sanskrit Suvarna Deva: the Golden God), a zealous Buddhist, in 630 gave a magnificent welcome to Hsüan-tsang, the Chinese pilgrim, despite the fact that he and his people adhered to that form of Buddhism known as the Lesser Vehicle (Hinayana), whereas Hsüan-tsang followed that of the Greater Vehicle (Mahayana).[44] In the same year, Swarnatep avowed himself vassal of the emperor T'ai-tsung, but later, displeased with the T'ang interventionist policy, he joined with the western T'u-chüeh in opposition to it. In 644 he refused to pay tribute, and helped the people of Kara Shahr in their revolt against China. He died before punishment could overtake him, and was replaced in 646 by his brother, whom Chinese historians call Ho-li Pu-shih-pi (in Sanskrit, Hari Pushpa: Divine Flower).[45] The new king, aware of the approaching storm, hastened to send protestations of loyalty to the Chinese court (647). It was too late. A-shih-na Shö-eul, the T'u-chüeh prince in Chinese service, set off for the west with an army of Chinese regulars and T'u-chüeh and Töläch auxiliaries.

A-shih-na Shö-eul began by depriving Kucha of expected support by crushing two Turkic tribes, allies of the rebel city: the Ch'u-yueh and the Ch'u-mi, the former living the life of nomads near Kucheng and the latter on the Manas River. From there he descended upon Kucha. King Ho-li Pu-shih-pi sallied forth with his army, and A-shih-na Shö-eul, following the old tactic of the hordes, pretended to retreat and lured him into the desert, where he inflicted a crushing defeat. This battle may well have been the Crécy and the Agincourt of that splendid chivalry of Iranian culture, of those paladins of the Kizil frescoes. The Turkic mercenary in the pay of China entered Kucha as its conqueror and then, pursuing King Divine Flower to the western outpost of Aksu (Pohuan), he laid siege to that place and captured him. Meanwhile a Kuchean lord (named Na-li in Chinese transcription), who had gone to fetch reinforcements from the western T'u-chüeh, returned unexpectedly and, under the initial effect of surprise, slew the Chinese general Kuo Hiao-k'o. In merciless reprisal, A-shih-na Shö-eul beheaded 11,000 people. "He destroyed five great towns and with them many myriads of men and women. The lands of the west were seized with terror" (647–648). The royal prisoner Ho-li Pu-shih-pi came to beat his brow on the floor before the emperor T'ai-tsung at Changan. A *yabghu* brother of this prince was placed by the Chinese on the throne of Kucha, but kept under strict tutelage.

The brilliant Indo-European society of Kucha and Kizil never recovered from this disaster. After a century of Chinese domination, when in the second half of the eighth century China once more lost interest in Kucha, it was not the Indo-European aristocracy of bygone days who assumed power but, as in Turfan, the Uigur Turks. This ancient Indo-European country—this Outer Iran—became an Oriental Turkestan. West of the Tarim lay the kingdom of Kashgar (Shufu in Chinese), inhabited no doubt by the descendants of the ancient Saka and probably speaking their language, eastern Iranian. The Chinese pilgrim Hsüan-tsang notes that the Kashgaris had blue eyes, or, as he puts it, "green eyeballs"—a precious piece of evidence of the persistence among this

people of what German writers were to call "Aryanism." Hsüan-
tsang also mentions that their writing was of Indian origin and
the predominant religion Hinayana Buddhism, although Sassanian
Mazdaism had its adepts also. In the kingdom of Yarkand (Soche
in Chinese), on the other hand, the prevailing form of Buddhism
was Mahayana. Lastly, the Khotan (Hotien) oasis, enriched by its
mulberry plantations cultivated for silkworms, its carpet manu-
factures, and its jade products, was also an important Buddhic
center where Sanskrit was zealously studied and where Mahayana
teachings prevailed. The name of the reigning dynasty is now
known only by its Chinese transcription, Wei-ch'ö.

Since the accession of the emperor T'ai-tsung, the three kingdoms had paid homage to China: Kashgar and Khotan in 632,
Yarkand in 635. In this latter year the king of Khotan sent his
son to the imperial court. In 648, when the imperial general
A-shih-na Shö-eul subjugated Kucha, he sent his lieutenant Sie
Wan-pei to Khotan, with an escort of light cavalry. The terrified
king of Khotan, called in Chinese Fu-shö Sin, was summoned to
appear at the court of China, whence he was sent home with
added titles and privileges.[46]

T'ANG CHINA, LORD OF CENTRAL ASIA

At the conclusion of these conquests, China's direct authority extended to the Pamirs. The pride of the emperor T'ai-tsung, conqueror of Central Asia, is understandable. "The only men who
in olden days subjugated the barbarians," the *T'ang Shu* reports
him as saying, "were Ch'in Shih Huang-ti and Han Wu-ti. But by
grasping my three-foot sword I have subjugated the Two Hundred Kingdoms and silenced the Four Seas, and one by one the
distant barbarians have come to make submission." [47] Among the
Turks too, his prestige was very great. If he had conquered them,
he had also rallied them, attaching them to himself with a bond
of personal loyalty in the Turko-Mongol manner. Indeed, as is
recorded by the Turkic inscription of Kosho-Tsaidam in the following century, he knew how to become the "Chinese khagan."

The most characteristic example of his faculty for gathering
Turks about him is shown in the story of A-shih-na Shö-eul, related in the *T'ang Shu*.[48] This khan, who belonged to the royal
family of the eastern T'u-chüeh (he was the brother of the

khagan Hie-li), had sided with China in 636. He became one of T'ai-tsung's best generals, and to reward him the emperor gave him a T'ang princess in marriage. We have seen the part played by him in the Chinese conquests—the capture of Kara Shahr, Kucha, and so on. Such was his devotion that on the death of T'ai-tsung, the old mercenary desired to kill himself on his tomb, in the nomad manner, "to guard the funerary couch of the Emperor."

To all these veterans of the Central Asian campaigns may be applied the celebrated lines of the poet Li Po in *The Man of the Marches:* "Throughout his life the man of the marches never so much as opens a book, but he can hunt, he is skillful, strong, and bold. In autumn his horse is fat, for the steppe grass suits it to perfection. When he gallops, how superb and haughty is his mien! His sounding whip slashes the snow or jingles in its gilded sheath. Elated by strong wine, he calls his falcon and rides far afield. His bow, bent with power, is never loosed in vain. Men make way for him, for his valor and his warlike mood are well known in the Gobi."

During the early part of his reign the emperor Kao-tsung (650–683), son and successor of T'ai-tsung, completed his father's work. He directed his efforts against the T'u-chüeh of the west— that is, against the two groups of tribes into which the western T'u-chüeh were now divided: the Nu-shih-pi southwest of the Issyk Kul and the Tu-lu to the northeast. This division naturally suited Chinese policy. A Tu-lu khan named Ho-lu (651–657) did obtain brief recognition from the Nu-shih-pi as well, thus restoring the khanate of the west, and he lost no time in rebelling against Chinese suzerainty. To counter this, the Chinese formed an alliance with the Uigur Turks—the former Tölös or Töläch—who roved in the neighborhood of the Khangai Mountains and whose khan P'o-juan ably seconded the imperial policy. Strengthened by this support, the Chinese general Su Ting-fang plunged into the bleak solitudes of the northwest. Winter was approaching and the ground was two feet deep in snow. Said the Chinese general to his troops: "The fog sheds darkness everywhere. The wind is icy. The barbarians do not believe that we can campaign at this season. Let us hasten to surprise them!" And surprise them he did, meeting Ho-lu on the River Borotala, near the Ebi Nor in Dzungaria; then he beat him again on the Chu, west of the Issyk Kul

(657), and forced him to flee to Tashkent. This was the end of Ho-lu, for the people of Tashkent handed him over to China.[49] The imperial court then appointed A-shih-na Mi-shö, a Turk loyal to Chinese service, as the new Tu-lu khan (657–662), while the Nu-shih-pi took as their khan another client of China, A-shih-na Pu-chen (659–665).

THE LAST BLAZE OF T'U-CHÜEH POWER: MO-CH'O KHAGAN

Just when T'ang China seemed to have achieved all her aims in Central Asia, the situation suddenly altered. During the latter half of his reign, from 665 to 683, Emperor Kao-tsung, a weak ruler swayed by harem intrigues, witnessed a general decline of Chinese influence in those regions. From 665 on, the two groups of western T'u-chüeh, Nu-shih-pi and Tu-lu, revolted against the khans appointed by China and regained their independence. Next the Tibetans, a people at that time little more than savages,[50] burst into the Tarim basin and seized from China what were called the "Four Garrisons": Kara Shahr, Kucha, Khotan, and Kashgar (670). More important still, the khanate of the eastern T'u-chüeh, destroyed in 630 by Emperor T'ai-tsung, was reconstituted under a descendant of the old royal family, the khagan Qutlugh ("The Happy"); he is celebrated in the Kosho-Tsaidam inscription under the name of Elterish Khagan.

This inscription, which we owe to Qutlugh's son, shows that the restoration of the Turkic khanate of the Orkhon came in response to a surge of something like national sentiment.[51] "The whole commonalty of the Turkic people spoke thus: 'I was a people with my own empire. Where is my empire now? I was a people with my own khagan. Where is my khagan now?' Thus did they speak, and in so speaking they became enemies of the Chinese khagan and began once more to cherish the hope of organizing and establishing themselves as a political state. Then said the Chinese: 'We will annihilate the Turkic people and cut off their posterity,' and they set forth to destroy them. But the god of the Turks in heaven above, and their revered terrestrial and aquatic sprites, did this: that the Turkic people might not be destroyed but might become once more a people, they raised up my father the khagan Elterish and my mother the khatun Ilbilgä, holding them at the summit of heaven." As is borne out by the inscription, the re-

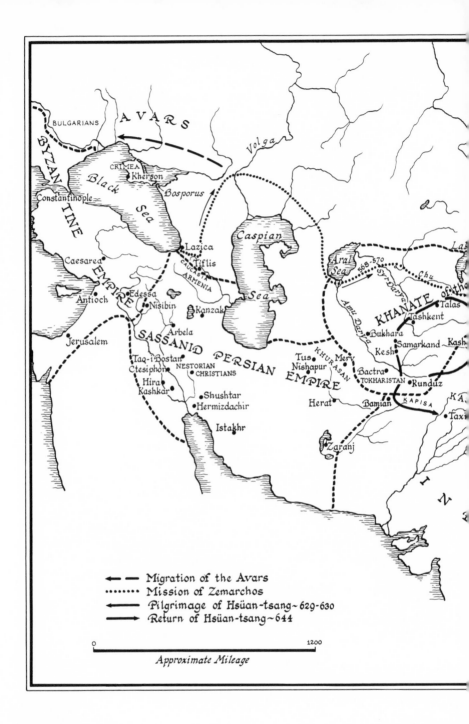

BULGARIANS

A V A R S

BYZANTINE

Volga

CRIMEA
Kherson
Black
Bosporus
Sea
Constantinople

Caspian

Caesarea

EMPIRE

Lazica
CAUCASUS
Tiflis
ARMENIA

Aral
Sea

558-570

Syr-Darya

Chu

Lak

Edessa
Nisibin
Kanzak

Sea

KHANATE

of the

Talas
Tashkent

Antioch

Jerusalem

SASSANID

Arbela

Taq-i-Bostan
Ctesiphon
Hira
Kashkar

NESTORIAN
CHRISTIANS

Shushtar
Hermizdachir

PERSIAN

Tus
Nishapur

KHURASAN

EMPIRE

Mery

Bactra
TOKHARISTAN

Amu Darya

Bukhara
Kesh
Samarkand
Kash

Runduz

Herat

Bamian

Istakhr

Zaranj

KAPISA

KA

Taxi

IN

←− − Migration of the Avars

· · · · · · Mission of Zemarchos

←−−−− Pilgrimage of Hsüan-tsang ~ 629-630

−−−−→ Return of Hsüan-tsang ~ 644

0   1200

Approximate Mileage

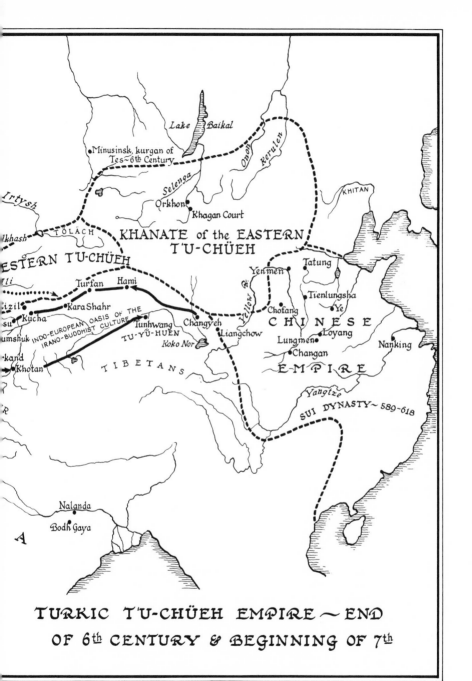

TURKIC T'U-CHÜEH EMPIRE ~ END
OF 6th CENTURY & BEGINNING OF 7th

storer of the Orkhon Empire started as leader of a simple band. "My father the khagan set off with twenty-seven men; then there were seventy. As Tängri gave them strength, my father's army was as wolves and his enemies as ewes. When the number of his men had grown to seven hundred, he dispossessed independent peoples, deposed khans, reduced men to slavery, governed them according to the laws of our ancestors, and fired their hearts. To the south the Chinese people were our enemies; to the north the Nine Oghuz (Toquz Oghuz) were our enemies, the Kirghiz and the Quriqan,[52] the Thirty Tatars and the Khitai, were enemies. My father the khagan made forty-seven campaigns and fought twenty battles. As Tängri favored him, he deprived of their empire those who had an empire, and those who had a khagan he deprived of their khagan. He pacified his enemies and made them bend the knee and bow the head." [53]

Thus the khanate of the eastern T'u-chüeh was restored in its traditional nucleus, by the headwaters of the Orkhon and in the Ötükän Mountains (presumably the Khangai range).[54] In this achievement Qutlugh had been closely supported by an astute politician, Tonyuquq (or Toñuqouq), a Turk whose family had at one time held a hereditary post in the Chinese administration in the frontier district of Yunchung, near present-day Kweihwa-cheng, north of Shansi. The inscription on Tonyuquq's funerary column, which was discovered in 1897 in the valley of the upper Tula, is of assistance in the reconstruction of this curious personality, particularly when supplemented by data from the *T'ang Shu*.[55] Like many Turkic nobles since T'ai-tsung's reign, Tonyuquq had received a Chinese education. But when Qutlugh restored Turkic independence, Tonyuquq joined him and became his adviser and best deputy, placing at the new khagan's service the knowledge he had gained of Chinese customs, mentality, and politics, and above all of the feeble state to which court intrigues had reduced the lamentable emperor Kao-tsung. In 682, therefore, Qutlugh and Tonyuquq opened hostilities against China by ravaging northern Shansi. In March, 683, Qutlugh laid waste the district of Kweichow (Hsailaihsien, north of the Nankow Pass, northwest of Peking).[56] Thenceforth, each succeeding year was marked by a raid on the borders of Shansi or Hopei. In April, 683, Qutlugh and Tonyuquq devastated the Shanyü district, the Suiyuan of today. In June, they killed the prefect of Yüchow or

Weichow (Lingkiu, southwest of Tatung), captured the governor of Fungchow (Yülin in northern Shensi), and ravaged the Lanchow area in northwest Shansi.[57] In the autumn of 684 they led raids in the direction of Suchow (Shoping [now Yuyü], north of Shansi). In may, 685, they thrust as far as Hinchow, north of Taiyüan, where a Chinese corps was defeated. In April, 687, they raided as far as Changping, northwest of Peking. In the autumn of that year, however, the Turks, who were still attacking near Shoping, in Shansi, at last suffered a reverse.

Meanwhile, on the death of the emperor Kao-tsung (December 26, 683), his widow Wu Hou (or Wu Tsö-t'ien) seized power. She was an unscrupulous, fiercely tyrannical woman, but full of energy and with a gift for government (684–705). Despotic though she may have been within her own borders, she revived the former Chinese external policy. In the Tarim basin, for instance, her generals recovered the Four Garrisons from the Tibetans: Kara Shahr and Kucha in 692, Kashgar and Khotan in 694.[58] She was less successful, as we saw, against the eastern T'u-chüeh, whose khagan Qutlugh raided and ravaged the frontier districts of Shansi and Hopei almost every year. She tried to outflank him by supporting the Türgish (Türgäch),[59] a Turkic tribe now resident in the Semirechye along the lower reaches of the Ili. The attempt was fruitless, for the Türgish khan Wu-che-lö was defeated and taken prisoner by Qutlugh, whose suzerainty he was forced to recognize (689).[60]

Qutlugh died between August and November 691.[61] He was succeeded not by one of his sons but by his brother Mo-ch'o, or Mo-cho (the Chinese transcription of the Turkic Bäk-chor, as Pelliot has established). This is the Mo-ch'o whom the Orkhon inscriptions designate by the name of Qapagan-khagan, the ruler who brought the fortunes of the eastern T'u-chüeh to their peak (691–716).[62] Assuming the role of arbiter in the palace dramas of the T'ang court, he contrived not unskillfully to figure as the protector of T'ang legitimacy against the usurping empress Wu Hou. She on her part tried to conciliate him by proposing the marriage of her nephew to his daughter. But when the young man presented himself at the khagan's court, then encamped at the Black Sands (Kara-Kum), south of present-day Sain Noyan, Mo-ch'o disdainfully rejected him (698). His daughter, he declared, was destined not for Wu Hou's nephew but for the rightful emperor, who had been set aside by the usurping empress dowager (703). He had already proclaimed that if she deposed the T'ang family he would invade the empire with all his hordes.

While feigning to defend the T'ang against the redoubtable widow, Mo-ch'o nevertheless continued his raids into Chinese territory. In 694 he devastated the Lingchow area near Ningsia, and in 698 the district of Weichow, in the region between Süanhwa and Lingkiu, west of Peking. In the interval he was persuaded into a brief collaboration with the court of China against the Khitan, Mongol nomads of Liaosi and Jehol, who were beginning a southward expansion by attacking the Chinese marches around Yungping. In 696, one of the Khitan chiefs, khan Li Tsinchung, had beaten a Chinese army in this region. This chief was Mo-ch'o's ally. On his death shortly afterward, the Khitan drove out his son and broke away from the Turkic alliance. Mo-ch'o entered Khitan territory with the object of reinstating the exile, but failed to do so. It was then that he joined China in a combined operation against the Khitan. For this he received lavish payment in the form of woven silk, rice, arms, breastplates, and so on. Caught between Mo-ch'o and the Chinese invaders, the Khitan were crushed (696–697).

The empress Wu Hou, believing Mo-ch'o to have been permanently won over to her side, complimented him on the aid he had given her. By way of reply, he resumed his raids in the Lingwu district, near Ningsia. The Chinese court rejected his insolent demands, whereupon he made a merciless expedition south of Süanhwa, stormed Weichow (in this case perhaps Lingkiu southeast of Tatung), sacked Tengkow in the heart of Hopei province between Paoting and Chengting, took Chaochow, and did not withdraw until he had removed thousands of captives, whom he caused to be put to death at the moment of his departure.[63] In 702 he devastated the district of Taichow in northern Shansi. In 706 he cut up the forces of the Chinese general Sha-ch'a Chung-yi in the Min Shan range, east of Tunhwang, and laid siege to the frontier post of Lingchow near modern Ningsia. The victory of Min Shan is celebrated in epic terms on the stele of Kosho-Tsaidam, which relates the part played in it by Mo-ch'o's nephew Kul-tegin: "We fought against Sha-ch'a *sengun*. First he [Kultegin] mounted the gray horse Tadiking-chur and charged. The horse was slain there. Next he mounted the gray horse Ishbara-

Yamatar and charged. That horse was slain there. Third, he mounted Kedimlig the bay, and charged. Clad in his armor, he struck more than a hundred foes with his arrows. His charge is in the memory of many of you, O Turkic nobles. But that [Chinese] army we destroyed there!" [64]

After each of these raids into Chinese territory, Mo-ch'o returned to Mongolia with long convoys of captives and fabulous booty. "In those days," says the Kosho-Tsaidam inscription, "slaves had become slaveowners, and serfs the owners of serfs; such were our conquests and our good order!" [65]

Mo-ch'o was no less successful against the Turkic peoples. In the east he vanquished the Bayirku folk of the upper Kerulen, and in the north the Kirghiz of the upper Yenisei. "Crossing snow that lay to the depth of our lances," says the stele of his nephew Kul-tegin, "we climbed the wooded mountains of Kögmän [modern Tannu-Ola], we swooped as conquerors upon the Kirghiz people and fought their khagan in the forest beyond. Kul-tegin charged, mounted upon a white stallion. He hit one man with his arrow and transfixed two in hand-to-hand encounter. In this charge the white stallion foundered, but the Kirghiz khagan was slain and we subjugated the people." [66] In the west, Mo-ch'o forced into temporary submission the two sections of the western T'u-chüeh: the Tu-lu and the Nu-shih-pi (699). With this, the Turks were welded once more into a formidable union, and the great T'u-chüeh empire of 550 was almost completely re-established. On the lower Ili, south of Lake Balkhash, the Türgish khan So-ko (706–711), son and successor of Wu-che-lö, attempted to resist and to rally the western T'u-chüeh against Mo-ch'o, but in 711 he was defeated and killed by the latter, who thus remained sole sovereign of the Turkic nations from the Chinese frontier to Transoxiana. [67] "The khagan of the Türgish," Kul-tegin's stele recounts, "was of my Turks, of my people. Because he was without wisdom, and failed us, he was slain. . . . We marched against the Türgish, climbing the wooded mountains of Altun [the Altai] and crossing the upper Irtysh. We swooped as conquerors upon the Türgish people. The army of the Türgish khagan came upon us like fire and tempest, and we fought. Kul-tegin charged, mounted on the gray horse Bashgu. We slew the Türgish khagan and subjugated the people." These triumphs were repeated against the Qarluq, another Turkic tribe of the Ili region. "We

fought at Karakol. Mounted on a white horse, Kul-tegin charged.
. . . We subjugated the Qarluq." [68]

But Mo-ch'o was growing old, and the Turks began to weary
of his cruelty and tyranny. Many chiefs offered their allegiance
to China, and the Bayirku of the upper Kerulen revolted. Mo-ch'o
cut them to pieces on the banks of the Tula, but while passing
through a forest on his return he was attacked by an enemy force
and killed (July 22, 716). His head was presented by the Bayirku
to the Chinese ambassador, who sent it to Changan.

KUL-TEGIN AND MO-KI-LIEN

Mo-ch'o's death was followed by serious unrest among the Turks.
His nephew, the energetic Kul-tegin, son of the old Khagan
Qutlugh, instigated a regular palace revolution. Strengthened by
the prestige he had acquired through his victories and notably by
the part he had played as his uncle's lieutenant, Kul-tegin put
Mo-ch'o's son Bögü to death, with all his family and indeeed all
the late khagan's advisers.[69] Tonyuquq alone was spared, being
the father-in-law of Kul-tegin's brother.

Kul-tegin did not seize the throne himself, but appointed his
elder brother Mo-ki-lien (in Chinese transcription) as khagan, a
man whom the Orkhon inscriptions call *bilgä khagan*, "the wise
emperor," who reigned over Mongolia from 716 to 734.[70]

Meanwhile, encouraged by Mo-ch'o's death and the family uproar that followed, all the vassal hordes had revolted against the
Orkhon dynasty. Kul-tegin and Mo-ki-lien wore themselves out
in the struggle to restore order and obedience among them. The
Kosho-Tsaidam stele, raised by Mo-ki-lien in honor of Kul-tegin,
enumerates a series of bloody battles against the Nine Oghuz
(Toquz Oghuz) and the Nine Tatar (Toquz Tatar),[71] who probably lived on the middle and lower reaches of the Kerulen respectively, and against the Uigur and Qarluq.[72] "The people of
the Toquz Oghuz were my own people. By a convulsion in heaven
and on earth they became our foes. In one year we fought five
times. Mounted on the white horse Azman, Kul-tegin charged. He
ran six men through the body. In the melee he drove his saber
into a seventh. We won, but the Turkic people were falling with
weariness and losing heart." Yet if amid these relentless battles
the eastern T'u-chüeh were forced to relinquish their suzerainty

over the T'u-chüeh of the west, they succeeded in holding the kingdom of the Orkhon. Mo-ki-lien congratulates himself, on Kul-tegin's stele, "Had I not toiled so manfully, together with my younger brother Kul-tegin, the Turkic people would have been lost." [73]

That he might bind up the last remaining wounds inflicted by civil war, Mo-ki-lien took counsel with old Tonyuquq, who was then seventy. Mo-ki-lien wished to inaugurate his reign by attacking China, but Tonyuquq dissuaded him. A great emperor, Hsüan-tsung (713–755), had just ascended the throne of the T'ang. Lacking the personal courage of T'ai-tsung the Great, and being seldom if ever disposed to tear himself away from court life (for this was the golden age, an epoch unparalleled at the court of Changan), the new Son of Heaven nevertheless displayed a keen appetite for glory, and he was eager to restore Chinese dominion in Central Asia. Tonyuquq, who was always well informed on the internal politics of China, made it clear to his lord that the Turks, exhausted as they were by civil strife, with their herds scattered, their horses emaciated, and their people famished, would be rash indeed to attack the reviving might of the T'ang. Going then to the opposite extreme, Mo-ki-lien desired to settle his Turks in a fixed abode, build a walled city in the Chinese manner on the Orkhon, and found Buddhist and Taoist monasteries. Tonyuquq showed him that this too would be a mistake. The chief advantage possessed by the Turks was their mobility as nomads, which enabled them to launch surprise attacks whenever the opportunity arose, and elude capture in the event of a reverse. "The T'u-chüeh," so the Chinese annalist reports the Turkic veteran's words, "number but one to every hundred of the Chinese. They seek water and pasture, they hunt; they have no fixed abode and they practice warfare. When they feel that they are strong, they advance. If they believe themselves weak, they retreat and hide. In this way they compensate for the advantage which the Chinese possess in their superior numbers, an advantage of which they can make no use. If you establish the T'u-chüeh in a walled town and are beaten, though it were only once, by the Chinese, you will become their prisoner. As for Buddha and Lao-tse, they teach men gentleness and humility, and such learning is unsuited to warriors." [74]

It was this exposition of the secret of Turkic strength that

Mo-ki-lien himself handed down to his descendants on the Kosho-Tsaidam stele. He recalled the demoralizing effect of Chinese customs on the eastern T'u-chüeh of the preceding century. "The enticements of the Chinese people, who without exertion give us so much gold, so much silver, so much silk, are sweet indeed, and their riches enervating. By these sweet enticements and by their wealth, the Chinese drew the Turkic people to them. Through yielding to the lure, many of your folk died, O Turkic people! Deserting the dark forest, many looked toward the south, saying: 'I would settle in the plain.'" Mo-ki-lien goes on to adjure the Turks to remain Turks: "If you go into that country, O Turkic people, you will perish! But if you remain in the forest of Ötükän [the Khangai and the Orkhon], where there are neither riches nor cares, you will preserve an everlasting empire, O Turkic people! . . . All that I have to tell you I have written on enduring rock." [75]

On the advice of Tonyuquq, Mo-ki-lien offered peace to China (718). Emperor Hsüan-tsung rejected his bid, however, and gave the order to attack. The Basmil, a Turkic tribe from the region of Kucheng (old Peiting), and the Khitan of Liaosi and Jehol, made common cause with China and prepared to take the T'u-chüeh on the flank, from southwest and southeast. Khagan Mo-ki-lien was anxious, but Tonyuquq reassured him, pointing out that the Basmil, the Chinese, and the Khitan were too far apart to be able to synchronize their attacks. Indeed Mo-ki-lien found time to cut the Basmil to pieces at Kucheng before going on to ravage the Chinese frontier of modern Kansu, near Kanchow and Liangchow (720). Peace was at last made in 721–722, and friendly relations were established between the T'u-chüeh and the empire. [76]

After the death in 731 of his brother Kul-tegin, to whom he owed his throne, Mo-ki-lien caused an elegy to be inscribed on his tomb, the site of which lay between the lake of Kosho-Tsaidam and the Kökshün Orkhon, about forty miles north of Karakorum. Several passages of this elegy have already been quoted, which may be thought of as the national epic of the ancient Turks. To it the emperor added in 732 a Chinese inscription in token of the friendship existing between the two courts. [77]

These inscriptions—the oldest dated monument of Turkic

literature—are written in what are erroneously known as "runic" characters. More properly, this writing is derived from Aramaean through the alphabet of ancient Sogdian (although, as Barthold contends, some of these "runes" have a separate origin and are of the ideographic kind). Other inscriptions in "runic" Turkic have been discovered in Siberia, in the Yenisei basin. Barthold judges that this first Turkic script may date from the seventh or even the sixth century A.D. As will be seen, it was to be replaced in the eighth century by the Uigur writing, similarly derived through Sogdian from northern Semitic alphabets.

DESTRUCTION OF THE EMPIRE OF THE EASTERN T'U-CHÜEH;
RISE OF THE UIGUR EMPIRE

By reason of their culture—to which the alphabet and inscriptions of the Orkhon bear witness—and of the relatively mild temper of their khagan Mo-ki-lien, the eastern T'u-chüeh seem to have been on the point of entering the mainstream of the great civilizations when Mo-ki-lien was poisoned in 734 by one of his ministers. His death gave rise to a series of disturbances at the end of which the T'u-chüeh empire would collapse. Soon afterward his son Yi-jan (Chinese transcription) also died, and was succeeded by his brother Tängri khagan, a young man who governed with Mo-ki-lien's widow as his adviser. In 741, however, Tängri khagan was put to death by one of his officers, the *shad* of the east, who is believed to have proclaimed himself king under the name of Ozmish khagan. This signaled the end of the T'u-chüeh empire, for Ozmish was at once faced with the revolt of the three principal vassal Turkic tribes, the Basmil, Uigur, and Qarluq, who respectively inhabited the region around modern Kucheng, the area between Kobdo and the Selenga, and the eastern end of Lake Balkhash near the Imil River. Ozmish khagan was killed in 744 by the Basmil, who sent his head to the court of Changan. The remnants of the royal clan of the eastern T'u-chüeh had already fled to China in 743.[78]

The empire of Mongolia was there for the taking. The Basmil attempted to seize it, but failed (744). The Uigur, apparently with Qarluq help, succeeded. The Uigur khan, known in Chinese transcription as Ku-li P'ei-lo, set himself up as khagan in the imperial province of the upper Orkhon under the name of

Qutlugh Bilgä (Ku-to-lu Pei-kia k'iu). His accession was approved by the T'ang court, and the emperor Hsüan-tsung bestowed upon him the title of Huai-jen. T'ang annals tell us that his dominion extended from the Altai to Lake Baikal. He died the following year (745), according to some sources—others give the date as 756—but his work survived him.

Thus the Uigur empire replaced that of the eastern T'u-chüeh. It was to last for a century (744–840). In fact, all that had happened was the substitution of one Turkic people for another, closely related, the hegemony of Mongolia. Nevertheless, in contrast to the T'u-chüeh, who had often proved dangerous neighbors for the Chinese, the Uigur were at first fairly loyal clients, then useful allies, and finally invaluable, though sometimes exacting, defenders of the T ang dynasty.

The capital of the Uigur khagans was at Karabalgasun, a town then known as Ordubaligh, "the city of the court," on the upper Orkhon near the old residences of the Hsiung-nu *shan-yü* and the T'u-chüeh khagans, in the neighborhood of what was later to be the Karakorum of the Jenghiz-Khanites.[79]

THE PEAK OF T'ANG POWER; THE SUBJECTION OF WESTERN TURKESTAN

In 714 the general A-shih-na Hien, Turkic mercenary in Chinese service, had won a resounding victory at Tokmak, west of the Issyk Kul, thus adding the Tu-lu tribes of Dzungaria and the Qarluq Turks of the Imil and Tarbagatai to the clients of China. The Türgish Turks, who presumably grazed their herds in the region of the Ili delta, south of Lake Balkhash in Semirechye, seem to have been made of sterner stuff. Their Khan Su-lu (717–738) found allies against China in the Tibetans and in a people who had newly surged forward as an unexpected invader on the Irano-Transoxianan borders: the Arabs. We shall later return to this new factor in Central Asian history. Here let us merely note that Su-lu, exploiting the disturbances caused by the onset of the Muslim legions, invaded the Tarim, which since 692–694 had been under a Chinese protectorate, besieged the town of Aksu (717), and for some months harassed the Four Chinese Garrisons of Kara Shahr, Kucha, Kashgar, and Khotan.

Though he could not reduce them, he was able, despite a campaign fought in that region by the imperial general A-shih-na (719), to hold Tokmak, west of the Issyk Kul, long an outpost of China in Turkestan. The Chinese court, despairing of holding these hazardous strong points, attempted to conciliate Su-lu by conferring titles and honors upon him (722). In 726 this inveterate plunderer was still ravaging the territory of the Four Garrisons. At last in 736 the Chinese general Kai Kia-yun, governor of Peiting, or Dzimsa, near Kucheng, inflicted a crushing defeat upon Su-lu. Shortly afterward, around 738, Su-lu was assassinated by Baga-tarkhan, the *kul-chur* of the Ch'u-mu-kuen, a small Turkic tribe which seems to have roamed between Türgish and Qarluq territories, southeast of Lake Balkhash.[80]

Baga-tarkhan joined with the Chinese general Kai Kia-yun in 739 to prevent the restoration of the Türgish pretender T'u-ho-sien, Su-lu's son. But the story of all these petty Turkic khans, all striving to reunite the western T'u-chüeh to their own advantage, is always the same. Baga-tarkhan soon broke with China and in 742 killed A-shö-na Hin, the Sinicized Turk whom the Chinese had sent to the Türgish country as viceroy.[81] Yet China as usual had the last word. In 744 the imperial general Fu-mung Ling-cha defeated and beheaded Baga-tarkhan.[82] By this victory China regained mastery of the Ili valley and of the Issyk Kul region. In 748 the Chinese general Wang Cheng-kien built a Chinese temple at Tokmak, on the upper Chu, northwest of the Issyk Kul.[83] In 751, another imperial general, the famous Kao Sien-chih, was to present yet another captured Türgish chief to the T'ang court.[84]

In the Tarim basin, the petty kingdoms of Kara Shahr, Kucha, Khotan, and Kashgar, occupied by the Chinese contingents known as the Four Garrisons, were loyal vassals. In 728, Chinese titles were bestowed upon the king of Kashgar, of the dynasty known in Chinese transcription as P'ei, and on the king of Khotan, known (also in Chinese transcription) as Wei-ch'ö Fu-shö of the Wei-ch'ö dynasty.[85] These ancient Indo-European inhabitants of the Tarim, once so rebellious against Chinese suzerainty, seem then to have rallied to it with alacrity, for the Chinese protectorate was a defense against the dual incursion of Arabs and Tibetans.

CHINESE AND ARAB RIVALRY WEST OF THE PAMIRS

About a century had passed since the Sassanid Persian Empire had fallen under the blows of the Arabs. As a result of the battles of Qadisiya (637) and Nehavend (642), the mighty Sassanid monarchy was overthrown and western Iran was conquered. In 651 Herat was occupied by the Arabs, and Yezdegerd III, the last Sassanid, died at Merv; in 652 the Arabs penetrated as far as Balkh. Satisfied with the conquest of the whole of the old empire, including Khurasan, the invaders for the time being advanced no farther. They resumed their forward march at the beginning of the eighth century, under the leadership of Qutaiba ibn Muslim, who governed Khurasan on behalf of the Ummayad caliphate from 705 to 715.[86] In 705 Qutaiba undertook an expedition against Tokharistan, the former Bactria, then ruled by a dynasty of Turkic Buddhist *tegins* founded by a junior branch of the old royal family of the western T'u-chüeh, a dynasty which according to Hsüan-tsang was usually resident near Kunduz. Qutaiba then took advantage of local quarrels to intervene in Khwarizm and Sogdiana. From 706 to 709 he waged war on the Irano-Turkic state of Bukhara, and in the latter year reduced it to vassalage. He then placed on the throne of Bukhara the lawful royal heir, Tugshada, who was to reign from 710 to 739, and who in the beginning at least was a loyal client of the Arabs and—in appearance—a follower of the Muslim religion.[87]

In 709 the local *tarkhan* of Samarkand made peace with Qutaiba in exchange for tribute and the return of hostages, but he was then overthrown by his subjects, who were incensed by his cowardice, and was replaced by Ikhshedh Ghurek. Qutaiba, after a prolonged siege of Samarkand, forced Ghurek to surrender, despite the intervention of the Turks of Tashkent and of the Ferganese, who were beaten (712).

In 707 the people of Bukhara, and in 712 those of Samarkand, appealed to Mo-ch'o, the powerful khagan of the eastern T'u-chüeh, who was then lord of all Mongolia. On each occasion Mo-ch'o sent an army to the relief of the Sogdians, under the command of one of his nephews, no doubt the famous Kul-tegin.[88] In 707 Qutaiba seems to have beaten and driven off the khagan's nephew in an engagement fought between Bukhara and Merv. In 712 the T'u-chüeh briefly occupied the whole of Sogdiana, the Arabs retaining only the city of Samarkand; but at length, in 713, Qutaiba forced them to retreat. The victorious Qutaiba kept Ghurek as vassal king in Samarkand, but installed an Arab garrison in the city. After expelling the T'u-chüeh in 712–713, he sent a punitive expedition against Tashkent and himself advanced into Fergana in the direction of Khodzhent. In 714 he was at Tashkent. In 715 he had just begun a second campaign in Fergana when civil strife in the caliphate resulted in his assassination by his own troops. (According to Tabari, Qutaiba had got as far as Kashgar, but this point is very doubtful.) [89]

The death of Qutaiba, the only Arab general of that day who had any real desire to conquer Central Asia, combined with the civil wars that weakened the caliphate of the last Ummayads, allowed the Sogdians a certain respite. At the same time, the restoration of Chinese power in Mongolia, on the Ili and in the Tarim, by the emperor Hsüan-tsung encouraged them to hope for support from that quarter. In 712 the king of Fergana,[90] expelled by the Arabs, had taken refuge in Kucha, whence he entreated China's aid in his restoration. In 715, no doubt immediately after Qutaiba's death, the Chinese general Chang Hiao-sung did indeed reinstate him after driving out of Fergana the king appointed by the Arabs.[91] In 718–719, Tugshada, the king of Bukhara, although confirmed on the throne by the Arabs, acknowledged himself a vassal of China, appealed for Chinese intervention, and, to this end, sent his brother Arslan ("The Lion" in Turkic) to the court of the emperor Hsüan-tsung in 726. Ghurek, king of Samarkand (ca. 710–739), albeit likewise compelled to recognize Arab suzerainty, repeatedly called for Chinese aid against his new masters (719, 731).[92] Farther south, the Turkic ruler or *yabghu* of Tokharistan (Kunduz and Balkh) made similar requests for Chinese protection from the Arabs (719, 727).[93]

Despite the emperor Hsüan-tsung's desire for territorial expansion, China hesitated to send an expeditionary force into Sogdiana or Bactria and to enter into open warfare against the Ummayad caliphate. The universal conflict between the court of the caliphs and the court of Changan, which the Turko-Iranians of Samarkand, Bukhara, and Kunduz were evidently dreaming of as the sole means of driving back the Muslim invasion, did not eventuate (at least before 751). Hsüan-tsung was content to stiffen the resistance of the Sogdians and Tokharians by conferring on them patents of nobility. It is true that a Turkic chieftain, the Türgish king Su-lu (717–738), being nearer to the country—he ruled over the Ili—also supported local revolts against Muslim domination. Thanks to such support and encouragement, a general uprising against Arab domination broke out in 728, and for a year (728–729) the Bukharan population maintained its rebellion with the help of the Türgish Turks. In 730–731, Ghurek, king of Samarkand, rose in rebellion, likewise with Türgish aid. Samarkand was not finally reconquered by the Arabs until about 737 or 738.[94]

THE CHINESE IN THE PAMIRS, 747–750

In effect, the emperor Hsüan-tsung had allowed Bukhara and Samarkand to relapse under Arab rule without intervening. The reason for this was that in Kansu and the Tarim the Chinese were at grips with more immediate adversaries, the Tibetans or T'u-fan.

The Tibetans, defeated in 700 by the Chinese general T'ang Hiu-ying, had sued for peace in 702, but war broke out again almost at once. In 737 the Chinese won a great victory over them west of the Koko Nor, and in 746 the Chinese general Wang Chung-tsu defeated them once more in the same region. The prize at stake was the fortress of Shih-pu-ch'eng, near Sining on the Kansu borders: a stronghold which had been snatched from the Tibetans by the Chinese general Li Yi, recaptured a little later on, and once more recovered by another imperial general, Ko Shu-han, in 749. At the other end of Tibet, the inhabitants were threatening the petty kingdoms of the Pamirs: Gilgit (in Chinese, Little Pulu), Baitistan (Great Pulu), and Wakhan (Humi), through which passed the road connecting the Chinese protectorate of the Tarim with India. To the China of the T'ang, linked to India by the bonds of trade and Buddhist pilgrimage, it was essential to maintain free passage through these high valleys of the Pamirs. The rulers of Kashmir, Chandrapida (d. 733) and Muktapida (733–769), opposed the Tibetan bands as loyal allies of the court of China, which conferred investiture

patents upon them (720, 733). The same is true of the Turkic
Buddhist dynasty of the Shahi, which reigned over Kapisa
(Ki-pin in T'ang Chinese) in the Kabul valley; Chinese patents
were conferred here in 705, 720, and 745.[95] The Tibetans having
attained suzerainty over Gilgit, the imperial general Kao Sien-
chih, second in command to the governor of Kucha, crossed the
Pamirs in 747 and came down into Gilgit by the Baroghil Pass
and imprisoned the Tibetan vassal king. In 749 the *yabghu* of
Tokharistan—that is, the Turkic Buddhist ruler of Kunduz, called
by the Chinese Shih-li-mang-kia-lo (from the Sanskrit Sri
Mangala)—sought the aid of the empire against a petty mountain chief (an ally of the Tibetans) who was cutting communications between Gilgit and Kashmir. Kao Sien-chih crossed the
Pamirs once more with a Chinese expeditionary force, and again
drove off the Tibetan partisans (750).[96]

Kao Sien-chih's two campaigns west of the Pamirs mark the
peak of Chinese expansion in Central Asia under the T'ang.
China at this time was mistress of the Tarim and Ili basins and
of the Issyk Kul region, and suzerain of Tashkent; she commanded the Pamir valleys and was protector of Tokharistan,
Kabul, and Kashmir. From his seat in Kucha, Kao Sien-chih
acted as virtual Chinese viceroy in Central Asia.

Suddenly all this collapsed, and through the agency of this
same Kao Sien-chih, who had carried the arms of China to such
distant regions.

The Collapse of T'ang Domination in Central Asia

The Turkic king or *tudun* of Tashkent, called in Chinese Kiu-pi-
shö, had repeatedly paid homage to China (743, 747, 749). Yet
in 750, Kao Sien-chih, then "protector"—that is, governor or
imperial commissioner—of Kucha, rebuked him for not fulfilling
his obligations as guardian of the marches. Kao Sien-chih arrived
in Tashkent, beheaded the *tudun*, and appropriated his treasury.
This act of violence provoked the revolt of the west. The victim's
son appealed for the support of the Qarluq Turks, whose territories were in Tarbagatai and on the River Urungu and extended from the eastern tip of Lake Balkhash to the Irtysh; he
also implored the aid of the Arab garrisons in Sogdiana. The
Arab general Ziyad ibn-Salih, who had just crushed a new rising

in Bukhara, hastened from the south, while the Qarluq forces came down from the north. In July, 751, Kao Sien-chih was crushed by these combined forces on the banks of the Talas, near present-day Aulie-Ata (Dzhambul). Tradition has it that Ziyad ibn-Salih brought thousands of captives back to Samarkand.[97] According to Barthold, this historic day determined the fate of Central Asia. Instead of becoming Chinese, as the general trend of earlier events seemed to presage, it was to turn Muslim. The Qarluq, after their victory, appear to have extended their possessions to the whole Ili region south of Balkhash and north of the Issyk Kul. The old royal residences of the western T'u-chüeh came under their sway, and their chief was content to take the lesser title of *yabghu,* no doubt to avoid offending the khagan of the Uigur.[98]

The Chinese disaster of the Talas might possibly have been repaired but for the internal strife and the revolutions which occurred at the end of Hsüan-tsung's reign. China, victim of a civil war of eight years' duration (755–763), lost at one stroke the empire of Central Asia.

THE UIGUR TURKIC EMPIRE

The revolt which came near bringing down the T'ang dynasty was led by a Khitan mercenary, a Mongol in Chinese service named An Lu-shan. This adventurer possessed himself in swift succession of the two Chinese capitals, Loyang (755) and Changan; the emperor Hsüan-tsung fled to Szechwan. Hsüan-tsung's son, the Emperor Su-tsung (756–762), undertook the task of reconquering his states and therefore appealed for aid to the Uigur Turks, at that time lords of Mongolia.[99]

In 744, as has been noted, the Uigur Turks had supplanted the eastern T'u-chüeh in the Mongolian empire. The Uigur khagan, called Mo-yen-cho [100] by the Chinese, or Ko-lo khagan (745–759), readily welcomed the request of the emperor Su-tsung, and in return was granted the hand of a Chinese princess in marriage. An Uigur army, arriving from Mongolia, thereupon co-operated with the imperial forces and afforded them vigorous aid in recapturing from the rebels the city of Loyang (757). The emperor Su-tsung loaded the Uigur chiefs with acknowledgments and titles, and before their departure promised them an annual present of 20,000 pieces of silk.

But civil war in China was not yet smothered, for other rebels imperiled the T'ang throne. Mo-yen-cho's successor, the new Uigur khagan, called in Chinese Teng-li Meu-yu (759–780), circumvented by the envoys of the rebels, thought at first to take advantage of the difficulties by which the T'ang were beset.[101] He even started for China with his army with the intention of co-operating with the rebels, but on the way an astute Chinese diplomat induced him to change his mind; he reverted to the imperial alliance and on the empire's behalf recovered Loyang from the rebels (November 20, 762). He also conscientiously plundered that city. Although the undoubted savior of the T'ang dynasty, he became a somewhat burdensome defender and a dangerous ally. In March, 763, however, he finally took the homeward road to Mongolia.

The Uigur khagan's prolonged stay in Loyang had important consequences in the spiritual sphere, for it was there that he became acquainted with Manichaean missionaries—no doubt of Sogdian origin—whom he took back with him to Mongolia and by whom he was converted to Manichaeism. This ancient Persian religion, born of a curious Mazdeo-Christian syncretism and persecuted both in Iraq and Iran by the Arabs, was thus the beneficiary of an unexpected stroke of luck: the conversion to its doctrine of the Uigur Empire, then at the height of its power as lord of Mongolia and the ally of China. Manichaeism indeed became the state religion of the Uigur. This same khagan is referred to in the Karabalgasun inscription as the "emanation of Mani" (*zahag i Mani*). An exalted Manichaean dignitary, a *mu-shö* (Chinese transcription of the title *mojak* in Sogdian and *moje* in Pahlavi), took up residence in Uigur territory as head of the new state church.[102] The Manichaean clergy quickly came to exert considerable political influence. A Chinese T'ang text of the period relates that "the Uigur always confer with the Manichaeans on government affairs."

The Uigur Empire remained the dominant power in Central Asia under succeeding khagans. Alp Qutlugh, whom the Chinese named Ho Ko-tu-lu (780–789), asked for and obtained the hand of a Chinese princess. The T'ang court could refuse nothing to these Turks whose hostility might destroy it, whose alliance had saved it, and who negotiated with it on equal terms [103]— something new in Sino-barbarian relationships.

The Karabalgasun inscription lists a number of other khagans designated by the same epithets: Tängridä bulmysh külüg bilgä (789–790), Tängridä bulmysh alp qutlugh ulugh bilgä (795–805), Tängri bilgä (805–808), Aï tängridä qut bulmysh alp bilgä (808–821). It was during the reign of this last "celestial khagan," and as a eulogy to him, that the celebrated inscription was carved in three languages—Chinese, Turkic, and Sogdian—near Karabalgasun on the left bank of the Orkhon.[104] He too had asked for the hand of a Chinese princess, but because of delays she married his son and successor Kün tängridä ulugh bulmysh kütshlüg bilgä ch'ung-tö, who reigned from 821 to 824.

The preaching of Manichaeism, with all that it conveyed of Christian and Mazdean philosophic elements, and Iranian artistic elements, was bound to contribute toward the civilizing of the Uigur. The Karabalgasun inscription explains that this "country of barbarous customs, full of the fumes of blood, was changed into a land where the people live on vegetables; from a land of killing to a land where good deeds are fostered.[105] At various times (770, 771, 807) Uigur embassies at the T'ang court constituted themselves the protectors of Manichaean communities already established in China and of those yet to be founded. In 768 the khagan obtained from the Son of Heaven a decree authorizing Manichaeans to preach in China; Manichaean temples were thereupon built for Uigur diplomatic residents (771) at Kingchow in Hopei, at Yangchow in Kiangsu, at Shaohing in Chekiang, and at Nanchang in Kiangsi. The Uigur embassy of 807 requested authority to build other Manichaean temples in Loyang and Taiyüan.

The land of Turfan,[106] incorporated with the Uigur possessions, could also boast of flourishing Manichaean communities, as is borne out by the frescoes and miniatures of this religion, especially at Idigutschai, discovered by the Le Coq mission. It is interesting to note in the miniatures, alongside likenesses of Uigur patrons, portraits of Manichaean priests in white robes, all the more so because these are the earliest-known Persian miniatures.[107] It was indeed from Persia that these Manichaean preachers had brought—together with their religion—this pictorial

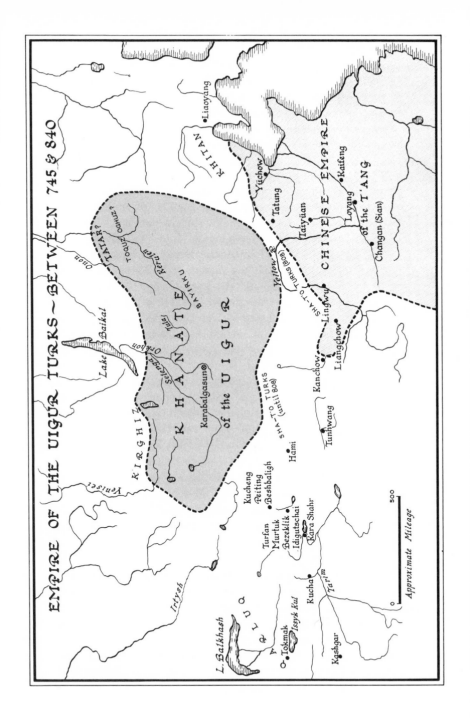

EMPIRE OF THE UIGUR TURKS ~ BETWEEN 745 & 840

Liaoyang

KHITAN

CHINESE EMPIRE

Yüchow

Tatung

Taiyüan

Loyang   Kaifeng

of the T'ANG

Changan (Sian)

Onon

TATAR?

TOQUZ OGHUZ?

Kerulen

Yellow R.

SHA-TO TURKS (808)

Lake Baikal

Selenga   Tula   Orkhon   BAYIRKU

KHANATE

of the UIGUR

Karabalgasun

Lingwu

KIRGHIZ

Kanchow   Liangchow

SHA-TO TURKS
(until 808)

Tunhwang

Yenisei

Hami

500

Kucheng
Peiting
Beshbaligh

Turfan
Murtuk
Bezeklik
Idigutschai
Kara Shahr

Irtysh

Kucha   Tar'im

Approximate Mileage

L. Balkhash

Tokmak
Issyk Kul

Kashgar

0

technique which they justly considered an excellent means of propaganda. Uigur patrons also figure in some of the Buddhic frescoes of the Turfan group, notably at Murtuk-Bezeklik.[108] Depicted in ceremonial dress, including handsome courtly robes and a miter as a headdress, accompanied by their ladies bearing flowers and by servants and musicians, they testify to the richness and splendor of Uigur culture. Farther on in these same Buddhic frescoes, other bearded patrons—of Turko-Iranian type, reminiscent of modern Kashgaris, wearing a flat helmet and followed by camels and mules in the manner of Buddhist magi —evoke the Sogdian caravaneers through whom the Uigur Empire made contact with the religions of Iran.[109] Lastly, in Uigur Turfan, one may still find some fine Nestorian frescoes. But it was above all in the succeeding period, after 840, in the second half of the ninth century and the beginning of the tenth, that this Uigur Turfanese art developed, notably at Bezeklik; for it was then that the Uigur were driven out of Mongolia and fled in great numbers to Turfan, where they founded a new principality. The finest patrons of the region seem to date from this second period.[110]

While borrowing their Manichaean religion from Iran or Outer Iran, the Uigur also took from the same area—precisely, from Transoxiana—the Sogdian alphabet, which derived from Syriac and from which they evolved their own Uigur script. In the ninth century, this script replaced the old Turkic (T'u-chüeh) alphabet of the Orkhon.[111] With its help they created a national literature: the earliest of the Turkic literatures, one into which they translated from Iranian several Manichaean texts, and from Sanskrit, Kuchean, and Chinese numerous Buddhist ones.[112] Thus the Uigur came to be greatly in advance of other Turko-Mongol peoples, of whom—up to the time of Jenghiz Khan—they were to be the mentors.

Nevertheless, in the process of acquiring civilization, the Uigur must have grown weaker. In 840 their capital city Karabalgasun was taken, their khagan slain, and their empire overthrown by those Turks who had remained in a more savage state, the Kirghiz of the upper Yenisei (between Minusinsk and Lake Kosogol.[113] The court of China, which for a hundred years had quailed before these all too powerful allies, took advantage of their fall to rid itself by systematic persecution of their protégés the Manichaeans (843).

The Kirghiz moved in to supplant the Uigur in "imperial Mongolia" on the upper Orkhon, in the neighborhood of the Karabalgasun and Karakorum of the present day. But these Siberian tribes caused a reversion to barbarism in Mongolia. The Kirghiz remained lords of those territories until about 920, when they were vanquished by the Mongol Khitan and thrust back to the steppes of the Yenisei.

The Uigur, dispossessed of the Mongolian empire, settled in the area of the northern Tarim oases, at Kara-khoja or Khocho—the old Turfan—at Dzimsa, which became the Turkic Beshbaligh, at Kara Shahr, and at Kucha (843).[114] Another Uigur group, since known by the name of Sari-Uigur, became established in western Kansu, round Kanchow,[115] in about 860 or 866. The Uigur principality of Kanchow lasted until 1028, when it was conquered by the Tangut. The flourishing state of Buddhism at Tunhwang in the tenth century provides evidence that this Uigur group must quickly have abandoned Manichaeism in favor of the local Buddhist faith.[116] The Uigur kingdom of Beshbaligh-Kucha was to endure until the Jenghiz-Khanite period, in the thirteenth century; and on the ancient Tokharian—or more accurately Kuchean (that is, Indo-European)—foundation upon which they had imposed themselves, the Uigur of this area produced an interesting Buddhic-Nestorian-Manichaean civilization, continuous with the culture of Kucha. Yet there too Manichaeism was to decline fairly quickly, and during the Jenghiz-Khanite period the Uigur of Beshbaligh-Kucha were either Buddhists or Nestorians.

It is quite possible that the settlement of the Uigur in Turfanese and Kuchean territory—a settlement which culminated in the Turkification of these ancient Indo-European lands—occurred in stages, the blend of Uigur and natives having perhaps produced a population which for a time was bilingual. Such is the apparent implication of Muslim sources, which state that besides their Turkic dialect the inhabitants of Uiguria had long possessed another language which they spoke among themselves.[117] However this may be, the Uigur benefited by literary acquisitions from the "Tokharian" of which they were a prolongation. Uigur literature—engraved on wood as often as written—which was discovered by the German, French, and English expeditions in modern Sinkiang, shows that while undergoing a Turkic transformation this country kept alive its former intellectual activity.[118] Thus the Uigur justly deserved their role of "teachers of civilization" to the Turko-Mongol states of the Altai and the Orkhon: to the Naiman of the twelfth century and to the Jenghiz-Khanites of the thirteenth, whom they provided with scribes, "offices," and a written language.

The Sha-t'o Turks

The Chinese T'ang dynasty, which was to be overthrown in 907, came near to falling in 880 as a result of a popular rising—a sort of Peasants' Revolt—led by one Huang Ch'ao. Changan, the imperial capital, like the great city of Loyang, fell into the hands of the rebel, and the court appealed for aid to a new Turkic horde, the Chöl—Ch'u-yueh in Chinese transcription, and in Chinese translation Sha-t'o: "the people of the desert of sand." [119]

Barthold is inclined to trace these Chöl, Ch'u-yueh, or Sha-t'o to the tribes of the Toquz Oghuz, of which at least a fraction roamed north of the Aral Sea from the tenth to the twelfth century.[120] In fact, the Sha-t'o had split off from the bulk of the western T'u-chüeh to live from the seventh century onward east of Lake Bar Kol. In 712, as Tibetan bands were ravaging the Barkol region, the Sha-t'o moved slightly to the west, in the direction of Kucheng. In 808, driven also from these encampments by Tibetan incursions, they appealed to China for protection. The T'ang court established them as confederates northeast of Lingchow (near Ningsia), in the northern part of the Ordos.

The Sha-t'o remained in the Ordos until 878. In that year, aided by the civil strife then devastating China, one of their leaders—Li K'o-yung—seized the frontier land of Tatung north of Shansi, where he was well placed to take a hand in the general anarchy. In 880, indeed, when the frightful rebellion led by Huang Ch'ao had wrested the capital, Changan, from the T'ang, the latter appealed to Li K'o-yung. This young leader (he was then twenty-eight) is described by Chinese historians as valiant and loyal. He seems to have taken his role of savior of the T'ang seriously, and his fidelity was never afterward in question. He drove the rebels from Changan in 883 and was rewarded by an appointment as minister to the imperial government which he had just saved. What was perhaps more important to him was that at the same time he was given the governorship of Taiyüan, that is, modern Shansi. For a while it seemed as if this Sinicized Turk would succeed to the expiring T'ang dynasty and ascend the throne of China; but from this, apparently, his sense of loyalty deterred him. Instead, a one-time bandit chief, Ch'u Wen, who had been won over to the Chinese, took power. Deposing the last of the T'ang, he proclaimed himself emperor, and founder of the Hou-Liang dynasty (907). Nevertheless, Li K'o-yung remained lord of Shansi, and after his death in 908 his son Li Ts'un-hsü (d. 926) succeeded him as emperor there under the title of king of Chin, with Taiyüan as his capital. In 923, Li Ts'un-hsü managed to overthrow the Hou-Liang dynasty and became emperor of China (his capital being Loyang) as founder of the ephemeral Hou-T'ang dynasty, which endured for no more than thirteen years (923–936). In 936, the last Hou-T'ang was deposed—thanks to the help of the Khitan horde— by general Shih King-t'ang, another Sha-t'o Turk, who proclaimed himself emperor of China and founded the Hou-Chin dynasty, with Kaifeng (P'ien) as his capital. But this house was to prove even more evanescent than the former, lasting only ten years (936–946). In 946 this ancient but over-Sinicized stock of Turks was overthrown by real barbarians, the Khitan, a Mongol people.

THE KHITAN

The Khitan (in Chinese transcription), or Khitai (in Arabo-Persian), or Kitat (in Mongol) are noted in Chinese annals from 405–6, at which time they were established west of the Liao, between that river and its branch the Shara Muren, in present-day Jehol.[121] They belonged to the Mongol family, their language being "a Mongol dialect, strongly palatalized by contact with Tungusic forms of speech." [122] In 696, via the pass of Shanhai-kwan, they had raided Hopei in the Yungping region, and even reached the plain of Peking; but the T'ang court (under the empress Wu Hou) summoned against them Mo-ch'o, the khagan of the eastern T'u-chüeh, then at the height of his power, who took them in the rear and inflicted upon them so disastrous a defeat in 697 that, as has been noted, their expansion was halted for three centuries. A border war between Khitan and Chinese in 734–35 in no way altered the situation. In 751 the Khitan defeated a Chinese army of invasion northeast of Pinglu (near modern Pingchüan), an army which incidentally was commanded by a man of their own stock, the notorious An Lu-shan, who had entered Chinese service and become the favorite of the T'ang Emperor Hsüan-tsung. It was this same An Lu-shan who afterward attempted to depose Hsüan-tsung and displace him as emperor (755).

The Khitan still occupied the northwest basin of the Liao and the region of its tributary the Shara Muren when at the beginning of the tenth century they were taken in hand by an energetic chief named (in Chinese transcription) Ye-lü (his clan name) A-pao-ki (d. 926), who succeeded in securing the dignity of khan for his own clan, the Ye-liu. According to later annalists, A-pao-ki had begun to introduce superficial Chinese ways among his horde, to which in 947 his successor was to give the dynastic name of Liao. It is indeed by this name that the Khitan are known in the history of China. In 924 he penetrated Mongolia, advanced as far as the upper Orkhon, entered Karabalgasun, and drove out the Kirghiz Turks who had inhabited that region since 840, thrusting them back toward the upper Yenisei and the steppes of the west.[123] It is strange that he should then have offered to restore the Orkhon country to the Uigur Turks of western Kansu. The old Uigur khagans had possessed those lands from 743 to 840, but their descendants, having adopted sedentary ways, rejected the idea of a return to nomadic life.[124] In the east, A-pao-ki —who died in the course of this expedition—destroyed in 926 the Tungus-Korean kingdom of Pohai, which comprised northern Korea (north of the 40th parallel) and the part of Manchuria lying east of Liaotung (from Harbin and Vladivostok to Port Arthur). The Jurchid Tungus of the Manchurian northeast, in the Ussuri forests, themselves became vassals of the Khitan.

A-pao-ki also tried to profit from the civil wars then ravaging China by seizing Hopei, but he was driven back at Wangtu, south of Paoting, by the aforementioned Li Ts'un-hsü, founder of the Chinese Hou-T'ang dynasty (922).

On the death of A-pao-ki, his widow,[125] a khatun of tireless energy like so many Turko-Mongol dowagers (including the mother of Jenghiz Khan), contrived to have her favorite second son elected khan. "She gathered together the Diet of her nation [the *quriltai* of the Jenghiz-Khanite Mongols], bade her eldest son T'u-yu and her second son Tö-kuang [Chinese transcriptions] mount their horses, and then said to the assembled nobles, who had been apprised of her wishes: 'I love these two sons of mine equally and cannot decide between them. Grasp the bridle of him who seems to you the worthier!'" Naturally they grasped Tö-kuang's bridle, and Tö-kuang became khan (927–47). At first his mother governed jointly with him, though according to her own ideas. Every time a chief displeased her, she sent him "to take news of her to her late husband." Guards posted at A-pao-ki's tomb then dispatched such messengers from life to death. A Chinese dignitary, Chao Ssu-wen, on being charged with this errand, declared that such an honor was due in the first place to the widow. The khatun replied that unfortunately her continued life was necessary to the horde; nevertheless, she sportingly cut off one hand and had it buried in the royal tomb.[126] This is a curious survival of a custom followed at family hecatombs on the death of a chief, an immemorial custom of the steppe, whether among Scythians, Huns, or Mongols. Notwithstanding these barbarous ways, the khatun did not hesitate to put her trust in the Chinese minister Han Yen-huei, who began to civilize the Khitan.

The new Khitan khan, Ye-lü Tö-kuang, soon found an opportunity to intervene in Chinese affairs. In 936 he took under his protection the imperial general Shih Ching-t'ang, who had revolted against the Hou-T'ang dynasty, descended on Hopei by the Kupehkow pass at the head of 50,000 men, and helped Shih Ching-t'ang to crush the imperial forces and ascend the throne of China as founder of the Hou-Chin dynasty.

Having thus become emperor of China by the favor of the Khitan, Shih Ching-t'ang ceded to them in gratitude the northern part of Hopei, including Yüchow or Yenchow—modern Peking— and the extreme north of Shansi, with Yünchow, the Tatung of today (936). In this way the barbarians came to be installed within the Great Wall, in those northern marches from which they were thenceforth able to keep watch over Chinese policy. Shih Ching-t'ang's treachery made the first breach in the integrity of the ancient empire, a breach destined to grow wider and to enable the hordes to conquer all north China in the twelfth century and the whole of China in the thirteenth. Peking, vanquished by Tö-kuang, passed from the Khitan to the Jurchid, from the Jurchid to the Jenghiz-Khanites, and thus remained in the power of the nomads from 936 until 1368. In 938, Tö-kuang made it his southern residence (*nanking* in Chinese), his northern one being at Linhwang on the Shara Muren and his eastern one at Liaoyang.[127]

Shih Ching-t'ang, emperor of China by the grace of the Khitan, remained their docile client until his death in 942, but his nephew and successor Shih Chung-kuei (943–46) tried to break free from this tutelage. It was a very rash move. The Khitan defeated his forces near Hokien, crossed the Yellow River, and appeared before Kaifeng (then Taliang), the imperial capital, where their khan Tö-kuang made his entry on the first day of the year 947.

The Khitan khan no doubt intended to proclaim himself emperor of China, and indeed in conquered Kaifeng he adopted Chinese dress. But behind him the Chinese revolted, massacring isolated Khitan groups, especially at Changteh. By way of reprisal Tö-kuang exterminated the inhabitants of Changteh, and then, faced with a general uprising, again took the road to Jehol, carrying with him the entire Chinese court as prisoners. After having come as far as Chengting, he died. His unexpected death in 947 spread confusion among the Khitan and so doubtless deprived them of the occasion to conquer China.

During the Khitan retreat, the Chinese general in command of Shansi province, Liu Chih-yüan, who furthermore was by origin a Sha-t'o Turk, was proclaimed emperor by his troops in February, 947. Actively supported by Chinese public opinion, he ascended the imperial throne at Kaifeng in April of the same year as founder of the Hou-Han dynasty.

Tö-kuang was succeeded as ruler of the Khitan by Ye-lü Yüan (947–51) and Ye-lü King (951–68). The Khitan would have lost all hope of intervening in Chinese affairs had not the Chinese themselves given them the opportunity of doing so. In 951 the imperial Hou-Han family, driven from the throne by a new dynasty—that of the Hou-Chou—took refuge in central Shansi, where they founded a local principality known as Pei-Han, which lasted from 959 to 979, with Taiyüan as its capital. Continuous war then broke out between the dynasties reigning successively in Kaifeng, on the one hand—the Hou-Chou (951–60) and the Sung (960)—and, on the other, the Pei-Han rulers of central Shansi, who ruled at Taiyüan. From rancor against those who had robbed them of the throne, and in order to defend their little realm in Shansi, the Pei-Han placed themselves under Khitan protection. The Khitan, of course, were willing enough to join in the game again, and their armies hastened to the aid of the Pei-Han whenever the imperial forces attempted to take Taiyüan.

This was the situation until a great national dynasty, that of the Sung, ascended the throne of China in 960 and by 975 restored the unity of all the Chinese states, with the sole exception of the Pei-Han kingdom of Taiyüan.

The founder of the Sung dynasty, the great emperor T'ai-tsu (his personal name was Chao K'uang-yin), had already tried in 968 to reconquer Taiyüan, but had been prevented by the Khitan, who as usual had hurried to its defense. The second Sung emperor, T'ai-tsung, was more fortunate. In 979, despite Khitan intervention, he succeeded in forcing Taiyüan to capitulate and annexing the Pei-Han kingdom of Shansi. He then resolved to deprive the Khitan of the territories that they had occupied since 936 south of the Great Wall: Tatung and Peking. But the reigning Khitan sovereign Ye-lü Hsien (968–82) and his generals put up so strong a resistance as to shatter this attempt at reconquest. The Chinese emperor advanced as far as Peking (then called Yüchow or Yenching) and laid siege to it, but was defeated by the Khitan general Ye-lü Hiou-ko near the River Kaoliang, northwest of Peking, and had to retreat hastily to Chochow, on the Peking-Paoting road (979). The Khitan in their turn tried to invade the Chinese part of Hopei, but their general Ye-lü Hiou-ko was defeated before Chengting.

In 986 the emperor T'ai-tsung made a fresh attempt. The Khitan khan Ye-lü Hsien had just died and was succeeded by a boy of twelve, Ye-lü Lung-sü (983–1031), under the regency of the queen mother, Hsiao-shih. The moment seemed favorable. The Chinese army, commanded by generals Ts'ao Pin, P'an Mei, and Yang Ye, was divided into a number of columns, of which some marched upon Tatung and the others upon Peking. The columns on the left succeeded in taking possession of the Tatung region, but those on the right could advance no farther than Chochow and were at last defeated by the Khitan general Ye-lü

Hiou-ko at Ki-kou-kuan, southwest of Chochow, near Yichow, and driven back to the River Kiu-ma, halfway between Peking and Paoting.[128] The remnants of the Chinese forces fled south. Ye-lü Hiou-ko caught up with them, relates the *T'ung-chien-k'ang-mu*, as they were crossing the Sha River, no doubt the river of that name that runs through Sinlo, north of Chengting and Hokien. He hurled the Chinese into the river, where they perished in great numbers. The Khitan took Shenchow (near Chengting), Töchow and Shuentö, but fortunately for China they did not press their advantage farther south. It was not until 989 that the Chinese were able to recover sufficiently to defeat them near Paoting.

China's troubles were increased by the Tangut, a people of Tibetan stock. At the beginning of the eleventh century, the Tangut founded a new state in the Ordos and the Alashan: the kingdom of Hsi-Hsia, which became a constant peril to the Chinese province of Shensi. The founder of this state, Chao Pao-ki, also designated by the name of Li Ki-ts'ien (d. 1003), was recognized as ruler of Hsi-Hsia in 990 by the Khitan, who were then suzerains of all the hordes of the eastern Gobi. In 1001 he robbed China of the important stronghold of Lingchow or Lingwu, near Ningsia. It was not far from here, at Halachar, that the kings of Hsi-Hsia had their capital. The Sung Empire thus found itself threatened simultaneously by the Khitan in the northeast and by the Hsi-Hsia in the northwest.

In 1004, during the reign of the third Sung emperor Chen-tsung, the Khitan king Ye-lü Lung-sü led a mounted expedition through southern Hopei, in the course of which he captured Paochow (modern Paoting), Kichow (Taming), and even Tötsing, or modern Tsingfeng, opposite Kaifeng the Chinese capital, from which he was separated only by the Yellow River (as it flowed in 1000; its course altered in 1007). At Kaifeng timorous courtiers advised Emperor Chen-tsung to move his residence to Nanking or into Szechwan. He not only refused to do this but took a courageous step. On the north bank of the Yellow River, the fortified place of Shenchow or Chenchow (the Kaichow of Manchurian nomenclatures, and the Puyanghsien of today) still held fast.[129] A brave Chinese captain, Li Ki-lung, besieged in this place by the Khitan, had lured them into an ambush where they sustained heavy losses. A glance at a map will show that Shenchow barred the road to Kaifeng. If Li Ki-lung had been over-whelmed, the Khitan would have attained the Yellow River, op-posite the capital. The emperor Chen-tsung was bold enough to leave Kaifeng and bring reinforcements to Shenchow at the "front." His resolute conduct impressed the Khitan, who in 1004 signed a peace treaty in that same city. The frontier remained as laid down in 936: Peking and Tatung were allotted to the Khitan, Paoting and Ningwu to the Chinese. This frontier cut through Hopei along the northern outskirts of Pachow (which remained in Chinese possession) and through Shansi north of the Wutai Mountains, which similarly continued to be part of Chinese territory.[130]

The peace of 1004 was preserved for a hundred years. The Khitan, content to rule in Peking and Tatung, made no further demands, and the Sung dynasty, which, with just about this ex-ception, possessed all China, gave up the idea of recapturing these two cities. The Khitan transferred their ambitions to Korea and the Gobi. But their attacks on Korea were repulsed since in 1014 the Koreans arranged for diversionary action to be taken by the Jurchid, a Tungus people of the Ussuri. In the Gobi the Khitan deprived the Uigur of Kanchow and Suchow, towns of west-ern Kansu. About 1017 they seem to have attempted the conquest of Kashgaria and of the Issyk Kul region, a country which, as will be seen, belonged to the Islamized Turkic ruling house of the Karakhanids. Having advanced to within eight days' march of one of the Karakhanid capitals, Balasagun on the upper Chu, west of the Issyk Kul, they were repulsed by the Karakhanid khan of Kashgar, Tughan.[131] The Tangut of Hsi-Hsia were also turning their eyes westward. Their king Chao Tö-ming (1006–32) in 1028 captured the town of Kanchow from the Uigur. (The Khitan, after their 1009 expedition, had failed to hold it.) In 1036, his son Chao Yüan-hao (1032–48) similarly took from the Tibetans the towns of Suchow and Tunhwang. In 1044 he repulsed an at-tack by the Khitan near the Ordos. During his reign, the Tangut acquired a writing of their own, the Hsi-Hsia script, derived from Chinese. A whole library of printed and manuscript works in Hsi-Hsia was discovered in 1908 by the Kozlov mission at Karakhoto, the old Yi-tsi-nai, Marco Polo's Etzina, in northern Kansu.[132]

The Khitan had similarly evolved a script of their own, but until recently no trace could be found of it.[133] At last, in 1922, two inscriptions in this Khitan writing, dating from the first years of the twelfth century, were discovered in Mongolia.[134]

THE JURCHID

The dream of reconquering from the Khitan the regions of Peking and Tatung still haunted the minds of the Chinese. Emperor Hui-tsung (1101–25)—one of the most brilliant of the Sung rulers, a lover of art, and himself a painter—made the mistake of "setting barbarians against barbarians, and those who are far against those who are near." In this may be recognized the traditional Chinese tactics, so often practiced with success, notably at the beginning of the T'ang period by T'ai-tsung the Great. In this case it was an error. The Khitan—those now tempered, civilized, and fairly Sinicized Mongols—had become tolerably good neighbors. To their rear, in the Ussuri forests, in the Manchurian northeast and in what is today Russia's maritime province, lived a Tungusk people called Jurchid (Ju-chen in Chinese transcription, Jurche in Arabo-Persian).[135] In 1124–25, the Chinese ambassador Hiu K'ang-tsung describes these Jurchid as sheer barbarians,[136] for the khan's headquarters was surrounded by pasture land and grazing herds. This cluster of dwellings had no streets or even alleys, and no defensive walls except for the one encircling the royal camp or barracks. The khan sat on a throne covered with twelve tiger skins. There was much barbaric revelry, with carousing, music, wild dances, and miming of hunts and battles; also— supreme luxury for these forest dwellers—painted women juggled with mirrors from which they projected flashes of light upon the spectators. (This was the game of the Thunderbolt Goddess, analogous to the Japanese scene of which Amaterasu is the heroine.) It was with these barbarians—"worse than wolves or tigers," according to Korean ambassadors at the court of China— that China allied herself in order to destroy the Khitan, who were her defense against this same hinterland of barbarism.

Just at this time an energetic chief named A-ku-ta, of the royal Wan-yen clan, was busy organizing the Jurchid (1113–23).[137] In 1114, having detected the hidden weakness of the Khitan rulers, who had absorbed too much of the Chinese way of life, he rebeled against their suzerainty and led his horde to conquer their dominions. Within nine years he deprived them of all their

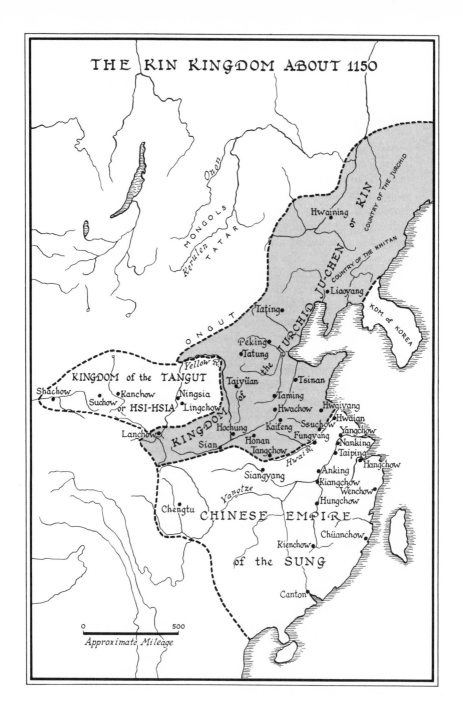

THE KIN KINGDOM ABOUT 1150

MONGOLS
TATAR
Kerulen
Onon

ONGUT

COUNTRY OF THE JURCHID
COUNTRY OF THE KHITAN
the JURCHID JU-CHEN or KIN

Hwaining●

Liaoyang●

KDM. of KOREA

Tating●
Peking●
●Tatung
Taiyüan●
●Tsinan

KINGDOM of the TANGUT
or HSI-HSIA

Shachow●
Suchow● ●Kanchow
Ningsia●
Lingchow●
Yellow R.

Lanchow●

KINGDOM
of the
KIN

Taming●
Hwachow●
Hochung● Kaifeng● Ssuchow●
Hwaiyang●
Hwaian●
Yangchow●

Sian
Honan
Tangchow●
Fungyang●
Nanking●
Taiping●

Hwai R.

Siangyang●
Anking●
Kiangchow●
Hangchow●
Wenchow●
Hungchow●

CHINESE EMPIRE

Chengtu●
Yangtze

of the SUNG

Kienchow●
Chüanchow●

Canton●

0   500
Approximate Mileage

strongholds, seizing from north to south the following centers: in 1114, Ningkiang (south of modern Harbin, on a tributary of the Sungari); in 1116, Liaoyang, the fall of which brought the whole of present-day Manchuria into Jurchid hands; in 1120, Linhwang, the northern capital of the Khitan (on the Shara Muren in the north of modern Jehol); in 1122, Tating, their central capital (near Tsifeng, northern Jehol); and in the same year, Tatung, in northern Shansi. In the treaty of alliance so rashly concluded by the emperor Hui-tsung of China with the Jurchid, it had been stipulated that in the partition of the Khitan realm Peking should revert to China. But the Chinese proved incapable of reducing the city, and it was the Jurchid who had to seize it (1122), after which they presented it somewhat contemptuously to China (1123). The last Khitan king, Ye-lü Yen-hsi, who had fled in the direction of Kuku Hoto, attempted a final stand around Wuchow (near Shoping, 1124) until his capture by Jurchid runners (1125).

Having thus conquered the Khitan kingdom, the Jurchid, under the astute guidance of the royal Wan-yen clan, strove to establish a regular state with a Chinese façade. In this effort they bestowed upon their Wan-yen dynasty the name of Golden: *Alchun* in Tungusic, *Kin* (or *Chin*) in Chinese, whence the designation Kin by which, with the Chinese historians, it will henceforth be called.[138]

The replacement of the Mongol Khitan—a people grown moderate and secured by pledges—by a Tungusic stock of fiery, untamed, barbaric temperament soon recoiled upon the Chinese, who had so rashly favored this reversal. The Kin ruler A-ku-ta, who died at the height of his triumph (1123), had been succeeded by his brother Wu-k'i-mai, a still more ambitious man, who reigned from 1123 until 1135. The court of China was unwise enough to bicker over the possession of some frontier towns north of Peking, and went so far as to lend secret support to risings against the Kin. This led to war. Within a few months the Kin general Nien-mo-ho seized Peking and the Hopei plain from the Chinese, then Taiyüan and the heart of Shensi (1125, 1126). Another Kin general, Wa-li-pu, rejoined by Nien-mo-ho, crossed the Yellow River and appeared before Kaifeng, the Chinese capital. Its defenders, the lamentable emperor Hui-tsung and his son Kin-tsung, surrendered (end of 1126). The two unhappy rulers, with all their suite, their baggage, and their treasure, were deported to the Kin "capital" at Ningkiang, south of Harbin, in the depths of Manchuria (beginning of 1127).[139]

One member of the imperial Sung family, Kao-tsung, escaped this disaster. He was proclaimed emperor in the south, at Nanking, beyond the protecting Yangtze (1127). Meanwhile, the Kin were completing the reduction of the last strongholds in northern China which were still in imperial hands: Hokien and Taming in Hopei, Tsinan in Shantung, Changteh in Honan, and Hochung (Puchow) in the southwest corner of Shansi—to say nothing of Kaifeng, which the imperial forces, profiting by the absence of a Kin garrison, had reoccupied and which now had to be retaken. (We shall see more of this unco-ordinated siege warfare under Jenghiz Khan, and in the same areas.)

After the north, it was the turn of central China. In 1129 the Kin, under the command of Nien-mo-ho, subjugated the country between the lower Hwai and the lower Yangtze. After a pause, they attacked the line of the lower Yangtze with two armies. The western army crossed the river at Hwangchow in Hupeh, descended on Kiangchow (Kiukiang in Kiangsi) north of Lake Poyang, and on Hungchow (Nanchang) south of the lake. From there it pressed on as far as Kienchow (Kanchow in southern Kiangsi), the limit of the advance. It had thus traversed, at a gallop, almost the whole of southern China. Not even the Mongols in the following century were to move so rapidly. The second Kin army, which operated on the lower Yangtze, crossed that river near Taiping and forced Nanking to capitulate. The emperor Kao-tsung had taken flight to Ningpo (then known as Mingchow) and later to the port of Wenchow, south of Chekiang. From Nanking the Kin general Wu-chu hastened in pursuit and captured Hangchow and Ningpo (end of 1129 and beginning of 1130).

However, the Kin army, consisting entirely of cavalry, had ventured too far into this China of the south with its flooded lands, intersecting rivers, paddy fields and canals, and dense population which harassed and encircled it. Wu-chu, leader of the Kin troops, sought to return north but was halted by the Yangtze, now wide as a sea and patrolled by Chinese flotillas. At last a traitor showed him how he might cross the river near Chenkiang, east of Nanking (1130). After the south was free of the Kin, the emperor Kao-tsung returned in 1130 and settled in Hangchow, and this town remained the capital of Chinese China until the Mongol conquest.

The Kin were disconcerted by this setback. The Chinese generals began to recover their bases between the Yangtze and Yellow rivers, and the bravest of them, Yo Fei, recaptured from the Kin the important town of Siangyang (1134). In 1138 he was on the point of marching on Kaifeng when Emperor Kao-tsung, a weak character who was becoming weary of this war, made peace with the Kin. The Kin king, Ho-lo-ma (1135–49), who had just succeeded his cousin Wu-k'i-mai, also wanted of peace because of a danger threatening him from the north. The Mongols, who now appear on the scene—at least under the name by which they are known to history—had just formed a federation under their khan Qabul and were attacking the Kin in the rear, in the region of the eastern Gobi (1135, 1139). In 1147 the Kin were forced to cede to them a number of frontier districts.[140]

Under this situation peace was readily concluded between the Kin realm and the Chinese empire of the Sung (1138). The frontier followed the course of the Hwai and the heights between the basin of the Yellow River (and of the Wei) and that of the upper Han, the Yellow River and the Wei basin being retained by the Kin and the Han basin by the Chinese. Thus the Kin kept Hopei, Shantung, Shansi, almost the whole of Shensi and of Honan, and a number of districts north of Anhwei and Kiangsu, so that their possessions in China were considerably more extensive than those of their predecessors the Khitan.

China, therefore, was now divided between a national Chinese empire in the south, that of the Sung, who retained Hangchow as their capital, and a Jurchid—that is, a Tungusic—kingdom in the north, that of the Kin. At first the Kin kept their northern capital (*pei-king* in Chinese) at Hwaining near Harbin, in Manchuria, which remained the chief residence of their kings until 1153. Our Peking was merely their secondary, southern capital (*nan-king* in Chinese); they had also a central capital (*chung-king*) at Tating, north of Jehol. In 1153, the Kin ruler Ti-ku-nai made Peking his principal residence, and from that time onward Tating in Jehol province was regarded as the capital of the north, Liaoyang as the capital of the east, Tatung as the capital of the west, our Peking as the central capital, and Kaifeng as that of the south.

It is interesting to note the part played in the founding of the Kin realm by a prince of the royal family, Wan-yen Wu-shih (no doubt Goshi in the Tungusic language of the Jurchids), an able statesman, who owed part of his influence to his position as shaman.[141] It was he who, adapting Chinese characters to Tungusic sounds, invented the Jurchid "great characters." His prestige made him suspect in the eyes of King Ho-lo-ma, who had him put to death in 1139.

King Ti-ku-nai, who ascended the Kin throne after assassinating his predecessor Ho-lo-ma and part of the royal clan (1149), was a barbarian whom civilization had merely perverted, a sensual brute whose rages were reminiscent of the savage temperament of the old Jurchid and whose taste for pleasure led him to forsake the Manchurian seat of the first Kin—his native forest—for the palaces of Peking. This was a grave error, amounting almost to desertion at a time when Tatars and Mongols showed an increasing tendency to raid the Manchurian region. But Ti-ku-nai's ambition was to become a true emperor of China and, to that end, to win southern China from the Sung. In 1161, therefore, he attacked the Sung, penetrated to the lower Yangtze, and attempted to cross the river at the head of the estuary opposite Yangchow, near the islet of Kinshan and the modern town of Chenkiang. But he met with disaster. His troops, maddened by his tyranny, murdered him, and another king, Wu-lo, was proclaimed at Liaoyang (1161).

The new Kin sovereign lost no time in making peace with the Sung, concluded as the result of negotiations carried on between 1163 and 1165, on the basis of the *status quo ante*. The annals describe him as a wise and moderate prince who from his throne in Peking yearned for the forests of northern Manchuria, his own land. He died very old, leaving the throne to his grandson Ma-ta-ku (1189).

Ma-ta-ku (1189–1208), as Chinese annals relate, allowed the military discipline of the Jurchid people to relax; the consequences of this were to become evident under his successor, at the time of the Mongol invasion. Meanwhile, in 1206, when the Sung had imprudently reopened hostilities, the Kin crossed the Hwai, which marked the frontier between the two states, and advanced as far as the Yangtze. Ma-ta-ku demanded the head of the Chinese minister who had wanted war, but in 1208 agreed to a return to the territorial *status quo* on condition that there should be an increase in the presents of silver and silk which the Chinese court sent to the Kin annually, and which were nothing but thinly disguised tribute. During the reign of his successor Chung-hei (1209–13), the Mongol invasion began.

Before going on to consider Mongol history, which has as much bearing on the Muslim Turkic world as on the Far East, it may be well to glance rapidly back at the history of the Turks who had been established on Islamic territory since the eleventh century.

3

The Turks and Islam to the Thirteenth Century

THE IRANIAN BARRIER AGAINST THE TURKIC WORLD IN THE TENTH CENTURY: THE SAMANIDS

The consolidation of Arab domination over Transoxiana after the battle of Talas in 751, already mentioned, proved after a century to have benefited the Iranian folk. In removing from Transoxiana the double Turkic (then pagan) and Chinese peril, the Arab governors thought that they were working solely in their own interest, in behalf of the caliphate. But in the third quarter of the following century, power in Bukhara and Samarkand passed from the Arab conquerors to the native Iranians, descendants of the old Sogdians of history. The purely Iranian Samanids, a ruling house originating in Saman near Balkh, thus from 875 to 999 found themselves masters of Transoxiana, with Bukhara as their capital. This shift of power occurred without revolution or violence, in the very bosom of Muslim society and within the still officially respected framework of the caliphate. The Samanids were satisfied with the modest title of emir, and pretended to be nothing more than the representatives of the caliph of Baghdad. In fact, everything went on as if they were completely independent, and their claim to be connected with Bahram Chobin, the ancient king of Persia, showed the true character of this national Iranian restoration, brought about under cover of the most orthodox Islam.[1]

The great period of the Samanid dynasty dates from Nasr ibn-

141

Ahmed, who in 874–75 received Transoxiana in fief from the caliph Mu'tamid, with Samarkand as his residence.[2] In the same year, Nasr appointed his brother Isma'il wali or governor of Bukhara. Conflict soon broke out between the two brothers, however (885, 886), a pernicious tendency common to the Transoxianian dynasties. On the death of Nasr in 892, Isma'il remained sole lord of Transoxiana, and from that time onward his royal seat of Bukhara became the Samanid capital.

This Isma'il (Isma'il ibn-Ahmed 892–907) was a great sovereign. Doubling the extent of his Iranian possessions through a victory won by his troops near Balkh in the spring of 900 over the Saffarid ruler 'Amr ibn el-Laith, lord of Khurasan, whom he took prisoner,[3] Isma'il followed up this triumph by annexing Khurasan. In 902 he won Tabaristan from another royal house, including Rai (present Teheran) and Kazvin. In the northeast he had been conducting a campaign since 893 against the Turkic region of Talas. Upon capturing the town (Talas or Aulie-Ata), he turned the church of the Christian community established there—probably Nestorian—into a mosque.[4] The Iranian prince returned from this expedition into the Turkic steppe with a huge booty of horses, sheep, and camels seized from the nomads. It is interesting to note that in so doing he was reverting to the policy of preventive counterraids followed by the old Sassanid kings on the north bank of the Oxus (Amu Darya). This watch on the Syr Darya (Jaxartes)—the "Watch on the Rhine" of the ancient lords of Iran—was now colored with a pious pretext: Persian Islam's war on the Turkic world, whether pagan or Nestorian. The situation was to be modified when the Turkic hordes of the frontier region were converted to Islam. This change of faith, for which the Samanid dynasty had so zealously striven, was to recoil upon its promoters, for it threw the gates of Muslim society wide open to the Turks, and in the mind of more than one chieftain this was the sole object of the conversion.

The peak of the Samanid dynasty from a territorial point of view was reached in the reign of Nasr II ibn-Ahmed (914–43). Tashkent (Shash) in the north, Fergana in the northeast, Rai in the southwest (this latter city until 928), all formed part of the Samanid state, which exercised an appreciable influence as far as Kashgaria. But the conversion of Nasr to Shi'a Islam gave rise to serious disturbances which resulted in his abdication. At that time, the Iranians of Transoxiana were already ardent Sunnites, and were inclined to make use of the religious difference to sharpen the distinction between themselves and the Persians proper.[5]

The reign of Nuh I ibn-Nasr (943–54) saw the beginning of the dynasty's decline. The Iranian military aristocracy took to fomenting incessant rebellion. In the southwest, the Samanids opened hostilities against another Iranian dynasty, that of the Buyids, who reigned over western Persia. The conflict was exacerbated by religious rifts, the Samanids being Sunnites and the Buyids Shi'ites; and it had as its pretext and aim the possession of the city of Rai, which changed hands several times. It was a monotonous struggle, affecting only the internal history of Iran, except in so far as it dangerously weakened the Samanid dynasty in its stand against the Turkic world. At that moment, however, the conversion to Islam of many Turkic bands entitled the Turkish converts to rights of membership in the community of Transoxiana, to which they were admitted as mercenaries, and thereby delivered into their hands the keys of the Iranian stronghold.

Such was the case with the future Ghaznavids. In the reign of the Samanid 'Abd al-Malik I (954–61), a Turkic slave named Alptigin, who had attained to the command of the guards, had himself appointed governor of Khurasan (January–February, 961). Under the succeeding Samanid, Mansur I ibn-Nuh (961–76), he was dismissed from his post and retired to Balkh. Then, driven from this city by the Samanid army, he took refuge at Ghazni, in Afghanistan (962).[6] His family succeeded in establishing themselves there by recognizing the Samanid suzerainty in this new realm. It is nevertheless true that this was the first state founded on Muslim Iranian territory by the Turks. Alptigin died shortly afterward (ca. 963?). The Turkic mercenary army which he had raised in Ghazni, and which was already profoundly influenced by Islam, was from 977 onward led by another Turkic ex-slave—another Mameluke—named Sebüktigin, who made himself master of Tokharistan (Balkh-Kunduz) and Kandahar, and embarked upon the conquest of Kabul.[7]

In the reign of the Samanid ruler Nuh II ibn-Mansur (977–97), the feudal anarchy resulting from the insubordination of the Iranian military nobility reached such a pitch that in 992 one of these barons, Abu 'Ali, appealed for help against his master to the

Karakhanid Turk Bughra-khan Harun, who reigned at Balasagun, on the Chu. Bughra-khan made a military expedition to Bukhara, which he entered in May, 992, though he did not attempt to remain there. To counter all these revolts and the menace of the Karakhanid Turks, Nuh II appealed to the Ghaznavid Turks, who at that time were commanded by the energetic Sebüktigin (995). Sebüktigin, having hastened from Ghazni, took the Samanid dynasty under his protection, but appropriated Khurasan.[8] Thus the Iranian principality was reduced to Transoxiana, flanked on the one side by the Ghaznavid Turks, masters of Afghanistan and Khurasan, and on the other by the Karakhanid Turks, who held sway over the steppes of the Chu and the Ili and of Kashgaria. The only question now was which of these two Turkic groups would strike the final blow.

It was during the reign of the Samanid ruler 'Abd al-Malik II (February–October, 999) that the blow fell, and from both sides. The Ghaznavid Mahmud, son and successor to Sebüktigin, defeated him near Merv and forced him to abandon Khurasan for good (May 16). That autumn, Transoxiana itself was invaded by the Karakhanid Arslan Ilek Nasr, king of Uzgen in Fergana, who entered Bukhara on October 23, 999, took 'Abd al-Malik prisoner, and annexed Transoxiana.[9]

Thus the Iranian realm of eastern Iran and Transoxiana was now divided between two Muslim Turkic powers: the Karakhanid khans of Kashgaria, who took Transoxiana, and the Ghaznavid sultans of Afghanistan, who took Khurasan. A summary of the history of these two groups, which played so large a part in the permanent Turkicizing of the two regions, is the subject of the next section.

The Turkicizing of Kashgaria and Transoxiana: The Karakhanids

The Uigur Turks, who, after losing their ascendancy in Mongolia, had settled in the northern part of the Tarim, at Khocho (Turfan), Beshbaligh (the Dzimsa of today), Kara Shahr, and Kucha, turned this old Tokharian country into a Turkic one; nevertheless, they did respect its Buddhist and Nestorian character. Unlike them, the Karakhanid Turks, who in the following century became established in the west and southwest of Kashgaria, and in the region of the Ili and the Issyk Kul, fundamentally altered the character of the region because of their conversion to Islam. This combined Muslim and Turkic influence allowed nothing of the past to survive in this part of Central Asia.

Little is known about the origins of the Karakhanid royal house, though it was destined to dominate Kashgaria from the middle of the tenth century to the beginning of the thirteenth. It is possible, as Barthold points out, that the Karakhanids were a Toquz Oghuz clan who captured the Balasagun region (west of the Issyk Kul) from the Qarluq Turks.[10] The first Karakhanid mentioned in Muslim literature is Satoq Bughra-khan, king of Kashgar, who died about 955 and who seems to have promoted the adoption of the Muslim faith among his people. For the rest of the tenth century and throughout the eleventh, the oases of the western Tarim and the Chu and Talas plains were shared out among members of his family, who by then were all Muslims. Despite their faith, however, the Karakhanids did not forget the hereditary struggle between Turk and Iranian and were not backward in waging war against the Samanid emirs of Transoxiana, although these were, at the gateway to Central Asia, the official champions of Sunnite Islam or Muslim orthodoxy. As has been seen, the Karakhanid Bughra-khan Harun, who reigned at Balasagun on the Chu, began the series of Turkic invasions in this area by a raid as far as Bukhara in May, 992, a raid, incidentally, without immediate results.[11] Another Karakhanid ruler, Arslan Ilek (or Ilig) Nasr of Uzgen in Fergana (d. 1012 or 1013), was more fortunate.[12] On October 23, 999, as noted, he entered Bukhara as victor, took the last Samanid ('Abd al-Malik II) prisoner, and annexed Transoxiana.

South of the Amu Darya, Khurasan, another remnant of the Samanid heritage, had fallen into the hands of a second Turkic dynasty: that of the Ghaznavids, represented at that time by the illustrious sultan Mahmud (998–1030), the conqueror of northwestern India. The relations between these two Turkic Muslim houses were at first correct and even harmonious. Arslan Ilek Nasr, the victor of Bukhara, gave Mahmud his daughter in marriage, but the concord was short-lived. The Karakhanids, a firmly established dynasty which ruled not only Kashgaria but also the old T'u-chüeh countries of the Ili and the Chu, regarded the Ghaznavids, those one-time slaves, as upstarts. Mahmud of

Ghazni, on the other hand, had just added the Punjab (1004–5) to his Afghan and Khurasani domains and had enriched himself with the treasures of India. Now thoroughly Iranized and at the height of his power, with the world of the rajas fallen at his feet, he looked upon the Karakhanid Turks, who had lingered too long in the meager northern steppes, as barbarian cousins and a constant threat to his magnificent Indo-Iranian empire. On this last point he was not mistaken. In 1006, while Mahmud was detained in India, the Karakhanid Arslan Ilek Nasr invaded Khurasan and sacked Balkh and Nishapur. On his return to Iran, Mahmud defeated Ilek Nasr at Sharkhiyan near Balkh (January 4, 1008) and drove him from the province.[13] In this battle, Ilek Nasr had been helped by his cousin Qadir-khan Yusuf, prince of Khotan; but a third Karakhanid, Tughan-khan, Ilek Nasr's brother, allowed himself to be won over to Mahmud's side.

Over and above these family rifts, the Karakhanids, while fighting along the line of the Amu Darya against Mahmud of Ghazni, were taken in the rear by the Khitan kings of Peking, who in 1017 sent an army into Kashgaria. This invasion was incidentally repulsed by the reigning Karakhanid in Kashgar, Tughan-khan. Minorsky has found evidence of an embassy sent by the Khitan court of Peking to Mahmud of Ghazni, no doubt to reach an agreement with him in opposing the Karakhanids.[14] It is true that Mahmud was for a long time engaged at the opposite end of his empire by the conquest of India (capture of Thanesar, 1014; sack of Mathura, 1019; siege of Gwalior, 1020–21; sack of Somnath, 1025). In 1025, after extending his dominions as far as the Ganges and the Malwa, he returned to settle accounts with 'Ali-tigin, the Karakhanid then reigning in Bukhara and Samarkand. Unable to resist, 'Ali-tigin beat a retreat and Mahmud entered Samarkand. At the same moment, another Karakhanid, Qadir-khan Yusuf, king of Kashgar, entered Transoxiana. He and Mahmud had a courteous meeting before Samarkand, with a view to dividing the country between them (1025). In fact, neither of them succeeded. As soon as Mahmud returned to Khurasan, 'Ali-tigin recovered both Bukhara and Samarkand (1026).[15] Mahmud's son and successor, the Ghaznavid sultan Mas'ud (1030–40), sent another army against 'Ali-tigin and again occupied Bukhara, but was unable to keep it (1032). 'Ali-tigin was to remain master of Transoxiana until his death in the same year. Shortly afterward, the country passed into the hands of a Karakhanid of a different branch: Buri-tigin, known as Tamgatch-khan, who reigned in Bukhara from 1041 (or 1042) to 1068.[16]

Meanwhile, as will be seen, a serious revolution had taken place in the Iranian east. On May 22, 1040, the Ghaznavids had been beaten at the battle of Dandanaqan, near Merv, by another Turkic band, the Seljuks, who had captured Khurasan from them and driven them back into Afghanistan and India. The Seljuk khan Togrul-beg, or Toghrul-beg, victor of Dandanaqan, then subjugated the rest of Persia, and in 1055 entered Baghdad, where he was recognized by the Abbasid caliph as sultan, king of East and West. This vast Turkic empire, which soon extended from the Amu Darya to the Mediterranean, was little inclined to tolerate the independence of the petty Karakhanid khans in Transoxiana. The Karakhanid Shams al-Mulk Nasr, Buri's son and successor, who reigned in Bukhara and Samarkand from 1068 to 1080, suffered the invasion of his domains in 1072 by the second Seljuk sultan, Alp Arslan. In this campaign Alp Arslan was killed, and his son, the great sultan Malikshah, marched on Samarkand, but granted peace to Shams al-Mulk, who became his vassal (1074). In 1089, Malikshah returned to the charge, occupied Bukhara, captured Samarkand, and imprisoned the Karakhanid Ahmed, nephew and second successor to Shams al-Mulk, whom he later reinstated as client-ruler. From that time forward, the Karakhanids who reigned in Bukhara and Samarkand did so as lieutenants of the Seljuk sultans. Transoxiana was now no more than a dependency of the Seljuk Empire.

While the Karakhanids of Transoxiana were thus struggling and succumbing, those of the Ili and of Kashgaria, remote from such great historical dramas, were pursuing a more obscure destiny. As noted, one of them, Qadir-khan Yusuf, had reunited his family's domains in that region: Balasagun, Kashgar, and Khotan. At his death, Balasagun, Kashgar, and Khotan passed to one of his two sons, Arslan-khan (ca. 1032–55?). The other son, Muhammad Bughra-khan, received Talas (ca. 1032–57). About 1055, Bughra-khan once more unified the country by taking Kashgaria from Arslan-khan, though further partitions followed. At the end of the eleventh century, Balasagun, Kashgar, and Khotan were presumably once more united under the Karakhanid Bughra-khan Harun (d. 1102), to whom the famous

Turkic book *Qudatqu bilig,* written about 1069 by Yusuf Khass
Hajjib of Balasagun, was apparently dedicated.

Thanks to the Karakhanids, Muslim Turkic domination had become deeply rooted in Kashgaria and in the Issyk Kul basin when
in 1130 these regions were conquered by a Mongol, "pagan"
people, the Khitan of Peking. But before describing this revolution of events, we shall return briefly to the history of the Seljuk
Turks in Western Asia.

ROLE OF THE SELJUKS IN TURKISH HISTORY

In the tenth century, the Persian geography of *Hudud al-Alam*
tells us, what is now the country of the Kirghiz-Kazakhs, north of
Lake Balkhash—that is to say, the steppe of the rivers Sary-Su,
Turgai, and Emba—was inhabited by Turkic peoples: the Oghuz
or Ghuzz, known to Byzantine chroniclers by the name of *Ouzoi.*[17]
Linguists rank these Ghuzz—together with the old Kimäks of the
middle Yenisei of the Ob, the old Kipchaks who later emigrated
to southern Russia, and the modern Kirghiz—in one particular
Turkic group, distinguished from the rest by the mutation of the
initial *y* sound to *j* (*dj*).[18] These are the same Ghuzz who have
been known since the Jenghiz Khan era as Turkmen: our Turkomans.[19]

The Ghuzz of the eleventh century, like the modern Turkmen,
formed a group of loosely linked tribes which were often at war
among themselves. In the second quarter of the eleventh century,
they sought their fortune in southern Russia and in Iran. Russian
chronicles first note their appearance in southern Russia about
1054. Harried by another Turkic horde, the Kipchaks—a branch
of the Kimäks of the middle Irtysh or of the Ob—these Uzes,
as the Byzantines called them (*Ouzoi*), penetrated as far as the
lower Danube, crossed it, and invaded the Balkans, where they
were finally crushed (1065). Another Ghuzz clan, that of the
Seljuks, moving in another direction, met with a more brilliant
fortune: it conquered Persia and Asia Minor.

The eponymous hero of the Seljuks, appropriately Seljuk[20] (or
Saljük), was the son of a certain Duqaq surnamed Timuryaligh
—"of the iron bow"—and either the chief or an eminent member
of the Ghuzz tribe of the Qiniqs. Before 985, he and his clan
split off from the bulk of the Ghuzz and set up camp on the

right bank of the lower Syr Darya, in the direction of Jend, near modern Perovsk (now Kzyl-Orda). The names of his sons —Mika'il, Musa, Isra'il—have led some to conclude that he professed the Nestorian faith. There are no grounds for this assumption, for these Biblical names are also Muslim ones; and it is likely that in settling on the borders of Samanid Transoxiana, the Seljuk clan was compelled to abandon its ancient Turko-Mongol shamanism for Islam.

In this period, the Iranian Samanid dynasty of Transoxiana was experiencing great difficulty in defending itself against the Turkic Karakhanid dynasty of the Issyk Kul and Kashgaria. Astutely, the Seljuks sided with the Iranian prince against their own kin. Nevertheless, as Barthold points out, these Ghuzz—who had barely emerged from the steppes of the Sary-Su and the Irgiz, and from paganism—must have been far greater barbarians than the Karakhanids, who had been followers of Islam for over a century and had become relatively civilized under the dual influence of the Samanids in the west and the Uigur in the east.

After the fall of the Samanids, when their heritage was being disputed between the Karakhanid Turks, lords of Transoxiana, and the Ghaznavids, who ruled in Khurasan, the Seljuk Turks advanced stage by stage, in the manner of modern Turkoman tribes, profiting by the general disorder, and camped in the heart of Transoxiana, where in 985 they pitched their tents northeast of Bukhara.[21] About 1025, one of their chiefs, Arslan ("The Lion," his Turkish name) Isra'il (his Muslim one), distinguished by the title of *yabghu*, acted as auxiliary to the local Karakhanid, 'Ali-tigin, against Mahmud the Ghaznavid. Mahmud took Arslan prisoner, carried him off to Ghazni, and attempted by stern repressive measures to subdue the rest of the tribe. But their manner of life enabled these nomads to escape any action by the sedentary peoples. The Ghaznavid was compelled in the end to leave 'Ali-tigin master of Transoxiana. On the latter's death (1032), the Seljuks, who seem to have been loyal to him until the end, rebelled against his sons and from then onward waged war on their own account. Their chiefs Togrul-beg, Daud, and Paighu ("the *yabghu*?") asked the Ghaznavid sultan Mas'ud for lands in Khurasan. On the sultan's refusal, Togrul-beg seized Nishapur (August, 1038) and inflicted upon him the disastrous defeat of Dandanaqan near Merv (May 22, 1040), after which the Ghaznavids were thrown back into Afghanistan and had to abandon the whole of Khurasan to Seljuk's descendants.[22]

The Seljuks—a horde without tradition, and the least civilized of all the nomad clans that had recently embraced Islam—found themselves, at a stroke, masters of eastern Iran. Their unexpected good fortune might have culminated in disaster for civilization had the clan not been led by a few intelligent chiefs who instinctively appreciated the superiority of Arabo-Persian culture and, instead of destroying it, constituted themselves its guardians. On entering Nishapur, Togrul-beg caused the *khutba* to be pronounced in his name, thus proclaiming that he intended to abide by Muslim institutions. The conquest proceeded in the manner of the steppes, each member of the family striving to win something on his own account. Togrul-beg's brother Chagri-beg, his paternal cousin Qutulmish or Qutlumish, and his maternal cousin Ibrahim ibn-Inal all acted in this way, while still recognizing the supreme authority of Togrul-beg himself. Chagri-beg, for example, in 1042–43 seized Khwarizm (Khiva). Ibrahim ibn-Inal settled in the Rai district, but the nomad temperament once more gained the upper hand, and his forces committed such excesses there that Togrul-beg had to intervene and restore order. As Togrul-beg penetrated farther into the Arabo-Persian world, he derived more and more benefit from the administrative ideas of these ancient civilized countries; they turned him from a leader of a band into a leader of a state, made of him a regular and absolute ruler with assurance of ascendancy over the other captains, his kinsmen.

Western Persia had long been ruled by a purely Persian house: that of the Buyids (932-1055). So Persian was the dynasty, indeed, that it had continued to profess the dissident Muslim doctrine of the country, Shi'a, notwithstanding the fact that the Buyid princes presided as emirs *el-omara* beside the Sunnite caliphs of Baghdad, whom they had reduced to idleness and for whom they acted as mayors of the palace. But in the eleventh century the Buyids were in decline. In 1029, Mahmud of Ghazni had deprived them of the greater part of Iraq 'Ajami. At the time of the Seljuk invasion, the last of them, Khosrau Firuz ar-Rahim (1048–55), still held—under the title of emir *el-omara* —Baghdad and Iraq 'Arabi, Shiraz, and Fars, while one of his brothers had Kerman. It is curious that this last Persian prince of the eleventh century, on the eve of the Turkic invasion, should have borne the name of two of the greatest kings of Sassanid Persia.

Togrul-beg was some time in conquering Iraq 'Ajami, for despite the anarchy prevailing in the country, his bands of Oghuz nomads did not know how to take cities. Ispahan did not capitulate for a year, and then only because it was starved out (1051). Togrul-beg, attracted by the sedentary life, made it his capital. Amid the prevailing political disruption, feudal disintegration, and intellectual anarchy, the Turk—rough and rude though he was—represented some principle of order, to which the people submitted no doubt with little regret. In 1054, Togrul-beg received the homage of the lords of Azerbaijan (Tabriz, Ganja, etc.). He was summoned to Baghdad by al-Qa'im himself, the Abbasid caliph, and by the caliph's commander of the guard, Besasiri, both of whom wished to throw off the yoke of the Buyids. Aided by all these conflicts, Togrul-beg entered Baghdad and deposed the last Buyid, Khosrau Firuz (1055).

In 1058 the caliph sanctioned this *fait accompli* by recognizing Togrul-beg as his temporal deputy, with the title of King of East and West. At the moment of attaining to this unprecedented honor, Togrul had to deal with the revolt of his cousin Ibrahim ibn-Inal, who allied himself with Besasiri. Profiting by this war between Seljuks, Besasiri briefly reoccupied Baghdad, where he proclaimed the fall of the caliph al-Qa'im—who was considered too well-disposed toward the Seljuks—and became a supporter of Sh'ia Islam (December, 1058). Faced by this danger, Togrul-beg showed himself to be levelheaded and resolute. He turned first against Ibrahim ibn-Inal, defeated him near Rai, and had him executed; then he beat and killed Besasiri before Baghdad and brought back the caliph in triumph to his capital (beginning of 1060). Thus the petty chieftain of the Oghuz band had succeeded not only in disciplining his horde, his clan, and his family and in assuming leadership of a regular government but also in winning recognition as the official representative of the

Arab caliphate. Better yet, he won the acclaim of the Sunnite world—that is to say, of orthodox Islam—as the savior and restorer of that caliphate.

The Turkish sultanate thus replaced the Persian emirate as the temporal counterpart of the Arab caliphate, a substitution that was the more lasting in that the Turks, newly converted though they were, had, unlike the "heretic" Iranians, the good fortune to profess orthodoxy. Not that they were fanatics. The first Seljuk sultans, descended from a line of pagan *yabghu*, were too rough and forthright to share these ideologies. But they found it convenient, when seeking conquest in the West, to justify the old Turkic expansion under the guise of the Holy War of Islam.

Almost without a struggle, and certainly without excessive violence, because of the exhausted state of Western Asiatic society, the Turks imposed their empire upon that of the Arabs, reinforcing without destroying it, lending it new vigor, and so justifying and legitimizing their own imperial existence.

Alp Arslan ibn Chagri-beg (1063–72), Togrul-beg's nephew and successor, was from the time of his accession faced with the task of abolishing the anarchical customs of his family clan, the members of which were evidently most unwilling to form themselves into a regular state. Alp Arslan therefore had to defeat his cousin Qutulmish, who was killed (1063–64), and his uncle Qawurd, who wanted to raise a revolt in Kerman, and whom he pardoned (1064). In the West he made the Mirdasid dynasty of Aleppo his vassal (1070). His greatest title to fame in Muslim history is his victory and his capture of the Byzantine emperor Romanus Diogenes at the battle of Malazgirt (Manzikert), in Armenia, on August 19, 1071.[23] This was a historic event which assured in the long run the conquest of Anatolia by the Turks. At the time, however, the battle did no more than set the seal on the conquest of Armenia by the Seljuks. Alp Arslan accorded chivalrous treatment to the basileus his prisoner, and soon gave him his freedom. In home affairs, this "uninstructed and probably illiterate" Oghuz chief was wise enough to leave administration to his Persian chief minister Nizam al-Mulk.

Alp Arslan's son and successor, Sultan Malikshah (1072–92), was only seventeen when his father died. His first campaign was against Shams al-Mulk, the Karakhanid ruler of Transoxiana, who had profited by the change of reign to invade eastern Khurasan and to occupy Balkh. As Malikshah was approaching Samarkand, the Karakhanid sued for peace and became his vassal. Malikshah made the usual Oghuz mistake of giving Balkh to his own brother Takash, who in due course rose in revolt. The sultan was compelled to lead two expeditions against him, and in the end he had his brother's eyes put out (1084). Malikshah's uncle Qawurd also revolted in Kerman. Malikshah made war upon him too and, upon capturing him, had him strangled (1078).

Such incidents show that in spite of Nizam al-Mulk's wise administration, Malikshah had difficulty in inducing the Oghuz horde of which he was the military commander to accept the framework of the Arabo-Persian state of which he was sultan. Nizam al-Mulk and Persian bureaucracy strove to reduce the role of the Turkoman bands to that formerly played by the Turkish guard, the Mamelukes of the tenth century under the old caliphs and Buyid emirs, but it was often a most delicate task to impose obedience on these turbulent compatriots of the new sultan and to tether such inveterate nomads to the soil.[24] The sultan alone saw eye to eye with his minister in the matter of putting the Seljuk adventure on a regular basis and, by imposing a sedentary and Iranian way of life on this onetime horde, of turning it into a Persian empire of traditional type. At the luxurious court of Ispahan, his capital, he himself took delight in ostensibly continuing the line of the shah-in-shahs of ancient Iran.

In the northeast, as has been observed, Malikshah led a second expedition into Transoxiana against the Karakhanid Ahmed, Shams al-Mulk's nephew and successor (1089). He took Ahmed prisoner, but later sent him to Samarkand as his vassal. In the west, also during Malikshah's reign, but independently of him, his cousin, the younger Seljukid Suleiman ibn Qutulmish, settled in Asia Minor at Nicaea, about 1081, to the detriment of the Byzantines, who had been rash enough to appeal to him for aid in their civil wars. This was the origin of the Seljuk sultanate of Rum (the Roman land), which was to endure from 1081 to 1302, with its capital first at Nicaea (1081–97) and then at Iconium (1097–1302).[25]

The Seljuk state, as a sedentary power, controlled only Persia.

In the old Byzantine territory of Asia Minor, which had been invaded in 1080, independent Ghuzz bands were active; they were led either by younger Seljuks like Suleiman or by Turkish captains of obscure origin, such as—apparently from 1084—the Danishmendid emirs of Cappadocia, who governed in Sivas and Caesarea. These ancient civilized lands were apportioned according to the movements of the roving bands, in the manner of the Kirghiz steppe. As Barthold so well puts it, in summarizing this story: "The Ghuzz or Turkomans, acting partly as independent bandits and partly under the command of their princes [the Seljuks], traversed all the countries lying between Chinese Turkestan and the Egyptian frontier and Byzantine frontiers." [26] Barthold adds that, to be rid of "their roving brothers"—the undisciplined bands of Ghuzz—and to prevent them from ravaging their fine Iranian domain, the Seljuk sultans apparently established them by preference in the marches of the sultanate, in Asia Minor. This fact explains why Persia proper escaped Turkification, while Anatolia became a second Turkestan.

The chieftains fought over their spoils. After conquering a good part of Asia Minor, Suleiman ibn Qutulmish descended upon Syria (1086). There he clashed with Malikshah's younger brother, Tutush, who in 1079 had carved himself a fief in Damascus. The two fought a great battle near Aleppo for possession of that city. Suleiman was killed and Tutush added Aleppo to Damascus (1086). Tutush was on the point of founding a separate Seljuk kingdom there when his brother, Sultan Malikshah, appeared in Syria that same year, forced him to return to Damascus, held court at Aleppo, and made a general redistribution of fiefs among his captains (1087).[27]

On the whole, Malikshah, like his predecessors, spent his life trying to regularize the Turkish conquest of the western areas. This conquest took the form of a surge of small Oghuz bands into Oqaylid or Fatimid territory round Syria, or into Greek territory in Asia Minor—as their nomadic journeys chanced to lead them—and of the exploitation of Byzantine and Arab internal broils. In Persia the appearance of unity was maintained entirely by the Arabo-Persian administration of the vizier Nizam al-Mulk; in the east and in Syria, only by the saber of Malikshah. In Asia Minor, where neither intervened, Oghuz anarchy prevailed.

At Malikshah's death in 1092 (his vizier had predeceased him), anarchy spread everywhere. Malikshah's eldest son, Barkiyaruk (1093–1104), was faced by the rebellion of all his kinsmen. His uncle Tutush, who in the meantime had added Aleppo to his possession of Damascus, attempted to seize Persia from him, but was defeated and killed near Rai, February 26, 1095. The remainder of Barkiyaruk's reign was spent in battles against his own brothers, with whom he was forced at last to divide Persia. From that time onward, the Seljuk possessions remained permanently split into three groups: the sultanate of Persia went to Barkiyaruk and his brothers, the kingdoms of Aleppo and Damascus to the sons of Tutush, and the sultanate of Asia Minor to Qyzyl Arslan, son of Suleiman.

The destinies of these three groups were to be very different. The Seljuk kingdoms of Syria (Aleppo and Damascus) rapidly assumed an Arab character. The two Seljuk houses of the Tutush family were very soon eliminated by their own Mamelukes—Turks also—whose history cannot be related here.[28] The Seljuk sultanate of Asia Minor, on the other hand, endured for two full centuries. Its achievement was of a lasting order, for it was from this realm that the Turkey of history was one day to emerge. In Persia, despite the founding of Turkic nuclei (in Khurasan, Azerbaijan, and near Hamadan), the population remained basically Iranian, as will be seen. In Syria, the Turkic elements were too scattered ever to encroach on the Arab mass, except round Antioch and Alexandretta.

In Asia Minor, however, not only the political conquest of the country may be followed but also the effective appropriation of its soil by the Turkic race. Here the Turkoman herdsman replaced the Byzantine peasant; for the Anatolian plateau, by its altitude, climate, and vegetation, forms a continuation of the steppe zone of Central Asia. Strabo describes Lycaonia—the modern region of Konya—as a grassland.[29] There was a natural affinity between this land and the nomads from the Kirghiz steppe. They settled there because they felt at home. Should one go further and accuse them, as some have done, of unconsciously helping the cultivated land to revert to pasture? Occupation of these ancient provinces of Cappadocia and Phrygia by the Ghuzz, who came from the solitudes of the Aral, may have given the country not only its Turkic but also its steppelike

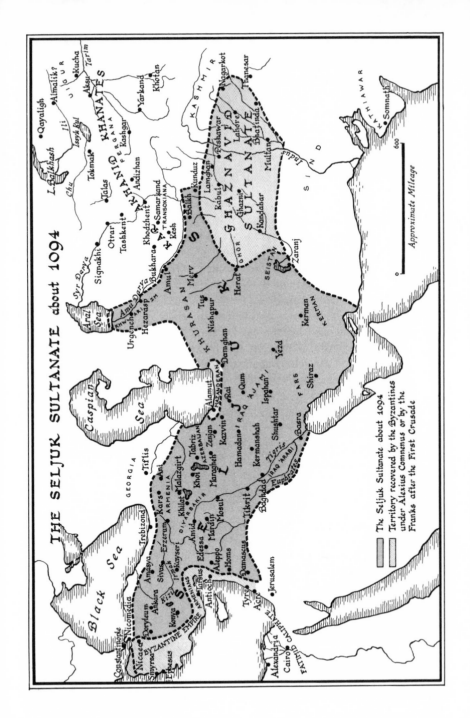

THE SELJUK SULTANATE about 1094

The Seljuk Sultanate about 1094

Territory recovered by the Byzantines under Alexius Comnenus or by the Franks after the First Crusade

Approximate Mileage

character. And when with the Ottomans the Turks extended their conquest to Thrace, did the steppe not follow them? Do we not find there its characteristic features—fallow lands and strings of camels—at the very gates of Adrianople? In fact, Strabo's testimony, just cited, proves that the Lake Tatta basin was already a semidesert steppe at the time of the Seleucids, the Attali, and the Romans. The desolate character of Thrace, however, results chiefly from its having been a perpetual battlefield.

To complete the picture, let us add that the Turkicizing of Anatolia was less the work of the Seljuk dynasty itself than of the regional emirs and the Turkoman clans, whose obedience to it was often far from perfect. From the cultural point of view, for instance, the Seljuks of Anatolia had as clearly defined a desire to Iranize themselves as their cousins of Persia. As no literary Turkish existed in Western Asia at that time, the Seljuk court of Konya adopted Persian as its official language. (It remained so until 1275.) Seljuk Turkey of the twelfth and thirteenth centuries therefore shows a layer of Persian culture superimposed on Turkoman foundations. Persian was spoken and above all written among the Kai-Khosraus and the Kai-Qobads, as Latin was spoken in Poland and Hungary. But this somewhat artificial veneer should not deceive us, nor conceal from us the fundamental Turkic transformation brought about by the Ghuzz bands in Cappadocia, Phrygia, and Galatia.

In Iran, as we said, the case was different, for the Iranian civilization and ethnic character were too strong to allow of the country receiving any serious Turkic influence. On the contrary, it was the Turkic invaders who were progressively Iranized: their ruling houses almost at once, their troops only after some generations. But politically Iran was thenceforth defenseless, and the whole steppe flooded in. The Seljuk conquest of 1040–55 had opened the country's gates to the nomads. It was in vain that the leaders of the stock of Seljuk, having become pan-Islamic sultans—Arab maliks and Persian shahs—sought to close those gates behind them, draw the bolts, and bar the road to all the Turko-Mongol clans of Central Asia who, tempted by their example, desired to make the same venture. The Seljuks who became Persians were not to succeed in defending Persia against the Turks who remained Turks. Notwithstanding their will to achieve this, and despite their "Watch on the Rhine" on the banks of the Amu Darya, they were never anything but the unwitting quartermasters of all the Khwarizmian, Jenghiz-Khanite, and Timurid invasions.

The cause of their failure to restore the stout framework of the Sassanid Persian state, or of the "neo-Sassanianism" of which the ninth century Abbasid Empire had consisted, must be sought in the incurable anarchy within the ruling families, a legacy from their Turkmen past. Despite the individual successes of a Togrul-beg or a Malikshah, they proved incapable of rising permanently to the Arabo-Persian concept of a state; just as, for all the brilliant genius of Charlemagne, the Carolingians were in the end incapable of rising to the concept of the Roman state.[30]

Barkiyaruk's brother and successor, Sultan Muhammad (1105–18), found himself at grips with the stealthy revolt of the Arab caliphate. Relations between the Seljuk court of Ispahan and the Abbasid court of Baghdad, officially close, now became tart, as the caliphs persisted in trying to free themselves from the political tutelage of the sultans. In this they succeeded in the second half of the twelfth century, at least in their little temporal domain of Iraq 'Arabi was concerned. This marks a widening breach between the Turkish sultanate and the Arab caliphate, which Togrul-beg claimed to have united indissolubly. The decline became more acute under the succeeding Seljuk sultans, Mahmud ibn Muhammad (1118–31) and Mas'ud (1133–52), who reigned amid civil strife.[31] These sultans, who ordinarily resided at Hamadan, had almost no possessions except Iraq 'Ajami. The other provinces—Azerbaijan, Mosul, Fars, and so on —had fallen under the sway of Turkish military and hereditary feudal lords known as atabegs. Among these atabegs, those of Azerbaijan ended by becoming mayors of the palace to the last of the Seljuks. Such was the case of the atabeg of Azerbaijan, Ildegiz (d. 1072), who served Sultan Arslan-shah (1161–75), and of Ildegiz' son atabeg Pehlewan (d. 1186), who served Sultan Togrul III (1175–94). Having tried to gain independence, Togrul III was imprisoned by the atabeg Qyzyl Arslan, Pehle-wan's brother and successor (1190). It was not until after Qyzyl Arslan's death (1191) that Togrul III, in whom burned something of the fire of the great Seljuks of the eleventh century, at last regained independence in his royal domain of Iraq 'Ajami. But this belated and quite local Seljuk restoration was to be of very brief duration. In 1194, Togrul III would succumb to the onslaught of the Khwarizmian Turks, who were destined at last to succeed the Seljuks to the empire of the Middle East.[32]

SULTAN SANJAR AND THE WATCH ON THE OXUS

One last great Seljuk, Sanjar, Malikshah's youngest son, had striven to halt the decay of his house. He was brave, generous, and chivalrous, a perfect example of an Iranized Turk, defender of Persian civilization. He even became one of its legendary heroes, like some character from the *Shah Namah*.

At the time of the division of the inheritance among the sons of Malikshah, Sanjar—who was then no more than ten or twelve years old—was given Khurasan to govern, his principal residence being at Merv (1096). In 1102 he had to defend his fief against an invasion by the Karakhanid khan of Kashgaria, Qadir-khan Jibra'il, whom he beat and killed near Termez. He then installed as vassal ruler of Transoxiana the local Karakhanid, Arslan-khan, who had fled before the invasion.[33] In 1130 he quarreled with his protégé Arslan-khan, took Samarkand, deposed the khan, and replaced him by other Karakhanid princes: first Hasan-tigin, then Rukn ad-Din Mahmud (the latter from 1132 to 1141).[34] Sanjar also intervened in Afghanistan in battles between the Ghaznavid princes of that country. In 1117, taking up arms against the Ghaznavid Arslan-shah, he seized Ghazni and enthroned another prince of the same line, Bahram-shah. At that time, therefore, he was suzerain of Ghaznavid Afghanistan and Karakhanid Transoxiana, lord of a vast sultanate of the Iranian East.

Among Sanjar's vassals was the shah of Khwarizm, the Turk Atsiz (1127–56). After an attempt to gain independence, Atsiz was beaten in 1138 at Hezarasp by Sanjar, who put him to flight. Atsiz returned in 1141, however, and by the generosity of the sultan received a pardon. But now Sanjar in his turn was to encounter reverses. In that same year, Transoxiana was invaded by the Kara-Khitai, who had migrated from China to the Issyk Kul. These Mongols were the more formidable as neighbors in that they had remained "pagan," that is to say, Buddhist, and were therefore regarded with horror by the Muslim world. Sanjar with his usual daring advanced to meet the Kara-Khitai, but on September 9, 1141, he sustained a serious defeat at Qatwan near Samarkand, and had to flee into Khurasan.[35] The whole of Transoxiana fell into the hands of the Kara-Khitai. Atsiz, the shah of Khwarizm, seized the opportunity to rise up in revolt. Entering Khurasan, he occupied Merv and Nishapur, but was unable to hold them against Sanjar's counterattack. Sanjar twice invaded Khwarizm (1143–44 and 1147); the second time, under the walls of Urgench, he succeeded in forcing Atsiz back into vassalage. But the heroism of the great sultan was worn down under these ever-recurring trials. Soon an unexpected peril arose. Tribes of Oghuz or Ghuzz—this is to say, people of the same ethnic stock as the Seljuks—from near Balkh rebelled against Sanjar when he tried to subject them to administrative and fiscal regulations of Persian type, took him prisoner, and plundered Merv, Nishapur, and the other towns of Khurasan (1153). Sanjar was unable to free himself until 1156, and died the following year, on the eve of the total ruin of his work.[36]

Sanjar had failed in his efforts to found a lasting Seljuk state in the Iranian east. The Ghuzz rebellion demonstrated the difficulty of bringing into the Arabo-Persian administrative framework those nomad tribes which had been associated with the Seljuk conquest of Iran. That traditionally Persian framework, adopted and maintained by the Seljuks, was not to survive the fall of the various branches of the dynasty (1157 in the Iranian east, 1194 in Iraq 'Ajami, 1302 in Asia Minor). When the setting changed and the neo-Persian sultanate disappeared, nothing was left of the conquests of Iran (1040) and of Asia Minor (1072 to 1080) but a movement of Turkoman tribes. All of these, from the Ghuzz of 1053 to the Qara-Qoyunlu and Aq-Qoyunlu bands of the fifteenth century, from the Karamans to the Ottomans, would wage war on each other for possession of Iran and Asia Minor, in the manner of all the ancestral hordes in the heart of the Central Asian steppes.

Despite the cultural inclinations of the Seljuks—those Turks who had so swiftly and fundamentally become Iranized—their triumph both in Iran and in Asia Minor resulted economically and socially in the transformation of both regions into an extension of the steppe. Here indeed, human geography had a disastrous effect on the geography of vegetation. Nomadism destroys cultivation and transforms the face of the earth. What has been said of Asia Minor is even truer of Iran. In the oases surrounding his cities, the Tadzhik could continue to cultivate the delightful gardens of cypress and roses sung by Omar Khayyam and Sa'adi. But at the gates of those cities, when the last of the gardens was left behind, the steppes took over; here migrant tribes drove their black herds and raised their black tents by the watering points.

Some especially astute tribal chief—for all these Turks had an innate sense of government—might from time to time win recognition and be hailed as king by the sedentary peoples whose internal squabbles he was able to quell. For some decades these two societies—the urban Tadzhik society and the nomad society of the black tents—would appear to complement each other and pull together, but then came dissolution. The tribal migrations resumed and the concept of state was forgotten, until the story began all over again with the sedentarizing of some nomad clan which had attained to kingship. The cycle was never closed, for it got new life from outside. Thus from the eleventh to the seventeenth century, fresh nomads appeared on the threshold of the Kirghiz or Turkoman steppe, at the fringe of cultivation, claiming their place in ordered partnership with the Tadzhiks.

This dual phenomenon occurred even within the lifetime of Sultan Sanjar. After him, the shahs of Khwarizm, who, like the Seljuks, were of Turkic stock, renewed the Seljuk attempt to found a great Turko-Persian empire in eastern Iran: Turkic in its military structure, Persian in its system of administration. At the same time, a people from the Far East, the Kara-Khitai— a Mongol rather than a Turkic people—seized eastern Turkestan; and their coming presaged, a hundred years in advance, the arrival of the main body of the steppe forces: the Jenghiz-Khanite Mongols themselves.

Before passing on to this new phase in the history of Asia, let us draw up the ethnic balance sheet of the Seljuk adventure. This balance sheet is, on the whole, somewhat paradoxical. It is to be noted that the Seljuks, those Turkomans who became sultans of Persia, did not Turkify Persia—no doubt because they did not wish to do so. On the contrary, it was they who volun-

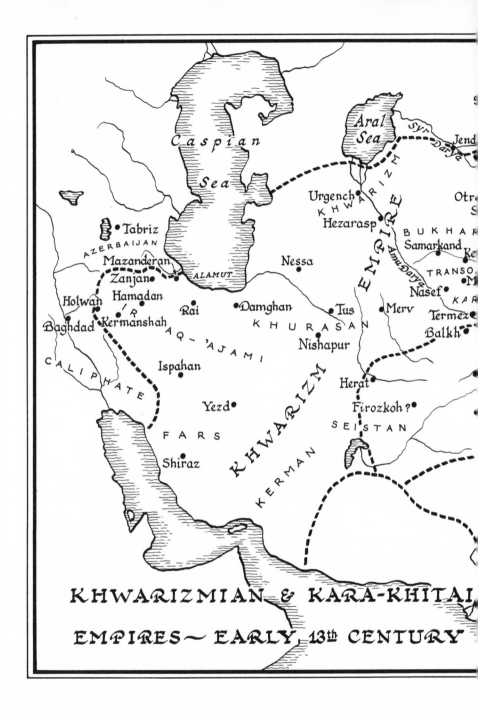

KHWARIZMIAN & KARA-KHITAI

EMPIRES ~ EARLY 13th CENTURY

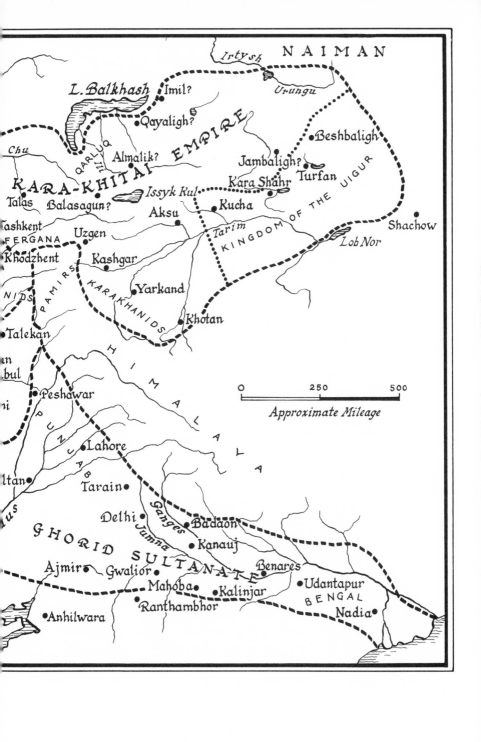

tarily became Persians and who, in the manner of the great old
Sassanid kings, strove to protect the Iranian populations from
the plundering of Ghuzz bands and save Iranian culture from
the Turkoman menace.[37] Nevertheless—and this is perhaps one
of the lasting results of Sanjar's defeat by the Ghuzz in 1153—
they were unable to prevent those Turkmen from establishing
themselves in a dense mass south of the lower Amu Darya, between the Ust-Urt plateau and Merv, in the ethnically de-Iranized
region which later became Turkmenistan. At the same time the
Turkoman bands led by junior Seljuks on the Anatolian plateau
unquestionably transformed those ancient Byzantine lands into
Turkic ones, and to such effect as to make of them—under the
rule of the Konya sultans, the Ottomans, and of Mustafa Kemal
Atatürk—the Turkey of modern history.

THE KARA-KHITAI EMPIRE

To understand the convulsion that occurred in eastern Turkestan
in the second quarter of the twelfth century, the contemporary
revolutions of northern China must be considered. From 936 until
1122 (see p. 129) a Mongol race, the Khitan, originating on the
west bank of the Liao River, had reigned at Peking in the
northern districts of Hopei and Shansi, as well as in Jehol and
Chahar, territories of theirs since an earlier period. Between
1116 and 1122, the Khitan had been dispossessed by the Jurchid,
or Kin, a people of Tungusic stock and succeeded them in the
domination of northern China.

The bulk of the Khitan continued to live as vassals of the
Kin in their own ancient domains between the Manchurian
southwest and the eastern portion of modern Jehol. But a portion
of the Khitan sought their fortune in the west, north of the
Tarim, where the Uigur Turks of Turfan, Beshbaligh, and
Kucha recognized their suzerainty. It seems that from there
one group of Khitan started in 1128 to penetrate Kashgaria,
only to be repulsed by the Karakhanid khan of Kashgar, Arslan
Ahmed. Khitan émigrés to the northwest, led by a prince of
their royal family named in Chinese Ye-lü Ta-shih, were more
fortunate. In Tarbagatai, near the Chuguchak of today, they
founded Imil.[38] West of the Issyk Kul, the Karakhanid reigning
at Balasagun [39] was threatened in this period both by the Qarluq

of the lower Ili and the Kankhli Turks situated north of the Aral Sea. He appealed to the Khitan chief Ye-lü Ta-shih, who came, deposed the rash Karakhanid, and took his place. Thus Balasagun became Ye-lü Ta-shih's capital, and he himself assumed the title of *gur-khan,* or king of the world, which his descendants bore after him.[40] Not long afterward, the new *gur-khan* subjugated the local Karakhanids ruling at Kashgar and Khotan. The new Khitan empire thus founded in eastern Turkestan is known in Muslim history by the name of "the Kara-Khitai empire" ("Black Khitan" or "Black Khitay"), and is so referred to here.

The Khitan were of the Mongol race, but in two centuries of rule at Peking they had become markedly Sinicized.[41] Their descendants, albeit settled thenceforth in Turkestan among Muslim Turks, remained hostile to Islam and to Arabo-Persian culture, for their orientation was toward Chinese civilization, whether Buddhist or Confucian; they were what the Muslims called "pagans." Taxation was assessed, as in China, on the importance of the household. In contrast to other nomads, the *gur-khans* did not create fiefs and appanages in favor of their kinsmen—plain evidence, it would seem, of the persistence of Chinese administrative ideas. Barthold even believes that the administrative language may have been Chinese. It should be noted also that Christianity flourished in the Kara-Khitai empire, side by side with Buddhism. "In Kashgar at this period we find a Christian bishop, and it is to this same period that the most ancient Christian inscriptions of the Chu belong." [42]

The foundation of the Kara-Khitai empire appears, then, as a reaction against the work of Islamization achieved by the Karakhanids.

The first Kara-Khitai *gur-khan,* Ye-lü Ta-shih (ca. 1130–42), having consolidated his power over the Issyk Kul region and in Kashgaria at the expense of the eastern Karakhanids, attacked the western Karakhanids established in Transoxiana and, beyond these, the Seljuk sultanate of eastern Iran over which Sanjar was still reigning. In May and June of 1137, he defeated the Karakhanid of Samarkand, Rukn ad-Din Mahmud, at Khodzhent, in Fergana. Sultan Sanjar, on coming to the rescue of his Transoxianian vassals, was himself beaten by the Kara-Khitai at Qatwan, north of Samarkand (September 9, 1141). Bukhara and Samarkand passed from Seljuk suzerainty to that of the *gur-khan,* who, however, allowed the local Karakhanids to remain as vassals in the second of these cities.[43] In the same year, 1141, the Kara-Khitai invaded Khwarizm. The shah of Khwarizm, Atsiz, was likewise compelled to acknowledge himself a tributary. His successor, Arslan (1156–72), although he cherished the ambition of succeeding to the Seljuks in eastern Iran, was forced to remain tributary to the *gur-khan* for almost all his life.[44]

The Kara-Khitai empire now extended from Hami to the Aral Sea and to Khodzhent, its suzerainty from the upper Yenisei to the Amu Darya. From a Muslim point of view, this hegemony of a pagan Mongol line in Muslim Turkic territory was a serious setback and a scandal. These people's eyes were fixed not upon the Muslim world but upon the China from which they derived their culture. Ye-lü Ta-shih, the most eminent among them, was known as an excellent Chinese scholar. China in turn continued to take an interest in these descendants of the ancient kings of Peking, whereas Arabo-Persian historiography alludes to them in somewhat contemptuous terms. As a result, they are known only by the Chinese transcription of their names. After the death of the *gur-khan* Ye-lü Ta-shih (about February, 1142), his widow Ta-pu-yen became regent of the empire (1142–50). Then followed the reign of their son Ye-lü Yi-lie (1150–63). After Yi-lie's death, his sister Ye-lü Shih (or Pu-su-wan) assumed the regency (1163–78), during which a Kara-Khitai army entered Khurasan to plunder Balkh (1165). Finally, Ye-lü Che-lu-ku, son of Yi-lie, ruled in his own right from 1178 to 1211. During his reign the Kara-Khitai empire was to fall foul of its own vassals, the shahs of Khwarizm; and this conflict, which broke out at the time of the Jenghiz-Khanite conquests, was shortly to bring about the downfall of both adversaries, to the advantage of the Mongols alone.[45]

THE KHWARIZMIAN EMPIRE

In opposition to the "pagan" and Sinicized Mongol world of the Kara-Khitai, the shahs of Khwarizm (in modern Khiva) represented the Muslim Turkic world, especially after the death in 1157 of the Seljuk Sanjar without a successor. The primary position of government in the Iranian east was thus left vacant. In fact, Sanjar's old kingdom of Khurasan was a masterless realm in which the Oghuz chiefs, since their unhoped-for victory in 1153, had been a law unto themselves, while still according recognition more or less to the suzerainty of the shahs of Khwarizm.[46]

On the death of Arslan (1172), the shah's two sons, Takash and Sultan-shah, competed for the throne.[47] Takash, the loser, sought refuge with the Kara-Khitai. The queen regent of the Kara-Khitai, Ye-lü Shih, charged her husband with the task of leading an army into Khwarizm in order to reinstate Takash and drive out Sultan-shah. This was done (December, 1172). But although he owed his throne to the Kara-Khitai, Takash lost no time in rebelling against them because of the exacting conditions they imposed for the payment of tribute; and the Kara-Khitai, reversing their policy, supported his brother Sultan-shah against him. Though they were unable to replace Sultan-shah on the throne of Khwarizm, they lent him an army with which he undertook the conquest of Khurasan (he captured Merv, Sarakhs, and Tus in 1181). Thus Sultan-shah reigned over Khurasan until his death in 1193, after which Takash reunited all Khurasan with his Khwarizmian possessions (1193).

Hardly had Takash become master of Khurasan when he invaded Iraq 'Ajami. This province, it has been noted, constituted the royal domain of the last Seljuk sultan, Togrul III. In a decisive battle fought near Rai on March 19, 1194, Takash defeated and slew Togrul.[48] The victory, which put an end to Seljuk domination in Persia, gave Iraq 'Ajami with Rai and Hamadan to the shah of Khwarizm.

The son of Takash, 'Ala ad-Din Muhammad, succeeded him (1200–20). 'Ala ad-Din Muhammad brought the Khwarizmian empire to its peak, and during his reign it became the dominant state in Central Asia. His first act was to capture Afghanistan from the Ghorids.

At the time when Muhammad's two predecessors were laying the foundations of the Khwarizmian empire on the lower Amu Darya, another great Muslim power had just arisen in Afghanistan. This country had until then belonged to the Turkic Ghaznavid line, who owned also the Punjab in India. About 1150 a clan of Suri Afghans rebelled against the Ghaznavid sultans in the Ghor Mountains between Herat and Bamian. That year the Ghorid chief Jahan Soz plundered Ghazni, the capital of the sultans, which in 1173 was occupied permanently by his successor Ghiyath ad-Din. The Ghaznavid sultans took refuge in Lahore, in the Punjab, abandoning Afghanistan to the Ghorids. During the reign of the famous Shihab ad-Din Muhammad of Ghor (1163–1206), the Ghorid empire made a remarkable eastward expansion. Muhammad dethroned the last Ghaznavids of the Punjab, annexed the province (1186), and seized the Ganges basin from the Hindu rajas (1192–1203). He had reached this point in his achievements when he was attacked by his namesake, Shah Muhammad of Khwarizm.[49]

The first battle between the two Muhammads, on the Amu Darya, was won by the Ghorid, who set forth to plunder Khwarizm proper (1204). Muhammad of Khwarizm appealed for help to his suzerain, the Kara-Khitai *gur-khan,* who sent him an army led by a certain Tayanku-Taraz and by his other vassal, Uthman, the Karakhanid prince of Samarkand. Thanks to these reinforcements, the shah of Khwarizm defeated the Ghorids at Hezarasp and drove them out of the country (1204). The Kara-Khitai pursued Muhammad of Ghor and dealt him a disastrous blow at Andkhoi west of Balkh (September–October, 1204). This victory conclusively demonstrated the ultimate superiority of the Khwarizmians over the Ghorids.[50] Yet it was not until after the death of Muhammad of Ghor (March 13, 1206) that Muhammad of Khwarizm seized Herat and Ghor itself from the Ghorids (December, 1206).[51] In 1215 the shah of Khwarizm would complete the conquest of Afghanistan by seizing Ghazni.

Muhammad of Khwarizm owed his victory over the Ghorids to the Kara-Khitai *gur-khan,* his suzerain. But his gratitude was short-lived. Having arrived at this peak of power, he, a Muslim emperor (for at about this time he assumed the title of sultan) and lord of two-thirds of Iran, felt it intolerable that he should remain the vassal and tributary of these "pagan" Mongols. The Karakhanid prince of Samarkand, Uthman ibn Ibrahim (1200–12), similarly a vassal of the Kara-Khitai, shared these sentiments. In 1207, Muhammad of Khwarizm, having come to an agreement with him, occupied Bukhara and Samarkand, where he substituted his own suzerainty for that of the Kara-Khitai. The Khwarizmian empire thus embraced all Transoxiana. The Kara-Khitai reacted, according to Juvaini, by entering Samarkand, but their general Tayanku was taken prisoner by the Khwarizmians in a battle fought either on the Ilamish steppe, near Andizhan in Fergana, or in the Talas steppe (1210).[52]

Muhammad had repulsed the Kara-Khitai with the co-operation of the prince of Samarkand, the Karakhanid Uthman, who had transferred his allegiance from the *gur-khan* to him. But in 1212, Uthman, tired of obeying the Khwarizmians, revolted. Muhammad marched on Samarkand, took it, sacked it, and executed Uthman (1212). Thus perished the last representative of the Karakhanid line, which had governed the Turkestans for over two centuries.[53]

Lastly, in 1217, Muhammad of Khwarizm made a triumphal progress on horse through Persia, in the course of which he received the homage of the atabegs, or independent and hereditary Turkish governors of the Persian provinces, notably the Salghurids of Fars. He advanced as far as Holwan in Zagros, on the borders of the Abbasid domain of Iraq 'Arabi. Having quarreled with the caliph, he was on the point of marching on Baghdad.[54] Even the atabeg of Azerbaijan (Tabriz), a country not included in his tour, spontaneously acknowledged himself Muhammad's tributary. At this time, 1217, the Khwarizmian Turkic empire, bounded in the north by the line of the Syr Darya, in the east by the Pamirs and the mountains of Waziristan, and in the west by Azerbaijan and the mountains of Luristan and Khuzistan, comprised Transoxiana, nearly all Afghanistan, and almost the whole of Persia.

It was then that he clashed with Jenghiz Khan.

Of the foregoing it should be borne in mind that, at the moment of the Mongol attack, the Khwarizmian empire was newly created and had existed in its final form for no more than a few years. It had not had time to stabilize itself and was still without any set organization. The collapse of this improvised structure at the first shock gives no reason to marvel at Jenghiz Khan's strategy. The only cohesive element between the various parts of the so-called Khwarizmian empire was Sultan Muhammad himself. And he, although he had been favored by the winds of fortune for longer than any other eastern ruler, was in fact as susceptible to discouragement as to enthusiasm. It must be remembered that when Jenghiz Khan embarked upon the conquest of this empire, Bukhara and Samarkand had belonged to the Khwarizmians for no more than eight years, the latter city only after capture by storm and a massacre. Afghanistan had not been completely attached to Khwarizm for more than four years before the Jenghiz-Khanite invasion (Ghazni in 1216); western Persia had been incontestably Khwarizmian for a mere three years (1217). In fact, then, contrary to the statements of historians, there was at the time of Jenghiz Khan's invasion no real Khwarizmian empire at all, but simply an embryo, an outline of an empire, still devoid of the bony structure of statehood. Jenghiz Khan was to have a task of a very different order when confronted by a true state, such as the Kin realm of northern China.

4

The Russian Steppe from the Sixth to the Thirteenth Century

THE AVARS

To the eyes of a geographer, the steppes of southern Russia are merely an extension of the Asiatic steppe. The historian takes the same view; we have seen the truth of it in antiquity, in connection with the Scythians, Sarmatians, and Huns, and it is no less valid in the case of the early Middle Ages, from the Avars to the Jenghiz-Khanites.

The migration of the Avars from Central Asia into southern Russia is known through the Byzantine historian Theophylactus Simocattes. Theophylactus distinguishes between true Avars and false Avars (*Pseudavaroi*). In the former he sees, as is noted by Marquart, the Juan-juan: a people of Mongol stock who had been masters of Mongolia throughout the fifth century, until crushed and superseded by the T'u-chüeh Turks in 552. By "false Avars" he denotes the Avars of European medieval history, who usurped that formidable name. These are said to have comprised two united hordes: that of the Uar (or Var), whence the name Avar, and that of the Kunni or Huni; the second term suggests a Hunnic origin.[1] The two linked names of Uar and Huni would thus stand for Avar and Hun. It is also claimed, however, that these Uars and Huni, from whom the Byzantines coined their word *Ouarkhonitai*, were two tribes of Ogor; that is to say, according to some Orientalists, Uigur. But the Uigur of history were Turks, whereas the Avars of Europe seem to have been Mongols.

171

Moreover, Albert Herrmann, in one of the maps in his atlas, continues to identify the Uar and the Huni with the Juan-juan, who were quite certainly Mongols.[2] Besides, as Minorsky [3] points out, the distinction between "true Avars" and "Pseudavars," based as it is on a single Byzantine source, appears somewhat slender. Again, as Herrmann suggests,[4] if the Avars who emigrated to Europe in the second half of the sixth century were not Juan-juan,[5] they must have been Ephthalite Huns. It may be recalled that the Ephthalites, who possessed Ili, Transoxiana, and Bactria in the fifth century and who were, like the Juan-juan, of Mongol stock, were overcome and dispossessed shortly after the Juan-juan, about 565, by the same adversaries, the T'u-chüeh, who had allied themselves with Sassanid Persia against them (see page 82).[6]

Whatever the rights and wrongs of this argument may be, it was toward the end of Justinian's reign (d. 565) that the Avars—*Abares, Abaroi* in Greek; *Avari, Avares* in Latin—moved into Europe, jostling and shoving ahead of them, as Theophylactus Simocattes says, "the Hunnugur and Sabir and other Hunnic hordes." The king of the Alans, called Sarosios by the Byzantines, contrived to remain on good terms with them. Their appearance reminded the Byzantines of the Huns of old except that, unlike the Huns, the Avars wore their hair in two long plaits down their backs. They were shamanists; Theophylactus mentions one of their sorcerers or *bocolabras* (from the Mongol *bögä*, sorcerer).[7] Their ambassador Kandikh, when received in audience by Justinian, demanded lands and tribute from him (557). Justinian then sent them his envoy Valentinos (the same who later visited the T'u-chüeh) and urged their khagan [8] to do battle with the other hordes, the Hunnugur and Sabir or *Viguri* and *Sabiri*, who were crushed. The Avars defeated also the Kutrigur and Uturgur Huns, who were both descendants of Attila's people, and who roamed as nomads northwest of the Sea of Azov and near the mouth of the Don, respectively (see page 79). They assimilated these Huns into their own horde. As the Huns in question must have been Turks and our Avars seem to have been Mongols, we see once again how each of the two great Turko-Mongol groups incorporated within its own empire the representatives of the other. The Avars, when acting as confederates of the Byzantine Empire, had destroyed these Hunnic kingdoms. In 560 their dominion already extended from the Volga to the mouth of the Danube. Their khagan pitched his camp of chariots on the north bank of the latter river. In the north he crushed the Slav tribes (Antes, Slovenes, and Wends); in the west he penetrated Germania and was beaten at last at a great battle in Thuringia by the Frankish king Sigebert of Austrasia, grandson of Clovis (562).[9] The Avars surged back again toward the Black Sea.

Shortly afterward (about 565), a very able khagan named Bayan ascended the Avar throne; his name, as Pelliot notes, seems specifically Mongol.[10] Like Attila before him and Jenghiz Khan after him, he seems to have been a calculating and astute politician rather than a strategist. In 567, in alliance with the Lombards—a Germanic race settled in Pannonia—he destroyed the Gepidae, another Germanic race (of Gothic stock), who were established in Hungary and Transylvania.[11] Hungary was occupied by the Avars, and Bayan set up his royal encampment near Attila's old capital. Thus, in this Hungarian plain which throughout history has figured as the extreme prolongation of the Asian steppe, the chain of Turko-Mongol empires was revived. The Avars now reigned from the Volga to Austria. This unlooked-for expansion of the Juan-juan or Ephthalite bands which had escaped the armies of the T'u-chüeh greatly displeased the latter; they therefore complained to the Byzantines about the treaty made between Justinian and the Avars. When Tardu, the king of the western T'u-chüeh, received the Byzantine ambassador Valentinos in 575–76 on the upper Yulduz north of Kucha, he reproached him bitterly for this pact. Menander [12] quotes him as having said: "Let those Uarkhuni [Varchonitae] but dare to await my cavalry, and the mere sight of our whips will send them fleeing into the bowels of the earth! Not with our swords shall we exterminate that race of slaves; we shall crush them like the meanest of ants beneath our horses' hoofs." [13]

In 576, to punish the Byzantines for their relations with the Avars, the T'u-chüeh sent a detachment of cavalry under the command of a certain Bokhan into the Russian steppe, where, together with the last chief of the Uturgur Huns, Anagai, they attacked the Byzantine city of Bosporus or Panticapaeum, near modern Kerch in the Crimea, at the entrance of the Sea of Azov.[14]

In 582, the khagan Bayan opened hostilities against the Byzantines and seized Sirmium (Mitrovica), a bridgehead on the

Sava. Under pressure from the Avars, some of the Bulgars—a people of apparently Turkic stock, who may have descended from the Kutrigur Huns—settled in Bessarabia and Wallachia, whence the arrival of the Magyars would later cause them to emigrate to Moesia, which they would make into a Bulgaria. In the west, Bayan—the *gaganus*, as Gregory of Tours renders his Mongol title—resumed his struggle with the Franks about 570, and this time beat Sigebert, the king of Austrasia. Bayan then attacked the Byzantine Empire once more, took Singidunum (Belgrade), and sacked Moesia as far as Anchialus (near Burgas).[15] In 587 he was defeated by the Byzantines near Adrianople, and for a time remained inactive. In 592 Bayan made a fresh raid, captured Anchialus, and ravaged Thrace as far as Zurulum (Corlu). An able Byzantine general named Priscus then succeeded in holding the khagan in check; he even crossed the Danube, attacked him in the heart of his empire, in Hungary, and conclusively defeated him on the banks of the Tisza, killing four of his sons (601). Shortly after this disaster, Bayan died (602).

The Avar khagan who followed turned against Italy, then in the power of the Lombards. The Avars had already taken advantage of the Lombards' migration from Pannonia to Lombardy to occupy Pannonia. In 610 their khagan seized and sacked Friuli. In 619,[16] on the occasion of an interview at Heraclea Pontica (Eregli) in Thrace, he resorted to treachery: a personal assault on Emperor Heraclius, followed by an attack on Constantinople. Both ambush and attack failed. However, the hostilities undertaken by Chosroes II, the king of Persia, against the Byzantine Empire soon provided the Avars with an unlooked-for opportunity. Persians and Avars combined to besiege Constantinople, the former through Asia Minor, the latter through Thrace. In June and July, 626, as the Persian general Shahrbaraz, having crossed Asia Minor from end to end, pitched his camp at Chalcedon at the entrance to the Bosporus, the Avar khagan sat down before the walls of Constantinople. Emperor Heraclius was then at the Caucasian front, and in his absence Constantinople was defended by the patrician Bonus. From July 31 until August 4, 626, the Avars launched assault after assault upon the city. This was the gravest peril that western civilization had faced for a very long time. What would have become of that civilization if the Mongol horde had moved into the capital of Christendom at that time?

But the Byzantine fleet, mistress of the Bosporus, prevented the Persians and Avars from co-ordinating their efforts. Repulsed with appalling losses at each of his attacks, the khagan raised the siege and returned to Hungary.

This reverse seriously impaired the prestige of the Avars. On the death of the khagan who had suffered it (630), the Bulgars—the Turkic people who had until then helped the Avars as allies rather than as subjects—demanded that the dignity of khagan should pass to their own khan, Kuvrat; and the Avars had to repress this claim to hegemony by force. Nevertheless, they were compelled to leave the Bulgars lords of modern Wallachia and of "Bulgaria" north of the Balkan Mountains, just as they had to allow the Slavs (Croats, etc.) to occupy the territory between the Danube and the Sava. They themselves remained in the Hungarian plain until the end of the eighth century.

It was left to Charlemagne to deal finally with the Mongol horde. In August, 791, in the course of his first campaign, he personally invaded the Avar khanate and penetrated as far as the confluence of the Danube and the Raab. In 795 his son Pepin, assisted by Eric, duke of Friuli, attacked the Ring—the walled citadel of the Avars—and captured part of the Avar treasure, the spoils of two centuries of raids through the Byzantine world. In 796, in a third campaign, Pepin demolished the Ring and removed the rest of the treasure. One of the Avar chiefs, who bore the ancient Turko-Mongol title of *tudun,* had come the year before to receive baptism at Aix-la-Chapelle (Aachen).[17] In 799 he rebelled against Frankish rule, but this was the final struggle. After his chastisement, a new Avar chief named Zodan came in 803 to make permanent submission. In 805, a khagan baptized with the name of Theodore ruled the Avars as a subject of Charlemagne.

But after so many disasters the Avars were unable to defend themselves against the dual pressure of Slavs and Bulgars. At the end of Charlemagne's reign, and with his authority, they and their khagan Theodore abandoned the north bank of the Danube for western Pannonia, between Carnuntum and Sabaria. At the end of the ninth century, the old Avaria was divided between (1) the Slavic empire of Sviatopolk (d. 895), known as Great Moravia, which extended from Bohemia to Pannonia, inclusively, and (2) the Turkic khanate of the Bulgars, which included southern Hungary, Wallachia, and Bulgaria north of the Balkan range. The Bulgarian tribe of the Onoghundur or Onogur, destined perhaps to give its name to Hungary, occupied in particular the region east and south of the Carpathians.[18]

The Avars were not without an important art of their own, as attested by archaeological finds in Hungary. It is a branch of steppe art, with distorted motifs of animals and above all of spiraling geometric or plant motifs gracefully interwoven, producing a solid decorative effect. The objects, usually in bronze, consist, like those of the traditional steppe, of belt plaques and buckles, ornaments of equipment or harness, hooks and fibulae. It is particularly interesting to note the close continuity of these Avar finds of Hungary with similar bronzes discovered in the Ordos, in the great loop of the Yellow River, and dating from the period of the Hsiung-nu, Juan-juan, and T'u-chüeh. Among the richest of the Hungarian sites may be noted those of Keszthely, Csuny and Nemesvolgy, Pahipuszta, Csongrad and Szentes, Szilagyi-Somlio, Dunapentele, Üllö, and Kiskörös.[19] Avar art, as Nandor Fettich observes, bears a particular affinity to the last Siberian style of Minusinsk, known as that of the Nomad Horsemen. The comparisons made by Fettich between this style and that of the finds of Mindszent, Fenek, and Pusztatoti are illuminating. Let us also note the strong possibility that the Avars introduced the use of the stirrup into the West.

BULGARS AND MAGYARS

After the decline of the Avars, the chief role in Turko-Mongol Europe belonged for a time to the Bulgars.[20] These people, who appear to have been of Turkic origin and related to the Kutrigur Huns, had, during the second quarter of the seventh century, built up a powerful realm northwest of the Caucasus, between the Kuban valley and the Sea of Azov, under the khan Kuvrat (d. 642), leader of the Bulgar tribe of the Onoghundur. After Kuvrat's death, the Khazar advance cut the Bulgar tribes in two. One portion, led by Bayan, one of Kuvrat's sons, remained in the territory under Khazar suzerainty. (The descendants of this branch are believed later to have moved northward in the direction of the Kama and Kazan, and there founded Great Bulgaria, which in the thirteenth century was destroyed by the

Jenghiz-Khanite Mongols; their latest descendants are thought to be the Chuvash of today.) The second Bulgar group, led by the khan Asparukh—another of Kuvrat's sons—moved westward, crossed the Danube in 679, and settled in ancient Moesia. Emperor Justinian II (705–11), protected amid the Byzantine civil wars by the khan Tervel (701–18), Asparukh's successor, officially recognized this appropriation. A century later, the Bulgars of Moesia, under their khan Teletz (ca. 762–64), marched on Constantinople; but the Byzantine emperor Constantine V crushed them at Anchialus, near modern Burgas (June 30, 762). In 811 another Bulgar khan, Krum, beat and killed the emperor Nicephorus I and had a drinking cup made of his skull in the ancient Hunnic manner; but in 813, when he laid siege to Constantinople, he failed like the Avars before him. His successor, the khan Omurtag (814–31), made peace with the Byzantines. The conversion of Czar Boris (852–89) in the middle of the ninth century and the increasing Slavic influence to which the Bulgars were subjected were to separate these people from the bulk of the Turkic nations and integrate them with Christian Europe.

The ancient territory of the Avars was occupied at the end of the ninth century by the Magyars or Hungarians. The Hungarian language belongs not to the Turko-Mongol but to the Ob-Ugrian section of the Finno-Ugrian group, and between these two linguistic groups no intimate connection has yet been found.[21] Nevertheless, it is possible that at the period in question, the Hungarians were politically organized by a Turkic aristocracy. Arab geographers such as the author of *Hudud al-Alam* (982) and Gardizi (1084) seem to distinguish (or confuse) two Magyar groups, one of which remained in the Ural Mountains, where the Vogul still live today,[22] while the other emigrated first to "Levedia" north of the Sea of Azov and later to "Atelkuzu," which is the plain between the lower Dnieper, the Carpathians, the Seret, the Danube delta, and the Black Sea. At this time, the same Arab geographers (as also Constantine Porphyrogenitus) speak of the "Majghari" as Turks, no doubt because both groups of these Finno-Ugrians had been organized by Bulgars: those of the Urals by the Bulgars of Kama, those of Atelkuzu by the Onoghundur or Onogur, who in the ninth century occupied the southeastern region of the Carpathians.[23] The name of Hungarians, to denote the Magyars, may have originated with these Onogur who mingled with them in the second half of the ninth century. Other sources link these Finno-Ugrian Magyars with another Turkic tribe, the Kabars, who are associated with the Khazars and who are believed to have given the Magyars their royal family, the Arpads. The presence of an Onogur or Kabar Turkic aristocracy among the Magyars would explain the Byzantine protocol by which, in the exchange of ambassadors under Constantine Porphyrogenitus, Magyar chiefs were always refered to as "Princes of the Turks, ἄρχοντες τῶν Τουρκων." [24]

Around 833 the Magyars were living in Levedia, between the Don and the Dnieper, within the clientele of the great Turkic empire of the Khazars. Toward 850 or 860, driven from Levedia by the Petcheneg Turks, they entered Atelkuzu. They reached the Danube delta around 880. In their new Danubian domain, the Hungarians continued to be clients of the Turkic kingdom of the Khazars (see below), and it is believed to have been a Khazar khan who, as suzerain, appointed a young noble of the Kabar tribe, named Arpad, to be prince among the Hungarians. Shortly afterward, the Byzantine emperor Leo VI, being then at war with Simeon, the Bulgarian czar, called the Hungarians to his aid. The Hungarians, led by Arpad, crossed the Danube and put Bulgaria to fire and the sword. But the Bulgarians then appealed to the Petchenegs, now masters of the Russian steppe, who attacked the Hungarians in the rear and forced Arpad and his people to take refuge in the mountains of Transylvania. At that moment, Arnulf, king of Germania, at war with the Slav ruler Sviatopolk, king of Great Moravia (Czechoslovakia, Austria, and western Hungary), decided like the Byzantine to appeal to the Hungarians. Arpad came in haste and overcame Sviatopolk, who disappeared in the conflict (895). Great Moravia collapsed, and the Hungarians took up permanent abode in the country which was subsequently named after them (899). From there, their bands sallied forth to ravage the West. They invaded Italy as far as Pavia (900). In Germany they crushed the last Carolingian king, Louis the Child (910). They launched a raid into Lorraine (919), set fire to Pavia, passed beyond the Alps to the Frankish kingdom of Burgundy and Provence (924); another raid followed, to Attigny in Champagne (926); they plundered the region of Rheims and Sens as far as Berry (937), and devastated Lorraine, Champagne, and Burgundy (954). The days of Attila had come again, never, it seemed, to end. At last, on August 10, 955, Otto I, king of Germania, overcame the Hungarians near Augsburg, a victory that put an end to the invasions. On that occasion the Germanic world saved Europe.

The conversion to Christianity of the Hungarian king Vaik, baptized as Stephen, was to change the destiny of his people. In the reign of "St. Stephen," first as duke and then as king (997–1038), Hungary entered upon a new vocation. Having been until then the terror of Europe, she was to become its surest defense against the assaults of Asiatic barbarism: "the shield of Christendom." From the Mongol invasion of the thirteenth century to the expulsion of the Ottomans in the seventeenth, the life of the Magyar people was to be one long, heroic, and glorious crusade.

THE KHAZARS

At the beginning of the seventh century, the southwestern part of the Russian steppe and Dagestan had witnessed the rise of the Khazar empire.

The Khazars were a Turkic people who worshiped Tängri and were governed by khagans and *tarkhans*. Barthold suggests that they represent a branch of the western Turks, or, perhaps more accurately, the western Huns.[25] They were already a powerful nation when in 626 their khan Ziebil, at the request of Heraclius at a meeting in Tiflis, lent the Byzantine emperor 40,000 men to make war on Persia, a reinforcement with which Heraclius laid waste the Sassanid province of Azerbaijan. The alliance thus formed between Byzantium and the Khazars was renewed many times by royal marriages. Emperor Justinian II, at the time of his exile (695–705), took refuge with the Khazars and married one of the khagan's sisters, who became the *basilissa* Theodora. Constantine V in his turn in 732 married a Khazar khagan's daughter who became the *basilissa* Irene. Their son, Emperor Leo IV, is known by the cognomen of Leo the Khazar (775–780). This system of alliance arrangements was most useful to the Byzantines in their battles against the Arabs, whom the Khazars would take in the rear in Transcaucasia (for example, in 764) while the Byzantine armies attacked in Asia Minor.

The cordial attitude of the Byzantine court toward the Khazars may be accounted for in other ways. The Khazars were by far the most civilized people of Turkic Europe, as the Uigur were to be of the Turks of Central Asia. Although they had never adopted a sedentary or agricultural way of life, as is sometimes said, they had built up a coherent state, enriched by trade and with a relatively high culture, thanks to their contact with Byzantium and with the Arab world. This state appears to have been centered at first in the area of the Terek steppes. The first Khazar "capital," Balanjar, has been located by Marquart at the source of the Sulak, a southern tributary of the Terek. After its destruction by the Arabs in 722–23, the royal residence was transferred to the town known to the Arabs as al-Baida, the White City, a name which Marquart seeks to amend to Sarigshar, the Turkic term for Yellow City (or better still, as Minorsky thinks, Sarigh-shin, that is to say, Saqsin). Marquart locates this city at the same site as that occupied by the later capital of Itil, at the mouth of the Volga. Itil, incidentally, was only the winter residence of the Khazar khagans. In summer they roamed, like their nomadic ancestors the Hsiung-nu, across the steppe, most likely in the direction of the Kuban. In 833, desiring to possess a headquarters less exposed to roving hordes, they appealed to the Byzantine emperor Theophilus for engineers to build them a fortified capital. Theophilus sent them the *protospathaire* (chief engineer) Petronas, who helped them to construct this third capital, Sarkel, which stood either at the mouth or, more probably, at the great bend of the Don.[26] On the ruins of old Phanagoria in the Taman Peninsula, opposite the Crimea, the Khazars further erected the trading post of Matarka.

The Khazar empire was the center of a brisk trade. Byzantine, Arab, and Jewish merchants flocked to Itil and Sarkel in quest of pelts from the north. With them, Christianity, Islam, and Judaism found foothold in the country. Between 851 and 863, Byzantium sent to the Khazars the apostle Saint Cyril, who was warmly welcomed. Biographies of Saint Cyril show him debating with Jewish rabbis at the khagan's table. In the reign of Leo VI, Matarka was the seat of a Byzantine bishopric, founded for the dissemination of the Gospel throughout Khazaria. Islam too, represented by numerous Arab residents, made many converts from 690 onward and, from 868 and above all after 965, was to become one of the major religions of the region. Judaism was in even greater favor. In 767, Isaac Sangari began his ministry among the Khazars. Mas'udi declares that under the caliphate of Harun ar-Rashid (786–809) the Khazar khagan and nobility embraced this religion. The persecution of the Jews instigated by the Byzantine emperor Romanus Lecapenus (919–44) drew a great number of Israelite refugees into the country.

A khagan who had assumed the Biblical name of Joseph is said to have written in 948 to the rabbi Shisdai to describe the thriving state of Khazar Judaism; but Marquart doubts the authenticity of this famous letter, which seems to date from no earlier than the eleventh century.[27] According to the *Risala* of Ibn-Fadhan, the khagan, the viceroy, the prince of Samandar (in Dagestan),[28] and other dignitaries professed Judaism. By way of reprisals for the destruction of synagogues on Islamic territory, one of the khagans demolished a minaret. Nevertheless, among the people, Muslims and Christians seem to have outnumbered the Jews. Around 965 a khagan is said to have embraced Islam for political reasons, but in 1016 the khan of the Taman Peninsula was a Christian Khazar by the name of "Georgios Tzoulos."

In the ninth century, the Khazars began to decline politically. These civilized Turks of Judaic faith were to be swept away by hordes of their own race who had remained untamed pagans. Once more the steppe was in a state of flux. The Oghuz Turks from the Aral steppes (the *Ouzoi* of Byzantine writers) drove the Petcheneg Turks of the Emba region and the River Ural toward the west. Around 850–60 the Petchenegs, crossing territories that were subject to the Khazar empire, dislodged the Magyars, who were clients of the Khazars, from the northern coasts of the Sea of Azov. As has been seen, the Magyars then withdrew to Atelkuzu, between the Dnieper and the lower Danube. Soon, between 889 and 893, the Petchenegs renewed their pursuit of the Magyars, dislodged them from their new area, and finally settled there themselves, thus occupying all that part of the Russian steppe lying between the mouth of the Don and Moldavia. The Khazars retained only the country between the lower reaches of the Don, the lower Volga, and the Caucasus.

In 965 the Russian prince of Kiev, Sviatoslav, attacked the Khazars and took possession of their capital, Sarkel, on the great bend of the Don. However, as Barthold observes, the

Khazar khanate survived this disaster, or at least it retained the territories of the lower Volga and of the Kuban and Dagestan steppe. In 1016 the Byzantine emperor Basil II sent a fleet, supported by a Russian army, against the last of the Khazars. These combined forces seized the Taman Peninsula and the Khazar dependencies in the Crimea. By 1030 the Khazars had disappeared as a political power. The Byzantines had miscalculated badly, however, in helping the Russians to crush these civilized Turks, the oldest and most faithful allies of the empire. In place of the Khazars, wild hordes were to seize control of the Pontic steppes.

PETCHENEGS AND KIPCHAKS

The Petchenegs (the Patzanakitai of Constantine Porphyrogenitus, and Ishthakri's Bachanak) were, as we have seen, a Turkic tribe which, according to Marquart, had once formed part of the confederation of western T'u-chüeh but had been driven back toward the lower Syr Darya and the Aral Sea by the Qarluq Turks.[29] Pursuing their westward migration, they were grazing their herds between the Ural (Yaik) and Volga (Itil) rivers when, around 913 (according to Constantine Porphyrogenitus), they were driven from the region by a combined attack of Khazars and Oghuz. Farther west, the Petchenegs had occupied "Levedia," north of the Sea of Azov, having wrested it from the Magyars. Shortly afterward, the Petchenegs, resuming their westward drive, expelled the Magyars from Atelkuzu, that is to say, the western part of the Russian steppe, between the Dnieper and the lower Danube. Thus about 900 the Petchenegs utilized the pastures between the mouth of the Dnieper and that of the Danube. In 934 they joined in the Hungarian invasion of the Byzantine Empire in Thrace; in 944 they were with Prince Igor on his descent upon Byzantium itself. In 1026 they crossed the Danube, but were repulsed by the able Constantine Diogenes. In 1036 the Russian prince Yaroslav of Kiev inflicted upon them a bloody defeat which put an end to their dominion over the steppe and forced them to aim once more at the Byzantine Empire. In 1051, under the impetus of their own ambitions and in reaction to the drive of the Oghuz, they again invaded the empire. There was a further

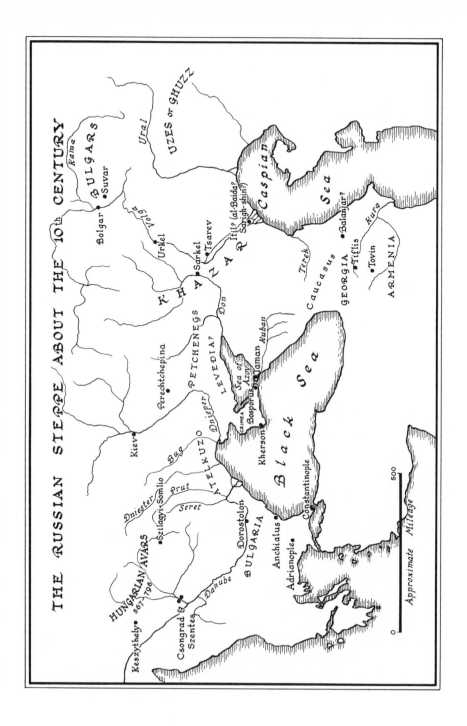

THE RUSSIAN STEPPE ABOUT THE 10th CENTURY

Kama
Ural
UZES or GHUZZ
BULGARS
Suvar
Volga
Bolgar
Urkel
Sarkel
Itil? (al-Baida?
Tsarev
Sarigh-shin?)
Caspian Sea
Balanjar?
Kura
KHAZAR
Tiflis
GEORGIA
Tovin
Don
Terek
Caucasus
ARMENIA
PETCHENEGS
Perechtchepina
LEVEDIA?
Dnieper
ATELKUZO
Kuban
Sea of Azov
Taman
Kiev
Bug
CRIMEA
Bosporus
Black Sea
Dniester
Szilagyi-Somlio
Prut
Kherson
Seret
Constantinople
HUNGARIAN AVARS
567-796
Dorostolon
Anchialus
BULGARIA
Danube
Adrianople
Keszythely
Csongrad & Szentes
500
Approximate Mileage
0

incursion in 1064, across Thrace to the gates of Constantinople. The drama for Byzantium lay in the fact that when it recruited mercenaries from among the pagan Turks of Europe to fight the Muslim Turks of Asia, the sense of Turkish kinship of the pagans 'was often stronger than their loyalty to the basileus. This was seen in 1071, on the eve of the battle of Malazgirt [Manzikert], when the Petcheneg corps deserted the service of Emperor Romanus Diogenes for that of Sultan Alp Arslan. In 1087 in Europe, during the reign of Alexius Comnenus, the Petchenegs once more invaded Thrace as far as Kule (between Enos and Constantinople), where at last they were put to flight, leaving their leader Tzelgu on the battlefield. Alexius Comnenus made the mistake of pursuing them, and was beaten at Dristra (Durostorum, Silistra) in the autumn of 1087. The empire was saved by the arrival of another Turkic horde, the Kipchaks or Polovtsy, who emerged from the Russian steppe behind the Petchenegs and defeated them on the Danube. But no sooner had all these hordes withdrawn into Russia again than the Petchenegs, under pressure from the Kipchaks, invaded Thrace once more in 1088–89, going as far as Ipsala, south of Adrianople, where Alexius had to buy them off. In 1090 the Petchenegs joined with the Seljuks of Asia Minor to attack Constantinople by the valley of the Maritsa, from Adrianople to Enos, while the Seljuk fleet, mistress of Smyrna, attacked the coasts and from Nicaea the Seljuk army threatened Nicomedia (Izmit).

It was a repetition of the situation at the time of Heraclius and the Avars, but now in both Asia and Europe Byzantium was confronted by Turks: pagan Turks in Europe, Muslim Turks in Asia, united against the empire by ties of kinship. The Petchenegs wintered near Luleburgaz, opposite the Byzantine lines, which had been withdrawn to Corlu. Once more Alexius Comnenus appealed to the Kipchaks, who, commanded by Togortak and Maniak, came down into Thrace from Russia and took the Petchenegs in the rear. On April 29, 1091, the combined Byzantine and Kipchak forces crushed the Petcheneg army at Mount Levunion. It was the decimation of a whole people.[30] The remnants of the Petchenegs, having reformed in Wallachia, made a fresh attempt in the succeeding generation, in 1121—an attempt which was confined to Bulgaria, north of the Balkan range. But they were surprised and massacred by Emperor John Comnenus in the spring of 1122.

The Petchenegs had given place in the Russian steppe to the Oghuz and the Kipchak.

The Oghuz, whose Asiatic descendants are now known as Turkmen and who were known to the Arabs as Ghuzz, were in the habit of roving northeast of the Caspian and north of the Aral Sea.[31] A clan of this nation, the Seljuks, embraced Islam and in the eleventh century went to seek its fortune in Persia, where it founded the great Turkic Muslim empire of Togrulbeg, Alp Arslan, and Malikshah (see page 148). Similarly in the eleventh century, another Oghuz clan, pagan in this case—the Ouzoi of Byzantine historians—overthrew Petcheneg supremacy in the Russian steppe. Russian chronicles first mention these Oghuz—under the simple name of Torks—in 1054, at the same time as the appearance of the Polovtsy or Kipchaks.[32] Byzantine historians report that in 1065, during the reign of the Byzantine emperor Constantine X Ducas, these Ouzoi crossed the Danube to the number of 600,000 and devastated the Balkan peninsula as far as Thessalonica and northern Greece, but that soon afterward they were annihilated by the Petchenegs and the Bulgars. The last of the Oghuz bands who had passed west of the Volga were finally subjugated, eliminated, or assimilated by the Kipchaks.

The people known in Turkic as Kipchaks were the same as the Polovtsy of the Russians, the Komanoi of the Byzantines, the Qumani (Cumans) of the Arab geographer Idrisi, and the Kun (Qoun) of the Hungarians.[33] According to Gardizi, they originally formed part of the group of Kimäk Turks who lived in Siberia along the middle reaches of the Irtysh, or perhaps— as Minorsky believes—along the Ob.[34] The Kimäks and Oghuz were in any event closely related. (Kashgari has remarked that the two differed from the rest of the Turkic nations by the mutation of the initial *y* to *j* [*dj*].) Around the midd¹e of the eleventh century, the Kipchaks, splitting off from the bulk of the Kimäks, departed in the direction of Europe. In 1054, the Russian chronicles first note their presence in the steppe north of the Black Sea, as well as that of the Oghuz, whom the Kipchaks pushed and drove ahead. The Kipchaks profited by the Oghuz' victory over the Petchenegs and, when the Oghuz were cut to pieces by Byzantines and Bulgars in the course of ill-fated expeditions into the Balkans (1065 and succeeding years), the Kipchaks remained sole masters of the Russian steppe. In 1120–21, Ibn al-Athir alludes to them as such, and as allies of the Georgians. At about this time, several Mongol clans, closely related to the Khitan and mingling to some extent with the westward migration of the Kara-Khitai, are believed to have come from the Sino-Manchurian borders to the region of the Ural and Volga rivers, there to join the main body of the Kipchaks, among whom they may have assumed the status and function of ruling class. Yet they must very soon have been assimilated, merging as they absorbed the Turkic way of life with the purely Kipchak element.[35] The Kipchaks remained masters of the Russian steppe until the invasion by Jenghiz Khan's lieutenants in 1222.[36] Then, under Russian influence, certain Kipchak chiefs began to adopt Christianity. Also, the Kipchaks were to bequeath their name posthumously to Mongolian Russia, since the Jenghiz-Khanite realm founded in that territory became known as the khanate of Kipchak.

What should be borne in mind of this summary is the achievement of the Byzantine Empire in resisting, throughout so many centuries, the succession of hordes that beat upon its frontiers. From Attila to the Oghuz, all these unpolished Turks and Mongols represented a far more formidable danger to Christian civilization than the crisis of 1453.

II

The Jenghiz-Khanite Mongols

5
Jenghiz Khan

MONGOLIA IN THE TWELFTH CENTURY

At the end of the twelfth century, the map of Asia was drawn thus: China was divided between the national empire of the Sung in the south, with its capital at Hangchow, and—in the north—the Tungusic kingdom of the Jurchids, Ju-chen, or Kin, of which the capital was Peking. In the northwestern part of China, the Ordos and Kansu of today, there had arisen the Tangut kingdom of Hsi-Hsia, which had Tibetan affinities. In the northwest of the Tarim, from Turfan to Kucha, lived the Uigur Turks, civilized Turks with a Buddhist and Nestorian culture. The Issyk Kul region of the Chu, and Kashgaria, formed the empire of the Kara-Khitai, a people of Mongol stock and Chinese culture. Transoxiana and almost the whole of Iran belonged to the sultans of Khwarizm, who were of Turkic stock but of the Muslim faith and of Arabo-Persian culture. Behind them, the rest of Muslim Asia was divided between the Abbasid caliphs at Baghdad, the Ayyubid sultans—of Kurdic stock and Arab culture—in Syria and Egypt, and the Seljuk sultans, of Turkic race and markedly Iranian culture, in Asia Minor.

This was sedentary Asia. Beyond to the north, on the Sibero-Mongol borders, in the steppes north of the Gobi toward the Altai, Khangai, and Kentei mountains, roved numerous tribes which had remained nomadic and which belonged to the three branches of the Altaic race: Turkic, Mongol, and Tungusic. Despite this linguistic division, most of the nomads of Central Asia, leading the same life in the same climate, had an ethnical

189

resemblance which has struck all travelers in those parts. The portrait drawn of them by Grenard hardly differs from the descriptions of Ammianus Marcellinus, William of Rubruck, or of the Chinese annalists: "They had broad faces, flat noses, prominent cheekbones, slit eyes, thick lips, sparse beards, and straight black hair; swarthy skins, tanned by sun, wind, and frost; they were short of stature and their stocky, heavy bodies were supported by bowlegs." This portrait of the eternal Hun or Mongol is not unlike that of the Eskimo or of the peasant of the Causses of France; for life on those vast wind-swept expanses, frozen in winter and scorched for a few week of summer, imposes on any race strong enough to withstand such conditions the same gnarled and stunted strength.

The exact location of many of these tribes is difficult to establish with any accuracy, and their probable position can only be estimated.

One of the principal Turko-Mongol peoples, the Naiman, seems to have inhabited what is now the district of Kobdo and the vicinity of Ubsa Nor, extending as far as the Black Irtysh and Lake Zaisan in one direction and the upper Selenga in the other. "Although their name seems Mongol (*naiman* means eight in Mongolian), their system of titles is Turkic, and the Naiman may well be Mongolized Turks." [1] Nestorianism had made many converts among them. The *Ta'rikh-i Jahan-gusha* even tells us that Nestorians were in the majority, and that at the beginning of the thirteenth century the heir of their kings—the famous Küchlüg—had been brought up in that religion. [2] Nevertheless, the *Secret History* shows that the shamans enjoyed an equal influence among the Naiman, for in war they were able to invoke the aid of storms and of the elements. The Naiman borrowed the principles of their culture from the Uigur, their neighbors to the south. At the beginning of the thirteenth century, the Naiman king had as his keeper of the seal and amanuensis an Uigur scholar named (in Chinese transcription) T'a-t'a-t'ung-a, for Uigur Turkic served as their chancellery language. Naturally China too (in the shape of Jurchid or Kin China) exerted its prestige among them, as is clearly proved by the title of *tayang*, borne during the period of Jenghiz Khan by their king: a title related to the words "great king" (*ta-wang*) in Chinese. In the previous generation, the Naiman king Inanch-bilgä, the father of our *tayang*, left behind him the reputation of a redoubtable chief.

North of the Naiman, on the upper Yenisei, were the Kirghiz, Turkic tribes whose leaders bore the title of *inal*. After they had been driven from the region of the upper Orkhon around 920 by a Khitan raid, they had played no further part in history.

The Kerayit people vied with the Naiman people for power.[3] Their exact abode is only vaguely identified.[4] A number of Orientalists have located it south of the Selenga, on the upper Orkhon and on the Tula and Ongkin, in the modern territory of Sain Noyan. According to others, the Naiman moved farther east, to the region of Karakorum, where the Kerayit zone is supposed to have begun. The Kerayit people are usually considered as Turks. "The legend of Mongol origins leaves no room for them, and it is hard to say whether the Kerayit were Mongols who had been strongly influenced by the Turks, or Turks who were becoming Mongolized. In any event, many Kerayit titles were Turkic, and Togrul is a Turkic rather than a Mongol name." [5] The Kerayit are thought to have been converted to Nestorianism soon after the year 1000, under circumstances related by the Syriac chronicler Bar Hebraeus. The Kerayit khan,[6] who had gone astray in the steppe, is said to have been saved by the apparition of Saint Särgis (Sergius). At the instigation of the Christian merchants who chanced to be in the country at the time, he asked Ebejesu, the Nestorian metropolitan of Merv, in Khurasan, either to come himself or to send a priest to baptize him, together with his tribe. Ebejesu's letter to the Nestorian patriarch (of Baghdad), John VI (d. 1011)—a letter dated from 1009 and quoted by Bar Hebraeus—states that 200,000 Kerayit Turks were baptized with their khan.[7] In the twelfth century the members of the Kerayit royal family continued to bear Christian names. This fact was to be one of the sources in the West of the legend of "Prester John," the other source relating to the negus of Ethiopia.[8] Two generations before the era of Jenghiz Khan, their khan, who called himself Marguz (that is, Marcus) Buyiruq, seems to have aspired to the hegemony of the eastern Gobi, as did the Tatars and, of course, the Kin kings of Peking. But, conquered by the Tatars, he was delivered by them into the hands of the Kin, and nailed upon a wooden donkey. His widow is said to have avenged him by arranging for the assassination of the Tatar khan. Marguz had left two sons, Qurjaquz (Cyriacus), with a name as Christian as his own, and Gur-khan. Qurjaquz succeeded him. After Qurjaquz' death, his son and successor Togrul ascended the Kerayit throne. He was faced by the necessity of struggling against his uncle Gur-khan, who was supported by Inanch, king of the Naiman, and who drove him temporarily from the country. But triumphing in this contest, he in his turn drove out Gur-khan, thanks to the support of the Mongol chief Yesugei, father of Jenghiz Khan.[9]

When in 1199 he had beaten the Tatars with the help and on behalf of the Kin court of Peking, Togrul was to be for a short time the most powerful ruler in Mongolia. The court of Peking set its seal on the authority of the Kerayit leader by conferring upon him the Chinese title of king: *wang*. It was under his dual kingly title—Chinese and Turkic—of *wang-khan* that he was to be known to history. Jenghiz Khan made his debut as client and vassal of this ruler.

North of the Kerayit, on the lower reaches of the Selenga, south of Lake Baikal, lived the Märkit, a Turkic or Mongol race among whom, in the course of this story, Christian elements will be found.[10] Still farther north than the Märkit, west of Lake Baikal, lived the Oyirad or Oirat, a people of Mongol stock. (Their name in Mongol means "the Confederates.") [11]

At the northern end of Manchuria, in the "pocket" between the Argun and the Amur, dwelt the Solang people, who were of Tungusic stock and whose descendants, the Solon, still live there today. Farther south, on the south bank of the Kerulen, near the Bor Nor and as far as the Khingan range, roved Tatars whom Pelliot believes to have been not Tungus (as has long been thought) but "apparently Mongolian-speaking." Tatars, confederated sometimes as the "Nine Tatars" (*Toquz Tatar*) and sometimes as the "Thirty Tatars" (*Otuz Tatar*), were already mentioned in the eighth-century Turkic inscriptions of Kosho-Tsaidam. Even at that time they may have been living in the region of the lower Kerulen.[12] The twelfth-century Tatars were redoubtable warriors and ranked among the fiercest of all these peoples. In the direction of Manchuria they constituted a serious danger to the Sino-Tungusic kingdom of the Kin. It was with a view to delivering a flank attack upon them from the northwest that the court of Peking gave its support to the early activities of Jenghiz Khan.

The Mongols proper, in the restricted, historical sense of the word,[13] of whom Jenghiz Khan was one, made their seasonal migrations in the northwest of modern Outer Mongolia, between the Onon and the Kerulen. As we have seen, history records the existence of peoples who almost certainly spoke Mongol tongues well before the appearance of tribes which, with Jenghiz Khan, were to give their name to the whole group, just as we found Turkic peoples before the rise of the T'u-chüeh proper. It is thus suggested that we should reckon among the Mongolian-speaking peoples the Hsien-pi of the third century, the Juan-juan and the Ephthalites of the fifth, and the Avars of Europe (sixth to ninth century). It has also been recognized that the Khitan, who played so great a part from the eighth to the twelfth century, spoke a Mongol dialect which, however, by contact with the Tungusic languages, had become strongly palatalized.[14] Yet although many of these "proto-Mongol" peoples founded vast dominions, not one achieved such worldwide fame as the Mongols proper, or Jenghiz-Khanites.

According to the Mongol legends collected by Rashid ad-Din, the Mongol people, conquered in the very earliest times by the Turks, had to take refuge in the mountains of Erkene-qun. At a time which Persian historians estimate as about the ninth century, these forebears of the Mongols are thought to have come down from the Erkene-qun into the plains of the Selenga and the Onon. The same legends relate the story of the mythical ancestress Alan-qo'a, who, after the death of her husband Dobun-mergen, is said to have conceived the progenitors of the Nirun Mongols through the intervention of a ray of light. Finally, it is added that the Nirun Mongol Bodunchar was the ancestor —eight generations back—of Jenghiz Khan.

In the twelfth century, the Mongols proper were divided into a great number of *ulus*, a word which, according to Vladimirtsov, signifies both tribe and small nation.[15] These independent tribes fought among themselves as well as with their neighbors, notably with the Tatars. The family into which Jenghiz Khan was to be born belonged to the clan (*oboq*) of the Borjigin and the subclan (*yasun*) of the Kiyat. Later, after Jenghiz Khan's triumph, it became the custom to divide the Mongol tribes into two categories, according to whether or not they were related to the Kiyat. The former constituted the Nirun, the sons of light, or the pure ones; the latter fell into the category of the Dürlükin, who were held to be of lesser lineage. Among the Nirun were included the Taijigot, Tayichi'ut, or Taiji'ut [16] (who seem to have lived somewhat apart from the bulk of the nation, farther north, and east of Lake Baikal); the Uru'ud and Manqud; the Jajirat or Juirat; the Barula or Barla; the Ba'arin; the Dörben (today Dörböt); the Saljigut or Salji'ut; and the Qadagin, Qatagin, or Qatakin. Among the Dürlükin were numbered the Arulat or Arlad, the Baya'ut, the Qorola or Qorla, the Suldu, the Ikirä, and the Qongirat, Ongirat, Qonqarat, or Qongrad. These last seem to have roved farther to the southwest, in the direction of the northern Khingan, near the Tatar country.[17] The Jelair tribe, often ranked among the Mongols and believed to have been situated either south of the confluence of the Khilok and the Selenga or nearer to the Onon, may have been a Turkic tribe reduced to vassalage and assimilated by the Mongols at the time of the legendary Mongol hero Qaidu.[18]

From the point of view of their way of life, the Mongols at the end of the twelfth century may be theoretically divided into the pastoral tribes of the steppe and the hunting and fishing tribes of the forest. Indeed, on the Mongol-Siberian borders, the home of the Mongols was on horseback between the steppe (soon to be the desert) zone in the south and that of the forest to the north. Grenard believes that originally the Mongols were not a steppe race but rather a people that came from the wooded hills. "Their forest origin is seen in the great use they make of wooden carts. Even today the Mongols, unlike the Kazakhs of the steppe, use wooden kegs instead of leather bottles." The steppe tribes, who were more especially nomadic, made periodic transhumance in search of pasture, and at the stopping places they would erect their felt tents which the French call (incorrectly, by the way) *yourtes*. Forest tribes lived in huts made of birchbark.

Barthold and Vladimirtsov find that the pastoral tribes—the richer of the two categories—were led by a very influential aristocracy, whose leaders bore the titles of *baghatur* or *ba'atur* (valiant) and *noyan* (chief), and of *sechen* or *setsen* (wise, in

Mongolian), *bilgä* (the same, in Turkic), and *t'ai-tsi* or *taishi* (prince, in Chinese). "The chief concern of this aristocracy of bagaturs and noyans," writes Vladimirtsov, "consisted in finding grazing lands (*nutuq*), and in securing the requisite number of clients and slaves to take care of their herds and tents." [19] This aristocracy wielded authority over the other social classes: the warriors or faithful, who were by definition free men *or noküd*, the commoners (*qarachu, arad*), and finally the slaves (*boghul*). This last category comprised not only individual slaves but also conquered tribes who had become the vassals or serfs of victorious ones, and who looked after their livestock, fought as auxiliaries in their wars, and so forth.

Among the tribes of forest hunters (*hoyin-irgen*), again according to the Russian experts on Mongolia, Barthold and Vladimirtsov, the aristocracy held a less important place than among the nomad herdsmen of the steppe (*ke'er-un irgen*). These scholars show that the forest tribes came particularly under the sway of a shaman. Vladimirtsov believes that when the shamans combined royal status with magical powers, they took the title of *bäki* or *bägi*, and indeed the chiefs of the Oirat and Märkit [20] at the time of Jenghiz Khan were so designated. But among all Turko-Mongol peoples an important part was played by the shamans or sorcerers (*qam* in old Turkic, *bögä* and *shaman* in Mongolian, *shan-man* in the Chinese transcription of Tungusic Juchen). [21] The role of the shaman Kökchü in the foundation of the Jenghiz-Khanite empire will be noted later.

In fact the division was far less sharp than might be deduced from the terms herdsmen and woodsmen. Among the Mongols proper, the Taiji'ut for instance belonged to the hunters of the forest, whereas Jenghiz Khan is supposed to have been born in a tribe of herdsmen. Besides, all these Turko-Mongols were hunters of one kind or another; the woodsmen, even in the depths of winter, when they wore their wooden or bone skates, [22] hunted marten and Siberian squirrel, which they traded, while the livestock breeders chased antelope or fallow deer with lasso or bow over the boundless steppe. The "steppe aristocracy" hunted with falcons. A clan might exchange one way of life for another according to the vicissitudes of its nomadic existence. During his youth, Jenghiz Khan, deprived of his father's herd by his paternal kinsmen, was reduced with his mother and brothers to leading a miserable life of hunter and fisherman before he was able to build up his fortune in horses and sheep.

On the whole, the forest tribes seem to have been more savage, without contact with civilized life except through the screen of the nomads, who benefited by their proximity to the Uigur of the central Gobi, the Khitan of the Liao River, or the Jurchids of Peking. They had no cities, but in the course of their migrations groups of camps (*ayil*) arose. Felt tents (*ger*) mounted on wheeled wagons (*qara'utai tergen, qasaq-tergen*) were drawn up in circles (*kuriyen*) or temporary clusters—a foreshadowing of future towns.[23] Ethnographers note the advance shown by the shift from the rude cabin of the forest Mongol to the *ger* or felt tent of the nomads, which was easy to fold and re-erect, and which among the Jenghiz-Khanite grand khans of the thirteenth century was to become so spacious and comfortable, with its piles of furs and carpets, that it would be a real traveling palace. However, since the decline of the Mongols in modern times, the *ger* has degenerated, and it no longer has the little pipe that in the thirteenth century served to ventilate it and let out the smoke.[24]

Lastly, the division of the Mongol peoples between the forest hunters and the nomadic herdsmen of the steppe may be seen in the two main classes of tents: (1) the *ger,* or round felt tent just described, which required a fairly large number of poles and laths, denoting a people living within reach of the forest zone; (2) a low, wide, woolen tent, the *maikhan,* easier of construction for nomads living in the treeless steppe. In the Jenghiz-Khanite period, the felt tents were often mounted on wagons, which facilitated transport—at least on the plains—and made possible the moving of real "nomadic towns," a mode of conveyance which has since been lost.[25]

Nevertheless, it is certain that by the twelfth century Mongolia had retrogressed culturally if one compares it with the ninth. At the time of their dominion on the Orkhon, the T'u-chüeh and above all the Uigur had begun to develop farming centers.[26] With their replacement by the Kirghiz, after 840, the country reverted to steppe life. The T'u-chüeh or Uigur inscriptions of the Orkhon give an impression of relative civilization that is no longer found in the history of Jenghiz Khan.[27] The occupation of the country by the Kirghiz in 840 had stifled the Syro-Sogdian civilization introduced by the Manichaeans. The expulsion of the Kirghiz in 920 had left the land in a state of anarchy, for the Uigur, as has been noted, refused to return to the Orkhon. What little civilization still filtered through came from these same Uigur, who had established themselves farther to the south, at Beshbaligh (the Dzimsa of today) and at Turfan; by that route also came Nestorian propaganda. Yet in Mongolia that very Nestorianism, as Rubruck's account shows, had declined almost to the level of the shamanism with which it competed for the minds of the chiefs.

First Attempts at Unity Among the Mongols

Tradition holds that there was, perhaps even before the twelfth century, a first attempt among the Mongols proper to form an organized nation (*ulus-irgen*). A Mongol chief named Qaidu is said to have distinguished himself by beating the rival Jelair tribe, and to have begun to reckon among his clientele a certain number of families belonging to different tribes. It was his great-grandson Qabul, already honored with the royal title of Qabul-khan and, rather posthumously, in the *Secret History*, with the imperial one of Qabul-khagan,[28] who first dared to oppose the powerful Jurchid sovereigns, the Kin rulers, masters of northern China. The Mongol legend shows him first as a vassal of the Kin, received at Peking by the Kin emperor and behaving in his presence like a savage in a civilized country. He astounded this potentate by his Pantagruelian appetite and thirst, and, when drunk, by pulling his host's beard. The emperor forgave him, and on his departure bestowed lavish gifts upon him. But the relations between them soon deteriorated. Qabul-khan, imprisoned by the Kin, escaped, slaying the officers sent in pursuit of him. It is possible that these anecdotes are figurative of the battles which the Kin had to fight against the nomads of Mongolia in 1135–39. In the course of these battles, the Kin general Hu-sha-hu, having advanced into the steppe, was beaten by the "Mong-ku," and to such purpose that in 1147 the court of Peking had to make peace, offering to the Mongols a number of cattle and sheep and certain quantities of grain. Sino-Ju-chen sources give the name of Ao-lo po-ki-lie to the leader who obtained these terms, a name which, according to Pelliot, might well be reconstituted as Oro bögilä.[29] Barthold has sought to relate this name to that of Qutula-khagan, the fourth son of Qabul and a celebrated figure in Mongol tradition.[30]

Qutula-khagan (note the term khagan, or emperor, even though it may have been conferred long after death at the time of the compilation of the *Secret History*, about 1240) is also a legendary hero. "His voice resounded like thunder in the mountains; his hands were like the paws of a bear and could snap a man in two as they would snap an arrow. On winter nights he slept naked by a fire built of great trees, and felt neither the sparks nor the brands that fell upon his body; at his awakening, he took his burns for the stings of insects." [31] But together with this fabled account, tradition maintains that one of his brothers, Okin-barqaq, and a cousin, Ambaqai, having been taken prisoner by the Tatars, were delivered by them into the hands of the Kin, who had them nailed to a wooden donkey, "a torture reserved for rebel nomads." To avenge them, Qutula raided and plundered Kin territory. Chinese annals relate that in 1161, following these devastations by the Mongols, the Kin emperor sent an expedition against them. Mongol tradition, on its part, speaks of a disaster sustained by the Mongols in a battle against combined Kin and Tatar forces near Bor Nor. It seems that in order to break the power of the Mongols, the court of Peking had appealed to the Tatars, and that their combined arms achieved their object. In consequence, Qutula's sons, Jöchi and Altan, seem to have held no truly royal rank, and the *Secret History,* although concerned with dynastic continuity, never bestows on Altan the title of khagan. After the first Mongol royalty had been destroyed by the Kin and Tatars, the people reverted to the old order of tribes, clans, and subclans.

It is true that Jenghiz-Khanite tradition links Yesugei, Jenghiz Khan's father, with the line of the ancient kings. It holds in particular that he was the son of Bartan-ba'atur, himself the second son of Qabul-khagan. Barthold is skeptical of this genealogy, perhaps wrongly so, for the evidence of the *Secret History,* of the *Yüan Shih,* and of Rashid ad-Din can hardly have been pure invention where such recent facts are concerned. What is certain is that Yesugei never figured as khagan, or even as khan, but only as chieftain of the Kiyat clan with the modest title of *ba'atur* or *baghatur.* He fought, like all his people, against the Tatars, who had become hereditary enemies of the Mongols. His adventures are those of a valiant clan chieftain and no more. He helped one of the Kerayit pretenders, Togrul, to triumph over a rival, Gur-khan, Togrul's uncle, an act which was later to afford Jenghiz Khan a valuable friendship. He abducted Oelun, the young wife of a Märkit chief, and married her; she became the mother of Temujin, our Jenghiz Khan. Before he died, he betrothed young Temujin to the little daughter of a Qongirat chief (for Mongols were exogamous). Around 1167, the Tatars succeeded in poisoning Yesugei at a meal in the steppe.

The Youth of Jenghiz Khan

Yesugei's eldest son Temujin, who was one day to be called Jenghiz Khan, was born about 1167 "on the right bank of the Onon, in the region of Dülün-Boldaq,[32] in what today is Russian [rather Outer Mongolian] territory, at approximately longitude 115 degrees east of Greenwich."[33] We know something about his physical appearance from the Chinese Chao Hung and the Persian Juzjani: he was tall, with a sturdy frame, broad forehead, "cat's eyes," and—at the end of his life—a long beard. The wanderings of his youth, his resistance to both frightful cold and stifling heat, his extraordinary endurance, his indifference to wounds and to ill-treatment in defeat, retreat, or captivity, all testify to his astounding vitality. His body was inured from adolescence to the sternest privations, under the discipline of the bleakest of climates and in the most precarious of circumstances. His spirit was tempered from the beginning by his ordeals. These experiences were to make of him a man of iron, a man to amaze the world.

When he was left an orphan, around 1179, he was only twelve or so, and his clan, deeming him too weak to rule, refused to obey him. Despite the energy of his mother, Oelun-eke, the last of his father's loyal adherents forsook him, taking the herds with them.[34] Robbed thus by his kinsmen, the boy remained alone with his mother, his three brothers Qasar,[35] Qachi'un, and Temuge, and his two half-brothers Bekter and Belgutai (sons of another wife). This little party, now fallen on evil times, was reduced to living by hunting and fishing in the Kentei Mountains (then known as the Burqan Qaldun) by the headwaters of the Onon. Temujin's position as head of the Borjigin clan had been claimed and seized by the leaders of the Tayichi'ut clan, Targhutai Kiriltuq [36] and his brother Tödöyän-Girte, sons of Ambaqai. They too, therefore, belonged—perhaps with more certainty—to the line of the Mongol khan Qaidu, who had fallen from his royal estate after the disaster of 1161.

Meanwhile, in the Kentei Mountains, Temujin and his brothers supplied their own needs by hunting and fishing. When his half-brother Bekter stole a lark and a fish from him, Temujin obtained the help of his younger brother Qasar and shot Bekter dead with arrows. Leading this rough life, young Temujin and Qasar grew hardy and fearless. The Tayichi'ut chief Targhutai Kiriltuq, who believed them to have perished, became uneasy and indignant at their stubborn survival; pursuing Temujin into the woods of the Kentei, he succeeded in taking him prisoner and subjected him to the cangue. Temujin escaped, thanks to the collusion of the Suldu chief Sorqan-shira and his sons Chila'un and Chimbai. Aided by his skill with the bow and the even greater skill of his brother Qasar, he began to restore the fortunes of his house. "He had now nine horses!" Eight of these were stolen by robbers of the steppe, but he recovered them with the aid of the son of an Arulat chief, young Bo'orchu (or Boghorchu), who from that time became his most loyal lieutenant and later, in the days of his greatness, one of his best generals. Having thus emerged from a life of want, he called upon Dai-Sechen, the Qongirat chief, to ask him for the hand of his daughter, young Börte, who had been promised to him since childhood. [37] Dai-Sechen consented, and gave as her dowry a cloak of black sables. Soon afterward Temujin moved his camp from the headwaters of the Onon to those of the Kerulen.

JENGHIZ KHAN, VASSAL OF THE KERAYIT

Bearing gifts of sables, Temujin went to the Tula to pay homage and court to the powerful ruler of the Kerayit, Togrul (ca. 1175?). Togrul, mindful that he had once been succored by Temujin's father, welcomed the young man and added him to the number of his clients. Thenceforth Togrul and Temujin were allies, though the latter remained clearly the vassal. This is evident from the title of "khan, my father," by which Temujin addressed the

Kerayit king in the famous message cited below (see the following section).

Shortly after this, Temujin was surprised by a band of Märkit, led by their chief Toqto'a-bäki.[38] Only by leaving his wife Börte a prisoner in their hands could he make his escape (to the Kentei).[39] Temujin secured the help of another Mongol chief of his own age, Jamuqa, of the Jajirat tribe, as well as that of the Kerayit ruler Togrul. The three together beat the Märkit on the Bu'ura, a tributary of the Selenga, and rescued the captive. The latter was restored to her honored place in the household, and Temujin never examined the question of whether the child born to her soon afterward, Jöchi—officially his eldest son—was in fact his or that of one of the Märkit abductors, Chilgerbökö. Nevertheless, this unspoken doubt about Jöchi's birth may well have been the factor that prevented the head of the "senior branch"—or rather his descendants—from playing a major part in the affairs of the Jenghiz-Khanite succession.

Meanwhile Temujin and Jamuqa, although they were *anda* or sworn brothers, soon quarreled. Each aimed at restoring the ancient royal house of the Mongols to his own advantage and being recognized as khan.

The *Secret History* relates how, after wandering together for a year and a half in the region of Qorqonaq Jubur [40] on the Onon, they parted. This was the place where the last Mongol khan, Qutula, had celebrated his election, and it may well have fired the ambitions of the two young chiefs. Temujin camped in the mountains, Jamuqa by the river. "On the slopes of the mountain," Jamuqa is alleged to have said, "the tents of the horse breeders; beside the river, the pasture land of the shepherds." Barthold and Vladimirtsov conclude from this that Temujin was supported by horsemen, the "steppe aristocracy," and Jamuqa by poor herdsmen, the common people or *qarachu*.[41] Farther on, the *Secret History* tells that Jamuqa "enjoyed novelty and despised tradition." Vladimirtsov infers therefrom that he was the representative of a sort of democratic party, while Jenghiz Khan stood for the nobility, an interpretation which seems singularly rash. Whatever the validity of the Russian scholar's argument, the fact remains that after Temujin and Jamuqa had separated, Temujin was followed by "men of the Jelair clan, the clan of the Kiyat, and the clan of the Ba'arin." The most exalted representives of Mongol aristocracy rallied to his side: his paternal uncle Daritai-ochigin and the senior branch of the descendants of the famous Qabul-khagan, among them Sächä-bäki, great-grandson of Qabul (and grandson of Okin-barqaq) and chief of the Jurkin clan,[42] and Altan-ochigin, son of Qutula-khagan. In other words, he won the support of the heirs of the last two Mongol kings. Vladimirtsov, interpreting a passage of the *Secret History*, believes that of the two pretenders to a new royal house, the representatives of ancient royalty preferred Temujin because they judged him to be the more traditional in outlook, and more docile, whereas the lively character and innovating tendencies of Jamuqa aroused their misgivings. Altan, the legitimate heir to the ancient kingship, declined the title of khan—no doubt for opportunist reasons—and somewhat hesitantly delegated the votes of what we might call the legitimist party to Temujin, who was elected.[43] Altan and Sächä-bäki were the first to proclaim Temujin khan—that is to say, king, king of the Mongols proper—in this election, which preceded by ten years his election, in 1206, as supreme khan or emperor of all the Turko-Mongol nations of Central Asia. As king, Temujin took the name of Chinggis-khan, transformed in our more usual histories to Jenghiz Khan. The exact meaning of this is still debated among scholars.[44]

Apart from political calculations, and serving to cloak them, a certain "religious" factor favored this election. Some time earlier the Ba'arin chief Qorchi had declared: "Heaven (Tängri) has ordained that Temujin should be our khan. This is what the Spirit has revealed to me, and I reveal it to you." Another announcement, of the same order, was what one may call the "prediction of Muqali." One day, when Temujin was encamped at Qorgonaq Jubur, the Jelair Muqali reminded him that at this same place, under the same tree, Qutula, the last Mongol chief to bear the title of khan, had once danced and feasted to celebrate his accession. "Since then the Mongols have known bad days and there was no longer a khan among them. But the Eternal Blue Heaven did not forget its people, the family of Qutula. A hero should rise among the Mongols, to be a dreaded khan and avenge their wrongs. . . ."[45] Apart from the religious aspect conveyed by these texts, Jenghiz Khan's election strikes us as that of a leader in war and hunting. The oath sworn by his "electors"—Altan,

Quchar, and Sächä-bäki—as reported by the *Secret History* is significant: "We have resolved to proclaim thee khan. We will march in the van into battle; if we carry off women and girls, 'twill be to give them to thee. We will be foremost in the hunt; if we catch game, 'twill be to give it to thee." [46]

There was one who might have—who ought to have—been disquieted by this new power: Togrul, the ruler of the Kerayit, who saw his client of yesterday on the way to becoming his equal. But Togrul was an unimaginative, vacillating, second-rate leader and failed to perceive the implications of this event. Moreover, the new Jenghiz Khan was very careful to declare himself more than ever the faithful and conscientious vassal. In addition, as a circumstance no doubt reassuring to Togrul, as yet Jenghiz Khan was far from having unified the Mongols proper. Opposite him, against him, his rival Jamuqa had his own partisans. Moreover, the Kerayit king had the same external enemies as Jenghiz Khan himself—the Tatars.

We have seen that one of the loyal adherents of Jenghiz Khan, the Jelair Muqali,[47] who had persuaded him to call himself khan, did so—according to the *Secret History*—by reminding him of the old feud between Mongols and Tatars. It was the Tatars who had handed over two members of the old Mongol royal family to the Kin to be ignominiously tortured; the Tatars who, in 1161, in conjunction with the Kin, had destroyed the first Mongol royalty; and the Tatars who, about 1167, had treacherously caused the death of Yesugei, Jenghiz Khan's father, at a friendly meal in the steppe, by giving him poisoned food. "Thou shalt be khan, O Temujin, to avenge us of our enemies the Tatars, and thou shalt raise up the glory of the Mongols!"

The opportunity came. The Tatars seem to have conquered the Mongols only with the aid of Peking. But once that victory made them masters of the eastern Gobi, they incessantly harassed the frontiers of the Kin realm. The court of Peking, reversing its system of alliances, decided to subsidize and to spur against them the Kerayit king Togrul. As his faithful client, Jenghiz Khan accompanied Togrul into war (ca. 1198), happy to be able to revenge himself upon the hereditary enemy. Caught by the Kin in the southeast and the Kerayit and Jenghiz Khan in the northwest, the Tatars of Bor Nor were badly beaten. The Kerayit king and Jenghiz Khan advanced along the River Ulja, according to the *Secret*

History, to kill the Tatar chief Megujin se'ultu. The court of Peking rewarded Togrul with the Chinese title of *wang* (king or prince), hence the name Wang-khan by which he is known to history. Jenghiz Khan too received a Chinese title, but a far more modest one, which proves that at this date the court of Peking saw in him no more than an obscure vassal of the Kerayit.

Vladimirtsov believes that it was after this campaign that Jenghiz Khan castigated a number of Mongol princes, descendants of the old royal house, for having refused to follow him and the Wang-khan against the Tatars, Sächä-bäki, great-grandson of the illustrious Qabul and chief of the Jurki or Jurkin clan, and two other princes, Taichu and Buri-bökö, were put to death. In his famous complaint to the Wang-khan, the Conqueror claims to have sacrificed "these well-loved brothers" to the vindictiveness of the Kerayit. In fact, he must have been very glad to find so excellent an excuse for ridding himself of the representatives of what one may term "Mongol legitimacy."

If we are to go by official Jenghiz-Khanite history, the alliance between Jenghiz Khan and the Wang-khan seems to have been chiefly to the latter's advantage. In any event, if at first the Wang-khan's protection enabled Jenghiz Khan to escape his enemies, the Mongol hero was soon able to render similar service to his suzerain. At an ill-determined date [48] the Wang-khan found himself dispossessed by his own brother, Erke-qara,[49] who was supported by Inanch-bilgä, king of the Naiman.[50] He fled to the southwest, as far as the River Chu, among the Kara-Khitai, whose aid he sought in vain. Having quarreled with the *gur-k'han* or king of the Kara-Khitai, he wandered miserably about the Gobi and, despairing of his cause, sought refuge with Jenghiz Khan. Jenghiz Khan succored his famished little troop and helped him to reconquer the Kerayit country. It was of this that the Conqueror was later to remind him, in his rough, näive turn of speech: "Weakened by hunger, you came on like a dying fire. I gave you sheep, horses, goods. You were thin. Within fifteen days I had fattened you again."

The Wang-khan's other brother, Jagambu,[51] had sought asylum in the Kin empire. Jenghiz Khan brought him back, having sent a troop to defend him against the Märkit, who were lying in wait for him. "And that was the second service I rendered you," Jenghiz Khan told the Wang-khan.[52]

Now, according to Jenghiz-Khanite tradition, the details of which are so precise in this matter that they must contain some kernel of truth, even though presented from one side only, the Wang-khan sometimes showed little gratitude for all these services. He broke the military pact of alliance as and when he chose. Without informing Jenghiz Khan, he undertook a profitable foray against the Märkit, forced their chief Toqto'a to flee by way of the mouth of the Selenga to the southeast shore of Lake Baikal (the country of Barghu, the Barqujin or Barghuchin of the *Secret History*), killed one of Toqto'a's sons, captured another, and amassed a great quantity of prisoners, livestock, and booty, of which—in further violation of military agreements—he omitted to give Jenghiz Khan any share.

Jenghiz Khan, as a loyal vassal, nevertheless accompanied the Wang-khan on a combined expedition against the Naiman. It seemed a good opportunity. After the death of the Naiman king Inanch-bilgä, a quarrel arose—over the possession of a concubine—between his two sons. Taibuqa (Taibugha or Baibuqa), better known by his Chinese title of *t'ai-wang* or *t'ai-yang* (in Mongol *tayang*), and Buyiruq. The *tayang* ruled the clans of the plain—probably near the lakes in the province of Kobdo—and Buyiruq those of the mountainous areas near the Altai. Taking advantage of this division, the Wang-khan and Jenghiz Khan came to raid Buyiruq's domain and forced him to retreat to the Urungu. Pursued, relates the *Secret History*, as far as Lake Qyzyl-bash—no doubt the Ulyungur Nor, into which the Urungu runs—he was at last killed. (However, Rashid ad-Din, corroborated by the *Yüan Shih*, states that he first took refuge near the upper Yenisei, in Kirghiz country.) But the following winter the Naiman general Köksegu (or Kökse'u) Sabraq, one of Buyiruq's men, launched a sudden counterattack against the two allies.[53] The clash was very violent. During the night the Wang-khan decamped without notifying Jenghiz Khan, who had to achieve a perilous withdrawal alone. Notwithstanding this act of near treachery, Jenghiz Khan—if we are to believe the official Jenghiz-Khanite history—never flinched in his loyalty to his suzerain. The Naiman in their turn came to plunder Kerayit territory and put to flight first the brother (Jagambu) and then the son (*Sängün*) of the Wang-khan. The latter appealed piteously to the ally whom he had wronged. Jenghiz Khan at once sent him his "four great warriors" (_dörben kulu'ud_): Bo'orchu, Muqali, Boroqul, and Chila'un, who just barely saved the _Sängün_ but drove the Naiman from Kerayit country and retrieved the captured live-stock.[54] Qasar, Jenghiz Khan's brother, ended the campaign with a great victory over the Naiman.

The _Yüan Shih_ records after this war a campaign fought by Jenghiz Khan and the Wang-khan against the Tayichi'ut, who were defeated on the upper Onon. It must have been then that Jenghiz Khan's bitter enemy and persecutor of his childhood, the Tayichi'ut chief Targhutai Kiriltuq, was killed by the hand of the gallant Chila'un.[55] There followed, according to the _Yüan Shih,_ a coalition, or rather conspiracy, between a number of clans that had been appalled by the defeat of the Naiman and the Tayichi'ut. It was joined by the Qatakin, the Salji'ut, the Dörben, the Qongirat, and by Tatar remnants. After sacrificing a white stallion, they all swore to take Jenghiz Khan and the Wang-khan by surprise. But Jenghiz Khan, warned in time by his father-in-law, the Qongirat Dai-Sechen, inflicted a crushing defeat upon the league of enemies near Lake Buyur. It was no doubt to this action that the Conqueror later alluded in his famous poetical message to the Wang-khan: "Like a falcon I flew upon the mountain and crossed Lake Buyur; for you I caught the blue-footed cranes with the ashen plumage, that is, the Dörben and the Tatars; passing then to Lake Kölö, I once more caught blue-footed cranes for you: the Qatakin, the Salji'ut, and the Qongirat."[56]

Officially the Wang-khan was the most powerful prince in Mongolia, but his power stood upon shaky foundations. Betrayed by his own family, as has been seen, he had to snatch the Kerayit throne from his uncle Gur-khan. He then had to contend for it with his brother Erke-qara. The _Yüan Shih_ adds that after his victory over the coalition referred to above, the Wang-khan was nearly deposed by his other brother, Jagambu, who, finding his plot discovered, took refuge with the Naiman.[57]

Mongolia was seething. The Jajirat chief Jamuqa formed a counterleague against the hegemony that the Wang-khan and Jenghiz Khan were striving to establish. He was an active and redoubtable adversary, and succeeded in gathering about him not only the clans of true Mongols that had rebelled against

Jenghiz Khan—the Jajirat, Tayichi'ut, Qongirat, Ikirä, Qorla, Dörben, Qatakin, and Salji'ut—but also the Märkit, the Oirat, the Naiman, and the Tatars. At a great assembly held in 1201 at Alquibula'a, on the banks of the Argun (lower course of the Kerulen), he had himself proclaimed *gur-khan*, "universal khan," that is, emperor of Mongolia.

The Mongol Empire was now on the way to becoming a reality. The question was which of the two rivals, Jenghiz Khan or Jamuqa, would win it. In this duel, Jenghiz Khan had the advantages of tenacity, political astuteness, the art of getting right on his side, and, in the beginning, the firm support of the Kerayit Wang-khan. Jamuqa had, it seems, remarkable if somewhat incoherent energy, a lively mind, and a gift for intrigue. But if Jenghiz-Khanite sources are to be believed, Jamuqa was an unreliable ally and did not hesitate to plunder the tribes of his own party, whereas Jenghiz Khan seems to have been an unswervingly loyal protector of those who had given him their faith.

Between these two it was the Wang-khan who tipped the scale. He came to the aid of Jenghiz Khan and with him defeated Jamuqa at Köyitän,[58] in spite of a storm raised by Oirat and Naiman magicians, and forced him to withdraw to the lower Argun. It is after this expedition that Vladimirtsov dates one last campaign of Jenghiz Khan's against the Tayichi'ut, his enemy brethren, as well as the famous episode of "Jelme's devotion." Repulsed in a first attack and wounded, Jenghiz Khan was tended by the faithful Jelme, who sucked the clotted blood from his wound. Whatever may be the chronological order of these various expeditions—for it is still very uncertain—in the end Jenghiz Khan utterly routed the Tayichi'ut, massacred a suitable percentage, and forced the survivors to obey him, thus restoring the unity of the Borjigin clan. A young Tayichi'ut, or rather Yesut, warrior, who had brought down Jenghiz Khan's horse with an arrow, expected execution. Jenghiz Khan pardoned him, and under the name of Jebe—"the arrow"—the marksman afterward became one of the finest of Jenghiz Khan's captains.[59] With his companion in honor Sübötäi, he was to be the most illustrious general in the Mongol epic.[60]

Jenghiz Khan could now settle accounts with the old enemies of the Mongols and his father's assassins, the Tatars Chaghan

Tatar and Alchi Tatar. For the better conduct of the operation, he forbade private looting. The Tatars, vanquished, were massacred and their survivors distributed among the Mongol tribes (1202). Jenghiz Khan himself selected two beautiful Tatar women, Yesui and Yesugän. Three Mongol princes, kinsmen of Jenghiz Khan—Altan, representative of the noble branch of the old royal house and son of the former Mongol khan Qutula; Quchar; and Daritai, Jenghiz Khan's paternal uncle—flouted the order and plundered on their own. But their booty was snatched from them. Altan and Quchar, and even Daritai, began to dissociate themselves from the Conqueror, and soon joined his enemies. Farther east than the Tatars, the Solons of the River Nonni were compelled to acknowledge themselves as a tributary people.

After the overwhelming of the Tatars, Toqto'a, king of the Märkit people, returned from Transbaikalia (from the Barghu country southeast of Lake Baikal), where he had been forced to take refuge, and, according to the *Yüan Shih*, made a fresh attack on Jenghiz Khan, who beat him.[61] Then, still in the chronological order given by the *Yüan Shih*, Toqto'a joined the Naiman antiking Buyiruq, to whose colors also rallied the Dörben, Tatar, Qatakin, and Salji'ut remnants. This new coalition fought against the combined forces of the Wang-khan and Jenghiz Khan in a series of marches and countermarches through the mountains, in blizzards unleashed—the *Yüan Shih* declares—by Naiman sorcerers. Although the topography, like the chronology, of these accounts is unreliable, both leave the impression of exceedingly mobile hordes which, in the course of their quarrels, moved from one end of Mongolia to the other, from the great Altai to the Khingan range. United for a seasonal campaign or for a brief engagement, they would thereupon disperse, whether the outcome was a reverse or a successful raid, for each clan reclaimed its freedom. Jenghiz Khan alone, among these chiefs of fluctuating purpose and unco-ordinated action, constituted a fixed pivot, not because he had formed any rigid plan of his future conquests, but because his strong personality enabled him to turn this perpetual state of guerrilla fighting to his advantage.

BREACH WITH THE WANG-KHAN: CONQUEST OF THE
KERAYIT COUNTRY

Until then, notwithstanding the Wang-khan's shabby treatment
of him on various occasions, Jenghiz Khan had remained consistently loyal to his lord. Considering that he had perfectly fulfilled his duties as vassal, the Mongol hero asked for the hand of
the princess Cha'ur-bäki,[62] the Wang-khan's daughter, for his son
Jöchi. The Wang-khan's refusal, the *Secret History* tells, deeply
wounded the hero.

The Kerayit king had certainly erred in failing to perceive a
rival in his client, and in neglecting to pounce upon him when
he proclaimed himself khan around 1196. By the time the Wang-
khan began to feel uneasy, it was already too late. It may be
that after reflecting a little, as we are told he did, he was vaguely
aware of this fact. He was old, his hair was white, and he would
have liked to end his days in peace. But he was urged to break
with Jenghiz Khan by his son Ilqa or Nilqa, better known by his
Chinese title of *tsiang-kiun, sängün* in Mongolian.[63] The *Sängün*
advised his father to support Jamuqa against Jenghiz Khan.
Bound to him by personal liens, the *Sängün* encouraged Jamuqa,
after the collapse of his ephemeral royalty, to take refuge at the
Kerayit court. Acting in concert with the *Sängün,* Jamuqa fomented the Wang-khan's distrust of his powerful vassal, accusing
the latter of contriving treachery. "I am the lark," he declared to
the Wang-khan, "living ever in the same place in the good season
and the bad. Jenghiz Khan is the wild goose which in winter
flies away." [64] Meanwhile Altan, the legitimate heir of the ancient
Mongol khans, who never ceased to regret having allowed the
kingship to pass into the hands of an upstart, had also come to
offer himself to the Wang-khan, and similarly encouraged him to
make war against his one-time ally.

In 1203 the breach between Jenghiz Khan and the Kerayit was
complete. This rift constituted the decisive turning point in the
life of the Mongol hero. Having up to then played the part of the
Wang-khan's brilliant second in command, he was now to fight
on his own account and for first place.

Encouraged by the *Sängün,* the Kerayit tried to rid themselves
of Jenghiz Khan by summoning him to an interview on the pretext

of reconciliation, but news of the trap leaked out. They then planned to make a surprise attack upon him. Two herdsmen, Kishiliq and Badai, who had heard the Kerayit general explaining the plot to his men, ran to warn Jenghiz Khan. For this he later ennobled them.[65]

Hastily Jenghiz Khan made preparations for war. The _Secret History_ relates that he first withdrew to the neighborhood of the heights of Mao'undur, where he left a small outpost. The next day he established himself farther to the rear, near the sand dunes which the _Yüan Shih_ calls "A-lan," which d'Ohsson (after Rashid ad-Din) designates as "Khalaldjin-alt," and which Hyacinthus identifies as "Khala-goun-ola." In other words, it was the "Qalaqaldjit-elet" (Qalaqaljit-elet) of the _Secret History_. More precisely, the position was near the spurs of the Khingan range, by the headwaters of the Khalka River.[66] Although warned in good time by his mounted patrols (men of Alchidai-noyan) of the enemy's approach, Jenghiz Khan here encountered what was probably the most severe ordeal of his career. The clash was furious indeed. Jenghiz Khan's lieutenants—old Jurchedäi-noyan, chief of the Uru'ud clan, and Quyildar-sechen of the Mangqud clan—performed marvels. Quyildar vowed to plan his _tuq_—his yak or horse-tail standard—on the hill in the enemy's rear. Penetrating the enemy's lines, he fulfilled his vow. Jurchedäi wounded the Kerayit _Sängün_ in the face with an arrow. But outnumbered by the Kerayit, Jenghiz Khan withdrew from the battlefield during the night. His third son Ogödäi (Ögedei) failed to answer the roll call, as did two of his most faithful officers, Bo'orchu and Boroqul. At last they reappeared, Boroqul mounted and holding in his arms Ogödäi, who had been wounded in the neck by an arrow. At this sight, says the _Secret History_, the man of iron shed tears.[67]

Jenghiz Khan, who was plainly having the worst of it, retreated along the Khalka [68] in the direction of the Bor Nor and the northern Dalai Nor, "near Lake Tung-ko" in the Chinese nomenclature of the _Yüan Shih_. At the mouth of the Khalka at Bor Nor lived the Qongirat, the tribe from which had issued Jenghiz Khan's wife. Jenghiz Khan appealed to them in the name of this kinship, and shortly thereafter succeeded in winning them to his cause.

It was from the region of the Bor Nor and Dalai Nor [69] that

Jenghiz Khan contrived to transmit a verbal message to the Wang-khan, reproduced or summarized in most of the sources, by which he strove to move the heart of his onetime suzerain by reminding him of their years of friendship and of the services he had rendered him.[70] He desired, he explained, no more than to be restored to favor. (On the contrary, he wished to lull the vigilance of the Wang-khan, the *Sängün* replied.) Jenghiz called the Wang-khan his father, *"khan echige,"* and pointed out that he had always scrupulously performed his duties as vassal. His loyalist character and his concern to put himself in the right are curiously stressed in the different versions of this famous passage. In the same spirit he reminded Altan, the descendant of the ancient Mongol khans who now numbered among Jenghiz' foes, that if he, Jenghiz Khan, had accepted the khanate, it was Altan's own doing, for Altan and the other representatives of the senior branches had declined the honor for themselves.[71] Under the epic and lyric form of this poem is a legal statement, stressing the correctness of Jenghiz Khan's attitude as man and ally, and addressed to his former suzerain. From the political point of view, it must be admitted that the Wang-khan—perceiving all too late the powerful personality of his former vassal—had been rash in supporting the early efforts of this masterful man. But in breaking the alliance without any valid reason and treacherously attacking Jenghiz Khan, he gave his opponent the right to do the same. And at this game the Kerayit ruler, fitful, vacillating, weak, cowardly, harassed by his entourage, and threatened by rebellion on the part of his son the *Sängün* unless he made an all-out effort, was no match for Jenghiz Khan.

For the moment, however, Jenghiz Khan, forsaken by some of his followers after the reverse at Qalaqaljit-elet, was enduring the most painful hours of his reign. Being greatly outnumbered, he found himself forced to withdraw northward in the direction of Siberia, to the extreme limit of Mongol territory and the frontiers of modern Transbaikalia. He retired, with a handful of loyal adherents, north of present-day Manchuria, not far from the Argun,[72] near the pool of the Baljuna, of which he was forced to drink the muddied waters.[73] On the Baljuna he spent the summer of 1203. The "Baljunians"—those who had shared these bitter hours with him—were afterward richly rewarded.

Once more, however, the coalition formed against Jenghiz

Khan disintegrated of its own accord, for the fickle nomads could conceive only of seasonal pacts. According to Rashid ad-Din, several Mongol chiefs who had rallied to the Wang-khan out of hatred for Jenghiz Khan—Daritai, Quchar, Altan, Jamuqa—joined in a plot to assassinate the Kerayit ruler. Warned in time, the Wang-khan fell upon them and seized their baggage as they fled. Jamuqa, Quchar, and Altan sought refuge with the Naiman, while Daritai made his submission to Jenghiz Khan.

For Jenghiz Khan, therefore, the situation had greatly improved when in the autumn of 1203 he marched from the Baljuna to the Onon to resume the offensive. He employed his brother Qasar, whose family had fallen into the power of the Kerayit, to allay the Wang-khan's suspicions by false messages. Reassured, the Wang-khan started peace negotiations, and to this end sent Jenghiz Khan "blood in the horn of an ox" for use at the swearing of the oath. At the same moment, Jenghiz Khan, after a secret march, fell upon the Kerayit army, which was taken utterly by surprise and scattered. This battle, which the *Secret History* locates at Jeje'er Undur (Mount Che-che yun-tu of the *Yüan Shih*),[74] no doubt between the sources of the Tula and the Kerulen,[75] ensured the decisive triumph of Jenghiz Khan. The Wang-khan Togrul and his son the *Sängün* fled westward. On reaching Naiman country, the Wang-khan was killed by a Naiman officer named Qorisü-bäki, who failed to recognize him.[76] His head was sent to the *Tayang;* the *Tayang's* mother, Gurbesu, offered sacrifice to the spirit of the dead man before this funereal trophy, "and made music in its honor." The *Sängün* crossed the Gobi, and for a time led a brigand's life on the borders of the Hsi-Hsia realm, near the Etsin Gol, and perhaps later near Tsaidam, and ended his life obscurely, being slain at Kucha among the Uigur.[77]

The Kerayit people made submission to Jenghiz Khan and thenceforth served him loyally. Nevertheless, he was cautious enough to resettle the Kerayit elements among the various Mongol clans, with a view to their absorption. He showed particular consideration for the people of Jagambu (the Wang-khan's brother), because he had married Ibaqa-bäki,[78] one of Jagambu's daughters, and because his youngest son Tolui had married another of Jagambu's daughters, the princess Sorghaqtani (who would play a considerable part in the Jenghiz-Khanite family).

CONQUEST OF THE NAIMAN COUNTRY; UNIFICATION OF
MONGOLIA

After Jenghiz Khan's subjugation of the Kerayit, only one independent power survived in Mongolia: the Naiman, under their
king or *Tayang*. Or rather at this time (the end of 1203), when
Jenghiz Khan had made himself master of eastern Mongolia, the
Tayang remained in possession of the west. Instinctively, all the
defeated and inveterate enemies of Jenghiz Khan gravitated
about the *Tayang*: Jamuqa the Jajirat chief, the Märkit chief
Toqto'a-bäki,[79] and Qutuqa-bäki the Oirat leader, to say nothing
of elements from broken and scattered tribes such as the Dörben,
Qatakin, Salji'ut, and Tatars, and even a rebel Kerayit clan. All
of these now prepared to make war upon Jenghiz Khan. In order
to outflank him, the *Tayang* sought the help of the Öngüt—Turks
who lived round Toqto (north of the modern Chinese province
of Shansi, in the northern part of modern Suiyuan) and acted as
frontier guards for the Kin empire, who incidentally were Nestorians. But the Öngüt chief Alaqush-tigin, when asked to make a
diversionary move against Jenghiz Khan, hastened to warn the
Mongol conqueror and joined his side.[80]

Before setting forth to war against the Naiman, according to
the *Secret History*, Jenghiz Khan issued various decrees concerning the organization of the Mongol army and state (see below,
page 220, particularly for what is said of the guard, *käshik*).[81]
Then, having resolved to forestall a Naiman attack, he summoned
a *quriltai* or assembly of his people in the spring of 1204, near the
river which the *Yüan Shih* calls the T'ie-mai-kai and the *Secret
History* designates as the Temeyen-ke'er. Most of the military
leaders considered that the horses were too thin at this season,
and that it would be better to postpone operations until the autumn. Jenghiz Khan's youngest brother Temuge and their uncle
Daritai-noyan were in favor of a sudden attack to gain the advantage of surprise. Jenghiz Khan praised their ardor and set off
for the Naiman country. Some sources, such as the *Yüan Shih*,
imply that he opened hostilities at once; others state that it was
not until the autumn that he entered Naiman territory. The
Tayang, with his allies Jamuqa, Toqto'a-bäki, and Qutuqa-bäki
—all the Naiman, Jajirat, Märkit, and Oirat forces—advanced to

meet the Mongols, says the *Yüan Shih*, from the Altai to the
Khangai. The clash was to occur in the Khangai, near present-day
Karakorum. It would be a mistake to accept Abu'l Ghazi's state-
ment that the battle took place near a river of the Altai—the
Altai-Su—or to seek this Altai-Su near the Kobdo River, for in-
stance, as Albert Herrmann does, not far from Lake Khara Usu.[82]
The *Tayang* was indeed thinking of withdrawing behind the
Altai, so as to exhaust the Mongol army by long marches and
then take it by surprise in some defile. His lieutenant Qorisü-
bächi shamed him out of such caution: When had his father
Inanch-bilgä, the old Naiman sovereign, ever turned his back
or his horse's rump to the enemy? Infuriated by this taunt, the
Tayang gave the order to attack.

It was a fierce and terrible encounter. Qasar, Jenghiz Khan's
brother, who commanded the Mongol center, showed consummate
leadership. By evening the Mongols were the victors. The *Tayang*,
gravely wounded, was carried by his men onto a hill. Here the
narrative of the *Secret History* takes on the tone of an epic. The
Tayang asks of his loyal followers: "Who are these who pursue
us as wolves pursue a flock?" Jamuqa replies: "They are the four
hunting dogs of my brother Temujin. They are fed on human
flesh and leashed with an iron chain; their skulls are of brass,
their teeth are hewn from rock, their tongues are like swords,
and their hearts are of iron. Instead of whips they have curved
sabers; they quench their thirst with dew and gallop with the
wind; in battle they devour human flesh. Now here they are un-
chained, their jaws slaver, they rejoice. These four hounds are
Jebe, Kublai, Jelme, Sübötäi!" The *Tayang* asks once more: "Who
is that in the rear, speeding forward like a hungry hawk?" "It is
my *anda* Temujin, wearing a coat of iron. You said that when
the Mongol came you would devour him as you would devour a
lamb, and leave no rag of flesh. And now . . . !"[83] The Mongol
tale goes on to relate that the last of the faithful followers asked
in vain of the *Tayang* what they should do. But their lord was
a dying man. In a fruitless effort to rouse him, Qorisü-bäki cried
to him that his wives and his mother Gurbesu[84] were awaiting
him in his tent. Weakened by loss of blood, the *Tayang* remained
lying on the ground. Then the last of his men, Qorisü-bächi at
their head, went down the hill again, to fight and to die. Jenghiz
Khan, admiring their dauntless courage, would have spared them,

but they refused to surrender and fought on until they were killed. Küchlüg,[85] the *Tayang's* son, was able to flee with some of his people, no doubt in the direction of the Irtysh. With the exception of these exiles, the greater part of the Naiman people had to make its submission to Jenghiz Khan.

The Märkit chief Toqto'a-bäki followed Küchlüg into flight.[86] A minor Märkit chieftain, Dayir Usun, surrendered of his own accord and gave his daughter, the lovely Qulan, to Jenghiz Khan in marriage. The episode, narrated in the *Secret History,* of the young Mongol officer Naya leading Qulan to Jenghiz Khan across country infested by marauders renders a revealing picture of the rough and ingenuous manners of the age.[87] The *Yüan Shih* assures us that the Naiman prince Buyiruq, the Wang-khan's brother, continued to hold ground and offer a fight, together with Küchlüg, Toqto'a-bäki, and Jamuqa, near the upper Irtysh, not far from Lake Zaisan and the Ulu-Tau range, that is to say, near the massif formed by the Siberian Altai, the Tarbagatai, and the Chingiz. All four men fell, one after another. Buyiruq was surprised hunting near the Ulu-Tau by Jenghiz-Khanite squadrons and killed (in 1206, according to the *Yüan Shih*). In the autumn of 1208,[88] Jenghiz Khan himself marched on the upper Irtysh to deal with the last of the "rebels." On the way he obtained the submission of the Oirat chief Qutuqa-bäki, who, being in no condition to resist him, joined him and served him as a guide. Küchlüg and Toqto'a were attacked on the banks of the Irtysh and routed. Toqto'a died in battle. Küchlüg succeeded in making his escape and in reaching the Kara-Khitai empire. Jamuqa, the Jajirat chief, who had been leading the life of an adventurer with a band of exiles turned brigands, was delivered by his own people into the hands of Jenghiz Khan. D'Ohsson confidently places this event immediately after the defeat and death of the *Tayang,* in 1204, although Rashid ad-Din gives no date for it. Vladimirtsov, on the contrary, following the sequence of the *Secret History,* places the capture of Jamuqa after Toqto'a's death, which was in 1208. Mindful that they were *anda,* sworn brothers, Jenghiz Khan let him die like a prince, without shedding his blood. "This was a mark of favor," Vladimirtsov notes, "for, according to shamanist beliefs, a man's blood is the seat of his soul." The tradition, passed on by Rashid ad-Din, that Alchidai (the nephew of Jenghiz Khan, to whom the latter had entrusted the guarding—or execution—of Jamuqa) tortured his captive by severing his joints one by one seems very fanciful. Let us bear in mind that Jamuqa, the man who had set himself up as anti-Caesar in opposition to Jenghiz Khan, had finally shown himself to be as much of a coward as an intriguer. Having drawn first the Kerayit and then the Naiman people into war against his rival, he deserted before the battle twice in succession, forsaking first the Wang-khan and later the *Tayang*. This adversary of the Conqueror was as inferior to him morally as he was in warfare.

The last of the Märkit bands were crushed soon afterward by the Mongol general Sübötäi.[89] Lastly, the Kirghiz of the upper Yenisei (Tannu-Ola and the Minusinsk region) submitted in 1207 without fighting.

All Mongolia was now subjugated. Jenghiz Khan's standard—the white standard with its nine flames—was to become the flag of all Turko-Mongols.

After the defeat of the Naiman in 1204, the *Tayang's* keeper of the seal, T'a-t'a-t'ung-a, an Uigur, entered Jenghiz Khan's service when he fell into the hands of the Mongols.[90] Thus was formed the embryo of a Mongol chancellery, with Uigur "bureaus."

JENGHIZ KHAN: EMPEROR

Jenghiz Khan did not wait to receive the last submissions or carry out the last executions in order to have his power confirmed by the tribes. In the spring of 1206, near the headwaters of the Onon, he summoned a great gathering or *quriltai* [91] of all the Turko-Mongols who had already submitted, that is, the nomads then present in what is now Outer Mongolia. On this occasion he was proclaimed supreme khan by all the Mongol and Turkic tribes, a title which the *Secret History* translates as khagan. This was the ancient title of the Juan-juan of the fifth century, afterward assumed by all the successive lords of Mongolia—the T'u-chüeh of the sixth century and the Uigur of the eighth.[92] Western travelers, such as Piano Carpini, Rubruck, Marco Polo, and Odorico da Pordenone, would render this same title as grand khan.

Since the fall of the Uigur in 840, the empire of the steppes had been virtually without heirs. Jenghiz Khan, upon proclaiming himself supreme khan of "all those who live in felt tents," announced that this old empire, possessed in turn by the ancestors of the Turks (the Hsiung-nu), then by those of the Mongols (the Juan-juan and Ephthalites), then again by the Turks (T'u-chüeh and Uigur), was now permanently restored to the Mongols. Both Turks and Mongols were thus incorporated within the new Mongol nation (*Monghol ulus, Mongholjin ulus*), and thenceforth it was by the name of Mongol that both victors and vanquished were to be known—Kerayit, Naiman, and Borjigin—"all generations dwelling in felt tents," and under this name that they were to win renown.[93]

A little-known part in the *quriltai* of 1206 was played by the shaman Kökchü, also called Täb-tängri.[94] Kökchü's father, the wise old Munglik, had been an important figure in the life of Jenghiz Khan, whose mother, the widowed Oelun-eke, he may have married, though the point is uncertain.[95] Kökchü, whose magical powers caused him to be held in superstitious fear (he was reputed to be in the habit of ascending to heaven on a dapple-gray horse and conversing with spirits), announced to the *quriltai* that the Eternal Blue Heaven had appointed Jenghiz Khan to be universal khagan. This celestial consecration was the divine right upon which the new emperor based his authority. He assumed the title of khagan (more accurately *qân, qaan*) by the power, order, or force of Eternal Heaven (*mongka tängri-yin küchün-dür*), and this is the protocol that was preserved under his successors, e.g., on the seal of his grandson the grand khan Güyük, when writing to Pope Innocent IV.[96] Vladimirtsov notes that there was a particular cult of Jenghiz Khan's banner, *tuq:* the White Banner with its nine yak tails,[97] which was regarded as the symbol and the dwelling place of the guardian genius (*sulde*) of the imperial or golden clan (*altan uruk*). "It was the Genius of the Banner," says Vladimirtsov, "the *sulde,* that led the Mongols to the conquest of the world."

The shaman Kökchü had helped Jenghiz Khan to establish the "religious" foundations of his power. Deeming himself inviolate, no doubt, by reason of his magical gifts and because of his father's position in the imperial family, his behavior soon became insolent, and he tried to rule emperor and empire by exploiting his prestige in the sphere of the supernatural. Having quarreled with Qasar, Jenghiz Khan's brother, he sought to rid himself of his enemy by announcing to the khan a strangely tendentious revelation. "The Spirit has revealed to me a command from Eternal Heaven. Temujin will reign at first, and after him Qasar. Unless you remove Qasar, you will be in danger!"

This pronouncement aroused suspicion in Jenghiz Khan's mind; he arrested his brother and deprived him of his cap and belt, the insignia of command. His mother Oelun-eke, when told of this, hastened to release Qasar; then, baring her breasts, as described by the *Secret History*, she pathetically cried out: "These are the breasts that suckled you. What crime has Qasar committed that you should desire to destroy your own flesh? You, Temujin, sucked this one, and your brothers Qachi'un and Ochigin the other. Qasar alone has fed from both. Temujin has genius, but Qasar strength, and he is the better archer. Each time the tribes have risen, his bow and his arrows have tamed them. But now that our enemies have all been removed, he is no longer wanted!" [98] Jenghiz Khan, abashed, gave Qasar back his titles and honors, depriving him only of a few of his men.

The shaman, however, still continued his efforts to rule the imperial family. He now turned against Jenghiz' youngest brother, insulting him in public. The wise Börte, Jenghiz Khan's wife, warned her husband: "If even during your lifetime your brothers are open to insult, after your death the people will rise against your sons!" This time Jenghiz Khan understood, and allowed Temuge to rid himself of the magician. The scene was a short one. Some days later, when Kökchü arrived with his father Munglik to visit Jenghiz Khan, Temuge seized the sorcerer by the throat. Jenghiz Khan ordered them to settle their affairs outside. As soon as Kökchü left the imperial tent, three guards posted by Temuge with the tacit consent of Jenghiz Khan broke his spine "without shedding his blood." Munglik, realizing that his son was dead, never flinched: "I served you, O khagan, long before your accession, and I shall continue to serve you. . . ." In Kökchü's place, Jenghiz appointed, as *bäki*, Usun "of the white horse and the white robe," eldest member of the Ba'arin tribe, who was a great and tranquil shaman. [99]

Thus beneath two felt tents on the plains had surged a virtual conflict between Church and State, between magician and grand khan. The struggle, however, came to an abrupt end when the grand khan literally broke the back of the sorceror.

The New Mongol Empire: State and Army

Despite the elimination of the shaman Kökchü, the new Jenghiz-Khanite empire preserved its religious basis: the ancient Turko-Mongol animism, mingled to a greater or lesser extent with Mazdean and Chinese elements. The divinity of which the grand khan was a manifestation was still Tängri, heaven or the god of heaven, similar in some respects to the Chinese T'ien, to say nothing of the Iranian Ormazd.[100] All the descendants of Jenghiz Khan who were not either entirely Sinicized in the Far East or Islamized in Turkestan, Persia, and Russia were to claim to be the representatives on earth of Tängri: their commands were his commands; rebellion against them was a rebellion against him.

Jenghiz Khan himself seems to have had a particular devotion to the divinity enthroned on Mount Burqan Qaldun, the Kentei of today, at the source of the Onon. When at the outset of his career he escaped—thanks to the swiftness of his horse—from the Märkit, who abducted his wife Börte, it was there that he took refuge. He at once climbed the mountain as a pilgrim. Having first, according to the Mongol custom, removed his cap and thrown his belt over his shoulders in token of submission, he genuflected nine times and made the ritual libation of kumiss, the fermented mare's milk that was the alcohol of the nomads. Similarly, later on, before undertaking the great "national" war against the Kin empire of Peking, he was to repeat this pilgrimage to Burqan Qaldun and, in the same suppliant attitude, his belt round his neck, to pray: "O Eternal Tängri, I am armed to avenge the blood of my ancestors, upon whom the Kin inflicted an ignominious death. If you approve of what I do, vouchsafe me the aid of your strength." Such is Rashid ad-Din's account of his words. Other sources show him shut up for three days in his tent on the eve of the campaign, alone with the Spirit, while around him his people supplicate Heaven: "Tängri! Tängri!" On the fourth day the khan-strength-of-Heaven emerges at last from his tent and announces that Eternal Tängri has promised him victory.[101]

From this ancient animist religion, with its cult of peaks and river sources, came the rites noted by both Muslim writers and Christian missionaries: the ascent ·of holy mountains to draw

near to Tängri and invoke him; the removal of one's cap and
the laying of one's belt over the shoulders in token of submission,
an obligation which fell upon the grand khan himself; the practice of hiding when it thundered, that is to say, when Tängri
showed his wrath; the care taken never to defile springs, for
they were the haunt of spirits, or to profane streams by washing
oneself or one's clothes in them (an act that at first gave rise
to serious misunderstandings with Muslim society, which adhered faithfully to its ritual ablutions).

In their superstitious awe of Heaven and of magical formulas,
the Mongols felt it wise to conciliate not only their own shamans
but also other possible representatives of the Divine—i.e., leaders
of any cult who might conceivably be possessed of supernatural
powers, such as Nestorian priests, whom they were to find
among the Kerayit and Öngüt, Buddhist monks among the
Uigur and Khitan, Taoist magicians from China, Tibetan lamas,
Franciscan missionaries, or Muslim mullahs.[102] Good will shown
toward representatives of these various cults provided an addi-
tional safeguard to their own Tängri worship; general superstitious dread thus engendered general tolerance. Not until they
lost this superstitious timidity did the descendants of Jenghiz
Khan in Turkestan and Persia become intolerant in outlook and
behavior.

The Mongol state, based on these principles, borrowed its
instruments of civilization—writing and official language—from
the Uigur. In 1204, as has been related, on the fall of the Naiman
kingdom Jenghiz Khan took into his service the Uigur T'a-t'a-
t'ung-a, the deceased *Tayang's* keeper of the seal. T'a-t'a-t'ung-a
was given the task of teaching Jenghiz Khan's sons to write
Mongolian in Uigur characters [103] and also to countersign official
decrees by affixing to them the *tamgha* or imperial seal.[104] In
these innovations may be discerned the germ of a chancellery.
From 1206 onward, Jenghiz Khan invested Shigi-qutuqu—a
Tatar whom he and his wife Börte had adopted as a baby and
brought up—with the functions of a great judge. Shigi-qutuqu
was charged with recording judicial decisions and sentences in
Uigur characters and in the Mongol tongue, and keeping registers known as "blue books" (*kökö däbtär*) showing the dis-
tribution of population among the various Mongol nobles. The
first activity resulted in the elaboration of a practical judicial

code, the second in the creation of a genealogical guide or, in Pelliot's terms, "a sort of Mongol Hozier."[105]

The *yasaq,* literally the "regulations," or common law code, of the Jenghiz-Khanites, also had its beginnings (or its imperial inauguration) at the *quriltai* of 1206.[106] Through the *yasaq,* the grand khan, "strength of Heaven," imposed strict discipline, ordained by Heaven, on both civilian society and the army. (These categories were barely distinguishable.) The code was severe indeed: it demanded the death penalty for murder, major theft, concerted falsehood (intrigue), adultery, sodomy, malicious witchcraft, receiving of stolen goods, and so on. Disobedience, whether civil or military, was equated with crimes under common law, the *yasaq* being at once a civil and an administrative code: a discipline valid for the government of the world. It was completed, in the sphere of jurisprudence, by the "wisdom" or "sayings" (*bilik*) of Jenghiz Khan, now lost to us like the *yasaq* itself.

The results of this Mongol discipline amazed western travelers. About forty years after the *quriltai* of 1206, Piano Carpini, the Franciscan, noted on returning from Mongolia: "The Tartars—that is, the Mongols—are the most obedient people in the world in regard to their leaders, more so even than our own clergy to their superiors. They hold them in the greatest reverence and never tell them a lie. There are no wranglings among them, no disputes, no murders. Only petty thefts occur. Should one of them lose any of his animals, the finder never keeps them, and may even return them to their owner. Their wives are very chaste, even when they make merry." If one compares this picture with that of the anarchy prevailing in Mongol territory on the eve of the Jenghiz-Khanite conquest, or with the moral level of the Mongols of today, one may appreciate the profound change which Jenghiz Khan's *yasaq* brought about in Mongol society.[107]

At the apex of the social structure was the family of Jenghiz Khan himself: the golden family (*altan uruk*) whose head was the grand khan (khagan, *qaan*), and whose princes were the grand khan's sons (*köbegün*). This family exercised rights of property over their vast domain of conquered lands in much the same way as the Conqueror's ancestors had held sway over their far smaller share of the native prairie. The grazing lands (*nutuq, yurt*) assigned to Jenghiz Khan's four sons were the germs of future Jenghiz-Khanite khanates. Mongol society—or rather Turko-Mongol, since Jenghiz Khan absorbed a number of Turkic tribes from the Altai—remained aristocratic in character. It was the ancient "aristocracy of the steppes" studied by Barthold and Vladimirtsov—the aristocracy of the brave (*ba'atur*, plural *ba'atut*) and of chiefs (*noyan*) [108]—which continued to officer and manage the various social classes: warriors or faithful men, who were pre-eminently free (*nökur*, plural *nökud*), commoners or plebeians (*arad, qarachu*), and lastly serfs (*unaghan boghul*), who theoretically were of non-Mongol stock. Vladimirtsov discerns in this all the elements of a feudal society whose various social groups, at different hierarchical levels, were linked by a hereditary bond of personal loyalty.

The same feudal principle obtained in the army. A bond of personal loyalty united the captains of tens (*arban*), of hundreds (*jaghun*), of thousands (*mingghan*), and of ten thousands (*tumen*). The centurions, millenaries, and commanders of myriads were furnished by the high aristocracy of the *noyan*. Beneath them, the backbone of the army was formed by the minor nobility of free men, who bore the old Turkic title of *tarkhan* (in Mongolian *darqan*) and who had the privilege, theoretically, of retaining their individual plunder in war and their game in the great hunting expeditions.[109] Incidentally, several *tarkhat*, for their valor, were promoted to *noyan*.

This army, "aristocratically organized," as Vladimirtsov describes it, had its own elite: the bodyguard of the grand khan. This guard (*käshik*) was composed of about ten thousand men. The soldiers of this guard (singular *käshiktü*, plural *käshiktän*) were in theory divided into day guards (*turghaq*, plural *turgha'ut*) and night guards (*käbtäül*, plural *käbtäwüt* or *käbtä'üt*).[110] To these should be added the *qorchin* or bowmen: "quiver bearers." "The *käbtä'üt* numbered from 800 to 1,000, the *qorchin* 400 to 1,000. The *turgha'ut* numbered 1,000. The effective strength of the guard amounted in the end to 10,000 men." [111] Only nobles and members of the group of privileged freemen known as *tarkhat* or *darqat* could join this corps. A private soldier of the guard took precedence over a captain of a thousand in the rest of the army, and it was from this guard that Jenghiz Khan selected the greater number of his generals.

In principle the Mongol army was divided into three wings, deployed according to the Mongol orientation, that is, facing south. The left wing (*jegün-ghar, je'un-ghar, jun-ghar*),[112] to the east, was commanded at first by the Jelair Muqali. The center (*qöl*) was led by the Ba'arin Naya, and Chagan—a young Tangut whom Jenghiz Khan had adopted and brought up as his son—commanded the thousand picked guardsmen. The right wing (*baraghun-ghar, bara'un-qar, barun-ghar*)[113] was commanded by the Arulat Bo'orchu, or Bogurji. On the death of Jenghiz Khan, the army was to attain an effective strength of 129,000 men. The left wing, for military reasons, consisted of 62,000 men, the right wing had 38,000, and the remainder was distributed between center and reserves.[114]

This southward-facing formation corresponded to Mongol objectives, facing fanwise as it did toward the various "southern" countries. These objectives were, to the left, China; in the center, Turkestan and eastern Iran; and, on the right, the Russian steppe.

What of the Mongol warrior, the hero of this epic? Chinese painters of the Chao Meng-fu school have admirably portrayed him, and reading the description given by Fernand Grenard, Jenghiz Khan's historian, after his travels in Mongolia is like unrolling a scroll by one of these old masters: "In camp the soldier wears a fur cap with ear flaps, felt stockings, boots, and a pelisse reaching below his knees. In battle he dons a leather helmet covering the nape of his neck and a strong, flexible cuirass made of strips of leather lacquered black. His offensive weapons consist of two bows and two quivers, a curved saber, a hatchet, and an iron mace suspended from his saddle, a lance furnished with a hook for unseating enemy horsemen, and a horsehair rope with a running noose."[115]

The Mongol cannot be dissociated from his steed. Indeed, they resemble each other; they were born of the same steppe, formed by the same soil and the same climate, broken in by the same exercises. The Mongol is short, stocky, big-boned, heavy-framed, and of prodigious stamina. His horse too is small and stocky, without grace; it has "a powerful neck, somewhat thick legs, and a dense coat, but is wonderful for its fiery spirit and its vigor, endurance, steadiness, and sureness of foot."[116] It was no doubt this charger of the northern nomads which at the dawn of history gave the Indo-European "horse-breakers" their superiority and, at the end of classical antiquity, carried the Huns to the conquest of China and of the Roman Empire. Now, in the Middle Ages, a fresh impulse was to hurl all this cavalry of the steppes toward the golden palaces of Peking, Tauris (Tabriz), and Kiev.

Much has been written about Mongol tactics. Some have compared them with those of Frederick II or Napoleon. Cahun sees them as the prodigious conceptions of genius, born at some war council of supermen. In fact, Mongol tactics were a perfected form of the old methods used by the Hsiung-nu and T'u-chüeh: the eternal nomad tactics, evolved from continual raids on the fringe of cultivation and from great hunting drives on the steppes. Tradition reports Jenghiz Khan as saying: "In daylight, watch with the vigilance of an old wolf, at night with the eyes of the raven. In battle, fall upon the enemy like a falcon." Patient stalking of herds of deer had taught the nomads to send forward a number of silent, invisible scouts to observe the quarry or the enemy while keeping out of sight. The use of a line of beaters in hunting taught them the heading-off movement (*tulugma*) which enabled them to outflank both wings of the hostile army, as one heads off a fleeing herd of wild animals on the prairie.

By means of this highly mobile cavalry, the nomads achieved an effect of surprise and ubiquity which, before any action began, disconcerted their adversary. If he stood his ground, the Mongol squadrons did not press home their attack; they scattered and disappeared in the manner of all steppe marauders, ready to return when the Chinese pikeman, Khwarizmian, Mameluke, or Hungarian horseman relaxed his vigilance. Woe to the enemy who made the mistake of pursuing the Mongol horsemen in their feigned retreat; they led him astray, lured him away from his base, over dangerous terrain and into some trap, there to be surrounded and felled like an ox. The Mongol light cavalry, placed in the vanguard and on the wings, had the task of harassing the enemy with flights of arrows, which hacked terrible gaps in his ranks. Like the Hun of old, the Mongol was the mounted archer—a rider and marksman from childhood—whose infallible arrow could bring a man down at 200, even at 400 yards or more. To his elusive mobility he added a tactical superiority unique in its day. Confident of their advantage, his advance guards were relieved at frequent intervals by echelons which slipped away after discharging a volley. Not until the enemy had been lured some way forward and had become demoralized by the long-distance shooting did the heavy cavalry at the center make its saber charge and cut him to pieces. In all these operations the Mongols made the fullest use of the terror inspired by their physique, their ugliness, and their stench. They appeared unexpectedly, deployed, and ringed the horizon. They advanced at a jog trot in an awe-inspiring silence, maneuvering without shouts of command, on signals from the standard bearers. Then suddenly, at the right moment, they charged, uttering diabolical shrieks and yells.[117]

These were the time-honored, traditional ruses of the hunter who seeks to madden and bewilder his prey in order to master it. The Mongol and his horse were to hunt the Chinese, the Persian, the Russian, and the Hungarian just as they hunted the antelope or the tiger. The archer of Mongolia struck down the knight where the latter was at his weakest, just as he brought down the eagle when it was in full flight. The "finest campaigns" of the Mongols, those of Transoxiana and Hungary, were to have the appearance of gigantic battues designed to tire the "game," to bewilder, exhaust, and surround it, before bringing the chase to an end by systematic slaughter.

All these tactics have been vividly described by that astute observer Piano Carpini: "As soon as they discover the enemy, they charge, each man shooting off three or four arrows. If they perceive that the opposing force is unbroken, they withdraw among their own people; but this is merely to invite pursuit and to entice the enemy into some ambush prepared beforehand. Should they find that the opposing army is too strong, they ride away, halting at the end of a day or two to ravage the districts in their path. . . . Or else they pitch camp at some well-chosen spot and, when the enemy forces start to file past, they spring out and take them by surprise. . . . Their tricks of war are many. They meet the first cavalry onset with a front consisting of prisoners and foreign auxiliaries, while the bulk of their own men take up their positions on the wings in order to encompass the enemy. They do this so effectively that he fancies them far more numerous than they are. If the adversary defends himself stoutly, they open their ranks and allow him to escape, where-

upon they dash in pursuit and slay as many of the fugitives as
they can. [This tactic was to be used by Sübötäi against the
Hungarians in 1241 at the battle of the Sajo.] But they engage in
hand-to-hand struggles as seldom as possible, their object being
merely to wound men and horses with their arrows." Rubruck
describes the same maneuver in the great Mongol hunting expeditions: "When they desire to hunt, they gather in great
numbers about the place where they know wild beasts to be,
and little by little advance upon them, enclosing them as in a
net, in order to shoot them down with their arrows."

CONQUEST OF NORTHERN CHINA

Having unified Mongolia, Jenghiz Khan embarked upon the
conquest of northern China.

He first attacked Hsi-Hsia, a kingdom founded by a Tangut
horde in Kansu, the Alashan, and the Ordos. These people were
of Tibetan stock. Buddhist by religion, who—thanks to Chinese
influence—had attained to some measure of culture, especially in
their writing, which was derived from Chinese characters. This
was against Hsi-Hsia was the first action by the Mongols against
a sedentary, civilized people, and in undertaking it their leader
was testing the quality of his army against the weakest of the
three states among which the lands of old China were divided.
Moreover, in becoming master of Hsi-Hsia territory, Jenghiz
Khan gained control of the road from China to Turkestan, and
at the same time surrounded, in the west, the Kin realm of
Peking, the traditional enemy of the Mongols. Yet quite certainly
the Mongols, admirably organized though they were for the
destruction of enemy forces in open country, were novices where
fortified positions were concerned. This was to be made glaringly
evident in their campaign against the Kin, and could be seen
even in their expeditions against Hsi-Hsia, when on various
occasions (1205–7, 1209) Jenghiz Khan devastated the country
without being able to reduce the Tangut capitals of Ningsia and
Lingchow. The Hsi-Hsia king, Li An-ch'uan (1206–11), temporarily saved his throne by acknowledging himself a tributary,
but in 1209 Jenghiz Khan returned and besieged Chunghing,
the Ningsia of today, which he attempted to capture by diverting
the course of the Yellow River. However, these dam-building

works were far too complicated for the Mongols, and they failed to direct the floods in the direction intended. King Li An-ch'uan again obtained peace, this time by giving one of his daughters to Jenghiz Khan (1209).[118]

Having made Hsi-Hsia his vassal, Jenghiz Khan turned against the Jurchid kingdom: the realm of the Tungus of northern China, or the Kin empire, as it was called. The vast extent of this state has been noted; it comprised Manchuria and that part of China lying north of the Han and the Hwai, with Peking as its chief capital and Tating in Jehol, Liaoyang and Tatung in Shansi, and Kaifeng in Honan as secondary capitals. It was also noted that in his youth Jenghiz Khan, together with the Kerayit, fought on the side of Peking against the Tatars. He was thus the client and vassal of the Kin, who had paid him as a mercenary and, in recognition of his services, had bestowed upon him a modest Chinese title. But the Kin king Ma-ta-ku (1189–1208), who might have reminded him of this bond of vassalage, died in the course of these events. Jenghiz Khan took advantage of the accession of Ma-ta-ku's successor Chung-hei (1209–13) to withdraw his allegiance in scorn. The Kin envoy desired Jenghiz Khan to receive the proclamation of his master's accession on his knees. The Conqueror flew into a rage: "Is an imbecile like Chung-hei worthy of the throne, and am I to humble myself before him?" And he "spat toward the south." Chung-hei was indeed a pitiful, incapable ruler, without authority or prestige, the plaything of his own generals. On this occasion, as in the Khwarizmian Empire, Jenghiz Khan was fortunate in being opposed by feeble and overrated adversaries.

The northern approaches to the Great Wall on the Mongol side, north of Shansi province, were guarded on behalf of the Kin by federated Turks: the Öngüt, who professed Nestorian Christianity.[119] In intertribal battles in Mongolia, the Öngüt chief Alaqush-tigin had, from 1204 onward, sided with Jenghiz Khan. The loyalty of the house of Alaqush was to prove a most effective aid to the Conqueror in his struggle against the Kin by opening the invasion routes and handing over to him in 1211 the frontier marches which were guarded by the Öngüt. Jenghiz Khan was to reward the Öngüt by giving one of his daughters, Alaghai-bäki, to Po-yao-ho, son of Alaqush.[120]

Jenghiz Khan turned this conflict between Mongols and Kin

into a sort of national war.[121] Solemnly he invoked Tängri, recalling the old Mongol khans whom the Jurchids had impaled
and nailed upon wooden donkeys: "O Eternal Heaven! I have
armed myself to avenge the blood of my uncles Okin-barqaq
and Ambaqai, whom the Kin put to an ignominious death. If
you approve of what I do, lend me from on high the succor
of your arm!" At the same time Jenghiz Khan presented himself
as the avenger of the former lords of Peking, the Khitan, later
dispossessed by the Kin. The Khitan, on their part, warmly
espoused his cause. One of their princes, Ye-lü Lü-ko—of the
ancient royal Ye-lü clan—rose in revolt in 1912 on his behalf in
the ancient Khitan country of the Liao River, southwest of Manchuria. Today it is known that the Khitan spoke the Mongolian
language. Between them and Jenghiz Khan some racial or kinship
bond must have existed to unite them against the Tungusic
dynasty of Peking. Jenghiz Khan received Ye-lü Lü-ko's oath of
allegiance and sent him a relieving army commanded by the
noyan Jebe. In January, 1213, Jebe helped Lü-ko to seize
Liaoyang from the Kin and to install himself in the ancient
domain of his ancestors as "king of Liao" under Mongol suzerainty. Up to his death (1220), this descendant of the old
Khitan kings was to prove himself the Mongol emperor's most
loyal vassal. Thus the Kin frontier was laid open in the northeast and northwest alike, on the Khitan as well as on the Öngüt
side.

Jenghiz Khan's war against the Kin, begun in 1211, was—
with only brief intervals—to be continued until after his death
(1227) and brought to an end by his successor (1234). The
reason for this was that although the Mongols, with their mobile
cavalry, excelled in ravaging the countryside and open towns,
they were for a long time ignorant of the art of capturing
strongholds defended by Chinese engineers. Moreover, they
waged war in China as in the steppe, launching repeated raids
but each time withdrawing with their booty and thus giving
the Kin time to reoccupy towns, rebuild ruins, repair breaches,
and reconstruct fortifications. Under such conditions, Mongol
generals were compelled to recapture certain fortresses two or
three times over. Lastly, the Mongols were accustomed to ridding
themselves of defeated foes in the steppe by massacres or wholesale deportations, or by collective enrollment under the White

Banner. In sedentary countries, however, and especially among the swarming people of China, massacres made little impression —there were always more inhabitants to take the place of those slain. In addition to this, the Kin—the ancient Jurchids, who had adopted the sedentary way of life barely a hundred years before —had retained all the vigor of their Tungusic blood. Thus against them the trials of siege warfare, to which the Mongols were unaccustomed, were redoubled by the fact that they found themselves opposed not only by the science of Chinese engineers but also by the valor of Tungus warriors. In any case, as will be seen, Jenghiz Khan himself did not take part in this war except at the beginning. Having launched it (1211–15), he was to withdraw the majority of his troops for the conquest of Turkestan. After his departure, his generals could do no more than carry on a slow-motion war which, though it destroyed the Kin forces, was incapable of putting an end to the Kin empire.

Yet in fairness it must be said that while he was present, the Mongol emperor conducted operations with his usual tenacity.[122] Those of 1211–12 were concentrated upon the systematic devastation of the frontier districts of the Tatung region (the Sian of the Kin rulers) in the extreme north of Shansi and of the region of Süanhwa (then Süan-tö) and Paoan in northern Hopei. The country was laid waste, but the fortresses held. And although in 1212 Jebe, one of the best of Jenghiz Khan's generals, succeeded by a feigned withdrawal in taking Liaoyang in southern Manchuria by surprise, Jenghiz Khan himself, in northern Shansi, failed to capture Tatung. Still less, therefore, could the Mongols hope to undertake a regular siege of Peking, the seat of the enemy court. In 1213 Jenghiz Khan, having at last conquered Süanhwa, divided his troops into three corps. The first of these, led by his sons Jöchi, Jagatai, and Ogödäi, penetrated to central Shansi, reaching and taking Taiyüan and Pingyang, says the *Yüan Shih,* only to evacuate them again in order to carry its plunder back to the north. The army of the center, in which Jenghiz Khan was accompanied by his youngest son Tolui, advanced down the plain of Hopei, seizing Hokien, Shantung, and Tsinan. Only a few other fortified cities besides Peking, for example, Chengting and Taming in Hopei, seem to have escaped the advancing flood, which rolled onward to the southern limits of Shantung. Lastly Qasar, Jenghiz Khan's brother and the finest marksman in the army, and their youngest brother Temuge Ochigin led a third corps along the Gulf of Chihli, toward the threshold of Yungping and Liaosi.[123]

After this three-pronged advance by horse, Jenghiz Khan regrouped his forces before Peking with the object of having a try at least at a blockade (1214). There a palace drama had just caused uproar at the court of the Kin. The Kin ruler Chunghei had been assassinated in 1213 by one of his officers, named Hu-sha-hu, who placed Wu-tu-pu, his victim's nephew, on the throne. The new king (1213–23) was unfortunately as inadequate as his predecessor. But Jenghiz Khan lacked the tools necessary for regular siege warfare. Prudent as ever, he acceded to Wu-tu-pu's request for peace, despite the impatience of his own generals. The Kin paid an enormous war indemnity—gold, silk, and three thousand horses, as well as young men and girls, including a Jurchid princess for Jenghiz Khan himself. The conqueror then took again the road to Mongolia with his booty, passing through the country of Kalgan.

Hardly had the Mongols left before King Wu-tu-pu, believing Peking to be too vulnerable, moved to Kaifeng (1214). This was desertion. Jenghiz Khan affected to believe that the departure indicated an early resumption of the war and forestalled this by breaking the truce himself. Once more he invaded Hopei and renewed the siege of Peking. A Kin army reinforcement with provisions was routed and dispersed at Pachow, between Peking and Hokien, and in despair the governor of Peking, Wanyen Ch'eng-huei, committed suicide. The Mongols captured the city, massacred its inhabitants, pillaged the houses, and then set the whole place on fire (1215).[124] The sack lasted a month.

It is clear that the nomads had no notion of what could be done with a great city, nor how they might use it for the consolidation and expansion of their power. Here is a most interesting situation for students of human geography: the bewilderment of steppe dwellers when, without a transitional phase, chance puts them in possession of ancient countries with an urban civilization. They burn and slay not so much from cruelty as from perplexity, and because they know of nothing better to do. Note that among the Mongol chiefs—or at least among those who faithfully observed the *yasaq*—pillaging was a disinterested affair. General Shigi-qutuqu, for example, refused to allot himself even a small portion of the Kin treasure.[125]

It was this conduct at the base of which was bewilderment that was so disastrous to civilization. Jenghiz Khan's Mongols, as shown in the texts or when considered as individuals, do not appear as wicked men; they obeyed a *yasaq* which (uncleanliness apart) was a code of honor and integrity. Unfortunately, they were markedly retarded compared with the old hordes that preceded them, especially the Khitan of the tenth century and even the Jurchids of the twelfth. The latter, with the minimum amount of slaughter, had at least immediately succeeded to the preceding dynasties and had avoided destroying anything which was thenceforth to be their property. The Jenghiz-Khanite Mongols, though doubtless no crueler than their predecessors (indeed, by their *yasaq*, they were more strictly disciplined and, because of Jenghiz Khan's personality, far more imperturbable and more greatly preoccupied by moral rules), were infinitely more destructive simply because they were far more barbarian, constituting indeed a levy en masse of barbarism, like the Hsiung-nu, Juan-juan, T'u-chüeh, and Uigur before them.[126]

The paradox of Jenghiz-Khanite history lies in the contrast between the wise, reflective, and moral character of a leader who regulated his own conduct and that of his people by maxims of sound common sense and well-established justice and the brutal reactions of a people newly emerged from primitive savagery, who sought no other means than those of terror for the subjugation of their enemies—a people for whom human life had no value whatever and who, as nomads, lacked all conception of the life of sedentary peoples, of urban conditions or farming culture, or of anything alien to their native steppe. The modern historian's astonishment is basically the same as that of Rashid ad-Din or the compilers of the *Yüan Shih* when confronted by this perfectly natural blend of wisdom—even moderation—in the leader and of ferocity in upbringing, in atavistic reversions, and in tribal traditions.

Among the prisoners taken after the capture of Peking and those who chose to support the Mongol regime, Jenghiz Khan singled out a Khitan prince, Ye-lü Ch'u-ts'ai, who pleased him "by his tall stature and handsome beard, his wisdom, and the impressive sound of his voice," and appointed him his counselor. It was a happy choice, for Ye-lü Ch'u-ts'ai combined a high degree of Chinese culture with the qualities of a statesman. Like the Uigur chancellor T'a-t'a-t'ung-a, he was exactly the right man to advise the new lord of Asia. At this stage the Jenghiz-Khanites were incapable of absorbing lessons in Chinese culture directly from the Chinese. But a Sinicized Turko-Mongol like Ye-lü Ch'u-ts'ai—who, being a Khitan, was of course Mongol—was able to bridge the gap and familiarize Jenghiz Khan and his successor Ogödäi with the elements of administration and political life as practiced in sedentary civilizations.

The Kin realm was now reduced, around its new capital of Kaifeng, to little more than the province of Honan and to certain fortified places in Shensi. In 1216 the Mongol general Samuqa ba'atur [127] cut Shensi off from Honan by capturing the stronghold of Tungkwan, which commanded the valley of the Yellow River at this point; but later the fortress fell once more into Kin hands. The fact was that Jenghiz Khan, preoccupied, as will be seen, by events in Turkestan, now paid only fitful attention to the war with China, and the Kin profited by this to regain a fair proportion of their provinces, with the exception of the Peking territory, which was retained by the Mongols.

Nevertheless, before turning his attention to the west, Jenghiz Khan entrusted operations in China to one of his best commanders, Muquli or Muqali. With relatively depleted forces (half the Mongol regular army, say, 23,000 Mongols and as many native auxiliaries),[128] Muqali was to achieve considerable success through tenacity and good planning. After seven years of incessant campaigning (1217–23), he succeeded in confining the Kin once more to Honan province.[129] In 1217 he captured Taming, a citadel in southern Hopei which had once held out against Jenghiz Khan himself.[130] In 1218 he recaptured the capitals of Shansi, Taiyüan, and Pingyang from the Kin; in 1220 he retook Tsinan, the capital of Shantung. In the part of Honan lying north of the Yellow River, one of his lieutenants captured Changteh in the same year. In 1221 Muqali seized a number of towns in northern Shensi, among them Paoan and Fuchow, and in 1222 the old capital of Shensi, Changan, south of the Wei, was in his hands. In 1223 he had just snatched from the Kin, who had reoccupied it by a surprise attack, the important fortress of Hochung (the Puchow of today), in the southwest corner of Shansi at the bend of the Yellow River, when he died, worn out. After his death Hochung reverted once more to the Kin. In this overpopulated country bristling with natural fortresses, the conflict thus degenerated into an interminable siege war. However, after their first groping efforts, the Mongols adapted themselves to the new type of warfare by enrolling large numbers of Khitan auxiliaries, Jurchid adherents, and Chinese engineers.[131]

Mongol Conquest of the Old Kara-Khitai Empire

When Jenghiz Khan began his conquest of northern China, Küchlüg, a personal enemy of his, the son of the last Naiman king, was making himself master of an empire in Central Asia: the empire of the Kara-Khitai *gur-khans*.

This realm, as we have noted (page 164), was founded on the Ili, Chu, and Talas, and in Kashgaria, by a branch of the northern China Khitan known in history as the Kara-Khitai or Black Khitan. We have also observed that these were a people (or rather an aristocracy) of Mongol race and Chinese culture superimposed on a local population which was ethnically Turkic and religiously Muslim. The Kara-Khitai rulers, whose capital was at Balasagun on the upper Chu, west of the Issyk Kul, and who bore the Turkic imperial title of *gur-khan*—"universal khan"— numbered the following among their vassals: (1) in the east, the Uigur, a Turkic people professing either Buddhism or Nestorianism and inhabiting the territories of Beshbaligh (the Dzimsa of today), Turfan, Kara Shahr, and Kucha;[132] (2) in the north, along the lower Ili, the Qarluq Turks, who were partly Nestorian; and (3) in the southwest, the shahs (later sultans) of Khwarizm, Muslim Turks whose history we have summarized and who ruled in Transoxiana and eastern Iran. Under the *gur-khan* Ye-lü Chih-lu-ku (1178–1211), the Kara-Khitai empire had declined. This sovereign, while lacking neither energy nor courage in emergencies, spent his life in pleasures and hunting, and allowed his empire to disintegrate. In 1209, the *idiqut* Barchuq, king of the Uigur, threw off Ye-lü's suzerainty in favor of Jenghiz Khan's. The *gur-khan's* representative in Uiguria, a certain Shaukam who resided at Turfan or Kara-khoja, was put to death.[133] Jenghiz

Khan, who seems always to have commiserated with the Uigur, promised their *idiqut* the hand of his daughter Al'altun, or Altun-bäki.[134] Thus the whole northeastern part of the Kara-Khitai zone joined the clientele of the Mongols. In 1211, Arslan, king of the Qarluq of the lower Ili (capital Qayaligh), and Buzar, a Turkic adventurer who had made himself ruler of Almalik (near modern Kuldja) on the upper Ili, likewise repudiated Kara-Khitai sovereignty and acknowledged themselves vassals of Jenghiz Khan. Such was the attraction of a united Mongolia for the petty Turkic princes of the Gobi and of Lake Balkhash. Yet it was not Jenghiz Khan who was to deliver the fatal blow against the Kara-Khitai, but a personal enemy of his, Küchlüg, the son of the last *tayang* of the Naiman.

Küchlüg had been driven from the Altai, his ancestral territory, by Jenghiz Khan's victory. After his father's death and the annihilation of his people, he had gone to seek his fortune in eastern Turkestan, as did his old associates, the remnants of the Märkit. The latter tried to settle in Uiguria, but the Uigur *idiqut* Barchuq drove them out.[135] Küchlüg was more fortunate. The old *gur-khan* Chih-lu-ku welcomed him at Balasagun, gave him his full confidence, and bestowed upon him his daughter's hand (1208). But the Naiman prince was impatient to rule. Noting the physical frailty of his father-in-law, he resolved—notwithstanding the favor shown him—to supplant him. In association with one of the former vassals of the Kara-Khitai, Muhammad the sultan of Khwarizm, he plotted to overthrow the *gur-khan* and divide the Kara-Khitai territory with his ally.[136] The Khwarizmians opened hostilities, but the Kara-Khitai made a vigorous counterattack and occupied Samarkand (1210). Meanwhile, in the region of the Ili, Küchlüg had rebelled against the *gur-khan* and set off to plunder the prince's treasure at Uzgen in Fergana, whence he marched on Balasagun, the Kara-Khitai capital. The *gur-khan,* disillusioned, opposed Küchlüg and indeed defeated him near Balasagun; but on the other front, near the Talas, his general Tayanku was taken prisoner by the Khwarizmians. The retreating Kara-Khitai army found the gates of their own capital closed against them by the treachery of the inhabitants, who were no doubt Turks and considered that the hour had come to throw off Khitan domination. The exasperated Kara-Khitai thereupon took Balasagun by storm and sacked it.[137]

Amid these disorders, the *gur-khan* Chih-lu-ku was at last surprised and taken prisoner by Küchlüg (1211). Küchlüg treated his father-in-law with humanity and deference, however, and up to the old man's death two years later pretended to regard him as sole sovereign while governing in his name.

Having gained effective control of the Kara-Khitai empire, the Naiman prince nearly came to blows with his old ally the sultan of Khwarizm over the demarcation of the frontiers. At one stage the sultan's authority was recognized north of the Syr Darya line, at the places of Otrar, Shash (Tashkent), and Sairam (Isfijab). But considering these points too difficult to defend, he soon transferred their inhabitants to the south side of the river.

Küchlüg's reign, *de jure* or *de facto*, over the Kara-Khitai empire lasted from 1211 to 1218. This nomad of the Altai had become the ruler of peoples of whom the greater part were sedentary, however, and he did not know how to govern them. Kashgaria, ruled by petty Muslim Turkic kinglets of the Karakhanid family, was a dependency of the Kara-Khitai empire. Not long before his fall, the *gur-khan* Chih-lu-ku had imprisoned the son of the Karakhanid khan of Kashgar.[138] Küchlüg released this young prince and sent him as his representative to govern Kashgar, but the Kashgari emirs refused to receive him and put him to death (ca. 1211). For two or three years after that, Küchlüg ravaged Kashgaria with his light troops (1211–13 or 1214) until famine forced the inhabitants to accept his authority.[139] This surrender was followed by savage religious persecution. Küchlüg, like many of the Naiman, must have been more or less of the Nestorian persuasion. Soon, under the influence of his wife, who was a daughter of the Kara-Khitai *gur-khan,* he tried to make the Muslims of Kashgar and Khotan abjure their faith and embrace either Buddhism or Christianity. When the chief imam of Khotan protested, Küchlüg had him crucified at the door of his madrasah (a religious school). After such violent persecution, Kashgaria, fundamentally a Muslim country, was to welcome the Mongols as liberators.

Küchlüg made himself no less unpopular with the peoples of the Ili. King Buzar of Almalik (Kuldja) had, as related, done homage to Jenghiz Khan. Küchlüg made a surprise attack on him while he was hunting and put him to death,[140] but he could not capture the town of Almalik, which was defended by Buzar's widow, Salbak-Turkan. Her son Suqnaq-tigin thereafter became one of Jenghiz Khan's most ardent partisans against Küchlüg.[141]

Jenghiz Khan could not allow his old enemy to remain lord of the Kara-Khitai realm, and in 1218 he ordered one of his best leaders, the *noyan* Jebe, to attack it with twenty thousand men. Jebe's instructions were, first of all, to defend Almalik and Suqnaq-tigin's inheritance, but when he arrived there Küchlüg had left the country and taken refuge in Kashgaria. Balasagun and what is today the Semirechye region surrendered to the Mongols without resistance. From there Jebe went down into Kashgaria, where the Muslim population welcomed him as their deliverer from persecution. Since Jebe had imposed the strictest discipline upon his troops and had specifically forbidden all looting, his passing was greeted, says Juvaini, as a blessing from Allah.[142] Küchlüg took flight in the direction of the Pamirs, but was overtaken by Jebe's runners and killed near the River Sarikol (1218).[143]

The whole of eastern Turkestan—the Ili, Issyk Kul, Chu, and Talas regions—was now annexed to the Mongol Empire.

DESTRUCTION OF THE KHWARIZMIAN EMPIRE

The empires of Jenghiz Khan and Khwarizm were now immediate neighbors.[144]

On Jenghiz Khan's side were all the Mongol and Turkic populations, whether shamanist, Buddhist, or Nestorian, of Mongolia. After the annexation of the Kara-Khitai realm, there was also Kashgaria, which, while Muslim by religion, was of purely Turkic culture, influenced hardly at all by Iran. On Muhammad's side there was a Muslim Turkic dynasty which was basically Iranian in its culture, with Turko-Iranian populations dwelling in Transoxiana and purely Iranian ones in Khurasan, Afghanistan, and Iraq 'Ajami.

Between the rulers themselves the contrast was complete. Jenghiz Khan was cool, prudent, tenacious, and methodical; Muhammad of Khwarizm an irresponsible fire-eater, inconsequent, with no sense of organization, but puffed up by his victories over the Ghorids and the Kara-Khitai. His first defeat was to demoralize him completely and deprive him of all resource, leaving him a piteous, almost cowardly, figure. Of the two, the nomad barbarian was the ruler, while the Iranized Turk, an emperor of

Islam and a king of the sedentary states, was nothing but a knight-errant.

Moreover, as was said before, this Khwarizmian empire which Jenghiz Khan was to destroy in 1220 dated from no earlier than 1194; indeed, it was only since 1212 that Muhammad, having slain the last Karakhanid of Samarkand, Uthman, transferred his capital to that city from Urgench (near Khiva). It was an empire in embryo, a dominion of recent date under a provisional ruler, with nothing corresponding to the Jenghiz-Khanite *yasaq* to stabilize it, or to counterbalance the tremendous prestige of the resurgent empire of the old khagans. Ethnically, between the Tadzhiks—the Iranian populations of the towns and cultivated areas—and the Turks, who made up the army, the Khwarizmian empire was in a perilous situation. It was not based, as were the Seljuks of an earlier day, on a whole Muslim Turkic clan able to supply a military feudal structure of atabegs. The Khwarizmian dynasty sprang from a house of Seljuk dignitaries, with no clan behind it. Khwarizm itself, the land of Khiva, was too small to support a solid Turkoman feudalism. As a result, the army consisted of mercenaries recruited at random from all the Ghuzz or Qanqli tribes of the Kirghiz steppe, who were bound by no feelings of loyalty, and of whom the majority had but one idea: to betray their masters and so earn admission into the great Jenghiz-Khanite army. Added to this, the sultan's family was split by implacable hatreds. His mother, the terrible Turkan-khatun, loathed and worked against her own grandson, Jalal ad-Din, Muhammad's favorite son and the only man of good will in that crumbling house.

The bond of Islam might have brought unity and cohesion to these clashing and discordant elements. As heir to the great Seljuks—to Sanjar, with whom he compared himself—Muhammad had no mean part to play. He had only to proclaim himself the deputy of Islam and invoke the Holy War, the jihad, against the pagan, Buddhist, or Nestorian Mongol. But to crown his folly, this prince, who aspired to resume the career of the great Seljuks and to become, like them, the sultan of Islam, had quarreled bitterly with the caliphate of Baghdad, which in 1217 he had been on the point of attacking. The caliph an-Nasir (1180–1225) regarded him as his worst enemy and would have declared for the Mongols rather than for him. This mortal enmity between

sultan and caliph was to expose the Muslim world, divided and
helpless, to the Mongol invasion.[145]

The rift between Jenghiz Khan and the Khwarizmians originated with the latter. Jenghiz Khan had sought to establish correct commercial and political relations with them. But in 1218 a
caravan from the Mongol Empire, consisting entirely of Muslims,
with the exception of the Mongol envoy Uquna, was stopped at
Otrar, a Khwarizmian frontier town on the middle Syr Darya,
robbed, and its hundred or so members put to death by the
Khwarizmian governor Inalchiq, also known by the title of Qadir-
khan.[146] Jenghiz Khan demanded compensation, and on being
refused it made ready for war.[147]

In the summer of 1219 the Mongol army concentrated on the
upper Irtysh. In the autumn Jenghiz Khan arrived at Qayaligh,
southeast of Lake Balkhash, among the Qarluq, whose king
Arslan-khan joined him, as did also Suqnaq-tigin, the new king
of Almalik, and the *idiqut* Barchuq, with their respective forces.
According to Barthold's estimate, the Mongol army comprised
between 150,000 and 100,000 men and, though greatly outnumbered by the Khwarizmian forces, was far better disciplined and
had a considerably more coherent staff.

Muhammad of Khwarizm had divided and scattered his troops
between the Syr Darya line and the fortified places of Transoxiana. As a result, despite their over-all numerical superiority,
they were outnumbered at each individual point. Jenghiz Khan
penetrated Khwarizmian territory near Otrar on the middle Syr
Darya. One Mongol division commanded by two of his sons,
Jagatai and Ogödäi, surrounded the town, but took it only after
a prolonged siege. A division under Jöchi, the conqueror's eldest
son, moved down the Syr Darya, capturing Signakhi (opposite
the modern town of Turkestan) and Jend (near modern Perovsk).
Five thousand Mongols, detached to the upper Syr Darya, took
Benaket (west of Tashkent) and laid siege to Khodzhent. The
governor of this place, the energetic Timur-malik, succeeded after
a courageous defense in escaping down the Syr Darya in a small
boat. Barthold points out in this connection that more acts of
individual heroism, more paladin figures, are found in this war
among the Muslims than among the Mongols, but that the latter
alone had the organization, unity of command, and discipline by
which victories are won.

Jenghiz Khan himself, with his youngest son Tolui, marched with the main body of the army straight to Bukhara, which he reached in February, 1220. The Turkic garrison tried to break the cordon of besiegers and make its escape, but succeeded only in being decimated. The inhabitants, forsaken by their defenders, surrendered (February 10 or 16, 1220). The citadel, in which four hundred men had sought refuge, was taken by assault and all its defenders were slaughtered. The city then underwent a methodical and thorough pillage. The people were robbed, mal-treated, bullied, and outraged in every way, but in general the only ones to be executed were those—especially among the Muslim "clergy"—who attempted to resist against the violence and sacrilegious acts of the victors. Juvaini's story of Jenghiz Khan entering the great mosque to harangue the crowd and proclaim himself the scourge of God is believed by Barthold to be no more than a legend.[148] Barthold also thinks that the great fire which completed the destruction of Bukhara was probably accidental.

From Bukhara, Jenghiz Khan marched on Samarkand, and was rejoined before the city by his sons Jagatai and Ogödäi, who had just taken Otrar. The population of Samarkand—still partly Iranian—bravely attempted a sortie, but was cut down. After five days, according to Juvaini, the town capitulated (March, 1220). Samarkand was thoroughly looted, the inhabitants having first been driven out in order to facilitate the operation. Many of them were put to death. Those of them who were considered use-ful—skilled craftsmen, for example—were deported to Mongolia. The Turkic garrison, although it had spontaneously rallied to the Mongols, was massacred to the last man. Unlike their colleagues of Bukhara, the Muslim religious leaders of Samarkand made no resistance and for the most part were spared.[149] Those so favored were at last allowed to re-enter Samarkand, but the massacre had been on so huge a scale that barely enough inhabitants were left to populate a single quarter.

The old capital of Khwarizm proper, Gurganj—the Urgench of today, near Khiva—was not taken until April, 1221, after a long siege which immobilized two of Jenghiz Khan's sons, Jöchi and Jagatai, and which toward the end required the presence even of a third son, Ogödäi.[150] The Mongols completed their destruction by submerging the city beneath the waters of the Amu Darya.

During the Mongol conquest of Transoxiana, the sultan Muhammad of Khwarizm, appalled by the disaster brought about by his own irresponsibility and arrogance, passed from vainglory to utter dejection and remained inactive; then he fled to Balkh. From there he went on to western Khurasan, where he sought refuge at Nishapur. Next, in increasing terror, he dashed to Kazvin in the northwestern part of Iraq 'Ajami, at the opposite end of his dominions. But Jenghiz Khan had sent a cavalry detachment in pursuit of him, commanded by his two best generals, Jebe and Sübötäi. It was a frantic chase. At the approach of Jebe and Sübötäi, Balkh bought itself off and received a governor. Nishapur also escaped with nothing worse than a control commission, for Jebe was in too great a hurry to linger. Tus (Meshed), Damghan, and Samnan, on the other hand, were sacked by Sübötäi. The two Mongol generals, still in pursuit of Muhammad, then entered Iraq 'Ajami and made a surprise attack on Rai, where they slaughtered the male population and enslaved the women and children. Passing Hamadan at a gallop, they reached Karun, where Muhammad nearly fell into their hands; then they lost track of him. They revenged themselves by the destruction of Zenjan and Kazvin. Meanwhile the luckless Muhammad had taken refuge on an islet in the Caspian, opposite Abeskun, where he died of exhaustion about December, 1220. Later we shall see Jebe and Sübötäi continue their raid through Azerbaijan into the Caucasus and the south of Russia.[151]

Having dealt with the sultan of Khwarizm, Jenghiz Khan crossed the Amu Darya in the spring of 1221 and began the conquest of Afghanistan and Khurasan from the remnants of the Khwarizmian forces.[152] He occupied Balkh, whose surrender could not save it from total destruction (massacre of the inhabitants and burning of the town). In Khurasan he dispatched his son Tolui to take Merv, which capitulated, and here too almost the whole population was slaughtered (end of February, 1221). Tolui, seated on a golden chair in the plain of Merv, witnessed this mass execution. Men, women, and children were separated, distributed in herds among the various battalions, and beheaded; "only four hundred artisans were spared." Sultan Sanjar's mausoleum was burned and his tomb emptied. (It was then, according to tradition, that an Oghuz clan whose grazing grounds were in the region of Merv emigrated to Asia Minor, where the Seljuks gave it land and where it laid the foundations of the Ottoman

Empire.) Tolui then went to chastise Nishapur, which shortly before (November, 1220) had had the misfortune to repel and kill the Mongol general Toquchar, Jenghiz Khan's son-in-law. This time Nishapur was taken by storm (April 10, 1221) and completely destroyed. Toquchar's widow presided at the massacre. To guard against deception, the corpses were beheaded and the heads of men, women, and children were stacked in separate pyramids; "even the dogs and cats were killed." Near Tus, the Mongols demolished the mausoleum of Harun ar-Rashid. His tomb and Sanjar's, and all that made the glory of that brilliant Arabo-Persian civilization, were systematically destroyed. Tolui then went on to take Herat, whose Khwarizmian garrison resisted, but whose civilian population opened the gates; he slaughtered the soldiers and—for once—spared the people. Tolui next rejoined Jenghiz Khan near Thaleqan. Jagatai and Ogödäi, who had just taken Urgench, did the same.

After destroying Thaleqan, Jenghiz Khan crossed the Hindu Kush to besiege Bamian. In this action the young Mütügen was killed; he was Jagatai's son and Jenghiz Khan's favorite grandson. The conqueror himself broke the news to the father at a meal, forbade him in the name of the *yasaq* to mourn his son, but honored the dead man with sanguinary obsequies. There was no plundering; everything was destroyed. No prisoner was taken, "every living creature was massacred," and the site upon which Bamian had stood was given the name of "accursed city." [153]

Meanwhile the Khwarizmian prince Jalal ad-Din Manguberti,[154] son of the late Sultan Muhammad, had escaped the disaster of Transoxiana and Khurasan by breaking through a cordon of Mongol troops at Nessa. Taking refuge in Ghazni, in the heart of the Afghan mountains, he organized a new army and then, at Perwan, north of Kabul, defeated a Mongol army corps commanded by Shigi-qutuqu.[155] Jenghiz Khan, burning to avenge his lieutenant's defeat, marched on Ghazni, where Jalal ad-Din did not dare to await him. Ghazni offered no resistance, and Jenghiz Khan, eager to overtake Jalal ad-Din, postponed the ritual destruction of the city. At last he caught up with the Khwarizmian prince on the banks of the Indus, where he cut his men to pieces (November 24, 1221, according to Nasawi). Jalal ad-Din himself made his escape by leaping fully armed onto his horse in midstream under a hail of arrows. He was lucky enough to reach the opposite bank

safe and sound, whence he went to seek refuge at the court of
the sultan of Delhi (December, 1221).[156] The Mongols did not
immediately continue the pursuit into Indian territory. (It was
not until the following year that one of their detachments, under
the orders of the Jelair *noyan* Bala, made a reconnaissance as far
as Multan, only to withdraw after a short time because of the
heat.) But in the absence of Jalal ad-Din, his family had fallen
into Mongol hands, and all the male children were killed.

The Mongol reverse at Perwan, however, had rekindled the
courage of the last towns left standing in eastern Iran. Jenghiz
Khan first settled accounts with the people of Ghazni, who were
all slain, with the exception of artisans whom he sent to Mongolia. After the battle of Perwan, Herat had risen in rebellion
(November, 1221).[157] The Mongol general Aljigidai captured
the city again after a six-month siege on June 14, 1222. The entire
population was massacred and the killing occupied a whole week.
Those people who had returned to Merv had been foolish enough
to kill the Persian prefect left there by Tolui and to acclaim Jalal
ad-Din. They were slaughtered meticulously to the last man by
Shigi-qutuqu. When the massacre was over, the Mongols took the
precaution of making a feigned departure. They moved to a distance, and such wretches as had been able to hide at the outskirts
of the town, or in cellars, reappeared one by one, believing that
the enemy had gone. The Mongol rearguard then returned, fell
upon them, and wiped them out.

It is evident that in general the Mongols found less difficulty
in taking fortified cities in Transoxiana and eastern Iran than
they did in China. This was partly because the terror they inspired as "pagans"—or as we should say today, "savages"—was
even more intense among Muslims than on Chinese territory,
where for centuries the inhabitants had been accustomed to having them as neighbors. Also, in these regions, they seem to have
made more use of local inhabitants. To capture a city the Mongols
would round up the male population of the surrounding districts—
from the countryside and from open towns—and drive it at the
point of the sword against ditch and wall. What if these wretches
were mown down by their fellow countrymen, so long as their
bodies filled in the ditch and their repeated attacks exhausted
the garrison? Sometimes they were disguised as Mongols, with a

Mongol flag to every ten, so that the garrison, seeing these multitudes deploying over the plain, believed themselves threatened by a huge Jenghiz-Khanite army. Thanks to this ruse, a small contingent of Mongols might force a capitulation, after which their human herds, being of no further use, were slaughtered. This horrible and almost universal practice, brought to perfection by Mongol discipline and organization, became one of their most habitual tactical procedures. It was with prisoners from Bukhara that Jenghiz Khan besieged Samarkand, the Samarkand captives in their turn were used at the siege of Urgench, and it was partly by means of the rural population of Khurasan that Tolui captured Merv. The terror and dejection was such that no one thought of resistance. When Nessa was taken, the Mongols herded the inhabitants together in the plain and ordered them to tie one another's hands behind their backs. "They obeyed," writes Muhammad of Nessa. "If they had scattered and fled to the nearby mountains, most of them would have been saved. As soon as they were bound, the Mongols surrounded them and dispatched them with their arrows—men, women, and children without discrimination."

Yet among the Mongols the administrative sense and the military sense of order were never in abeyance. After slaying four-fifths of the population, they left behind them, to manage the affairs of the surviving fifth, a civilian official—the *darugachi* or *daruqachi*—who was often an Uigur and sometimes even a Persian, and with him scribes competent to keep registers in the Uigur and Persian languages.

Eastern Iran never quite recovered from the Jenghiz-Khanite tempest. A city such as Balkh still bears the marks of Mongol destruction. The Timurid renaissance in these regions in the fifteenth century, under Shah Rukh, Olugh-beg, and Husain-i Baiqara, could not altogether restore a land turned upside down. Yet, although Jenghiz Khan may have behaved like the worst enemy of Arabo-Persian civilization, liked the Damned and Accursed stigmatized by Muslim writers, he felt no hostility to Islam itself. If he forbade the practice of ablution and the Muslim manner of killing livestock, it was merely because they were contrary to Mongol custom or superstition. If in eastern Iran he destroyed the brilliant urban civilization produced by a Firdausi or an Avicenna, it was because he meant to create a sort of no man's land or artificial steppe in the southwestern marches to serve as a glacis or protective barrier to his empire. It was with this object that he "killed the land." In him there was both the sensible man of government, who could never have approved of a religious war, and a nomad with an imperfect conception of sedentary life and an inclination to destroy urban civilization, abolish agriculture (on leaving eastern Iran, he destroyed its granaries), and turn fields into steppe, because the steppe suited his way of life and was less difficult to administer.

Jenghiz Khan stayed for some time in Afghanistan, south of the Hindu Kush. In May, 1222, he received a visit from the famous Taoist monk K'iou Ch'ang-ch'uen, whom he had summoned from China in 1220, and who had just arrived via Uiguria, Almalik, the Talas, and Samarkand. The Conqueror was eager to learn of the drugs of immortality of the Taoist magicians.[158]

But he was now also thinking of returning to Mongolia. He recrossed the Amu Darya in the autumn of 1222 and continued by way of Bukhara, where he had the curiosity to inquire into the principal tenets of the Muslim faith. He approved of them, except in the matter of the pilgrimage to Mecca, which he considered unnecessary, seeing that the whole world was the house of God (or of Tängri, the "Eternal Heaven" of the Mongols). At Samarkand he commanded that the Muslim public prayers should be conducted in his name, since he had replaced Sultan Muhammad. He even exempted the Muslim "clergy"—imams and cadis— from taxation, which substantially proves that the atrocities he committed against the Muslim world were acts of war, and no part of a religious campaign. He wintered at Samarkand and spent the spring of 1223 north of the Syr Darya. It was near Tashkent, probably in the valley of the Chirchik, a small northern tributary of that river, that he held a sort of barbarian "court," seated on a golden throne among his *noyat* and *ba'atut*. Then, still in the spring of 1223, he presided at a *quriltai* with his sons in the Qulan-Bashi steppe north of the Alexander (Kirghiz) Range. Meanwhile, his army amused itself with huge hunting expeditions. He spent the summer of that year in the steppes of the Talas and the Chu, and the summer of the following year apparently on the Irtysh. He returned to Mongolia in 1225.

Before we follow Jenghiz khan on his last Chinese campaign, it may be well to recall the expedition made by his two lieutenants, Jebe *noyan* and Sübötäi *ba'atur,* round the Caspian Sea.

We saw how these two generals, the best strategists in the Mongol army, had been sent with a corps of cavalry—25,000 men, as Grenard estimates—in pursuit of Muhammad of Khwarizm on his flight across Persia. After the sultan's death, they continued their ride westward. Having sacked Rai, a city renowned for its marvelously decorated pottery which was never to recover from this disaster,[159] they were entreated by certain Sunnite Muslims, says Mirkhond, to destroy the Shi'ite center of Qum, which they readily did. As Hamadan had surrendered, they exacted from it no more than a ransom, after which they demolished Zenjan and had to take Kazvin by storm, for which the inhabitants were punished by massacre. The last Turkic atabeg of Azerbaijan, the old Özbeg—of the dynasty of local Mamelukes which, toward the end of the twelfth century, came near to succeeding the Seljuks—bribed them lavishly to spare Tauris (Tabriz). Jebe and Sübötäi went on across the Mugan plain, in the depths of winter, to invade Georgia. This Christian kingdom, then ruled by Giorgi III Lasha, or the Brilliant (1212–23), was at the height of its power, but in February, 1221, the two Mongol generals cut the Georgian army to pieces near Tiflis (Tbilisi).[160] From there they returned to Azerbaijan to sack Maragheh, after practicing their usual mode of attack: they forced prisoners to lead the assault of the citadel and slaughtered them if they retreated; then, after the fall of the city and the massacre of the population, they made a false departure so as to restore confidence among those who had escaped, followed by a whirlwind return of the rear guard, who beheaded them (March, 1221). The two Mongol generals were then on the point of marching on Baghdad to destroy the Abbasid caliphate. The outcome doubtless would have been catastrophic for the Arab world, for at the same moment, as Ibn al-Athir observes, the Crusaders had invaded Egypt and occupied Damietta.[161] The little Abbasid army concentrated at Daquqa would have been hardly inadequate to defend Iraq 'Arabi. That year of 1221 might have seen Jebe and Sübötäi in Baghdad and King John of Brienne in Cairo at one and the same time. Fortunately for the caliph, Jebe and Sübötäi were content to return and hold Hamadan to ransom once more. This time the citizens resisted. The Mongols took Hamadan by assault, massacred the entire population, and burned the city. From there, passing by Ardebil, which they also sacked, the two Mongol commanders returned to Georgia.

The Georgian knighthood was one of the finest of the time. But by a feigned retreat, Sübötäi drew it into an ambush where Jebe was awaiting it and cut it to pieces. The Georgians doubtless considered themselves fortunate in being able to save Tiflis, though to do so they had to allow the Mongols to lay waste the southern part of the country. The invaders then went on to Shirvan, where they sacked Shamakha. Then, via Derbent, they descended upon the steppes north of the Caucasus, where they clashed with a coalition of the peoples of the region: Alans (who were descendants of the old Sarmatians and were Christians of the Greek confession),[162] Lezghians (Lezginy), and Circassians —all three of Caucasian race—and Kipchak Turks. Jebe and Sübötäi cunningly engineered the defection of the Kipchaks by invoking their common Turko-Mongol brotherhood and by giving them part of their plunder. They then defeated the other members of the coalition, one by one, and lastly sped in pursuit of the Kipchaks, cut them to pieces, and recovered their booty.[163]

Meanwhile the Kipchaks had appealed to the Russians. One of the Kipchak khans named Kutan, whose daughter had married the Russian prince Mstislav (the Bold) of Galich, secured the intervention of his son-in-law and other Russian princes against the Mongols. A Russian army of 80,000 men, led by the princes of Galich, Kiev, Chernigov, and Smolensk, came down the Dnieper to concentrate near Khortitsa, in the neighborhood of Aleksandrov. The Mongols drew back and refused to fight until the enemy was sufficiently weary and its various military units conveniently widely spaced. The action took place near the Kalka or Kalmius, a small coastal river flowing into the Sea of Azov near Mariupol.[164] The prince of Galich and the Kipchaks, who charged without waiting for the men of Kiev, were routed and had to flee (May 31, 1222). The prince of Kiev, left alone, defended his camp for three days and was allowed an honorable surrender. Nevertheless, he was afterward put to death with all his men.[165]

This first Russian disaster had no immediate political consequences. Grand Duke Yurii of Vladimir, who had not had time to reach the Kalka with his troops, preserved his army intact. The Mongols were content to rob the Genoese countinghouses of Sudak or Soldaia in the Crimea (though there is nothing to support Cahun's theory of an agreement between them and the Venetians).[166] Jebe and Sübötäi crossed the Volga near Tsaritsyn (Stalingrad, Volgograd), beat the Bulgars of the Kama and the Qanqli Turks of the Urals, and, after this fantastic foray, rejoined Jenghiz Khan's grand army in the steppes north of the Syr Darya.

The Last Years of Jenghiz Khan

Jenghiz Khan was back in Mongolia in the spring of 1225 and spent the winter of 1225–26 and the following summer in camp on the Tula, a tributary of the Orkhon. From Peking to the Volga the world trembled before him. His eldest son Jöchi, who had been detached to the government of the Aralo-Caspian steppes, seemed toward the end to be pursuing a separate policy. This alarmed the Conqueror; but before an open breach could occur between father and son, Jöchi died, in February, 1227.

Jenghiz Khan led yet another campaign against the Tangut kingdom of Hsi-Hsia in Kansu. The king of Hsi-Hsia, although a vassal, had evaded his obligation to send a contingent for the war against Khwarizm. To the formal request for aid, the *Secret History* relates, a Tangut dignitary named Asha-gambu had the insolence to reply in the name of his master that if Jenghiz Khan had not troops enough, he did not deserve to wield supreme power. Such bravado could not be overlooked and, having settled the affairs of Khwarizm, the Conqueror retaliated. Furthermore, as Vladimirtsov points out, Jenghiz Khan must have perceived that in order to achieve the conquest of the Kin realm of northern China, where his subordinate Muqali had just died in attempting it, it was essential for the Mongols to obtain direct possession of Kansu, the Alashan, and the Ordos. He therefore opened his campaign in the autumn of 1226, took Lingchow at the end of the year, and, in the spring of 1227, began the siege of the Hsi-Hsia capital, the modern city of Ningsia.[167] The method of "Mongol terror" was applied here as pitilessly as in Afghanistan. "In

vain the inhabitants hid in mountains and caves to escape the
Mongol might. The fields were covered with human bones."
While Ningsia was being besieged, Jenghiz Khan camped during
the summer of 1227 in the region of the River Tsingshui and in
the district of Lungtö, northwest of modern Pingliang. There, in
the area west of Pingliang, he died on August 18, 1227, at the
age of sixty.[168] Soon afterward, Ningsia, the enemy capital, was
taken and, in accordance with the Conqueror's last commands,
the whole population was slain. A portion of the Tangut people
was given to the Empress Yesui, one of Jenghiz Khan's wives, who
had accompanied him on this campaign.

The body of Jenghiz Khan was buried near the sacred mountain of Burqan Qaldun (Kentei), where Tängri had once spoken
to him, by the headwaters of the Onon and the Kerulen. In 1229
his successor was to offer great ceremonial sacrifices in his honor,
in the Mongol manner. "He commanded that for three days dishes
should be offered, according to custom, to the manes of his father.
He chose from among the families of *noyans* and generals the
loveliest girls, to the number of forty; they were adorned with
rich garments, and jewels of great price, and, in Rashid ad-Din's
phrase, they were sent to serve Jenghiz Khan in the next world.
In addition to this barbaric homage, splendid horses were sacrificed." [169]

JENGHIZ KHAN: HIS CHARACTER AND ACHIEVEMENTS

Jenghiz Khan has been regarded as one of the scourges of humanity. He is the personification of twelve centuries of invasion
of ancient sedentary civilizations by nomads of the steppe. Indeed, none of his predecessors left so terrifying a reputation. He
made terror a system of government and massacre a deliberate
and methodical institution. His destruction of eastern Iran ex-
ceeds in horror anything attributed by Europe to Attila, or by
India to Mihirakula. Nevertheless, we should bear in mind that
his cruelty arose chiefly from the harshness of his milieu, the
crudest of all the Turko-Mongol levies, rather than from any
natural ferocity. (In this respect Tamerlane, another slaughterer,
has far more to answer for, because he was more civilized.[170] The
collective executions imposed by the Mongol conqueror formed
part of a system of warfare. It was the nomad weapon wielded

against sedentary peoples who did not submit promptly enough and, above all, against those who rebelled after making submission. The sad thing was that this nomad could barely apprehend the nature of an agricultural and urban economy. Having conquered eastern Iran and northern China, he found it natural to reduce these countries to steppeland by demolishing their cities and destroying their fields. A thousand years of nomad tradition, of raids on the threshold of civilization and on the fringe of age-old cultivation, spoke in him when he gave this definition of supreme joy: "to cut my enemies to pieces, drive them before me, seize their possessions, witness the tears of those dear to them, and embrace their wives and daughters!" [171] Conversely comes his rueful reflection at the thought that his grandsons would forsake the hardy life of the steppe for the life of sedentary peoples: "After us, the people of our race will wear garments of gold; they will eat sweet, greasy food, ride splendid coursers, and hold in their arms the loveliest of women, and they will forget that they owe these things to us. . . ." [172]

A Taoist stele of 1219, engraved at the instigation of the monk Li Chih-ch'ang, who in 1220–23 accompanied the famous K'iou Ch'ang-ch'uen on his visit to the Conqueror, gives a curious rendering, in the Taoist philosophical vocabulary, of the impression made upon the Chinese by the emperor of the nomads, by his way of life and his achievements: "Heaven is weary of the inordinate luxury of China. I [Jenghiz Khan is speaking] remain in the wild region of the north; I return to simplicity and seek moderation once more. As for the garments that I wear and the meals that I eat, I have the same rags and the same food as cowherds and grooms, and I treat the soldiers as my brothers. In a hundred battles I have been in the forefront. Within the space of seven years I have performed a great work, and in the six directions of space everything is subject to a single rule!" [173]

In the framework of his way of life, his milieu, and his race, Jenghiz Khan appears as a man of a reflective cast of mind and sturdy common sense, remarkably well-balanced and a good listener. He was also firm in friendship and, for all his sternness, generous and affectionate. He had the qualities of a true administrator—an administrator, that is, of nomadic peoples, not of sedentary ones, of whose economy he had only the vaguest conception. Within these limits he displayed an innate sense of order and good government. Combined with ruthless barbarian sentiments, there is in him a certain nobility and loftiness of mind whereby the "Accursed" of Muslim writers regains his proper status as a human being. One of the most characteristic features of his attitude of mind is his instinctive horror of traitors. Servants who hoped to ingratiate themselves with him by betraying their unfortunate masters were executed by his order.[174] On the other hand, he would often reward or take into his own service those who had remained faithful throughout to their lords, his enemies. Rashid ad-Din and the _Secret History_ ascribe to him a number of similar traits and emphasize not only his respect for courage in misfortune but also the sound moral basis of his rule. Weaker characters whom he had taken under his protection he defended to the end and followed through life with unshakable loyalty. Alaqush-tigin, the Öngüt chief, had been murdered for siding with him against the Naiman. He restored the chief's family, took the son into his service, gave him his own daughter in marriage, and assured the fortunes of his house.[175] Vanquished adversaries of former wars—the Uigur and Khitan—found in him the most loyal of protectors, just as later the Syriac Christians and the Armenians had no more sure defenders than his grandsons. In Liaotung, the Khitan prince Ye-lü Lü-ko, who had been his vassal from the beginning, died during the war with Khwarizm. His widow sought out the Conqueror at the time of his last campaign in Kansu. He welcomed the princess with the greatest kindness and showed her and Ye-lü Lü-ko's two sons the most affectionate and fatherly consideration.[176] In all such circumstances, this skin-clad nomad, this exterminator of peoples, displayed a natural majesty, a sublime courtesy, and a true nobility which surprised even the Chinese. Being a gentleman of good family, he was in soul a king, and therefore less elated than anyone by his meteoric rise to fortune.

Lastly, inflexible though Jenghiz Khan was in his policy, he was not deaf to the voice of civilized experience. He took many advisers into his confidence: Uigur like T'a-t'a-t'ung-a, Muslims like Mahmud Yalavach, and Khitan like Ye-lü Ch'u-ts'ai. T'a-t'a-t'ung-a, who had performed the same function at the court of the last Naiman king, became his chancellor as well as tutor in Uigur writing to his sons.[177] Mahmud Yalavach became his deputy to the Transoxianian populations, the first "Mongol" governor of

Transoxiana.[178] The Sinicized Khitan Ye-lü Ch'u-ts'ai succeeded in giving his master some tinge of Chinese culture, and even sometimes in preventing massacre. One of his chief concerns, his biography explains, was to rescue precious texts from towns sacked or burned by the Mongols; another, to search for medicinal drugs to combat the epidemics born of such carnage.[179] Notwithstanding his devotion to the Mongol state and the Jenghiz-Khanite family, he could not always conceal his emotion when imploring mercy for some condemned city or province. "Are you going to weep for the people again?" Ogödäi would ask him. Tactful and judicious intervention on his part often prevented irreparable damage. "Tatar by origin and Chinese by culture," writes Rémusat, "he was the natural intermediary between oppressors and oppressed." [180] He could not plead the cause of humanity with the Mongols; they would not have listened to him. He endeavored to prove to them that clemency was good policy, and in this he did wisely, for the barbarity of the Mongols was born chiefly of ignorance.

At the time of Jenghiz Khan's last campaign in Kansu, a Mongol general pointed out to him that his new Chinese subjects would be useless to him, since they were unsuited to warfare, and that therefore he would do better to exterminate them—there were nearly ten million—so that he might at least make use of the soil as grazing land for the cavalry. Jenghiz Khan appreciated the cogency of this advice, but Ye-lü Ch'u-ts'ai protested. "He explained to the Mongols, to whom any such idea was unknown, the advantages to be gained from fertile soil and hard-working subjects. He made clear that by imposing taxes on land and exacting tribute on merchandise, they might collect 500,000 ounces of silver yearly, 80,000 pieces of silk, and 400,000 sacks of grain." He won his point,[181] and Jenghiz Khan ordered Ye-lü Ch'u-ts'ai to draw up a system of taxation on these lines.

Thanks to Ye-lü Ch'u-ts'ai and Jenghiz Khan's Uigur advisers, there arose, amid all the carnage, the rudiments of Mongol administration. In this there must have been a contributing factor in the Conqueror himself, a general inclination toward culture. Jenghiz Khan appears to have felt particularly drawn toward the Khitan and Uigur, the two most civilized peoples of the Turko-Mongol world. The Khitan could, without depriving it of its nationhood, initiate the Jenghiz-Khanite empire into Chinese culture, while the Uigur were in a position to give the Mongols a share in the ancient Turkic civilization of the Orkhon and Turfan, and in a whole heritage of Syriac, Manichaeo-Nestorian, and Buddhist traditions. Indeed, it was from the Uigur that Jenghiz Khan and his immediate successors derived the framework of their civil administration, as they did the language and writing of their chancellery. Later the Uigur writing, with little alteration, was to provide the Mongols with their national alphabet.

Massacres were forgotten, while the administrative accomplishment—a blend of Jenghiz-Khanite discipline and of the Uigur system of bureaus or departments—continued. And this work was in the end, after so much early devastation, to be to the advantage of civilization. It was from this point of view that Jenghiz Khan was judged by his contemporaries. "He died, and this was a great pity, for he was a just man and a wise one," says Marco Polo. "He kept the people at peace," says Joinville.[182] This verdict is paradoxical in appearance only. By unifying all the Turko-Mongol nations into a single empire, by imposing iron discipline from China to the Caspian, Jenghiz Khan suppressed the endless intertribal wars and afforded the caravans a security they had never known. Abu'l Ghazi writes: "Under the reign of Jenghiz Khan, all the country between Iran and Turan [the lands of the Turks] enjoyed such peace that a man might have journeyed from the land of sunrise to the land of sunset with a golden platter upon his head without suffering the least violence from anyone." [183] His *yasaq* established throughout Mongolia and Turkestan a "Pax Jenghiz-Khana," no doubt a terrible one in his own day, but one which under his successors became milder and rendered possible the achievements of the great travelers of the fourteenth century. In this respect Jenghiz Khan was a sort of barbarian Alexander, a pathfinder who opened up new roads to civilization.[184]

6

The Three Immediate Successors to Jenghiz Khan

Distribution of Appanages Among Jenghiz Khan's Sons

Each of Jenghiz Khan's four sons had received during his life-time an *ulus*—that is, a certain number of tribes—together with a *yurt*, or territorial appanage of grazing land sufficient to support these tribes. With this went an *inju*, a revenue proportionate to the needs of his court and servants, in which were included the dues payable by the sedentary peoples of the subjugated areas of China, Turkestan, and Iran.[1] It is proper to comment here that the only divisible asset was the Turko-Mongol prairie, the nomads' grazing grounds. The cultivated country round Peking and Samarkand remained imperial territory. It would never have occurred to Jenghiz Khan's sons to count the countries of the sedentary peoples in the division among them of their possessions, or to become respectively emperor of China, khan of Turkestan, and sultan of Persia. Such ideas, which suggested themselves to their successors from 1260 onward, were to them entirely alien. Indeed, to their mind, the partition of the prairies in no way entailed that of the Jenghiz-Khanite empire. This would continue, under the regime of *concordia fratrum*, the harmony of brothers. Moreover, as Barthold observes, by nomad law, regardless of the khagan's absolute power, the state belonged less to him than to the whole royal family.

Jenghiz Khan's eldest son Jöchi[2] predeceased him by six months, about February, 1227, in the steppes north of the Arals.

253

Although Jenghiz Khan had never officially held Jöchi's dubious birth against him, the rift between them had widened toward the end. During the years 1222–27, after the capture of Urgench, in which he had taken part (April, 1221), Jöchi had dwelt in retirement on his own appanage of Turgai and Uralsk, and had taken no part in his father's campaigns. This gloomy withdrawal somewhat perturbed the conqueror, who began to wonder whether his eldest son was plotting against him. Jöchi's death may have prevented a painful conflict between them.

Batu, one of Jöchi's sons, inherited control of his father's appanage. Characterized in Mongol tradition as a wise and gentle prince (he was given the cognomen of *Sain-khan*, "the good khan") and known to the Russians as a ruthless conqueror, he was later to play an important role as chief of the Jenghiz-Khanite family in disputes arising over possession of the imperial throne. In these disputes he figured as a "maker of grand khans." [3] In the meantime his comparative youthfulness, his father's death, and the unspoken doubt cast upon the legitimacy of his line allowed "the house of Jöchi" no more than an obscure role in the affairs of the empire. Nevertheless, by virtue of the Mongol law which reserved for the eldest son the domain farthest away from the paternal residence, the house of Jöchi faced Europe and constituted the attacking wing of the Mongol Empire. To it had accrued the steppes west of the Irtysh "as far as Mongol hoofs had beaten the ground"—that is to say, Semipalatinsk, Akmolinsk, Turgai or Aktyubinsk, Uralsk, Adaj, and Khwarizm proper (Khiva), plus the expectation of all conquests west of the Volga from the Kipchaks, conquests prefigured in the expedition of Jebe and Sübötäi.

Jenghiz Khan's second son Jagatai [4] (d. 1242), whom the Conqueror had appointed to administer the *yasaq* and be responsible for Mongol discipline, was a stern and dreaded judge, a scrupulous and meticulous executor of the Jenghiz-Khanite code, a seasoned soldier who felt at home in the ranks, and somewhat unimaginative. He made no protest when his father appointed his younger brother Ogödäi to the highest place. Jagatai received as his portion the steppes of the former Kara-Khitai empire, extending from Uigur country to Bukhara and Samarkand in the west, thus essentially the region of the Ili, the Issyk Kul, the upper Chu, and the Talas. He also received

Kashgaria and Transoxiana, but it should be borne in mind that these were lands of sedentary peoples and that in Transoxiana the cities of Bukhara, Samarkand, and so on, were directly administered by the functionaries of the grand khan. On the evidence of Ch'ang-ch'uen, Jagatai's usual residence was south of the Ili.

Ogödäi,[5] Jenghiz Khan's third son, received territory east and northeast of Lake Balkhash, namely, the region of the Imil and the Tarbagatai, the Black Irtysh and the Urungu. The latter region was situated near the old Naiman country, while the Ogödäi camp was usually set up on the Imil.

Lastly, in accordance with Mongol custom, Tolui,[6] the youngest son of Jenghiz Khan, was, as such, the *ochigin*—or better, *otchigin* —or the guardian of the hearth. In other words, he was heir to the original patrimony comprising the region between the Tula, the upper Onon, and the upper Kerulen. Tolui is described to us as a daring soldier, dreaming only of conquests, and a good general (his Honan campaign of 1232 was to be most ably conducted). He was addicted to alcohol (of which he prematurely died in October, 1232, at the age of forty), however, and wanting in any great personal insights. But he had married an exceptionally intelligent woman, the princess Soyurghaqtani or Sorghaqtani, of the ancient Kerayit royal family (she was the niece of the last *Wang-khan*), who like all the Kerayit people was a Nestorian, and who was later to secure the empire for her sons.

In addition, the families of two of Jenghiz Khan's brothers, Qasar and Temuge Ochigin, also received appanages. Qasar's was near the Argun and the Hailar, and Temuge's at the eastern end of Mongolia, near the old Jurchid lands in the modern province of Kirin.

In accordance with Mongol law and in his capacity as guardian of the hearth, Tolui was charged with the regency (1227–29) after Jenghiz Khan's death, until the election of a new grand khan. As regent he received the *ordus* or tented palaces of his father, which constituted the court, and 101,000 men out of the 129,000 who made up the Mongol army in 1227. (The remaining 28,000 men were allocated as follows: 4,000 to each of Jenghiz Khan's other sons; 5,000 to Temuge, Jenghiz Khan's younger brother; 3,000 to the sons of Qachi'un, another brother; 1,000 to the sons of a third brother, Qasar; and 3,000 to the family of his mother Oelun-eke.)

It was not until the spring of 1229 that a *quriltai* or general assembly of Mongol princes gathered on the banks of the Kerulen for the election of a grand khan. This congress did no more than ratify the wishes of Jenghiz Khan, who had appointed his third son Ogödäi to be his successor.[7]

THE REIGN OF OGÖDÄI (1229–41)

Ogödäi, whom Jenghiz Khan had chosen as his successor, was the most intelligent of his sons. While he had inherited none of his father's genius, passion for ruling, or energy, he had the same good sense and steadiness. He was a clumsy, easygoing, jovial sot, lenient and generous in the extreme, and he took advantage of his absolute power to drink and amuse himself in his own fashion. Thanks to the *yasaq*, the affairs of the Mongol Empire ran themselves.

Ogödäi took up residence in Karakorum. His choice of site had historical signficance, for it was in this region of the upper Orkhon that most of the old Turko-Mongol empires had had their "capital," from the Hsiung-nu of antiquity to the eastern T'u-chüeh of the high Middle Ages. Nearby, at Karabalgasun, the Uigur khagans of the eighth century had established their *ordu-baligh*, and it was by this same name of Ordubaligh (city of the court) that the Jenghiz-Khanite capital was at first known. Already during the reign of Jenghiz Khan, at least from 1220 onward, Karakorum or some neighboring site was probably chosen as a theoretical capital, but it was Ogödäi who in 1235 made our Karakorum the true capital of the new empire by surrounding it with a defensive wall.[8]

Ogödäi put full trust in the Sinicized Khitan Ye-lü Ch'u-ts'ai, who strove to establish an administrative counterpart to the purely military government in the Chinese manner. In agreement with the Uigur literati, he set up Chinese, Tangut, Uigur, and Persian departments within the Mongol chancellery (the Uigur being for a long time the most important). The Mongols had long had a system of couriers to serve their military needs, and Ye-lü Ch'u-ts'ai and his emulators organized storehouses of grain at regular stages along these routes.[9] Above all, Ye-lü gave the Mongol Empire a sort of fixed budget, whereby the Chinese paid taxes in silver, silk, and grain, assessed by households, and the Mongols contributed 10 per cent of their horses, cattle, and sheep. To this end, the conquered parts of China, which up to that time had been regarded merely as a source of random plunder, were in 1230 divided into ten districts, each with its administrative staff of Mongol officials and Chinese literati. Ye-lü Ch'u-ts'ai also opened schools in Peking and Pingyang for the "Confucian" education of young Mongol lords, and at the same time recruited into the Mongol civil service a great number of Chinese. "The empire," he told Ogödäi, "was created on horseback, but it cannot be governed on horseback." [10]

In addition to Ye-lü Ch'u-ts'ai, Ogödäi put his faith in the Nestorian Kerayit Chinqai, whom Jenghiz Khan had already honored and whom Piano Carpini describes as a "protonotary," that is, a chancellor of the empire. Pelliot writes: "No edict could be promulgated in northern China without a line written in Uigur writing by Chinqai." [11]

In the military sphere, Ogödäi's reign witnessed the completion of the Mongol conquest of northern China, Persia, and southern Russia.

DESTRUCTION OF THE KIN REALM BY THE MONGOLS

In China, fresh efforts were called for. After Muqali's death and while Jenghiz Khan was busy in the west, the Kin had regained some of their territory. This ancient Jurchid people, in whom the Tungus blood still ran strongly, displayed an astonishing vitality. Not only had they remained in Honan, round Kaifeng, their new capital, but they had recovered from the Mongols almost the whole of the Wei basin in central Shensi, including the important stronghold of Tungkwan, which covered the entrance to Honan. They also took possession of the fortress of Hochung (Puchow), which was situated north of the Yellow River in the southwest corner of Shansi, facing Tungkwan. The last Kin ruler, Nin-kia-su (1223–34), could begin to hope again.[12]

In 1231 the Mongols reopened hostilities by seizing the towns of the Wei basin: Pingliang, Fengsiang, and so on. For the campaign of 1232, they conceived a plan on the grand scale.[13]

Unable to force the Tungkwan pass, they outflanked it in the northeast and southwest. While Ogödäi, with the main body of the army and abundant supplies of war material, captured Hochung—an act which later enabled him to cross the Yellow River downstream—his brother Tolui with 30,000 horsemen performed a huge circular sweep through the southwest. Deliberately violating Sung territory, he passed from the Wei valley into the valley of the upper Han, captured Hanchung (Nancheng; in Sung territory), and proceeded along the valley of the Kialing River in Szechwan, where he devastated the Paoning district. Then, turning his forces northeastward, he moved across the middle basin of the Han (which he traversed in January, 1232) and suddenly appeared on Kin territory in southern Honan, near Nanyang. At the same time Ogödäi and the bulk of the army, having taken Hochung, crossed the Yellow River and invaded Honan from the north (February, 1232). The two Mongol armies made their junction in the heart of Honan, at Künchow (the Yüchow of modern times), near which town Tolui had crushed the Kin some days earlier.[14]

In this supreme and final battle, the Kin gave proof of a courage that aroused the admiration of the Mongol staff officers, who were experts in the subject. Their generals submitted to torture rather than join forces with the victors. But their situation was desperate. In the northwest the Mongols had now at last occupied Tungkwan (March, 1232). Ogödäi ordered his best strategist, Sübötäi, the victor of Persia and Russia, to besiege Kaifeng, the Kin capital. The city was taken, only after prolonged resistance, in May, 1233. Ye-lü Ch'u-ts'ai persuaded the emperor Ogödäi not to destroy the place, which thenceforth would form part of the Mongol possessions. Before the end came, the king Nin-kia-su had left Kaifeng to try to organize resistance in the provinces. At first he took refuge at Kweiteh, and then in the little stronghold of Ts'aichow (Juning). In this latter town he committed suicide as the Mongols were launching their final assault (February–March, 1234).[15] Seeking revenge against its ancient enemies the Kin, the Sung dynasty had lent the Mongols some contingents of infantry who helped in the capture of the city.

The fall of Ts'aichow completed the annexation of the Kin realm by the Mongol Empire. From that time on, the Mongols were immediate neighbors of the national Chinese empire of the Sung. In return for their aid in the final battle against the Kin, Ogödäi allowed the Sung to retain certain districts in the southeastern point of present-day Honan. The emperor Li-tsung (1225–64)—or rather, his government—dissatisfied with the reward and coveting the whole of Honan, was foolish enough to attack the Mongols.[16] At first the Chinese troops reoccupied Kaifeng and Loyang (July–August, 1234) without fighting. They were of course immediately driven out by the Mongols, and at a *quriltai* held at Karakorum in 1235 Ogödäi decided upon the conquest of the Sung Empire.

Three Mongol armies invaded it. The first, commanded by Godan,[17] Ogödäi's second son, penetrated Szechwan and captured Chengtu (October, 1236); the second, under the orders of Kuchu, another of Ogödäi's sons, and of General Temutai, occupied Siangyang in Hupeh in March, 1236. The third, led by Prince Kün-buqa[18] and General Chaghan, marched as far as Hwang-chow, downriver from present-day Hankow, on the Yangtze, but were unable to remain there. In 1239 Siangyang also was to revert to the Sung. In fact, a forty-five-year war was beginning (1234–79), and Ogödäi was to see no more than the early part of it. A fourth Mongol army had marched to subjugate Korea. In December, 1231, the Korean capital Kaesong, northwest of modern Seoul, had been taken by the Mongols, who placed the country under their protectorate with seventy-two *darughachi* to run it; but in the following year all these Mongol residents had been massacred by the order of the king of Korea, Ko-tjong, who in July, 1232, took refuge on the little island of Kanghwa, west of Seoul. The new army dispatched by Ogödäi effectively occupied Korea, or at least the mainland, in 1236. The Korean court, on the other hand, declared its submission (it sent envoys to acknowledge its vassaldom from 1241 onward), but remained for another thirty years ensconced on its island.[19]

Conquest of Western Persia by the Mongols

When Ogödäi ascended the throne, Iran had yet to be reconquered.

In November, 1221, Jenghiz Khan forced Jalal ad-Din Manguberti, heir to the Khwarizmian empire, to take refuge in India (page 241). The sultan of Delhi, the Turk Iltutmish, welcomed the exile and gave him his daughter in marriage, but Jalal ad-Din plotted against him and was banished (1223). Jenghiz Khan and the Mongol grand army had just returned to Turkestan, leaving Khurasan and Afghanistan in ruins behind them and almost entirely depopulated, at least so far as cities and towns were concerned. These regions formed a sort of no man's land in which they had created before their departure no regular form of administration; while after Jebe's and Sübötäi's raid, central and western Persia were in a state bordering on anarchy. This was not a conquest in the true sense, although it was the work of a regular army operating in a regular manner, and the Mongols had remained there for three years; it was the whirlwind passage of a horde.

Jalal ad-Din took advantage of the Mongols' seeming indifference toward the affairs of Iran to return to that country in 1224.[20] As representative of the last legitimate power preceding the Mongol storm, he found no difficulty in being recognized as sultan by the atabegs or hereditary Turkic governors of Kerman (Kirman) and Fars (in Kerman, Boraq Hajjib, founder of the local Qutlugh-khan dynasty; in Fars, Sa'd ibn-Zengi, 1195–1226, of the Salghurid dynasty). From Shiraz, Jalal ad-Din went on to seize Ispahan and Iraq 'Ajami from his own brother Ghiyath ad-Din, who had carved himself out a principality there (1224); he then set forth to subjugate Azerbaijan. The atabeg of Azerbaijan, Özbeg (1210–25), of the powerful Turkic feudal house which had governed that province since 1136, had contrived in return for substantial tribute to survive Jebe's and Sübötäi's invasion; with Jalal ad-Din, he was less fortunate. The new invader forced Tabriz to capitulate and was recognized throughout the province (1225). From there the Khwarizmian prince went on to attack Georgia. Four years earlier, this Christian kingdom had suffered the onslaught of Jebe and Sübötäi, and was painfully recovering from this under the rule of the famous Queen Rusudan (1223–47), sister and heiress of Giorgi III, when Jalal ad-Din appeared. The sultan defeated the Georgians at Karni (or Garni) in August, 1225. In a second raid the following year he sacked Tiflis, where in March he destroyed all the Christian churches. In 1228 he returned a third time and, at Mindor near Lore, defeated the Georgian army of the high constable Ivane.[21] These Caucasian expeditions consolidated Jalal ad-Din's power in Azerbaijan.

He now found himself master of the whole of western Iran: Kerman, Fars, Iraq 'Ajami, and Azerbaijan, with Ispahan and Tabriz as his capitals. This constituted a partial restoration of the old Khwarizmian empire with a shift toward the west. But this illustrious knight was strangely lacking in political sense. With all the dash and daring that made him one of the most dazzling paladins of the Muslim world, this heir of the sultans of Khwarizm, while occupying the throne of Persia, continued to behave like a knight-errant. Instead of consolidating his new Persian realm in preparation for the inevitable return of the Mongols, this champion of Islam quarreled with the chief Muslim princes of Western Asia, who were his natural allies. In 1224 he threatened the caliph of Baghdad with invasion, and then, on April 2, 1230, after a prolonged siege, seized the fortress of Khilat (northwest of Lake Van, in Armenia) from the Ayyubid sultan of Damascus, al-Ashraf.[22] Finally, he brought upon himself the coalition of al-Ashraf and the Seljuk sultan 'Ala ad-Din Kai-Qobad (Kaykobad) I, king of Turkic Asia Minor (the Konya sultanate). In August, 1230, these two princes inflicted a crushing defeat upon him near Erzincan. It was precisely at this juncture that the Mongols launched a fresh invasion.

To put a stop to this unexpected restoration of the Khwarizmian empire, Ögödäi had just sent an army of 30,000 men into Persia, commanded by the *noyan* Chormaghan or Chormaqan.[23] During the winter of 1230–31, the Mongols arrived at lightning speed by way of Khurasan and Rai before Jalal ad-Din had time to muster his troops, and made straight for Azerbaijan, his usual residence. At this news the illustrious paladin lost his head. Leaving Tabriz, he fled toward the plains of Mugan and Arran, near the mouth of the Aras (Araxes) and the Kura; then to Diyarbakir, trailed all the way, like his father before him, by Mongol light horsemen. In the end he perished obscurely, murdered in the mountains of Diyarbakir on August 15, 1231, by a Kurdish peasant.

For ten years, 1231–41, Chormaghan remained at the head of the Mongol army encamped in northwestern Persia. He established his regular headquarters in the plains of Mugan and Arran, on the lower reaches of the Kura and Aras,[24] because this steppe with its lush grass suited his cavalry. For the same reason the Mugan and Arran country was, from 1256 onward, one of the favorite places of sojourn of the Mongol khans of Persia. It was from these pasture lands in the northwest of Azerbaijan that for a hundred years the Mongols governed ancient sedentary Iran with its polished urban civilization.

After Jalal ad-Din's disappearance, Chormaghan sent his little army to pillage the Irano-Mesopotamian borderlands. In Armenia the Mongols massacred the inhabitants of Bitlis and Ercis (Arjish). In Azerbaijan they took possession of Maragheh, where they also indulged in their customary slaughter. Profiting by example, the people of Tabriz surrendered, paid all that was demanded, and appeased Chormaghan by manufacturing precious fabrics for the grand khan Ogödäi (1233). In the south, Diyarbakir and the country of Erbil were horribly devastated. Ibn al-Athir describes some of these scenes of carnage:

A man of the Nisibin region told me that, when hidden in a house, he watched through an opening what was going on outside. Each time the Mongols were about to kill someone, they shouted [in derision that Muslim formula]: *"la ilaha illa allah."* The massacre over, they plundered the town and carried off the women. I saw them frolicking on their horses, he said; they laughed, they sang in their own language, and they said: *"la ilaha illa allah."*

Here is another anecdote, narrated by the same Ibn al-Athir:

I have been told things that are hard to believe, so great was the terror that Allah had struck into all hearts. It is related, for example, that a single Tatar horseman rode into a densely populated village and began killing the inhabitants one after the other, without anyone trying to defend himself. I have heard that one Tatar, having no weapon on him and wishing to kill someone whom he had taken prisoner, ordered the man to lie down on the ground, then went and fetched a sword and slew the wretch, who had not stirred. Someone told me this story: "I was on the road with seventeen others; we saw a Tatar horseman arrive who told us to tie each other's hands behind our backs. My companions began to obey him, and I said to them: 'This man is alone; we must kill him and run away,' 'We're too frightened,' they answered. I then urged them: 'But this man is going to kill you. Let us kill him! It may be that Allah will save us.' But upon my soul not one of them dared to do it. So I stabbed him to death with my knife, and we fled to safety." [25]

In the Caucasus the Mongols destroyed Ganja and then invaded Georgia and forced Queen Rusudan to flee from Tiflis to Kutaisi (ca. 1236). The Tiflis region was taken under the Mongol protectorate, and the Georgian feudal lords had to serve as auxiliaries in the Mongol wars. In 1239, in Great Armenia, Chormaghan seized and sacked the towns of Ani and Kars, which belonged to the family of the Georgian high constable Ivane.[26]

Despite his acts of war committed in Georgian and Armenian territories, Chormaghan was not hostile in principle to Christianity, for there were Nestorians among his own kinsmen.[27] Moreover, during the period of his command, between 1233 and 1241, when he was in Azerbaijan, the grand khan Ogödäi sent to him the Syriac Christian Simeon, called Rabban-ata, as commissioner for Christian affairs. This man did much to protect the Armenian communities.[28]

Chormaghan was succeeded as leader of the Mongol army in Persia (that is, the army of Mugan and Arran) by the *noyan* Baiju, who was to hold this appointment from 1242 to 1256.[29] Baiju made an important contribution to the Mongol conquest by attacking the Seljuk sultanate of Konya. This great Turkic kingdom of Asia Minor, ruled by the sultan Kai-Khosrau (1237–45), seemed then to be at the height of its power. But Baiju, having taken and plundered Erzurum in 1242, inflicted a crushing defeat on the Seljuk army, commanded by the sultan in person, in Közädagh, near Erzincan (June 26, 1243). After this victory he occupied Sivas, which surrendered promptly and was merely plundered. Tokat and Kayseri, which attempted resistance, were completely sacked. Kai-Khosrau begged for peace and obtained it by acknowledging himself the vassal of the grand khan. This campaign extended the Mongol Empire to the borders of the Greek Empire.[30]

The astute ruler of Armenia (that is, Cilicia), Hethum I (1226–69), was clever enough to place himself voluntarily under Mongol suzerainty in 1244. This policy, followed by all his successors, secured to the Armenians the new lords of Asia as defenders against Seljuk or Mameluke Islam.[31] In 1245, Baiju consolidated Mongol domination in Kurdistan by occupying Khilat and Amid. The Mongols then handed over Khilat to their Georgian vassals of the Ivane clan. The atabeg of Mosul, Badr ad-Din Lulu, who was as prudent a politician as Hethum, acknowledged Mongol suzerainty of his own accord.

BATU'S AND SÜBÖTÄI'S CAMPAIGNS IN EUROPE

At this time, by command of the grand khan Ogödäi, a great Mongol army, 150,000 strong, was active in Europe. It was nominally under the leadership of Batu, khan of the Aral steppes and of the Urals, around whom were grouped the representatives of all the Jenghiz-Khanite branches: Orda, Berke, and Shayban, Batu's brothers; Güyük and Qada'an, his sons; Qaidu, Ogödäi's grandson; Mongka, Tolui's son; Baidar and Büri, son and grandson of Jagatai.[32] The real leader was Sübötäi, the victor of Persia, Russia, and China, who was now about sixty years of age.

According to Muslim sources, the campaign opened in the autumn of 1236 with the destruction of the Turkic realm of the Kama Bulgars. Sübötäi sacked and destroyed their capital, the trading center of Bolgar, situated near the Volga, south of its confluence with the Kama.[33] (Russian sources give the date of these events as the autumn of 1237.)

In the early spring of 1237, the Mongols attacked the pagan, nomad, and half-savage Turks of the Russian steppe, who were called Kipchaks by the Muslims, Cumans by the Hungarians and Byzantines, and Polovtsy by the Russians. Some of the Kipchaks surrendered; it was this element that was later to form the ethnic and geographic basis of the Mongol khanate known to the former lords of the country as the "Kipchak khanate." Known also as the "Golden Horde," the Kipchak khanate belonged to one of the branches of Jöchi's house. A Kipchak chief named Batchman lay in hiding for some time on the banks of the Volga, but was captured at last on an island in the lower part of the river (winter 1236–37).[34] Mongka had him cut in half. According to the evidence of Rashid ad-Din, Berke led a third campaign in 1238 which inflicted final defeat on the Kipchaks. It was then that the Kipchak chief Kutan (mentioned earlier in connection with Jebe's campaign of 1222) emigrated with forty thousand "huts" to Hungary, where he was converted to Christianity. In the winter of 1239–40 (more precisely, around December, 1239), the Mongols completed the subjugation of the steppes of southern Russia by capturing, under Mongka's leadership, the city of Maghas (Mankas or Monkas), which seemed to have been the capital of the Alans or As (Asod in Mongolian).[35]

It was between these two campaigns in the steppes of southern Russia that the expedition against the Russian principalities themselves took place. The territorial fragmentation of these principalities facilitated the task of the Mongols. The two brothers Yurii and Roman, princes of Ryazan, shut themselves up in Ryazan and Kolomna respectively. Ryazan was taken, Yurii was killed, and the entire population was slaughtered (December 21, 1237). The most powerful of the Russian princes, Yurii II, grand duke of Suzdalia, sent reinforcements in vain to the defenders of Kolomna: Roman was defeated and killed before the fortress, and Kolomna in its turn was captured. Moscow, then a secondary town, was sacked (February, 1238). The grand duke Yurii II could not prevent the Mongols from destroying his cities of Suzdal and Vladimir. Suzdal was burnt. Vladimir, taken by assault on February 14, 1238, witnessed scenes of horror; the people were massacred in the churches in which they had taken refuge amid the conflagration. Yurii II himself was defeated and killed in a decisive battle on the Sita or Siti (Syas), a tributary of the Mologa (March 4, 1238). Other Mongol detachments sacked Yaroslavl and Tver. Novgorod in the north was most likely saved only by the thaw.

Operations were resumed at the end of the following year, this time against the southern and western (now mostly Ukrainian) lands of medieval Rus. After sacking Chernigov, the Mongols captured Kiev and destroyed it almost completely (December 6, 1240). They then devastated the Russian principality of Galich or Galicia, and its ruler Daniel took refuge in Hungary.

In the course of these expeditions, dissension had arisen among the Mongol princes. Güyük, one of Ogödäi's sons, and Büri, a grandson of Jagatai, both of whom resented Batu's superior position, were guilty of such insubordination toward him that Ogödäi had to recall them. Büri even had a violent altercation with Batu. Mongka, Tolui's son, also left the army, but remained on good terms with Batu. Batu's disagreement with Güyük and Büri and his friendship with Mongka were to have a considerable effect on subsequent Mongol history.

From what is now the Ukraine, part of the Mongol army, under Baidar and Qaidu, launched an attack on Poland.[36] During the winter of 1240–41 the Mongols crossed the frozen Vistula (February 13, 1241), sacked Sandomierz, and advanced as far as the outskirts of Cracow. They defeated a Polish army at Chmielnik on March 18, 1241, and marched on Cracow, whence the Polish king Boleslav IV fled to Moravia. Finding Cracow deserted by its inhabitants, the Mongols set fire to it. They penetrated Silesia under the command of a prince whom Polish historians call Peta—no doubt Baidar—crossed the Oder (Odra) at Ratibor, and clashed with the Polish duke Henry of Silesia, who commanded an army of 30,000 consisting of Poles, German crusaders, and Teutonic Knights. On April 9 this army was annihilated and the duke killed at Wahlstatt, near Liegnitz (Legnica). After this victory the Mongols went into Moravia and laid waste the country, but were unable to take the town of Olomouc (Olmütz), defended by Yaroslav of Sternberg. From Moravia this corps rejoined the other Mongol armies operating in Hungary.

Indeed, during this time the other Mongol forces, under Batu's command and Sübötäi's direction, had penetrated Hungary in three detachments: one, led by Shayban, came by the north, between Poland and Moravia; the second, under Batu, coming from Galicia, forced the Carpathian defiles between Ungvar (Uzhgorod) and Munkacs (Mukachevo), and on March 12, 1241, routed the count palatine whose task was to defend them; the third, under the command of Qada'an, advanced from Moldavia to Oradea and Csanad, which were then destroyed and the inhabitants massacred with every sort of atrocity. These forces assembled, at least partially, opposite Pest between the 2nd and 5th of April.[37] At Pest, Béla IV, king of Hungary, hastily gathered together his army. When he advanced to meet the enemy on April 7, the Mongols slowly withdrew as far as the confluence of the Sajo and the Tisza. It was there, south of Mohi, upstream from the confluence, that on April 11 Sübötäi won one of his finest victories. Juvaini and Rashid ad-Din describe Batu on the eve of the battle, ascending a height in the manner of Jenghiz Khan, to invoke Tängri—Heaven, the supreme deity of the Mongols—for a day and a night.

The two armies were separated by the River Sajo. During the

night of April 10–11, Sübötäi brought his troops across the river between Girines and Nagy Czeks.[38] On the following morning, he sent forward his wings, which outflanked and encircled the enemy camp as far as Szakald. According to Juvaini, the decisive charge was led by Shayban, Batu's brother. The Hungarians were utterly defeated and were either massacred or put to flight.

The Mongols stormed and burned Pest, while King Béla took refuge on the Adriatic. The population was subjected to unspeakable atrocities, most often followed by mass execution. The *Rogerii carmen miserabile* is full of tragic stories, all alike: the Mongols treacherously encourage the fleeing inhabitants to return to their homes, with the promise of a complete amnesty; having thus reassured them, they cut them down to the last man. At other times they drive their captives before them to storm fortified cities. "They stayed behind these unfortunates, laughing at those who fell, slaying those who retreated." Having compelled the peasants to harvest their crops for them, they killed them as they killed—after violating them—the women of the areas they evacuated, before going on to continue their ravages elsewhere.[39] The entire country as far as the Danube came under their yoke, with the exception of a few citadels like Gran (Strigonium, Esztergom) and Alba-Iulia, which resisted. In July, 1241, Mongol forward troops even reached Neustadt, near Vienna. Batu himself crossed the frozen Danube on December 25, 1241, and went on to capture Gran.

The Mongols remained at rest in the Hungarian *puszta*, which doubtless reminded them of their native steppe, throughout the summer and autumn of 1241. At the beginning of 1242 they did no more than send Prince Qada'an in pursuit of King Béla, who had taken refuge in Croatia. On the approach of the Mongol advance guard, Béla escaped to the Dalmatian archipelago. Qada'an pressed on to Split (Spalato) and Kotor (Cattaro) on the Adriatic, and did not return to Hungary until he had sacked the latter city (March, 1242).

Meanwhile in Mongolia, on December 11, 1241, the grand khan Ogödäi had died. The question of the succession which then arose caused the Mongols to evacuate Hungary. Güyük and Mongka had already returned to Mongolia, and the other army leaders were in haste to do the same. There is no doubt that this saved the West from the gravest danger it had faced since Attila. The Mongols began to withdraw, not, however, without instilling a false sense of security in their prisoners, who were told that they were free to return home, only to be overtaken and cut down. In the spring of 1242, Batu slowly took the route to the Black Sea via Bulgaria, whence, after passing through Wallachia and Moldavia, he arrived in the winter of 1242–43 at his encampments on the lower Volga.

The result of the Mongol campaigns of 1236–42 was to increase considerably Jöchi's domains west of the Volga. This *ulus*, in Jenghiz Khan's will, was to include all territories west of the Irtysh trodden by Mongol horses; and now their hoofmarks had printed the soil from the Irtysh to the lower Dniester, and even to the mouths of the Danube. These huge territories became Batu's, the more legitimately in that he had been at least the nominal chief of the 1236–42 campaign. Thenceforward he was to be known to history by the name of the conquered country, as "Khan of Kipchak."

Törägänä's Regency (1242–46)

At Ogödäi's death on December 11, 1241, the regency was entrusted to his widow, the energetic khatun Törägänä.[40] This princess, whose first husband had been a Märkit [41] and who is said to have been a Märkit herself, though she was more probably a Naiman, held power from 1242 to 1246. Ogödäi had first intended as his successor his third son Kuchu; then, when Kuchu was killed in the war against the Sung (1236), his choice fell upon Kuchu's eldest son, the young Shirämön. But Törägänä wanted her own son Güyük to be grand khan, and prolonged her regency to prepare for his election.

Törägänä's regency was marked by the lapse from favor of a number of Ogödäi's advisers, especially that of the Nestorian Kerayit Chinqai, the chancellor of the deceased emperor,[42] and of the Sinicized Khitan Ye-lü Ch'u-ts'ai, who had been Ogödäi's finance minister, but whom she replaced by the Muslim 'Abd ar-Rahman. 'Abd ar-Rahman promised to double the revenue from taxation. Ye-lü Ch'u-ts'ai, finding his wise counsels scorned and foreseeing the excessive burden that would be laid upon the people, died of grief shortly afterward at Karakorum, aged only fifty-five (June, 1244). Törägänä dismissed two other great ad-

ministrators: one, the Muslim Mas'ud Yalavach, governor of
Turkestan and Transoxiana, she got rid of temporarily; the other,
Körgüz the Uigur, governor of eastern Persia, she put to death
and replaced by the Oirat Arghun Agha.

The regent's power, although protected by old Jagatai, was
based on shaky foundations.[43] Shortly after the beginning of her
rule, Jenghiz Khan's youngest brother Temuge Ochigin, whose
appanage extended, as we saw, from eastern Mongolia to the
Kirin region, advanced with his troops upon the imperial *ordu*
with somewhat dubious intent. Güyük's return from Europe to
his own *ulus* of the Imil caused these evil designs to evaporate.
More serious was the hostility of Batu, khan of Kipchak and the
personal enemy of Güyük, toward whom he felt bitter resentment because of Güyük's disobedience during the Russian campaign, for which he had had to be recalled. Batu therefore did all
he could to delay the *quriltai* at which Törägänä hoped to have
Güyük elected. When the assembly was at last called, he feigned
illness to avoid attending it.[44]

Güyük's Reign (1246–48)

The *quriltai* was held in the spring and summer of 1246 near the
little Koko Nor and the sources of the Orkhon, not far from
Karakorum. Here sprang up the great tent city of the *sira-ordo*,
the Yellow (Golden) Residence, at which all the Jenghiz-Khanite
princes—with the exception of Batu—made haste to appear, together with many provincial governors and vassal kings. Among
the dignitaries present were Mas'ud Yalavach, once more administrator of Turkestan and Transoxiana; Arghun Agha, administrator of Persia; the two Georgian pretenders David Narin and
David Lasha; the Russian grand duke Yaroslav; Sempad the high
constable, brother of Hethum I, king of Armenia (Cilicia); [45] the
Seljuk Qilich Arslan IV, afterward (1249) sultan of Asia Minor;
envoys from the atabegs of Kerman; and even an embassy from
the caliph of Baghdad. In compliance with the wishes of the
queen regent Törägänä, the *quriltai* elected as grand khan her
son by Ogödäi, prince Güyük, who was enthroned on August 24,
1246.[46] The new grand khan accepted power only on condition
that the empire should remain hereditary in his line. "Then the
Mongol princes removed their caps, unbuckled their belts, caused

Güyük to be seated on a golden throne, and saluted him with the title of *qaan*. The members of the assembly did homage to the new monarch by nine prostrations, while the multitude gathered in the plain—vassal princes and foreign ambassadors, who remained respectfully outside the precincts of the imperial pavilion —prostrated themselves likewise, their faces to the ground." [47]

The *quriltai* of 1246 is known through the account written by the Franciscan friar Piano Carpini; he had been sent to the Mongols by Pope Innocent IV as the bearer of pontifical letters entreating them to attack other nations no longer and to become Christians. Starting from Lyons on April 16, 1245, he journeyed across Germany, Poland, and Russia. (He left Kiev on February 3, 1246.) On April 4, 1246, he was received on the lower Volga by Batu the khan of Kipchak. Batu sent him on to the grand khan by way of the old Kara-Khitai country, south of Lake Balkhash— the usual route was by Otrar, the lower Ili, and the Imil—and through the former Naiman country. On July 22, 1246, Piano Carpini arrived at the imperial camp (*sira-ordo*), half a day's journey from Karakorum, where the *quriltai* was in session. He witnessed the election of Güyük, of whom he has left this vivid portrait: "At the time of his election, he was forty or forty-five years old at the most. He was of middle height, very wise, astute, serious, and most grave in his air and manner. He was hardly ever seen to laugh or make merry." In religion, Güyük favored Nestorianism. Piano Carpini bears witness that the Nestorians celebrated mass before Güyük's tent. His chief ministers, his tutor Qadaq and the Kerayit chancellor Chinqai, were themselves Nestorians.[48] Another of his counselors was the "Syrian rabban," Rabban-ata (in Chinese: Li-pien-a-ta), "who was in charge of affairs relating to his religion." [49] It was by the mediation of Chinqai and Qadaq that Piano Carpini expounded the purpose of his visit to the Mongol court. However, Güyük's reply to the pontifical message—recently discovered by Pelliot in the Vatican archives—was hardly encouraging to Christianity. In it, in a threatening tone, the Mongol sovereign invites the Pope and the Christian princes, before making any attempt to preach the Gospel, to come and pay him homage at his very dwelling. Güyük claims to hold his power by divine right, and speaks in the name of Eternal Heaven (*Mängü Tängri* in Turkic, *Mongka Tängri* in

Mongolian) as supreme representative of the deity and arbiter of the various cults.[50]

Piano Carpini, having received Güyük's reply, left the tent city of the *sira-ordo* on November 13 and made the return journey via the lower Volga and Batu's residence, which he reached on May 9, 1247. From there he re-entered the West by way of Kiev.

Sempad, the Armenian high constable, envoy to Güyük on this same occasion for his brother Hethum I of Armenia (Sempad's journey lasted from 1247 to 1250), seems to have understood better than Piano Carpini the advantages to be gained for Christendom by a Mongol alliance. Güyük received him cordially and handed him a document assuring King Hethum of his protection and friendship. A letter written by Sempad, while on his return trip, to his brother-in-law, King Henry I of Cyprus, has come down to us. In this letter, dated Samarkand, February 7, 1848, he stresses the importance of the Nestorian factor in the Mongol empire and court. "The Christians of the East," he writes, "have placed themselves under the protection of the khan, who has received them with much honor, granted them immunity, and publicly forbidden anyone to molest them." [51]

The impression of sternness that Güyük made upon Piano Carpini is confirmed by Rashid ad-Din. Energetic, masterful, very jealous of his power, and believing that during the reign of the good-natured Ogödäi and of his own mother's regency the sinews of the state had slackened, he had resolved to restore the power relationship between grand khan and princes to what it had been under Jenghiz Khan. He made an inquiry into the somewhat suspect attitude of his great-uncle Temuge Ochigin, who had planned to attack the regent, and punished his entourage. Jagatai, khan of the Ili, on his death in 1242, had chosen as his heir his grandson Qara-Hulägu (son of Mütügen, who had been killed in 1221 at the siege of Bamian). Güyük, intervening as overlord in the affairs of this *ulus,* replaced the young man by a younger son of Jagatai and personal friend, Yissu-Mangu (1247). To Persia he sent a trusted man, Eljigidäi, a sort of high commissioner who, from 1247 to 1251, held a parallel or superior appointment to that of general Baiju, commander of the Mongol army in Mugan.[52] In the Far East, 'Abd ar-Rahman, financial administrator of the conquered Chinese provinces, was put to death for embezzlement and replaced by Mahmud Yalavach. Chinqai, the Nestorian Kerayit, was reappointed chancellor of the empire, a position he held when Piano Carpini met him. Among his tributary peoples Güyük divided Georgia between two rival pretenders: David Lasha, who was given Kartlia, and David Narin, son of Queen Rusudan, who kept only Imeretia. In the Seljuk sultanate of Asia Minor (Konya), Güyük gave the throne to Qilich Arslan IV, in preference to his elder brother Kai-Kawus II, who had reigned up to that time.[53]

In his determination to stamp out the growing autonomy which had begun to be enjoyed by the other Jenghiz-Khanite branches, Güyük clashed with Batu, the chief of the Jöchids, that is, the senior branch. At the beginning of 1248, relations between them were so strained that both began to prepare for war. Under the pretext of visiting his hereditary domain of the Imil, Güyük marched westward out of Karakorum. Meanwhile, Batu had been secretly warned by Princess Sorghaqtani, the directing spirit of Tolui's house, and had advanced to Semirechye. He got as far as Alaqmaq, seven days' journey short of Qayaligh (near the present town of Kapal); Barthold interprets this to mean that he reached the Ala-Tau, between Lake Issyk Kul and the Ili River. The clash appeared inevitable, until Güyük, prematurely worn out by drink and debauchery, died within a day's march of Beshbaligh. Barthold believes this may have occurred in the Urungu region; Pelliot says it was northeast of Beshbaligh (the Dzimsa of today).[54] Chinese sources place the date of Güyük's death between March 27 and April 24, 1248.[55] He was then only forty-three.

It may be that this death saved Europe from a formidable peril. Güyük dreamed not only of defeating the khan of Kipchak but also—on Piano Carpini's evidence—of subjugating Christendom. In any case, he seems to have turned his attention particularly to the West. The accession, however, of the princes of the Tolui house—first Mongka and then above all Kublai—was to direct the main Mongol effort toward the Far East.

REGENCY OF OGHUL QAIMISH

On Güyük's death his widow Oghul Qaimish, believed by d'Ohsson to have been of Oirat birth, though Pelliot amends this to Märkit, assumed the regency in the normal way.[56] In 1250, in the

Imil and Qobaq sector of the Tarbagatai or patrimonial lands of the house of Ogödäi, she received the envoys of Louis IX of France: the three Dominicans André de Longjumeau, his brother Guy or Guillaume, and Jean de Carcassonne. They arrived by way of Persia (Tabriz) and the Talas. She accepted as tribute the presents they brought her from the king of France and demanded that he should make more explicit submission to her. This embassy would not rejoin King Louis in Caesarea until April, 1251, at the earliest.

Oghul Qaimish would have liked the throne to pass to a prince of the line of Ogödäi, either to Shirämön,[57] Güyük's nephew, or even better (but he was too young) to her own son by Güyük, Qucha.[58] But as head of the Jenghiz-Khanite family, Batu played the chief part in such affairs, and he was determined to set the Ogödäi line aside. More precisely, he joined forces with Soyurghaqtani or Sorghaqtani, Tolui's widow. This princess, who was a Kerayit (the niece of the *Wang-khan* Togrul) and therefore of the Nestorian faith, was as intelligent as she was shrewd.[59] Earlier, when Güyük had prosecuted a stern inquiry into certain abuses of power of which a number of Jenghiz-Khanite princes had been guilty, to the detriment of the state, it had been established that thanks to her the conduct of the house of Tolui had always been beyond reproach.[60] Now it seemed to her that her own family's turn had come. She was able to persuade Batu to nominate as grand khan the eldest of her sons by Tolui, Prince Mongka.[61] It was therefore Mongka whom Batu chose and imposed upon a *quriltai* summoned for that purpose at his Alaqmaq camp, north of the Issyk Kul, apparently in 1250. The only representatives to vote for Mongka, however, had been the delegates of the Jöchi and Tolui families. As Barthold has shown, the representatives of the houses of Ogödäi and Jagatai either had not attended the assembly or had left Alaqmaq before the matter was settled. When they learned of Mongka's nomination, they flatly refused to ratify it, on the grounds that the gathering had been held to far away from the sacred places of the Jenghiz-Khanites, and that in any case it had been inadequately attended. Batu therefore decided to call another, fuller *quriltai* in the venerated holy region of the Onon, or of the Kerulen. He invited members of the Ogödäi and Jagatai families to attend, but of course his invitation was refused.

Ignoring this opposition, Batu charged his brother Berke with the reunion of a *quriltai* at Ködä'ä-aral, or Kötö'ü-aral,[62] on the Kerulen. Despite the protests of the house of Ogödäi, whose members refused to ratify their own eviction, and of their supporter Yissu-Mangu, chief of the Jagatai *ulus*, Berke proclaimed Mongka grand khan (on July 1, 1251, according to Juvaini). The imperial authority thus passed definitively from the house of Ogödäi to that of Tolui.[63]

The relative ease with which this *coup d'état* was brought off is accounted for by the fact that compared with Mongka, the very model of the strong man, the legitimate Ogödäi princes were both young and undistinguished. Moreover Batu, as dean of the Jenghiz-Khanite family and head of the senior branch, was in a position during an interregnum to wield a sort of dictatorship. Nevertheless, the relegation of the Ogödäi house in favor of Tolui's was a violation of legitimacy which the principal victims could not accept without some attempt at opposition. The ousted Ogödäi princes, most prominent among them Shirämön, arrived toward the conclusion of the *quriltai* as if to render homage to the new grand khan, but in reality, it appears, to take him by surprise and depose him. But their plans were discovered. Their escort was disarmed, their counselors—among them, Qadaq and Chinqai —were executed,[64] and they themselves were placed under arrest.

Mongka punished these unhappy cousins severely. The former regent Oghul Qaimish, whom he hated (she was "more contemptible than a bitch," he told Rubruck), was stripped of her clothes for questioning and then sewn up in a sack and drowned (May–July, 1252). Kublai, Mongka's younger brother, temporarily saved Shirämön by taking him away to the army in China, but later he was unable to prevent Mongka from having the wretched young man drowned. Güyük's young son Qucha was banished to an area west of Karakorum. Qada'an, who had submitted of his own accord, was spared (most likely it was a namesake of his who carried out Mongka's revenge on Güyük's high commissioner to Persia, Eljigidäi), as was Qaidu. Both therefore retained the Imil *ulus*. Later Qaidu was to raise the standard of Ogödäi legitimacy and give a great deal of trouble to Mongka's successor. Finally, Mongka put to death the chief of the Jagatai *ulus*, Yissu-Mangu, who had sided against him, and replaced him by another prince of the same line, Qara-Hulägu, and afterward by the latter's widow, Princess Orghana (1252). Büri, another of Jagatai's grandsons, was handed over to Batu, who put him to death for some offense committed against him at the time of the European campaign.[65]

MONGKA'S REIGN (1251–59)

After Jenghiz Khan, Mongka, who began his reign at forty-three, was the most notable of the Mongol grand khans. Taciturn, an enemy to luxury and debauch, with hunting as his only recreation, he restored to the *yasaq* and to the precepts of his ancestor their original stringency. He was an energetic leader and a stern but just administrator (he honored to the last fraction the huge bills signed by his predecessors and never paid),[66] a hardheaded but intelligent politician, and a good soldier. As such, he entirely restored the strong and effective machine set up by Jenghiz Khan. Without in any way renouncing his racial character (as his successor Kublai was to do), he strengthened the administrative structure and made of the Mongol Empire a great and regular state. At the beginning of his reign, his obligations toward Batu (who had literally made him emperor) resulted *de facto* if not *de jure* in a sort of division of power, as Barthold has noted, by which Batu was practically independent west of Lake Balkhash.[67] But Batu's death (in 1255 at the latest) once more left Mongka the sole effective lord of the Mongol world. The various chiefs of *ulus* or of Jenghiz-Khanite appanages considered themselves authorized to grant tax exemptions and to share the revenues of the country with the agents of the central power. Mongka forbade these practices. It is clear that, if he had lived longer and if his successors had continued his policy, the Mongol Empire, instead of splitting up into khanates of the Far East, Turkestan, Persia, and Russia, would have remained a relatively united realm.

Mongka, who had been brought up by a Nestorian mother, the Kerayit princess Sorghaqtani, favored the Nestorian faith. He chose a Nestorian, the Kerayit Bolghai,[68] as his chancellor. But he was also favorably disposed toward Buddhism and Taoism. In 1251–52 he appointed to his immediate entourage a leader of the Taoist religion and a Buddhist "master of the kingdom." The former was the monk Li Chih-ch'ang, the latter a lama "from the western lands" named Na-mo.[69] At first, Li Chih-ch'ang was especially favored by the sovereign. In 1255, Mongka attended a debate at Karakorum between the Buddhist monk Na-mo and some Taoists.[70] In 1256 a sort of Buddhist council sat at his court in Karakorum. "All religions," he told Rubruck, "are like the five fingers of one hand." But to the Buddhists he said that Buddhism was the palm of the hand, of which other religions were the fingers. Indeed, it seems as if, having kept the balance level between Buddhists and Taoists, Mongka in the end inclined slightly in favor of the former, especially after the convocation of 1255 at which the Taoists were convicted of having spread apocryphal stories misrepresenting Buddhist origins. In the main the Mongol ruler made use of all cults for his political ends. It was for this reason that he gave to the Buddhists as their chief the bonze K'ai Yüan, and to the Taoists a man equally devoted to Mongol interests.

RUBRUCK'S JOURNEY

During Mongka's reign, Louis IX of France (Saint Louis) sent the Franciscan William of Rubruck (near Cassel) on a mission to the Mongols.[71] Rubruck left Constantinople on May 7, 1253,[72] and crossed the Black Sea to the Italian countinghouses of the Crimea, arriving at Sudak on May 21. Upon penetrating beyond the Crimea into the Russian steppe—that is, into the khanate of Kipchak—Rubruck felt that he had entered another world, the nomad world. Since the wholesale massacres of the old Kipchak Turks, it was even more a desolate world, a grassy desert on whose horizon Mongol cavalry patrols would brusquely sweep into view. "And when I found myself among the Tatars, it seemed to me truly that I had been carried into another time, another world." Rubruck's description of the Mongol hordes remains a classic: "They have no permanent abode, for they have divided amongst themselves the whole of Scythia, which stretches from the Danube to the Far East; and each captain, according to the number of men under his command, knows the limits of his pasture land and where he must abide at one season or another. At the approach of winter they go down to the warmer countries of the south; in summer they return toward the north." Rubruck goes on to describe the Mongol felt tents mounted on wagons and often gathered into mobile villages. As for the Mongols themselves, no one has portrayed them better than the Franciscan: "The men shave a little square on the top of their heads, and what is left of their hair they braid into plaits which hang down each side as far as their ears." Enveloped in furs during the winter, in summer they array themselves in silks from China. Lastly, he mentions their tremendous drinking bouts of kumiss—fermented mare's milk—and wine.[73]

On July 31 Rubruck arrived at the camp of Sartaq, Batu's son, three days' march short of the lower Volga. Although the Franciscan did not realize it, Sartaq was a Nestorian and Rubruck was introduced to him by "a certain Nestorian Christian named Coyat, who is one of the principal men at this court."[74] And although it may be untrue that Rubruck discovered a Knight Templar at court, Sartaq was rather well-informed on the affairs of the West. To Rubruck, who told him that the emperor was the most powerful sovereign of Christendom, he replied that the hegemony had now passed to King Louis. After leaving Sartaq's encampment and crossing the Volga, Rubruck was received in Batu's *ordu,* which was situated on the east bank of that river. "Batu was seated on a high gilt chair or throne the size of a bed, approached by three steps; near him was one of his wives. The other men were seated to the right or left of this lady." Batu in his turn sent Rubruck on to the court of Mongka, the grand khan. The Franciscan crossed the Yaik or Ural River and set foot on the Asiatic steppe, "this vast solitude which resembles a great sea." He continued along the Chu, passed within six days of Talas, crossed the Ili, and went north of it by way of the town of "Equius," inhabited by Persian-speaking Tadzhiks, who, according to Barthold's ingenious suggestion, might have been identical with the Iki-ögüz of Kashgaria.[75] Rubruck then passed via "Cailac" (Qayaligh, near present-day Kapal), where flourished an important Nestorian center as well as an Uigur Buddhist one, in whose midst he listened to the recital of *Om mani padme hum.*[76] Rubruck tells us that it was from the Uigur that "the Tatars [Mongols] have taken their letters and their alphabet, and the letters that the khan Mango [Mongka] sends your Majesty [Louis IX] are written in the Mongol language but in Uigur characters."

On November 30, 1253, Rubruck left Qayaligh and, having rounded the eastern point of Lake Balkhash, crossed the Imil

Liegnitz• •Breslau
•Olmütz• •Ratibor
POLAND
•Novgorod
•Cracow• •Szydlow
•Buda• •Pest
HUNGARY
RUSSIAN
PRINCIPALITIES
•Tver •Suzdal
Moscow• •Vladimir
•Kolomna
•Galich •Chernigov •Ryazah
SERBIA
•Kiev
BULGARIA
Danube
ULUS
Dnieper
Don
of
Volga
Ural
BATU
•Bolgar

GREEK
EMPIRE
LATIN
EMPIRE
Soldaia•
Black Sea
Constantinople•
Tana
Kuban
MONGOL
VENETIANS
•Ankara
GREEKS
ALANS
Caspian
ULUS of ORDA
Aral
Sea
Syr Darya
Chu
SELJUK
SULTANATE
Trebizond•
•Kutais
•Tiflis
•Lori •Ani
KHWARIZM
Otrar•
•Talas
Uzg
•Konya
Sivas
•Erzincan
Kars
•Ganja
Derbent•
ULUS of JAGATAI
•Chinaz
•Samarkand
ARMENIA
•Sis
•Antioch
•Amid
Shamakha•
•Tabriz
Sea
•Bukhara •Kesh •Khodzhen
KINGDOM of CYPRUS
FRANKS
•Aleppo
•Tripoli
•Mosul •Arbela
•Daqouqa
AZERBAIJAN
•Zenjan •Alamut
•Merv
•Balkh
•Tyre
•Acre
•Kazvin •Rai
•Isfarain •Tus •Sarakhs
•Bamian
Cairo•
•Jerusalem
AYYUBID SULTANATE
•Baghdad
•Hamadan •Damghan •Nishapur
•Kabul
KHUZISTAN
•Qum
Kashan•
IRAQ 'AJAMI
•Herat
KHURASAN
•Ghazni
•Ispahan •Yezd
•Kandahar
•Shushtar
FARS
•Shiraz •Kerman
SEISTAN
Indus

 o   450   900
Approximate   Mileage

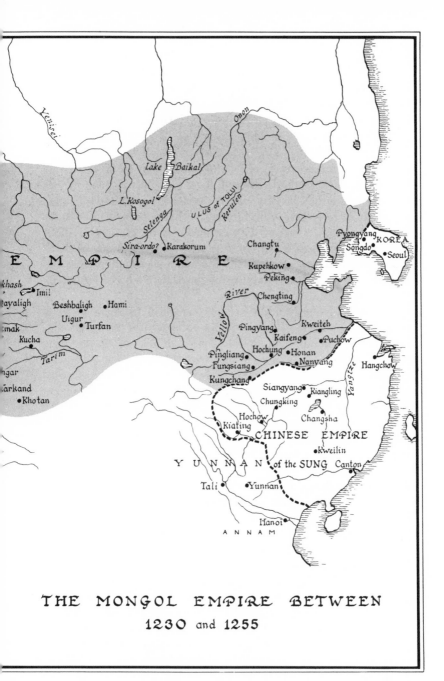

THE MONGOL EMPIRE BETWEEN
1230 and 1255

or Tarbagatai region, a fief of the Ogödäi family at the fringe
of the old Naiman country among the southern foothills of the
Altai. At last, he reached the *ordu* of Mongka, who gave him
audience on January 4, 1254. "We were led into the palace, and
when the felt before the doorway was raised we entered, chanting
the hymn *A solis ortu*. This place was all hung with cloth of
gold. In the middle stood a brazier in which burned a fire of
thorns, wormwood roots, and cattle dung. The grand khan was
seated on a little bed, dressed in a rich furred robe which
glistened like the skin of a seal. He was a man of middle height,
aged about forty-five, with a somewhat flattened nose. The khan
ordered us to be served with *cerasine*, made of rice, as clear
and sweet as white wine. He then sent for many kinds of birds
of prey, which he set upon his fist and viewed attentively for
some time. After that he ordered us to speak. He had a Nestorian
as his interpreter."

At Mongka's *ordu* Rubruck was surprised to come upon a
woman from Lorraine called Paquette, who had been brought
from Hungary and was in the service of one of the prince's
Nestorian wives; she herself had married a Russian who was
employed as architect. At the Karakorum court Rubruck also
found a Parisian goldsmith named Guillaume Boucher, "whose
brother dwelt on the Grand Pont, in Paris." This man was employed first by the dowager Sorghaqtani and then by Mongka's
youngest brother Ariq-böga, who was also sympathetic toward
Christianity. Rubruck found that at the great court festivals the
Nestorian priests were admitted first, with their regalia, to bless
the grand khan's cup, and were followed by the Muslim clergy
and "pagan" monks, that is, Buddhists and Taoists. Mongka
himself sometimes accompanied his Nestorian wife to the services
of this church. "He came, and a gilded bed was brought for him,
upon which he sat with the queen his wife, opposite the altar." [77]

Rubruck had followed the court to Karakorum, where he
arrived on April 5, 1254. Guillaume Boucher, who was exceedingly well-treated as court goldsmith, received him "with great
joy. His wife was the daughter of a Saracen and had been born
in Hungary. She spoke good French and Cumanian. We found
there also a man named Basil, the son of an Englishman, likewise
born in Hungary and speaking the same languages."

At the festival of Easter, 1254, Rubruck was allowed to cele-

brate mass in the Nestorian church of Karakorum, where
"Guillaume the goldsmith had caused an image of the Virgin
to be made, in sculpture, after the fashion of France." Besides
the Nestorian church, Karakorum had two mosques and twelve
pagodas or other temples of "idolaters." Rubruck had occasion
to receive Ariq-bögä at divine service; he was one of the imperial princes most favorably disposed toward Christianity, "and
he extended his hand to us, making the sign of the cross in the
manner of our bishops." One day, when controversy arose in
front of Rubruck between Muslims and Christians, Ariq-bögä
sided openly with the latter. In Karakorum, on May 30, 1254,
the eve of Pentecost, in the presence of three arbiters appointed
by Mongka, Rubruck held a great religious debate in public.
In the course of this, taking his stand on theism, he sided with
the Muslim doctors against the Buddhist philosophers.[78]

Rubruck left Karakorum on August 18, 1254, bearing Mongka's
reply to Louis IX: "This is the commandment of Eternal Heaven.
There is but one God in heaven, and on earth one sovereign:
Jenghiz Khan, son of God." And in the name of Eternal Heaven
and of the *qaan*, his earthly representative, Mongka commanded
the king of France to acknowledge himself vassal.[79] Carrying
this letter, Rubruck made the journey from Karakorum to the
Volga in two months and six days. His path crossed that of
Hethum I of Armenia, who was on his way to pay court to the
grand khan. In September he reached the *ordu* of Batu, who at
that time seems to have been at his new residence of Sarai.
Thence, by the Alan country and the Derbent pass, Rubruck
came to the Mugan plain, where he was received by the *noyan*
Baiju, commander of the Mongol army in Persia, while his
interpreter went to Tabriz to visit Arghun Agha, civil administrator of Persia. Then, by way of Nakhichevan, where he celebrated Christmas, Erzincan, Kayseri, and Konya in the Seljuk
sultanate, he arrived at Little Armenia (Cilicia) and embarked
at Lajazzo (Latakia?) for the kingdom of Cyprus.

The king of Armenia (that is, of Armenianized Cilicia),
Hethum I, whom Rubruck had passed on his journey, showed
himself to be the better diplomat.[80] Rubruck had lived in terror
of provoking Mongol intervention, whereas the astute Armenian
did all he could to obtain it, so as to strengthen the Christian
world against Islam. With this object he went first to Kars, where

Baiju, commander of the Mongol army in Persia, was at that time encamped (1253). From there, via Derbent, he came to Batu's camp on the lower Volga, and then to Mongka's *ordu* near Karakorum. He was received in audience by this ruler, "enthroned in the splendor of his glory," on September 13, 1254.

Mongka gave a warm welcome to this faithful vassal and handed him a *yarligh* or diploma of investiture and protection,[81] "a diploma," says the Armenian chronicle of Kirakos, "bearing his seal and explicitly forbidding any action against the person or states of Hethum. He also gave him a charter enfranchizing churches everywhere." Another Armenian historian, the monk "Hayton," in his *Flor des estoires d'Orient*, states in addition that Mongka gave his visitor an assurance that a great Mongol army under his brother, Hulägu khan, would attack Baghdad; destroy the caliphate, their "mortal enemy"; and restore the Holy Land to the Christians.[82] This promise was to be at least partially fulfilled. Full of confidence, Hethum left the Mongol court on November 1 and, traveling by the usual route—Beshbaligh (Dzimsa), Almalik (near Kuldja), the Amu Darya, and Persia—arrived back in Cilicia in July, 1255.[83]

MONGKA'S WAR AGAINST THE SUNG EMPIRE

Mongka gave fresh impulse to the Mongol conquests, which had come almost to a standstill since the death of Ogödäi. First, in a *quriltai* held in 1253 at the source of the Onon, he decided that his younger brother Hulägu should complete the conquest of Persia by subjugating the caliphate of Baghdad and Mesopotamia, and then go on to conquer Syria. Second, Mongka himself, with his other brother Kublai,[84] renewed the offensive against the Chinese empire of the Sung.

Notwithstanding the flabbiness of the court of Hangchow, the incompetence of the ministers, and the personal feebleness of the Sung princes, the Chinese met the invading Mongols with unexpected resistance. A gallant Chinese general, Meng Kung (d. 1246), had recaptured from the Mongols in 1239 the important town of Siangyang, which commanded the middle reaches of the Han and had long struggled with them for possession of central Szechwan, where Chengtu, twice sacked by them, did not fall permanently into their hands until 1241.[85]

In the vast human beehive of southern China, checkered by many rivers and mountain ranges, and with many thickly populated urban areas, the only possible war was a war of siege, in which the horsemen from the steppe found themselves somewhat at a loss. The conquest of northern China had been achieved by other Turko-Mongol hordes before the Jenghiz-Khanites: the Hsiung-nu and Hsien-pi in the fourth century, the Toba in the fifth, the Khitan in the tenth, and the Kin in the twelfth. But in their attempts upon southern China, all, from the Toba to the Kin, had failed. To succeed there, Chinese warfare was necessary, with large contingents of Chinese infantry and a whole "artillery" apparatus of siege engines served by Chinese or Muslim engineers.

Mongka concentrated all his attention on Chinese affairs, so as to co-ordinate the hitherto somewhat scattered efforts of the Mongol armies. His younger brother Kublai, whom he made responsible for this task, took the problem even more to heart, being personally drawn toward Chinese civilization and, it seems, having already made up his mind to seek his fortune in that quarter. In 1251, Mongka had entrusted him with the government of the conquered parts of China and had then given him Honan as his appanage. This was a zone of administration far exceeding in area the modern province of that name, since it comprised all that lay between the old course of the Yellow River and the Yangtze, and extended westward as far as 110 degrees east.[86] In addition, Mongka gave him the Kungchang (Lungsi) district on the upper Wei in present-day Kansu. For the discharge of his duties, Kublai availed himself of the advice of the Chinese scholar Yao Chu, who in Kublai's youth had taught him the rudiments of Chinese letters. In Honan he strove to revive agriculture, which had been ruined by war, by distributing seed and tools to the peasants and turning even the soldiers into cultivators.

Before making a frontal attack on the Sung empire on the lower Yangtze, Kublai outflanked the enemy by Mongka's order. With Uriangqatai,[87] son of the great Sübötäi, he left Shensi about October, 1252, crossed Szechwan, and entered Yunnan. This latter country, then alien to China, had since the eighth century constituted a separate realm, the kingdom of Nanchow or Tali, which was a non-Chinese state inhabited by Lo-Los or

Thais, and which had always been able to preserve complete independence within its complex of mountains. Kublai seized Tali, the enemy capital, and Shanshan (Yunnanfu or perhaps Pingtinghsiang?), where the king of Tali, called by the Chinese Tuan Hing-chih, had taken refuge (1253).[88] He allowed this ruler to retain his throne like a maharaja, but placed at his side a "Mongol" administrator, the naturalized Chinese Lü Shih-chung. Although the old dynasty was maintained, all Yunnan was divided into Mongol commanderies.[89] Next Uriangqatai attacked the Tibetans and forced them—or those at least of the neighborhood—to recognize Mongol suzerainty

At the end of 1257, Uriyangqatai attacked the kingdom of Annam (capital Hanoi). From Yunnan he came down into the Tonkin plain and plundered Hanoi (December, 1257), after which Tran Thaitong, the king of Annam, found it wise to acknowledge himself vassal (March, 1258).

In September, 1258, at a *quriltai* held in Mongolia, Mongka decided to take over the leadership of the war against the Sung empire. In October he passed from Shensi to Szechwan with the main Mongol army and took Paoning around December, 1258, but despite all his efforts he was unable to capture Hochow, the Hochwan of today—a place of some importance, owing to its situation at the confluence of the Kialing and its two tributaries. He died near that city of dysentery contracted during the siege on August 11, 1259.

At the time of Mongka's death, his brother Kublai, having come down from Hopei with another Mongol army, was laying siege to Wuchow, modern Wuchang, on the middle Yangtze opposite Hankow in Hupeh province. At the same moment Uriyangqatai (who had returned to Yunnan from Tonkin at the end of 1257) left Yunnan for Kwangsi, where he attacked Kweilin, and then went on to Hunan to besiege Changsha.[90] Thus the Sung empire found itself beset simultaneously in the north, west, and south when Mongka's death allowed it a momentary respite. Indeed, Kublai in his desire to have his hands free for the Jenghiz-Khanite succession, hastened to make peace, or truce, with the Sung minister Chia Ssu-tao—the Yangtze serving as common frontier to the two empires—and returned with his army to Hopei.

7

Kublai and the Mongol Dynasty of China

RIVALRY BETWEEN KUBLAI AND ARIQ-BÖGÄ

Mongka left three brothers: Kublai, Hulägu, and Ariq-bögä.[1] Hulägu, who since 1256 had been khan of Persia, was too far away to press his claim to the succession. Kublai and Ariq-bögä remained. Ariq-bögä, as the youngest, had been governor of the native land and resident in Karakorum, the Mongol capital. As ruler of Mongolia, he made ready to summon a *quriltai* in that country and so secure his election as grand khan. But Kublai forestalled him. Bringing his army northward from Wuchang, he set up his headquarters on the borders of China and Mongolia, at Shangtuho, where only somewhat earlier he had established his summer residence (near the present-day Dolonnor, between Chahar and Jehol). There on June 4, 1260, he was proclaimed grand khan by his partisans, that is, his army.[2] He was then forty-four years old.[3]

According to Jenghiz-Khanite law, this precipitate election was irregular. Traditionally, the *quriltai* should have been held in Mongolia, in the presence of the representatives of the four Jenghiz-Khanite *ulus* properly summoned in advance. At Karakorum, Ariq-bögä also had now no hesitation in assuming the title of grand khan, encouraged in this enterprise by the Kerayit Nestorian Bolghai, who had been Mongka's chief minister. In China itself, the Mongol generals commanding in Shensi and Szechwan were inclined to side with him, but Kublai was soon

285

able to rally the troops of those two provinces to himself. A victory won by Kublai's lieutenants over those of Ariq-bögä east of Kanchow (in Kansu province) confirmed him in the possession of Mongol China. Pressing home his advantage, Kublai wintered at the end of 1260 on the River Ongkin, south of Karakorum, while Ariq-bögä withdrew to the upper Yenisei. Kublai then made the mistake of assuming the war to be over and returned to China, leaving an ordinary garrison in Karakorum. At the end of 1261, Ariq-bögä came back, drove out the garrison, and advanced to meet his rival. Two battles were fought on the fringe of the Gobi. The first was won by Kublai, who, however, repeated his mistake of not pursuing Ariq-bögä; the second, ten days later, though fiercely fought, was indecisive.

Ariq-bögä had on his side Prince Qaidu, chief of the house of Ogödäi and ruler of the Imil in Tarbagatai, and Alghu or Alughu, a Jagatai prince whom he had helped in the capture of the *ulus* of Jagatai from his female cousin Orghana. Thanks to this support, Ariq-bögä's forces matched those of his adversary until toward the end of 1262, when Alghu deserted Ariq-bögä for Kublai (see below, page 331). This unexpected defection altered the situation. While Kublai reoccupied Karakorum, having driven out Ariq-bögä's men, the latter chief was forced to contend with Alghu on the Ili. Caught between the two foes, Ariq-bögä finally surrendered to Kublai in 1264. Kublai pardoned him, but executed some of his chief supporters, including the Nestorian minister of state Bolghai.[4] As a precaution, he kept Ariq-bögä a virtual captive until his death in 1266.

CONQUEST OF THE SUNG EMPIRE

Having put an end to the family rivalries, Kublai was free to renew his attempt upon the Sung empire. The Sung emperor Tu-tsung (1265–74) relied on a baleful minister, Chia Ssu-tao, who rendered ineffective the efforts of his ablest commanders. At Tu-tsung's death, Chia Ssu-tao arranged for the succession to go to a four-year-old child, Kung-ti (1275–76), and ruled in his name. In the war against Sung China, Kublai was fortunate in being served by two remarkable officers: Bayan [5] and A-chu (the latter being the son of Uriyangqatai and grandson of Sübötäi), supported by the Uigur Ariq-qaya. In 1268, A-chu undertook the siege of the twin cities Siangyang and Fancheng, which commanded the lower Han basin in Hupeh. This famous siege lasted five years (1268–73) and was the scene of many heroic episodes, such as the attempt to bring in supplies to Siangyang by water, a task entrusted to two gallant Chinese captains, Chan Kue and Chang Shuen, who lost their lives in so doing (1271). Lü Wen-huang, the defender of Siangyang, made stubborn resistance notwithstanding. Ariq-qaya then (1272) brought in from Mesopotamia two renowned Muslim engineers, 'Ala ad-Din of Mosul and Isma'il of Hilla, with siege engines which at last crushed the resistance of the beleaguered inhabitants.[6] Fancheng was taken in February, 1273, and in March, annoyed by the intrigues of the Sung court, Lü Wen-huang surrendered Siangyang.

Being now in control of the lower course of the Han River, Bayan and A-chu moved down the Yangtze and in 1275 succeeded in subjugating the strongholds of eastern Hupeh (Hanyang, Wuchang, and Hwangchow), of Anhwei (Anking, Chichow, Wuhu, Taiping, and Ningkwo), and of Kiangsu (Nanking and Chinkiang).[7]

Bayan next invaded Chekiang, took Changchow, and reached the Sung capital, the great city of Hangchow. The empress regent, daunted, handed it over in January–February, 1276. On February 25, 1276, Bayan sent the little emperor to Kublai, who treated him kindly.[8] From this may be judged the progress made by the Mongols since the days of Jenghiz Khan: in two generations the half-savages of the Onon had raised themselves to the level of the ancient civilized races.

The south, where the Chinese resisted to the end, still remained to be subjugated. Ariq-qaya took the important city of Changsha in Hunan and Kweilin in Kwangsi (1276). The war which Kublai then had to wage in Mongolia against his rebel cousins allowed the stubborn Sung partisans a brief respite, and they attempted to re-form on the coasts of Fukien and Kwangtung. But the Mongols, returning to the charge under the command of general Sögätü, captured, one after the other, the ports of Fukien (Fuchow and Chüanchow, 1277) and Kwangtung (Canton, 1277, and Chaochow, 1278) provinces. The last of the Chinese "patriots," under the leadership of the heroic Chang Shih-kie, took refuge aboard their fleet with a new little Sung prince,

Ti-ping, aged nine. On April 3, 1279, this fleet, attacked by the Mongol squadron near the islet of Yaishan southwest of Canton, was destroyed, taken, or scattered, and the child Ti-ping was drowned.

This was the first time that the whole of China, including the south, had fallen into the hands of a Turko-Mongol conqueror. What neither the Toba Turks of the fifth century nor the Jurchid Tungus of the twelfth had been able to accomplish, Kublai at last achieved. It was he who fulfilled the dream dimly cherished for ten centuries by "all who dwelt beneath felt tents," by countless generations of nomads. With him the roving herdsmen of the steppe, "all the sons of the Gray Wolf and the Hind," became at last the lords of China—that is, of the densest community of sedentary farmers in all Asia. Nevertheless, the conquest had been slow enough to neutralize its worst effects. And indeed, though Kublai, the offspring of nomads, may have conquered China, he himself had been conquered already by Chinese civilization. He was thus able to realize the constant objective of his politics: to become a true Son of Heaven and make of the Mongol Empire an empire of China. For this the way lay open. No sooner had the Sung disappeared than he became legitimate lord of an empire fifteen centuries old. His house, which took the name of Yüan (1280–1368), aspired only to follow in the footsteps of the twenty-two Chinese dynasties of the past. A visible sign of this Sinicization was the fact that, having snatched Karakorum from Ariq-bögä, Kublai never went to live there. In 1256–57 he had chosen as his summer residence the site of Shangtuho near the Dolonnor in the eastern Chahar of today, where he built a group of palaces. In 1260 he established his capital at Peking. In 1267 he began to build, northeast of the old urban complex of Peking, a new city which he called Tatu, "Great Capital," known also as the city of the khan, Khanbaligh —the Cambaluc of western travelers. This became the winter quarters of the Mongol sovereigns, while Shangtuho remained their summer residence.[9]

WARS IN JAPAN, INDOCHINA, AND JAVA

As the new emperor of China, Kublai claimed homage from the other states in the Far East which—rightly or wrongly—traditional Chinese policy had regarded as natural satellites.

Korea, although garrisoned by Mongols, remained in a state of permanent insurrection. The Korean dynasty had withdrawn to the little island of Kanghwa, opposite Seoul, whence it directed its resistance.[10] However, in 1258 the old king Ko-tjong entrusted his son Wen-tjong to Mongka as hostage. On his accession, Kublai sent the young prince to rule Korea. He also made him his son-in-law, and the Korean dynasty, through this alliance with the Yüan ruling house, was thenceforth an obedient vassal.[11]

Kublai also demanded homage from Japan. The regent of Japan, the shikken (regent) Hojo Tokimune (1251–84), twice refused it (1268 and 1271). Kublai in 1274 thereupon sent against the Japanese archipelago a fleet of 150 vessels carrying an expeditionary force, which embarked from the coast southeast of Korea, laid waste the islands of Tsushima and Iki-shima, and landed in Hakozaki (Hakata) Bay in the island of Kyushu, in Shikuzen Province, near Shimonoseki Strait. But the steppe warriors were not at home on these maritime expeditions. Moreover, they were intended to form no more than the nucleus of the army of invasion, the bulk of which consisted of Chinese and Korean auxiliaries, who were not particularly warlike. At any rate, the daimyos of Kyushu, ensconced about the fortress of Mizuki, put up so vigorous a resistance that after a momentary setback —due, it is said, to Chinese firearms—they forced the invader to re-embark.

In 1276, Kublai reiterated his demand, and was once more refused by Hojo Tokimune. In June, 1281, after long preparation, Kublai sent a more powerful armada against Japan, consisting of 45,000 Mongols and 120,000 Sino-Koreans, who landed at Kyushu in Hakozaki Bay and on the islands of Taka-shima and Hirado-shima in Hizen Province. Yet this time too the Mongol troops, being so entirely out of their element, and the Sino-Koreans, who were of little military value, could not stand up to Japanese fury. Above all, on August 15, 1281, a terrible typhoon dispersed or destroyed the Mongol squadron, and the Mongol troops, cut off from their base, were either captured or massacred.[12]

Kublai fared little better in Indochina. This region was then divided among four great states: the kingdom of Annam (Tonkin and the north of what much later became French Annam and is now North Vietnam), much influenced by Chinese culture; the kingdom of Champa (the central and southern parts of one-time French Annam, the South Vietnam of today), Malayo-Polynesian by race and of Indian (Brahman and Buddhist) culture; the empire of Khmer or Cambodia, of Mon-Khmer stock and of the same Brahman and Buddhist culture; and the Burmese Empire, Burmano-Tibetan by race, Indian by culture, and Buddhist by religion, of which Pegu, of Mon-Khmer race and Buddhist religion, was a dependency. In 1280 the Maharaja of Champa, Indravarman IV, intimidated by Kublai's ambassadors, accepted the Mongol protectorate, but his people refused to allow the country to be divided up into Chinese districts (1281). Kublai then sent by sea, from Canton to Champa, a small army commanded by Sögätü (So-tu in Chinese), who seized the Champa capital Vidjaya (Vijaya) or Chaban, near modern Binhdinh (1283). This force failed to overcome the Champa guerrilla troops, however, and was compelled to re-embark. In 1285, Kublai sent a larger army into Indochina—this time through Tonkin, via Langson—commanded by one of his sons, Prince Toghon or Toghan, who attacked the Annamese. Toghon triumphed near Bacninh and advanced as far as Hanoi, but was afterward defeated at Chuong-duong in the delta and driven back into China. Meanwhile Sögätü had tried to attack Tonkin in the rear, from the south. Landing in Champa, he moved up to Nghean and Thanhhoa to meet Toghon, but was taken by a surprise attack and killed by the Annamese at Tay Kiet (1285). A fresh Mongol expedition in 1287, via Tonkin, occupied Hanoi once more, but was unable to hold it and had to evacuate the country. Tran Nhon-ton, king of Annam (1278–93), having successfully withstood all attacks, re-entered his capital in triumph. Nevertheless, in 1288 he deemed it wise to acknowledge himself Kublai's vassal. Because he refused to come in person to Peking, Kublai decided in 1293 to detain his envoy, Dao-tu Ki. The emperor Temür, Kublai's successor, was in the end to become reconciled with his former "rebel vassal" (1294). The king of Champa too had made the act of vassalage.[13]

In 1277, in Burma, the Mongols had seized the defile of Bhamo, which opened up to them the valley of the Irrawaddy. (Marco Polo gives a lively description of the battle in which the Mongol bowmen got the better of the Burmese war elephants.) In 1283–84 they invaded the country again, and the Burmese ruler, Narasihapati, king of Pagan (1254–87), fled from his capital. Yet it was not until 1287, in the course of a third campaign, that the Mongols came down the valley of the Irrawaddy as far as Pagan, the Burmese capital, which they plundered. In 1297 the new king of Pagan, Kyozwa, acknowledged himself Kublai's vassal in order to check the devastation. In 1300 the Mongols were to intervene yet again in Burma in order to restore order among the petty Shan chiefs, who were quarreling over the royal succession of Pagan.[14]

Mongol influence was to make itself felt as far as Cambodia. In 1296 Kublai's successor, the emperor Temür, sent an embassy to that country, a party which included Chou Ta-kuan, who has left an account of the journey.[15] From 1294, even the two Thai (Siamese) kingdoms of Chiangmai (Xiengmai) and Sukhotai became vassal states.[16]

Lastly, in January, 1293, Kublai sent an expeditionary force of 30,000 from Chüanchow to Java. The chief Javanese ruler was the king of Kediri, in the eastern part of the island. The Mongol army, commanded by the Chinese leaders Shih Pi and Kao Hing, defeated him near Majapahit, thanks to the aid of another Javanese chief named Raden Vijaya. The Mongols captured the enemy capital, Kediri or Daha. But Raden Vijaya afterward turned against them and forced them to re-embark. Having thus liberated the island, he founded the Majapahit Empire.[17]

STRUGGLE WITH QAIDU

These "colonial" expeditions were less important to Kublai than the battles he was called upon to fight against the other Jenghiz-Khanite branches, and especially against Qaidu, Ogödäi's grandson, who ruled the paternal domain of the river Imil and the Tarbagatai Range.[18] This Mongol, who had remained faithful to the old traditions and to the way of life of his race, was the living antithesis of Kublai, and already partially Sinicized Mongol. There is little doubt that many Mongols and Mongolized Turks beheld with amazement the transfer of government to conquered China and the transformation of the grand khan into a Son of Heaven. Ariq-böga had been the first representative of this opposition, and Qaidu was to adopt the same role, but he brought to it a much stronger personality and dauntless energy.

In defiance of the house of Tolui, which, in the person of Kublai, seemed to be forsaking the pure Jenghiz-Khanite tradition, he set himself to restore the fortunes of the house of Ogödäi, which had been divorced from power since 1251. In other words, Qaidu aimed to assert himself as the legitimate heir or, in any event, to carve himself a vast khanate in Central Asia at the expense of Kublai in Mongolia and of the Jagatai house in Turkestan.

It was against the latter that Qaidu first turned. Between 1267 and 1269 he defeated Baraq and seized the Ili and Kashgaria, leaving him only Transoxiana. Baraq's successors were no more than Qaidu's vassals, chosen or rejected at his pleasure. Being now lord of Central Asia, Qaidu took the title of *qaan* and attacked Kublai.

Kublai gave his fourth son, Prince Nomokhan or Nomoqan,[19] the task of waging war against Qaidu, and in 1275 sent him with an army to Almalik (near modern Kuldja, on the Ili). Nomokhan was accompanied by a brilliant staff of princes, among whom were Toqtemür and his first cousin Shirki,[20] Mongka's son. But in 1276 Toqtemür, dissatisfied with Kublai, persuaded Shirki to join him in a conspiracy. The two men treacherously seized Nomokhan and declared for Qaidu, handing over Nomokhan to an ally of Qaidu's, the khan of Kipchak, Mangu Timur. They also induced Jagatai's second son Sarban and other Jenghiz-Khanites princes to join the revolt. From Almalik, Qaidu advanced in 1277 to Karakorum. The situation was a serious one for Kublai, and he recalled Bayan, his best general, from China. Bayan defeated Shirki on the Orkhon and drove him back upon the Irtysh, while Toqtemür fled to the Kirghiz country, in Tannu-Ola, from which he was chased out again by attacking imperial advance troops. After this setback Shirki, Toqtemür, and Sarban fell out among themselves. Toqtemür was put to death by Shirki, and Shirki and Sarban took hostile action against each other. After leading somewhat desultory operations, Sarban—who had taken Shirki prisoner—surrendered to Kublai and handed over his captive to him. Kublai pardoned Sarban, but banished Shirki to an island. Soon thereafter, in 1278, Prince Nomokhan was released. The coalition against Kublai had failed through the inferior quality of its members.

Qaidu, however, remained in a state of war with Kublai, and

he at least had the soul of a leader. Master of the Imil, of the Ili, and of Kashgaria, and suzerain of the Jagatai princes, whose possessions he had reduced to Transoxiana, he was the true khan of Central Asia, as Kublai was that of the Far East. In 1287 he formed a fresh alliance against Kublai, bringing into it the leaders of the collateral Mongol branches: the descendants of Jenghiz Khan's brothers. Among these were the princes Nayan, Shiktur or Shinktur, and Qada'an. Nayan, a descendant either of Jenghiz Khan's youngest brother Temuge Ochigin or of his half-brother Belgutai,[21] held domains in the Manchurian region; he was a Nestorian and, maintains Marco Polo, displayed the cross on his standards or his *tuq*. Shiktur was the grandson of Qasar, the eldest of Jenghiz Khan's brothers. Qada'an was a descendant of Qachi'un, the second brother.[22] They too held appanages in the region of eastern Mongolia and Manchuria. If Qaidu, bringing contingents from Central Asia and western Mongolia, were to succeed in joining with the troops that Nayan, Shiktur, and Qada'an were assembling in Manchuria, the situation would become dangerous for Kublai.

Kublai acted swiftly. He ordered Bayan to take up his position in the Karakorum area and to halt Qaidu. He himself set off for Manchuria at the head of another army. He had with him general Yissu-Temür, grandson of Bo'orchu, Jenghiz Khan's most faithful companion. From Chinese ports on the lower Yangtze, the imperial fleet had landed huge quantities of supplies at the mouth of the Liao River for the waging of the campaign by which the fate of the Mongol Empire would be decided. Nayan's army was encamped near the Liao and protected in the Mongol manner by a line of wagons. Kublai, who was seventy-two, followed the battle on a wooden tower carried or drawn by four elephants. Rashid ad-Din relates that the action was hard-fought and for a time indecisive. Kublai won, no doubt, as Chinese history tells us, thanks to his numerical superiority and also to his effective combination of Chinese and Mongol contingents. Nayan was taken prisoner. As befitted a grand-nephew of Jenghiz Khan, Kublai had him put to death without bloodshed by smothering him under felt carpets (1288). The Nestorians who had committed themselves on Nayan's side had reason to fear reprisals, but Kublai refused to hold Christianity responsible for the rebellion.²³ Temür Oljaitu, grandson and future successor of Kublai, stifled all further insurrection by crushing Qada'an and pacifying Manchuria and the adjoining Mongol districts.

Qaidu had lost hope of intervening in the affairs of the Far East, but he still remained master of western Mongolia west of the Khangai Mountains, and of Turkestan. One of Kublai's grandsons, Prince Kamala,²⁴ given the task of defending the frontier of the Khangai Mountains against Qaidu's men, was defeated and surrounded near the Selenga, and only narrowly escaped. Kublai, despite his great age, felt it necessary to come and retrieve the situation in person (July, 1289). But Qaidu, in the nomad fashion, had ridden away. In 1293, Bayan, left in command of the imperial army in Mongolia, with Karakorum as his base, led a victorious expedition against the rebel troops. In that same year he was replaced in his command by Prince Temür, a grandson of Kublai. Bayan became Kublai's prime minister, and died shortly after him in 1295.

Kublai did not live to see the end of the war against Qaidu. When this great emperor died, on February 18, 1294, the head of Ogödäi's house was still master in Mongolia west of the Khangai and in Central Asia. Kublai's grandson and successor, Emperor Temür Oljaitu (1295–1307), continued the fight. Qaidu's chief ally and vassal was then Duwa, chief of the Jagatai *ulus* in Turkestan. In the course of the years 1297 and 1298, Duwa launched a surprise attack and captured the gallant Öngüt prince Körgüz (that is, George, for it will be remembered that the Öngüt were Nestorians), who was in command of the imperial armies of Mongolia and was the son-in-law of emperor Temür Oljaitu.²⁵ Duwa then attempted to surprise another imperial army, that of Prince Ananda, who was guarding the frontiers of the Tangut country (western Kansu). But he himself was unexpectedly attacked and put to flight. He took revenge by having his prisoner Körgüz executed (1298).

In 1301, Qaidu made one last effort against the empire. Attended by many princes of the Ogödäi and Jagatai houses, he marched on Karakorum, where Prince Khaishan, Emperor Temür's nephew, was in command. A great battle was fought in August, 1301, in the region between Karakorum and the River Tämir, a left-bank tributary of the Orkhon. Qaidu was defeated and died during his retreat.

Chäpär, Qaidu's son, succeeded him as leader of the *ulus* of Ogödäi, on the Imil in Tarbagatai, and played the same part of anti-Caesar against the imperial rights of Kublai's house. Duwa, chief of the Jagatai *ulus,* at first accepted him as suzerain; but soon, wearied of these incessant wars against the empire, he persuaded his lord to acknowledge in his turn the suzerainty of Emperor Temür. In August, 1303, the ambassadors of these two princes came to pay homage at the court of Peking, a most important act, which restored Mongol unity by once more placing the *ulus* of Ogödäi and Jagatai under the vassalage of that of Tolui. Then, as will be seen, Duwa and Chäpär quarreled; Duwa took Chäpär prisoner and forced him to hand over the two Turkestans (ca. 1306). After Duwa's death (ca. 1306–7), Chäpär attempted to restore the hegemony of Ogödäi's *ulus* over Jagatai's around 1309 by attacking the khan Kebek, Duwa's son and successor, but was beaten by Kebek and had no choice but to take refuge with the grand khan of China.

Thus ended the *ulus* of Ogödäi, which, from its base on the Ili in Tarbagatai, had for forty years (1269–1309, approximately) dominated Central Asia and counterbalanced the fortunes of Kublai's house.

Kublai's dynasty, the Mongol dynasty of China, remained sole suzerain of the other Mongol khanates. Peking was the capital of the world as far as the Danube and the Euphrates.

To render more intelligible the struggle between the houses of Kublai and Qaidu, we have been obliged to follow it to its end, fifteen years after the death of Kublai himself. We may now turn back and consider what one may call the "internal policy" of this ruler.

KUBLAI'S GOVERNMENT: MONGOL AND CHINESE POLICY

Kublai pursued a dual policy, its aspect depending upon whether one considers him—or he considered himself—as grand khan and heir to Jenghiz Khan or as Son of Heaven and successor to nineteen Chinese dynasties. From the Mongol point of view, he consistently maintained in principle (if not in reality) the moral unity of the Jenghiz-Khanite empire. As supreme khan, inheritor of Jenghiz Khan's and Mongka's authority, he never ceased to demand obedience from the great Jenghiz-Khanite appanages, which had become as many autonomous khanates. To impose this obedience on the houses of Ogödäi (Qaidu) and Jagatai, he spent his life waging war in Mongolia. Persia, where his brother Hulägu was ruler, was for him simply a province of his empire. The khans of Persia—Hulägu (1256–65), Abaqa (1265–81), and Arghun (1284–91)—were in his eyes mere *il-khans,* or subordinate khans: governors of high rank, who held their appointments from him and remained in close contact with him.[26] Kublai, possessor of all China, theoretical suzerain of Turkestan and of Mongol Russia, and actual suzerain of Iran, was truly, as Marco Polo observed, "the great Lord," "the most powerful master of men, lands, and treasures that has ever been in the world, from the time of Adam until today."[27]

While in the rest of Asia, Kublai was Jenghiz Khan's heir, in China he sought to be the loyal continuator of the nineteen dynasties. No other Son of Heaven took his role as seriously as he did. His healing administration bound up the wounds of a century of war. After the fall of the Sung, he not only preserved the institutions and administrative personnel of that dynasty, but made every effort to secure the personal loyalty of the officials functioning at the time. Having conquered the soil, he achieved also the conquest of minds, and his greatest claim to fame is perhaps not that he was the first man in history to conquer the whole of China, but that he pacified it.

The problem of communications, so important for the administration and provisioning of that vast empire, received his close attention. He repaired the imperial roads, planted shade trees along them where practicable, and built caravansaries at regular stages. More than two hundred thousand horses, distributed among the various relay stations, are thought to have been employed in the service of the imperial mails. To assure the food supply of Peking, he repaired and completed the great canal by which rice was brought to the capital from central China.[28] To combat famine, he revived state control, long established in China, which the famous Wang An-shih, under the Sung of Kaifeng, had perfected. In good years, surplus crops were bought by the state and stored in public granaries. With the advent of famine and high prices, these granaries were opened and the grain distributed gratis.[29] Public assistance was also organized. An edict of 1260 ordered viceroys to provide relief and assistance for old scholars, orphans, and the sick and infirm. Another of 1271 called for the setting up of hospitals. Over and above the Chinese administrative tradition, these acts were quite probably the result of Buddhist influence—apparently very strong—on the mind of Kublai. Rice and millet were regularly distributed to needy families, and Kublai himself, Marco Polo tells, fed 30,000 paupers daily.[30]

The only inferior side to Kublai's administration was in the field of finance. Among the Sung institutions, Kublai had discovered the use of *ch'ao,* or paper currency. This he brought into general circulation and made the basis of his financial policy. In 1264 he promulgated a decree setting forth the value, in paper money, of the principal goods. His first finance minister, the Muslim Sayyid Ajall of Bukhara (d. 1279), seems to have maintained the issue of currency within reasonable limits.[31] Rashness began with subsequent ministers, first with the Transoxianan Ahmed Fenaketi (d. 1282) and then with Sanga the Uigur.[32] Both these men pursued a policy of uncontrolled inflation which rapidly devalued the *ch'ao.* In their search for money, they resorted to repeated conversions and established burdensome monopolies. Ahmed, who was assassinated in 1282, was posthumously degraded by Kublai. Sanga was condemned to death for malversation (1291). In 1303, after Kublai's reign, it became necessary to check the fall of previous issues and introduce new notes, which in their turn depreciated.

RELIGIOUS POLICY OF KUBLAI AND HIS SUCCESSORS: BUDDHISM

Kublai, as Marco Polo expressly states,[33] was widely tolerant of all cults, although in 1279 he did for a time revive Jenghiz Khan's regulations relating to the slaughter of livestock—regulations which offended against Muslim custom—and once displayed extreme annoyance at the obligation imposed upon Muslims by the Koran to wage a Holy War against "infidels." [34] Furthermore, his sympathies for the Buddhists caused him for a short time to show a measure of personal hostility toward the Taoists, their traditional rivals. Buddhism indeed benefited very markedly from his favor, and it is under this aspect that he is known to Mongol tradition. That devout Buddhist, the Mongol historian Sanang Sechen, went so far as to add to Kublai's titles those of *qutuqtu*

(venerable, divine) and *chakravartin* ("universal monarch," in
the vocabulary of Buddhism).[35] Even before his accession, during
Morigka's reign, he had called a conference at Shangtuho at which
Buddhists debated with Taoists and triumphed (1258). At this
famous disputation, Buddhist doctrine was expounded by Na-mo,
who had already debated in the presence of Mongka, and by the
young Tibetan lama Phags-pa. As at the debate of 1255, they
convicted the Taoists of spreading apocryphal tales which distorted the history of Buddhist origins and made Buddhism appear
a mere satellite of Taoism. After this controversy, Kublai issued
edicts ordering the burning of suspect works, and compelled the
Taoists to hand back the monasteries that they had taken from
the Buddhists (edicts of 1258, 1261, 1280, and 1281).[36] After becoming emperor, Marco Polo tells us, he accorded a magnificent
ceremonial reception to the relics of the Buddha, sent him by the
raja of Ceylon.

Kublai's chief assistant in the domain of Buddhism was the
Tibetan lama Phags-pa, who was born about 1239 and died most
probably on December 15, 1280. Phags-pa was the nephew and
successor of the celebrated Sas-Kya pandita, abbot of the monastery of Sas-Kya in the province of Tsang.[37] Kublai, who had
sent for him in Tibet, employed him both to convert the Mongols
and to ensure Tibetan vassalage. He named him "master of the
realm" (*kuo-shih*), a title borrowed from ancient Chinese Buddhism,[38] and about 1264 placed the Tibetan provinces under his
politico-religious authority. Up to that time the Mongols had
known no other alphabet than the Uigur. By Kublai's order, in
1269 Phags-pa produced for them a new writing called *dür-
bäljin*, or square, inspired by the Tibetan alphabet. However, the
part played in this by Phags-pa is thought by Pelliot to have been
somewhat overestimated; and in any case this square writing
enjoyed only temporary success, for the Mongols continued to
use characters copied from the Uigur alphabet (differing only in
the style of writing and in having more angular characters),
which became their national writing. It was in Uigur characters
that the Mongols' chancellery texts in the French Archives Nationales were written.[39] In this connection, Pelliot points out that
Uigur writing has the defect of conveying only imperfectly the
sounds of thirteenth-century Mongolian, in that it fails to distinguish between the sounds *o* and *u,* omits the initial *h,* and so

on. For guttural sounds, too, the Uigur alphabet is less rich than Phags-pa's.[40]

Most of Kublai's successors were equally fervent Buddhists, the first of these being his grandson Temür, who reigned after him (1294–1307). However, another of Kublai's grandsons, Prince Ananda (despite his essentially Buddhist Sanskrit name), inclined toward Islam. "He knew the Koran by heart, excelled in Arabic writing," and was an enthusiastic propagator of the Muslim faith in the Tangut country (Ningsia), of which he was viceroy. Temür tried to bring him back to Buddhism, but in vain, and for a time he imprisoned him. At Temür's death (February 10, 1307), Ananda attempted to seize the throne, but his cousin Khaishan secured it and had him put to death.[41] During his reign (June 21, 1307–January 27, 1311), Khaishan showed himself to be a devout Buddhist and caused many texts of the Buddhic canon to be translated into Mongolian. The Chinese literati, of Confucian culture, reproved him for the favor he bestowed upon the lamas, and it may have been as a reaction to this favoritism that the administration withdrew from both Buddhist and Taoist foundations the fiscal immunity which they had enjoyed until that time.[42] In the reign of Yesun Temür, Kublai's great-grandson, who was emperor from October 4, 1323, to his death on August 15, 1328, the minister Chang Kuei made a public protest on behalf of Confucian communities against the favor shown the lamas. Shensi especially was the resort of numbers of Tibetan monks. A contemporary report runs: "These lamas are to be seen riding about the western provinces, carrying at their girdles passports written in letters of gold. They overrun the towns and, instead of lodging at the inns, they move into private houses and drive out the householders, the more readily to take advantage of and ravish their wives. Not content with debauchery, they remove from the people what little money they have. Action must be taken against these public bloodsuckers, who are more cruel even than the tax gatherers."[43] Emperor Yesun had to regulate the entry of lamas into China proper.

The excessive Buddhist "clericalism" for which Chinese literati held the Mongol dynasty responsible was no doubt a contributing cause to that dynasty's downfall. However, the inordinate influence exerted by the Buddhist "church" on Kublai's house was nothing new in the history of Turko-Mongol dynasties on Chinese soil. The same thing had happened with the famous Fu Chien at the end of the fourth century, and with the last of the Toba at the beginning of the sixth (pp. 59 and 65). Buddhism at first made these fierce barbarians gentler and more humane, then sluggish, and at last deadened in them the instinct of self-preservation. Then old Confucian China, which had endured these terrible masters, perceived that they had grown harmless, and either absorbed them, as in the case of the Toba, or expelled them, as with the Jenghiz-Khanites. The situation would have been far more serious if the house of Kublai had embraced Islam, as might have happened if Ananda had had his own way in 1307. The triumph of Islam would have been a terrible blow to the old Chinese civilization. The two greatest dangers that threatened it in the course of its long history were perhaps Ananda's attempt in 1307 and Tamerlane's invasion, fortunately averted by that leader's death in 1404.[44]

RELIGIOUS POLICY OF KUBLAI AND HIS SUCCESSORS:
NESTORIANISM

Kublai's preference for Buddhism had in no way prevented him from showing sympathy for the Nestorian faith. At the great Christian celebrations he, like his predecessors, caused the Nestorian priests attached to his *ordu* to bring before him the Gospels, which he censed and piously kissed.[45] "In 1289 he even instituted a special department, the *ch'ung-fu-ssu*, for administering the Christian cult throughout the empire." His edicts, like those of Ogödäi and Mongka, laid down exemption from taxation and bestowal of various privileges upon Nestorian priests, as upon Buddhist and Taoist monks and Muslim doctors. It will be remembered in this connection that the Mongols followed Syriac etymology in designating Christians by the names of *tarsa* and *ärkägün* or *ärkä'ün* (the plural is *ärkägüd* or *ärkä'üd* and the Chinese transcription is *ye-li-k'o-wen*), while priests and monks were called *rabban-ärkägün* and bishops were known as *marhasia*.[46]

Among Mongols and assimilated groups, Nestorians were proportionately numerous, especially among the Kerayit and the Öngüt Turks. The Öngüt Turks, who had taken over the place of the old Sha-t'o Turks north of the Great Wall on the fringe of modern Shansi, employed a nomenclature which reveals itself, despite the heavy veil of Chinese transcription, as being often Nestorian: Shen-wen (Simeon), K'uo-li-ki-ssu (George), Pao-lu-ssu (Paul), Yo-nan (John), Ya-ku (James), T'ien-ho (Denha), Yi-sho (Isho: Jesus), Lu-ho (Luke).

The majority of the Öngüt people lived in what is now the province of Suiyuan, in the region of modern Toqto or Kweihwa-cheng, an area known in the Mongol period by the name of Tung-sheng. Pelliot thinks that from this name derives that of Koshang, that is, Toshang, by which the country is designated in the life of Mar Yahballaha III and of Rabban Sauma.[47] The name *Tanduc*, Marco Polo's name for the same region, originates, according to the same scholar, from an ancient name current under the T'ang (T'ien-tö, formerly pronounced Thiän-tak).[48] This was the true home of the Öngüt dynasty, a line of Turkic princes originally greatly attached to Nestorianism and at the same time closely related to the Jenghiz-Khanite family. The house of Jenghiz Khan owed these Nestorian princes a debt of gratitude which it apparently never forgot. The Öngüt chief Alaqush-tigin [49] had rendered the Mongols a vital service at a decisive moment when, invited to join the alliance formed by the Naiman against them, he did the opposite and stood firmly by Jenghiz Khan.[50] He paid for his devotion with his life; for when he returned home after the war with the Naiman, certain members of his tribe who favored an alliance with the Naiman assassinated him, and with him his eldest son Buyan Shiban. His widow was able to escape to Yüncheng with their second son Po-yao-ho. When Jenghiz Khan entered Yüncheng as conqueror of the Kin, his heartfelt wish was to restore his faithful vassal's family to the leadership of the Öngüt country. Young Po-yao-ho went with him on his campaign against Khwarizm, and on their return Jenghiz Khan gave the young man his own daughter, Alaghai-bäki, in marriage. At Po-yao-ho's death, as a true daughter of Jenghiz Khan, Alaghai-bäki governed the Öngüt country with a forceful hand. Having no children of her own, she treated the three sons whom her husband had had by a concubine—Kün-buqa, Ai-buqa, and Choligh-buqa—as her own. The first two in their turn married Jenghiz-Khanite princesses: Kün-buqa married Yelmish, daughter of the grand khan Güyük, and Ai-buqa married Yüräk, Kublai's daughter.[51] Ai-buqa's son Körgüz or Görgüz—that is, George—

married first Princess Qutadmish, the daughter of Kublai's son Chen-kin, and then Princess Ayamish, the grand khan Temür's daughter. It has been related earlier how he was killed in Temür's service in 1298.[52]

It is thus evident how closely this Nestorian princely house was allied to the Mongol dynasty. And, within the limits of Mongol religious tolerance, it did not fail to use its favored position to protect Christianity. The life of Mar Yahballaha and of Rabban Sauma shows us Kün-buqa and Ai-buqa showering tokens of good will and presents on the two Nestorian pilgrims at the moment of their departure for "Jerusalem." [53] "Prince George" indeed, toward the end of his life, was converted to Catholicism by the Franciscan missionary Giovanni da Montecorvino.[54]

Mar Yahballaha's and Rabban Sauma's biography makes it clear that Nestorianism on the northern boundaries of Mongol China was not confined to the Öngüt country, for at their departure for the West they were given the most moving welcome by Christians in the Tangut country—that is, Kansu—and more particularly in the "city of the Tangut," Ningsia.[55] Indeed, Nestorian communities existed all over that region, at Ningsia, Sining, Kanchow, Suchow, and Tunhwang. Marco Polo mentions three Nestorian churches in Ningsia alone.[56]

But the Nestorians did not remain confined to these outer marches of old China, where no doubt they had dwelt in obscurity since the T'ang dynasty. Thanks to the Jenghiz-Khanite conquest, the interior of China was now open to them. One might even say that Nestorianism, having been expelled from China after the fall of the T'ang, re-entered it with the Mongols. In 1275 the Nestorian patriarch of Baghdad created an archbishopric at Peking. In the wake of the Mongols, the Nestorian faith penetrated even the region of the lower Yangtze. In 1278 Kublai entrusted the government of Chenkiang (Marco Polo's *Cinghianfu*) in modern Kiangsu to a certain Mar Särgis (Ma Sie-li-ki-ssu in Chinese transcription), who, as his name suggests, was a Nestorian, and who was prompt in building a church in that place (1281).[57] Other Nestorian churches were built in Yangchow and Hankow.[58]

There is a celebrated piece of evidence of Mongol Nestorianism in the Syriac bibliography of Mar Yahballaha III and Rabban

Sauma. Rabban Sauma (d. 1294) and his friend the future patriarch Mar Yahballaha, Markus by name (1245–1317), were two Nestorians of whom at least the second was an Öngüt.[59] Markus' father was archdeacon of the Öngüt town of Koshang or Toshang, which Pelliot identifies, as we saw, with medieval Tungsheng or modern Toqto, on the frontier of present-day Suiyuan and Shansi. Rabban Sauma was the son of a "visitor" from the Nestorian church of Khanbaligh, or Peking. He was the first to embrace the monastic life; he received the tonsure at the hands of the metropolitan of Peking, Mar Guiwarguis, after which he withdrew to a hermitage, where he was joined by Markus, on a mountain a day's journey from the city. At Markus' suggestion, the two monks resolved to make the pilgrimage to Jerusalem. The two Öngüt princes, Kün-buqa and Ai-buqa, who were also Nestorians and whom the monks visited near Toqto to tell them of their plan, welcomed them most warmly, at the same time trying to dissuade them from it: "Why should you set off for the West, when we take so much trouble to bring hither bishops and monks from those places?" But seeing that Rabban Sauma and his campanion were determined to go, the Öngüt princes gave them horses, money, and everything required for their journey across Central Asia.

The pilgrims first passed through the Tangut country, that is, the northern part of present-day Kansu, near Ningsia, a land where Nestorian communities were numerous. "Men, women, and children came out to meet them, for the faith of the inhabitants of Tangut was very ardent." Journeying along the trails south of the Lob Nor and the Tarim, they reached Khotan and the domains of the khan of the Jagatai house, who at this time was Duwa; for this was in 1275–76, according to Pelliot's estimate.[60] The warfare then prevailing in Central Asia among the Jenghiz-Khanite princes prevented Rabban Sauma and Markus from traveling directly from Kashgaria to Persia. They found Khotan in the grip of famine, Kashgar depopulated by war, and the road leading westward from Kashgar closed to travelers. They therefore turned north and went to Talas (the Aulie-Ata, or Dzhambul, of today), where the khan Qaidu of Ogödäi was encamped.[61] He gave the two Nestorians a cordial reception, and provided them with safe-conducts which enabled them to pass through the lines of the combatant armies and at last arrive in the Mongol khanate of Persia, of which the ruler was at that time Khan Abaqa (1265–82).

A Nestorian named Ai-sie in Chinese transcription—that is, 'Isä or Jesus (1227–1308)—who was probably an Arabic-speaking Christian from Syria, occupied an important position under Kublai. Multilingual and a physician and astronomer, he had been in Güyük's service. In 1263 Kublai appointed him director of the department of astronomy, and he appears to have been one of the inspirers of the edict of 1279 by which Kublai sought to curb Muslim propaganda in China. In 1284–85, 'Isä accompanied a high-ranking Mongol official, the *ch'eng-hsiang* Bolod, when Bolod was sent as ambassador to Arghun, the khan of Persia. On his return to China, 'Isä was appointed commissioner for the Christian cult in 1291 and minister of state in 1297. His sons Elya, Denha, Hei-ssu, George, and Luke, Nestorians like himself, also performed important functions at the court of Peking.[62]

Lastly, Kublai and his successors reckoned among their personal guard in Peking 30,000 Christian Alans of the Greek rite, who had come from the Caucasus in Mongka's time. In June, 1275, as we saw, a corps of these Alans was treacherously massacred by the Sung at the siege of Chenchow, north of the lower Yangtze. The revenues of Chenchow were then made over by Kublai to the families of the Alans who had died in his service. On July 11, 1336, the descendants of these Alans sent a letter of submission to Pope Benedict XII. The embassy that presented it to the Avignon pope in 1338 included, besides Andrew and William of Nassio, Thogay the Alan.[63]

Pelliot has established, moreover, the fact that the Manichaeism of old became active once again in Fukien, where it had given signs of revival already under the Sung.[64]

MARCO POLO'S JOURNEY

Niccolo Polo and his brother Maffeo Polo were Venetian merchants who had lived for a long time in Constantinople. In 1260 they left that city on a trading expedition to the Mongol khanate of Kipchak in what later became southern Russia. They were received at Sarai on the lower Volga (the "Tigris" of Marco Polo) by Berke (*Barca*), the khan of Kipchak, Batu's brother and successor, and they sold him their assortment of jewelry. Then they took the Khwarizm road to Bukhara, in the Jagatai khanate, where they remained for three years, for their return was hindered by warfare among the Mongol princes. At last they decided to accompany the embassy from Hulägu the khan of Persia to his brother Kublai in China. In doing so they had to follow the usual caravan route via Otrar on the Syr Darya, Almalik in the Ili valley, and Uiguristan (Ioguristan), in which were the two towns of Beshbaligh (near Kucheng) and Turfan, the latter being then known as Kara-khoja (Marco Polo's *Carachoço*).[65] Finally, via Hami (his *Camul*) and Tunhwang or Shachow (*Saciu*), they arrived in China and reached Peking or Khanbaligh (*Cambaluc*).

Kublai gave them the best possible reception and, as they were leaving, urged them to ask the Pope to send him a hundred doctors learned in the seven arts.[66] The Polos left China in 1266, and arrived at Layas, Lajazzo, or Ayas on the Mediterranean, the chief port of the Armenian kingdom of Cilicia. From there, in April, 1269, they went on to Acre, and thence to Rome. Unable to obtain the missionaries and doctors requested by Kublai, they re-embarked for Acre, and left there again at the end of 1271 for China. This time they took with them Niccolo's son Marco Polo, who has left us an immortal account of his journey.

Marco, with his father and uncle, left Lajazzo and, traveling by the Sivas route through the Seljuk sultanate of Asia Minor, reached the Mongol khanate of Persia. They were prevented from taking the Transoxiana road by the war then going on between Abaqa the khan of Persia and his cousins, the Jagatai khans of Turkestan who had sided with Qaidu; they therefore took the direct diagonal route through Persia by way of Tabriz, Sultaniyeh, and Kashan, and then no doubt via Yezd and Kerman (Kirman) to Hormuz (Ormuz).[67] They had probably intended to take ship for China from Hormuz, but, as Pelliot points out, the coasts of southern China and the great ports of Canton, Chüanchow, Fuchow, and Hangchow still belonged to the Sung at that time, and not to the Mongols. So at Hormuz the Polos changed their plans. Giving up hope of reaching the Far East by sea, they went up into Central Asia via Khurasan (which Marco Polo calls "the country of the Dry Tree" or of "the Lone Tree"),[68] passing through Nishapur, Sheburgan (*Sapurgan*), and Balkh (*Balc*).

Avoiding Transoxiana, the scene of incessant wars between the khan of Persia and the Jagatai *ulus,* the Polos set off northeastward from Balkh across the Badakhshan (*Badascian*) and over the Pamirs (*Pamier*) by way of the high valley of the Wakhan (*Vocan*) north of Bolor (*Belor*). By the old Silk Road (Tash Kurghan, Ptolemy's "stone tower"), they came down into Kashgar (*Cascar*), whose beautiful gardens and vineyards Marco Polo praises, as well as the commercial sense of its inhabitants, "who travel and trade all over the world." At Kashgar too he notes the existence of a Nestorian community with its own church. From there the Polos took the no less ancient route along the south of the Tarim basin by way of Yarkand (*Yarcan*), Khotan (*Cotan*), Keriya (*Pem*), and Cherchen (*Charchan* or *Ciarcian*). Skirting the Lob Nor, they passed through Lop, a town identified by Sir Aurel Stein as the Charkhlik of today.[69] They came next to Tunhwang or Shachow (*Saciu*). Then, in the old Tangut country, they came upon Suchow of Kansu Province (*Succiu*)[70] and Kanchow (*Campiciu*), an important trading center where the Venetians stayed for nearly a year, awaiting instructions from the Mongol court. Marco Polo notes that the Nestorians had three churches in Kanchow and that there were also in the town a number of Buddhist monks, whose virtues he praises in an objective manner.[71]

After this sojourn at Kanchow, the Polos resumed their eastward journey through Liangchow (*Erginul* or *Ergiuul*)[72] and Ningsia (*Egrigaia*).[73] In this latter city, the old Tangut capital, the majority of the population were Buddhists. But Marco Polo notes a Nestorian community there also, with three churches. The travelers then penetrated the Öngüt country, which Marco Polo calls *Tanduc* (see above), and of which the center may be sought near the modern town of Toqto or Kweihwacheng. Marco Polo does not omit to mention the Nestorian faith of the Öngüt princes, whom for that reason he confuses with the family of Prester John, that is to say, of the old Kerayit rulers. This mistake was repeated by Odorico da Pordenone. Marco refers specifically to "Prince George" (Körgüz), who then ruled over the Öngüt under the suzerainty of the grand khan. He alludes also to the marriage alliances between the Mongol dynasty and the princely house of the Öngüt.

Leaving this country, the Polos entered China proper or, more accurately, northern China, which Marco Polo calls *Cathay*, in the Mongol manner, from the name of the Khitan or Khitai, the lords of eleventh-century Peking. From the Toqto region they reached Kublai's summer residence of Shangtuho (*Cyandu, Chandu*), the modern Dolonnor, in May, 1275.

The Polos handed Kublai a letter from Pope Gregory X. Kublai seems to have taken a liking for Marco, whom he took with him to his winter court at Khanbaligh (*Cambaluc*), our Peking. On Marco Polo's own testimony, he found him a place in the government and, as will be seen, entrusted him with various confidential missions. Nevertheless, it appears that Marco Polo never acquired a serious appreciation of the Chinese language; on the other hand, he knew Persian and often used Persian transcriptions for the geographical names of China.[74] The functions which he, his father, and his uncle were able to perform cannot have been as important as some people, through false interpretations, have been tempted to suggest. From the information Marco gives about the exploitation of salt deposits, Pelliot infers that he may have been employed in the Chinese administration of the salt tax; it may have been in that capacity that he worked for three years as assistant to the local subprefect at Yangchow.[75] What he says of the part played by his father and uncle in the siege of Siangyang in 1268–73 does not correspond to the statements in Chinese sources. But if the renowned Venetian did somewhat exaggerate his kinsmen's role, the important fact remains that his own duties, however minor, gave him the opportunity of visiting the principal Chinese cities.

Marco Polo's book describes two itineraries: one from Peking to Yunnan, the other from Peking to Fukien. In the first he mentions Taiyüan (*Taianfu*), capital of what is now Shansi; Pingyang (*Pianfu*), the second city of the province; Sian, then called Fengyüanfu or Kingchaofu (*Quengianfu*) in Shensi—a son of Kublai's named Mangala was viceroy there (1272–80) and he mentions Marco Polo; [76] and then Chengtu (*Sindufu*) in Szechwan. From there the journey is described with an abundance of detail, indicating that Marco Polo was indeed sent on some errand to these parts. In Yunnan or the ancient realm of Tali (*Caraian, Caragian*), he mentions the two towns of Tali (*Caragian*) and Yunnan (*Yachy, Iaci*), where already he notes a large Muslim community.[77] Yunnan formed a separate viceroyalty governed by a suc-

cession of Jenghiz-Khanite princes: Kublai's son Ugechi (1267),
Tughlugh (1274), and Ugechi's son Esen or Yesen Temür (1280).
Marco Polo tells that at the time of his journey Esen Temür (*Essantemur*) was in power. The details he gives of the Mongol wars
in Burma or the country of Mien (Mongol expeditions of 1277,
1283–84, and 1287) suggest that he may have gone as far as the
frontier of that country in the wake of the Mongol armies. In
any event, he gives a detailed description of the battle of 1277,
in the course of which the Mongol archers caused panic among
the king of Pagan's war elephants, and forced the Bhamo pass on
the upper Irrawaddy. He also speaks of the Mongols' entry into
Pagan, which did not take place until 1287.[78]

The second itinerary described by Marco Polo passed through
eastern China from north to south, parallel to the China Sea. From
Peking he went via Hokien (Marco Polo's *Cacianfu*) [79] to Tsanglu
(*Cianglu*); Tsiyang (*Ciangli*); Tsining in Shantung (*Singiu-
matu*); Hwaian (*Coigangiu*), near the mouth of the Hwai (at
that time the mouth of the Yellow River); [80] Yangchow (*Yangiu*);
Suchow (*Sugiu*); Hangchow (*Quinsai*); Wuchow (*Vugiu*) in
Chekiang Province; south of Lanchi and, quite close by, Küchow
(*Ghiugiu*) in Chekiang; Chuchow (*Cugiu*), also in Chekiang;
Kienning (*Quenlinfu*) in Fukien; Fuchow (*Fugiu*), the capital
of modern Fukien Province; and Chüanchow (*Çaiton*). It will be
noticed that this itinerary went no farther south than Chüanchow
and therefore makes no mention of Canton.

It appears that Marco Polo also had occasion to join two Mongol embassies sent by Kublai to Champa (*Ciamba, Cyamba*) [81]
and Ceylon, the latter to fetch some Buddhist relics, including the
famous Tooth of the Buddha. In Ceylon the Venetian traveler
asked to be told the life of the Buddha Sakyamuni (*Sagamoni
Burcan*),[82] of which he has left us a faithful and delightful summary.[83]

In the spring of 1291, Marco Polo and his relatives were
enabled to sail for Europe. Arghun, khan of Persia, Kublai's great-
nephew, had asked Kublai to give him a Mongol princess of the
Baya'ut tribe in marriage. Kublai sent him princess Kökächin
(*Cocachin* in Marco Polo's account) of that tribe. But the Central
Asian routes were blocked by the war between Kublai and Qaidu.
Kublai therefore asked the Polos to escort the Mongol fiancée
to Persia by sea, at the same time giving them letters for the

Pope and for the kings of France, England, and Castile. The Polos probably had to put in at Vijaya or Chaban (near Binh-dinh), the capital of Champa, and then make for the Straits. Off the coast of Sumatra, however, they were held up for five months by contrary winds. No doubt, like all navigators of that time, they then called at Quilon or Kollam (*Coilum*), the great spice market of Travancore. From there they skirted the coast of the Deccan plateau to the Gulf of Cambay and then, following the Persian coast, landed at Hormuz. Thence they must have traveled into Persia by Kerman (*Cherman*) and Yezd (*Yasd*). Arghun, the khan of Persia, had just died. The Polos delivered the princess Kökächin to his son Ghazan, governor of Khurasan, and then went to call upon the new khan of Persia, Gaikhatu, in Tabriz. For three months they remained in Azerbaijan, after which they embarked at Trebizond for Constantinople. They arrived home in Venice in 1295.

ECONOMIC PROSPERITY IN CHINA UNDER MONGOL RULE

One of the most interesting features of Marco Polo's book is the picture he gives of the economic activity of the two Chinese regions: northern China, which he continues to call *Cathay*, from the name of the old Khitan; and southern China, the former Sung empire, which he calls *Manzi*. We learn from him that in northern China coal was mined, "a kind of black stones which are extracted from the hills in veins and burnt like faggots, and they are so fit for this purpose that all over Cathay no other fuel is used." The use made of waterways surprises him no less, and he notes above all the commercial importance of the Yangtze (the *Quian* or *Kian*), the main artery of the Chinese economy. "More vessels and more rich merchandise pass up and down this river than upon all the rivers and all the seas of Christendom." He adds that "two hundred thousand boats pass up the river every year, to say nothing of those that come down." He notes also the economic function of the imperial canal, adapted and completed by Kublai, whereby rice might be brought to Peking from the lower Yangtze.

To control this enormous internal commerce and to carry on trade with India and Indonesia, powerful merchant guilds had been formed in the ports of central China and in the Cantonese

region. These guilds equaled and surpassed the Métiers of
Flanders and the Arti of Florence. Of the guilds of *Quinsai*
(Hangchow), Marco Polo writes: "So many merchants were
there, and such rich ones, and they carried on so vast a commerce,
that no one could assess their wealth. Know also that neither
the masters of trades, who were heads of enterprises, nor their
wives turned their hands to anything, but led lives of such luxury
and elegance that one would have fancied them kings." The general use of paper currency, which Marco Polo jestingly calls the
true philosopher's stone, facilitated commercial transactions:
"And I tell you that everyone willingly accepts these notes because to whatever part of the grand khan's territories people go,
they may buy and sell with them as readily as if they were fine
gold." [84] The excellent business sense of the Chinese race filled
the Venetian with admiration. He continually evokes the spectacle of all these riches: vessels returning from India laden with
spices—with pepper, ginger, and cinnamon; junks going down
the Yangtze or up the Grand Canal with their cargoes of rice;
the shops of Hangchow or Chüanchow, overflowing with precious
wares—raw and damask silk, gold camacas (heavy silk fabrics) and
brocades, samites (silk richly embroidered with gold or silver),
tartarines and satins, or clothes of "Çaiton" (satin) fabrics. [85]

In the same vein, Marco Polo describes the chief Chinese
markets: *Cambaluc* (Peking), the center for silks from the north
("no day passes without the entry of a thousand cartloads of silk,
of which quantities of cloth of gold and woven silk are made");
Sindufu (Chengtu in Szechwan), which manufactured sendal
silks and exported its silken wares from China to Central Asia;
Nangin or *Namghin* (Anking or Kaifeng?) and *Sugiu* (Suchow
in Kiangsu), which made cloth of gold; *Yangiu* (Yangchow in
Kiangsu, the great rice market of the lower Yangtze. An especially busy place was *Quinsai* [86] (Hangchow in Chekiang), the
old Sung capital, which had lost none of its former commercial
activity under the Mongols. Indeed, it may have gained, for it
was now linked up with all the trade of the vast Mongol Empire.
Marco Polo describes it as a sort of Chinese Venice. It was noted
above all as the great sugar market. Countless vessels brought to
it the spices of India and the East Indies, and carried from it silk
for India and the Muslim world. It thus contained a large colony
of Arab, Persian, and Christian merchants. Lastly, there were

the two great ports of *Fugiu* (Fuchow) and *Zayton* or *Çaiton* (Chüanchow) in Fukien. The *Fugiu* merchants "possess incredible stocks of ginger and galingale. In this city too there is a very considerable traffic in sugar and a great market for pearls and precious stones brought hither by vessels from the Indies."

The greatest storehouse of Mongol China was still Marco Polo's *Çaiton*, "where all the ships come in from India so laden with spices, precious stones, and pearls that it is a wonder to behold. This is the port at which all the merchants of *Manzi* come together, the great import center for the whole of China. And I tell you that for one ship from the Indies laden with pepper and bound for Alexandria or any other port in Christendom, more then a hundred come to *Çaiton*." These statements are corroborated by the Arab traveler Ibn-Batuta, who speaks of Zayton around 1345.[87]

It is evident that during the Mongol period the Chinese market was closely associated with the Indian and Malayan market. On Marco Polo's testimony, great numbers of Chinese ships put in regularly at the ports of Java and brought back "black pepper, nutmeg, galingale, cubebs, cloves, and other spices, from which the merchants of Caiton derive great wealth."[88] From other sources it is known that Kublai and his successors concluded genuine commercial treaties with the rajas of Travancore and of the Carnatic. The Chinese merchant flotillas put in regularly at Kaveripatnam, Cail or Kayal, Kollam or Quilon, and Ceylon with bales of raw silk, colorful silken fabrics, satins, sendals, and gold brocades, and returned to China carrying cargoes of pepper, ginger, cinnamon, nutmeg, muslins, cottons from the Hindu world, pearls from the Indian Ocean, and diamonds from the Deccan.

In addition to this, the establishment in Persia of a junior branch of the Mongol dynasty of China stimulated a brisk traffic between the two countries. The Persian khans of the house of Hulägu, who amid their Muslim surroundings had remained quite Mongol in their tastes, sent to China for luxuries such as silks and porcelain, and Persian miniatures of the day began to show the influence of Chinese masters. Conversely, Mongol Persia exported carpets, harness equipment, armor, bronzes, and enamel work to China.

Lastly—Marco Polo's journeys and Pegolotti's *Pratica della mercatura* [89] bear witness to this—the Mongol conquest had put the Chinese world into touch with Europe. By the end of the thirteenth century, two great transcontinental routes linked the West with the Far East. First was the route from Kipchak to Tunhwang, which for Westerners started from the Genoese and Venetian countinghouses of the Crimea, or more accurately, from Tana at the mouth of the Don. Of this the principal stages were Sarai on the lower Volga, capital of the Mongol khanate of Kipchak, followed by Otrar on the middle Syr Darya and by Talas and Balasagun west of the Issyk Kul. From the Issyk Kul, one trail led up into Mongolia via the Imil, the Black Irtysh, and the Urungu rivers to Karakorum on the upper Orkhon, whence it descended upon Peking. Another trail from the western point of the Issyk Kul led to Almalik (near Kuldja) on the upper Ili, Beshbaligh (the Dzimsa of today), Hami and Suchow in Kansu, and thence into China proper. A second route passed through the Mongol khanate of Persia, from either Trebizond on the Black Sea, capital of the Greek state of that name, or from Lajazzo (Layas, Ayas), the busiest port of the Armenian kingdom of Cilicia, near Frankish Syria. From either starting point the road ran through the eastern part of the Seljuk sultanate of Asia Minor, which was linked in close vassalage to the Mongol khanate of Persia, to Tabriz, the khanate's effective capital. From there the chief stages were usually Kazvin, Rai, Merv, Samarkand, Tashkent (then called Shash), Kashgar, Kucha, Turfan, Hami, and Kansu. An alternative way of passage led from Merv to Balkh, Badakhshan, Kashgar, Khotan, Lob Nor, and Tunhwang. By way of these various caravan routes, merchandise from the Far East was conveyed directly to Europe.

In addition to these continental routes, which corresponded to the old Silk Road, the Mongol conquest reopened the sea route or spice route. While Arab and Seljuk Iran had remained practically closed to the West, the Mongol khans of Persia freely opened their states to merchants and Christian missionaries who wanted to go to China by sea. From the fall of the Baghdad caliphate until the final triumph of Islam in the khanate of Persia, Latin travelers could pass without difficulty through Iran from Tabriz to Hormuz, the embarkation point for Thana, Quilon, and Zayton. Odorico da Pordenone's journey, as will be seen, was typical in this respect. Conversely, silk from China and spices from the East Indies were unloaded at Hormuz to be carried by caravans through Mongol Persia to the great market of Tabriz, and from there to the Christian ports of Trebizond or Lajazzo.

The point must be stressed, for this freedom of passage was the one great beneficial result of the Mongol conquest, at the price of so much massacre. The union of China, Turkestan, Persia, and Russia in one huge empire, regulated by a strict *yasaq* under princes who were concerned for the safety of the caravans and tolerant of all cults, reopened by sea and by land the world routes that had been blocked since the end of antiquity. But the Polos' journeys testify to a far greater activity than that of which Maes Titianos' name has remained the symbol. For the first time in history, China, Iran, and the West came into real contact with one another. Such was the result, as unexpected as it was fortunate, of the appalling Jenghiz-Khanite conquest.

CATHOLICISM IN CHINA UNDER THE MONGOL DYNASTY

The Polos' journey was not unique. In 1291, Petrus da Lucalongo, an Italian merchant, arrived in China from Tabriz by way of the Indian Ocean. He settled in Peking, where he must have prospered, for in 1305 he gave the Franciscan Giovanni da Montecorvino a piece of land near the imperial palace. About twenty years later, the Genoese Andalo da Savignano also went to China, where he won the trust of the grand khan. He returned to the West as Mongol ambassador, and then left for China once more in 1338, probably by the Tana route.[90]

Simultaneously with these adventurous traders came the missionaries. In 1289 Pope Nicholas IV, who had just learned from Rabban Sauma of the existence of many native Christian communities in the Mongol Empire, sent Giovanni da Montecorvino to the Far East with letters for Arghun the khan of Persia and the grand khan Kublai. Montecorvino stayed some time in Tabriz with Arghun and then left in 1291 for India, where he remained for thirteen months in Mylapore in company with the merchant Petrus da Lucalongo. After this sojourn, he took ship for China, where the grand khan Temür, Kublai's grandson and successor, gave him a warm welcome. Odorico da Pordenone writes of this:

"We have one of our Friars Minor as bishop at the emperor's court. He pronounces a benediction whenever the emperor goes riding, and the emperor kisses the cross with great devotion."

At Peking, Montecorvino built two churches, one through the generosity of the Italian trader Petrus da Lucalongo, who had come with him from Mylapore (1305). Within a few years, he baptized "more than ten thousand Tatars" [91] and began to translate the Psalter into one of the languages current among his flock. A notable convert to Catholicism was Prince Körgüz of the Öngüt, that is, George, who had been born and bred a Nestorian.[92] This conversion was of inestimable value, for after it "Prince George" was bound to afford even more effective protection to the Catholic missionaries, whom, as Emperor Temür's son-in-law, he appointed to exalted positions at court. Körgüz' young son was baptized under the name of Shu-an—John—in Montecorvino's honor.

In 1307, Pope Clement V appointed Montecorvino archbishop of Cambaluc (Peking). In 1313, there arrived in this city three Franciscans who were to be his suffragans: Andrew of Perugia, Gerard, and Peregrino.[93] At about the same time, the Pope also sent the brothers Thomas, Jerome, and Peter of Florence to the Mongols. Jerome was made archbishop of the Crimea (Gazaria, Khazaria), with jurisdiction over the khanate of Kipchak. Gerard became bishop of Zayton (Chüanchow in Fukien), where a rich Armenian lady provided funds for the building of a church. At his death, the bishopric of Zayton passed to Peregrino. Peregrino, who died in 1322 or 1323, was replaced in his turn by Andrew of Perugia. The favor shown these missionaries at the Mongol court is stressed in a letter which Andrew sent from Zayton in January, 1326, to the superiors of his monastery at Perugia. In it he tells that the grand khan—at that time Yesun Temür—had granted him a pension valued at a hundred golden florins. Andrew adds that he has built near Zayton a house for twenty-two monks and that he divides his time between his church and his mountain hermitage.

After Montecorvino and Andrew of Perugia, the most famous Catholic missionary in Mongol China was the Franciscan Odorico da Pordenone (born about 1265, died in 1331). Odorico embarked at Venice around 1314 (some authors say not until 1318) and landed at Trebizond. From there he went first to the Mongol khanate of Persia. He visited Tabriz and noted its commercial importance, observing that it brought in more revenue to the khan of Persia than the king of France received from his whole realm. He remarked also upon the many Nestorian and Armenian communities of Azerbaijan. He intended originally to reach India by way of eastern Iran, but at Yezd he had to turn back owing to the violence of Muslim fanaticism in that area. In these years, 1313–15, eastern Iran was the scene of a fratricidal conflict. Oljaitu, the khan of Persia, was at war with the Jagatai khan of Turkestan, Esen-buqa, and with Esen-buqa's nephew Dawud-khoja, lord of Afghanistan. Moreover, communications between eastern Iran and India were rendered difficult by the plundering expeditions which, from 1305 to 1327, the Jagatai Mongols of Turkestan continually led against the Punjab. Odorico therefore turned back and headed westward for Iraq 'Arabi, where at Basra he embarked for Hormuz. From Hormuz, he sailed for India, landing at Thana near Bombay either in 1322 or at the end of 1323 or beginning of 1324. Here he collected the relics of four Franciscans who had been massacred a short time before (April 9–11, 1321) by Muslims. He visited the Malabar coast, which was the true land of spices, the kingdom of pepper, and made valuable notes on this subject, which was of such great importance to the commerce of his day.[94] Going on to St. Thomé or Mylapore, where the body of the Apostle Thomas was said to lie,[95] and where there was a large Christian colony, he comments on the degeneration of these old Nestorian communities which, amid their essentially idolatrous surroundings, had reverted almost to paganism. In Mongolia, Rubruck had similarly observed the Nestorian clergy fighting the shamans on their own ground and stooping almost to their level. It was above all the monstrous divagations of Hinduism, the blood-drenched madness of fanatics who flung themselves beneath the chariot of their idol, that drew from our saint the same cry of revulsion as it did from Hsüan-tsang, the seventh-century Buddhist pilgrim. Odorico then visited Ceylon and Java and called at Champa, whence he took ship for China.

Odorico landed at Canton, which he calls *Sincalan,* from the Arab name *Sinkalan* or *Sinikalan.* He was impressed by the great density of the population, the wealth of the country, and the plentifulness and cheapness of the wares, as well as by the hard-working character of the inhabitants, who were all born traders and wonderful craftsmen. He was struck too by the number of deities revered by the people.[96] He was no less interested in Chüanchow or Zayton, which in his manuscripts is spelt *Caitan:* a city "twice as large as Rome." Where he was received at the Franciscan monastery already mentioned and could admire the cathedral built by his brethren in St. Francis, as well as the hermitage that they had made in the hills. Hangchow, called in Odorico's manuscripts *Cansay* or *Guinzai,* astonished him even more. It is, he says, "the greatest city in the world, situated between two lakes and among canals and lagoons, like our Venice." [97] The sight of such a diversity of peoples—Chinese, Mongol, Buddhist, Nestorian, Muslim—dwelling together in this enormous city filled him with admiration for Mongol administration. "The fact that so many different races are able to live together peaceably under the control of a single power seems to me one of the greatest wonders of the world." At Hangchow Odorico met a Mongol dignitary who had been converted (almost certainly from Nestorianism) to Catholicism by Franciscans, and who greeted him by the title of *ata,* that is, father, in the Turkic language.[98] Thanks to this man, he was allowed to visit a Buddhist monastery, where he discussed metempsychosis with the bonzes.

From Hangchow, Odorico went on to *Quelinfu,* known to Cordier as Kin-ling-fu and to us as Nanking, and then to *Ianzu* or Yangchow, where he found a Franciscan monastery as well as a number of Nestorian churches. Next he visited *Sunzumatu,* Marco Polo's *Singiumatu* (most probably modern Tsining in Shantung), which he identifies as an important silk market. Finally he arrived at the "khan's city," *Khanbaligh,* or Peking.

It is here that the grand khan resides, in a palace so huge that its walls are at least four miles in circumference, and enclose a number of secondary palaces. The imperial city is thus composed of several concentric enclosures, all inhabited; and it is in the second enclosure that the grand khan lives with his whole family and all his court. Within this enclosure rises an artificial knoll on which stands the principal palace. This hill has been planted with very beautiful trees, from which it takes its name of Green Hill. It is encircled by a lake and a pond. The lake is spanned by a wonderful bridge, the most beautiful that I have ever seen, both in the quality of its marble and the subtlety of its architecture. In the pond may be seen a multitude of fishing birds, such as ducks, swans, and wild geese. Nor need the grand khan leave the enclosures of his palaces to indulge in the peasures of the chase, for the encircling walls contain also a large park, full of wild beasts.

Odorico next describes the receptions at the Jenghiz-Khanite court. (The grand khan at this time was Kublai's great-grandson Yesun Temür, who reigned from October 4, 1323, to August 15, 1328.)

When the grand khan is seated upon his throne in imperial majesty, the first empress sits at his left hand, one step lower than himself; then, on the third step, are three other concubines. After them come other ladies of the blood royal. On the grand khan's right hand sits his eldest son, and below him in degree the princes of the blood. . . . And I, Brother Odorico, stayed in this city [of Peking] for three years and a half in the company of our Friars Minor, who have a monastery there and who even hold rank at the grand khan's court. And as we went there from time to time to give him our blessing, I took the opportunity to learn what I could and observed all things closely. . . . Indeed, one of our brethren [Giovanni da Montecorvino] is archbishop at court, and pronounces benediction over the grand khan whenever the latter is about to travel. One day when this ruler was returning to Peking, our bishop, our Friars Minor, and I went forth to meet him at two days' journey from the city. We advanced in procession toward the sovereign, who was enthroned in his chariot, bearing before us a cross affixed to a long staff and singing the anthem *Veni Sancte Spiritus*. When we had come near to the imperial chariot, the grand khan recognized our voices and summoned us to his immediate presence. As we then approached, with the cross held high, he removed his headdress, which is beyond price, and bowed in reverence before the cross. The bishop pronounced his blessing and the grand khan kissed the cross with great devotion. I then placed incense in the thurible and our bishop censed the prince. But as etiquette requires that no one should come before His Majesty without offering him a gift, we presented a silver dish full of fruit which he very cordially accepted, even making as if to taste of it. We then stepped aside lest we be hurt by the cavalry escort that followed him, and withdrew among certain exalted persons of that escort who had been baptized [Nestorian Turks who had been converted to Catholicism]. They in turn received our modest offering with as much joy as if it had been a magnificent present.[99]

Odorico also gives an account of the colossal battues organized for the grand khan in an imperial forest twenty days' journey from Peking. The description of the hunt, with the grand khan mounted upon an elephant and the Mongol lords discharging arrows of their own colors, is most picturesque. "The cries of the animals and the barking of dogs make such a din that no one can hear another speak." Once the climax was reached and the scene properly set, Yesun Temür, like Jenghiz his ancestor, broke the ring of beaters and in the spirit of Buddha allowed the surviving animals to escape.

Lastly, Odorico notes the excellence of the postal service in the Mongol Empire. "Couriers speed at full gallop on prodigiously swift horses, or on racing dromedaries. On coming within sight of a relay station, they sound a horn to announce their arrival. Thus warned, the wardens call out a relief rider with a fresh mount. Seizing the dispatches, this man leaps into the saddle and gallops to the next stage, there to be relieved in his turn. Thus within twenty-four hours the grand khan receives news from lands normally reckoned at three days' journey on horseback."

After staying in Peking for two or three years, Odorico da Pordenone seems to have left the capital about 1328 to return to Europe by way of Central Asia. He passed through the territory of the Öngüt Nestorian Turks, one of whose princes, George (d. 1298), had been converted to Catholicism by Giovanni da Montecorvino. Like Marco Polo before him,[100] Odorico confuses these Öngüt princes with the Kerayit "Prester John," but it is quite certainly the Öngüt princes that he has in mind when he mentions their frequent intermarriage with Jenghiz-Khanite princesses (see above). The town of *Thozan,* as he calls the Öngüt capital, is, as Pelliot has established, medieval Tungsheng, that is, the Toqto or perhaps the Suiyuan of modern times. From the Öngüt country, Odorico set off for the land of *Kansan*—that is to say, Kanchow, in Kansu—of which he notes that the towns and villages were so closely strung along the great caravan route that on leaving one the traveler could spy the walls of the next. After that Odorico must have taken one of the trails across the Gobi, either to the north or the south of the Tarim basin, collecting interesting information about

Tibet and the Lamaist theocracy as he went. He never actually entered Tibet, however, despite statements to the contrary.[101] He was back in Padua in May, 1330, and died on January 14, 1331, in his monastery of Udine, after having dictated the story of his mission.

Giovanni da Montecorvino, archbishop of Peking, who had received Odorico, died shortly after the latter's departure, in 1328 or 1329.[102] In 1333 Rome replaced him by another Friar Minor named Nicholas, who took the Central Asian route. News of Nicholas' arrival at Almalik, near modern Kuldja in the Ili region, reached Europe in 1338, but he seems to have died before reaching China.[103] In 1339, Pope Benedict XII sent the Franciscan Giovanni da Marignolli to China. Having arrived in Constantinople from Naples in May, 1339, Marignolli re-embarked for Caffa (Feodosiya) in the Crimea. He then paid a visit to Özbeg, khan of Kipchak, to whom he presented a number of gifts from the Pope. In the spring of 1340, he went from Kipchak to Almalik, in the Jagatai khanate, where he regrouped the Christian communities which had been decimated· by the persecutions carried out during the previous year (see p. 342). He then crossed Central Asia and arrived in Peking in 1342. On August 19 he was received in audience by the grand khan Toghan Temür, tenth successor to Kublai, and presented him with a big horse from the West, a gift much appreciated by the royal recipient.[104] On December 26, 1347, Marignolli sailed from Chüanchow, breaking his voyage on the coast of India for one year at Mylapore and Quilon. He returned to Avignon in 1353.[105]

In 1370, Pope Urban V appointed as archbishop of Peking a professor at the University of Paris, Guillaume da Prato, and next year he named as his legate to China Francesco da Podio. But the Mongol dynasty had just been overthrown (see below). The victorious Chinese—the Ming—included Christianity in the proscription which they imposed on all foreign doctrines introduced or approved by the Mongols. Christianity had the disadvantage of being considered a Mongol religion by national Chinese reactionaries. The same thing had happened in 840, at the time of the downfall of the Uigur khagans, when the Manichaeism protected under their regime was proscribed overnight in the belief that it had been imposed by the barbarians (see p. 124).

In order to consider the various religions of the Mongol Empire of China, we have had to anticipate certain events and to interrupt the history of the Kublai dynasty. To this we now return.

Emperor Temür (1294–1307) was the last able member of the Mongol dynasty of China. After him, degeneration set in at once. As Jenghiz Khan had foreseen—if the statement attributed to him is authentic—the descendants of the steppe hunters had forgotten their hardy origins and the causes of their rise to power, and had succumbed to the pleasures of the sedentary life and to the luxury of which Marco Polo and Odorico da Pordenone have given us some idea. Mongka had been the last to try to bring the conquerors back to the simple ways of the steppe. Kublai, who succeeded him, decisively reoriented his dynasty toward the Chinese way of life: a sedentary existence among civilized pleasures. Under a man of his personality (or that of his grandson Temür), this was all to the good, for to Mongol hardihood—which in him remained unimpaired—he added Chinese ability. But with the coming of weak, second-rate emperors, this combination proved wholly detrimental. The last Jenghiz-Khanites of China were over-Sinicized, softened by court life and its voluptuous excesses, and cut off from the outer world by a screen of favorites and mistresses, literati and bureaucrats, and so lost virtually every vestige of their Mongol vigor. These descendants of the most redoubtable and terrible conqueror known to history dwindled away into feebleness, ineptitude, tearful vacillation, and, in the hour of disaster, lamentation. Of the barbarian character they retained only the inability to accustom themselves to the Chinese idea of the state as an abstract entity. Although occupying the throne of the Sons of Heaven, they remained a clan whose members wrangled in public, snatched power from one another, and destroyed one another. At the time of the Chinese rebellion, they were so hopelessly divided among themselves and so bitterly jealous that, rather than unite in the face of danger, they let the Chinese overcome them one by one.

In addition, their lives were shortened by their hedonistic

excesses. Kublai died on February 18, 1294, at the age of seventy-nine. His favorite son (the second) Chen-kin—Rashid ad-Din's Chinkim—died in January, 1286. Temür, Chen-kin's son, was able to cure himself of the inveterate drunkenness of the Jenghiz-Khanites and proved a better sovereign than his grandfather had expected; but he died prematurely, without issue, on February 10, 1307, at the age of forty-two. The throne was then disputed, as has been shown, between a grandson and great-grandson of Kublai: Prince Ananda, viceroy of Tangut (Kansu),[106] against Prince Khaishan, viceroy of Karakorum and Mongolia, who on the Khangai frontier commanded the strongest army in the empire. Khaishan won the struggle and had his rival put to death. Having given proof of his military ability, notably in the war against Qaidu, he aroused the hopes of his subjects; but owing to his addiction to alcohol and women, he died at thirty-one (January 27, 1311). His brother Buyantu (Ayurparibhadra), "mild, beneficent, and persevering," who wanted to subject Mongol candidates to the same examinations as those given to the Chinese literati, died at thirty-five (March 1, 1320). Buyantu's son Suddhipala, aged seventeen, was assassinated three years later by a clique of Mongol dignitaries who proclaimed his cousin Yesun Temür emperor (September 4, 1323).

Yesun Temür, who commanded the army in Mongolia, was proclaimed emperor in his camp on the banks of the Kerulen, and ceremonially crowned in Peking on December 11, 1323, at the age of thirty, but five years later (August 15, 1328) he died, worn out by his debauches. Chinese history depicts him as an ineffectual, sluggish prince, the prisoner of a huge and extravagant court. At his death, civil war broke out. Togh Temür, Khaishan's son, seized power on November 16, 1328, but ceded the throne to his elder brother Kusala, viceroy of Mongolia. Kusala died suddenly on February 27, 1329, and Togh Temür rose again to the throne, but he too, worn out by his excesses, died on October 2, 1332, at the age of twenty-eight.[107] Rinchenpal, Kusala's younger son, was proclaimed emperor at the age of six (October 23, 1332), but he died two months afterward (December 14). Toghan Temür, Rinchenpal's thirteen-year-old elder brother, succeeded him on July 19, 1333.

Toghan Temür's reign saw the fall of the Mongol dynasty. During his youth the Mongol lords squabbled for power amid

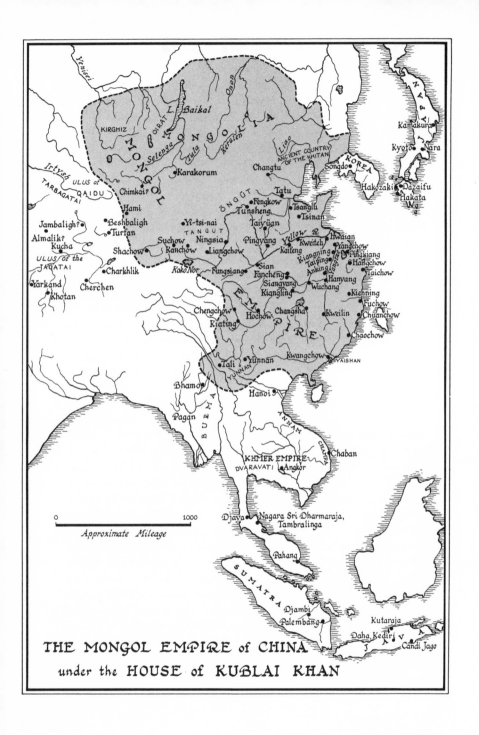

THE MONGOL EMPIRE of CHINA
under the HOUSE of KUBLAI KHAN

court dramas and intrigues. At first this power was wielded by a lord of Märkit origin named Bayan. After his fall from favor and his death in 1340, the struggles between the Mongol factions completed the ruin of the dynasty's prestige and the erosion of the central power. Toghan Temür, a weak, vacillating person, found delight only in the company of his favorites and of Tibetan lamas. Dulled by debauchery, he took no interest in affairs of state and ignored the Chinese national rebellion now rumbling in the south.

This spectacle of decadence encouraged Chinese "patriots" to rebel against foreign domination. The revolt, like that of 1912, began on the lower Yangtze and in the Canton region. It was spontaneous and sporadic, led by a great number of half-patriot, half-bandit chiefs, who quarreled among themselves while making war on the Mongols. A typical example was Hsü Chou-huei, who seized Hanyang and Wuchang, the twin towns in Hupeh, from the Mongols (1352), then Siangyang (1356), finally gaining control of the greater part of the two Hu (Hupeh and Hunan) and of Kiangsi. In 1359, however, he was supplanted by his lieutenant Ch'en Yu-liang, son of a simple fisherman now playing the part of a candidate to empire who maintained residence at Kiukiang, north of Lake Poyang. Another of the same stamp was Liu Fu-t'ung, an adventurer who in the name of alleged descendants of the Sung dynasty achieved brief mastery of Kaifeng in 1358, but was driven out by the Mongol prince Chaghan Temür in 1359. A fourth rebel leader, Chang Shih-ch'eng, had possessed himself of Yangchow at the mouth of the Yangtze (1356), while the coasts of Chekiang and Fukien were ravaged by a bold pirate named Fang Kuo-chen.

All these desperadoes were to be eclipsed by the cleverest of them all, Chu Yüan-chang, the future emperor Hung-wu, founder of the Ming dynasty. He was the son of a poor farm laborer of Anhwei and had formerly been a bonze. In 1355 he had taken up arms in the Taiping area on the banks of the lower Yangtze. Although at first he was merely the leader of a group, like all his competitors, he distinguished himself from the rest by his political sense and by tactfulness and humanity in his dealings with local inhabitants, whom he was able to attach to himself without the use of force. In 1356 he seized Nanking from the Mongols and made it his capital. It was not long before he established there, amid all the prevailing anarchy, a regular government. In 1363, he beat and slew his rival Ch'en Yu-liang near Jaochow on the eastern shore of Lake Poyang and appropriated his hereditary domains: Hupeh, Hunan, and Kiangsi. He thus became master of the entire Yangtze basin. In 1367 he snatched Chekiang from his other rival Chang Shih-ch'eng, and in 1368 he won the Fukien ports from Fang Kuo-chen the corsair. In the same year, Canton and the two towns named Kuang accepted him without a struggle, and with that the Ming were masters of the whole of the south.

The Mongol court appears to have remained relatively indifferent to the loss of southern China, the former Sung empire, conquered by Kublai a century earlier and lost through the apathy and ineptitude of his feeble descendants. The Jenghiz-Khanites were far more interested in northern China, the former Kin realm and their first conquest, which up to this time had remained intact. But to defend it, some measure of cohesion was needed, and the Mongol princes had never been more divided than they were now. In 1360, two of the most energetic among them, the best generals of the imperial army—Chaghan Temür, who had reconquered Kaifeng, and Bolod Temür, governor of the Tatung marches in Shansi—almost came to blows over the allocation of the governorship of Taiyüan (then Tsining). Next, from Mongolia, an Ogödäi prince tried to take advantage of the situation to overthrow the house of Kublai. He marched on the Great Wall and defeated an imperial army near Shangtuho (Dolonnor), but was then killed by treachery (November, 1361). Among the imperial leaders themselves, civil war was raging. In 1363, as the empire was losing southern China, Bolod Temür resorted to armed force in an attempt to seize the government of Taiyüan—that is, Shansi—from Kökö Temür, Chaghan's heir. Prince Ayurshiridhara, the heir to the throne, sided against Bolod and ordered Kökö Temür to remove him from his governorship of Tatung. Then, on September 9, 1364, Bolod entered Peking at the head of his army and forced the emperor Toghan to appoint him generalissimo, while the heir to the throne fled to Kökö Temür's army at Taiyüan. But Bolod failed to overcome these two adversaries, and in September, 1365, he was assassinated at Peking as the result of a court conspiracy to which the emperor himself was a party. Kökö Temür then returned to

Peking with the prince imperial and was appointed generalissimo in his turn, until the day when he too fell into disgrace (1367). Small wonder, then, that while the Mongol court and nobility were engaged in this civil strife, the Chinese insurgents were able to win possession of the whole of southern China. It was against a demoralized foe that the Ming leader undertook the conquest of the north.

It was a triumphal march. Chu Yüan-chang left Nanking in August, 1368, and entered Hopei by way of Kwangping and Kwantao. The Mongol general Buyan Temür tried to defend the approaches of Peking, but was defeated and killed at Tungchow by Hsü Ta, the best commander of the new Ming ruler. Ayurshiridhara, the heir to the throne, fled to Mongolia, carrying with him the tablets of his ancestors. The emperor Toghan Temür himself left Peking for Shangtuho (Dolonnor) on the night of September 10. A Mongol prince, Temür-buqa, died gallantly in trying to defend the capital. The Ming then made their entry into Peking.

One last Mongol army still occupied Shansi, under the command of Kökö Temür, viceroy of Taiyüan, who, acting as an independent prince, had refused to help his sovereign, preferring to concentrate all his forces in defense of his own fief. But at the approach of the Chinese army under Hsü Ta, he too succumbed. Taiyüan was taken, while Kökö Temür fled to Kansu. The miserable emperor Toghan Temür, feeling no longer safe in Dolonnor, fled to Yingchang (Kailu) on the Shara Muren. There he died on May 23, 1370, filled with despair at having lost the empire of China, or rather the delights of the imperial demesnes: "My great city of Tatu [Peking], adorned with varied splendor; Shangtuho, my delectable cool summer retreat; and those yellowing plains, the delight and refreshment of my divine ancestors! What evil I have committed to lose my empire thus!" [108]

The khanate founded in China by Jenghiz Khan's descendants had lasted no more than a hundred years, from Kublai to Toghan Temür. The similar khanate that they had founded in Turkestan was destined, with varying fortunes and despite the break in continuity caused by Tamerlane, to endure until the seventeenth century.

8

Turkestan Under the House of Jagatai

Jagatai,[1] Jenghiz Khan's second son, had inherited the Issyk Kul region, the basin of the river Ili southeast of Lake Balkhash, and the steppes of the Chu and the Talas—or at any rate, the eastern part of them. According to Juvaini, his winter camp was at Marawsik-ila and his summer one at Quyash, both places being in the Ili valley, the latter one near Almalik (not far from modern Kuldja). As dependencies he had Kashgaria and Transoxiana. In about 1260, Uiguria, the old Uigur country of Beshbaligh (modern Dzimsa), Turfan (Kara-khoja), and Kucha, became a direct dependency of the Jagataites, although up to that time it seems to have been attached to the grand khans of Karakorum. It was also from the court of Karakorum that the Transoxianan towns of Bukhara and Samarkand were for some time administered.

The khanate of Jagatai—for the territory took its name from the prince—corresponded to the ancient kingdom of the Kara-Khitai *gur-khans*. And like the Kara-Khitai state, it was a Turkic country under Mongol domination: the Mongol realm of Turkestan. But the Jagatai rulers, resembling in this the Kara-Khitai *gur-khans* and the even earlier seventh-century khans of the western T'u-chüeh, had no conception of how to establish a regular state on our western pattern, or on that of China or

326

Persia. For this they lacked the historical background. Their cousins of Kublai's house, or of the house of Hulägu in Persia, had found at their disposal the age-old tradition of ancient centralized empires—a whole history of administrative custom, of yamens and divans. They became Sons of Heaven here, sultans there. They could identify themselves with states that were sharply defined, geographically and historically as well as culturally. Jagatai's sons had nothing like this. Their realm with its shifting boundaries had as its center no Peking or Tabriz, but a prairie. It never occurred to them to settle in Kashgar or Khotan, in the Tarim oases, for these were gardens enclosed, too small for their herds and cavalry. Nor would they settle among the Tadzhiks and the more or less Iranized Turks of Bukhara and Samarkand, in those crowded cities whose Muslim fanaticism and mob turbulence must have been utterly repugnant to their nomadic natures. For far longer than their kinsmen of other *ulus,* they remained entirely ignorant of urban life and lacking in any understanding of its needs or its uses. Thus the khan Baraq did not hesitate to order the pillage of Bukhara and Samarkand—his own cities!—simply to obtain funds for the raising of an army.[2] Until the end, in the fifteenth century, the Jagataites continued to roam as nomads between the Ili and the Talas, and remained men of the steppes. In a family that had produced statesmen like Arghun, Ghazan, Oljaitu, Kublai, and Temür, they represented Mongol cultural backwardness. Not that they were any more resistant to their surroundings than Kublai's line, which became Chinese, or Hulägu's, which turned Persian. Living as they did in a Turkic country, they became Turks from the fourteenth century onward, to such an extent that the Turkic language spoken in the East became known as Jagatai Turkic. But these Turks of the Ili, remnants of the old Türgish and Qarluq Turks, had no more cultural past than the Mongols themselves. Between the Uigur Buddhic-Nestorian culture of Beshbaligh and the Arabo-Persian culture of Bukhara and Samarkand, the house of Jagatai remained suspended, incapable of choosing. No doubt, at the beginning it was subjected more to Uigur influence, like Jenghiz Khan himself, the influence of the ancient Turko-Mongols who remained faithful to the Buddha and to the Nestorian cross. Then at the beginning of the fourteenth century, the Jagataites turned to Islam, though in the Mongol fashion, without fanaticism and without scripture; so that even then, in the eyes of the devout Muslims of Samarkand, they appeared half-pagan, while Tamerlane's campaigns against them were to assume the aspect of a Muslim Holy War.

Jagatai, founder of the khanate which he ruled from 1227 to 1242, was, as we have seen, a Mongol of the old type. His father Jenghiz Khan, whom he admired and feared, had appointed him guardian of the *yasaq*—of the code and of discipline —and he spent his life in observing this legislation himself and in ensuring that those about him did so too. One day, having ridden a race with his younger brother Ogödäi, who was then grand khan, and beaten him, he came next day to ask his forgiveness, like a criminal.[3] Incidentally, he felt no resentment at his younger brother's elevation to the position of grand khan, because this had been their father's decision. For the same reason, although he ruled over Muslim peoples, he showed some hostility toward Islam, particularly in regard to the matter of ablutions and the slaughter of cattle, where the precepts of the Koran were contrary to Mongol customs and to the *yasaq*.[4] In spite of this, one of his ministers, Qutb ad-Din Habash 'Amid of Otrar (d. 1260), was a Muslim.[5] Moreover, Jenghiz Khan had entrusted the administration and the fiscal affairs of the cities of Transoxiana—Bukhara, Samarkand, and so on—to another Muslim, Mahmud Yalavach, who set up residence at Khodzhent in Fergana. This did not deter Jagatai from dismissing Mahmud from his post, but (as Mahmud was directly responsible to the grand khan) Ogödäi, who was then in power, pointed out the irregularity of Jagatai's conduct and reinstated Mahmud.[6] Mahmud was succeeded by his son Mas'ud Yalavach or Mas'ud-beg, who continued to administer the Transoxianan cities in the name of the grand khan and also, Barthold thinks, the other "civilized provinces" of Jagatai, all the way to the Chinese frontier. He was present in this capacity at the *quriltai* of 1246, where he was confirmed in his functions. In 1238–39, a popular Muslim movement, aimed against both the proprietary classes and the Mongol administration, broke out in Bukhara. Mas'ud crushed it and at the same time managed to save the town from the vengeance of Mongol troops.[7]

At his death (1242), Jagatai left the throne to his grandson Qara-Hulägu, the son of Jagatai's eldest son Mütügen, who had been killed in 1221 at the siege of Bamian and whose death had caused such sorrow to his family. Qara-Hulägu reigned from 1242 to 1246 under the tutelage of the widowed khatun Ebuskun. In 1246 the new grand khan Güyük replaced him by a younger brother of Jagatai and personal friend, Prince Yissu-Mangu,[8] a personal friend of his whose wits were dulled by drink and who left the government of the country to his wife and to his Muslim minister of state the Beha ad-Din Marghinani, a man whom Juvaini praises as a Maecenas.[9] But Yissu-Mangu also ruled only for a very short time (1246–52), and for similar reasons. In the quarrels over the imperial succession, which in 1249–50 divided all the Jenghiz-Khanite houses, he sided with the house of Ogödäi against Mongka's candidature. After his accession, Mongka deposed Yissu-Mangu and replaced him in August, 1252, by that same Qara-Hulägu whom Yissu-Mangu had removed five years before. Qara-Hulägu was even given the task of putting Yissu-Mangu, his own uncle, to death, after having seized power. It is clear from this series of palace dramas that the *ulus* of Jagatai was hardly autonomous at this time and that it was merely a dependency of the Karakorum court, exposed to all the repercussions of the family revolts occurring there. It was in fact a viceroyalty, closely linked to the central power, a collateral branch treated as a junior one, although in fact senior to the houses of Ogödäi and Tolui.

Qara-Hulägu died, however, while on his way to reclaim his fief (1252), and it fell to his widow Orghana to carry out the imperial command to have Yissu-Mangu executed.[10] The old minister Habash 'Amid, who as Qara-Hulägu's adherent had suffered under Yissu-Mangu, took his own revenge on Beha ad-Din Marghinani and had him put to death.[11] Orghana took over control of the khanate of Jagatai and held it for nine years (1252–61).

The old pre-Jenghiz Khan dynasties existing under the suzerainty of the house of Jagatai were likewise affected by the palace revolutions at Karakorum. The Uigur kingdom of Beshbaligh (Kucheng), Turfan, and Kucha provides an example of this. Barchuq the Uigur ruler had been, as was noted, a faithful vassal to Jenghiz Khan throughout his life, and had supported him against Küchlüg, against the shah of Khwarizm, and against the Hsi-Hsia. As a reward, Jenghiz Khan intended to give him one of his daughters—his favorite one, it is said—Al'altun-bäki or Altun-bäki. The marriage never took place, however, first because of Jenghiz Khan's death and then because of the death of the princess herself. Barchuq himself died shortly afterward and was succeeded as *idiqut*—that is, king of the Uigur—by his son Kishmain, who went to the Mongol court for his investiture by Ogödai the grand khan.[12] Similarly, on Kishmain's death, the Mongol queen regent Törägänä conferred Uigur royalty upon Salendi, his brother.[13] A Buddhist, Salendi seems to have been hostile to Islam, and Muslims complained of his severity. In the quarrel between the Ogödäites and Mongka over the succession, in 1251, at least some of Salendi's entourage sided with the house of Ogödäi. Indeed, one of his chief officers, named Bala or Bela, was condemned to death with Oghul Qaimish's accomplices by the triumphant Mongka, and escaped only by a lucky chance. Salendi, whose conscience may not have been altogether easy, hastened to pay court to Mongka (1252), and had just returned from the imperial *ordu* when the storm broke. The Muslims of Uiguria accused him of wanting to slaughter them, and gave details. The massacre was to take place, they held, "on a Friday, in the mosques during prayer," at Beshbaligh and all over the country. One of Mongka's representatives—as it turned out, a Muslim named Saif ad-Din who was at Beshbaligh at the time—received the accusation and made Salendi return to Karakorum to give an account of the affair to the grand khan. The unfortunate Uigur prince, on being questioned and put to torture, ended by making the desired confession. Mongka sent him back to Beshbaligh to suffer his punishment. D'Ohsson comments: "He was beheaded on a Friday by his own brother Ukenj[14] in the presence of a huge throng and to the great satisfaction of the Muslims, who seem to have been determined to bring about the execution of this Buddhist prince." In fact, Salendi was executed as a partisan of the house of Ogödäi, and his brother was put in his place as Mongka's adherent; but this family quarrel gave the Muslim minority in Uiguria the opportunity of revenge upon the Buddhist majority (1252).[15]

Orghana, who is described as a beautiful, wise, and discerning princess, governed the khanate of Jagatai from 1252 to 1261. At this latter date, the khanate began once more to feel the repercussions of conflicts in Mongolia over the supreme khanate—in this case, the rivalry between the grand khan Kublai and his brother Ariq-böga. Ariq-böga, who at the moment was lord of Mongolia, nominated as "khan of Jagatai" a grandson of Jagatai and son of Baidar, Prince Alghu or Alughu, and gave him the task of guarding the Amu Darya frontier to prevent Hulägu the khan of Persia from sending reinforcements to Kublai. Alghu therefore went to Beshbaligh, removed Orghana from power, and was accepted without opposition from Almalik to the Amu Darya. His reign was to last from 1261 to 1266, but it followed a very different line from that intended by Ariq-böga.

Taking advantage of the struggle between Kublai and Ariq-böga, Alghu acted as an autonomous khan, and was the first of his house to do so. His suzerain Ariq-böga had sent commissioners into Jagatai to levy taxes and collect arms and livestock. Alghu, coveting this wealth, seized it, put the envoys to death, and declared for Kublai (ca. 1262). Ariq-böga was infuriated by this treachery and marched against Alghu. But Alghu made a successful beginning, beating the enemy advance guard near Pulad or Bolod, between the Sairam Nor and the Ebi Nor. Then, believing himself safe after this victory, he made the mistake of disbanding his troops and returning peacefully to his Ili headquarters. At this moment another of Ariq-böga's lieutenants arrived with a fresh army, invaded the Ili basin, occupied Almalik, and forced Alghu to flee toward Kashgar and Khotan. Ariq-böga then came himself to winter in the Almalik country, the heart of the Jagatai *ulus*, while Alghu withdrew to Samarkand (ca. 1262–63). So savagely did Ariq-böga behave in this beautiful Ili region, devastating the countryside and slaying all his enemy's partisans, that famine ensued and a number of his own officers deserted him with their troops. Seeing his army melting away, he tried to make peace with Alghu. He had with him princess Orghana, who had come to protest against her removal from the khanate of Jagatai, and therefore assigned her and Mas'ud Yalavach the mission of carrying peace proposals to Alghu in Samarkand. But here events took a dramatic turn. On Orghana's arrival, Alghu married her and appointed Mas'ud as his finance minister. Mas'ud's support was invaluable. This wise administrator succeeded in levying substantial contributions from Bukhara and Samarkand, thus allowing Alghu and Orghana to recruit a good army. Alghu was then able to repulse an invasion by the Ogödäi prince Qaidu, who had come down from his Imil domains. Meanwhile, deprived of resources and attacked in the west by Alghu and in the east by Kublai, Ariq-bögä was forced in 1264, as was seen, to surrender to Kublai.[16]

The result of these events was *de facto* if not *de jure* liberation of the khanate of Jagatai from the rigid control under which up to that time it had been held by the grand khans. Mas'ud Yalavach (d. 1289), who until then had administered Bukhara and Samarkand on behalf of the grand khans, thenceforth gathered the tax levies there for the benefit of Alghu. Alghu also enlarged the territories of his khanate by making war on Berke the khan of Kipchak, from whom he seized Otrar—which he destroyed—and the province of Khwarizm.[17]

At Alghu's death (1265 or 1266), his widow Orghana placed on the throne her son by her first marriage (to Qara-Hulägu), Mobarek-shah, who was the first Jagataite to be converted to Islam under Transoxianan influence. (Jamal Qarshi gives the date of his accession as March, 1266.) But Baraq, another Jagataite, grandson of Mütügen, obtained a *yarligh* from the grand khan Kublai appointing him coregent with his cousin Mobarek.[18] Once on the Ili, Baraq subverted the troops, seized Mobarek himself at Khodzhent (September, 1266, according to Jamal Qarshi), deposed him, and reduced him to the position of master of the royal hunt. Although he owed his throne to Kublai, Baraq soon quarreled with him. The grand khan had appointed his agent Mogholtai to the governorship of Chinese Turkestan. Baraq drove out this dignitary and replaced him by one of his own men. Kublai sent a detachment of 6,000 horsemen to reinstate the deposed governor, but Baraq met them with 30,000 men, forcing Kublai's cavalry to retire without fighting. Baraq also sent troops to plunder the city of Khotan, which was under Kublai's authority.

Against Qaidu, Baraq was less fortunate. It has been noted how Qaidu, head of the house of Ogödäi and ruler of the Imil in Tarbagatai, competed with Kublai for the title of grand khan and for suzerainty over the other Jenghiz-Khanite *ulus*. He began by demanding homage from Baraq, and attacked him. In an early battle, near the Amu Darya, Baraq lured the enemy into an ambush and took many prisoners and much booty. But Qaidu obtained the support of Mangu Timur, khan of Kipchak, who sent an army of 50,000 against Baraq under Prince Berkejar. Defeated by this leader in a great battle, Baraq withdrew into Transoxiana, where, by means of further extortions at the expense of Bukhara and Samarkand, he was able to re-equip his army. He was preparing for a supreme effort when Qaidu offered him peace. Qaidu, who wanted his hands free to tackle Kublai in Mongolia, allowed Baraq to keep Transoxiana. In return, Baraq had to leave Qaidu in virtual command of the Ili and of eastern Turkestan, and even in Turkestan he had to acknowledge himself as Qaidu's vassal. A great *quriltai* of reconciliation on this basis was held, according to Wassaf, in the Qatwan steppe north of Samarkand in about 1267, though Rashid ad-Din states that it took place on the Talas in the spring of 1269.[19] Barthold writes: "An empire completely independent of the grand khan Kublai was thus set up in Central Asia, under the suzerainty of Qaidu. All the princes [who took part in this agreement] had to consider themselves as blood brothers (*anda*). The property of town and country populations was to be protected, and the princes had to be content with grazing lands in the steppes or mountains, and alert to keep the nomads' herds away from cultivated areas. Two-thirds of Transoxiana were left to Baraq, but there too the administration of farm lands was entrusted to Mas'ud [Yalavach] by Qaidu."

To keep Baraq away from eastern Turkestan, Qaidu, now his suzerain, sent him to win the khanate of Persia from the house of Hulägu, represented at this time by the khan Abaqa, Hulägu's son and successor. Once more, in spite of Mas'ud's expostulations, Baraq overtaxed the townsmen of Bukhara and Samarkand in order to fit out his army and, but for Mas'ud's entreaties, would have sacked the two cities completely. He then crossed the Amu Darya and pitched camp near Merv, at the head of an army distinguished by a whole staff of Jenghiz-Khanite princes, including Büri and his cousins Nikpai Oghul and Mobarek-shah (the predecessor whom he had deposed).[20] His first objective was the conquest of Afghanistan, which he no doubt claimed on the strength of his grandfather Mütügen's death at the siege of Bamian in 1221.

The campaign opened well. Near Herat, Baraq defeated Prince Buchin, brother of Abaqa and governor of Khurasan. He occupied the greater part of the province (about May, 1270), sacked Nishapur, and forced Shams ad-Din Muhammad Kert of Herat to render him homage and pay tribute. But Abaqa the khan of Persia, who had hastened from Azerbaijan, enticed him into a trap near Herat and, on July 22, 1270, inflicted a crushing defeat upon him. Baraq returned to Transoxiana with the remnants of his army. Crippled by a fall from his horse, he spent the winter in Bukhara, where he was converted to Islam under the name of Sultan Ghiyath ad-Din.

Baraq's disaster persuaded his princely kinsmen and vassals to withdraw their support. He therefore went to Tashkent to beg help from his suzerain Qaidu. Qaidu took the field with 20,000 men, less to help him than to profit from his misfortunes. Baraq, it is said, died of fright—or was discreetly eliminated by Qaidu's men—at the moment of his suzerain's arrival (August 9, 1271, according to Jamal Qarshi).[21]

After Baraq's death, his four sons joined with the two sons of Alghu in an effort to rid Transoxiana of Qaidu's armies, but they were continually defeated, although they too had occasion to loot the Transoxianan cities which had begun to flourish under Mas'ud Yalavach's wise administration. It was thus not to any of them that Qaidu gave the khanate of Transoxiana in 1271, but to another Jagataite named Nikpai Oghul. When Nikpai Oghul tried to shake off his yoke, Qaidu had him put to death and replaced him as khan with Tuqa Timur, another prince of the same house and grandson of Büri (ca. 1274?).[22] Tuqa Timur died soon thereafter, however, and Qaidu then gave the throne to Baraq's son Duwa (ca. 1274?). Meanwhile, Abaqa the khan of Persia, who had not forgotten the aggressive act of 1270, had taken his revenge. At the end of 1272, he sent an army into Khwarizm and

Transoxiana, where it sacked Urgench and Khiva and, on January 29, 1273, entered Bukhara. The pillage and burning lasted for a week, and such of the population as had not fled was decimated.[23] The army of the house of Hulägu carried 50,000 captives back to Persia.

From such events may be seen the appalling conditions imposed on urban populations by nomad domination. The nomad chiefs, when they were not ruining their own cities, made their disjointed family squabbles the pretext for descending at intervals upon towns dependent upon the opposite party and destroying them.

After the departure of the invaders, Mas'ud once again rebuilt the ruins which Mongol civil wars periodically left behind them in the luckless Transoxianan towns. He was to continue this task until his death in October or November, 1289. His work was then carried on by his three sons, who in turn administered Bukhara and Samarkand: Abu Bakr until May or June, 1298, Satilmish-beg until 1302 or 1303, and then Suyunitch.[24] But they too, by-passing the Jagataites, depended on the terrible Qaidu, who appointed the first two, while the third was put in power by Chäpär, Qaidu's son and successor.

Duwa, who had no doubt learned his lesson from the example of his predecessors, showed himself to be a loyal vassal of Qaidu. As the Uigur *idiqut* had maintained his allegiance to the grand khan Kublai, Qaidu and Duwa invaded Uiguria in 1275 in order to compel him to change sides. They then marched on his capital (Beshbaligh), but an imperial army came up in time and delivered the Uigur territory.[25] In 1301 Duwa again acted as Qaidu's brilliant second in the latter's battles against the armies of the emperor Temür, Kublai's successor, in the region of the Khangai Mountains, west of Karakorum. It was thus that in September, 1298, Duwa captured Temür's son-in-law, the Christian Öngüt prince Körgüz, whom he barbarously put to death. After this success, Duwa prepared to attack the imperial frontier between Turfan and Kansu, but his own army was taken by surprise and cut to pieces by the imperial forces.[26] At that moment, Qaidu and Duwa found themselves threatened by a flank attack from the khan of the White Horde (the eastern branch of the Jöchi family), Bayan or Nayan, who reigned northwest of Lake Balkhash and north of the Aral Sea. At last, in 1301, Duwa

attended Qaidu on an expedition launched in order to reconquer
Karakorum from the imperial forces and was thus involved in the
defeat inflicted upon the Ogödäite anti-Caesar between Karakorum and Temir in August of the same year.[27] As was related,
Qaidu died during the retreat.

Qaidu, of whom only fugitive glimpses are seen in the history
of the Yüan dynasty, seems to have been a most remarkable
prince, with a powerful personality: a sort of Güyük *manqué*.
This last great member of the house of Ogödäi at any rate had
in him the stuff of a sovereign. The wise measures that he had
imposed upon Alghu for the protection of the farming population
and of the towns of Transoxiana prove that his vision extended
beyond the usual plundering raids of the nomads.[28] The forty-one
battles in which he took part (and he had been a member of the
great expedition to Poland and Hungary in 1241) showed him to
be a true leader in war.[29] He alone in all of Asia had been able to
impede the fortunes of the great Kublai, who, even at the height
of his power, had never succeeded in vanquishing him. The
welcome he gave to the Nestorian pilgrims Rabban Sauma and
Markus, and the hope that Pope Nicholas IV placed in him (he
wrote to him on July 13, 1289, urging him to embrace Catholicism), prove that, like all the old Mongols, he was sympathetic
toward Christianity.[30] His misfortune was that he came too late,
when Kublai was firmly established in China and when the other
Jenghiz-Khanite branches were already half Sinicized, Turkicized,
or Iranized. In many respects, this last khan of Central Asia was
also the last of the Mongols.

THE KHANATE OF JAGATAI AT ITS ZENITH: DUWA, ESEN-BUQA, AND KEBEK

Duwa had faithfully followed Qaidu to the last. The death of his
formidable suzerain may have come as a relief, but he saw to it
that the transition should be gradual. Qaidu left a son, Chäpär,
who inherited all his titles. Duwa recognized his suzerainty, but
the great Ogödäite's successor lacked the stature to preserve the
empire artificially created by his father. Duwa began by sug-
gesting that he should recognize the suzerainty of Emperor
Temür, and in August, 1303, both of them acknowledged submission to Peking, thus putting an end to the civil strife which

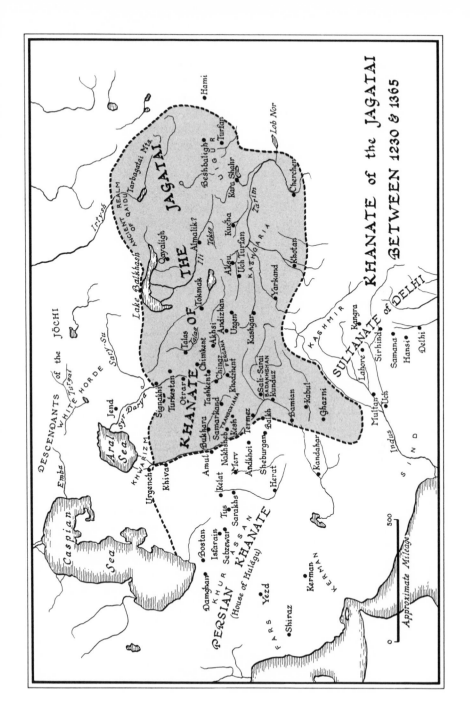

KHANATE of the JAGATAI
BETWEEN 1230 & 1365

• Hami

THE JAGATAI

Tarbagadai Mts

ANCIENT REALM OF QAIDU?

Beshbaligh
Turfan

UIGUR

Lob Nor

Irtysh

Qayaligh
Almalik?
Ili

Kara Shahr
UIGUR

Kucha

Tarim

KASHGARIA

Cherchen

Tokmak
Talas
Ilas
Chimkent
Andizhan
Ugen
Kashgar
Yarkand
Khotan

Tekes

Aksu
Uch Turfan

DESCENDANTS of the JŌCHI

WHITE Turgat

WHITE HORDE

Sary-Su

KHANATE OF THE

Signakhi
Otrar
Turkestan
Tashken
Khojhent
FERGANA
Sadi-Sarai
BADAKHSHAN
Kunduz
Bamian
Kabul
Ghazni

KASHMIR

Kangra

SULTANATE of DELHI

Lahore
Sirhind
Samana
Hansi
Delhi
Multan
Uch

Emba

Caspian

Jend
Syr Darya
Aral Sea
KHWARIZM
Urgench
Khiva

Amul
Kelat
Nakhshab
Merv

Bukhara
Samarkand
Kesh
Termez
Balkh
Andkhoi
Sheburgan

TRANSOXIANA

Chinaz
Khojhent

Tus
Sabzewar
Sarakhs

Indus

SIND

Damghan
Bostan
Isfarain
KHUR
ASSA
KHANATE
Herat
Kandahar

PERSIAN KHANATE
(House of Hulagu)

Kerman

FARS
KERMAN

Yezd
Shiraz

500

Approximate Mileage

0

had ravaged Central Asia for the past forty years and re-establishing Mongol unity.[31] But as soon as he was sure of the empire's support, Duwa broke with Chäpär. The armies of the two princes met between Khodzhent and Samarkand, and Chäpär was at first defeated. In a second battle, however, Chäpär's brother Shah-Oghul was victorious. Duwa then proposed to Chäpär that they should resume their old friendship, and it was agreed that Duwa and Shah-Oghul should meet to discuss the matter at Tashkent. But Shah-Oghul, with typical nomad rashness, disbanded some of his troops. Duwa arrived at Tashkent with all his forces, took Shah-Oghul by surprise, and routed him. He then seized Chäpär's cities of Benaket and Talas. Chäpär, who was then encamped between the Black Irtysh and the Yulduz, seems not to have known of this foul play when a fresh blow fell: Emperor Temür's troops from Karakorum crossed the southern Altai and took him in the rear. The unfortunate Chäpär had no choice but to surrender to Duwa. Duwa treated him honorably, but seized all his possessions. It was thus that the Jagataites, once confined to Transoxiana by the house of Qaidu, recovered the Ili and Kashgaria and repossessed themselves of the whole of their original inheritance (ca. 1306).[32]

Duwa had little time to enjoy his new fortune, for he died toward the end of 1306. His eldest son Kunjuk (Kundjuk) occupied the throne for no more than a year and a half. At his death Taliku, a grandson of Büri, seized power. D'Ohsson writes of him: "He was a prince grown old in battle. Professing Islam himself, he strove to propagate it among the Mongols." [33] But the partisans of Duwa's family rebelled against him, and one of them assassinated him at a banquet (1308 or 1309). The conspirators then proclaimed Kebek, Duwa's younger son, as khan. Meanwhile these disturbances had somewhat encouraged the Ogödäi pretender Chäpär, who had earlier been vanquished and despoiled by Duwa. Chäpär attacked Kebek but was beaten; he recrossed the Ili and took refuge at the court of Khaishan, the Mongol emperor of China. After this victory, which put a final stop to the final struggles of the house of Ogödäi, the Jagataite princes held a great *quriltai* at which they decided to appoint as khan one of Duwa's sons then at the court of Peking, Prince Esenbugha or Esen-buqa. Esen-buqa then came of his own free will, says Wassaf, to take possession of the throne ceded to him by his brother Kebek. At Esen-buqa's death, about 1320, Kebek returned to power.[34]

Despite these changes among individuals, the Jagataites, restored by Duwa to the height of their sovereignty, began to exercise an influence on the outside world. Any expansion in the direction of China or of the Aralo-Caspian steppes and Persia (where the houses of Kublai, Jöchi, and Hulägu were firmly entrenched) being barred to them, they looked to Afghanistan and India. The khans of Persia, whose court was at the other end of Iran, in Azerbaijan, paid little attention to Afghan affairs. The Jagataites took advantage of this to move into Badakhshan, to Kabul and Ghazni. It is true that in western Afghanistan a strong and adaptable form of native government had been created, that of the Afghan-Ghorid dynasty of the Kerts, who, under the suzerainty of the khans of Persia, were virtually autonomous. Unable to achieve anything here, the Jagataites made for eastern Afghanistan and from there made profitable raids into northwest India. In 1297, Duwa devastated the Punjab, but was repulsed. The empire of Delhi, ruled at this time by Sultan 'Ala ad-Din Khilji (1295–1315), was in fact a powerful military monarchy against which all assaults by the Jagataites crumbled; yet there is no doubt that at one time the danger was very great, and it took all the efforts of the sultan and his Mamelukes to counter it. Contemporaries even believed that at last, after three-quarters of a century, India would succumb to the Jenghiz-Khanite conquest.

Qutlugh-khoja, one of Duwa's sons, had settled in eastern Afghanistan. Hardly had he taken possession of his domains when he led a plundering expedition to the very gates of Delhi (ca. 1299–1300?). In 1303 came another Jagataite invasion, led by Prince Turghai with 120,000 men.[35] The Mongols camped under the walls of Delhi and blockaded it for two months. Then, having devastated the whole region, this vast army withdrew—perhaps for lack of siege engines—and returned to Afghanistan. In 1304 another incursion was made. Forty thousand Mongol horsemen ravaged the Punjab north of Lahore and advanced as far as Amroha, east of Delhi, where they were at last crushed by Tughlugh, Sultan 'Ala ad-Din's lieutenant. Nine thousand Mongol prisoners were trampled to death by elephants. To avenge their death, the Jagataite prince Kebek (later to be khan) devastated the Multan region, but when returning was taken by surprise on the banks of the Indus by Tughlugh, who did great slaughter among the Mongols (1305–6). Once more the prisoners were sent back to Delhi to be trampled by elephants.[36]

To the khans of Persia, the formation of this Jagataite fief in eastern Afghanistan, headed by Qutlugh-khoja's son and successor Dawud-khoja, was an encroachment. In 1313, Oljaitu, the khan of Persia, sent an army which drove out Dawud-khoja and forced him to withdraw into Transoxiana. Dawud-khoja went to beg help of his uncle and suzerain Esen-buqa, khan of Jagatai. Esen-buqa sent an army against the khanate of Persia, commanded by his brother Kebek and by Dawud-khoja. The two commanders crossed the Amu Darya, beat the enemy army on the Murgab, and ravaged Khurasan as far as Herat (1315).[37] But they were compelled to relinquish their conquest, for the khanate of Jagatai had been attacked in the rear by the Mongols of China. Esen-buqa had in fact simultaneously encumbered himself with another war, against the court of Peking, and had been beaten by imperial troops commanded by the *ch'eng-hsiang* Togachi "near the Tengri hills," no doubt between Kucha and the Issyk Kul. In revenge he had slain ambassadors of the grand khan (who at that time was Buyantu [or Ayurparibhadra]) as they were returning from the Persian court to Peking, whereupon Togachi's imperial army invaded the khanate of Jagatai and devastated Esen-buqa's winter quarters on the Issyk Kul as well as his summer residence on the Talas. A final complication was that a Jagatai prince named Yassawur quarreled with Esen-buqa and Kebek; crossed the Amu Darya with all his adherents, among whom were many of the persons from Bukhara and Samarkand; and offered himself to the khan of Persia, who settled these new arrivals in the already Jagataite fief of eastern Afghanistan: Balkh, Badakhshan, Kabul, and Kandahar (1316).[38] Soon afterward, however, Yassawur rebelled against the khan of Persia and took possession of part of Khurasan (1318). But Kebek, the khan of Jagatai, who had just succeeded his brother Esen-buqa, was a personal enemy of Yassawur, and he offered to help the khan of Persia to overthrow him. Thus while the Persian army moved to attack Yassawur in the rear, the Jagataite forces crossed the Amu Darya and made a frontal attack upon him. Deserted by his troops, Yassawur was killed as he fled (June, 1320).[39]

According to the coins that are extant, Kebek seems to have reigned until 1326. The importance of his reign, as Barthold observes, was that, unlike his predecessors, he took an interest in the ancient civilized country of Transoxiana and in the life of the cities: "In the neighborhood of Nakhsheb or Nasef [southwest of Samarkand] he built himself a mansion to which the town owes its modern name, Qarshi [Karshi]: a Mongol word for palace. It was he who set in circulation the coins later called *kebeki*, first official currency of the state of Jagatai. Until that time the only currencies had been those of individual towns or local dynasties." [40] Yet, despite the charms of life in Transoxiana, Kebek did not turn Muslim.

SCHISM IN THE KHANATE OF JAGATAI:
TRANSOXIANA AND MOGHOLISTAN

Kebek was succeeded by three of his brothers: Eljigidäi, Duwa-Timur, and Tarmashirin. The first two reigned for only a few months. Tarmashirin's reign seems to have been an important one (ca. 1326–33?). In 1327 he revived the tradition of great plundering expeditions into India. He penetrated as far as Delhi and, according to some sources, withdrew only on payment of heavy tribute. Other sources state that the sultan of Delhi, Muhammad ibn-Tughlugh, repulsed him and pursued him as far as the Punjab.[41]

It is also noteworthy that Tarmashirin, despite his Buddhist name (derived from the Sanskrit Dharmasri), was converted to Islam and became Sultan 'Ala ad-Din. But while this conversion may have suited the inhabitants of Transoxiana, it aroused the disapproval of the nomads of the Issyk Kul and the Ili, who regarded it as an infringement of the Jenghiz-Khanite *yasaq*. An insurrection broke out in those areas against Tarmashirin (ca. 1333–34) and ended in the elevation of a new khan, Duwa's grandson Jenkshi (Djenkshi), who reigned in the valley of the Ili from about 1334 to 1338. The anti-Muslim reaction that characterized this reign favored the Nestorians, always numerous in the old Christian communities of Almalik and Pishpek.[42] It was also of benefit to the Catholic missionaries, who for a few months could once more preach and build churches. One of Khan Jenkshi's sons, aged seven, is said even to have been baptized (by the name of John) with his father's consent.[43] In 1338, Pope

Benedict XII could again appoint a bishop of "Armalech," that is to say, Almalik: the Franciscan Richard of Burgundy. Yet almost at once, about 1339 or 1340, Richard died a martyr's death at the hands of the Ili Muslims along with the campanions of his apostolate—Francis of Alexandria, Pascal the Spaniard, Laurence of Ancona, and Brother Peter, an "Indian" brother who acted as interpreter—and the merchant Gilotto.[44] The following year, it is true, Giovanni da Marignolli, a papal legate, arrived in the Ili valley. He had been sent, as we have seen, on an official mission to the grand khan of Peking via Caffa, the khanate of Kipchak, and the khanate of Jagatai. During his stay at Almalik, he preached, built or rebuilt a church, and baptized a great number of people.[45] His position as ambassador to the grand khan must certainly have won him respect in a place where his predecessors had been massacred, but after his departure the Christianity of Almalik was destined to melt rapidly away. What remained of the ancient Nestorian center of the Ili was not to survive the Timurid persecution.[46]

TRANSOXIANA UNDER THE RULE OF EMIR QAZGHAN

The old Jagatai khanate now split in two under different branches of the royal family, and became Transoxiana and, in the Issyk Kul country between the Talas and the Manas, Mogholistan.

The ruler of Transoxiana was the khan Kazan (ca. 1343–46), Yassawur's son, whose capital was Karshi. The *Zafer-name* portrays him as a tryrant,[47] and indeed he seems to have tried to quell the insubordination of the Turkic nobility of Transoxiana, who had set him upon the throne. The leader of these nobles was at that time the emir Qazghan, whose fief lay about Sali-Sarai on the north bank of the Amu Darya, a little to the southeast of modern Kabadian (Mikoyanabad) and due north of Kunduz. He rebelled against Kazan, who won the first battle, fought north of the Iron Gates between Termez and Karshi, and struck Qazghan, it is said, in the eye with an arrow. But instead of following up his advantage, Kazan went to spend the winter at Karshi, where some of his troops abandoned him. This carelessness proved fatal. He was attacked once more by Qazghan, who defeated and killed him near that city (1346–47).[48]

Qazghan, now the true lord of Transoxiana, did not hesitate to break with the legitimate Jagatai line and give the Transoxianan throne—a puppet throne, in any case—to a descendant of Ogödäi named Danishmendiya (ca. 1346–47). However, the kingmaker then put his king to death and, turning once more to the Jagataites, chose Buyan-quli, Duwa's grandson, to take his place (1348–58). The praises heaped upon Buyan-quli by the *Zafername* indicate that he proved as docile a tool as Qazghan had desired.[49]

In fact, the Jagataites of Transoxiana were no longer anything but figureheads. Power had passed into the hands of local Turkic nobles: Qazghan today, tomorrow Tamerlane. This so-called Mongol khanate was in fact a Turkic realm. Qazghan's reign (1347–57) was not inglorious. He began to make the strength of Transoxiana felt in Iran. The Iranian king of Herat, Husain Kert, had made bold to plunder the districts of Andkhoi and Sheburgan which, although south of the Amu Darya, were dependencies of Transoxiana. Qazghan, taking with him his puppet king, Buyan-quli, blockaded Herat (1351) and compelled Kert to acknowledge himself as vassal and in that capacity to pay him court shortly afterward at Samarkand.[50] Thus at the very moment when the disappearance of the Mongol khanate of Persia brought about an unlooked-for Iranian restoration in eastern Iran (Kerts at Herat, Sarbedarians at Sebzewar, and Muzaffarids at Shiraz), Qazghan, true precursor of Tamerlane, intervened at the head of the Transoxianan nobility to re-establish Turkic supremacy.

Qazghan was assassinated in 1357,[51] and his son Mirza 'Abdallah proved incapable of continuing his work. Coveting the wife of the khan Buyan-quli, he had this prince assassinated in Samarkand (1358), thus arousing the displeasure of the Transoxianan feudal lords and the hostility of Bayan Selduz—and even more, that of Hajji Barlas, Tamerlane's uncle, lord of Kesh, modern Shahr-i Sebz ("Green City"), south of Samarkand. These two nobles drove 'Abdallah as far as Andereb, north of the Hindu Kush, where he died.[52] Such conflicts between Transoxianan lords undermined their power and provoked an unlooked-for Jenghiz-Khanite reaction.

TUGHLUQ TIMUR: REINTEGRATION OF JAGATAI

While the Jagataite branch of Transoxiana was deteriorating into a line of puppet kings in the service of Turkic feudal lords, the nomads of "Mogholistan"—that is, of the Talas, upper Chu, Issyk

Kul, Ili, Ebi Nor, and Manas—had, after a period of anarchy, re-established Jagataite royalty. The chief Mongol clan of the region was that of the Dughlats or Duqlats, who possessed large domains both in Mogholistan, round the Issyk Kul, and in Kashgaria, which was then known as Alti-shahr, "the Six Cities." [53] In the middle of the fourteenth century, the Dughlat clan was led by three brothers, Tulik, Bulaji or Puladshi, and Qamar ad-Din; and these were the true lords of the land. Around 1345, according to the *Ta'rikh-i Rashidi,* Bulaji dominated the Issyk Kul to Kucha and Bugur, and from the Fergana frontier to Lob Nor, with Aksu as his base. [54] It was he who took the initiative in seeking out some member of the Jagataite line who was not enfeoffed with the Transoxianans in order to place him at the head of a restored khanate of the Ili, then known as Mogholistan.

A certain Tughlugh Timur, alleged to be the son of Esen-buqa, was then living obscurely in the eastern part of Mogholistan, with a series of fabulous adventures behind him. This was the Jagataite, whether genuine or spurious, whom Bulaji now summoned. [55] He received him formally at Aksu and proclaimed him khagan. Tulik, Bulaji's elder brother, became *ulus-begi,* or first emir of the empire.

If the Dughlats had wanted no more than a figurehead to rally Jagataite legitimacy against the opposition—the Jagataite legitimacy of Transoxiana—they may well have been disappointed. Tughluq Timur seems to have been a man of strong character and made himself felt in every sphere of life. His reign (1347–63) was one of great importance, first from the religious point of view. Though the Turko-Tadzhiks of Transoxiana or townsfolk of Bukhara and Samarkand were fervent Muslims, the Turko-Mongols of Mogholistan or seminomads of the Ili and of Aksu remained for the most part "pagans," i.e., Buddhists or shamanists. But there too, Muslim propaganda was beginning to prevail. The eldest of the Dughlats, Emir Tulik, then living in Kashgar, was himself a convert to Islam. Three years later, Tughlugh Timur followed his example, in fulfillment of a vow, the *Ta'rikh-i Rashidi* tells, made in the days of his distress. "He received circumcision, and on the same day 160,000 people shaved their heads and confessed Islam." [56] Tughlugh Timur, as he appears in the memoirs of Muhammad Haidar II Dughlat, was a shrewd and energetic leader. Irrespective of any spiritual attraction that Islam may have had for him, he must certainly have calculated the advantage to be gained by conversion in his goal to acquire Transoxiana. Bukhara and Samarkand were well worth a Koranic prostration. In any event, once he had consolidated his position in Mogholistan, Tughlugh Timur intended to press his claims on the western part of old Jagatai. Conditions were favorable. Since the exile of the emir 'Abdallah ibn-Qazghan, Transoxiana had relapsed into partition and anarchy. The two emirs Bayan Selduz and Hajji Barlas had triumphed over 'Abdallah, but were incapable of firm and consistent rule. Bayan Selduz, whom the *Zafer-name* describes as "merciful and good-natured," was incapacitated by habitual drunkenness. Hajji Barlas, although firmly installed in his fief of Kesh, was later to show himself a somewhat feeble character. Finally, the rest of Transoxiana was split up among countless local Turkic feudal lords. To Tughlugh Timur the time seemed ripe. In March, 1360, he invaded Transoxiana, marching straight from Tashkent to Shahr-i Sebz. Hajji Barlas, with troops from Shahr-i Sebz and Karshi, intended at first to resist; then, in the face of enemy superiority, he crossed the Amu Darya and withdrew into Khurasan.[57]

So complete was Tughlugh Timur's triumph that Hajji Barlas' nephew, our Tamerlane, then aged twenty-six, deemed it wise to rally to the side of the victor. That Timurid panegyric known as the *Zafer-name* makes extravagant efforts to show that it was merely in order to resist the invasion more effectively that Tamerlane accepted the yoke, and that he did so by agreement with his uncle, the voluntary exile.[58] These statements are contradicted, however, by the context. Tamerlane, in return for his submission to Tughlugh Timur, received the fief of Shahr-i Sebz, which until then had belonged to Hajji Barlas. When shortly afterward Tughlugh Timur left for Mogholistan, Hajji Barlas returned to Transoxiana from Khurasan, beat Tamerlane, and forced him not only to restore Shahr-i Sebz to him but to return as a tractable client, even as the younger Barlas would do.[59] However, Tughlugh Timur was not long in returning to Transoxiana from Mogholistan, and from the moment of his entry into Khodzhent the Transoxianan nobility received him with all submission. Bayan Selduz escorted him as far as Samarkand, and this time Hajji Barlas came to pay court to him; but when soon after the khan put the emir of Khodzhent to death, Hajji Barlas became alarmed and fled to Khurasan, where he was assassinated by brigands near Sebzewar

(Shindand).[60] The result of this dramatic episode was that Tamerlane became the head of the Barlas clan, as well as undisputed lord of the Shahr-i Sebz domain, under the acquiescently accepted suzerainty of Khan Tughlugh Timur. A grandson of Qazghan, Emir Husain, had carved himself a domain in northeastern Afghanistan, including Balkh, Kunduz, Badakhshan, and Kabul, on both sides of the Hindu Kush. Tughlugh Timur marched against him, beat him on the River Vakhsh, entered Kunduz, pressed on to the Hindu Kush, and, in the manner of his ancestor Jenghiz Khan, spent spring and summer in that country. On his return to Samarkand, he put Bayan Selduz to death and went back to Mogholistan, leaving his son Ilyas-khoja as viceroy with Tamerlane as his adviser. Tamerlane's conduct appeared a sufficient guarantee of his loyalty.[61]

Thus the unity of the old khanate of Jagatai was restored under a forceful and dreaded khan. No one at that time could have foreseen that not many years later the Tamerlane whom he had given his son as mentor and minister would bring this Jagataite restoration to an end and replace it by a new empire. But before beginning the history of the Transoxianan conqueror, we must retrace our steps to study the formation and fall of the Mongol khanate of Persia.

9

Mongol Persia and the House of Hulägu

THE MONGOL REGIME IN PERSIA UNTIL THE COMING OF HULÄGU: CHORMAGHAN, BAIJU, AND ELJIGIDÄI

After its conclusive conquest by the Mongols and the destruction of the neo-Khwarizmian kingdom of Jalal ad-Din (p. 261), Persia remained under a makeshift and somewhat disjointed regime. The Mongol army of the west, quartered on the lower Kura and lower Aras (Araxes) in the Arran and Mugan steppe, was still under the command of generals who held full powers: first Chormaghan, destroyer of Jalal ad-Din's kingdom (1231–41), and then Baiju, conqueror of the Seljuks of Asia Minor (1242–56). The vassals of the west—Georgian princes, Seljuk sultans of Asia Minor, Armenian kings of Cilicia, and atabegs of Mosul—were directly dependent on this military government of the marches, as were, in the early stages at least, some of the communications with the Latin world.

Chormaghan, who, as Pelliot points out, had two Nestorian brothers, was quite well disposed toward Christianity.[1] During the period of his command, between 1233 and 1241, the grand khan Ogödäi sent a Syriac Christian to Tabriz, a man named Simeon but better known under his Syriac title of Rabban-ata (Li-pien-a-ta in Chinese transcription). Rabban-ata would later become the grand khan Güyük's official chargé d'affaires in matters concerning the Christian religion.[2] He arrived in Persia furnished by Ogödäi with extensive powers and handed to Chor-

347

maghan imperial decrees forbidding the massacre of disarmed Christian communities that accepted Mongol authority. The Armenian chronicler Kirakos of Ganja reports: "The arrival of Rabban-ata brought much relief to the Christians, and saved them from death and servitude. He built churches in Muslim towns where, before the coming of the Mongols, it had been forbidden so much as to pronounce the name of Christ, notably in Tabriz and Nakhichevan. He built churches, erected crosses, caused the gong to be sounded night and day [the equivalent among eastern Christians of our bell], and the dead to be buried with the reading of the Gospel, with crosses, candles, and chanting. Even the Tatar generals gave him presents." Rabban-ata's mission meant that the Mongol regime, after the first massacres, brought far more favorable conditions to the Christian populations of western Iran than any they had previously known.

Around 1241, Chormaghan was stricken with dumbness (no doubt the result of paralysis). Baiju,[3] who replaced him in 1242, was perhaps less in sympathy with Christianity, or so it appears from the reception he gave the Dominican Ascelin and his four companions, who had been sent by Pope Innocent IV. Ascelin had made a detour via Tiflis, where he was joined by another monk, Guichard of Cremona (for since 1240 there had been a Dominican monastery at Tiflis). On May 24, 1247, he arrived at Baiju's camp in the Arran region, north of the Aras and east of Lake Gokcha (Sevan).[4] Somewhat undiplomatically, he exhorted the Mongols to cease their massacres and to submit to the spiritual authority of the Pope; he also refused to make the triple genuflection due to Baiju as the khan's representative. Enraged, Baiju threatened to have the Dominicans executed. At this juncture there arrived at Baiju's camp, on July 17, 1247, a sort of Mongol missus dominicus, Eljigidäi, who had been sent by the grand khan Güyük.[5] Baiju charged Ascelin to carry a reply to the Pope based on that given by Güyük to Piano Carpini in November, 1246, of which Eljigidäi knew the text. The Mongols claimed that theirs was a universal empire by divine right, and enjoined the Pope to come in person to render homage to the khan, failing which he would be treated as an enemy. Ascelin left Baiju's camp on July 25, 1247, accompanied by two "Mongol" envoys, one bearing the name of Aibeg (Pelliot thinks he may have been an Uigur official in the service of the Mongol administration) and the other Särgis, a Christian, no doubt Nestorian.[6] This caravan party must have taken the usual route by way of Tabriz, Mosul, Aleppo, Antioch, and Acre. From Acre, in 1248, the Mongol envoys sailed for Italy, where Innocent IV gave them a long audience and where, on November 28, 1248, he handed them a reply for Baiju.

Despite the negative result of Ascelin's embassy, Eljigidäi, who had far more sympathy with Christianity than Baiju, sent two eastern Christians, David and Mark, to Louis IX of France at the end of May, 1248, carrying a curious letter probably written in Persian, of which we have the Latin translation. In it, Eljigidäi gives an explanation of the mission entrusted to him by the grand khan Güyük to liberate the eastern Christians from Muslim servitude and to enable them to practice their religious rites without hindrance. In the name of the grand khan, "the king of the earth," he informs his "son" the king of France that it is the Mongols' intention to protect all Christians—Latin, Greek, Armenian, Nestorian, and Jacobite—without distinction. Louis IX received this "embassy" during his stay in Cyprus, in the second half of December, 1248.[7] Although some doubt has been cast on the authenticity of this mission, it does appear that, as Pelliot thinks, Eljigidäi was then planning to attack the caliphate of Baghdad— an action which Hulägu would bring to a successful conclusion ten years later—and that with this object in mind he intended to join forces with the crusade that Saint Louis was about to launch against the Arab world in Egypt. On January 27, 1249, the two "Mongol" Christians took leave of Louis and sailed from Nicosia in Cyprus, accompanied by three Dominicans: André de Longjumeau, his brother Guillaume, and Jean de Carcassonne. André and his companions, having no doubt reached Eljigidäi's camp in April or May, 1249, were sent by him to the Mongol court, then headed by the queen regent Oghul Qaimish, and located in the old Ogödäite appanage of the Imil and Qobaq in Tarbagatai. They were to return to Saint Louis in Caesarea in April, 1251, at the earliest.[8]

Eljigidäi, the grand khan Güyük's confidential adviser, was included in the general proscription introduced at the election of the grand khan Mongka and aimed at the partisans of the Ogödäi branch [9] (see page 274). Between mid-October, 1251, and mid-

February, 1252, Mongka had him arrested and put to death.[10] Baiju was left in sole charge of the military government of the marches, in which post he remained until the arrival of Hulägu in 1255.

Baiju's actions were decisive in the affairs of Georgia and Asia Minor. On the death of Rusudan, the queen of Georgia, who had always irritated him by her stubborn refusal to yield to the Mongols, he intended to give the crown to her nephew, David Lasha, who was more pliable. But Batu the khan of Kipchak had taken Rusudan's son David Narin under his protection. The two pretenders went to plead their cause before the grand khan Güyük in Mongolia (1246). It has already been related he allocated a realm to each, giving Kartlia to Lasha and Imeretia to Narin.[11]

There was a similar arbitration in the Seljuk sultanate of Asia Minor. In 1246 the grand khan Güyük awarded the throne to the young prince Qilich Arslan IV (who had visited him in Mongolia) in preference to his elder brother Kai-Kawus II. At the same time, Güyük fixed the annual tribute to be paid by the Seljuks: "1,200,000 hyperpers, 500 pieces of stuff woven of silk and gold, 500 horses, 500 camels, 5,000 head of small livestock [sheep, goats, etc.], and, in addition to this, presents equal in value to the tribute itself." In 1254, the grand khan Mongka decided that Kai-Kawus should rule west of the Kizil Irmak and Qilich Arslan to the east; however, the two brothers fought and the victorious Kai-Kawus took his brother prisoner. In 1256, impatient at Kai-Kawus' delay in paying tribute, Baiju attacked and defeated him near Aksaray, after which the sultan fled to the Greeks of Nicaea and the Mongols replaced him by Qilich Arslan. Not long afterward, however, Kai-Kawus returned and in the end agreed to divide the kingdom with his brother on the basis of Mongka's decision.[12]

On the whole, Mongol suzerainty made itself felt only by fits and starts in these marches of the southwest. Both Chormaghan and Baiju, while bearing hard upon the vassal states, were compelled to refer continually to the court of Karakorum, where, owing to the distances involved, decisions were delayed for months on end, and where client princes, like ambassadors, went to plead their cause amid all the hazards of Jenghiz-Khanite family revolutions.

During this time, the rudiments of a civil administration were appearing in Khurasan and in Iraq 'Ajami. In 1231, the Mongol general Chintimur had wiped out the last pockets of Khwarizmian resistance in Khurasan, while in the northwest Chormaghan was ousting Jalal ad-Din. It was this Chintimur whom the grand khan Ogödäi appointed governor of Khurasan and Mazanderan in 1233.[13] At this time the function was a purely fiscal one. Tax revenues, which were divided between the grand khan and the chiefs of the three other Jenghiz-Khanite *ulus,* were extorted from this unhappy province with a brutality intensified by the fact that the massacres and persecutions of the preceding years had entirely ruined the land. However, even such a governor as Chintimur was beginning to employ Iranian scholars: his *sahib-divan* or finance minister was the father of the historian Juvaini.[14]

Chintimur, who died in 1235, was succeeded after a brief interval by the Uigur Körgüz (1235–42), who despite his Christian name (George) was a Buddhist. He came from the region of Beshbaligh (Kucheng), and was reputed a scholar among the Uigur. It was for this reason that he had been marked out during Jenghiz Khan's lifetime by prince Jöchi and given the task of instructing the children of the Conqueror's household in Uigur writing. Thanks to the protection of the Nestorian "chancellor" Chinqai, Ogödäi charged Körgüz with the task of taking a census and raising taxes in Khurasan. "Each *noyan,* each officer, acted as absolute lord in his district, and appropriated the greater part of the revenues to his own use. Körgüz put an end to this regime and compelled them to disgorge. He protected the life and property of the Persians against the tyranny of the Mongol officials, who thenceforth might no longer behead people at their own pleasure." [15] Buddhist though he was, he became the protector of the Muslim element and in the end turned Muslim himself. Having settled in Tus, which he rehabilitated, this intelligent, skillful, and energetic Uigur tried to institute a regular administration and what one may call a civil service, as much for the benefit of the Iranian population as for that of the Mongol treasury. It was largely at his prompting that the grand khan Ogödäi ordered the rehabilitation of Khurasan in 1236. As a result, Herat now began to be repopulated. But after Ogödäi's death the Mongol officials whose depredations Körgüz had stopped brought him before the queen regent Törägänä, and then sent him to Qara-Hulägu, Jagatai's grandson, whom he had offended and who put him to death (1242).[16]

Törägänä entrusted the administration of Khurasan and Iraq 'Ajami to the Oirat Arghun Agha, likewise chosen for his knowledge of written Uigur, and who because of this had served in Ogödäi's chancellery.[17] During his governorship (1243–55), Arghun Agha tried, like Körgüz, to protect the Iranian population from the fiscal abuses and extortions of Mongol officials. To the grand khan Güyük's satisfaction, he revoked the bills, exemptions, and patents that the junior Jenghiz-Khanites had issued so blindly and in such profusion, and thanks to which they had been able to dip into the Mongol treasury. He found a no less firm supporter in the grand khan Mongka, whose court he visited in 1251. At his request, Mongka extended to Persia the system already established in Transoxiana by Mahmud and Mas'ud Yalavach in place of the chaotic finances of the early days of the conquest. That is, he introduced a capitation tax proportionate to the means of the taxpayer, the revenues from this to be used to maintain the army and the imperial postal service. Arghun Agha died near Tus in 1278 at an advanced age. His son was the famous emir Nauruz, who for a short time became viceroy of Khurasan.[18]

In 1251, the grand khan Mongka entrusted the province of Herat, then rising again from its ruins, to a lord of the Ghor district, Shams ad-Din Muhammad Kert, Afghan by race, Sunnite Muslim by religion, who had come to Mongolia to pay his respects at court. Shams ad-Din was the grandson of a dignitary attached to the last Ghorid sultans of eastern Afghanistan, and had himself inherited the Ghor district in 1245. The Kert princes, who bore the title of *malik* (king), were compelled to retain the good will of their Mongol masters by prudent and adroit behavior, to navigate without shipwreck amid the Jenghiz-Khanite wars, and finally, in their little kingdom of Herat, to survive Mongol domination (1251–1389). Shams ad-Din's lengthy reign (1251–78) established the authority of his house firmly in the land. This Ghorid Iranian restoration is the more interesting in that it came about under cover of Mongol rule and in harmony with it.[19]

The Mongols also tolerated, at least in the beginning, the existence as vassals of the dynasty of the atabegs of Kerman of the house of the Qutlugh-shah, as well as the Salghurid atabegs of Fars. The house of the Qutlugh-shah had been founded by Boraq Hajjib (1223–35), a wily character who had succeeded in surviving the Khwarizmian squalls of Jalal ad-Din. His son Rukn ad-Din Khoja (ca. 1235–52) was prompt in paying court to the grand khan Ogödäi in Mongolia (1235). Qutb ad-Din, who went there later (ca. 1252–57), after serving in the Mongol army of China, was in his turn invested with the principality of Kerman by the grand khan Mongka. Similarly, at Shiraz the Salghurid Abu Bakr (1231–60) was able to win the favor of Ogödäi and of the succeeding grand khans, who allowed him to keep his throne.[20]

HULÄGU'S REIGN: DESTRUCTION OF THE ASSASSINS, CONQUEST OF BAGHDAD, AND ANNIHILATION OF THE CALIPHATE

Not until twenty years after their conquest of Persia did the Mongols think of putting an end to their provisional regime there and to the dual form of government (the purely military rule in Arran and Mugan and the fiscal administration of Khurasan and Iraq 'Ajami) by superimposing a regular political power. At the *quriltai* of 1251, the grand khan Mongka decided to give the viceroyalty of Iran to his younger brother Hulägu.[21] In addition, Hulägu was charged with the task of suppressing the two spiritual powers that still survived in Persia: the principality of the Isma'ili imams in Mazanderan and the Abbasid caliphate of Baghdad. A further task assigned to him was to conquer Syria: "Establish the usages, customs, and laws of Jenghiz Khan from the banks of the Amu Darya to the ends of the land of Egypt. Treat with kindness and good will every man who submits and is obedient to your orders. Whoever resists you, plunge him into humiliation." [22]

Having journeyed from Mongolia by short stages via Almalik and Samarkand, Hulägu crossed the Amu Darya on January 2, 1256. On the Persian bank of the river, he received the compliments of the representatives of his new vassals, from the men of Shams ad-Din Kert the *malik* of Herat and of Abu Bakr the Salghurid atabeg of Fars to those of the Seljuks of Asia Minor, Kai-Kawus II and Qilich Arslan IV. In accordance with the program drawn up by Mongka, he went first to attack the Isma'ilis or Assassins in their aeries of Mazanderan, Meimundiz, and Alamut. The grand master of the Isma'ilis, Rukn ad-Din Kurshah, was besieged by Hulägu in Meimundiz and capitulated on November 19, 1256.[23] Hulägu sent him to the grand khan Mongka in Mongolia, but on the way the prisoner was murdered. The defenders of Alamut surrendered on December 20. The terrible sect which in the twelfth century had defied the efforts of the Seljuk sultans, had caused sultanate and caliphate to tremble, and had been a contributing factor in the demoralization and disintegration of the whole of Asian Islam was at last wiped out. In achieving this, the Mongols rendered an incalculable service to the cause of civilization and good order.

Hulägu next attacked the Abbasid caliph of Baghdad, the spiritual leader of Sunnite Islam and lord of a small temporal domain in Iraq 'Arabi. The reigning caliph al-Musta'sim (1242–58) was characterless and fancied he could deal with the Mongols by trickery, as his predecessors had dealt with the hegemonies that had succeeded one another in Iran: the Buyid, Seljuk, Khwarizmian, and Mongol.[24] In the past, whenever the masters of the moment had proved too powerful, the caliph had yielded. In the tenth century he had accepted as coruler the Buyid emir *el-omara,* and in the eleventh the Seljuk sultan. For the time being he confined himself to his spiritual functions and awaited the passing of these ephemeral masters. When the opportunity came, the caliph re-emerged, arbitrated their disputes, and helped to deliver the *coup de grâce.* His was a quasi-divine power which would outlive these lords of a day or a century, having eternity on its side—or so he believed. But the terrestrial empire which the Jenghiz-Khanites declared to have been bestowed upon them by Tängri, Eternal Heaven, would admit of no derogation. The correspondence between Hulägu and the caliph, as reconstructed by Rashid ad-Din, is as loftily phrased as any in history. From the heir to the thirty-six caliphs of the house of Abbas, the khan demanded the temporal power once conceded in Baghdad to the Buyid *el-*

omara emirs and later to the great Seljuk sultans: "You have learned the fate brought upon the world since Jenghiz Khan by the Mongol armies. What humiliation, by the grace of Eternal Heaven, has overtaken the dynasties of the shahs of Khwarizm, of the Seljuks, of the kings of Daylam, and of the different atabegs! Yet the gates of Baghdad were never closed to any of these races, which all established their domination there. How then should entry into this city be refused to us, who possess such strength and such power? Beware of taking arms against the Standard!" [25]

The caliph defied this solemn warning and refused to hand over the Abbasid temporal domain, which his ancestors had won back from the last Seljuks of Persia. To the universal empire of the Jenghiz-Khanites he opposed the no less universal sovereignty of the Muslim "papacy": "O young man, who have barely entered upon your career and who, drunk with a ten-day success, believe yourself superior to the whole world, do you not know that from the East to the Maghreb, all the worshipers of Allah, whether kings or beggars, are slaves to this court of mine, and that I can command them to muster?" [26] Vain threats. The Ayyubid sultanate of Syria and Egypt, terrified of the close approach of the Mongols, never stirred, and Hulägu and his shamanist, Buddhist, and Nestorian generals were quite unmoved by the Muslim prophecies which the caliph hurled against them.

The descent of the Mongol armies on Baghdad began in November, 1257.[27] Baiju's army approached by the Mosul road to take Baghdad from the rear on the west bank of the Tigris. Hulägu's best commander, the Naiman Kitbuqa (a Nestorian), led the left wing along the Luristan route to the Abbasid capital. Finally, Hulägu himself came down from Hamadan on the Tigris via Kermanshah and Holwan. By January 18, 1258, the Mongol forces were reassembled and Hulägu set up his camp on the eastern outskirts of Baghdad. The caliph's little army, having tried to prevent the city's being surrounded, had been cut to pieces on the previous day (January 17). On the 22nd, the Mongol generals Baiju, Buqa Timur, and Sugunjaq or Sunjaq moved in to take up their positions in the suburb west of the Tigris, while on the other side Hulägu and Kitbuqa pressed forward their encirclement. In an attempt to pacify the Mongols, the caliph sent them his vizier, who was a zealous Shi'ite and may have shared their feelings; [28] and he also sent the Nestorian Catholikos Makikha. But it was too late. The Mongols had carried the whole of the eastern sector of fortifications by vigorous assault (February 5 and 6), and the beleaguered townsfolk had no choice but to surrender. The soldiers of the garrison tried to escape, but the Mongols caught them, distributed them among their companies, and slew them to the last man. On February 10, the caliph came in person to surrender to Hulägu, who told him to order all the people to leave the city and to lay down their arms. "The inhabitants, disarmed, came in groups to give themselves up to the Mongols, who massacred them on the spot." [29] The Mongols then entered Baghdad, subjected those townsfolk who had not obeyed the order to another massacre, and set fire to the city (February 13).[30] The sack lasted seventeen days, during which 90,000 inhabitants are thought to have perished.

As for the caliph, the Mongols forced him to hand over his treasures and disclose all his hiding places, but they seem to have avoided shedding his blood out of respect for his dignity. Instead, they sewed him up in a sack and then had him trampled upon by horses (about February 20).[31] "They set fire to the greater part of the city, notably the *jami* mosque, and destroyed the tombs of the Abbasids."

HULÄGU'S SYMPATHY WITH CHRISTIANITY

To the eastern Christians the capture of Baghdad by the Mongols seemed like divine retribution. Moreover, the Mongols, whose ranks included many Nestorians, such as the Naiman Kitbuqa (to say nothing of the Georgian auxiliaries led by Hasan Brosh, the Armeno-Georgian prince of Kakhetia), consistently spared the Christian elements in Baghdad at the time of the sack. The Armenian chronicler Kirakos of Ganja writes: "At the capture of Baghdad, Hulägu's wife Doquz-khatun, who was a Nestorian, spoke on behalf of the Christians of the Nestorian or any other confession, and interceded for their lives. Hulägu spared them and allowed them to keep all their possessions." [32] In fact, as Vartan confirms, at the time of the assault the Christians of Baghdad shut themselves up in a church by order of the Nestorian patriarch Makikha, and the Mongols spared both church and flock.[33] Hulägu even gave the patriarch Makikha one of the caliphal palaces: that of the little *dewatdar* or vice-chancellor.[34]

The Armenian Kirakos of Ganja has spoken of the joy and even triumph of all these eastern Christians at the fall of Baghdad. "Five hundred and fifteen years had passed since the founding of this city. Throughout its supremacy, like an insatiable leech, it had swallowed up the entire world. Now it restored all that had been taken. It was punished for the blood it had shed and the evil it had done; the measure of its iniquity was full. The Muslim tyranny had lasted 647 years." [35]

In the eyes of the Nestorians too, and of the Syrian Jacobites and Armenians, the terrible Mongols appeared as the avengers of oppressed Christendom, as providential saviors who had come from the depths of the Gobi to attack Islam in the rear and shake it to its foundations. Who could have imagined that those humble Nestorian missionaries who in the seventh century left Seleucia on the Tigris, or Beit Abe, to spread the Gospel in the bleak lands of eastern Turkestan and Mongolia would sow the seed of so great a harvest? [36]

The favor enjoyed by the Christians within Hulägu's sphere of influence was largely due, as noted, to his chief wife, Doquz-khatun. She was a Kerayit princess, the niece of the last Kerayit king, the *Wang-khan* Togrul.[37] Mongka, who greatly respected her wisdom, had advised Hulägu to consult her in his affairs.[38] "As the Kerayit had long ago embraced Christianity," writes Rashid ad-Din, "Doquz-khatun made it her constant care to protect Christians, and throughout her lifetime they prospered. To please his princess, Hulägu heaped favors upon them and gave them every token of his regard, so that all over his realm new churches were continually being built, and at the gate of Doquz-khatun's *ordu* there was always a chapel, where bells were rung." [39] The Armenian monk Vartan confirms this: "The Mongols of Persia carried with them a canvas tent in the shape of a church. The *jamahar* [rattle] called the faithful to prayer. The offices of Mass were celebrated every day by priests and deacons. Here ecclesiastics drawn from among Christians of every language could live in tranquillity. Having come to ask for peace, they obtained it, and returned home with gifts." [40]

Doquz-khatun's niece Tuqiti-khatun, who was also a wife of Hulägu, was no less devoted to Nestorian Christianity.

With Doquz-khatun it was more than a matter of ancestral tradition. Vartan the monk, who was in her confidence, says: "She hoped to see Christianity increase in luster, and its every advance is to be attributed to her." Hulägu, although himself a Buddhist, shared this sympathy, and nothing is more significant of this than the continuation of Vartan's account. "In 1264, the *il-khan* Hulägu summoned us: myself, the *vartabeds* Sarkis [Serge] and Krikor [Gregory], and Avak the priest of Tiflis. We arrived in the presence of this powerful monarch at the beginning of the Tatar year, in July, the time of the *quriltai*. When we were admitted to the presence of Hulägu, we were excused from bending the knee and prostrating ourselves according to Tatar etiquette, since Christians bow only to God. They bade us bless the wine, and received it at our hands. Hulägu said to me: 'I have summoned you that you might learn to know me and that with all your heart you may pray for me.' After we were seated, the brethren who had accompanied me sang hymns. The Georgians celebrated their office and so did the Syrians and the Greeks. The *il-khan* said to me: 'These monks have come from everywhere to visit me and bless me. This is proof that God is inclined in my favor.'" [41] Hulägu once spoke to Vartan in memory of his mother, the Nestorian Sorghaqtani: "One day he caused all the people of his court to withdraw and, attended by two persons only, he conversed with me at length upon the events of his life and childhood and upon his mother, who was a Christian." Hulägu himself never embraced Christianity. We know that he remained a Buddhist, and was in particular a devotee of the boddhisattva Maitreya in particular. But his Iranian kingdom included no Buddhists, whereas Christians— whether Nestorian, Jacobite, Armenian, or Georgian—were numerous, and it was natural that in the absence of his own coreligionaries he should favor those of his mother and of his wife. During the interview he granted to the monk Vartan, he owned that his sympathy with Christianity had begun to create a rift between himself and his cousins the Jenghiz-Khanite khans of southern Russia and Turkestan (the Kipchak and Jagatai khanates): "We love the Christians," Vartan reports, "while they [his cousins] favor Muslims." [42]

EXPEDITION OF HULÄGU TO SYRIA

After the capture of Baghdad and the destruction of the caliphate, Hulägu took the Hamadan route to Azerbaijan and, like the Mongol generals Chormaghan and Baiju before him, established the seat of his dynasty in the north of that province. The cities of Azerbaijan—Tabriz and Maragheh—were his capitals, in so far as this still nomadic court ever halted near towns. Hulägu had a number of buildings erected in the region of Lake Urmia, his favorite resting place: "an observatory on a hill north of Maragheh, a palace at Alatagh, and some pagan temples (*butkhanaha*) at Khoi." The booty taken from Baghdad was deposited in a fortress on an island in the lake.[43] The Arran and Mugan plains served Hulägu and his successors as winter quarters, where, as Chormaghan and Baiju had done, they turned their horses out to grass. In summer, the princes of Hulägu's house went up to the Alatagh hills, a spur of Mount Ararat.

The fall of Baghdad had plunged the Muslim world into a state of terror. The old atabeg of Mosul, Badr ad-Din Lulu (1233–59), who was over eighty, did not confine himself to exposing the heads of the Baghdad ministers on the city wall, as commanded, but came in person to pay court to Hulägu at his camp in Maragheh. Next, the atabeg of Fars, Abu Bakr, sent his son Sa'd to felicitate the khan on his capture of Baghdad. At the same time, there arrived at Hulägu's camp, then situated near Tabriz, the two Seljuk sultans of Asia Minor, the rival brothers Kai-Kawus II and Qilich Arslan IV. Kai-Kawus trembled, for in 1256 his troops had tried to withstand the Mongol general Baiju, who crushed them at Aksaray. He pacified Hulägu by a truly remarkable piece of flattery. Having had his own portrait painted on the soles of a pair of boots, he offered these to the incensed khan, saying, "Your slave dares to hope that his king will condescend to honor his servant's head by placing upon it his august foot."[44] This incident illustrates the degree of abasement to which Islam was reduced.

To complete the program laid down for him by Mongka, Hulägu had now to subjugate Syria and Egypt. Syria was divided between the Franks and the Muslim dynasty of the Ayyubids. The Franks possessed the coastal zone, divided into two distinct states: in the north, the principality of Antioch and the county of Tripoli, both belonging to Prince Bohemund VI; and in the south, the kingdom of Jerusalem, which had been long since deprived of Jerusalem itself and of any effective rule and which in fact consisted of a federation of baronies and communes, such as the barony of Tyre, the commune of Acre, and the county of Jaffa.[45] Bohemund VI, prince of Antioch-Tripoli, was the intimate ally of his northern neighbor the king of Armenia (i.e., Cilicia), Hethum I, whose daughter he had married.[46] Following Hethum's lead, he at once joined the Mongol alliance. Opposite Christian Syria lay the interior of the country, with its cities of Aleppo and Damascus; this territory belonged to the old Ayyubid dynasty, which was of Kurdish origin but was now entirely Arab in character, and which had been founded by the great Saladin. The ruler at this time was the sultan an-Nasir Yusuf (1236–60), a timid, inferior character, who made his act of vassalage in 1258, when he sent his own son al-'Aziz to Hulägu.[47]

Notwithstanding these tokens of submission, Hulägu was resolved to win western Mesopotamia and Muslim Syria from the Ayyubids. The campaign opened with a local expedition against the emirate of Maiyafariqin, in Diyarbakir, which belonged to a junior Ayyubid named al-Kamil Muhammad.[48] One of the Mongols' grievances against al-Kamil was that, as a fanatical Muslim, he had crucified a Jacobite Christian priest who had entered the country on a Mongol passport. Hulägu besieged Maiyafariqin with a Mongol detachment supported by a Georgian and Armenian corps under the Georgian leader Hasan Brosh. An Armenian prince, Sevata of Kachen, was killed during this siege, or—as the Armenian chronicle of Vartan says—"won the immortal crown, ever faithful to God and the *il-khan;* he will share the triumph of those who shed their blood for Christ." [49] This association of cross and Jenghiz-Khanite standard should be borne in mind: the eastern Christians felt that in marching with the Mongols against Muslims of Syria, they were taking part in a sort of crusade.

After a long siege, Maiyafariqin was taken, and al-Kamil perished under torture. The Mongols tore off pieces of his flesh and crammed them into his mouth until he died. His head, impaled on a lance, was carried in triumph by the Mongols through the great cities of Muslim Syria, from Aleppo to Damascus, preceded by singers and tabor players. A large part of the Muslim population of the Maiyafariqin emirate was massacred. The Christians alone were spared; and there were many of these, for the city was a very ancient Jacobite bishopric and also an Armenian center. Kirakos of Ganja notes: "The churches were respected, as were the countless relics collected by St. Maruta." [50]

While the siege of Maiyafariqin was in progress, Hulägu conquered Muslim Syria. According to the Armenian historian Hayton, the Mongols' plan of campaign had been settled in the course of an interview between Hulägu and his faithful vassal the king of Armenia (Cilicia), Hethum I. "The khan had asked Hethum to join him with the whole Armenian army at Edessa, for he desired to go to Jerusalem to deliver the Holy Land from the Mussulmans and restore it to the Christians. King Hethum, joyful at this news, gathered together a great army and marched to join Hulägu." Vartan tells us that the Armenian patriarch came to give the khan his blessing. [51] Thus the expedition led by Jenghiz Khan's grandson took on the aspect of an Armeno-Mongol crusade. In some respects, it even had the appearance of a Franco-Mongol crusade. For, as noted earlier, in his relations with the Mongols the Armenian king Hethum negotiated not only for himself but for his son-in-law Bohemund VI, prince of Antioch and count of Tripoli. This is borne out by the Templar of Tyre in the *Gestes des Chiprois:* "Hethum, king of Armenia, spoke to Hulägu on behalf of Bohemund his son-in-law, and thereafter Bohemund stood high in Hulägu's favor." [52]

The great Mongol army marched out of Azerbaijan for Syria in September, 1259. The *noyan* Kitbuqa, that Nestorian Naiman, last noted at the siege of Baghdad, departed with the advance troops. The right wing was commanded by old Baiju and by Sonqor, the left by Sugunjaq (or Sunjaq), and the center by Hulägu in person, accompanied by his Christian wife Doquz-khatun. [53] Descending by way of Kurdistan into the province of Al Jazira, the khan took Nisibin (Nusaybin), received the submission of Haran and Edessa, and massacred the people of Seyhan, who had opposed him. After occupying Birecik, he crossed the Euphrates, sacked Menbij, and laid siege to Aleppo. The sultan an-Nasir, instead of putting up resistance in that city,

had remained in Damascus. The Jacobite metropolitan of Aleppo,
Bar Hebraeus the historian, came to meet the Mongols and
render homage to Hulägu.[54]

On January 18, 1260, the Mongol army, commanded by Hulägu
and reinforced by Hethum's Armenians and the Franks of
Bohemund VI, began the siege of Aleppo, which was defended
by an old Ayyubid prince called Turan-shah.[55] "They moved
twenty catapults into position and on January 24 entered the
city, which they occupied at one sweep save for the citadel,
which held out until February 25." The massacre was thorough
and methodically carried out, in the Jenghiz-Khanite manner,
and lasted six full days, until the 30th, when a word from Hulägu
brought it to an end. The great mosque was set on fire by King
Hethum of Armenia, but the Jacobite church was of course
spared. Hulägu gave Hethum some of the plunder and restored
to him several districts and castles which the Muslims of Aleppo
had once seized from the Armenian kingdom. To Bohemund VI
he gave the lands belonging to the principality of Aleppo which
had been in Muslim hands since the days of Saladin.[56]

Wild panic spread throughout Muslim Syria, and several
Muslim princes came to make submission without awaiting the
Mongols' arrival. Before Aleppo itself, Hulägu received the
Ayyubid al-Ashraf Musa, former king of Homs, who had been
dispossessed by his own people and whom Hulägu now reinstated.
The fall of Aleppo caused that of Hama, which capitulated
without a struggle. The sultan an-Nasir Yusuf made no more
effort to defend Damascus than he had Aleppo, and at the news
of the latter's fall he fled to Egypt. Damascus, abandoned by its
defenders, surrendered in advance. On March 1, 1260, Kitbuqa
arrived in the city with a Mongol occupation corps, accompanied
by the king of Armenia and Bohemund VI. The administration of
Damascus was placed in the hands of a Mongol governor assisted
by three Persian secretaries. The citadel, which resisted, surrendered on April 6, and by Hulägu's order Kitbuqa beheaded
the governor with his own hand.[57]

In the course of the next three weeks, Kitbuqa completed the
conquest of Muslim Syria. The Mongols penetrated Samaria and
put the Nablus garrison to the sword for having offered resistance.
Unhindered, they advanced as far as Gaza. The sultan an-Nasir
Yusuf was taken prisoner in Bilqas; Kitbuqa used him to force

the capitulation of the 'Ajlun garrison, and then sent him to Hulägu. The junior Ayyubid, who reigned in Baniyas, rallied to the side of the conqueror.[58]

To the native Christians, whether of the Syriac-Monophysite or Greek rite, the entry of the Mongols into Damascus appeared as just retribution for six centuries of oppression. They organized street processions in which they sang psalms and carried crosses before which the Muslims were forced to stand up in respect. They went so far as to "ring bells and cause wine to flow even in the mosque of the Umayyads." The Templar of Tyre relates that Hethum, king of Armenia, and his son-in-law Bohemund, prince of Antioch, having helped the Mongols to subdue Damascus, were allowed by Kitbuqa to deconsecrate a mosque, or rather to restore to Christian use an old Byzantine church which the Muslims had appropriated to their own worship. The Muslims complained to Kitbuqa; but he, freely following his devotional bent, visiting churches and the prelates of the various Christian confessions, complied with none of their requests.[59]

These conquests seemed permanent until an unexpected event supervened. On August 11, 1259, the grand khan Mongka died in China, and a war of succession broke out between his two brothers Kublai and Ariq-bögä (p. 285). Hulägu the fourth brother, being so far away and in any case sufficiently provided for, did not offer himself as candidate, but his sympathies were with Kublai and his support or mediation might be required. Hulägu also knew that his cousin Berke, the khan of Kipchak, who favored Islam as Hulägu favored Christianity and blamed him for the Baghdad massacre, was threatening him on the Caucasian frontier.[60] For these reasons, Hulägu returned to Persia, leaving under Kitbuqa's command in Syria and Palestine an army of occupation reduced to 20,000, according to Kirakos, though Hayton gives it as no more than 10,000.[61]

Kitbuqa, now in control of Mongol Syria and Mongol Palestine, was well-disposed toward the Christians there, not only because he himself was a Nestorian, but also, it seems, because he appreciated the advantage to both parties of the Franco-Mongol alliance.[62] Unfortunately, though Bohemund VI, prince of Antioch-Tripoli, might share his views on this subject, the barons of Acre continued to see in the Mongols mere barbarians to whom even the Muslims were to be preferred.[63] One of these barons,

Count Julien of Sidon, attacked a Mongol patrol and killed
Kitbuqa's nephew. The enraged Mongols replied by sacking
Sidon. This was the end of the alliance, explicit or tacit, between
Franks and Mongols.[64]

The clash inspired the Muslims with fresh courage; for although
the Ayyubid sultanate of Aleppo-Damascus had been conquered,
there still remained a great Muslim power, that of the Mamelukes,
the lords of the sultanate of Egypt. The Mamelukes were mercenaries, chiefly of Turkish origin, who had formed the armies
of the Ayyubid sultans of Egypt and who in 1250 had overthrown that dynasty and remained masters of the country, their
generals becoming its sultans. The Mameluke sultan Qutuz, then
reigning in Cairo (1259–60), realized that the situation was
turning to his advantage. Once Hulägu and the main Mongol
army had departed for Persia, it would be impossible for Kitbuqa,
whose forces were reduced to 20,000 men at most, to maintain
the conquest except with the aid of the coastal Franks. Now
that these had broken with him, the Mamelukes could act. On
July 26, 1260, their advance troops, led by the emir Baibars, left
Egypt for Palestine. The small Mongol detachment occupying
Gaza under Baibars' command was overwhelmed.[65] The Franks
of Acre, instead of making peace with Kitbuqa, authorized the
Mamelukes to cross their territory and to revictual under the
very walls of their city.[66]

This permission to march through the Frankish coastal region
and refresh and replenish their army gave the Mamelukes a great
initial advantage. Their numerical superiority did the rest.
Kitbuqa, trusting to the invincibility of the old Jenghiz-Khanite
bands, had put up a brave resistance. The Mamelukes left Acre
and marched through Frankish Galilee toward the Jordan.
Kitbuqa, with his cavalry and a few Georgian and Armenian
contingents, came out to meet them.[67] The encounter occurred
at 'Ain Jalud, near Zerin, on September 3, 1260. Kitbuqa was
crushed by the force of numbers, but saved the honor of the
Jenghiz-Khanite banner: "Spurred on by his zeal and courage,"
writes Rashid ad-Din, "he ran to right and to left, delivering
mighty blows. In vain men tried to induce him to retreat. He
shunned this counsel, saying: 'It is here that I must die! Some
soldier will reach the khan to tell him that Kitbuqa refused to
make a shameful retreat and that he sacrificed his life to his duty.

Nor must the loss of one Mongol army grieve the khan too deeply. Let him reflect that for a year the wives of his soldiers have not conceived, that the horses of his stud have sired no colts. A happy life to the khan!'" Rashid ad-Din continues: "Deserted though he was by all, he sustained the fight against a thousand foes; but at last, his horse being brought down, he was taken prisoner." His hands were bound behind him and he was led before Qutuz, who insulted the vanquished conqueror: "After overthrowing so many dynasties, behold you now, caught in the trap!" The Nestorian Mongol's reply is worthy of the Jenghiz-Khanite epic: "If I perish at your hand, I acknowledge that God and not you will be the author of that deed. Do not be intoxicated by a moment's success. When the news of my death reaches the ears of Hulägu-khan, his wrath will boil like a stormy sea. From Azerbaijan to the gates of Egypt the land will be crushed by the hoofs of Mongol horses!" In a final outburst of loyalty to the Mongols and to the majesty and legitimacy of the Jenghiz-Khanites, he flouted these Mameluke sultans, these chance-come kings to whom the murder of a predecessor was the usual road to the throne: "Since I was born I have been the khan's slave: I am not, like you, the murderer of my master!" His captors then cut off his head.[68]

The sultan Qutuz made a triumphant entry into Damascus, and the Christians of the city paid a heavy price for their pro-Mongol sentiments; for the whole of Muslim Syria as far as the Euphrates was annexed to the Mameluke sultanate of Egypt. Hulägu made one more attempt. At the end of November, 1260, a Mongol detachment again entered Syria and plundered Aleppo for the second time, but was repulsed by the Muslims near Homs (December 10) and thrown back once more east of the Euphrates.

HULÄGU'S LAST YEARS

Hulägu failed, then, in his attempt to subjugate Muslim Syria, for he was at a serious disadvantage in view of the threat posed by his cousin Berke, the khan of Kipchak. This Jenghiz-Khanite of the senior branch who ruled the steppes of southern Russia favored Islam even more perhaps than Hulägu favored Christianity; consequently, Hulägu's victories appalled him. Rashid ad-Din reports him as saying of the khan of Persia: "He has sacked all the cities of the Muslims and, without consulting his kinsmen, has brought about the death of the caliph. With the help of Allah I will call him to account for so much innocent blood!" [69] Feeling as he did, Berke had no hesitation in joining the Mamelukes— who, though nominally enemies of the Mongols, were defenders of the Muslim faith—in order to oppose his cousin the khan of Persia, who was a protagonist of the Mongol conquest yet at the same time a protector of Christians. The new Mameluke sultan Baibars (1260–77), himself a Turk of Kipchak origin, encouraged this move. In 1262, Berke and Baibars began to exchange embassies, and Berke declared war on Hulägu. [70] In November and December of that year, Hulägu took the offensive; crossed the Derbent pass, which marked the Caucasian frontier between the two khanates; and advanced into Kipchak territory beyond the Terek. Soon after, however, he was met by a surprise attack on the Terek by Berke's army under the command of Berke's nephew Nogai and thrown back into Azerbaijan. [71] The hostility of the Kipchak khans, which was evident from the beginning, and later the hostility of the khans of the Jagatai branch, soon resulted in the encirclement of the khanate of Persia, which was paralyzed by continual flank attacks from the Caucasus or the Amu Darya and prevented from expanding in the direction of Syria. This civil warfare among the Jenghiz-Khanites put a final stop to the Mongol conquest.

Hulägu did at least achieve the territorial unity of Persia by abolishing a number of provincial dynasties. The atabeg of Mosul, old Badr ad-Din Lulu (1233–59), had saved his throne by his acknowledgment of servility to the Mongols. But after his sons rashly sided with the Mamelukes, Hulägu took possession of Mosul, sacked it, and annexed the principality (1262). [72] Seljuk-shah of the Salghurid dynasty, atabeg of Fars from 1262 to 1264, also rebelled and was killed by the Mongols when they took Kazerun (December, 1264). Hulägu then gave the throne of Fars to the Salghurid princess 'Abish-khatun and had her marry his fourth son, prince Mangu Timur, an act equivalent to annexation. [73] Another of Hulägu's sons, his heir Abaqa, similarly married Padsha-khatun, the heiress of the Qutlugh-shah dynasty of Kerman. [74]

An interesting feature, but one about which there is little information, relates to Buddhist activity in Persia at the time of Hulägu and his early successors. All that is known is that a certain number of Buddhist monks came from Uiguria, China, and Tibet to settle in Hulägu's kingdom, where they built many pagodas adorned with paintings and statues.[75] In particular, Hulägu's grandson Arghun khan embellished such pagodas with paintings in which he himself was represented.[76] What is known of the Chinese paintings of the Yüan gives reason to deplore the loss of these works, whose influence might explain certain characteristics of the later Persian miniatures.

Although, after the sack of Baghdad, Hulägu was regarded by the Muslims as the scourge of God, he was nonetheless a patron of Persian literature. The great Persian historian 'Ala ad-Din Juvaini is the best example of this. His father, Beha ad-Din (d. 1253), whose family originated in the Nishapur country, was himself a member of the Mongol administration and had been put in charge of the finances of Khurasan. Juvaini too became an administrator. In 1256 he dissuaded Hulägu from burning the precious library collected by the Isma'ilis at Alamut. Having twice visited Mongolia (1249–51 and 1251–53), and being familiar with Central Asian questions, he wrote around 1260 his invaluable *History of the Conqueror of the World (Ta'rikh-i Jahan-gusha)*, that is, the history of Jenghiz Khan and his successors down to 1258. In 1262–63, Hulägu appointed him governor (*malik*) of Baghdad. To his credit be it noted that in 1268, during a wave of Muslim fanaticism, the Nestorian patriarch Mar Denha found safe refuge in his house.[77] His brother Shams ad-Din Juvaini was finance minister (*sahib-divan*) to the khans Hulägu, Abaqa, and Tekuder from about 1263 to 1284.

ABAQA'S REIGN

Hulägu died near Maragheh on February 8, 1265, followed shortly afterward by his queen Doquz-khatun. Their loss was felt by all eastern Christians, who mourned in them "the two great stars of the Christian faith" and "another Constantine, another Helen," as Bar Hebraeus wrote feelingly in the name of the Jacobite Syriac Church and Kirakos of Ganja on behalf of the Armenian Church.[78]

Hulägu was succeeded by his eldest son Abaqa (1265–82).

The new khan continued to live in Azerbaijan; but whereas, under Hulägu, Maragheh had served as capital, Tabriz was now chosen and was to continue as such until the end of the dynasty, except for the period of Oljaitu's reign (1304–16), when it was transferred to Sultaniyeh. Like Hulägu, Abaqa never considered himself as more than the lieutenant of the grand khan Kublai, who at his request sent him a *yarligh* of investiture.

Abaqa, like his father, was probably more Buddhist than anything else; yet he too showed good will toward the Christian communities—Armenian, Nestorian, or Jacobite—at home, and favored the alliance with Christendom against the Mamelukes of Egypt and Syria abroad. In the year of his accession he married the *despoina* Mary, daughter of the Byzantine emperor Michael Palaeologus. On the Syriac side, Abaqa was the protector of the Nestorian patriarch Mar Denha.[79] Later, he became the friend of the patriarch's successor, the famous Mar Yahballaha III.

We spoke earlier (page 303) of the pilgrimage made by the two Nestorian monks, Rabban Sauma and Markus, who came from Peking and from the Toqto region in northern Shansi, respectively, and who desired to visit Jerusalem. We saw how, after crossing Kashgaria between 1275 and 1276, they arrived in Persia. Their Syriac biography shows the important position held by the Nestorian Church in Persia under the Mongols. On their arrival in Khurasan, they came upon a Nestorian monastery near Tus, that of Mar Sehyon.[80] Near Maragheh in Azerbaijan, they met the patriarch Mar Denha, who, as has been said, was highly esteemed by the Mongol authorities.[81] From there they went down to Baghdad, where the Nestorian patriarchal see was situated—it was still designated by the ancient name of Seleucia—and then into Assyria, with its famous sanctuaries and monasteries of Arbela, Beth Garmai, and Nisibin.[82] Rabban Sauma and Markus had withdrawn into the monastery of St. Michael of Tarel near Nisibin when the patriarch Mar Denha summoned them to undertake a mission to the khan Abaqa. The khan not only gave them the most cordial reception but furnished them with letters patent to facilitate their pilgrimage to Jerusalem. However, they were unable to make this journey owing to the state of war that existed between the khanate of Persia, on the one hand, and the khanate of Kipchak and the Mamelukes, on the other.

The patriarch Mar Denha then appointed Markus metropolitan

of the Öngüt and Khitan countries—that is, of northern China—
with Rabban Sauma as his coadjutor.[83] But before they had set
off for their new sees, Mar Denha died (February 24, 1281), and
a Nestorian council which met near Baghdad elected Markus
patriarch under the name of Mar Yahballaha III. It is clear that
this election was largely a matter of policy. Despite his great
piety, the new pontiff had only a slight knowledge of the Syriac
language and none at all of Arabic. But he was a "Mongol" and
at any rate belonged to that Turko-Öngüt people whose princes
were closely allied to the Jenghiz-Khanite family. The Nestorian
Fathers felt that they could have no patriarch more acceptable
to the khan of Persia. And indeed, when Mar Yahballaha went
to seek investiture at the hands of Abaqa, the Mongol ruler welcomed him as a friend. "He put upon his shoulders a coat and
offered him his own chair, which was a small throne. He gave
him also a parasol of honor and a *paiza* or golden tablet bearing
the royal insignia and the great seal of the patriarchs." [84] On November 2, 1281, the prelate from Peking was consecrated patriarch
of the Nestorian Church in the cathedral of Mar Koka near Seleucia, in the presence of Mar Abraham, metropolitan of Jerusalem; Mar James, metropolitan of Samarkand; and Mar Jesusabran,
metropolitan of Tangut, i.e., Kansu in China.[85]

Abroad, Abaqa ended the war started by his father against
Berke, khan of Kipchak. In the spring of 1266, Berke's nephew
Nogai had resumed the offensive, crossing the Derbent pass and
the Kura, but he was beaten on the Aksu by Abaqa's lieutenants
and thrust back into Shirvan. Berke himself then came through
the Derbent with a larger army and was marching up the Kura in
order to make the crossing when he died (1266). At his death,
his forces withdrew.[86]

In the northeast, as has been seen, Abaqa had to face the onslaught of the Jagataite Baraq, khan of Transoxiana, who in 1269–
70 invaded Khurasan and occupied Merv and Nishapur. After a
feinted retreat to deceive the enemy, Abaqa also crushed Baraq
near Herat on July 22, 1270.[87] The skill with which Shams ad-Din
Kert, the *malik* of Herat, avoided committing himself in these
inter-Mongol wars should be noted. To save his city, this adroit
Afghan, faced with an invasion of Jagataites, consented to render
them homage; but when Abaqa arrived in Khurasan with his
army, Shams ad-Din rallied to him again and, by his energetic

defense of Herat, enabled the khan of Persia to draw the invaders into an ambush, where they were crushed.

In January, 1273, Abaqa completed his revenge. Carrying the war into Transoxiana, he sent an army to sack Bukhara (see above). Notwithstanding the loyalty displayed in 1270 by Shams ad-Din, *malik* of Herat, Abaqa mistrusted him. In 1277, having showered titles and honors upon him, he lured him to Tabriz and there had him discreetly poisoned (January, 1278). Yet in 1279 it was the son of his victim, Rukn ad-Din, whom he made prince of Herat under the name of Shams ad-Din II.[88]

In the west, Abaqa had to continue his father's struggle against the Mamelukes, who were now masters not only of Egypt but also of Muslim Syria. The Mameluke sultan Baibars, Islam's protagonist and one of the most redoubtable warriors of his time (1260–77), took the offensive by devastating time and again the Armenian kingdom of Cilicia, client and close ally of the Mongols. In April, 1275, he plundered its principal cities—Sis, Adana, Tarsus, and Lajazzo—after which he intervened in the affairs of the Seljuk sultanate of Asia Minor. This state was closely bound in vassalage to the khanate of Persia. During the minority of the young sultan Kai-Khosrau III (1265–83), it was administered, under the Mongol protectorate, by the *pervane* (chancellor) Mu'in ad-Din Suleiman. This minister, a great intriguer, appears to have entered into secret correspondence with Baibars, whom he was no doubt urging to deliver the country from Mongol control. In 1277, at any rate, Baibars entered the Seljuk sultanate and on April 18 overcame the Mongol army of occupation at Albistan on the upper Jihun, at the entrance to Cappadocia, while the *pervane,* who was in command of the Seljuk contingent, took flight. Baibars made a triumphal entry into Kayseri in Cappadocia (April 23) and then returned to Syria.

At the news of this defeat, Abaqa hastened to Anatolia (July, 1277); sternly punished the Seljuk Turks, who, more loyal to the Muslim faith than to the Jenghiz-Khanites, had put up a poor fight; and, after an inquiry, executed the *pervane* (August 2).[89]

Abaqa would have liked to conclude a firm alliance with the Latin powers against the Mamelukes, and in 1273 he wrote to this effect to the Pope and to Edward I of England. In May–July, 1274, two of his ambassadors had an audience with Gregory X and were received by the Fathers of the Council of Lyons.

Other envoys from the same khan are mentioned as appearing in Italy in November, 1276 (John and James Vasellus), and in England, at the court of Edward I, in 1277. But neither the Papacy nor France nor England responded to the Mongol offers.[90]

Abaqa determined to act alone. At the end of October, 1271, he had sent 10,000 horsemen to harry the countryside in the province of Aleppo. In September and October, 1280, he sent a larger detachment which for a short time occupied the city of Aleppo, except for the citadel, and set fire to the mosques (October 20). This was no more than a reconnaissance. In September, 1281, a Mongol army of 50,000 men penetrated Syria. The king of Armenia (Cilicia) Leo III, as loyal a vassal to the Mongols as his father Hethum, rallied to this army with his own forces. Thus to the 50,000 Mongols were added 30,000 Armenians, Georgians, and Franks. All these troops were commanded by Prince Mangu Timur, Abaqa's brother. On October 30, 1281, near Homs, they encountered the Mameluke army, led by the sultan Qalawun. The Mongol right wing, headed by King Leo III with the Armenians and Georgians, put the forces opposite them to flight, but at the center Mangu Timur retired wounded from the battlefield, and his withdrawal demoralized his men. Once more the Mongols had to retreat across the Euphrates,[91] and shortly after this setback, on April 1, 1282, Abaqa died.

ARGHUN'S REIGN

Tekuder,[92] Abaqa's brother and successor (May 6, 1282), broke with the traditional policy of his house. Although his mother (Princess Qutui-khatun) may have been Nestorian and although he himself was baptized in his youth, according to the monk Hayton, he embraced the Muslim faith after his accession, took the name of Ahmed and the title of sultan, and set about reorientating the khanate of Persia to Islam. The monk Hayton writes: "He devoted all his understanding to bring about the conversion of the Tatars to the false law of Muhammad." [93] In August, 1282, Tekuder sent the Mamelukes an offer of peace and alliance. The Buddhist and Nestorian "Old Mongol" party protested to Kublai, grand khan of China, Tekuder's uncle and still suzerain of the khanate of Persia. Greatly displeased, according to Marco Polo, Kublai threatened to intervene. Tekuder blamed the leaders of the Nestorian Church, the patriarch Mar Yahbal-laha III and his coadjutor Rabban Sauma, for these appeals to the court of Peking. The patriarch was thrown into prison and might have lost his life but for the queen mother, Qutui-khatun, who obtained his release.[94]

Meanwhile the whole of the old Mongol party of malcontents, Buddhists and Nestorians alike, rallied to Prince Arghun, Abaqa's son and governor of Khurasan, and soon civil war broke out. The stakes were high. Would Mongol Persia remain Mongol or become a mere Muslim sultanate? Would Nestorians and Jacobites at home and Armenians and Franks abroad continue to receive favorable treatment, or would the country enter into an alliance with the Mamelukes? At first the struggle went against Arghun. He had stirred to rebellion his own territory of Khurasan, whence he marched on Iraq 'Ajami. But beaten at Aq-khoja, near Kazvin, on May 4, 1284, he was forced to surrender to Tekuder. However, shortly afterward a conspiracy among the army leaders resulted in a palace revolution. Tekuder, deserted by his troops, was put to death on August 10, 1284, and on the following day Arghun ascended the throne.

Arghun halted the national trend toward Islam. Being himself something of a Buddhist, like Abaqa and Hulägu, he entrusted many of the civil appointments to Christians or Jews, especially in the financial administration. He chose as finance minister and chief adviser the Jewish physician Sa'd ad-Daula, who from 1288 until Arghun's last illness (February, 1291) enjoyed the prince's entire confidence. Being intelligent, adaptable, fluent in Turkish and Mongolian, and an able courtier (he owed his favor to a timely purge administered to his sovereign), Sa'd made himself agreeable to Arghun, who also appreciated his devotion to the welfare of the state. He was an outstanding administrator, and restored order in the financial sphere by preventing the depredations of the lords. He forbade military commanders to flout sentences passed by the tribunals and issued orders to the purveyors of the great to refrain from imposing crushing requisitions on the people. In short, he hunted down abuses and tried to introduce into the purely military government of the Mongols the practice of a regular civil administration. Instead of interfering with the Muslim religion, he caused lawsuits between Muslims to be conducted according to Koranic law and not Mongol custom. He also increased the endowments of pious institutions and encouraged and subsidized scholars and men of letters. The Muslims could complain of nothing beyond the fact that he reserved the chief administrative posts for his fellow Jews, and especially that he farmed out all taxation to his kinsmen, except for that of Khurasan and Asia Minor, these provinces being the appanages of the princes Ghazan and Gaikhatu, son and brother of Arghun. Nevertheless, the Jewish minister aroused fierce hostility. The Mongol lords were angry with him for stopping their pillage, and devout Muslims claimed that he and Arghun were going to start a new religion, force the faithful to become "pagans," and turn the Kaaba of Mecca into a temple of idols—probably a Buddhist sanctuary—and so on. The accusations were of course absurd, but in the end they were to deprive the state of a great man.[95]

One of Arghun's wives, Uruk-khatun, Kerayit by birth and niece of the late queen Doquz-khatun, was a Nestorian. In August, 1289, she had one of her sons, the future khan Oljaitu, baptized by the name of Nicholas, in honor of Pope Nicholas IV. The monk Hayton writes: "Arghun greatly loved and honored the Christians. He rebuilt the Christian churches that Tekuder had pulled down." The life of the Nestorian patriarch Mar Yahballaha tells that he was now able to rebuild a number of former sanctuaries, including the church of Mar Shalita at Maragheh.

RABBAN SAUMA'S EMBASSY TO THE WEST

Wishing to resume the struggle against the Mamelukes, Arghun tried to win anew an alliance of Christendom. He proposed to make a concerted attack: an invasion of Muslim Syria to coincide with the landing of a crusade at Acre or Damietta, followed by the partition of Syria. Aleppo and Damascus were to be given to the Mongols, Jerusalem to the crusaders. With this object, Arghun sent a letter in 1285 to Pope Honorius IV, the Latin translation of which has been preserved at the Vatican and which sets forth a detailed plan. In this famous document, the khan of Persia, after invoking the name of Jenghiz Khan, "the ancestor of all the Tatars," and mentioning the grand khan Kublai—emperor of China and his great-uncle, suzerain, and ally—recalls the bonds which had united the Jenghiz-Khanite dynasty with Christendom: his Christian mother, his grandfather Hulägu, and his father Abaqa, all protectors of Christians. The grand khan Kublai, he says, has charged him to deliver and take under his protection "the land of the Christians." He ends by asking that a crusading army may be landed while he himself invades Syria. "As the land of the Saracens will lie between yourselves and us, together we will surround and strangle it. . . . We will drive out the Saracens with the help of God, the Pope, and the Grand Khan!" [96]

In 1287, Arghun sent another embassy to the West, with the same object, led by Rabban Sauma, the Nestorian prelate. The extraordinary odyssey of this Öngüt or Uigur monk, born near Peking, from China to Persia was described earlier. Rabban Sauma took ship on the Black Sea, no doubt at Trebizond, and landed at Constantinople. The Byzantine emperor Andronicus II (1282–1328) gave a cordial welcome to Arghun's representative, the more so as Seljuk Anatolia, which bordered upon the Byzantine Empire, was a dependency of the khan of Persia. [97] After performing his devotions at the church of Saint Sophia, Rabban Sauma sailed for Italy and went ashore at Naples, where he witnessed a naval battle fought in the bay on June 23, 1287, between the Angevin and Aragonese fleets. [98] From Naples he went on to Rome. Unfortunately, Pope Honorius IV had just died (April 3, 1287) and his successor had not yet been elected. Rabban Sauma was received by the assembled cardinals. He explained to them the importance of Mongol Christendom: "Know that many of our Fathers [the Nestorian missionaries of the seventh and succeeding centuries] have gone into the lands of the Turks, Mongols, and Chinese and have taught them. Today, many Mongols are Christian, among them children of kings and queens, who have been baptized and confess Christ. They have churches in their camps. King Arghun is united in friendship with my lord the Patriarch. He desires to possess himself of Syria and entreats your aid to deliver Jerusalem." [99]

After devotional visits to Saint Peter's and the other churches of Rome, Rabban Sauma left for France by way of Genoa. The Genoese, who had important countinghouses in the Crimea and in Trebizond, and many merchants in Mongol Persia, were also prompt and warm in their welcome to Arghun's envoy. [100] Rabban Sauma arrived in Paris about September 10, 1287, and was received by Philip the Fair, who conducted him in person to the Sainte-Chapelle. After having seen Paris from the Sorbonne to the abbey of Saint-Denis, Rabban Sauma went to Bordeaux to visit Edward I of England (end of October and beginning of November). Like the king of France, Edward gave the Mongol ambassador the most flattering welcome; yet neither monarch would conclude the definite military pact which it was Rabban Sauma's mission to secure.[101] Somewhat discouraged, Rabban Sauma returned to Rome, where a new Pope, Nicholas IV, had at last been elected on February 20, 1288. Nicholas listened to the Mongol prelate with the greatest interest and affection; he admitted him to the ceremonies of Holy Week, reserving a place of honor for him everywhere and giving him communion with his own hand. Rabban Sauma departed filled with consolation; from the account of his mission, it is clear that this prelate born near Peking had never dreamed of experiencing such warmth and such religious satisfaction.[102] But from the political point of view, his mission had failed. The western powers would not organize the crusade which, in conjunction with the Mongol army of Persia, might have saved the Frankish colonies of Syria. Rabban Sauma's complaint to the cardinal of Tusculum at the time of his second call at Genoa speaks for itself: "What can I tell you, dear and venerable lord? I came hither on an embassy on behalf of King Arghun and the Patriarch concerning Jerusalem. A whole year has elapsed. . . . What am I to say; what answer shall I make to the Mongols on my return?" [103]

Rabban Sauma went back to Persia carrying letters from Nicholas IV, Philip the Fair, and Edward I for Khan Arghun.[104] He must have returned to court about the end of the summer of 1288. Arghun expressed deep gratitude and attached him to his *ordu* as Nestorian chaplain: "Arghun caused a chapel to be erected very near to the royal tent, so that the ropes of the two tents intertwined. And he commanded that the sound of the bell should never cease to be heard in this church." [105]

After the Easter celebrations (April 10) of 1289, Arghun sent a new ambassador, the Genoese Buscarel de Gisolf, to Pope Nicholas IV and to Philip the Fair and Edward I. Buscarel arrived in Rome between July 15 and September 30, 1289. On being received by Nicholas and later (November and December) by Philip, he reiterated his sovereign's offer of an offensive alliance with the object of delivering the Holy Land. We have the text of the letter addressed to Philip, written in Mongolian in Uigur characters: "By the power of Eternal Heaven and under the auspices of the supreme khan [Kublai], this is our word: King of France, we invite you to set forth on campaign in the last winter month of the year of the panther [January, 1291] and to pitch camp before ·Damascus about the fifteenth day of the first month of spring [about February 20, 1291]. If you on your part will send troops at the time fixed, we will recapture Jerusalem and give it to you. But it will be useless for our troops to march if you fail at the rendezvous." Attached to this letter was a document written in French and handed to Philip the Fair by Buscarel, by which Arghun promised to supply the necessary provisions and 30,000 remounts for a French crusade landing in Syria.[106] In 1290, Arghun sent a fourth ambassador to the Pope and to Philip and Edward, a certain Chagan or Zagan, whose Christian name was Andrew and who was accompanied by Buscarel de Gisolf, whose second mission this was.[107] But once again the western powers returned no answer beyond formal compliments, and the Franco-Mongol expedition against the Mamelukes never took place.

Arghun had to turn his attention instead to the defense of his northern frontiers alone in Khurasan and Transcaucasia. He had appointed his eldest son Ghazan governor of Khurasan, with Emir Nauruz, son of the Oirat administrator Arghun Agha, as his deputy. From 1243 to 1255, Arghun Agha, as we saw, had administered eastern and central Persia for the krand khan with almost unlimited powers, and even after the accession of the Hulägu dynasty he had retained considerable authority until his death, near Tus, in 1278. Nauruz, born and bred to honors, regarded Khurasan as virtually his own property. In 1298 he rose in revolt and almost succeeded in capturing Prince Ghazan himself. But after a successful beginning, he was pursued by Arghun's armies and had to take refuge in Transoxiana with the khan Qaidu, chief of the house of Ogödäi (1290).[108] In the Caucasus, the·khan of Kipchak attacked the Persian frontier by the Derbent pass, but Arghun's lieutenants defeated the enemy vanguard on May 11, 1290, on the banks of the Kara-Su in Circassia, and the invasion was repulsed.[109]

THE REIGNS OF GAIKHATU AND BAIDU

The reaction against Arghun's policy of centralization began at the time of his last illness. He died on March 7, 1291. On February 30, his courtiers removed and executed the Jewish minister Sa'd ad-Daula. The most influential of the military leaders nominated Arghun's brother Gaikhatu—then governor of Seljuk Anatolia—as khan. This was a prince of little merit, addicted to wine, women, and sodomy, wildly extravagant, and lacking in any sense of government. He and his minister, *sadr-jihan* Ahmed al-Khalidi, were so misguided as to introduce in Persia in May, 1294, the use of paper currency, or *ch'ao*, in imitation of what the grand khan Kublai had done in China.[110] The first issue was made in Tabriz on September 12 of the same year. The result was even more disastrous than in China and, in the face of a kind of merchants' strike and of bazaar riots, the paper money had to be withdrawn.

In the matter of religion, the life of Mar Yahballaha III assures us that Gaikhatu treated that patriarch, no less than Rabban Sauma, with great benevolence, and that he did them the pleasure of visiting the Nestorian church built by the latter at Maragheh.[111] Nevertheless the policy of the *sadr-jihan*, the all-powerful minister whose aim it was to remove Mongol emirs from government posts, favored chiefly the Muslims, as Barthold points out.

Gaikhatu was overthrown by a party of Mongol lords, who objected to such tendencies. On April 21, 1295, he was strangled in his Mugan encampment with a bowstring, "without bloodshed." In his place the nobles appointed his first cousin Baidu, another of Hulägu's grandsons. The new khan was a somewhat insignificant person who accepted power only under compulsion.[112] According to Bar Hebraeus, he was very favorably inclined to Christianity. "From being in the company of the Greek princess, Abaqa's wife, he had conceived a good opinion of the Christians, and he allowed them to have chapels and ring bells in his *ordu*. He even told them that he was a Christian himself and wore a cross about his neck, but he dared not show his liking for them too openly. . . . The Muslims nonetheless resented his partiality for the Christians, who during his very brief reign received many civil appointments." [113]

Prince Ghazan, Arghun's son and viceroy of Khurasan, whose ambition it was to succeed to his father's throne, rebelled against Baidu. In this he was supported by Emir Nauruz, who, having become reconciled with him in 1294, now served as his lieutenant. Nauruz, a zealous Muslim, persuaded Ghazan to forsake Buddhism for Islam, so that in the struggle against Baidu he might

obtain the support of the Persian element. This was a natural
enough policy, since Baidu was backed by the Christians.[114] Baidu,
as it turned out, was a victim of his own clemency. In the course
of a meeting with Ghazan, his followers had urged him to rid
himself of this prince; but, moved by a long-standing affection,
he had refused. His enemies were less scrupulous. Owing to
Nauruz' intrigues, he found himself gradually deserted by his own
followers and was vanquished without a fight. He tried to flee
from Azerbaijan to Georgia, but was taken prisoner near Nakhichevan and put to death on October 5, 1295.

GHAZAN'S REIGN

Ghazan at last ascended the throne which he had coveted ever
since the death of his father Arghun. For all his conversion to
Islam, he was a thorough Mongol. He is described by the monk
Hayton as short and ugly—uglier than anyone in his army. His
energy was tireless; he was crafty, dissembling, patient, as will be
seen in his dealings with Nauruz; he was ruthless to his enemies
and held human life as of no account where the pursuit of his
policy was concerned; yet he was a sound administrator and
to that extent humane. He was also a good general and a brave
soldier. (This was proved at the battle of Homs, which he won,
so to speak, singlehanded when his men were routed.) In short,
allowing for changing times, he recalls somewhat his ancestor
Jenghiz Khan. Moreover, he was very intelligent and well-informed. Rashid ad-Din says that "Mongolian was his mother
tongue, but he knew a little Arabic, Persian, Hindi, Tibetan,
Chinese, and Frankish. His special field of knowledge was Mongol
history, which, like all of his nation, he held in highest esteem.
Better than any other Mongol except Bolod Agha, he knew by
heart the genealogy of his ancestors and of all the Mongol chiefs
and army leaders." [115] No Jenghiz-Khanite was ever more conscious of his race than this prince, who by force of circumstance
would start all unawares the denationalization of his people by
leading them on to the path of Islam.

At the outset of his reign, despite the strength of his personality, Ghazan was compelled to follow not his own policy but that
of his partisans. Having attained the throne through the support
of Emir Nauruz and of the Muslim party, he had first to satisfy

them. The Mongol state of Persia became officially Muslim; and as an outward and visible sign of this, the Mongols assumed the turban. A violent Muslim reaction, inspired by Nauruz, now ran counter to the entire policy of Hulägu, Abaqa, and Arghun. From the moment he entered Tabriz, his capital, Ghazan, a prisoner of his adherents, gave orders for the destruction of Christian churches, Jewish synagogues, Mazdean fire temples, and Buddhist pagodas. Buddhist idols and Christian icons, smashed and tied together, were paraded in mockery through the streets of Tabriz. Buddhist bonzes were ordered to embrace Islam. Arghun, Ghazan's father, had had his portrait painted on the walls of a pagoda; nevertheless, Ghazan caused these paintings to be destroyed.[116] Christians and Jews might no longer appear in public except in a distinctive dress. Nauruz, exceeding his sovereign's instructions, even instituted massacres among bonzes and Christian priests. Many Buddhist monks had to abjure their faith. Despite his great age and "Mongol" origin, the venerable Nestorian patriarch Mar Yahballaha III was arrested in his Maragheh residence, imprisoned, hung head downward, and beaten, while the Muslim populace sacked the Nestorian sanctuary of Mar Shalita. Mar Yahballaha, whom Nauruz wanted to put to death, was saved by the intervention of Hethum II, king of Armenia (Cilicia), who happened to be staying at the court of Tabriz and interceded with Ghazan in behalf of the old man. Notwithstanding the violence of the persecution, the Mongol court dared not oppose the loyal Armenian vassal who provided the empire's defense on the frontier of the Mameluke sultanate. Ghazan had turned Muslim for good, no doubt because he felt that the conversion of the dynasty was essential to rulers of a Muslim country, but he shared none of the religious hatreds of his minister Nauruz; he was too much of a Mongol for that.[117] As soon as he gained some freedom of movement, he reinstated Mar Yahballaha, whose Mongol origins cannot have failed to engage his sympathy (March–July, 1296). Nevertheless, in March, 1297, the unleashed Muslims of Maragheh fomented a new riot, sacking both the patriarchal residence and the Nestorian cathedral. At the same time, the Kurdish hillmen, stirred up by Nauruz' agents, besieged the citadel of Arbela, the Nestorians' place of refuge.[118]

Meanwhile Ghazan, who was a strong character and very jealous of his authority, had become irked by the dictatorship of

Nauruz. Nauruz was the son of a Mongol who had been the almost independent viceroy of eastern Persia, and was himself the husband of a royal princess, Khan Abaqa's daughter. Since placing Ghazan on the throne, he had fancied himself inviolable and free to act as he pleased. In recognition of his services, Ghazan had made him lieutenant general of the realm. Now his arrogance and insolence knew no bounds. Suddenly the hand of the monarch fell upon him. In March, 1297, without warning Ghazan arrested and executed all Nauruz' clients who happened to be at court. Nauruz himself, then at the head of the Khurasan army, was attacked by loyalist troops and beaten near Nishapur. He took refuge with the *malik* of Herat, Fakhr ad-Din Kert, Rukn ad-Din's son and successor, whom he thought he could trust. But Kert policy consisted in surviving amid the Mongol wars by means of timely adherence to the stronger side. Was it likely, then, that this astute family of Afghans would clash with the Jenghiz-Khanite dynasty for the sake of a fallen minister? When the imperial army came to lay siege to Herat and seize Nauruz, Fakhr ad-Din cynically handed over the fugitive, who was executed then and there (August 13, 1297).[119]

Freed now from Nauruz' tutelage, Ghazan threw himself into his task. He had remained a true Mongol for all his conversion to Islam, and he was an energetic ruler, both enlightened and strict. He restored authority to the central power by merciless execution—sometimes on mere suspicion—of princes of the blood, emirs, and officials who might hinder his purpose. "As sovereign and legislator," Barthold writes, "he displayed tremendous activity, completely free from bigotry. He devoted his attentions on state finance, particularly to the currency. On his coins, inscribed in three languages (Arabic, Mongolian, and Tibetan), Ghazan no longer figures, as did his predecessors, as representative of the grand khan of Peking, but as sovereign by the grace of God: *tängri-yin kuchundur* (literally, by the virtue of Heaven)."[120] Nevertheless, despite this declaration of sovereignty, Ghazan's ambassadors in China continued to render homage to the grand khan Temür as head of the Jenghiz-Khanite family and, more especially, of the house of Tolui.

Pitiless though Ghazan may have been in his measures against conspiracy and the peculations of the great, his ever-watchful administration "protected the rural population from molestation and extortion." He said one day to his officials: "You want me to let you plunder the Tadzhiks [Persian cultivators]. But when you have destroyed the farmers' cattle and crops, what will you do? If you come to me seeking provisions, I will punish you cruelly!" [121] After so much harrying and devastation, a large part of the arable land in Khurasan and Iraq 'Ajami lay waste. Nomad rule was killing the soil. Rashid ad-Din notes: "The fields remained largely untilled. Whether they belonged to the public domain or to individuals, no one dared tend them for fear of being dispossessed after having spent much labor and money on their cultivation." Ghazan set about "remaking the land." Rashid ad-Din goes on: "He felt the need for encouraging such enterprise and issued an edict guaranteeing to cultivators the fruit of their toil under fair conditions. Public lands which had remained uncultivated for some years were to be given to those who would till them, with exemption from tax for the first year. By the same edict, hereditary estates that had been neglected for a certain number of years might be appropriated by new settlers without the consent of the original owners." [122] The watch kept upon depredations by the nobles raised state revenues from 1,700 to 2,100 tomans.

Ghazan's minister was the great Persian historian Rashid ad-Din (Fadl Allah Rashid ad-Din Tabib, of Hamadan, born about 1247, died in 1318, raised to the dignity of *sadr* in 1298). [123] It was Ghazan who asked Rashid ad-Din to write the history of the Mongols, and so the immortal *Jami-ut-Tavarikh* by that famous scholar came into being. Ghazan, who, as seen, had a remarkably thorough knowledge of his people's past, was one of Rashid ad-Din's chief sources of information, as was the *ch'eng-hsiang* Bolod, envoy of the grand khan of China to the court of Persia.

Ghazan also covered Tabriz his capital with splendid buildings: mosques, madrasahs (mosque schools), charitable institutions, and so on. As Rashid ad-Din observed: "The Mongols, who until then had only destroyed, now began to build." Ghazan's reign marks the point at which in Persia these perpetual nomads took to an almost sedentary life. Unfortunately, this trend had its drawbacks. In abandoning their universal tolerance in order to adopt an increasingly sectarian form of Islam (recall Rashid ad-Din's ordeal), the Mongols of Persia soon lost their national characteristics and qualities; they merged with the rest of the inhabitants, and finally disappeared.

There was neither time nor opportunity for these regrettable tendencies to develop during the energetic Ghazan's reign. In Asia Minor, for instance, this prince dealt sharply with separatist manifestations. Sulamish, grandson of the *noyan* Baiju, sought to create for himself an independent principality, helped by the Turkoman emir Mahmud-beg, true founder of the Karaman dynasty in old Lycaonia (southeastern Cappadocia). On April 27, 1299, this revolt was crushed by the royal army at Aksehir near Erzincan. And the last Seljuk sultans of Konya, appointed and deposed at the whim of the court of Tabriz, had less authority than any Mongol prefect. Thus Ghazan removed Sultan Mas'ud II (1295), enthroned Kai-Qobad II (1297) and dethroned him (1300), and restored Mas'ud II (d. 1304), the last prince of that illustrious house.

Ghazan, following in this respect the foreign policy of Hulägu and Abaqa, launched a fresh invasion of the Mameluke empire, in Syria. He occupied Aleppo except for the citadel (December 12, 1299), defeated the Mameluke army before Homs (December 22), and entered Damascus (January 6, 1300). Hethum II, king of Armenia (Cilicia), a loyal vassal of the Mongols like all of his house, supported him with some of his own forces. But after the fall of the last Frankish possessions and the permanent conversion of the Persian Mongols to Islam, these Mongol victories had little significance, being in a sense "posthumous." In any event, after this brilliant cavalcade, Ghazan returned to Persia (February, 1300) and the Mamelukes were able to reoccupy Syria.

It is true that a Jagataite diversion in the Iranian East had once more paralyzed the khanate of Persia. Prince Qutlugh-khoja, son of Duwa the khan of Turkestan, had carved himself out a fief at Ghazni and Ghor in Afghanistan, and during Ghazan's expedition into Syria he had ravaged Kerman and Fars. In the spring of 1303, Ghazan sent a fresh army into Syria, but Qutlugh-shah, the general whom he had put in charge of the expedition, was beaten by the Mamelukes in Marj as-Soffar, near Damascus (April 21, 1303). This was the last Mongol intervention in Syria.

One may say that Ghazan had succeeded in combining an entirely Muslim internal policy with a foreign policy derived from Hulägu, Abaqa, and Arghun. It has been seen—and Rashid ad-Din provides sufficient testimony thereto—that there is no reason to doubt the sincerity and permanence of his conversion to Islam. He had irrevocably broken with Buddhism, the religion of his family, and so compelled Buddhist bonzes and lamas either to abjure their faith or to leave the country. On the other hand, no doubt to suit his foreign policy, he put a stop to the persecution of Nestorians and gave his friendship to their patriarch Mar Yahballaha III. In June, 1303, the latter had visited the old pontiff in the monastery he had just rebuilt at Maragheh and loaded him with honors, gifts, and tokens of his regard.[124]

Oljaitu's Reign

Ghazan died on May 17, 1304, and was succeeded by his younger brother Oljaitu (1304–16).[125] Although son of the Nestorian princess Uruk-khatun and baptized by her with the name of Nicholas, Oljaitu was later converted to Islam under the influence of one of his wives. For a time he was even an adherent of Persian Shi'ism.[126] During his reign, Islam made fresh strides in Persia. The Nestorian patriarch Mar Yahballaha, who had hoped to enjoy the same favor from Oljaitu as he had from Ghazan, was received with no more than strained politeness, so the biographer says. The Muslims took advantage of this to persecute the Nestorians. The church in Tabriz would have been turned into a mosque but for the intervention of the Mongol emir Iranjin, a prince of Kerayit origin—Doquz-khatun's nephew and brother of Oljaitu's mother—who like all the Kerayit had held on to the Christian sympathies of old. The Nestorians, as noted, had one stronghold, the citadel of Arbela or Erbil. In the spring of 1310, the governor of the region attempted to seize it from them with the help of the Kurds. Despite Mar Yahballaha's efforts to avoid irreparable disaster, the Christians of Arbela resisted. The citadel was at last taken by royal troops and Kurdish hillmen on July 1, 1310, and all the defenders were massacred. Mar Yahballaha was to outlive his work; he died at Maragheh on November 13, 1317, full of bitterness against these Mongols whom he had served so faithfully and who disowned him in being false to themselves.[127]

Notwithstanding his abandonment of traditional Jenghiz-Khanite sympathies toward the Nestorians, Oljaitu followed his brother Ghazan's policy in general; and although his was a less powerful personality, he maintained the solid administrative framework that Ghazan had founded. Muslim sources describe him as a man of liberality and integrity.[128] He retained as minister the great historian Rashid ad-Din, an outstanding administrator and wise statesman who under this reign exercised a yet greater influence than he had under Ghazan. He even succeeded in converting Oljaitu to the Shafi'ite doctrine. Oljaitu bestowed his patronage also upon the other historian of the day, Wassaf. Lastly, Oljaitu was a great builder. In 1305–6 he established his capital at Sultaniyeh, in the northwestern part of Iraq 'Ajami, on a site which had been chosen by his father Arghun and which he embellished. He also displayed interest in the observatory of Maragheh. Rashid ad-Din too was a builder, and in 1309 he laid out a whole new quarter in the city of Ghazaniyeh, east of Tabriz.[129]

Despite his Muslim piety, Oljaitu's foreign policy, like Ghazan's, followed the same line as that of his ancestors: he opposed the Mamelukes and sought an alliance with Christian Europe. To the courts of the West he sent the Christian Thomas Ilduchi as ambassador. The letters that he addressed on this occasion to Pope Clement V, Philip the Fair of France, and Edward II of England have been preserved. The French Archives Nationales contain notably Oljaitu's letter to Philip the Fair, dated May, 1305, in which he congratulates himself upon the harmony prevailing between him, the khan of Persia, and the other chiefs of the Jenghiz-Khanite *ulus:* Temür, grand khan of China; Chäpär, head of the *ulus* of Ogödäi; Duwa, chief of the Jagatai *ulus;* and Toqtai, khan of Kipchak. Oljaitu also expresses the desire to preserve his predecessors' good relations with the leaders of Christendom.[130]

Meanwhile, the frontier war between the khanate of Persia and the Mameluke sultanate of Egypt had begun again. During the years 1304 and 1305, the Mamelukes carried out plundering raids in the Armenian kingdom of Cilicia, a vassal state of the Mongols. On the second of these raids, they were met by the Mongol garrisons of Asia Minor and sustained considerable losses.[131] In 1313, Oljaitu besieged the fortress of Rahiba, a Mameluke frontier post on the middle Euphrates, but the heat obliged him to abandon the siege before the city capitulated.[132]

In Asia Minor, the Seljuk dynasty had become extinct in 1302, so that the Mongol viceroys of Konya were now the rulers there. In reality, the disappearance of the convenient Seljuk "screen" left the Mongols confronted by petty Turkish emirs who were all trying to take advantage of the absence of a central power to gain their independence. This was the case with the Karaman emirs, Turkoman chiefs established in the mountainous region of Ermenak who at this time were seeking to take the place of the Seljuks in Konya and whom Ghazan had had to castigate in 1299 (see above). Between 1308 and 1314, the Karaman emir Mahmud-beg made himself lord of Konya. Oljaitu sent out against him General Chopan, who forced him first to flee and then shortly afterward, in 1319, to come and make his submission.[133] The Ottomans, on their part, who were established in northwestern Phrygia and in Bithynia, were beginning to expand at the expense of Byzantium. The founder of the Ottoman Empire, 'Uthman I, threatened especially the great Byzantine city of Nicaea. The Byzantine emperor, Andronicus II, sought the alliance of Oljaitu and offered him his sister Maria in marriage.[134] It appears to have been in consequence of this alliance that a force of Mongols invaded the Ottoman district of Eskisehir, from which it was repulsed by Uthman's son Orkhan.[135]

The Turko-Byzantine confines of northwestern Anatolia were only of modest interest to the Mongols of Persia. How could they have supposed that the petty Ottoman emirate so recently founded there would within a century become the greatest Muslim power in the world? They paid far closer attention to the affairs of the Iranian East, for there they had continually to guard against the encroachments of their cousins, the Jagataite khans of Transoxiana, and at the same time put down the stealthy attempts of their own vassals, the Afghans of the Kert family of Herat, to achieve independence.

In 1306, Oljaitu sent General Danishmend Bahadur to besiege the city of Herat, where the *malik* Fakhr ad-Din, third prince of the Kert dynasty, was acting like an independent sovereign.

Fakhr ad-Din consented to withdraw into the fortress of Amankoh, and Danishmend was able to occupy the city itself; but
the citadel, held by a lieutenant of Fakhr ad-Din's named
Muhammad Sam, remained impregnable. In September, 1306,
Muhammad Sam lured the overconfident Danishmend into the
place and killed him. Oljaitu then sent a fresh army commanded
by Emir Yassawur and Danishmend's son Bujai. After a long
blockade and some dramatic incidents, the town and citadel
of Herat surrendered, as much from starvation as through
treachery and betrayal (1307). Fakhr ad-Din in the meantime
had died at Amankoh.[136] But instead of taking advantage of
this situation to dispossess the Kert dynasty, Oljaitu at once
gave the principality of Herat to Ghiyath ad-Din, Fakhr ad-Din's
brother (July, 1307). Suspected for a time of wishing to foment
a new revolt, Ghiyath ad-Din came before Oljaitu to exonerate
himself and was then left permanently in possession of Herat
(1315).[137]

In 1313 (see page 315), Oljaitu took eastern Afghanistan
from the junior Jagataite Dawud-khoja, an action which led to
an invasion by the khan of Jagatai, Esen-buqa himself, who
upon conquering Murgab occupied part of Khurasan (1315).
But Persia was soon released from this struggle, thanks to a
diversion undertaken by the grand khan of China, whose armies,
attacking the Jagatai territory in the rear, penetrated as far as
the Talas (ca. 1316).[138] However, Khurasan was threatened
again shortly afterward by an exiled Jagataite prince named
Yassawur, whom Oljaitu had been rash enough to welcome, and
who now tried to become independent (1318). Luckily for
Persia, Yassawur was killed in June, 1320, by a personal enemy,
Kebek, the khan of Jagatai.[139] In the course of this war, Ghiyath
ad-Din Kert, emir of Herat, who had been besieged in his city
by Yassawur during May, 1319, had held out against him. He
thus appeared to be a defender of the loyalist cause of the house
of Hulägu, and the court of Tabriz felicitated him warmly. In
fact, he was merely tightening his grip on the principality of
Herat.[140] By the end of his life (he died in 1329) he had
become virtually independent, though the court of Tabriz still
thought of him as the indispensable frontier guard of the northeastern marches.

These last events occurred in the reign of Abu Sa'id, who at the age of twelve had succeeded his father Oljaitu on the latter's death at Sultaniyeh, December 16, 1316. He occupied the throne from 1317 to 1334, but throughout his life he remained the puppet of the Mongol lords who governed in his name and quarreled with one another for power and possessions. The great historian Rashid ad-Din, who as minister had always defended the interests of the state, fell a victim to this camarilla and was executed on false and hideous charges (July 18, 1318).[141]

For the first part of Abu Sa'id's reign, power lay in the hands of a Mongol emir named Chopan or Juban.[142] From 1317 to 1327, Chopan was the real ruler of Persia, and he ruled it firmly. In 1322, he quelled a revolt led by his own son Timurtash, viceroy of Asia Minor; in 1325, he led a victorious expedition as far as the Terek against the khanate of Kipchak; in 1326, near Ghazni, his son Husain beat Tarmashirin, khan of Jagatai, who had invaded Khurasan, and drove him back into Transoxiana. But by 1327, Abu Sa'id was weary of his tutelage and broke with him.[143] Chopan, then in Khurasan, raised the flag of rebellion and prepared to march from Meshed upon Azerbaijan. He was deserted by his troops, however, and compelled to seek refuge at Herat with *malik* Ghiyath ad-Din. The *malik* had him strangled and "sent his finger" to Abu Sa'id (October–November, 1327).[144] Timurtash, one of Chopan's sons and viceroy of Asia Minor, fled to Cairo, where the Mamelukes, for fear of displeasing Abu Sa'id, put him to death.[145]

The fall of a strong man like Chopan, following so closely upon the legal assassination of the great minister Rashid ad-Din, struck a mortal blow to the khanate of Persia. When after a few years Abu Sa'id himself had gone, there was no leader, either military or civil, to hold the Mongolo-Persian state together, and the *ulus* of Hulägu was dissolved.

Chopan's downfall had another consequence: the abandonment of Turkic Anatolia to its own fate. Ever since the disappearance of the Seljuk sultanate of Konya after the death of Mas'ud II in 1304, the Mongol viceroys appointed by the court of Persia had shown a tendency to behave like autonomous

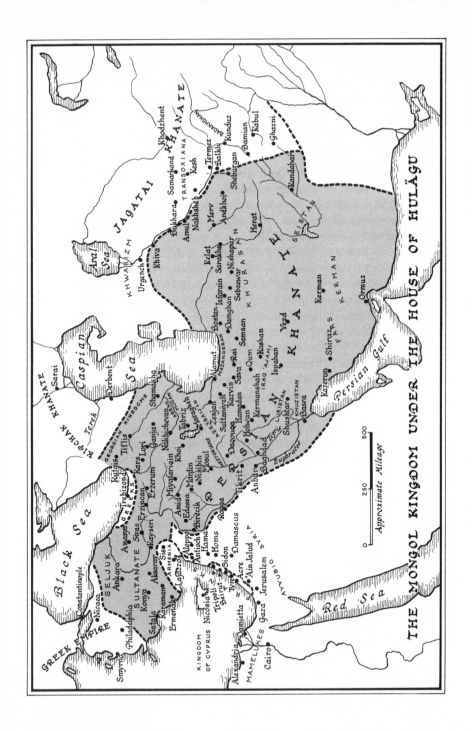

THE MONGOL KINGDOM UNDER THE HOUSE OF HULÄGU

princes. We have seen how Chopan's son Timurtash was already aiming at independence. It is very probable that but for the disaster to his family he would, after Abu Sa'id's death, have founded a Mongol sultanate of Anatolia at either Konya or Kayseri, and that this sultanate would have proved a stumbling block to the expansion of the Ottoman Empire.[146] As it was, Timurtash's fall in 1327, followed eight years later by the death of Abu Sa'id, left Anatolia masterless and freed the local Turkic emirs of the house of Karaman in the southeast and of the house of Ottoman (Osman) in the northwest. Thus the rise of the Ottoman Empire resulted indirectly from the conflicts at the Mongol court of Persia during the crucial years 1327–35.

DISSOLUTION OF THE MONGOL KHANATE OF PERSIA

Abu Sa'id's death (November 30, 1335) led to the dissolution of the Mongol khanate of Persia. Instead of choosing a new khan from the house of Hulägu, the nobles elected a Jenghiz-Khanite of another branch: Arpagaon or Arpakawan, a descendant of Ariq-bögä, the brother of Mongka, Hulägu, and Kublai. In 1336, this unforeseen khan was defeated and killed by a rebel governor.[147] After this, two feudal lords, each drawing to his side a portion of the Mongol nobility, struggled for power under cover of puppet kings. One of these rivals was the governor of Asia Minor, Hasan Buzurg (the Tall) or Hasan the Jelair, as he was also called, after the Mongol tribe from which he descended.[148] The other, Hasan Küchük (the Small), also of Mongol stock, was a grandson of Chopan and had escaped the massacre of his kinsmen.[149] In 1338, Hasan the descendant of Chopan succeeded in snatching Tabriz, the current Persian capital, from his rival, Hasan the Jelair. He then carved himself a kingdom in the northwest, including Azerbaijan and Iraq 'Ajami. At his death in 1343, his brother Ashraf succeeded to these domains, still with Tabriz as the capital.[150] Meanwhile, the Jelair reigned in Baghdad, where in 1340 he proclaimed himself an independent king and from which in 1347 he repulsed all of Ashraf's attacks.

On top of this anarchy came foreign invasion. In 1355, Janibeg, khan of Kipchak (southern Russia), penetrated Azerbaijan and killed Ashraf the Chopanian; he then returned to Russia without troubling to establish his domination on a solid basis.[151]

This disaster turned to the advantage of the Jelairs. Hasan Buzurg had just died (1356), but his son Uweis, who succeeded him on the throne of Baghdad, marched on Azerbaijan and captured it after a preliminary setback (1358).[152] As ruler now of both Baghdad and Tabriz, he reigned over western Persia until his death in 1374, when he was replaced by his son Husain Jelair (1374–82). Later, as will be seen, Husain's brother and successor Ahmed Jelair disputed possession of Tabriz and Baghdad with Tamerlane.

Meanwhile in Herat and eastern Khurasan the Afghan kingdom of the Kert rulers was becoming entirely independent. The astute Ghiyath ad-Din had died in October, 1329, and his two elder sons, Shams ad-Din II and Hafiz, reigned only for a few months. But the third son, Mu'izz ad-Din Husain, who was proclaimed king despite his youth, reigned from 1332 to 1370 and during that time made his kingdom a relatively powerful state, which at one time was bold enough to intervene in the affairs of Transoxiana (see above, p. 343).[153]

In western Khurasan, a brigand chief named 'Abd ar-Razzaq, who in 1337 had seized the fortress of Sebzewar, founded a new principality, that of the Sarbedarians. His brother Wajih ad-Din Mas'ud, who killed him (1338), continued his work by at once capturing Nishapur.[154] In the general uproar, a Mongol prince named Toghul Timur, a descendant of Jenghiz Khan's brother Qasar, had been proclaimed khan in 1337.[155] He established himself at Bistam in northwestern Khurasan and reigned over Mazanderan as well. He improved the city of Meshed, and it is known that he spent his summers nearby, at Radkan, and his winters on the Gurgan not far from the Caspian. The Sarbedarians recognized no more than his nominal suzerainty. About December, 1353, they assassinated him and so remained masters of the whole northwest of Khurasan, the southeast remaining in the possession of the Kerts. Naturally, these two Iranian dynasties waged savage war upon each other, embittered by religious differences, the Kerts being Sunnite Afghans, the Sarbedarians Shi'ite Persians.

A third Iranian—or, more accurately, Arabo-Iranian—dynasty, the Muzaffarid, had established itself in Kerman and Fars.[156] Its founder, the Arab Mubariz ad-Din Muhammad, who was already in power at Yezd and in Kerman, won control of Shiraz in 1353 and Ispahan in 1356–57. In 1358 he was deposed and blinded by his son, Shah Shuja (d. 1384), who succeeded him at Shiraz, while Ispahan passed to other Muzaffarids.

To complete the picture, it should be noted that beside these lords of the moment, those of the morrow were already emerging. They included, in western Persia, the still nomadic Turkoman tribe known from its emblem as the tribe of the Black Sheep: Qara-Qoyunlu. At the time of the partition of the Hulägu khanate, the Qara-Qoyunlu dwelt in the Armenian district of Mus and were encroaching upon Mosul, whence Uweis Jelair drove them out (ca. 1336). On Uweis' death in 1374, the Qara-Qoyunlu chief Bairam Khwaja reoccupied Mosul and Zenjan. His grandson Qara-Yusuf was to found the fortunes of his house by capturing Tabriz from the Jelairs and remaining there until the coming of Tamerlane.[157]

In the former realm of Seljuk Asia Minor, which had fallen into abeyance since the disappearance first of the Seljuk house (ca. 1304) and then of the suzerain khanate of Persia, two Turkoman principalities were disputing possession of Cappadocia. At Sivas and Kayseri, it was the Artena-oghlu clan, whose ruler from 1380 to 1399 was the famous poet-prince Burhan ad-Din,[158] followed in 1400 by another Turkoman clan, known as the White Sheep (Aq-Qoyunlu).[159] At Laranda (the Karaman of today), there arose the dynasty of the Karaman emirs (likewise Turkoman), who for a time were to fight the Ottoman Turks of the Bithyno-Phrygian borders for the hegemony of Asia Minor and the Seljuk succession.[160]

Later Tamerlane was to irrupt into the midst of these bitter contests.

10

The Khanate of Kipchak

Jenghiz Khan had given his son Jöchi—who predeceased him by six months, in about February, 1227—the plains west of the Irtysh: that is to say, Semipalatinsk, Akmolinsk, Turgai, Uralsk, Adaj, and Khwarizm proper (Khiva). At his death, he left this domain to Jöchi's sons, more particularly to the second son Batu, who, after the successful campaigns of 1236–40, added to it the whole of the former Kipchak and Bulgar territories, besides the suzerainty of the Russian principalities.

The European part alone of Batu's khanate was a vast domain, consisting first of the longitudinal belt of steppes north of the Black Sea, namely, the Ural basin, the lower reaches of the Don, the Donets, the Dnieper, and the Bug, the mouth of the Dniester, and the lower Prut. It also comprised the steppes that continued north of the Caucasus across the basins of the Kuban, the Kuma, and the Terek. In short, it included the whole of ancient European Scythia. Beyond this, it stretched to the Bulgar country, or zone of forest and cultivation watered by the middle Volga and its tributary the Kama. Like the ancient Scythia described by Herodotus, the limitless steppes of this "Mongolia in Europe" were empty expanses. Rubruck's account gives some idea of this: "traveling ever eastward, we found nothing along our way but sky and earth, and sometimes to our hand the sea, and now and again the burial places or *kurgans* of the Cumans, which we could discern at a distance of two leagues." [1] Over these lonely ex-

392

panses roved Mongol hordes, or rather Turkic troops officered by Mongols, for, according to Rashid ad-Din, Jenghiz Khan's "will" allocated no more than four thousand genuine Mongols to Batu, all the rest of his armies consisting of Turks who had rallied to the Mongol cause—Kipchaks, Bulgars, Oghuz, and so on—which explains how the Jöchid khanate acquired a Turkic character so rapidly.[2]

Batu's nomadic sojourns took him along the Volga, upstream in spring to the old Bulgar country of the Kama and the trading town of Bolgar, where the Mongol coinage was minted. In August, he began the descent to the mouth of the river, where his encampment foreshadowed the founding of the later capital, the great Sarai.[3] It was on the lower Volga that Rubruck was admitted to his tent: "Batu was seated upon a high chair or throne the size of a bed, gilded all over and approached by three steps. Near him was one of his wives. The other men were seated to the right and left of this lady. At the entrance, there was a bench upon which stood some kumiss and several large cups of gold and silver enriched with precious stones. Batu looked at us intently. His face was somewhat ruddy." [4]

One of Batu's brothers, Orda, who although the eldest of the family played only a minor part in its affairs, had received an appanage in what is today Kazakhstan.[5] In the south, his lands comprised the right bank of the Syr Darya from approximately the town of Signakhi, near the Kara-Tau Mountains, to the delta of that river in the Aral Sea, including also, it seems, a strip of territory on the left bank of the same delta extending as far as the delta of the Amu Darya. He thus controlled almost the whole of the eastern shore of the lake. In the north, he held the basin of the Sary-Su and the Ulu-Tau massif which separates this basin from that of the Turgai. In 1376, Orda's last successor, Toqtamish, acquired the towns of Signakhi and Otrar, points of contact with the sedentary world.[6] Batu's khanate was to be known to history as the khanate of Kipchak and as the Golden Horde (Altan-ordo, Altun-ordu), and Orda's as the White Horde (Chaghan-ordo, Aq-ordu).

Shayban, another of Batu's brothers (heard of during the Hungarian campaign in 1241), had received as his share the territories to the north of Orda's, that is, the country east and southeast of the southern Ural, notably, in this latter quarter, a good part of the modern Russian regions of Aktyubinsk and Turgai. In summer, it appears that his *ordu* camped between the Ural Mountains, the River Ilek (tributary of the River Ural south of Orenburg, now Chkalov), and the River Irgiz; in winter, he must have moved south toward Orda's *ulus*. Later the Shaybanids no doubt would extend their dominion into western Siberia.[7]

BATU AND BERKE

To return to the principal horde, Batu, who reigned from 1227 to 1255, exerted considerable influence on Mongol policy in general as head (no doubt with Orda's approval) of the senior Jenghiz-Khanite branch.[8] Yet it is to be noted that he never laid any claim to the supreme khanate. In the beginning, he even respected the decisions of his grandfather, who had bequeathed the empire to the house of Ogödäi. This abstention may be explained by the doubt relating to Jöchi's birth. Jenghiz Khan's wife Börte, the mother of the four imperial princes, had been abducted by a Tatar chief about the time of Jöchi's conception. The question of his legitimacy seems to have been deliberately shelved. The lack of affection felt by Jenghiz Khan for his eldest son has been noted, as well as Jöchi's strange behavior after the siege of Urgench, when he spent the last five years of his life in his appanage of the Turgai, Emba, and Ural without taking part in Jenghiz Khan's campaigns. By the end, the disagreement between them was almost public knowledge. These circumstances at first condemned the house of Jöchi to a somewhat inconspicuous role.

In 1250–51, Batu took his revenge by bringing about the fall of Ogödäi's house and the accession of Tolui's. His decisive intervention at Alaqmaq in 1250 has been noted, and how in 1251 he sent his brother Berke to Mongolia to enthrone Mongka, Tolui's son, at the expense of the house of Ogödäi. Unquestionably Mongka owed him his throne, and he never forgot this obligation. He told Rubruck in 1254 that his power and Batu's extended over all the earth, like the rays of the sun, a remark that seems to imply a sort of condominium or joint empire. Rubruck observes that in Mongka's territories Batu's representatives were treated with far more deference than was shown in Batu's domains to Mongka's men.[9] On the whole, as Barthold points out, between 1251 and 1255 the Mongol world was virtually divided between the grand khan Mongka and the "doyen" Batu, their joint boundary running across the steppes between the Chu and the Talas.[10] Among the other members of the Jenghiz-Khanite family, Batu enjoyed the position of supreme arbiter and king-maker. The man himself has been very variously assessed. The Mongols called him *Sain-khan,* "the good prince," and praised his good nature and generosity. To Christendom, however, he appeared as the instigator of the nameless atrocities that character-ized the campaigns of 1237–41 in Russia, Poland, and Hungary. Piano Carpini summed up these contradictions by describing him as "mild, affable, and benign to his own people, but very cruel in warfare." [11]

This "European campaign" of 1237–41, through Slavic Russia, Poland, Silesia, and Moravia, and into Hungary and Rumania, in which representatives of all the Jenghiz-Khanite branches had taken part, had been organized mainly to Batu's advantage. He had been commander in chief, at least officially (the direction of strat-egy fell to Sübötäi, though in Batu's name), and he alone gained by it in the end. Not only had the last of the Kipchak Turks been crushed, but the Russian principalities of Ryazan, Suzdal, Tver, Kiev, and Galicia had been conquered, and were to remain vassals of the Golden Horde for more than two hundred years. And a strict vassalage it was, down to the end of the fifteenth century, for the khan appointed and deposed at his pleasure the Russian princes who were under obligation to come to "strike their foreheads" before him in his encampments on the lower Volga. This policy of humble dependence originated with the Grand Prince Yaroslav of Vladimir, who came first in 1243 to render homage to Batu and to be recognized by him as "dean of the Russian princes." [12] In 1250, Prince Daniel of Galicia (who in 1255 took the royal title) also came to confirm his submission and to request consecration. Grand Prince Alexander Nevsky (1252–63), Yaroslav's son and successor, made the best of the stern Mongol protectorate in order to be able at least to face Russia's enemies in the Baltic region. Acceptance of this servitude was the only means by which the country could come through those terrible times. Muscovy was to remain in bondage until its liberation by Ivan III at the end of the fifteenth century.

The history of the khanate of Kipchak is fundamentally different from that of the other Jenghiz-Khanite khanates. In the other lands which they conquered, the Mongols adapted themselves in some degree to their surroundings and learned lessons from the vanquished. In China, Kublai and his descendants became Chinese; while in Iran, the descendants of Hulägu, represented by Ghazan, Oljaitu, and Abu Sa'id, became sultans of Persia. Their cousins the khans of southern Russia, on the other hand, refused to be won over by the Slavo-Byzantine civilization and become Russians. They remained, as their geographic nomenclature implies, "khans of Kipchak," that is, heirs of the Turkic horde of that name. They were thus mere continuators of those "Cuman" Turks or Polovtsy, without a past or remembrance of things past, whose sojourn on the Russian steppe might, so far as history is concerned, never have occurred. The Islamization of the Kipchak khans—at once so superficial from a cultural point of view and, from a European point of view, so isolating—in no way altered the situation. On the contrary, their Islamization, without enabling them really to share in the ancient civilization of Iran and Egypt, severed them finally from the western world and made of them—as it later made of the Ottomans—foreigners encamped on European soil, never to be assimilated.[13] While the Golden Horde endured, Asia began at the southern outskirts of Kiev. Piano Carpini and Rubruck well convey the impression made on Westerners entering Batu's khanate: they felt they were entering another world.[14] There were certainly many more manifestations of "Westernism" among the Khazar Turks of the tenth century than among Jöchi's heirs.[15]

It must be recognized, however, that events might have taken another course. Whatever Rubruck may say—and he was too greatly shocked by the ignorance and drunkenness of the Nestorian clergy to be fully aware of the political importance of Nestorianism in the Mongol Empire—Christianity was rooted in Batu's own household.[16] Batu's son Sartaq was a Nestorian, despite the Franciscan's statements to the contrary.[17] Armenian (Kirakos), Syriac (Bar Hebraeus), and Muslim (Juzjani and Juvaini) sources all agree on this point.[18] Only certain unpredictable deaths prevented a Nestorian prince from succeeding his father. When Batu died in 1255 at the age of forty-eight at his camp on the lower Volga, Sartaq was in Mongolia, where he had gone to pay court to the grand khan Mongka, his father's friend. Mongka appointed him khan of Kipchak, but Sartaq died, either on his homeward journey or shortly after his arrival on the Volga. In his place, Mongka then nominated the young prince Ulaqchi, whom Juvaini identifies as a son and Rashid ad-Din as a brother of Sartaq. The regency was placed in the hands of Batu's widow Boraqchin. But Ulaqchi died, mostly probably in 1257, and Batu's brother Berke became khan of Kipchak.[19]

Berke's reign (approximately between 1257 and 1266) impressed upon the khanate a decisive reorientation.[20] If Sartaq had lived, it is reasonable to suppose—Rubruck notwithstanding—that Christianity would have benefited by royal protection. But Berke inclined rather toward Islam. Not that he would have departed from the religious tolerance that was characteristic—especially among Mongols—of the Jenghiz-Khanites. Nestorianism was one of the religions of his people, and he would certainly not have banned it. Nevertheless, in foreign affairs especially, his sympathies were chiefly with the Muslims. It is to this fact that, bearing in mind Barthold's exposition, the beginnings of a trend toward Islam in the khanate of Kipchak should be attributed.[21]

Berke, as we have seen, was involved in all the inter-Jenghiz-Khanite wars. We know that he sided with Ariq-bögä against Kublai, though without giving him any very effective help. He then fought, unsuccessfully, against Alghu, the Jagatai khan of Turkestan, who between 1262 and 1265 deprived him of Khwarizm. Regarded until then as a dependency of the Kipchak khanate, Khwarizm would thereafter form part of the khanate of Jagatai. Not long afterward (before 1266), Alghu captured, either from Berke or from Berke's brother Orda, the fort of Otrar (an important relay station for caravans on the north bank of the middle Syr Darya) and destroyed it. In this way, the western steppe of the Chu was added to the khanate of Jagatai at the expense of Jöchi's descendants. Berke, whose forces, as we shall see, were engaged in the Caucasus, could do nothing against this adversary.

Though Berke's Muslim sympathies may not have caused the breach between him and Hulägu the khan of Persia, as Arabo-Persian historians have declared, they did at least serve as a diplomatic pretext at that juncture. According to Persian writers, indeed, the khan of Kipchak rebuked Hulägu for having slaugh-

tered the population of Baghdad and tortured the caliph without
consulting the other Jenghiz-Khanite princes.[22] In fact, Jöchi's
house must have considered Hulägu's occupation of Azerbaijan
as a sort of usurpation and as an encroachment.[23] Berke thus did
not scruple to ally himself with the traditional enemies of the
Jenghiz-Khanites and protagonists of Muslim resistance, the
Mamelukes of Egypt, then governed by the sultan Baibars,
against his cousins the Mongols of Persia. From 1261, ambassadors were exchanged between the two courts, those from Baibars
landing at Sudak in the Crimea, and those of Berke at Alexandria.
In 1263, a specific alliance was concluded between the two sovereigns against the khanate of Persia.[24]

Baibars gained doubly by this arrangement. Thenceforth he
could recruit new Mamelukes for his armies from among the
Turks of Kipchak, subjects of the Golden Horde (he himself, it
will be remembered, was a Kipchak Turk). More important still,
by the most fortunate of diplomatic victories, he was helping the
Jenghiz-Khanites to neutralize one another. Thanks to the support of the house of Jöchi, and to the diversionary actions carried
out by Berke in the Caucasus, he succeeded in permanently block-
ing the advance of the house of Hulägu toward Syria. Threatened
at the Derbent pass, the khans of Persia could not take their
revenge at Aleppo for the disaster of 'Ain Jalud (see p. 364).
Hulägu, as mentioned earlier, bitterly resented the injury done
him by Berke. In November–December, 1262, he crossed the
Derbent pass, which served as the Caucasian frontier between
the two khanates, and advanced as far as the Terek. Soon afterward, he was surprised near this river and thrown back into
Azerbaijan by the enemy army commanded by Nogai (or
Noghai), Berke's great-nephew. Many horsemen of Hulägu's
army were drowned in attempting to recross the Terek over ice
that broke under the hoofs of their mounts. These inter-Jenghiz-
Khanite quarrels had deplorable consequences: Hulägu caused
all Kipchak merchants in Persia on whom he could lay hands to
be put to death, and Berke did the same with Persian merchants
trading in Kipchak.[25] In 1266, Nogai in turn crossed the Derbent
pass and then the River Kura, thus directly threatening Azerbaijan, the heart of the Persian khanate. But he was beaten on
the Aksu by Abaqa, Hulägu's successor, and wounded in the eye,
and his army retreated in disorder to Shirvan. Berke himself

made haste to bring reinforcements in person. But while moving up the north bank of the Kura in the same year 1266, in order to cross the river near Tiflis, he died.

In Christian Europe, the Russian prince Daniel of Galicia had rebelled against Mongol domination (1257). He even ventured an attack upon the frontiers of the khanate, but was brought back into subjection without Berke having to intervene in person. By the khan's order, he was forced to pull down most of the fortresses that he had built. Elsewhere, under the heading of the year 1259, the chronicle of Cromerus tells of another Mongol expedition to the West. After an incursion into Lithuania, where the invaders slaughtered all the inhabitants who had not had time to hide in the woods or swamps, the Mongols entered Poland with Russian auxiliaries whom they forced to accompany them. "After burning Sandomierz for a second time, they besieged the citadel in which the population had taken refuge. The commander, Peter of Crempa, refused to surrender. The Mongols then sent to him the brother and son of Daniel of Galicia, who persuaded him to yield on very favorable terms. But the Mongols broke their oath in their usual fashion and massacred all those unhappy people. From there they went on to Cracow, which they set on fire. King Boleslav the Chaste had fled to Hungary. The Mongols ravaged the country as far as Bytom, in the Oppeln district, and after three months returned to Kipchak laden with spoils."

During Berke's reign, the Kipchak Mongols were called in by Constantine Tych, czar of the Bulgars, to intervene in Balkan affairs against the Byzantine emperor Michael Palaeologus. The Mongol prince Nogai, Berke's great-nephew, crossed the Danube with 20,000 horsemen, and Michael Palaeologus came to meet them. But, Pachymeres acknowledges, on their arrival at the Bulgarian frontier the Greeks were seized with panic at the sight of the Mongols. They broke and fled, and almost all of them were cut down (spring of 1265). Michael Palaeologus returned to Constantinople in a Genoese vessel, while the Mongols ravaged Thrace.[26] In the course of this expedition (though other sources state that it was not until the winter of 1269–70), Nogai delivered the former Seljuk sultan Kai-Kawus II from his semi-captivity in Constantinople. Kai-Kawus followed the Mongols on their way home with their plunder and married a daughter of Khan

Berke, who, in the course of the years 1265–66, bestowed upon him as appanage the important Crimean trading center of Sudak (Soldaia).[27] Meanwhile, Michael Palaeologus had begun to appreciate the importance of the Mongol factor. To the powerful Nogai he gave his natural daughter Euphrosyne in marriage and sent him magnificent silken fabrics—upon receiving which, incidentally, the Jenghiz-Khanite observed that he preferred sheepskin.[28] But the alliance thenceforth subsisting between Michael Palaeologus and the khanate of Kipchak proved greatly to the advantage of the former, as will be seen. For a time, they and the Mameluke sultanate of Egypt constituted a real Triple Alliance, in opposition both to the Latins (Charles of Anjou and Venice) and to the khanate of Persia.[29]

Mameluke ambassadors have left a most vivid portrait of Berke. He was a true Mongol, with a yellow skin, sparse beard, and hair gathered into plaits behind his ears. He wore a tall cap and in one ear a gold ring set with a precious stone. He was girded with a belt of green Bulgarian leather, gilded and jeweled, and was shod with red leather boots.

The first Kipchak Mongols had had no other dwelling place than those huge camps of felt tents and wagons which, according to the season, changed their location along the banks of the Volga, giving Rubruck the impression of a town on the march. Berke ordered the building of a sedentary capital, Sarai, or he completed what may have been begun by Batu. This town, which must have sprung up round one of Batu's usual camps, was situated on the east bank of the lower Volga, near its mouth on the Caspian; unless, as Barthold says, Batu's Sarai corresponds to modern Selitrennoe and should be distinguished from the Sarai of Berke at the site of Tsarev, somewhat to the north.[30] However this may be, Berke's Sarai was the capital of the Kipchak khanate, from its foundation in approximately 1253 until 1395, the date of its destruction by Tamerlane. It acquired even more importance than the old Khazar capital situated in the same region as a starting point for caravans bound for Central Asia and the Far East via Otrar, Almalik, Beshbaligh, and Hami and the Tangut and Öngüt countries to Peking.[31] Berke and his successors, particularly the khans Özbeg and Janibeg, drew Muslim doctors, both Hanefites and Shafi'ites, to Sarai, and these gave fresh impetus to the Islamization of the country.[32]

Berke's successor was Mangu Timur (in Turkic) or Mongka Temür (in Mongolian), Batu's grandson by Tutuqan or Tuquqan.[33] In the inter-Jenghiz-Khanite civil wars of Central Asia, Mangu Timur, who reigned over Kipchak from 1266 to 1280, sided with Qaidu of Ogödäi against Baraq of Jagatai, the khan of Turkestan. In 1269, as noted, he sent 50,000 men into Central Asia under the command of Prince Berkejar to help Qaidu triumph over Baraq. In Qaidu's struggle to wrest the empire from the grand khan Kublai, Mangu Timur took Qaidu's part, at least in the realm of diplomacy. We have seen that it was to him that Prince Nomokhan, Kublai's son, was delivered after he had been made prisoner in Mongolia; Mangu Timur later restored him to his father. Owing to this conflict, the khanate of Kipchak was able to reaffirm its independence in relation to the grand khan. The coins of the Golden Horde, which were minted in Bolgar and which up to that time had borne the names of the grand khans, were thenceforth inscribed only with the name of Mangu Timur or of his successors.

In his relations with the Mameluke sultanate of Egypt, on the one hand, and the Byzantine Empire, on the other, Mangu Timur preserved the policy of friendship introduced by Berke. He issued an edict to safeguard the privileges of the priests of the Greek Orthodox Church, and on various occasions employed Theognostes the bishop of Sarai as ambassador to the court of Constantinople.[34]

NOGAI AND TOQTAI

According to Nowairi, Mangu Timur's brother and successor Tuda Mangu (1280–87) was a very devout Muslim, "observing strict fasts and always surrounded by sheikhs and fakirs," but he was an incapable ruler. He had to abdicate and was replaced on the throne by Tula-buqa (1287–90), nephew of the two preceding khans. The real master of the khanate was Nogai, that Jöchid of a junior branch who led armies on Berke's expeditions to Persia in 1262 and 1266, and against the Byzantine Empire in 1265.[35] The Franciscan Ladislas, leader of the mission of Gazaria (Crimea), in reporting to the general of his order, April 10, 1287, speaks of Nogai as of equal rank with Tula-buqa, and even as coemperor.[36] It appears that whereas Tuda Mangu's domain, and later Tula-buqa's, was in the Sarai area on the lower Volga, that of Nogai should be sought in the region of the Don and the Donets.[37] The correspondence between the Franciscans proves also that Nogai was not hostile to Christianity. One of his wives, for example, whom the Franciscans call Djaylak (that is, Jaylak) and Pachymeres identifies as Alaka, had come to be baptized by the Franciscans at Kirki or Chufut-Kale. Then, when Muslims had removed the bell from the Catholic chapel of Solhat or Solgat in the Crimea, a Mongol dignitary arrived to punish the culprits.

To the Byzantines, Nogai proved a dependable ally. In 1279, he helped them to overthrow Ivailo or Lakhanas, king of the Bulgars, who was succeeded after various vicissitudes by a boyar of "Cuman" origin, that is to say, a Kipchak Turk by the name of George Terter.[38] During Terter's reign (1280–92), as P. Nikov and G. Cahen have shown, Bulgaria was a true Mongol protectorate, bound by close personal relationships to Nogai himself. Terter's son Svetoslav came to live at Nogai's court as hostage, and his sister married Chaka or Jeku, a son of that redoubtable chief.[39]

At length Nogai's power disquieted the young khan Tula-buqa, who mustered his troops to remove him. But the old warrior succeeded in allaying his suspicions and invited him to a so-called friendly meeting, which was in fact a trap. In the course of their conversation, Tula-buqa found himself surrounded by Nogai's troops, who threw him off his horse and bound him. Nogai handed him over to a son of Mangu Timur named Toqtai, Toqta, or Toqtoa, who was a personal enemy of the unfortunate young man and put him to death. Nogai then placed this same Toqtai on the throne (1290), confident that the new khan, if anyone, would be an obedient tool in his hands. But Toqtai soon tired of being at the kingmaker's orders. He attacked Nogai and, at a first battle near the Don in 1297, was completely defeated. The aging Nogai made the mistake of not marching at once on Sarai, whither his adversary had withdrawn.[40] In 1299, in a second battle fought near the Dnieper, he was beaten by Toqtai and deserted by his own men. "His sons and his troops took flight at the end of the day. He was far advanced in age and his long eyebrows covered his eyes. He was accosted by a Russian soldier of Toqtai's army, who wanted to kill him. Nogai made himself known to the soldier and asked him to lead him to Toqtai, but the Russian cut off his head and carried it to the khan. Toqtai was grieved by the old man's death and had the murderer executed." [41]

Nogai's sons each tried to seize the inheritance, but their quarrels enabled Toqtai to defeat them. Nowairi relates that one of them, Chaka, pursued by Toqtai, took refuge first with the Bashkirs, then with the As or Alans, and lastly in Bulgaria, where his brother-in-law Svetoslav was ruler. But fearing reprisals from Khan Toqtai, Svetoslav killed Chaka at Tirnovo (1300).[42]

While these civil wars were disturbing the Golden Horde, says Rashid ad-Din, the White Horde of the steppes of Sary-Su and Turgai were struggling—under its Khan Nayan or, more appropriately, Bayan (1301–9), grandson of Orda the founder—to quell the revolt of Bayan's cousin and rival Kuilek or Kobluk, who was supported by Khan Qaidu of Ogödäi and Khan Duwa of Jagatai, the two lords of Turkestan. Bayan sought help from Temür, grand khan of China, but the distance was too great for him to obtain material aid. Nevertheless, he succeeded in remaining master of his native steppes.[43]

For the past fifty years, trading agencies had been established by the Genoese and Venetians in the Crimea, or Gazaria (Khazaria), so named after the Turkic people who had once lived there. Apparently, around 1266, the Mongol government ceded a piece of land to the Genoese of Caffa on which to build a consulate and some warehouses; this must have been the starting point of the great Genoese colony in the Crimea.[44] Italian merchants were active also in Sarai on the lower Volga, capital of the Kipchak khans and the great market for furs from the North. It is known that they also bought young Turkish slaves for resale as recruits to the Mamelukes of Egypt. Displeased by a traffic which deprived the steppe of its best soldiers, Khan Toqtai adopted a hostile attitude toward these Italian merchants. In 1307, he arrested the Genoese residents in Sarai and then sent an army to besiege the Genoese colony of Caffa. On May 20, 1308, the Genoese settlers set fire to their own city and escaped aboard their ships. The situation remained tense until Toqtai's death in August, 1312.[45]

ÖZBEG AND JANIBEG

Toqtai was succeeded by his nephew Özbeg (1312–40). The available information concerning Özbeg's religious outlook is somewhat contradictory. According to Rashid ad-Din, he had displeased the Mongol chiefs during Toqtai's reign by his ill-considered Muslim propaganda. "Be content with our obedience," was their reply. "How does our religion concern you? And why should we forsake Jenghiz Khan's *yasaq* for the Arab faith?" At Toqtai's death, therefore, before nominating his son as khan, the Mongol chiefs resolved to set aside Özbeg's candidature by enticing him to a feast and there assassinating him. But Özbeg, warned of this, had time to gallop off and return with troops. Surrounding the plotters, he massacred them, along with Toqtai's heir, and then ascended the throne himself. When the Mameluke sultan of Egypt an-Nasir asked Özbeg for a Jenghiz-Khanite princess in marriage, Özbeg gave his consent, though after much vacillation. It was an unprecedented favor in Mongol eyes, and it sealed the bond between the Kipchak khanate and the official defenders of Islam (1320).[46]

Yet generally speaking, Özbeg's Mohammedanism did not prevent him from treating Christians liberally.[47] A letter from Pope John XXII dated July 13, 1338, thanks the khan for his kindness to Catholic missions.[48] In 1339, Özbeg received the Franciscan Giovanni da Marignolli, who had been sent by Benedict XII and who made him a present of a magnificent charger before going on through Kipchak to Jagatai and Peking.[49] At that time, Özbeg also concluded a trade agreement with the Genoese and Venetians and granted the ambassadors from Genoa, Antonio Grillo and Nicolo di Pagana, authorization to rebuild the walls and warehouses of Caffa. By 1316, this colony was again in a flourishing state.[50] In 1332, Özbeg allowed the Venetians to found a colony at Tana, at the mouth of the Don.[51]

In Russia, however, on August 15, 1327, the people of Tver massacred the Mongol commissioners charged with the levying of tribute, and even killed a cousin of Özbeg's; Özbeg therefore sent 50,000 men to Prince Ivan of Moscow, commanding him to take repressive measures. It was as executors of the khan's wishes that the princes of Moscow took their first steps toward future greatness.

Khan Janibeg (1340–57), Özbeg's son and successor, at first confirmed the privileges of the Italian merchants (1342); but after a brawl at Tana in 1343 between Italians and Muslims, he drove the Venetians and Genoese from that town and twice laid seige to Caffa (1343, 1345).[52] The Genoese colony put up so stout a resistance that he was compelled to raise the siege.[53] Genoa and Venice then started to blockade the Mongol coasts of the Black Sea, east of Kerch. Finally, in 1347, Janibeg had to authorize the re-establishment of the Tana colony.[54] Hostility to Westerners went hand-in-hand with a fresh wave of Islamization. The advance of Islam, so noticeable under Özbeg, now bore fruit and the influence of Mameluke Egypt made itself felt in every sphere of political and social life. From the traditional religious tolerance of the Jenghiz-Khanites, the Golden Horde was swinging over to the "totalitarian" Muslim fanaticism of the Mamelukes.[55]

Janibeg took advantage of the anarchy that had prevailed in Persia since the fall of the Hulägu khanate to realize the old ambition of his family: the conquest of Azerbaijan. This he achieved in 1355, capturing also Tabriz, the former capital of the khans of Persia. He killed the local chief Ashraf the Chopanian and hung his head at the gate of the great mosque of Tabriz. But his son Berdibeg, whom he left as viceroy in Tabriz, was soon recalled to Kipchak by his father's illness, and in 1358 the Kipchak troops were driven from Azerbaijan by the Jelairs.[56]

MAMAI AND TOQTAMISH

Berdibeg's reign was short (1357–59). After him, Kipchak fell into a state of anarchy, while several Jöchids struggled for the throne. Power lay chiefly in the hands of a new kingmaker, the energetic Mamai or Mamaq, who from 1361 to 1380 was, as Nogai had once been, the true master of the Golden Horde.[57] However, the Mongols' prestige had not survived their civil wars, and from 1371 onward the Russian princes ceased to render homage at the court of Sarai, or even to pay tribute. Grand Duke Dimitrii Donskoi of Moscow repulsed a Mongol punitive invasion (1373) and in his turn opened retaliatory campaigns in the direction of Kazan (1376). On August 11, 1378, he defeated Mamai's armies for the first time on the Vozha. On September 8, 1380, he fought a second and more important battle on the field of Kulikovo, at the confluence of the Don and the Nepryadva. The fighting was fierce and the issue at first uncertain, but in the end, weakened by his losses, Mamai retreated. Despite his activity, he was no more fortunate against the Genoese colony of the Crimea, and after a fruitless assault the Mongols were compelled to recognize Genoese possession of the whole of "Gothia" between Sudak and Balaklava (1380).[58]

From that moment, it seemed as if the khanate of Kipchak was bound to collapse beneath the vengeance of the Christian powers, but it was unexpectedly stiffened and renewed by the appearance on the scene of a fresh actor from the East: Toqtamish, khan of the White Horde.

The Sary-Su steppes, from Ulu-Tau in the north and the lower Syr Darya in the south to Signakhi (near present-day Tyumen), as has been related, had been allocated at the division of the inheritance among Jöchi's sons to the White Horde, of which the first chief was Orda, elder brother of Batu and Berke. The sixth in succession from Orda, Khan Urus (ca. 1361–77), went to war with a kinsman named Toqtamish. Some sources state that this man was a nephew of Urus, but Abu'l Ghazi mentions him as a distant cousin, the descendant of Tuqa Timur, the brother of Orda, Batu, and Berke.[59] Toqtamish went to Samarkand to entreat the support of Tamerlane, king of Transoxiana. Tamerlane was pleased to receive the Jenghiz-Khanite pretender into his clientele and gave him the cities of Otrar, Sabran, and Signakhi on the north bank of the middle Syr Darya, at the frontier of Transoxiana and the White Horde territory.[60] Nevertheless, Toqtamish was not left in peaceful possession, and was driven out several times by Urus and Urus' three sons, Qutlugh-buqa,[61] Tokhta-qiya, and Timur-malik. Qutlugh-buqa beat him and put him to flight, but was killed at the moment of his victory. Toqtamish returned to Transoxiana to implore Tamerlane's help, and was enabled to enter Sabran once more, though for only a short time, for Tokhta-qiya again chased him out without difficulty. Tamerlane himself then came into the steppe and at the beginning of 1377 inflicted a severe defeat on the White Horde. Old Khan Urus died soon afterward and was succeeded by his two sons in turn: Tokhta-qiya first, then Timur-malik. No real decision had been reached. As soon as Tamerlane withdrew into Transoxiana, Timur-malik again beat Toqtamish in that same year 1377. Finally, during the winter of 1377–78, Toqtamish, still with Tamerlane's help, succeeded in triumphing over Timur-malik and making himself khan of the White Horde.

Toqtamish, who until then had been Tamerlane's somewhat feeble confederate, now became more ambitious. West of the Ural River, the Golden Horde—or khanate of Kipchak—was struggling to quell the revolt of its Russian vassals. Taking advantage of these troubles, and adding to them by his interference, Toqtamish proclaimed himself a candidate for the Kipchak throne. In the spring of 1378, according to Barthold's chronology, he left Signakhi with the intention of conquering Mongol Russia. This conflict, of which little is known, lasted several years. Mamai, leader of the Golden Horde, was attacked from the north by the Russian princes; on September 8, 1380, as noted, he was beaten at Kulikovo by Dimitrii Donskoi, grand duke of Russia. Shortly afterward, Toqtamish, attacking Mamai on the southern front, overwhelmed him in a battle fought near the Sea of Azov, in the Mariupol area by the River Kalka or Kalmius, where 158 years earlier Sübötäi had won his famous victory. Mamai fled to Caffa in the Crimea, where he was killed somewhat treacherously by the Genoese.

Toqtamish then ascended the throne of the Golden Horde. Being already leader of the White Horde, he thus reunited the possessions of his ancestor Jöchi. From his capital Sarai he would reign over all the steppes lying between the mouth of the Syr Darya and the mouth of the Dniester.

Toqtamish at once used his power to claim from the Russian princes the homage traditionally paid by them to the khans of Kipchak. Elated by their victory at Kulikovo, they refused (1381). Toqtamish then invaded the Russian principalities, put them to fire and the sword, and sacked the towns of Suzdal, Vladimir, Yuriel, Mozhaisk, and, in August of 1382, Moscow, which he razed to the ground. The Lithuanians, who had sought to intervene in Russian affairs, suffered in their turn a bloody defeat near Poltava. For another century Christian Russia was forced back under the Mongol yoke.

By an unexpected recovery, Toqtamish had completely restored the power of the khanate of Kipchak. The union of the Golden Horde with the White Horde and the annihilation of Muscovy made of him a new Batu, a new Berke. His recovery had the greater impact in that by now the Jenghiz-Khanites had been driven out of China, eliminated from Persia, and annihilated in Turkestan. Alone of that illustrious family, Toqtamish stood firm. As the restorer of Mongol greatness, he felt himself naturally enough called upon to follow in the footsteps of his ancestor Jenghiz Khan, and it was no doubt with this in mind that he set about the reconquest of Transoxiana and Persia. Twenty years earlier, amid the anarchy then prevailing in those two lands, he might well have succeeded. But for some years now Transoxiana and Persia had been the property of a leader of the first magnitude, the very man indeed who had helped Toqtamish to rise: Tamerlane. The war that broke out between them in 1387 and lasted until 1398 would show whether the empire of the steppes was to remain with the ancient Mongol dynasty or pass to the new Turkic conqueror.

11

Tamerlane

THE KINGDOM OF TRANSOXIANA DELIVERED FROM THE
MONGOLS BY TAMERLANE

Timur, known as Timur *lenk* (the Lame), whence our Tamerlane, was born on April 8, 1336, at Kesh, modern Shahr-i Sebz (the Green City), south of Samarkand. Timurid historians have attempted to trace his descent from a companion or even a kinsman of Jenghiz Khan. In fact, he was no Mongol but a Turk. He belonged to a noble Transoxianan family of the Barlas clan, with estates round Kesh, which it governed.

In connection with the khanate of Jagatai, we observed the conditions prevalent at this time in its dependency of Transoxiana (page 343). Spurred on by the energy of Qazghan, "mayor of the palace," this country, which in theory was a Mongol khanate and in reality a Turkic confederation, had begun once more to play some part in Central Asia. But the assassination of Emir Qazghan in 1357 brought back anarchy. His son, Mirza 'Abdallah, was driven out by Tamerlane's uncle Hajji Barlas, lord of Kesh, and by another local Turkic noble named Bayan Selduz (1358). Neither of these men had sufficient political skill to control the Turkic nobility of Transoxiana. Moreover, a grandson of Qazghan, Mir Husain, made himself master of an important principality in Afghanistan, including Kabul, Balkh, Kunduz, and Badakhshan. This was a feudal partition of the country. The Jagataite khan of the Ili, Tughlugh Timur, took advantage of this anarchy to invade Transoxiana, subjugate it, and thus reunite to his own advantage the former Jagatai *ulus*

409

(in March, 1360, according to the *Zafer-name*).[1] Hajji Barlas, Tamerlane's uncle, gave up the hopeless struggle and fled from Kesh to Khurasan.

Tamerlane was much cleverer. This young man of twenty-five saw that now was the moment to emerge from obscurity. Not that he played the role of the desperate champion of the Transoxianan Turks against the renewed offensive of the Ili Mongols. On the contrary, in the events then taking place, he saw a means of succeeding legally to his uncle Hajji Barlas as head of the Barlas clan and of the government of Kesh. With this object in view, he made a timely act of vassalage to Tughlugh Timur, the invading khan. The speech that Sharif ad-Din puts into his hero's mouth on this occasion is a little masterpiece of seemly hypocrisy: in submitting, at whatever personal cost, he was sacrificing himself to the public interest in place of his uncle, whose flight threatened the downfall of their house.[2] Tughlugh Timur, glad of so valuable a supporter, rewarded Tamerlane and confirmed him in the possession of Kesh. Meanwhile, Hajji Barlas profited by a temporary withdrawal of Jagataite troops to return to Kesh. The virtuous Tamerlane did not shrink from attacking him, but despite a first successful battle he was deserted by his troops and had no choice but to make *amende honorable* to Hajji Barlas, who pardoned him.[3] Tughlugh Timur's return from the Ili retrieved the situation for Tamerlane (1361).[4] On the khan's arrival, all the Transoxianan nobles—Mir Bayezid, the emir of Khodzhent, Bayan Selduz, Tamerlane, and Hajji Barlas himself this time—came to pay court to him. But the Mongol wanted to make an example, to impress these all too turbulent Turks, and, for no apparent reason, executed Mir Bayezid.[5] At this Hajji Barlas took fright and departed as a dissident. He suffered for his action; on arriving in Khurasan, he was assassinated near Sebzewar. Tamerlane at once set out to punish the murderers; but in fact, he was now conveniently rid of a rival and once more became permanent and sole lord of Kesh and head of the Barlas clan. Tughlugh Timur, pleased by the mature astuteness of the young man, appointed him adviser to his son Ilyas-khoja, whom, on his own return to the Ili, he made viceroy of Transoxiana.[6]

Up to this time, Tamerlane had played the card of loyalty

to the Jagataites, no doubt hoping to win for himself the leading post in the Jagataite administration. Instead, he was given second place when the khan appointed another emir, Begjik, to wield the supreme power at his son's side. Tamerlane thereupon broke with the khan's representatives and went to join his brother-in-law Mir Husain, king of Balkh, Kunduz, and Kabul, whom he had once helped in the subjugation of Badakhshan. Both then went to Persia, where they led the life of adventurers and placed their swords at the service of a prince of Seistan. After this experience, they returned to re-form their forces in Afghanistan, near Kunduz, within Mir Husain's possessions, and then re-entered Transoxiana.[7] A Jagataite army attempted to stop them at the Stone Bridge (Pul-i Sengi) over the Vakhsh.[8] By a ruse Tamerlane crossed the river, beat the enemy, and went on by way of the Iron Gates to liberate his city of Kesh. The Jagataite prince Ilyas-khoja made one more effort, but he was defeated in a great battle which the *Zafer-name* places between Tash Arighi and Kaba-matan, or Mitan, near Kesh and Samarkand. Narrowly escaping capture, he fled with all speed to the Ili.[9] Tamerlane and Mir Husain pursued him beyond Khodzhent and did not stop until they reached Tashkent. Transoxiana was thus delivered from the Mongols (1363). Between the battle of the Stone Bridge and that of Kaba-matan, Ilyas-khoja learned that his father Tughlugh Timur had died on the Ili.

Transoxiana was delivered from the Mongols and freed from Jagataite authority, but neither Tamerlane nor Mir Husain nor any other leaders of the local Turkic nobility felt able to do without a Jagataite sovereign. So unquestioned did Jenghiz-Khanite legitimacy remain, at least formally, that the conquerors deemed it necessary to sanction their victory by a Jagataite figurehead, under whose cover, of course, they themselves would rule. They found a great-grandson of Duwa named Kabil-shah or Kabul-shah, who was hiding in the disguise of a dervish. This was the man they needed. "They set him on the throne, they presented him with the royal goblet, and all the lords together made the nine ritual genuflections before him," after which they paid him no further attention. But his presence at the head of the kingdom of Transoxiana sufficed to legitimize and consecrate that kingdom by Jenghiz-Khanite law.[10] Ilyas-khoja, the Jagataite of the Ili, had no further reason to meddle in Transoxianan affairs, since at Bukhara and Samarkand there was another authentic Jagataite, another khan by divine right, in whose name Tamerlane and Mir Husain could act with a clear conscience and satisfy all their legalistic scruples.

After gathering the reins of succession into his hands following his return to the Ili, Ilyas-khoja made one last attempt. In 1364 he returned with a new army and at first defeated Tamerlane and Mir Husain on the north bank of the Syr Darya, between Tashkent and Chinaz, in what is known as the Battle of the Marshes (1365). Mir Husain and Tamerlane retreated as far as the Amu Darya, the former toward Sali-Sarai (north of Kunduz), the latter to Balkh, leaving Transoxiana open to invasion by Ilyas-khoja, who laid siege to Samarkand.[11] Then the tide turned. The population of Samarkand, stimulated by its Muslim "clergy," put up a spirited defense, while the ranks of the besiegers were thinned by an epidemic. At last, in 1365, Ilyas-khoja evacuated Transoxiana and returned to the Ili. As will be seen, he barely survived his defeat, for soon afterward he fell a victim to the rebellion of a Dughlat emir.

DUEL OF TAMERLANE AND MIR HUSAIN

Tamerlane and Mir Husain had effectively liberated Transoxiana. This duumvirate, which was further united by Tamerlane's marriage to Husain's sister, showed signs of strain from the beginning. Husain appeared the more powerful; in addition to Transoxiana, he had his own Afghan kingdom with its cities of Balkh, Kunduz, Khulm, and Kabul.[12] But Tamerlane, firmly in control in his domain of Kesh and Karshi, at the very gates of Samarkand, had the more forceful personality. After Ilyas-khoja's flight, both men went to Samarkand to reorganize their state. Husain played the overlord, levying taxes on even the most exalted nobles. Tamerlane, to win them to his cause, was prompt in supplying them with the necessary sums from his own coffers. He went further and, with a feigned submission as insulting as any accusation, returned to Husain the jewels belonging to his wife, Husain's sister.[13] The princess's death completed the rift between the two rivals. At first, Husain had the upper hand and drove Tamerlane from Karshi. Tamerlane then recaptured the city by escalade and through this same action became master of Bukhara. Husain retaliated by setting forth from his residence at Sali-Sarai, north of Kunduz, to reconquer Transoxiana with a larger army. From the Timurids he took Bukhara and Samarkand, while Tamerlane, believing his forces too greatly outnumbered, fled shamelessly to Khurasan.[14]

This flight, following upon the earlier withdrawals or retreats from Tughlugh Timur and Ilyas-khoja, puts the finishing touch to our impression of Tamerlane's character. Not that he can be accused of cowardice. His military valor is beyond question. Yet notwithstanding the dash and daring that impelled him to the assault like one of his own soldiers when the need arose, Tamerlane was politically shrewd and knew when to break off and bide his time. Meanwhile, he again led the life of a knight-errant, galloping from adventure to adventure, from Khurasan to the Tashkent region, where, incidentally, he did not shrink from making a second pact with the Mongols of the Ili, his people's hereditary foes. Worse still, he strove to provoke an invasion by them, to occur the following spring.[15] Thus, having swept Transoxiana clear of the Jagataite Mongols of the Ili, he made ready to recapture the country from Husain at the head of their army. The *Zafer-name* becomes quite breathless in its efforts to find excuses for this period of the great adventurer's life. We should add that Tamerlane was never called upon to implement this meditated treachery; for when threatened by another Mongol invasion, led this time by his rival, Mir Husain took fright. He offered peace to Tamerlane, appealing of course to the Muslim faith that bound them both and to the need to unite and to prevent the half-"pagan" Mongols of the Ili and the Yulduz from coming to plunder the sacred soil of Transoxiana.[16]

This was what Tamerlane had been waiting for. He professed himself to be moved by these pious considerations and claimed even to have had a dream to act accordingly. Peace was made; the *status quo*—that somewhat ill-defined condominium between him and Husain—was re-established. He thus also recovered his domain of Kesh.

The sequel presents a rare comedy of Oriental hypocrisy, complete with protestations of friendship, conciliatory embraces, and pious maxims from the Koran ejaculated at every turn,

followed by betrayals, surprise attacks, and summary executions
à la turque.

Tamerlane appeared to be playing his part loyally as Husain's
ally; he helped him to subdue the citadel of Kabul when it
revolted and then the equally rebellious hillmen of Badakhshan.
But this help now assumed the aspect of supervision, coercion,
even menace. Husain, conscious that Transoxiana would remain
in his rival's hands, confined himself more and more to Afghanistan and hurriedly rebuilt the citadel of Balkh, an act, we are
told, that was "displeasing to Tamerlane." [17]

"When God wills something," the *Zafer-name* announces
piously, "He furnishes the causes by which it may be brought
about according to His providence. To Tamerlane and his
posterity, He had destined the empire of Asia, foreseeing the
mildness of his rule, which would bring happiness to his subjects." [18] This godly tone, which may seem somewhat paradoxical,
is in fact most appropriate. Sharif ad-Din goes on to moralize
upon Mir Husain's greed, upon the inflexibility that alienated
him from the other feudal lords, and upon his impolitic behavior. There follows a tangle of intrigue in which of course
Husain is consistently in the wrong and is accused of planning
a trap for Tamerlane. Nevertheless, it was Tamerlane who,
without declaring war, launched a sudden attack upon Husain.
On leaving Kesh, he crossed the Amu Darya at Termez and
invaded Bactria, his adversary's fief. Husain's garrison at Kunduz,
taken unawares, surrendered, as did the lord of Badakhshan,
and Tamerlane appeared unexpectedly before Balkh, where
Husain, all unprepared, found himself besieged. Thus trapped,
without hope of relief, this unfortunate man was forced to
capitulate, relinquish power, and set forth on pilgrimage to
Mecca. Tamerlane generously pardoned him and indeed shed
tears of emotion on seeing him again; but, "unknown to him,"
declares the *Zafer-name,* the conqueror's entourage put the
fugitive to death. The inhabitants of Balkh, guilty of fidelity to
Husain, for the most part suffered the same fate.[19]

RULER OF TRANSOXIANA AND THE TIMURID EMPIRE

This classic tragedy was an expression of Tamerlane's very self.[20]
Its dominating feature was a farsighted Machiavellianism, a

consistent hypocrisy based on and identified with reasons of state. He is a Napoleon with the soul of a Fouché, a Philip II descended from Attila. "Grave and somber, a foe to mirth," like the man in the Escorial; as devout as he, yet a dashing soldier and an experienced and prudent leader; the friend of artists and men of letters, savoring Persian poetry like a Shirazi —such was the man who by the capture of Balkh became supreme lord of Central Asia. The deliberateness of his rise to power, with the cold calculation that enabled him to yield when necessary and go into exile when the game required it, is reminiscent of Jenghiz Khan. Like the Mongol conqueror, the leader of Transoxiana had obscure beginnings and submitted to working as a subordinate under a feudal lord lacking in boldness and firmness like Husain, just as Jenghiz Khan had served under the inept *Wang-khan*. Tamerlane's flight to Khurasan and his adventurous life from Seistan to Tashkent are reminiscent of Jenghiz Khan's days of misfortune on the Baljuna. He was as legalistically scrupulous—ostensibly, at any rate—in his breach with Husain as Jenghiz Khan had been in breaking with the Kerayit king: the Livy-like discourse of the *Zafer-name*, plus the pietistic Muslim tone and minus the rough simplicity of the Mongol herdsman, recalls the famous poetic complaint of the *Secret History*. But as soon as he had law on his side, backed up with invocations from the Koran, Tamerlane defended himself against the betrayals, real or supposed, of his old ally by resorting in his turn to treachery; he surprised and brought him as low as Jenghiz Khan had brought down Togrul.

Jenghiz Khan, however, had completed his work. He had proclaimed himself *qan*, sole and supreme emperor. It did not occur to him to maintain above him some figurehead, some direct descendant of the ancient Mongol kings, of a more solidly established legitimacy than his own; even less did he think of conquering the Far East under the aegis of a younger brother of the Kerayit king or of the Kin emperor. Tamerlane did indeed proclaim himself king in conquered Balkh. On April 10, 1370 (he was then thirty-four), "he ascended the throne, placed the crown of gold upon his head, and girded himself with the imperial belt in the presence of the princes and emirs, who fell upon their knees." The *Zafer-name* assures us that he declared himself as the heir and continuator of Jenghiz Khan and Jagatai.

But his title remained indeterminate, and it was not until 1388 that he clearly adopted that of sultan. Above all, he dared not abolish the puppet emperors of Jenghiz Khan's house, although Khan Kabul-shah, whom he and Husain had placed on the throne, had sided openly with Husain against him. In reality, as the *Ta'rikh-i Rashidi* confides, he did think of ridding himself of the burden of a khan, but he soon reflected that in order to exact obedience from the Transoxianan nobility he must exert his authority from behind the screen of an undisputed legal principle.[21] He therefore confined himself to bringing about the death of Kabul-shah and replacing him by another Jenghiz-Khanite, Soyurghatmish, who was faithful to him and reigned as khan of Timurid Transoxiana from 1370 to 1388.[22] After his death, Tamerlane named as successor this prince's son, Mahmud khan (1388–1402).[23] With all due respect and according to protocol, the firmans issued by the Timurid government bore the names of these descendants of the illustrious family.[24] No doubt they were mere shadow kings, entirely subservient to Tamerlane and appointed at his pleasure, poor, obscure men of straw whom no one ever thought or cared about. "In my day," Muhammad Haidar II Dughlat was to write, "khans are treated in Samarkand like political prisoners."

It is nevertheless true that Tamerlane approached the question of political sovereignty obliquely and casuistically. He dared not create an entirely new law; instead, he was content to produce a new situation, substituting in fact Turkic rule for Mongol, a Timurid empire for a Jenghiz-Khanite. In law he claimed to have changed virtually nothing. Thus he never said that he would abolish the Jenghiz-Khanite *yasaq* in favor of the *shari'a*, or Muslim law. Indeed, strange though it may seem, Ibn 'Arabshah calls him a bad Muslim for having "preferred Jenghiz Khan's law to the law of Islam."[25] This of course may be a purely formal accusation, since in the eyes of the Central Asian populations Tamerlane had sought to figure as Jenghiz Khan's successor, even as a new Jenghiz Khan. In practice the reverse was true. It is the Koran to which he continually appeals, the imams and dervishes who prophesy his success. His wars were to influence the character of the jihad, the Holy War, even when—as was almost always the case—he was fighting Muslims. He had only to accuse these Muslims of lukewarmness, whether the Jagataites of the Ili and Uiguria, whose conversion was so recent, or the sultans of Delhi, who tolerated—and refrained from massacring—their millions of Hindu subjects.

From the beginning, Tamerlane's empire was out of balance and lacked the solidity, soundness, and stability of Jenghiz Khan's. Its culture was Turko-Persian, its legal system Turko-Jenghiz-Khanite, and its politico-religious discipline Mongolo-Arab. In this respect, Tamerlane comprised as many characters as the European emperor Charles V. But in him these contradictions were not apparent; or rather their shifting lights heightened his personality, one quite without parallel, that of a superman peregrinating through several civilizations at the confines of two great periods. Tall, with a large head and a deep reddish complexion, this lame man ever coursing about the world—this cripple with his hand ever clasped about his sword, this bowman whose marksmanship, as he "drew the bowstring to his ear," was as infallible as Jenghiz Khan's—dominated his age like Jenghiz Khan before him. But, though Jenghiz Khan vanished, his empire—even under mediocre rulers—survived. Tamerlane's empire, to which men of talent and even genius succeeded, such as Shah Rukh, Olugh-beg, Husain-i Baiqara, and Baber, was to disappear immediately, to dwindle to the little native land of Transoxiana and annex of Khurasan.

The Jenghiz-Khanite survival may be accounted for by the foundations upon which the empire had been built. Jenghiz Khan had raised up the ancient empire of Mongolia, that eternal empire of the steppes which, centered upon the Orkhon, had endured from the time of the old Hsiung-nu; the empire that the Huns had handed on to the Juan-juan and the Ephthalites, the Juan-juan to the T'u-chüeh, the T'u-chüeh to the Uigur, and which at the time of Jenghiz Khan's birth was passing into the hands of the Kerayit. Here was a physical framework, that of the steppe; an ethnic and social framework, that of Turko-Mongol nomadism, the firmer for being simple, and for being based solely on the law of nature which impels the nomad herdsman to seek plunder and, if possible, to subject sedentary farmers to his control. The foundation and periodical resurrection of the empire of the steppes was in this respect a law of human geography. Until the still distant day when the sedentary peoples upon its borders would acquire an artificial superiority by means of scientific weapons, they would be dominated by the nomad, whose empire was regenerated at shorter or longer intervals, like the flooding of a river.

There was nothing like this about the empire that Tamerlane was to found. His Transoxiana was a geographical center in appearance only, which means that it was not in itself a source of dynamism. Circumstances which at the end of the fourteenth century made it a storm center were purely accidental. In the course of Asia's history there have been two kinds of domination. One was that of the ancient sedentary civilizations on the periphery—China, India, Iran—which, little by little and in spite of everything, overcame one "Barbary" or zone of barbarism after another by assimilation, a more powerful process in the long run than force of arms. The second, surging from the heart of the continent, was the rude strength of the nomads, exerted because they were hungry and because the ravening wolf will always, by some means and at some time, get the better of domesticated animals. But the Transoxianan empire of Tamerlane fell into neither category. If for some years he was able to disrupt the Old World, it was above all by virtue of his exceptional personality, so well expressed by the Turkic meaning of his name: Timur, the man of iron.

There is also the fact that the crossing of this iron, Turkic race of the Old World with the Mongol race, or at least its training under Jenghiz-Khanite discipline, produced by the end of the fourteenth century a formidable military power between Tashkent and the Amu Darya. It must be stressed again that it was a transient phenomenon. Who were more undisciplined, for all their bravery, than the Transoxianan Turks before Jenghiz Khan? The fact is illustrated vividly enough by those lamentable knights-errant of the thirteenth century: Muhammad of Khwarizm and Jalal ad-Din, for example, to say nothing of Sanjar before them. Nor need the anarchy of the Turkmens and Kirghiz of more modern days be emphasized. In contrast to this, according to the comment in the *Zafer-name,* the Transoxianan Turks of the Timurid period had military discipline in their blood; ranks formed without word of command, orders were anticipated before drum or trumpet sounded, and the young men were broken to the profession of arms by two centuries of *yasaq,* rigorously applied. Tamerlane's marches through Siberian winters or the heats of India give striking evidence of this. These forces, born of Jenghiz-Khanite discipline imposed upon Turkish valor, endured for two hundred years without ever having an opportunity to give free rein to their warlike temperament. Men of the Orkhon under Kublai had the whole of the Far East as their theater of conquest; those of the Golden Horde galloped to the gates of Vienna; those of Hulägu strove to reach the waters of the river of Egypt. Only the Turko-Mongols of this "middle kingdom" of Turkestan in Jagatai, encircled by the other three Jenghiz-Khanite *ulus*, were forced to mark time. But now suddenly the barriers about them were down. Westward, no khanate of Persia hemmed the Transoxianans in; the northwest was held by a Golden Horde in decline, incapable now of barring the way; in the direction of the Gobi the way was open, for "Mogholistan" lay in ruins; the sultanate of Delhi was in momentary collapse and in no state to guard the Indus as in the days of the first Jagataites. Tamerlane's Transoxianans sped forth in all directions. They had a long period of enforced idleness to make up for, during which conquest had been enjoyed by the outer Turko-Mongol *ulus* alone, while the men of Transoxiana had been cut off from the glories and rewards of Mongol warfare. Now at last their hour had come.

The Timurid epic—if one may so describe that series of betrayals and massacres—while ethnically Turkic, was still part of the Mongol epic, though a belated part.

CONQUEST OF KHWARIZM

Tamerlane's conquering activities were carried on from the Volga to Damascus, from Smyrna to the Ganges and the Yulduz, and his expeditions into these various regions followed no geographical order. He sped from Tashkent to Shiraz, from Tabriz to Khodzhent, as enemy aggression dictated; a campaign in Russia occurred between two in Persia, an expedition into Central Asia between two raids into the Caucasus. There is nothing here of Jenghiz Khan's straightforward planning: campaigns in Mongolia, campaigns in the Far East, campaigns in Turkestan and Afghanistan, and a return to the Far East. Tamerlane's expeditions followed upon one another higgledy-piggledy because, unlike Jenghiz Khan, who made a clean

sweep wherever he went, Tamerlane at the end of every successful campaign left the country without making any disposi-
tions for its control except in Khwarizm and Persia, and even
there not until the very end. It is true that he slaughtered all
his enemies as thoroughly and conscientiously as the great
Mongol, and the pyramids of human heads left behind him
as a warning example tell their own tale. Yet the survivors
forgot the lesson given them and soon resumed secret or overt
attempts at rebellion, so that it was all to do again. It appears,
too, that these bloodsoaked pyramids diverted Tamerlane from
the essential objective. Baghdad, Brussa (Bursa), Sarai, Kara
Shahr, and Delhi were all sacked by him, but he did not overcome the Ottoman Empire, the Golden Horde, the khanate of
Mogholistan, or the Indian sultanate; and even the Jelairs of
Iraq 'Arabi rose up again as soon as he had passed. Thus he
had to conquer Khwarizm three times, the Ili six or seven times
(without ever managing to hold it for longer than the duration
of the campaign), eastern Persia twice, western Persia at least
three times, in addition to waging two campaigns in Russia
and other expeditions.

Tamerlane's campaigns "always had to be fought again,"
and fight them again he did. Despite their meticulous strategy
and impeccable tactics, they seem from the viewpoint of political
history to be lacking in all cohesion. Chronological study de-
prives them of interest, beyond the purely personal interest
one may feel in the character of the hero. Historical clarity is
best achieved by grouping them according to the great regions
of conquest, starting from Transoxiana and working outward.
Thus we shall study Tamerlane's activity in Khwarizm, eastern
Turkestan, Persia, Russia, Turkey, and India.

Comprising the lower course of the Amu Darya and its delta
on the Aral Sea, Khwarizm or the present land of Khiva had
played a considerable if ephemeral part in the history of the
Orient at the end of the twelfth century and for the first eighteen
years of the thirteenth under the great Khwarizmian dynasty
of Turkic stock which Jenghiz Khan expelled in 1220. It had
afterward been attached in principle to the Kipchak khanate
until captured from Khan Berke of Kipchak by Alghu the khan
of Jagatai (between 1260 and 1264). Khwarizm then became
an integral part of the khanate of Jagatai, as was geographically

appropriate. But this conquest was apparently of short duration. Shortly afterward, according to Barthold, Khwarizm was divided between Kipchak and Jagatai, with the Kipchak khanate in control of the Syr Darya delta and Urgench and the khanate of Jagatai ruling the southern region, including Kath (Shah Abbaswali) and Khiva.[26] Soon after 1360, a Turkic chief of the Qungrad tribe named Husain Sufi took advantage of the anarchy prevailing in Kipchak to found an independent kingdom of Khwarizm. He next profited by the wars in Transoxiana to take Kath and Khiva from the Transoxianans. But as soon as Tamerlane became ruler of Transoxiana, he reclaimed the territory of these two cities (1371).[27] Defied by Husain Sufi, he took Kath and laid siege to his enemy in Urgench.[28] Husain Sufi died during the siege, and his brother Yusuf Sufi, who succeeded him, sued for and was granted peace in return for restoring to Tamerlane the land of Kath (Khiva region).[29] Yusuf Sufi soon regretted this cession and devastated the country of Kath.[30] Tamerlane again opened hostilities in 1373,[31] but relented on obtaining Yusuf's daughter, the beautiful Khanzade, for his son Jahangir. War broke out again in 1375,[32] but Tamerlane was recalled to Samarkand by the revolt of two of his lieutenants.

The peace that followed was brief. While Tamerlane was fighting the White Horde north of the lower Syr Darya, Yusuf Sufi seized the occasion to devastate the country about Samarkand deep in Transoxiana. This dangerous neighbor, who threatened the capital as soon as the Timurid army was engaged elsewhere, had to be removed. In 1379,[33] provoked by Yusuf, Tamerlane arrived at the gates of Urgench to meet his adversary in single combat. "He donned his light cuirass, girded his sword about him, slung his shield upon his shoulder, and, wearing the royal helmet, he mounted his horse and advanced toward the city. Placing his trust in God, he went forward alone to the edge of the ditch and summoned Yusuf to match his strength with him. But Yusuf, preferring life to honor, returned no answer."[34] The siege of Urgench lasted three months. Yusuf, increasingly hard-pressed, died of despair. The city was finally taken by assault, followed by the usual massacre (1379).[35]

The annexation of Khwarizm completed the formation of the Transoxianan realm.

Scarcely had Tamerlane assured himself of the throne of Transoxiana when he was called forth again to wage war in the old khanate of eastern Jagatai (the Ili and Yulduz regions).

Revolution had recently broken out in that country. We have seen the dominant position acquired there by the Mongol Dughlat family, which was almost entirely in control of Kashgaria, with Aksu as its center, and which possessed in addition large estates in the specifically Jagataite zone of the Ili, where the khans had their headquarters.[36] Also, the Dughlat emir Puladshi or Bulaji in 1347 took the initiative—after several years of anarchy—in replacing on the Ili throne the Jagataite Khan Tughlugh Timur.[37] After Bulaji's death, which occurred during the reign of Tughlugh Timur (1347–63), the post of *ulus-begi* (approximating to that of mayor of the palace) was given to his young son Khudaidad. Bulaji's brother, Emir Qamar ad-Din, who coveted the appointment, protested in vain to Khan Tughlugh Timur and at the latter's death took his revenge by killing the deceased khan's son Ilyas-khoja, who had just returned from Transoxiana, driven thence by the victorious Tamerlane (ca. 1365–66). Qamar ad-Din, overthrowing the Jagataite dynasty, usurped the title of khan and ruled over Mogholistan (that is, over the region of the Talas, Issyk Kul, Ili, Yulduz, and Manas, and most likely also over the greater part of the Alti-shahr or Kashgaria) from about 1366 to 1392.[38] A younger brother of Ilyas-khoja named Khizr-khoja escaped the fury of Qamar ad-Din, thanks to Khudaidad, who helped him to flee from Kashgar into the Pamirs, where the young man went into hiding until the dawn of better days.[39]

It was against Qamar ad-Din that Tamerlane launched a series of expeditions, far less celebrated than those of Persia, Delhi, or Ankara, yet perhaps more remarkable; for they were conducted in more difficult country against an elusive enemy. These were preventive expeditions, designed to protect Transoxiana from periodical nomad invasions. Tamerlane's officers made a reconnaissance in the direction of Alma-Ata, later also known as Verny, north of the Issyk Kul, and returned after having made a peace or truce with the enemy, which Tamerlane repudiated. Leaving Tashkent, Tamerlane marched from Sairam (north of that city) to a place referred to in the *Ta'rikh-i Rashidi* as Tanki and believed by Elias and Denison Ross to be Yangi, that is, Talas, also known as Aulie-Ata. Here he put the nomads to flight and captured much plunder.[40]

In 1375, Tamerlane fought his third campaign.[41] He left Sairam and crossed the Talas and Tokmak regions by the headwaters of the Chu. Qamar ad-Din, adopting the usual nomad tactics, retreated before him to a place called Birkeh-i Gurian or Arshal Atar according to the *Zafer-name,* believed by Elias and Denison Ross to represent Otar, near the upper basin of the Ili, by one of the northern spurs of the Ala-Tau.[42] It seems at any rate that the site should be looked for in the mountains northwest of the Issyk Kul. Jahangir, Tamerlane's eldest son, took the enemy by surprise here and they scattered toward the Ili. Tamerlane devastated that part of the Ili region (Ap-ili) which constituted the heart of old eastern Jagatai and then, it seems, went on into the valley of the upper Naryn, where the *Zafer-name* shows him operating by the rivers Arpa and Yazi, northwest of Kashgar.[43] He had captured Princess Dilshad Agha, Qamar ad-Din's daughter, and added her to his harem. He returned to Samarkand by way of Uzgen and Khodzhent in Fergana.

But Qamar ad-Din was not beaten. When the Timurid army had gone back to Transoxiana, he attacked Fergana, a province belonging to Tamerlane, and sacked the city of Andizhan. Enraged Tamerlane hastened to Fergana and chased him beyond Uzgen and the Yassy Mountains as far as the valley of the At-Bashi, a southern tributary of the upper Naryn.

In entering this area of the T'ien Shan, Tamerlane fell into an ambush where Qamar ad-Din was awaiting him. He escaped, thanks solely to his personal courage, "with his lance, his war club, his sword, and his lasso," and returned to put his enemy to flight once again. He then regained Samarkand, where his son Jahangir had just died (1375 or 1376).[44]

During the years that followed (1376–77), Tamerlane led a fifth expedition against Qamar ad-Din. He fought him in the gorges west of the Issyk Kul and pursued him to Kochkar, at the western point of the lake.[45] The *Zafer-name* mentions even a sixth expedition sent by Tamerlane to the Issyk Kul against

Qamar ad-Din around 1383, but again the khan was not to be caught.[46]

In 1389–90, Tamerlane made a decisive effort to rid himself of the nomads of Mogholistan.[47] In 1389, he crisscrossed the Ili and Imil regions in all directions, south and east of Lake Balkhash (the Atrek-Kul of the *Zafer-name*) and round the Ala-Kul, territories which have since become the Russian province of Semirechye and the Chinese protectorate of Tarbagatai, and which were then the heart of Mogholistan. Playing the role of lord and conqueror, he sent his mobile squadrons speeding across the historic steppes where the khans of Jagatai and Ogödäi had once held their nomadic court, in the region of modern Kuldja and Chuguchak, while his vanguard galloped in pursuit of Mongols as far as the Black Irtysh, south of the Altai.[48] Then his army, moving in separate columns across the T'ien Shan massif, passed from the Balkhash basin to that of the Bagrach Kol. The general rendezvous was the valley of the Yulduz, which Tamerlane reached by way of the Kunges valley.[49] On the evidence of the *Zafer-name*, the Timurid advance troops pushed farther eastward to Kara-khoja, or almost to Turfan.[50]

Among the Mongol chiefs whom Tamerlane fought in that region, the *Zafer-name* mentions Khizr-khoja, heir to the house of Jagatai, who had been temporarily driven from his throne by the usurping Qamar ad-Din. We know from the *Ta'rikh-i Rashidi* that Khizr-khoja had fled to the most easterly part of eastern Turkestan (first to the Khotan, then the Lob Nor area), where he strove to found a new realm, meanwhile forcibly converting the last Uigur of Turfan to Islam.[51] Although Tamerlane's chief enemy, Qamar ad-Din, was also the enemy of Khizr-khoja, Tamerlane did not hesitate to attack the latter, evidently fearing lest the house of Jagatai might recruit new strength in Uiguristan. Khizr-khoja was beaten and fled into the Gobi.[52] The victorious Tamerlane held a military assembly at Chalish or Jalish, modern Kara Shahr, and shared out among his men the booty taken from the nomads.[53] The *Zafer-name* creates the impression that, having thus established himself in the heart of Central Asia, he assumed the pose of successor to Jenghiz Khan. Yet in fact, he destroyed Mongol domination in eastern Turkestan at the very moment when the accession of the Ming had overthrown it in China.

Before returning to Samarkand, Tamerlane sent his son 'Umar-shaikh on ahead from the Yulduz by the Uch Ferman (Uch Turfan) and Kashgar route.[54] We do not know whether he himself with the main body of the army chose this way, or whether he came back from the Yulduz via the Ili, the Chu, and the Talas.

Yet this time too, although Tamerlane had carried devastation to the heart of the Gobi, his great foe Khan Qamar ad-Din remained undefeated. Scarcely had the Timurid army re-entered Transoxiana when Qamar ad-Din built up his power again in the Ili valley. In 1390, therefore, Tamerlane again sent an army against him. From Tashkent these forces marched by the Issyk Kul, crossed the Ili at Almalik, advanced beyond the Kara-Tal, and trailed Qamar ad-Din to the Black Irtysh, where they lost him. Qamar ad-Din vanished into the Altai, "into the country of martens and sables," and was heard of no more. Tamerlane's men amused themselves by burning their leader's name with red-hot irons into the pine trunks of the Altai; then, skirting the banks of the Atrek-Kul—i.e., Lake Balkhash—they returned to Transoxiana.[55]

The disappearance of the usurper Qamar ad-Din enabled Khizr-khoja of Jagatai to recover the throne of Mogholistan. The new chief of Dughlat's house, Emir Khudaidad, Qamar ad-Din's nephew, who had always been a "legitimist," was the first to summon Khizr-khoja and to support and ensure his restoration.[56] The new khan was a wholehearted Muslim. We have seen that, having subjugated Turfan, he forcibly converted the last of the Uigur elements there.[57] This outlook drew him nearer to Tamerlane, and peace was ultimately concluded between the two princes. Around 1397, as a result, Khizr-khoja gave his daughter in marriage to Tamerlane, who greatly valued the alliance since it brought him into the great Jenghiz-Khanite family.[58]

Khizr-khoja died in 1399. The *Ta'rikh-i Rashidi* reports that he was succeeded on the Ili throne by his three sons, Shama-i Jahan or Sham-i Jahan (ca. 1399–1408), Naksh-i Jahan, and Muhammad-khan (d. ca. 1428), the latter being praised in this same text for his Muslim piety.[59] All three lived under the surveillance and protection of the Dughlat emir Khudaidad. Tamerlane could not refrain from taking the opportunity offered by his father-in-law's death to send a fresh expedition, if not to the Ili itself, at least into Kashgaria (1399–1400). This army, led by the conqueror's grandson Mirza Iskander, entered Kashgar, plundered Yarkand, seized the fortified city of Aksu—whose inhabitants ransomed themselves by handing over the rich Chinese merchants dwelling among them—and then sent a detachment to the northwest to pillage Bai and Kucha. Mirza Iskander then proceeded to Khotan, where the inhabitants welcomed him with presents and declared themselves Tamerlane's subjects. He finally returned to Samarkand by the Andizhan route through Fergana.[60]

CONQUEST OF EASTERN IRAN

When Tamerlane had established his kingdom of Transoxiana—an essentially Turkic kingdom, though under the fiction of being a Jenghiz-Khanite khanate—he resumed in Iran the struggle of the Turko-Mongol against the Tadzhik.

The general splitting up of the country meant that the Iranian people were at the mercy of the first resolute invader. Jenghiz Khan in his day had at least been faced with a united power, the Khwarizmian Empire, which extended from Kabul to Hamadan. Facing Tamerlane, on the contrary, were four or five rival powers, among which the former Hulägid empire had been parceled out at random; these states were very deeply divided and their rulers never even thought of uniting against the Turk. The Kert were Afghan by race and Sunnite by religion, and lived in Herat. They were the sworn enemies of the Sarbedarians of Sebzewar, who were Shi'ite Persians. The Arabo-Persian Muzaffarids of Fars were rivals of the Jelairids, the Mongol masters of Tabriz and Baghdad. Moreover, in that Muzaffarid family, where sons thought nothing of putting out their fathers' eyes, all the princes detested and betrayed one another, and fought among themselves for a mere village. Tamerlane, who had had to make such strenuous efforts in his battles with the nomads of Mogholistan and Kipchak, here found his opponents delivered into his hands. The Persia of 1380 invited conquest.

Indeed, after the fall of the Hulägid khanate, eastern Iran soon felt the weight of the Transoxianan Turkic threat. In 1351, as has been noted, the famous emir Qazghan, chief of the Transoxianans, had come to lay siege to Herat and had reduced the reigning Kert to a state of vassalage. This act was now repeated by Tamerlane.

In 1380, he summoned the *malik* or king of Herat, Ghiyath ad-Din II Pir 'Ali, to appear as a vassal at his *quriltai*. Ghiyath ad-Din II (1370–81), son and successor to Mu'izz ad-Din Husain and seventh prince of the Kert dynasty, no doubt lacked the political adaptability which had enabled his father and earlier forebears to tack about amid the Hulägid wars and then to be accepted by Qazghan. While declaring his submission, he yet delayed. In the spring of 1381, Tamerlane marched on Herat. Ghiyath ad-Din had just captured Nishapur from the other eastern Iranian dynasty, the Sarbedarians, and this war, which set the Kert and the Sarbedarians at each other's throats, added to the confusion and tumult in Khurasan.[61] Moreover Ghiyath ad-Din's brother, who commanded the fortress of Sarakhs south of Herat, made submission to Tamerlane of his own accord "and was admitted to the honor of kissing the imperial carpet." Bushang fortress, northeast of Herat, was taken by assault. In Herat itself, where Ghiyath ad-Din had shut himself up, the garrison, composed of rough Afghans from Ghor, was all for resisting, and even made a sortie. But the townsfolk "preferred peace for their homes, which were adorned with beautiful pottery from Kashan," and refused to fight. Ghiyath ad-Din had to capitulate.[62] Tamerlane received him well and "admitted him to the honor of kissing the carpet of his throne," but caused all the riches of the city to be handed over to himself. One of the *malik's* sons, who held the impregnable fort of Amankoh or Ishkalcha, was persuaded by his father to surrender.

Tamerlane left Ghiyath ad-Din as titular ruler of Herat, but the city, its walls demolished, was now no more than a dependency of the Timurid Empire. Ghiyath ad-Din himself, reduced to the role of a humble vassal, was sent into compulsory residence at Samarkand. This situation might have been prolonged indefinitely but for bands of Afghans from Ghor who, at the end of 1382, helped by the people of Herat, made a surprise assault on the city and took possession of it.[63] Prince Miranshah, Tamerlane's third son, sternly repressed this revolt, and towers were built of human heads. The *Zafer-name* relates laconically that after these events Ghiyath ad-Din and his family, no doubt suspected of complicity, received the order to die.[64] Thus ended the Afghan dynasty of the Kert, who by their adroitness had managed to survive amid all invasions for nearly a hundred and thirty years in this fortress of Herat, exposed though it was to the rapacity of all conquerors.

Having subdued the Kert realm of Herat, Tamerlane marched on eastern Khurasan in 1381. Two states were then quarreling over possession of this country: the Sarbedarian principality headed by 'Ali Mu'ayyad (1364–81), with Sebzewar as its capital,[65] and Mazanderan. Mazanderan, including the territories of Astera-bad, Bistam, Damghan, and Samnan,[66] was then under the control of the adventurer Emir Wali, who after Tugha Timur's death had made himself king (1360–84). There was also a third lord, 'Ali beg, ruler of Kelat and Tus. At Tamerlane's approach, 'Ali beg submitted of his own accord.[67] 'Ali Mu'ayyad, threatened by Emir Wali, had appealed to Tamerlane. He thus welcomed the conqueror, did him homage in Sebzewar, and declared himself his subject (1381).[68] Thenceforth he attached himself to Tamerlane and in 1386 died fighting in his service. After a brief siege, Tamerlane captured Isfarain from Emir Wali and destroyed it.[69]

Tamerlane then returned to Samarkand for a short time before continuing operations in Iran. During the winter of 1381–82, he besieged 'Ali beg in the eyrie of Kelat and again forced him to submit.[70] Not long afterward, 'Ali beg was sent to Transoxiana and executed (1382). Tamerlane continued the campaign against Emir Wali, prince of Jurjan and Mazanderan, who ended by sending him tribute.[71]

In 1383, Tamerlane returned from Samarkand to Persia and inflicted an appalling punishment on rebellious Sebzewar. "Nearly two thousand prisoners were piled alive, one on top of the other, with mud and brick, to form towers," [72] Rebellious Seistan suffered the same fate. "Our soldiers made a mountain of dead bodies, and built towers with the heads." At Zaranj, capital of Seistan, Tamerlane "put the inhabitants to death, men and women, young and old, from centenarians to infants in the cradle." [73] Above all, Tamerlane destroyed the irrigation system of the Seistan country-side, which reverted to desert. "And when they had come to the banks of the River Helmand, they destroyed the dam called the Dam of Rustam, and no vestige of this ancient work was left." [74] The desolation that strikes the traveler in this region even today is the result of these acts of destruction and massacre.[75] The Timurid chiefs were finishing what the Jenghiz-Khanite Mongols had begun. Both, through their ancestral nomadism and their system of methodical devastation, made themselves the active agents of this "Saharifying" process, to which the center of Asia, by its geographic evolution, is already too prone. By destroying cultivation over a vast area and turning the land into steppe, they were unconscious collaborators in the death of the soil. Especially on the high plateau of Iran, where water and trees are rarities, where diligent cultivation preserves one by means of the other, and where conservation of arable land is a constant battle, the nomad killed the trees, dried out the gardens, and reduced the meager trickle of water to bog and the plowed field to desert.

From Seistan, Tamerlane went into Afghanistan to possess himself of Kandahar (1383). After a three months' rest in his beloved Samarkand, he returned to Persia to deal finally with Emir Wali, prince of Mazanderan. This man bravely defended every step of his ground, from the Atrek River to the heart of the forest; indeed, he nearly succeeded in a surprise attack by night on the Timurid camp,[76] but Tamerlane in the end got the upper hand and in 1384 seized Asterabad, the enemy capital, where everyone was slaughtered, "even infants at the breast." [77] Wali fled to Azerbaijan. Tamerlane then entered Iraq 'Ajami.

CONQUEST OF WESTERN IRAN

Iraq 'Ajami, Azerbaijan, and Baghdad belonged (p. 389) to the Mongol dynasty of the Jelairs, represented as of 1382 by Sultan Ahmed Jelair ibn-Uweis. Ahmed was a typical example of a Mongol noble modified by his surroundings and transformed into an Arabo-Persian sultan, like the Seljuks and Khwarizm-shahs of the twelfth century: "a cruel and faithless despot, yet at the same time a brave warrior and the protector of scholars and poets." [78] He had achieved power by executing his elder brother Husain in 1382 and then, in 1383 and 1384, overcoming his other brothers. He was in Sultaniyeh, the principal city of Iraq 'Ajami at that time, when Tamerlane advanced upon it. He left in all haste and Tamerlane set up his court there.[79] Ahmed Jelair had fled to Tabriz, but Tamerlane did not pursue him, returning instead by the Amul and Sari route to Samarkand, where he was in the habit of resting after each campaign (1385).

It was not until 1386 that Tamerlane embarked upon the conquest of western Persia, which required a campaign of two years. One pretext for the expedition was his sudden pious impulse to chastise the mountaineers of Luristan, who had plundered the caravan to Mecca. And he did indeed carry through this police action with success—"the greater number of these robbers having been captured, he caused them to be hurled from the mountaintops." [80] Tamerlane then marched into Azerbaijan and entered Tabriz; at his approach, Ahmed Jelair fled to Baghdad.[81] Tamerlane then held court at Tabriz, where he spent the summer of 1386, before going on by way of Nakhichevan to invade Georgia.

As the Georgians were Christians, Tamerlane was able to give his campaign the color of a Holy War. Leaving Kars, which he had just destroyed, in the winter of 1386 he took Tiflis by assault and there made prisoner the king of Georgia, Bagrat V, who shortly afterward obtained his release by a pretended conversion to Islam.[82]

Tamerlane then returned to winter quarters at Karabakh, in the steppes of the lower Kura. Here he had the surprise of being attacked by his protégé Toqtamish, khan of Kipchak, who at the beginning of 1387 crossed the Derbent pass with a strong army to dispute possession of Azerbaijan. A great battle was fought north of the Kura. The army corps sent by Tamerlane was at first beaten, but his son prince Miranshah arrived with reinforcements, overcame the enemy, and drove him back north of Derbent. Merciless in the castigation of Afghans and Persians, Tamerlane here showed unwonted clemency, and sent all the prisoners back to the khan of Kipchak, to whom he addressed no more than a fatherly rebuke. The upstart Turk still stood in awe of the legitimate Jenghiz-Khanite line, represented by Toqtamish.[83]

After holding court on the shores of Lake Gokcha, Tamerlane undertook the conquest of the western areas of Great Armenia. This country was then divided among a number of Turkoman emirs, all good Muslims, but against whom, comments the *Zafername,* Tamerlane proposed to conduct a Holy War, giving as his excuse that these Turkomans had attacked the Mecca caravan.[84] He captured Erzerum in one day. The Turkoman emir Taherten, lord of Erzincan, acknowledged himself tributary and Tamerlane confirmed him in his lordship. Next Tamerlane sent his son Miranshah to Mus and Kurdistan to fight the Turkoman horde named the Black Sheep or Qara-Qoyunlu, then commanded by

Qara-Muhammad Turmush. Tamerlane himself sacked the Mus district, but the Turkomans escaped among inaccessible gorges.

After completing the conquest of Armenia by taking Van and hurling its inhabitants from the crags, Tamerlane headed for the Muzaffarid states of Fars (Shiraz), Ispahan, and Kerman. The Muzaffarid prince Shah Shuja, whom Ibn 'Arabshah depicts as a model of all the virtues (except in so far as he had caused his old father to be blinded and to perish in prison), had shortly before been summoned to make submission to Tamerlane.[85] He at once recognized the latter's suzerainty and so preserved his domains from the threat of invasion. When he died in his capital of Shiraz, he left it and Fars to his son Zain al-'Abidin and Kerman to his brother Ahmed, while Ispahan and Yezd were quarreled over by his nephews Shah Yahya and Shah Mansur. (In the end, the former was able to keep Yezd and the latter ultimately seized Ispahan.)[86] Before he died, Shah Shuja had placed all his family under Tamerlane's protection. Despite the confident tone of this letter (of which the *Zafer-name* claims to reproduce the text), it is evident that the writer was anything but reassured.[87]

Indeed, Tamerlane at once took advantage of his vassal's death to invade the Muzaffarid territory (October–November, 1387), marching directly upon Ispahan by way of Hamadan. The Muzaffarid governor of Ispahan, Muzaffar-i Kashi, hastened to bring him the keys of the city; Tamerlane made a triumphal entry and then camped outside. Everything seemed peaceful until during the night the inhabitants rose up and slaughtered the Timurid officers appointed to collect taxes, as well as any Transoxianan soldiers whom they could seize. Tamerlane in fury ordered a wholesale massacre. Each army unit had to contribute a fixed number of heads to the general "pool." The *Zafer-name,* Tamerlane's official apologia, speaks of 70,000 heads, "which were piled in heaps outside the walls of Ispahan and of which towers were then built in various parts of the town." The scenes of horror described by Ibn 'Arabshah are worse than those reported by Jenghiz Khan's historians in connection with the massacres of Balkh, Herat, and Ghazni in 1221; for the early Mongols were simple savages, whereas Tamerlane was a cultured Turk and a great lover of Persian poetry who yet destroyed the flower of Iranian civilization, a devout Muslim who sacked all the capitals of the Muslim world.[88]

From Ispahan, now reduced to a charnel house, Tamerlane marched on Shiraz, whence the Muzaffarid Prince Zain al-'Abidin had just fled. The terrified city strove to placate him, and Tamerlane held court there. The Muzaffarids of Kerman and Yezd, Shah Ahmed and Shah Yahya, came trembling to "kiss the royal carpet"; in return, Shah Ahmed was left in possession of Kerman, and Shah Yahya of Fars. The most highly skilled of Shirazi artisans were deported to Samarkand to contribute to the embellishment of the Timurid capital.[89]

Tamerlane himself was compelled at this moment to return to Samarkand because of the khan of Kipchak's invasion of Transoxiana at the end of 1387. He did not revisit Persia until 1392 for the so-called Five-Years' War of 1392–1396. His first campaign opened in Mazanderan. He captured Amul, Sari, and Meshed-i-Sar (Babulsar) from a local branch of Sayyids, blazed trails through the virgin forests that cover this strange country, and tried to convert the Shi'ite inhabitants—whose faith was still corrupted by Isma'ili survivals—to the orthodox Sunnite doctrine.[90] After wintering in Mazanderan, he took the Nehavend road to Luristan, where he punished the Lur for their inveterate banditry. Then, traveling by way of Dizful and Shushtar, he went on to subjugate the rebel Muzaffarids.

After Tamerlane's departure, one of the Muzaffarid princes, Shah Mansur, more energetic than the rest, had removed his fellow princes and reintegrated the ancestral domain in opposition to Tamerlane. He had blinded his cousin Zain al-'Abidin, forced his brother Yahya to withdraw from Shiraz to Yezd, and then seized Shiraz, which he made his capital, along with Ispahan. Treacherous like all his kin but active and energetic and of extraordinary courage, he defied even Tamerlane. In April, 1393, after mustering his army at Shushtar, Tamerlane marched on Shiraz. On his way, at the beginning of May, he took the fortress of Qal'a-i-Sefid, until then considered impregnable. Mansur came out to meet him and fought a savage battle with him on the outskirts of Shiraz. By sheer bravery, the Muzzaffarid succeeded in breaking through the ranks of the Transoxianan guard. He then went up to Tamerlane and struck him two blows with his sword, but the blows were deadened by Tamerlane's massive helmet. At last, Mansur was killed. Tamerlane's seventeen-year-old son

Shah Rukh is said to have cut off his head and thrown it at the victor's feet (May, 1393).[91]

Tamerlane made a triumphal entry into Shiraz. He commanded all the treasures of the ancient city to be handed over to him, as well as a huge war contribution. "He spent there a month of feasting and rejoicing," exults the *Zafer-name*. "There was playing of organs and harps, and the good red Shiraz wine was presented in golden cups by the prettiest girls of the city." The surviving Muzaffarids—Shah Ahmed, prince of Kerman, and Shah Yahya, prince of Yezd—came humbly to pay their court, but soon afterwards Tamerlane had almost all the members of that family put to death and gave their fiefs to his captains.[92] Artists and men of letters from Fars were deported to Samarkand, which Tamerlane intended to make the capital of Asia.

In June, 1393, Tamerlane left Shiraz for Ispahan and Hamadan, where he held court, and then opened his campaign to seize Baghdad and Iraq 'Arabi from Sultan Ahmed Jelair, last representative of the Mongol dynasty of that name. At the beginning of October, he appeared before Baghdad, and at his approach Ahmed Jelair fled westward. He was nearly caught near Karbala by Miranshah, who had been sent in pursuit, but he contrived to escape and to flee to Egypt, where he was received by the Mameluke sultan Barquq. Tamerlane entered Baghdad without a fight. "The Tatar troops," sings the *Zafer-name*, "hurled themselves upon Iraq like armies of ants and grasshoppers; they overran the countryside and sped in all directions, plundering and ravaging." Tamerlane spent three months in relaxation at Baghdad, "delighting in the houses of pleasure situated on the banks of the Tigris."[93]

After this, Tamerlane returned north. In passing, he reduced the stronghold of Tikrit (Tekrit) and went on to subjugate the fortresses of the provinces of Kurdistan and Diyarbakir. In this campaign he lost his second son 'Umar-shaikh, who was killed by an arrow before a Kurdish fort (February, 1394).[94] After a hard siege, he took Mardin (March, 1394) [95] and Amid (Diyarbakir), and then, moving upward again into Great Armenia, he drove out from the Mus region the Turkoman Qara-Yusuf, chief of the Black Sheep (Qara-Qoyunlu) horde. Next he advanced along the Van route to fight in Georgia (end of 1394).

In 1395, while Tamerlane marched via the Caucasus to wage

war upon the khan of Kipchak in southern Russia, the Georgians defeated his third son Miranshah, who had laid siege to Alinjaq near Nakhichevan.[96] When Tamerlane returned to the Caucasus in 1399, he avenged Miranshah by devastating the region of Kakheth (eastern Georgia). Even sterner was his vengeance in the spring of 1400, when he marched on Tiflis, installed a garrison there, and completely devastated the country, while the king, Giorgi VI, fled into the mountains. In 1401, Tamerlane granted him the *aman* (clemency) in return for tribute. Nevertheless, in 1403, he returned to ravage the country again, destroying some seven hundred great villages and minor towns, massacring the inhabitants, and demolishing all the Christian churches of Tiflis.[97] It has been noted that the Jenghiz-Khanite Mongol invasion of the thirteenth century was less cruel, for the Mongols were mere barbarians who killed simply because for centuries this had been the instinctive behavior of nomad herdsmen toward sedentary farmers. To this ferocity Tamerlane added a taste for religious murder. He killed from piety. He represents a synthesis, probably unprecedented in history, of Mongol barbarity and Muslim fanaticism, and symbolizes that advanced form of primitive slaughter which is murder committed for the sake of an abstract ideology, as a duty and a sacred mission.

The last attempts at resistance to Timurid domination in Iran were made by the former sultan Ahmed Jelair and by the Turkoman chief Qara-Yusuf, emir of the Black Sheep. In December, 1393, and January, 1394, upon being driven from Baghdad by Tamerlane, Ahmed Jelair had, as noted, taken refuge in Egypt with the Mameluke sultan Barquq. With the latter's aid, after the withdrawal of the Timurid army, he succeeded in reinstating himself at Baghdad in the same year 1394. Since Tamerlane was engaged elsewhere, he was able to remain there, partly owing to the support of the emir of the Black Sheep Qara-Yusuf, until the summer of 1401. When Tamerlane returned to Iraq 'Arabi at that time, Ahmed Jelair again fled to the Mamelukes, but his officers stayed on by their own wish to defend the city. Baghdad was taken by Tamerlane on July 10, 1401. The defenders had fought with the energy of despair, and Tamerlane's vengeance was merciless. Whereas seven years before he had treated Baghdad with some moderation, he now ordered a general massacre. Each soldier had to bring the head of an inhabitant, says Sharif ad-Din;

two heads, says Ibn 'Arabshah.[98] Amid all the carnage, the literary-minded Tamerlane spared certain men of letters and even offered them coats of honor. Apart from these men, the entire population was slaughtered, and all buildings except mosques demolished. Ibn 'Arabshah estimates the number of victims at 90,000. July heat under the sky of Iraq soon bred epidemics from the heaped corpses and forced the victor to withdraw.

In the course of the war between Tamerlane and the Ottoman sultan Bajazet, discussed below, the stubborn Ahmed Jelair took the opportunity to return yet again to Baghdad, but was soon defeated and driven out by his former ally Qara-Yusuf, chief of the Black Sheep horde. Qara-Yusuf himself was then expelled by a renewed attack from the Timurid army under the command of Abu Bakr, Tamerlane's grandson (1403). Qara-Yusuf and Ahmed Jelair both fled to Egypt, not to return until after Tamerlane's death.[99]

TAMERLANE AND KIPCHAK

In 1376, Tamerlane had received a visit in Samarkand from Toqtamish, a Jenghiz-Khanite of the Jöchi branch. Toqtamish came to ask for support against his suzerain Urus, khan of the White Horde, which held sway north of the lower Syr Darya, in the Sary-Su steppe, and around the Ulu-Tau Mountains.[100] It is uncertain whether Toqtamish was a nephew or a more distant kinsman of Urus khan.[101] Glad to include among his clientele this Jenghiz-Khanite pretender, who might prove useful to him, Tamerlane gave him the cities of Otrar, Sabran, and Signakhi on the north bank of the middle Syr Darya, opposite the steppes of the White Horde, Toqtamish was twice driven from this little domain by Urus khan, and on each occasion was succored by Tamerlane at Samarkand. According to the *Zafer-name*, Urus demanded his extradition. Far from acceding to this demand, Tamerlane advanced to defend the Syr Darya line. He beat Urus between Signakhi and Otrar and thrust him back into the steppe (beginning of 1377).[102]

Urus died the same year and was succeeded in turn by his two sons, Tokhta-qiya first, then Timur-malik. No sooner had Tamerlane returned to Transoxiana than Toqtamish was again defeated by Timur-malik. Once more Tamerlane restored him to Signakhi

and lent him reinforcements with which Toqtamish at last took
the enemy by surprise in their winter quarters, a region named
Kara-Tal in the *Zafer-name*.[103] This victory was decisive and enabled Toqtamish to ascend the throne of the White Horde (winter
1377–78).[104]

Up to that time, Toqtamish seems not to have displayed any
great personal qualities, in any case, according to the *Zafer-name,*
which holds that he owed his elevation solely to Tamerlane's support. Yet once he became khan of the White Horde he seems of a
sudden to have become remarkably active. Almost at once he
sought to subjugate the Golden Horde or khanate of Kipchak,
that is, the Mongol empire of southern Russia. In 1380, he vanquished Mamai, leader of the Golden Horde, in a decisive battle
near the Kalka or Kalmius, in the Mariupol district not far from
the coasts of the Sea of Azov. He was then acknowledged as khan
by the Golden Horde, and thus reunited Golden and White
Hordes, which together constituted almost the whole of the former
Jöchi domain. Thenceforth he reigned from the lower Syr Darya
to the Dniester, from Signakhi and Otrar to the gates of Kiev.
From Sarai, his capital on the lower Volga, he now stood forth
as one of the greatest potentates of his century. Reviving the
tradition of his Jenghiz-Khanite ancestors, he launched great
mounted expeditions; invaded Christian Russia; burned Moscow
in August of 1382; sacked Vladimir, Yuriel, Mozhaisk, and other
Russian towns, even defeating near Poltava the Lithuanians, who
had attempted to intervene; and forced Muscovy back under the
Mongol yoke for another hundred years.

These triumphs turned his head. What was Tamerlane, this upstart Turk without a past, without any well-defined lawful title,
compared to himself, the true scion of the Jenghiz-Khanite line?
Moreover, his indisputable rights now had the backing of all the
hordes of the northwest, an immense reserve of steppe fighters.
To him, the commander of the northern nomads, Tamerlane, king
of Transoxiana and Iran, must have appeared a mere Tadzhik. As
a Mongol, Toqtamish must have felt for this three-quarters sedentary, this builder of a Turk, something of Tamerlane's secret con-
tempt for the people of Ispahan and Shiraz. Energetic, active,
and of good stature, and famed among the Mongols for his justice,
he wearied of behaving as the client of an upstart Turk who called
him his son. He was wrong to forget that he owed his rise to that

same Turk, and doubly wrong in failing to assess the formidable force that he represented.

Like his predecessors the Kipchak khans since the time of Berke, Toqtamish laid claim to Azerbaijan. It will be remembered that never, from 1260 to 1330, had the lords of Sarai been entirely reconciled to the fact that neither Transcaucasia nor north-western Persia was a dependency of their *ulus*. In 1385, there-fore, while it still belonged to Sultan Ahmed Jelair and before Tamerlane had intervened there, Toqtamish invaded Azerbaijan by the Shirvan route and captured and plundered Tabriz (winter of 1385–86).[105] He then retired with his booty in the Mongol fashion, while Ahmed Jelair repossessed himself of the province. It was at this juncture that Tamerlane, who had just subjugated Persia, annexed Azerbaijan to his empire (1386). This annexation caused a breach between the two former allies, or, rather, it led Toqtamish to launch a sudden attack upon his benefactor without any declaration of war, and to come near to catching him un-awares.

Tamerlane had spent the winter of 1386–87 north of Azerbaijan in the province of Karabakh, and he was still there when in the spring of 1387 Toqtamish unexpectedly crossed the Derbent pass and marched straight upon him in Karabakh. Tamerlane, en-camped at Bardhaa, south of the Kura, had no time to do more than send a strong advance guard north of the river. This little army engaged Toqtamish's forces and had just been defeated when Prince Miranshah, Tamerlane's third son, arrived with re-inforcements, retrieved the situation, and put Toqtamish to flight. Tamerlane's behavior on this occasion is significant. Many prison-ers were brought to him from the vanquished army, and his grim way with such people is known; yet this time he not only spared them but sent them back to Toqtamish, having supplied them with food and necessary equipment. Meanwhile, attests the *Zafer-name*, he reproached Toqtamish—whom he persisted "in regarding as his son"—in a tone of affectionate grief rather than anger.[106] Comparing this attitude to the cold and haughty con-tempt and the implacable vindictiveness with which he treated his Turkic or Iranian adversaries gives a measure of the prestige which for him the legitimate Jenghiz-Khanite line still retained. It is true that in reality Tamerlane had overthrown the achieve-ments of Jenghiz Khan, or at least substituted his own; yet in theory, he dared not admit this openly, or even perhaps to himself. He resorted to subterfuge, gave his Turkic empire a Mongol front, and showed to Jenghiz Khan's descendants—whenever they gave any sign of energy—a surprising and perhaps involuntary respect. He must also have felt the Transoxianan's unconscious but fundamental dread of the northern hordes.

Not only did Toqtamish remain deaf to these appeals, but as Tamerlane lingered in Persia, he took advantage of his absence to attack him at the heart of his empire: in Transoxiana itself. Toward the end of this same year, 1387, he assailed the Syr Darya line near Signakhi and threatened Sabran; then, being ill-equipped for a siege, began to ravage the countryside. 'Umarshaikh, Tamerlane's second son, tried to halt the invaders, but was beaten near Otrar and nearly taken prisoner.[107] The attack was all the more serious in that Transoxiana, stripped of troops, had been taken in the rear by a foray of nomads from Mogholistan into Fergana. Toqtamish's troops spread through Transoxiana, plundered all open towns, and even ventured to blockade Bukhara. Their devastations extended as far as the outskirts of Karshi and even to the banks of the Amu Darya.[108]

Tamerlane had to return with all speed from Persia (beginning of February, 1388). Toqtamish did not wait for him but regained the steppes of the White Horde. At the end of 1388, having levied a powerful army in Kipchak—an army which the *Zafer-name* declares to have included contingents from Muscovy—Toqtamish renewed his attack on Transoxiana, this time by a detour to the east, near Khodzhent in Fergana. Tamerlane advanced to meet him with what few troops he could muster and, amid snow and bitter cold, drove him back north of the Syr Darya (about January, 1389).[109] Toqtamish still continued to prowl north of the middle Syr Darya, however, besieging Sabran and looting Yasy (the modern town of Turkestan). But when Tamerlane crossed the Syr Darya, the enemy army scattered over the steppe.[110]

This experience convinced Tamerlane that he could not pursue his conquests in Western Asia, leaving Transoxiana to be invaded by Toqtamish. He resolved to carry the war into the enemy's camp, into the steppes of the White Horde. Leaving Tashkent in January, 1391,[111] he met ambassadors from Toqtamish, who in an attempt to avert the storm offered him coursers and a falcon. "He took the falcon upon his wrist and looked at it, but gave no other sign of cordial welcome." After his experiences of 1387 and 1388, Tamerlane had reason to suppose that Toqtamish's forces were preparing in his ancestral domain: in the steppes of the White Horde, the Sary-Su basin, the Ulu-Tau massif, and the basin of the Turgai. He therefore headed in that direction. From Yasy he marched northwestward through the solitudes of the lower Sary-Su and then of the Ulu-Tau (*Ulugh tagh*) Mountains, which separate the basins of the Sary-Su and the Turgai. "He went to the top of the mountain," says the *Zafer-name*, "and beheld with wonder those vast plains which in their verdure and extent resembled the sea" (end of April, 1391).[112] But there was no sign of the White Horde. Toqtamish had left a void before Tamerlane, in the manner of the old Hsiung-nu and T'u-chüeh. Hunting for food as it went forward over these vast expanses, the Timurid army reached and crossed the River Jilanchik (Pétis de la Croix's Ilanjouc), which flows into the Jaman Aq-köl.[113] This army then crossed the River Kara-Turgai (which Howorth identifies with the River Ataqaroghai of the *Zafer-name*, Pétis' Anacargou).[114] It was now four months since its departure from Tashkent. An enormous battue was organized on May 6 and 7 to bring in game.[115] Then, to raise the morale of his troops, Tamerlane held a solemn review with the same meticulous ceremony as on the maidan of Samarkand.[116] The whole enterprise might in fact have ended in disaster. Had Toqtamish really continued to withdraw northward, he would have succeeded at last in exhausting the Timurid forces and then, when they were half dead with cold and hunger, could have turned back and overwhelmed them. Tamerlane, who believed that the enemy was indeed retreating before him, advanced ever farther toward Siberia. From the Turgai, he reached the headwaters of the River Tobol, in the modern district of Kustanai.[117] At last, from the other side of the Tobo' his patrols spied some fires. Tamerlane crossed the river, but found nothing. "All the scouts who were sent out strayed at random through these huge wastes, finding no trace of men, and learning nothing of the enemy." At last, a prisoner told Tamerlane that Toqtamish was in the Ural region. At once the army headed west, crossed the Yaik or Ural River, no doubt in the Orsk area, and reached its tributary the Sakmara, which according to Howorth is the Semmur of the *Zafer-name*.[118] Toqtamish appears to have concentrated his army near Orenburg.

At last Tamerlane succeeded in pinning him down. The decisive battle was fought on June 9, 1391, in an area placed by Howorth near Kondurchinsk on the Kondurcha, a tributary of the Sok, not far from Samara (present-day Kuibyshev), or better at Kunduzcha, according to Barthold's emendation.[119] After a hard-fought engagement, Toqtamish was beaten, and fled. His men, trapped between the victorious Transoxianans and the Volga, were either slaughtered or captured.[120]

Part of the defeated army sought refuge in the islands of the Volga, according to the *Zafer-name,* but Timurid patrols took them prisoner. The *Zafer-name* complacently describes the rejoicings of the Timurid army in the Urtupa plains beside the Volga: "This part of the Volga was the seat of the empire of Jöchi, the great Jenghiz Khan's son, and his successors had always resided here. Tamerlane had the satisfaction of ascending their throne. The most beautiful ladies of his seraglio were beside him, and each lord had his own lady and each person held a goblet in his hand. The whole army took part in the entertainments, which caused the soldiers to forget the hardships of war. For twenty-six days they enjoyed all the pleasures that were destined for them." [121]

It is remarkable that after this tremendous effort and hard-won victory, Tamerlane, content with having carried destruction to the heart of the Golden Horde, did nothing to consolidate his conquest. Certainly he conferred power and position on a number of Toqtamish's Jenghiz-Khanite enemies within the khanate of Kipchak, including Timur Qutlugh, grandson of the late Khan Urus.[122] Timur Qutlugh at once set off in search of his new subjects and succeeded in gathering some of them together; but instead of bringing them to Tamerlane, he expressed his dissidence by taking them away with him across the steppe.[123] Another Jöchid prince named Idiqu, who up to that time had also followed the fortunes of Tamerlane, played the same game. He obtained the task of organizing some of the Kipchak hordes, but once free worked only for himself.[124] Tamerlane did nothing to bring them back into submission and, satisfied with the huge quantities of plunder amassed by his soldiers, he returned to Transoxiana by way of the later Russo-Turkestan province of Aktyubinsk.

No doubt Tamerlane's only aim had been to inspire enough

terror among the men of the Golden Horde to ensure that they would make no further attack on his domains. Once that object had been achieved—as he hoped—he took no further interest in Kipchak's fate. The result was that Toqtamish soon regained his throne. In a letter written on May 20, 1393, from Tana (Azov) to Jagiello, king of Poland, and studied by Barthold, Toqtamish himself explains his defeat and restoration: "Tamerlane had been called by the khan's enemies; Toqtamish was late in learning of this, and at the beginning of the battle he was deserted by the plotters. His empire had thus been thrown into disorder, but now all was well again. Jagiello was to remit the tribute due." At the same time, during 1394 and 1395, Toqtamish was entering into an alliance with Barquq, the Mameluke sultan of Egypt, against Tamerlane. By 1394, he had recuperated enough to attempt an assault south of Derbent upon the province of Shirvan, which formed part of the Timurid Empire; but the mere approach of Tamerlane was enough to put a stop to it.[125]

This renewed aggression determined Tamerlane to make a second expedition to Kipchak in the spring of 1395. Experience had taught him to shun the deceptive and exhausting route across the Turkestano-Siberian steppe and to take the Caucasus road, which led directly to the "capitals" of the Golden Horde, Sarai and Astrakhan. At Samur south of Derbent, he received an embassy from Toqtamish, but was dissatisfied with the explanations and excuses offered. He crossed the pass and on April 15, 1395,[126] attacked Toqtamish's army on the banks of the Terek. Tamerlane, who fought like a common soldier, "his arrows all spent, his spear broken, but his sword still brandished," was nearly killed or captured. At last Toqtamish was beaten and fled to the Bulgar country of the Kazan region. The *Zafer-name* states that he vanished into the forests of this area before the galloping Timurid vanguard could overtake him. The pursuers then returned, looting the country on their way. "There were gold, silver, furs, rubies, and pearls, there were young boys, and there were girls of great beauty." Tamerlane himself went on northward as far as the Russian town of Yelets, in the upper Don basin, on the borders of Mongol Kipchak and Slav Russia. Contrary to what is asserted in the *Zafer-name*, he did not attack Muscovy. Instead, after reaching Yelets, he began to retrace his steps southward on August 26, 1395.[127] At the mouth of the Don, he entered Tana (Azov), a commercial center frequented by many Genoese and Venetian traders, who sent him a deputation laden with gifts and were gullible enough to believe his promises. The sequel proved how misplaced had been their confidence. Only the Muslim inhabitants were spared. All Christians were enslaved; their shops and countinghouses, churches, and consulates were destroyed. This dealt a terrible blow to the trade between the Genoese colonies of the Crimea and Central Asia.[128] From there, Tamerlane went on to Kuban to sack the country of the Circassians, then into the Caucasus amid forests and inaccessible gorges to devastate the land of the Alans or As (*Asod* in Mongolian), the forebears of the present-day Ossetians.[129] During the winter of 1395–96, he advanced to the mouth of the Volga to demolish the city of Hajji-tarkhan, later known as Astrakhan, and to burn Sarai, the capital of Kipchak. Barthold thinks that the headless, handless, and footless skeletons found by Tereshcenko in the Tsarev excavations on the Akhtuba are relics of the atrocities committed by Tamerlane on this occasion. The *Zafer-name* simply says that while their city burned, the Sarai survivors, in appalling cold, were "driven before the army like sheep." [130] In the spring of 1396, Tamerlane returned to Persia by way of Derbent.

Tamerlane had ruined Kipchak. By the destruction of Tana and Sarai he had dealt a paralyzing blow to commerce between Europe and Central Asia; he had closed the ancient intercontinental routes described by Marco Polo and erased such vestiges of the Jenghiz-Khanite conquest as might have been of advantage to Europe. In Kipchak, as elsewhere, he had destroyed everything and rebuilt nothing.[131] On Tamerlane's return to Persia, Toqtamish reascended the throne of the Golden Horde. A passage from Ibn Hajar Asqalani, noted by Barthold, shows him waging war against the Genoese colonies of the Crimea between September, 1396, and October, 1397. Meanwhile, his rival Timur Qutlugh challenged his right to the throne. He had also to contend with another local chief named Idiqu, and Ibn 'Arabshah narrates the vicissitudes of this new war, so exhausting to the country.[132] Of all these pretenders, Timur Qutlugh was the victor, at least for some years. He felt it prudent to acknowledge himself Tamerlane's client and sent him an embassy which was received on August 17, 1398. Beaten, Toqtamish took refuge with Witowt (Vitovt, Vitautas), grand duke of Lithuania. Witowt espoused his cause but was beaten by Timur Qutlugh on the Vorskla, a tributary of the Dnieper, on August 13, 1399.

Toqtamish, reduced to the life of an adventurer, tried to regain favor with Tamerlane, who in January, 1405, received an embassy from him at Otrar. Tamerlane, who had always had a soft spot for this thankless friend, is thought to have promised to reinstate him, but Toqtamish's death prevented this. Timur Qutlugh was succeeded as khan of Kipchak by his brother Shadibeg (ca. 1400–07). According to Russian sources, it was Shadibeg's troops who killed Toqtamish in 1406 at Tyumen in Siberia, whither he had fled.

EXPEDITION TO INDIA

Tamerlane also found inspiration in the tradition of the khans of Jagatai to make plundering expeditions into India. Northwestern India—the Punjab and the Doab—was regarded as the hunting ground of the Jenghiz-Khanite princes. From 1292 to 1327 (see pp. 339 and 341), they never ceased to make sudden periodic cavalry raids to ravage Lahore and Multan, destroying all before them and galloping to the very gates of Delhi, which at various times they attempted to blockade. These invasions all ebbed away after a few months, first because almost their only purpose was pillage, and second because the Jagatai Mongols found themselves confronted by a strong state. The sultanate of Delhi, Turkic or Turko-Afghan in its command framework and Muslim by religion, with such vigorous sovereigns as 'Ala ad-Din Khilji (1296–1316) and Muhammad ibn-Tughlugh (1325–51), was always able by means of gold or of cold steel to halt the Mongol troops that descended upon it through the Afghan passes.

In adopting this Jagataite custom, Tamerlane had really no other purpose than to resume profitable forays into one of the richest lands in the world. But as was his habit, he found religious pretexts for his actions. It is true that the Turkic sultanate of Delhi was essentially Muslim, and several of its rulers had attempted the mass conversion to Islam of their Hindu subjects by means of systematic persecution; but Tamerlane considered that they had been too lenient with paganism. The *Zafer-name* insists that it was solely to make war on the enemies of the Muslim faith that he set forth to conquer India. "The Koran emphasizes that the highest dignity to which man may attain is to wage war in person upon the enemies of the Faith. This is why the great Tamerlane was always concerned to exterminate the infidels, as much to acquire merit [for good deeds done] as from love of glory." [133]

Underlying these devout protestations was a very exact knowledge of the political situation in India. The sultanate of Delhi, which in 1335 had comprised almost the whole of India, shortly afterward fell into rapid decline, followed by territorial disintegration. The governors of a number of large provinces threw off the sultan's authority and set up their own autonomous Muslim states. Thus the empire lost the Deccan, which was made into a Bahmanid subsultanate (1347), and Bengal (1358–59), the Oudh or kingdom of Jaunpur (1394), and finally Gujarat (1396). The secession of these local Muslim kingdoms reduced the sultanate of Delhi to no more than the Punjab and the Doab, and even the Punjab was disturbed by the revolt of the Khokhar tribe of the Salt Range. Moreover, the sultan then reigning in Delhi, Mahmud Shah II (1392–1412), was a weak ruler, under the thumb of his all-powerful minister Mallu Iqbal. [134]

Tamerlane, then, would be faced in India by no more than a sultanate in decline, deprived of its richest provinces by the secession of local governors. At the beginning of 1398, he sent ahead an advance guard commanded by his grandson Pir Muhammad. The latter crossed the Indus and attacked Multan, which he took after a six months' siege. Tamerlane himself with the main army crossed the Indus on September 24, 1398; ordered or allowed his troops to sack the town of Talamba, northeast of Multan; and rejoined Pir Muhammad. On the Sutlej River, he defeated Jasrat, chief of the Khokhars, and then marched upon Delhi by the direct Multan-Delhi route, slightly south of the 30th parallel. On this road stood Bhatnair fort, defended by the Rajput chief Ray Dul Chand. Tamerlane captured and demolished it, occupied Sirsuti, and took the fort of Loni, seven miles north-northeast of Delhi, and here on December 10, 1398, he set up his headquarters. Before fighting the decisive battle, he thought it wise to slaughter the hundred thousand or so Hindu prisoners that were hampering him. The *Malfuzat-i*

Timuri[135] states that this order was meticulously carried out. On December 17, on the banks of the Jumna, between Panipat and Delhi, Tamerlane engaged the enemy army, which was commanded by Sultan Mahmud Shah and his minister Mallu Iqbal. Once more he was victorious. The Indians' war elephants could no more withstand the Timurid cavalry than they had withstood the Macedonian, "and soon one saw the ground strewn with elephants' trunks mingled with the bodies and heads of the dead."[136] The sultan took refuge in Gujarat while Tamerlane made his triumphal entry into Delhi. At the request of the Muslim "clergy," he granted the inhabitants their lives, but his soldiers requisitioned their supplies with such brutality that the population was goaded into resisting. This aroused the fury of the troops, who put the city to pillage, massacre, and fire. The booty was colossal, for it was at Delhi that for two hundred years the Turko-Afghan sultans had amassed the treasure they had plundered from the India of the rajas. This vast collection of gold and precious stones fell at one stroke into the hands of the Transoxianans. The massacre was in proportion, and pyramids of severed heads arose at the four corners of the city.[137] So far as was possible under the circumstances, however, Tamerlane as usual spared qualified craftsmen and sent them to beautify Samarkand.

Tamerlane spent fifteen days in Delhi. He took his place solemnly upon the throne of the sultans of India and delighted in summoning the hundred and twenty war or ceremonial elephants. "These well-trained elephants bowed their heads and knelt before him in obeisance, and all trumpeted at the same moment, as if rendering homage."[138] They were sent off in long strings to the cities of the Timurid empire: Samarkand, Herat, Shiraz, and Tabriz. Tamerlane performed his devotions in the great mosque of Delhi, where the khutbah was pronounced in his name. In general, he behaved like an emperor of India; yet, there as elsewhere, having destroyed everything, he departed without establishing anything new. On January 1, 1399, he left a gutted Delhi. He went on to sack Miraj in the same way, pulling down the monuments and flaying the Hindu inhabitants alive, an act by which he fulfilled his vow to wage the Holy War.[139] He then set his face toward home, following a very northerly route along the Siwalik Range and the high Punjab.

On the upper Chenab, he took the raja of Jammu prisoner and had the joy of making him forsake Hinduism for Islam, and eat beef.[140] On his way, he received acknowledgment of vassalage from the Muslim king of Kashmir, Sikander-shah. Without entering Kashmir, he returned to Afghanistan. Before leaving, he had appointed an Indo-Muslim lord as governor of Multan and the Punjab, Khizr khan the Sayyid, who thirteen years later was to become sultan of Delhi.

In fact, in his usual fashion, having shaken the Indo-Muslim empire of Delhi to its foundations, Tamerlane departed, leaving the country in the grip of total anarchy, with everything destroyed and nothing set in order. Though he professed to have come to fight Brahminism, it was at Indian Islam that he had struck. This relatively cultured man, a lover of Persian literature and Iranian art, in making contact with one of the most polished civilizations of the Old World behaved like the leader of a horde, plundering for the sake of plunder, massacring and destroying through blindness or closed-mindedness to a certain set of cultural values. This strange champion of Islam had come to deliver a stab in the back to the vanguard of Islam at the fringe of India. He was to adopt the same attitude toward the Ottoman Empire on the marches of Rumania.

TAMERLANE AND THE MAMELUKES

In the traditional Near East, Tamerlane was confronted by two great Muslim powers, the Mamelukes and the Ottoman Empire.

The Mameluke Empire, comprising Egypt since 1250 and Syria since 1260, was an essentially military state. The Turko-Circassian Mameluke force was a Praetorian Guard which had abolished the legitimate dynasty in 1250 and placed its own generals on the throne of Cairo, governing and exploiting the Arab population as a warrior aristocracy. It will be remembered that in 1260, at the battle of 'Ain Jalud, the Mamelukes had halted the Mongol conquest and thrown the Mongols of Persia east of the Euphrates.[141] But by the end of the fourteenth century, the powerful military machine that had driven crusaders and Mongols out of Syria was beginning to falter as a result of the incessant quarrels between the Mameluke generals over their Egypto-Syrian fiefs and over the throne itself. The energetic Mameluke sultan Barquq

(1382–99) spent his life quelling insurrections among his lieutenants. Tamerlane sought an alliance with him. But Barquq, conscious of the threat to the Mameluke empire represented by this new power forming in the East, executed one of Tamerlane's ambassadors in 1393 and more than once gave asylum to Ahmed Jelair, sultan of Baghdad, who had been put to flight by Tamerlane. Barquq's son and successor, the young sultan Faraj (1399–1412), refused from the moment of his accession to acknowledge Tamerlane's suzerainty or to return certain fugitives to him. Tamerlane decided then to make war.

He was at that time near Malatiya and descended upon Syria by the 'Aintab route in October, 1400, to march on Aleppo. Before this city, he beat a Mameluke army commanded by the governor Timurtash, the elephants which he had brought back with him from India contributing to the spread of panic among the enemy (October 30).[142] Aleppo was taken instantly, and four days later Timurtash surrendered the citadel itself. Once master here, Tamerlane appeared in his customary dual aspect of sophistical littérateur and mass murderer. Maliciously he put this thorny problem before the teachers of Islam: Which of those who had died in the war—his own soldiers or the Mamelukes— had the right to the title of martyr? Then he discussed theology with them and embarrassed these orthodox Sunnites worse than ever by forcing them to add 'Ali to the number of legitimate caliphs.[143] When not engaged in learned discourse with the doctors of law, he massacred the garrison of the citadel, built "towers of severed heads," and sacked the town. The pillage of this great city, whose bazaar was one of the great trading centers of the Levant, lasted three days.

Tamerlane next took Hama, Homs, and Baalbek, and then appeared before Damascus, whither the young Mameluke sultan Faraj had come from Cairo to encourage its defenders by his presence. On December 25, 1400, Faraj tried to take advantage of the fact that the Timurid army was changing camp, and moved into Ghuta to attack it as it was on the move; but after a hard battle he was repulsed.[144] Threatened by sedition in his own entourage, Faraj returned to Egypt, leaving Damascus to its fate. The authorities of the city, discouraged, resigned themselves to capitulating. In the delegation that waited upon Tamerlane for this purpose was the great historian Ibn-Khaldun

of Tunis. "Tamerlane, struck by the distinguished air of the
historian and dazzled by his discourse, invited him to be seated
and thanked him for affording him the opportunity of knowing
so learned a man." [145] The conqueror, rosary in hand and speaking nothing but piety and mercy, reassured the negotiators, and
the city opened its gates. The citadel held out and did not
surrender until after a regular siege. No sooner was Tamerlane
in control of Damascus than he demanded ten times the agreed
ransom from the inhabitants and confiscated all their wealth.
The *Zafer-name* assures us that in proceeding at last to the total
sack of the city and the massacre of part of the population, he
was merely punishing the Damascenes for their impiety toward
'Ali, the son-in-law of the Prophet, in the year 659. [146] In the
midst of all these brutalities, a terrible fire broke out and destroyed the greater part of the city, causing the death of countless people and devouring the great mosque of the Ummayads,
where thousands of fugitives perished in the flames. On March
19, 1401, Tamerlane at last left Damascus, taking with him all
the craftsmen that he had been able to gather together: silk
weavers, armorers, glassworkers, and potters to engage in the
embellishment of Samarkand. He also forced a great number of
writers to accompany him, along with the multitudes who had
been reduced to slavery. [147] Among these deported people was
the future historian Ibn 'Arabshah, then aged twelve, [148] who was
later to take his revenge by writing a pitiless book about the
conqueror.

Tamerlane, having ruined Syria, evacuated it without attempting to establish any regular form of rule, and it was immediately
reoccupied by the Mamelukes.

TAMERLANE AND THE OTTOMAN EMPIRE

Tamerlane had beaten the Jenghiz-Khanites of Kashgaria and
southern Russia and the sultan of India. We have just seen how
little trouble the sultan of Egypt gave him. Only one great power
now survived in the lands around him: the Ottoman Empire.

The Ottoman sultan Bajazet (Bayezid, Bayazid, 1389–1403)
had carried the Ottoman Empire to the zenith of its might. [149]
After being proclaimed sultan at his father's death in 1389 on

the battlefield of Kosovo, where the Serbian army had been crushed, he completed the conquest of Serbia and annexed Bulgaria (1394). In Asia Minor, he annexed the Turkish emirates of Aydin and Saruhan (1390), the great Turkoman emirate of Karaman (1390),[150] the Turkish emirates of Mentese and Kermian (1391), and finally the Kastamonu emirate and the former emirate of Burhan ad-Din at Tokat, Sivas, and Kayseri in Cappadocia (1392).[151] In 1396, at Nicopolis, he crushed the famous crusade led by King Sigismund of Hungary and the Burgundian heir Jean sans Peur.

Bajazet the Lightning, as he was called (Bayezid Yildirim), reigned over a huge empire, which in Europe included Thrace without Constantinople, Macedonia without Salonika, Bulgaria, and the Serbian protectorate. In Anatolia, his dominions extended to the Taurus (which separated Bajazet's lands from Mameluke Cilicia), the Armenian massif (which constituted the boundary with Tamerlane's dominions), and the Pontic range (the boundary with the Greek empire of Trebizond). His army, which had vanquished the dazzling Franco-Burgundian chivalry, was with justice regarded as the best in the Near East. He seemed now on the point of crowning his triumphs by capturing Constantinople from the Greeks, and had already begun the blockade of that city.

For once Tamerlane met an adversary of his own stature. Both leaders, aware of this, watched and spied upon one another, hesitant to engage in battle and so hazard what they had gained, one from the conquest of Asia, the other from that of the Balkans. It was Bajazet who committed the first act of hostility by trying to impose his suzerainty on the emir Taherten, lord of Erzincan and Erzerum, who was Tamerlane's vassal. Tamerlane had a high regard for this Turkoman chief who guarded the frontiers of Asia Minor for him, and he had presented him with a war elephant after the sack of Delhi. Conversely, Bajazet had welcomed into his own territories another Turkoman chief, Qara-Yusuf, leader of the Black Sheep horde and an enemy of Tamerlane, who had driven him out. The battle was thus to be fought on a dual issue of clientele, Tamerlane protecting Taherten and Bajazet supporting Qara-Yusuf. The *Zafer-name* claims to reproduce the exact text of the letter sent by Tamerlane to Bajazet on this subject.[152] After some biting insults concerning the obscure origins of the Ottoman dynasty, Tamerlane consents to take into consideration the part played by the Ottoman Empire as the bulwark of Islam in Europe, and the Holy War so victoriously fought there by the sultan. He would therefore spare his rival. Nevertheless, his attitude to this Romanized Turk, this *qaisar* (Caesar) of Rum, is that of an overlord, the legitimate sovereign of the Turkic race. In comparing the extent of the two empires, he ends with this threat: "Can a petty prince like yourself measure himself against us?" Bajazet took up the challenge: "We will pursue you to Tabriz and Sultaniyeh!" [153]

On receiving this reply, Tamerlane marched upon Asia Minor in August, 1400. At the beginning of September, after his vassal Taherten had paid him homage at Erzerum and Erzincan, he entered Ottoman territory and laid siege to the fortified city of Sivas.[154] Faced by the entrenchments and by the bombardment of siege engines, Sivas did not await the final assault but capitulated after about three weeks. Tamerlane spared the lives of Muslims, but the four thousand Armenian soldiers in the Ottoman garrison he either buried alive or threw into wells. He then pulled down the city walls.

On this occasion, Tamerlane went no farther. He could not advance into Asia Minor since he was being threatened in the rear by the Mameluke army and by the momentary restoration of Ahmed Jelair in Baghdad. It was at this point (see above) that he went to wipe out the Mamelukes in Syria and to reconquer Baghdad. This task accomplished, he returned to Asia Minor. Meanwhile, Bajazet had taken Erzincan from Taherten and captured the emir's family.[155] Tamerlane did not retaliate immediately. Instead, after returning from Syria and Baghdad, he went to spend the winter of 1401–2 in Karabakh and the spring on the frontiers of Georgia while his armies were concentrating. It was not until June, 1402, that he invaded the Ottoman Empire. After reinstating Taherten in Erzincan, he reviewed his army on the Sivas plain. "A certain number of squadrons had red standards; their breastplates, saddles, saddlecloths, quivers, and belts, their lances, shields, and war clubs were red also. Another army corps was yellow, another white. One regiment wore coats of mail, another cuirasses." Then by way of Kayseri, Tamerlane marched on Ankara, where he had learned Bajazet was.

The decisive battle was fought northeast of the city, at Cubuk, on July 20, 1402. It lasted from six in the morning until nightfall and involved nearly a million men.[156] Bajazet had brought contingents from among the peoples he had conquered. But although the Serbs and their king Stephen remained loyal to him, to Tamerlane's admiration, the Turks of Aydin, Mentese, Saruhan, and Kermian, beholding their princes among Tamerlane's forces, changed sides.

Tamerlane seems to have made good use of the war elephants he had brought from India.[157] At the head of 10,000 Janizaries and Serbs, Bajazet fought all day, and it was not until he had seen his guard annihilated that he decided at sunset to retreat. But his horse fell and he was taken prisonor with one of his sons.[158]

Tamerlane treated his enemy with courtesy.[159] Nevertheless, because the sultan tried to escape, he made him travel in a barred litter, which gave rise to the exaggerated story of the "iron cage." Bajazet, broken by disaster and humiliation, died a few months later (at Aksehir on March 9, 1403).

Once the Ottoman army was destroyed and the sultan a captive, the conquest of western Anatolia was no more than a route march for Tamerlane. He called a halt at Kutahya while his vanguard raced on to plunder Bursa, the Ottoman capital. Ibn 'Arabshah and Sharif ad-Din describe the conquerors behaving like a horde of savages, and that lovely city was set on fire. Tamerlane's grandson Abu Bakr galloped as far as Nicaea (Iznik), "slaying and looting everywhere," as Sharif ad-Din tells with relish. Tamerlane himself went to lay siege to Smyrna (later Izmir), which belonged to the Knights of Rhodes. Before attacking, he exhorted the governor, Brother Guillaume de Munte, to turn Muslim. The governor naturally refused with vehemence. The siege began, says the *Zafer-name*, on December 2, 1402,[160] and ended after two weeks, when the place was taken by storm. The massacre was general, except for such few knights as could be picked up by the Christian fleet. The *Zafer-name* attaches great importance to this victory on Christian territory. It served to justify Tamerlane to the devout Muslims, who with reason accused him of having struck a crippling blow at Islam by destroying the Ottoman Empire. The taking of Smyrna and the massacre that followed transformed the Ankara campaign—after the event—into a Holy War.

"Smyrna, which the Ottoman sultan had besieged in vain for seven years, was conquered by Tamerlane in less than two weeks! . . . The Muslims entered the city praising God, to whom they offered the heads of their enemies in thanksgiving." [161] Phocaea, an important Turko-Italian commercial center which the Timurid army went on to besiege, ransomed itself in time by offering to pay tribute. The Genoese "Mahone," a trading company which owned the island of Chios opposite, also made an act of homage,[162] while the Byzantine regent John VII, when he was required to acknowledge Tamerlane's suzerainty, at once sent an embassy in token of his compliance.[163]

Notwithstanding the Smyrna massacre, Tamerlane's triumph over Bajazet saved Christendom. Since Bajazet's victory over the crusaders of Nicopolis, Byzantium, rigidly blockaded by the Ottomans, was doomed, and its fall seemed only a question of months. The sudden disaster suffered by the Ottomans at Ankara allowed the Byzantine Empire an unhoped-for respite of half a century (1402–53). Thus by a singular turn of events it was Byzantium that benefited most from the Transoxianan's conquest in Western Asia, as Muscovy was to benefit from his victories over the Golden Horde.

This stroke of good fortune for Balkan Christendom was enhanced by the fact that, having overcome the Ottoman Empire, Tamerlane did all he could to prevent its resurgence. In Turkish Asia Minor, he ceremonially restored the various emirates that Bajazet had destroyed ten years earlier. Bajazet had stripped 'Ala ad-Din, emir of Karaman, of his possessions in eastern Phrygia and Lycaonia; Tamerlane appointed 'Ala ad-Din's son Muhammad II as ruler of Konya and Laranda (Karaman).[164] Similarly he reinstated the emir of Kastamonu, of the Isfendiyar-oglu house, in Paphlagonia; the Saruhan emirs, in the person of Khidr-shah, in Magnesia ad Sipylum (now Manisa); the emir Ya'qub of Kermian in Kutahya and Karahisar; [165] Isa, emir of Aydin, in his fief of Ionia, near Ephesus; Ilyas, emir of Mentese in Caria; and 'Uthman, emir of Tekke, in Lycia. The Ottoman domain in Asia was again reduced to little more than northern Phrygia, Bithynia, and Mysia. To weaken the Ottomans still further, Tamerlane took care to fan the flames of discord among Bajazet's sons, who were quarreling over their inheritance.

THE CONQUEST OF CHINA

Tamerlane returned to Transoxiana in 1404. At Samarkand he received Clavijo, who had been sent by Henry III of Castile and who has left a valuable account of his journey. Traveling by way of Constantinople, Trebizond, Tabriz, and Rai, Clavijo arrived in Samarkand on August 31, 1404, and was received by Tamerlane on September 8.

Tamerlane now contemplated the conquest of China, where the national dynasty of the Ming, who had driven out the Jenghiz-Khanites, was at the peak of its power. The first Ming emperor, Hung-wu (the former Chu Yüan-chang), as successor to the Jenghiz-Khanite grand khans, had claimed homage from the former khanate of Jagatai. In 1385, therefore, he sent ambassadors into Central Asia, Fu An (Chih Tao) and Liu Wei, who visited Hami, Kara-khoja (Turfan), and Ilibaligh, where without any difficulty they obtained the homage of the khans of the house of Jagatai or of the Dughlat emirs. But at Samarkand they were arrested by the Timurid authorities and were not released until after long parleying. However, Tamerlane more than once sent embassies to the court of China bearing gifts which might pass as tribute (1387, 1392, 1394). In 1395, the emperor Hung-wu sent Fu An back to Samarkand with a letter of thanks addressed to Tamerlane. Emperor Yung Lo (1403–24), brother and second successor to Hung-wu, had just ascended the throne when Tamerlane announced his intention of conquering China so as to convert it to Islam, and began assembling a huge army at Otrar.

This was surely one of the gravest dangers that had ever threatened Chinese civilization, for now it was not a question of invasion by a Kublai who respected Buddhism and Confucianism and desired to become a true Son of Heaven, but the irruption of a fanatical Muslim who, by turning the country to Islam, might have utterly destroyed Chinese civilization and eroded Chinese society. Yung Lo, the most warlike of the Ming

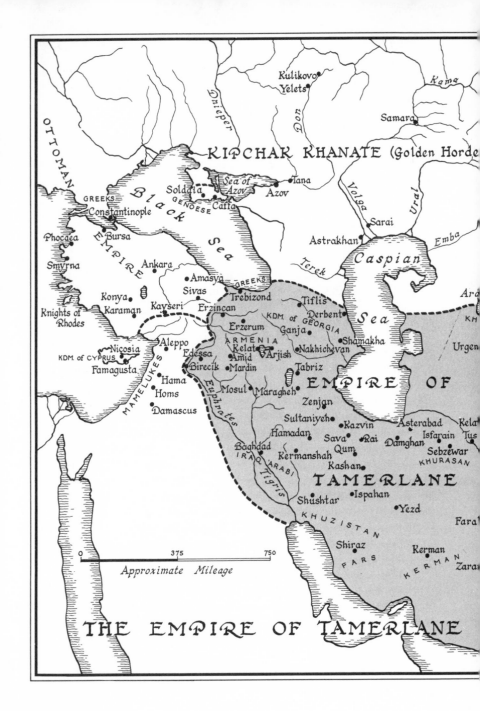

THE EMPIRE OF TAMERLANE

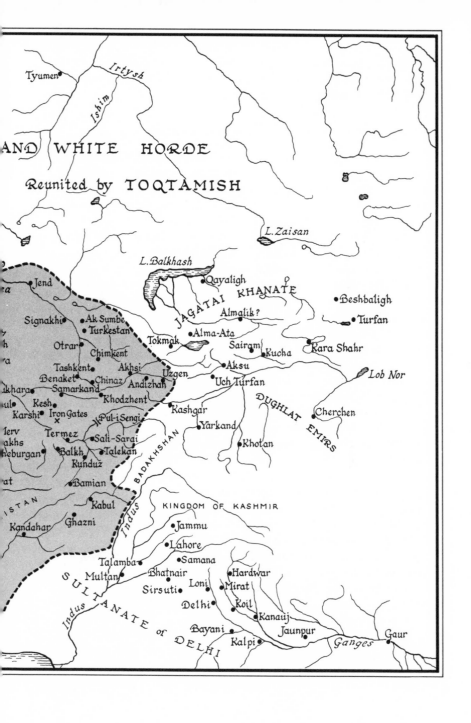

AND WHITE HORDE

Reunited by TOQTAMISH

Tyumen

Irtysh

Ishim

L. Zaisan

L. Balkhash

Jend

JAGATAI KHANATE

Qayaligh

Beshbaligh

Signakhi
Ak Sumbe
Turkestan

Almalik?

Turfan

Otrar

Chimkent

Tokmak

Alma-Ata

Sairam

Kucha

Kara Shahr

Tashkent

Akhsi

Aksu

Lob Nor

Benaket
Chinaz
Andizhan
Uzgen

Uch Turfan

Bukhara
Samarkand

Khodzhent

Kesh

Kashgar

Karshi
Iron Gates
Pul-i Sengi

Yarkand

Cherchen

Merv
Termez
Sali-Sarai

Khotan

DUGHLAT EMIRS

Talekan

Balkh

Kunduz

Bamian

BADAKHSHAN

Indus

KINGDOM OF KASHMIR

Kabul

Kandahar
Ghazni

Jammu

Lahore

Samana

Hardwar

ISTAN

Talamba
Multan
Bhatnair
Loni
Mirat

Sirsuti

Koil

Indus

Delhi

Kanauj

SULTANATE of DELHI

Bayani

Jaunpur

Kalpi

Gaur

Ganges

emperors, might have proved a worthy adversary; yet the danger was great until Tamerlaine fell ill at Otrar and died on January 19, 1405, at the age of seventy-one.

THE TAMERLANE SUCCESSION: SHAH RUKH'S REIGN

After the death of Jenghiz Khan, the Mongol Empire had known thirty years of internal peace (1227–59), until the period of rivalry between Kublai and Ariq-böga. After Tamerlane's death, however, the Turkic empire of Transoxiana was torn by quarrels among the sons and grandsons of the deceased.

Tamerlane left a numerous family.[166] In his last will and testament, he bequeathed a fief to each of his sons and grandsons, but at the same time sought to retain the principle of primogeniture. His eldest son Jahangir, as we saw, predeceased him by many years, around 1375.[167] The conqueror therefore chose Jahangir's eldest son to succeed him at the head of the empire. This was Pir Muhammad ibn-Jahangir, the twenty-nine-year-old governor of eastern Afghanistan (Balkh, Kabul, and Kandahar). At the same time, all the rest of the family received huge fiefs, so that under the theoretical authority of Pir Muhammad ibn-Jahangir the empire was in fact already split up.

Tamerlane's second son 'Umar-shaikh had also died before his father, having been killed in 1391 during a campaign in Diyarbakir; but his sons Pir Muhammad ibn-'Umar-shaikh,[168] Rustam, Iskander, and Baiqara had kept the inheritance: Fars (Shiraz) and Iraq 'Ajami (Hamadan and Ispahan).

Miranshah, Tamerlane's third son, then aged thirty-eight, had been given Mugan, Azerbaijan (Tabriz), and Iraq 'Arabi (Baghdad), but a fall from his horse had injured his brain and caused him to display such wildness and cruelty that Tamerlane placed him under the tutelage of a sort of family council, in this particular case of Miranshah's own son 'Umar-mirza, aged twenty-two, who governed the territory in his father's name. Miranshah's other two sons, Abu Bakr and Khalil, were soon to reveal their ambitious aims.

Tamerlane's fourth son Shah Rukh, aged twenty-eight at his father's death, had received Khurasan. His was the steadiest temperament and the only political mind in the family.

On the very morrow of Tamerlane's death, the quarrels, coups, and palace revolutions began. His grandson Pir Muhammad ibn-Jahangir, to whom he had left the supreme power and who was at that time too far from Transoxiana, in Kandahar, to take any action, found his rights being trampled upon. Another grandson, Khalil, Miranshah's fourth son, who was only twenty-one, was acclaimed by the army at Tashkent. He marched on Samarkand and there ascended the imperial throne (March 18, 1405).[169] Pir Muhammad ibn-Jahangir marched out of Afghanistan through Transoxiana, but was beaten by Khalil's armies near Nesef (Karshi).[170] Although left in possession of his Afghan domain (Balkh, Kabul, and Kandahar), he was assassinated six months later by his own vizier (1406). Khalil, once he had secured the throne of Samarkand, behaved as one might expect of anyone of his age, squandering the imperial treasure in wild extravagance and using his power only to gratify the whims of his favorite, the lovely Shad al-Mulk.[171] He soon goaded the emirs into revolt; they deposed him (1406, 1407) and acknowledged as king of Transoxiana Tamerlane's fourth son Shah Rukh, who was already the ruler of Khurasan. Shah Rukh consoled the young scapegrace Khalil with the Rai region in Iraq 'Ajami, where he died in 1411.

Shah Rukh was the most remarkable of the Timurids.[172] This son of the terrible Tamerlane was a good leader and a brave soldier, though of a peaceful disposition; he was humane, moderate, a lover of Persian letters, a great builder, a protector of poets and artists, and one of the best rulers Asia ever had. The evolution followed the same pattern as that from Jenghiz Khan to Kublai. His long reign from 1407 to 1447 was decisive for what in the cultural sphere has been called the Timurid renaissance, the golden age of Persian literature and art. Herat, which he made his capital, and Samarkand, the residence of his son Olughbeg (whom he had made governor of Transoxiana), became the most brilliant centers of this renaissance.[173] By one of the paradoxes that occur so often in history, the sons of the butcher who had ruined Ispahan and Shiraz were to become the most active protectors of Iranian culture.

Shah Rukh's direct authority did not extend beyond Transoxiana and eastern Iran. Ispahan and Fars belonged to his nephews Pir Muhammad ibn-'Umar-shaikh, Rustam, Iskander, and Baiqara. These princes had recognized Shah Rukh's suzerainty from the outset, and they appealed to him at various times to arbitrate in their quarrels. In 1415, especially, he had to go to Ispahan, where he deposed Iskander and left Rustam as his deputy; then he went to Shiraz to punish an insurrection by his nephew Baiqara, whom he sent into exile.[174]

The anarchy and the random quarrels of the Timurid successors had no disturbing effect on eastern Iran because Shah Rukh, that strong and wise administrator, was able to put an end to them, arbitrate effectively, and restore unity. This was not the case in western Persia, Azerbaijan, and Iraq 'Arabi. This region, as noted, had been bequeathed to Tamerlane's third son Miranshah, who was much incapacitated by his mental troubles, and to Miranshah's two sons Abu Bakr and 'Umar-mirza, who loathed each other and were constantly at loggerheads. Their quarrels favored the return of the former rulers of that country, who had been driven out by Tamerlane: Sultan Ahmed Jelair, one-time ruler of Baghdad, and Qara-Yusuf, chief of the Turkoman horde of the Black Sheep. Ahmed Jelair re-entered Baghdad (1405). Qara-Yusuf, having returned from exile in Egypt, went back to Azerbaijan, defeated the Timurid Abu Bakr near Na-khichevan, and reoccupied Tabriz (1406). Abu Bakr and his father Miranshah tried to recapture Azerbaijan, but on April 20, 1408, Qara-Yusuf inflicted a decisive defeat on them in which Miranshah was killed.[175] This battle, one of the most important in the history of the Orient, nullified all the results of Tamerlane's conquests in the West. Four years later, his heirs were driven from western Persia.

Qara-Yusuf, chief of the Black Sheep, now firmly established as ruler of Azerbaijan with Tabriz as his capital, fell foul of his former ally Ahmed Jelair, sultan of Baghdad. Ahmed tried to seize Azerbaijan, but was defeated near Tabriz on August 30, 1410, and assassinated next day.[176] Baghdad and Iraq 'Arabi passed into the hands of Qara-Yusuf, who thus found himself lord of a vast realm extending from the Georgian frontier to Basra. Within a few months this Turkoman kingdom of the Black Sheep (Qara-Qoyunlu), with Tabriz and Baghdad as capitals, became one of the principal powers in the East. In 1419, Qara-Yusuf took advantage of further inter-Timurid quarrels to occupy Sultaniyeh and Kazvin in Iraq 'Ajami.

These events caused Shah Rukh some anxiety. Determined to avenge his brother Miranshah and to re-establish Timurid dominion in western Persia, he left Herat for Azerbaijan at the head of a powerful army.[177] Qara-Yusuf died in December, 1419, before it arrived. Iskander, Qara-Yusuf's son, attempted resistance but was beaten by Shah Rukh, who subjugated Azerbaijan (1421). If Shah Rukh had pursued his advantage, the Timurid restoration might have been permanent, but soon afterward he returned to Khurasan, and Iskander immediately reoccupied Azerbaijan. Shah Rukh came back in 1429 and beat Iskander again, but once more Iskander reoccupied the country after the departure of the Timurid army.

In 1434, Shah Rukh sent a third expedition to Azerbaijan, and Iskander was put to flight with no more difficulty than before; but instead of appointing a Timurid viceroy in Azerbaijan, Shah Rukh entrusted the government to Iskander's own brother Jahan Shah (1435). This was to confirm the seizure of Azerbaijan and Baghdad by the Turkomans of the Black Sheep. After Shah Rukh's death, Jahan Shah was to deprive the Timurids of Iraq 'Ajami (1452), Ispahan, Fars, and Kerman (1458). When he died, it was not from Timurid reprisals but under the onslaught of another Turkoman tribe, that of the White Sheep (Aq-Qoyunlu) encamped in Diyabakir, whose chief, Uzun Hasan, took Jahan Shah by surprise and killed him on November 11, 1467, in the Mus region, and then succeeded him as king of western Persia. Thus, despite the efforts of Shah Rukh, western Persia had permanently eluded Tamerlane's heirs and fell under Turkoman dominion.

Where China was concerned, Shah Rukh gave up Tamerlane's ideas of conquest. He exchanged several ambassadors with the emperor Yung Lo. In 1417, for example, he sent Ardashir Togachi to Peking, while Fu An, who had already visited Transoxiana during the reign of Tamerlane, returned to Samarkand and to Herat, Shah Rukh's court. The purpose of these various missions, in part, was to re-establish between the Timurid empire and Ming China the trade relations that had existed between the two Mongol khanates of Kublai and Jagatai.[178]

Elsewhere, Shah Rukh followed Tamerlane's example and sent an expedition led by his son Olugh-beg against the Jagataite khanate of Mogholistan (1425). Olugh-beg, by what is known from the *Matla' es-sa'dein*, beat the Jagataite Shir Muhammad.[179] The head of the powerful Dughlat family, Khudaidad the kingmaker, lord of Kashgar and Yarkand, had been impelled by Muslim piety to ally himself with Olugh-beg, whom he joined beyond the Charin, a southern tributary of the Ili northeast of the Issyk Kul.[180]

Shah Rukh died on March 2, 1447, and was succeeded by his son Olugh-beg. Olugh-beg, who had long been viceroy of Transoxiana, was a cultured man, a scholar—he was particularly interested in astronomy—and a poet, and he made his court in Samarkand a brilliant center of Persian letters. But he was entirely lacking in authority. The Uzbeks—that is, the Mongols of Shayban's horde who were established in the Sibero-Turkestani provinces of Aktyubinsk and Turgai—made a foray into Transoxiana in the course of which they ravaged Samarkand, smashed Olugh-beg's famous porcelain tower, and destroyed his picture gallery. Olugh-beg, who was so easygoing as to be the plaything of his kinsmen, fell victim to his own son 'Abd al-Latif, who had rebelled in Balkh. 'Abd al-Latif imprisoned his father and had him executed on October 27, 1449. The parricide himself was assassinated some months later (May 9, 1450).

ABU SA'ID

Olugh-beg's death was followed by a further period of inter-Timurid warfare. One of his nephews, 'Abd-Allah, became ruler in 1450–51 of Samarkand and Transoxiana, while a second nephew, Babur-mirza, reigned over Herat and Khurasan (1452–57). In 1452, 'Abd-Allah was defeated and killed by another Timurid, Abu Sa'id, Miranshah's grandson.[181] It is interesting to note that this victory, by which Abu Sa'id won the throne of Samarkand, was achieved with the help of Abu'l Khair, khan of the Uzbeks, who, having made himself master of the Syr Darya line from Signakhi to Uzgen, now acted as arbitrator in Timurid quarrels. This was an unexpected Jenghiz-Khanite resurgence against the grandsons of Tamerlane.[182] A similar reaction seemed imminent from the princes of the house of Jagatai, or khans of Mogholistan (Ili and Yulduz region).

Esen-buqa or Esen-bugha II, khan of Mogholistan (1429–62), whose residence was at Aksu, between the Issyk Kul, Kucha, and Kashgar, had revived the traditional Jagataite incursions on the frontiers of Transoxiana, ravaging Sairam, the city of Turkestan, and Tashkent (1451 and after). But Abu Sa'id, who had just ascended the throne of Samarkand, raced in pursuit of Esenbugha, overtook him near Talas, and scattered his army.[183]

In 1457, after the death of the Timurid Babur-mirza, king of Khurasan, Abu Sa'id seized that province. On July 19, 1457, he made his entry into Herat.[184] Being now ruler of both Khurasan and Transoxiana, he set about restoring the Timurid Empire insofar as the rivalries and risings among his kinsfolk allowed. To weaken Esen-bugha II, the Jagataite khan, he resorted to traditional methods. In 1429, Esen-bugha had driven out his elder brother, Yunus-khan, who had taken refuge with Olugh-beg in Samarkand. In 1456, wishing to raise up a rival to Esen-bugha, Abu Sa'id recognized Yunus as the rightful khan. With the forces lent him by the Timurid, Yunus returned to Mogholistan and won recognition for himself in the western part of the country, round the Ili, while Esen-bugha continued to hold sway over the east: the Yulduz and Uiguristan region. A little later, Yunus marched on Kashgar. He was stopped and routed between that city and Aksu by Esen-bugha, who had hastened from the Yulduz, and by the Dughlat emir of Kashgar, Sayyid 'Ali. Yunus again fled to Transoxiana and Abu Sa'id (about 1458), and again the latter lent him reinforcements with which he appears to have re-established himself in the western part of Mogholistan, near the Ili and in the direction of the Issyk Kul. Meanwhile, eastern Mogholistan (Yulduz and Uiguria as far as Turfan) continued to belong to Esen-bugha (d. 1462) and then to his son Dust Muhammad-khan (1462–69), who usually lived at Aksu. Abu Sa'id had thus succeeded in annihilating the resurgent forces of the Jagataites by splitting up their possessions between two rival branches.[185]

Abu Sa'id was equally active in Persia. The western part of the country—Azerbaijan, Iraq 'Arabi, and Iraq 'Ajami, with Ispahan, Fars, and Kerman—had come under the sway of Jahan Shah, chief of the Turkoman horde of the Black Sheep (Qara-Qoyunlu). In 1458, Jahan Shah marched on Khurasan and occupied Herat (July, 1458). But six months later Abu Sa'id, who had withdrawn to Balkh, inflicted a savage defeat on Jahan Shah's son Pir Budaq at the banks of the Murgab and so liberated Khurasan. The city of Samnan between Damghan and Rai was recognized as the frontier separating Timurid from Black Sheep territory (about December, 1458). In his own states, Jahan Shah clashed with a rival Turkoman horde, the White Sheep (Aq-Qoyunlu), established in Diyarbakir; since the days of Tamerlane, this horde had been the traditional ally of the Timurids. In 1467, in the hope of ridding himself of these rivals, Jahan Shah marched on Diyarbakir; but on November 11, 1467, he was surprised and beaten at Kigi, between Mus and Erzincan, by Uzun Hasan, chief of the White Sheep, and was killed while running away.[186] As a result of this catastrophe, the domains of the Black Sheep passed to the rival horde.

Uzun Hasan hoped that this change would be regarded with a favorable eye by the Timurids, who were old allies of his house. But Abu Sa'id thought he might take advantage of the conflict between the two Turkoman hordes to recover western Persia. And indeed he had been asked to intervene by Jahan Shah's son Hasan 'Ali, who was trying to wrest Azerbaijan from the victorious Uzun Hasan. At Hasan 'Ali's request, Abu Sa'id declared war on Uzun Hasan, crossed Iraq 'Ajami, entered Azerbaijan, and marched on Karabakh in the steppe of the lower Aras and the lower Kura, Uzun Hasan's headquarters. As cold weather set in and Uzun Hasan, in the Turkoman fashion, had slipped away, Abu Sa'id made up his mind to winter in Karabakh, which was known for the mildness of its climate. His march to the Aras was disastrous, however, and at Mahmudabad he found his way blocked by Uzun Hasan. Being short of provisions, he tried to retreat but was captured on February 11, 1469, by the Turkomans. Six days later, Uzun Hasan had put him to death. He was only forty.

Abu Sa'id was the last Timurid to try to restore Tamerlane's empire from Kashgar to Transcaucasia. His failure, which was due less to his enemies abroad than to the ceaseless rebellion of his kinsmen at home, put a final stop to Tamerlane's achievement. His death delivered the whole of western Persia into the hands of the White Sheep horde. Uzun Hasan, who thenceforth was the undisputed ruler of Tabriz, Baghdad, Shiraz, Ispahan, Sultaniyeh, Rai, and even Kerman, appeared to the world as the king of Persia (1469–78) and his family was to remain in possession of that country, with Tabriz as capital, until the rise of the national Persian dynasty of the Safavids in 1502.[187]

With the powerful Turkoman kingdom of Persia as their neighbor, the last of the Timurids were now no more than local princelings of Transoxiana and Khurasan; and even that limited domain was split up among hostile kinsmen. Abu Sa'id's son Ahmed-sultan succeeded him only in Transoxiana, with Samarkand as his capital (1469–94), and he was forced to wage war against his own brothers. Meanwhile, the Jagataite khanate of Mogholistan, which Abu Sa'id had weakened by dividing it between two rival branches, recovered its unity and strength. The Jagataite ruler of Yulduz and Uiguristan, Kebek II (ca. 1469–72), son and successor to Dust Muhammad, had been assassinated, and his great-uncle Yunus, who was already khan of western Mogholistan (Ili) and to whom the Dughlat emirs of Kashgar had rallied some time before, now reintegrated the Jagataite possessions. Assured of the support of his vassal the Dughlat emir of Kashgar, Muhammad Haidar I (1465–80), Yunus-khan had become the mightiest ruler in Central Asia. The situation was reversed. It was now he who acted as mediator among the last Timurids, in quarrels between Ahmed, king of Transoxiana, and his brother 'Umar-shaikh, lord of Fergana. On several occasions, Yunus protected 'Umar-shaikh from attempted attacks by Ahmed; thus the Timurid of Fergana became a real vassal of the khan, who castigated him when he rebelled, then pardoned him and came to hold his court with him in Andizhan.[188] The reversal in the positions of the Jenghiz-Khanite and Timurid houses could not have been more complete. Fresh quarreling broke out between the brothers Ahmed and 'Umar-shaikh over the possession of Tashkent and Sairam, and Yunus, called in to arbitrate, resolved their differences by having both cities ceded to himself (1484).[189] Yunus died at Tashkent in 1487 after having successfully accomplished this brilliant Jenghiz-Khanite restoration. Ahmed tried to take advantage of his death to recover Tashkent from Mahmud, Yunus' son and successor, but was defeated near the city on the Chirchik or Parak. Tashkent remained the seat of the Mongol khan.

'Umar-shaikh, the Timurid prince of Fergana (1469–94), who had been able to reign only under the protection of the Jagataite khans of Mogholistan, died on June 8, 1494. His elder brother

Ahmed, king of Transoxiana, at once tried to seize Fergana, but died near Ura Tyube in the course of his campaign (July, 1494). Fergana remained the property of 'Umar-shaikh's son, young Baber, the future "Great Mogul."

Ahmed left a brother, Mahmud, and three sons, Mas'ud, Baysonqor (Baysonkur), and 'Ali, who quarreled over the possession of Transoxiana. Their tenure of the throne of Samarkand was fleeting. Mahmud (1494–95) was a dissipated tyrant, and died in July, 1495. Mas'ud is said by Mirkhond to have reigned in Samarkand, and by Baber in Hissar. In any event, he spent that brief period in fighting his brothers, until blinded by a treacherous minister. Baysonqor, who held brief sway in Samarkand amid general turmoil, soon perished at the hand of the traitor who had killed his brother. Their cousin Baber, prince of Fergana, who was only fourteen at this time, profited by the uproar to make himself lord of Samarkand (end of 1497), but was unable to remain there. Samarkand passed in 1498 to a cousin of Baber's named 'Ali, Ahmed's last remaining son. But these domestic conflicts encouraged invaders. The "Mongol" khan Muhammad Shaybani, a descendant of the senior Jenghiz-Khanite branch and chief of the Uzbek horde, had already turned his eyes toward Transoxiana and settled on the north bank of the lower Syr Darya, awaiting a favorable opportunity to cross the river. The foolish disputes of the last Timurids gave him that opportunity. In 1500, he entered Bukhara and then appeared before Samarkand. The Timurid king 'Ali was rash enough to come out and parley with him. Shaybani, who under the veneer of a cultured prince retained all the instincts of a steppe marauder, had the ingenuous young man put to death and ascended the throne of Transoxiana.

During this time another Timurid descendant, Husain-i Baiqara, had remained in Khurasan, and in the course of the general war among the members of his family, he made himself ruler of Gurgan and Mazanderan, with Asterabad as his capital (September, 1460). Driven from this principality in 1461 by his cousin Abu Sa'id of Transoxiana, he was forced into exile until Abu Sa'id's death brought about a sudden change in his fortunes. He was recognized as king by the inhabitants of Herat on March 25, 1469, and ruled Khurasan until his death on May 4, 1506.

Despite the limited size of his domain, his long thirty-seven-year reign was one of the most fruitful in Oriental history.[190] Husain-i Baiqara, who contrasts strongly with his contemporaries in his gentleness and clemency, made the court of Herat a brilliant intellectual center. Among those he invited to it were the Persian poet Jami, the two Persian historians (grandfather and grandson) Mirkhond and Khondemir, the great Persian painter Bihzad, and Sultan 'Ali of Meshed, the calligrapher. As minister he had the celebrated Mir 'Ali Shir Newa'i (1441–1501), who is one of the first great poets of Jagatai Turkic literature. Writing with equal facility in Persian and Turkish, he was concerned to prove that as a literary language Turkish could equal and even surpass Persian.[191] Herat during this exceptional reign was the Florence of what has justly been called the Timurid renaissance.

Thus the fourth-generation descendant of one of the most bloodthirsty Turkic conquerors of history and one of the most savage destroyers was a Persian prince, poet, and dilettante, under whose protection Iranian civilization shone with a new brilliance. More than that, 'Ali Shir gave the budding Jagatai Turkic literature a share in this Iranian renaissance. Herat, the city so brutally destroyed by Jenghiz Khan, so badly treated by Tamerlane himself, became once more, even as did Bukhara and Samarkand, what it had been under the Samanids, with an added quality resulting from the vast blending of civilizations that had taken place since the thirteenth century. Chinese influences, introduced by the Mongol conquest, gave a discreet flavor to the decorative arts. One has only to think of the miniatures of a Bihzad to evoke these glories, flowering amid what were thought to be eternal ruins.

But this was no more than a brief interlude between invasions, as Herat itself is an oasis in the midst of desolation. Badi' az-Zeman (1506–7), Husain-i Baiqara's son and succesor, was faced at the outset by an invasion of the Uzbeks, who since 1500 had been rulers of Transoxiana. The Uzbek conqueror Muhammad Shaybani sent Badi' az-Zeman fleeing to Koh-i-Baba, near the River Murgab, and entered Herat (1507).

Khurasan, like the country of Bukhara and Samarkand, thus fell into the hands of the Uzbek khans of the Shaybanid house. Within a hundred years, the race of Jenghiz Khan had won a final and permanent victory over that of Tamerlane.

III

The Last Mongols

12

The Mongols of Russia

Mongol power did not melt away all at once. Through the example of the final Jenghiz-Khanite reaction against the Timurids, it had from time to time and over a long period shown sudden bursts of vitality and activity which astonished contemporary observers and at times led them to believe that the days of Jenghiz Khan had come again. Long after the sixteenth-century restoration of a Jenghiz-Khanite—if Turkicized—dynasty on Tamerlane's throne, in the second half of the seventeenth century and down to the middle of the eighteenth, the western Mongols tried to revive Jenghiz-Khanite ambitions at the expense of the Chinese Empire. These last attempts form an epilogue to the great medieval epics, and a brief summary of them is presented here.

The result of Tamerlane's last operations in Russia had been to set at the head of the Golden Horde or Kipchak khanate, in place of Toqtamish, his rival Timur Qutlugh, who was also of the line of Orda or the house of the White Horde.[1] Timur Qutlugh had consolidated Mongol dominion in Russia by his victory of August 13, 1399, near the Vorskla, a tributary of the Dnieper, over Witowt (Vitovt, Vitautas), grand duke of Lithuania, who, spurred on by the former khan Toqtamish, had tried to interfere in the affairs of the horde. He was succeeded by his brother Shadi-beg[2] (ca. 1400–1407), who reigned over Kipchak proper, while the eastern steppes passed to another descendant of the White Horde named Koirijak, who enjoyed Tamerlane's protection. Under Shadi-beg's leadership, the Golden Horde ravaged the frontiers of the Russian principality of Ryazan, Similarly, during the reign (ca. 1407–12) of Khan Pulad (Bolod in Mongolian), son of Timur Qutlugh and nephew of Shadi-beg, the army of the Golden Horde commanded by Idiqu marched in December, 1408, against the principality of Muscovy, set fire to Nizhni Novgorod and Gorodets, and blockaded Moscow, but withdrew on the promise of a war contribution.

Under Shadi-beg and Pulad, the real power was wielded by that same Idiqu, chief of the Nogai or Mangit [3] horde, whom Ibn 'Arabshah describes as a true "mayor of the palace." The same writer adds that civil war broke out when a new khan named Timur refused to submit to this dictatorship (ca. 1412–15?). In the end Timur won and killed Idiqu.[4]

Khan Kuchuk Muhammad's long reign (between 1423 and 1459) was to end in the dismemberment of the Golden Horde and the founding of the khanates of Kazan and the Crimea. It is true that during this time similar family disputes paralyzed Muscovy in the reign of Grand Prince Basil II the Blind (1425–62). A decisive trial of strength occurred during the following reigns between Khan Ahmed (ca. 1460–81), Kuchuk Muhammad's son and successor, and the Russian Grand Prince Ivan III the Great (1462–1505). To shake off the suzerainty of the Golden Horde, Ivan III sought the friendship of the dissident khan of the Crimea, Mengli Girei (Geray),[5] and was also able to make friends at the court of Kazan. In 1476, he gave the Venetian Marco Ruffo the task of concluding a third pact with the Turkoman Uzun Hasan, king of western Persia, against the court of Sarai. Having thus more or less isolated or surrounded the Golden Horde, he omitted to pay tribute. In 1474, Khan Ahmed commanded him to do so and sent him his ambassador Qarakuchum. In 1476, another embassy was sent, ordering Ivan III to appear before the Horde. Ivan refused. Ahmed, who on his side had tried to encircle Muscovy by an alliance with Casimir IV, king of Poland, marched on Moscow. Ivan, to bar the way, took position on the Oka and then, as the Mongols pushed on westward, on the Ugra (1480). There the two armies kept watch upon each other for a long time. Ivan refused to come and "kiss the stirrup" of the khan, but hesitated to stake Russia's fate on a single battle. Ahmed was no less hesitant, for he was afraid of being taken in the rear by the khan of the Crimea. In October, faced by a cold that bore hard upon his troops, he left the Ugra and returned to Sarai with his booty. This battleless campaign led in effect to the liberation of Russia (1480).

Shortly afterward, Ahmed was surprised and killed by Ibak, chief of the Shaybanid horde that roamed east of the Ural (1481). Shaikh 'Ali, Ahmed's son and successor, resumed hostilities against Muscovy by allying himself with the Lithuanians (1501), but Ivan III could bring his own alliance with the khan of the Crimea to bear against him. In 1502, Mengli Girei attacked Sarai and destroyed it.

This was the end of the Golden Horde. Its place was taken by the three "subkhanates" which had already seceded from the Horde: the khanates of the Crimea, of Kazan, and of Astrakhan.

The Khanates of the Crimea, Astrakhan, and Kazan

The khanate of the Crimea was founded around 1430 by Hajji Girei, a descendant of Tugha Timur, Batu's brother. The first coins of his reign date from 1441–42 and it is known that he ruled until 1466.[6] The khanate that he formed was bounded in the east by the lower Don and in the west by the lower Dnieper, and extended northward as far as Yelets and Tambov. In 1454, Hajji Girei established the capital of the khanate at Bakhchisarai, the former Qirq-yer, in the south of the Crimea. The Girei dynasty founded by Hajji was to last until the Russian conquest of 1771 and the definitive annexation of 1783. Being profoundly Muslim, the family imposed a strongly Islamic character on the Crimea. Nevertheless, after a preliminary clash, Hajji Girei perceived the financial benefits to be gained from the Genoese colony of Caffa, and he remained on excellent terms with it until his death in 1466. His sons then quarreled over the succession. The second son, Nur Daulet, was at first the winner (1466–69 and 1475–77), but in the end it was the sixth son, Mengli Girei, who triumphed (1469–75 and 1478–1515). In 1468, Mengli Girei paid a visit of thanks to the Genoese of Caffa, who had helped him by keeping Nur Daulet prisoner.[7] Meanwhile, Mehmed II, sultan of Turkey, sent a squadron commanded by Göduk Ahmed-pasha to seize Caffa, which he did on June 4–6, 1475. Mengli Girei held staunchly by the Genoese and was shut up with them in Caffa, where he was taken prisoner by the Ottomans. Two years later, however, they sent him back to the Crimea as the sultan's vassal. The southern coast of the Crimea came under direct Ottoman administration, with a resident pasha in Caffa; and from the accession of Islam Girei II (1584–88), the name of the sultan of Turkey was pronounced in the khutbah. Nevertheless, the coinage continued to be struck in the name of the khans of the Girei dynasty, and in 1502 Mengli Girei delivered the *coup de grâce* to the Golden Horde.

The second khanate formed as a result of the disintegration of the Golden Horde was that of Kazan. During the reign of Kuchuk Muhammad of the Golden Horde (1423–59), a luckless pretender, Ulu Muhammad (a descendant of Tugha Timur, Batu's brother), had settled with his son Mahmudek in Kazan, where he founded an independent khanate that was to last from 1445 until 1552. This new state corresponded roughly to the old Bulgar kingdom of the middle Volga and the Kama. The basis of the population consisted of Turkic-speaking Cheremis and Bashkir peoples and Finno-Ugrian Mordvinians and Chuvash. Ulu Muhammad was assassinated in 1446 by his son Mahmudek, whose reign (1446–64) completed the foundation of the new state. Mahmudek's brother Qasim (d. 1469) fled to the Muscovites, who around 1452 gave him the town of Kasimov, named after him, on the Oka. The subkhanate of Kasimov, thus subject from the beginning to the rigid suzerainty of the grand dukes of Moscow, served the latter as a means of intervening in the affairs of the khanate of Kazan. Qasim himself took part with the Russians in wars against Kazan.[8]

The third khanate born of the dismembered Golden Horde was founded about 1466 by a prince, also named Qasim, who was the grandson of Kuchuk Muhammad, khan of the Golden Horde. Although Astrakhan had inherited some of the commercial importance of old Sarai, the khanate of this name, hemmed in between the lower Volga in the east, the lower Don in the west, and the Kuban and the Terek in the south, played only an insignificant part in history. It was also torn between the khans of the Crimea and the khans of Nogai (region of the Ural River), who took turns in imposing a khan of their choice on Astrakhan.[9]

All the Jenghiz-Khanates of southern and eastern Russia are known as Mongol (rendered improperly in classical history as Tatar). Yet although the dynasties were indeed genuinely

Jenghiz-Khanite by descent, the Kipchak Mongols had never constituted more than a handful of chiefs in the native Turkic mass, and had become thoroughly Turkic in character. Their Mongol framework apart, the khanates of the Crimea, Kazan, and Astrakhan were nothing but Muslim Turkic khanates, as were the Kirghiz hordes of Turkestan.

The history of these three khanates is that of their resistance to Russian counterinvasion. The khanate of Kazan was the first to suffer Russian blows. Ibrahim its khan, Mahmudek's son and successor, made a fair beginning against the Russians, even subjugating Viatka in 1468, but he was soon forced to make peace and return the prisoners he had taken. His two sons, Ilham and Muhammad Amin, quarreled over the succession. Ilham won and Muhammad Amin appealed to the Russians, who brought him back to Kazan at the head of an army and set him on the throne in his brother's place (1487). But in 1505, Muhammad Amin rebelled against Russian authority and the following year he defeated a Muscovite army.

On Muhammad Amin's death, the dynasty founded by Ulu Muhammad at Kazan became extinct (1518). Possession of the throne was now disputed between the Russian and Crimean factions. Vasili Ivanovich (Basil III), grand prince of Moscow (1505–33), gave the khanate to a prince of a junior branch of the house of Astrakhan, Shah 'Ali, who since 1516 had been reigning in Kasimov under his supervision. Muhammad Girei, khan of the Crimea (1515–23), Mengli Girei's son and successor, now made a move and in 1521 contrived to place his own brother Sahib Girei on the throne of Kazan and to drive out the client of the Russians. Indeed, after uniting the two hordes, Muhammad Girei and Sahib Girei launched a sudden invasion into Muscovy, surprised and wiped out a Russian army on the Oka, and reached the outskirts of Moscow (1521). They dared not make an assault on the Russian capital, but extracted from the voivodes the promise of an annual tribute. They took back with them countless prisoners to be sold as slaves in the Caffa markets. In 1523, Muhammad Girei again tried to invade Russia, but was stopped on the Oka by a Muscovite army supported by artillery.

Muhammad Girei scarcely had time to profit by his successes, for in 1523 he was surprised and assassinated by a Nogai khan named Mamai, who cruelly devastated the Crimea. In 1524,

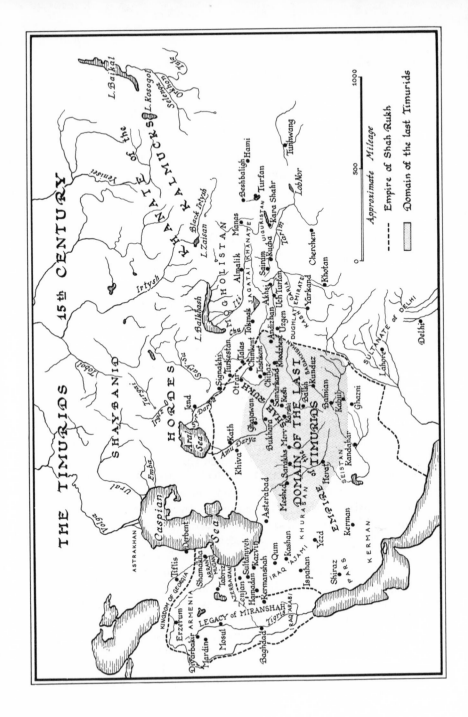

THE TIMURIDS
15th CENTURY

Approximate Mileage

- - - Empire of Shah Rukh

▨ Domain of the last Timurids

KINGDOM OF GEORGIA
ASTRAKHAN
Caspian Sea
Tiflis
Erzerum
Mardin
Diyarbakir ARMENIA
Shamakha
Derbent
ARRAN MUGAN
AZERBAIJAN
Tabriz
Zenjan
Sultaniyeh
Qazvin
Kermanshah
Hamadan
Mosul
Baghdad
Tigris
LEGACY of MIRANSHAH
IRAQ 'ARABI
IRAQ 'AJAMI KHURASAN
Qum
Kashan
Ispahan
Yezd
Shiraz
PARS
Kerman
KERMAN

Volga
Ural
Emba
Tobol
Irgiz
Turgai
Or
Or-Darya
SHAYBANID
HORDES
KHANATE of the KALMUCKS
L. Baikal
L. Kosogol
Selenga
Orkhon
Tula
Yenisei
Irtysh
Black Irtysh
L. Zaisan
L. Balkhash
Ili
Chu
MOGHOLISTAN
JAGATAI KHANATE
Talas
Syr-Su
Aral Sea
Khiva
Kath
Amu Darya
Jend
Signakhi
Turkestan
Otrar
Sauran
Yagwan
Bukhara
Merv
Sarakhs
Asterabad
Mashad
Meshed
HERAT
EMPIRE of TIMURIDS
Seistan
DOMAIN OF THE LAST TIMURIDS
Balkh
Bamian
Kunduz
Ghazni
Kandahar
Kabul
BADAKHSHAN
DUGHLAT EMIRATE
KASHGARIA
Yarkand
Khotan
Kashgar
Uch Turfan
Uzgen
Khojend
Andijan
Akhsi
Ferghana
Chinaz
Tashkent
Shimkent
Sairam
Kucha
UIGURISTAN
Turfan
Manas
Beshbaligh
Hami
Turfan
Kara Shahr
Turfan
Cherchen
Lob Nor
Tunhwang
Delhi
Lahore
SULTANATE of DELHI
Samarkand
Kesh
Korshi
Khojend

Muhammad's brother Sahib Girei returned to the Crimea from Kazan, leaving his son Safa Girei in that city. In 1530, the Muscovites drove out Safa Girei and replaced him by Jan 'Ali, Shah 'Ali's brother. Having become khan of the Crimea, Sahib Girei (1532–51) made a fresh attempt, as a result of which a "national" insurrection broke out in Kazan, in which Jan 'Ali perished and Safa Girei was recalled, supported by his father Sahib (1535). In 1546, the Russians brought back their old protégé Shah 'Ali, but immediately after their departure Safa Girei returned. He kept the throne of Kazan until his accidental death in 1549. After that the Russians deposed his son Otemish, once more substituting Shah 'Ali.

A new "national" movement overthrew Shah 'Ali and called in from the Nogai country a prince of the house of Astrakhan, Yadiyar. The czar of Muscovy, Ivan IV the Terrible (1533–84), made up his mind to put an end to Kazan's independence. In June, 1552, he came and laid siege to the town with some strong artillery.[10] On October 2, he took it by assault, massacred a large part of the male population, enslaved the women and children, pulled down the mosques, and annexed the territory of the khanate.

The destruction of the khanate of Kazan marks the turn of the tide in Russia's relations with the Jenghiz-Khanites. The conquest of the khanate of Astrakhan followed almost at once. In 1554, Ivan the Terrible sent to Astrakhan an army of 30,000, which installed as tributary khan a Jenghiz-Khanite named Dervish, who was a member of the reigning house (that of Kuchuk Muhammad). In the following year, Dervish rebelled and drove out the Russian resident or diplomatic agent, Mansurov. In the spring of 1556 the Russian army reappeared, put Dervish to flight, and annexed Astrakhan.

The last Jenghiz-Khanite khanate, that of the Crimea, was to survive for over two hundred years because the Girei dynasty, having accepted Ottoman suzerainty, was protected by the fleets and armies of the Sublime Porte. Thus, although Peter the Great occupied Azov by the Treaty of Karlowitz (1699), he had to restore it by the Treaty of the Prut (1711). In 1736, the Russians once more took possession of Azov and even of Bakhchisarai, but by the Treaty of Belgrade (1739) they once more gave back their conquests. At last, by the Treaty of Kuchuk Kainarji (1774),

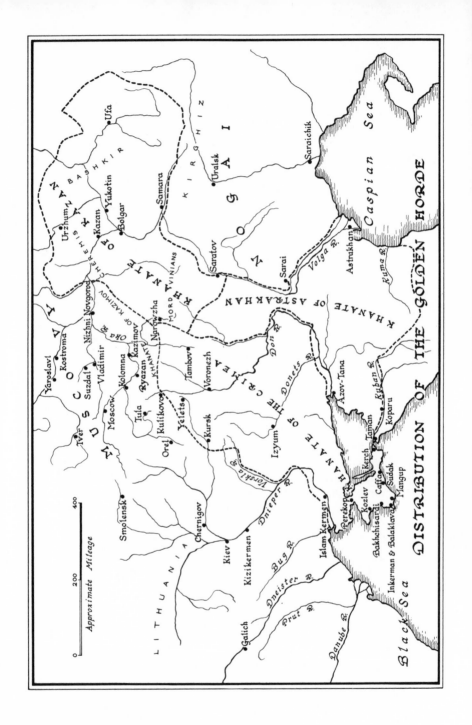

Russia compelled the Porte to recognize the "independence" of the Crimea. Russian agents then brought about the fall of khan Daulet Girei III and replaced him by his cousin Shahin Girei, who at once made himself a dependent of Catherine II (1777). The Crimean nobles soon rebelled against Shahin, who appealed to the Russians for help. Potemkin arrived in the Crimea at the head of 70,000 men and annexed the country (1783). The unfortunate Shahin Girei was banished and driven across the Ottoman frontier. The Turks took revenge upon him by sending him to Rhodes, where he was beheaded. Thus, on the eve of the French Revolution, the last Jenghiz-Khanite of Europe met his end.

13

The Shaybanids

FROM SHAYBAN TO ABU'L KHAIR

As the Jenghiz-Khanite families of Persia, China, Transoxiana, and southern Russia dwindled and died out, other branches of the same house—left behind and forgotten in the northern steppe —came to take their place and to claim their share of the historic empires. The Shaybanids are a case in point.[1]

It has been noted that the Shaybanid house descended from a grandson of Jenghiz Khan, Shayban, brother of the Kipchak khans Batu and Berke. Shayban distinguished himself in 1241 during the Mongol campaign in Hungary—so much so indeed, according to Rashid ad-Din, that if the Mongols had remained in possession of that country, he would have stayed on as governor. At Jenghiz Khan's death, Shayban was allotted the territories east and southeast of the southern Ural River, including —in the last direction—a large part of the province of Aktyubinsk and Turgai. These are the lands occupied today by the Kirghiz of the Middle Horde (between the headwaters of the Tobol in the west and the Semipalatinsk region on the upper Irtysh in the east) and of the Little Horde (between the Ural and the Sary-Su. It appears that Shayban and his successors camped in summer between the Ural Mountains, the River Ilek (tributary of the Ural River south of Orenburg), and the River Irgiz; in winter, his *ordu* may have moved nearer the Sary-Su. Until the end of the fourteenth century, the Shaybanid horde was not alone in these parts; its neighbors were the White Horde, which roamed the Sary-Su steppe and the Ulu-Tau Mountains. But

478

when in 1380, with the reign of Toqtamish, the leaders of the White Horde became khans of the Golden Horde, almost all the White Horde moved to southern Russia; such at least is the impression created by the account of the "exploration" of the steppe by Tamerlane in 1391.[2] The whole of this Sary-Su and Ulu-Tau region, like Turgai, must then have been occupied by the Shaybanids. About the middle of the fourteenth century, the hordes subject to the Shaybanids took the name of Özbeg or, in the spelling now usual, Uzbek, by which they are known to history, although the origin of the name is still obscure.

The true founder of Uzbek power was the Shaybanid prince Abu'l Khair, who led a most adventurous life.[3] In 1428, at the age of seventeen, he was proclaimed khan of his horde on the Tura, west of modern Tobolsk in Siberia. Immediately after this, he seized from other Jöchids the whole of the former *ulus* of this branch east of the River Ural and north of the Syr Darya. In 1430–31, he even took possession of Khwarizm and sacked Urgench. Shortly before 1447, at the Timurids' expense, he gained control of the fortified towns along the line of the Syr Darya, from Signakhi to Uzgen. Barthold believes that Signakhi was his capital. Yasy, on the other hand, the modern city of Turkestan, remained in Timurid hands. Abu'l Khair took advantage of the disputes between Timurid descendants to intervene in Transoxiana. It was thus that he helped the Timurid Abu Sa'id to win the throne of Samarkand (1451).

Abu'l Khair's power was at its height. His empire extended from the neighborhood of Tobolsk to the Syr Darya when about 1456–57 it was invaded by the Oirat or Kalmucks, that is, eastern Mongols. The Oirat owned a vast territory that included the Great Altai and the Khangai Mountains from Tarbagatai and Dzungaria to the southwest shore of Lake Baikal, across the lands of the Black Irtysh, Urungu, Kobdo, and Uliassutai, and the sources of the Selenga and Kosogol. They were expanding at this time, and their plundering bands ranged from the outskirts of Peking to western Turkestan. Abu'l Khair, having been defeated by them in a great battle, was forced to flee to Signakhi and let them devastate the whole of the north bank of the middle Syr Darya (1456–57).

This disaster greatly impaired Abu'l Khair's authority. Even before this, two vassal chiefs named Qarai and Janibeg—both,

like himself, of the house of Jöchi—had deserted him for Esen-
bugha II of Jagatai (d. 1462). They asked Esen-bugha for land,
and he settled them on the marches of Mogholistan. In the years
that followed, notably around 1465–66, a great number of nomad
clans formerly subject to Abu'l Khair left him to join Qarai and
Janibeg and enjoy an independent life. After their separation
from the Uzbek khanate, these nomads became known as Qazaqs
(or Kazakhs, "adventurers" or "rebels"), or Kirghiz-Kazakhs, as
they will henceforth be called.⁴ Their secession was of considerable historic importance, as may be realized by a consideration
of the extent of the territory which they soon occupied and
which even today is traveled by their descendants; the territory
of the Middle Horde, or the steppes between Aktyubinsk and
Semipalatinsk, the territory of the Little Horde from the mouth
of the Ural to the Sary-Su, and that of the Great Horde from
the town of Turkestan to the south shores of Lake Balkhash.⁵
Abu'l Khair was killed in 1468 (date emended by Barthold) in
a final battle against the Kirghiz-Kazakhs, whom he was trying
to bring back into his fold. About three years later, Yunus, the
Jagataite khan of Mogholistan, scattered the last remnants of
the Uzbek loyalists. As for the dissident Uzbeks, or Kirghiz-
Kazakhs, they formed a purely nomadic state, which after the
death of their two first chiefs was governed by the chiefs' sons,
Qarai's son Baranduk (ca. 1488–1509) and Janibeg's son Qasim
(ca. 1509–18).⁶ At one point Qasim tried to take Tashkent. He
failed and seems not to have persevered in the attempt. He was,
in fact, a perfect example of the pure nomad according to his
own definition in a curious speech reported by Haidar-mirza:
"We are the men of the steppe; all our wealth consists of horses;
their flesh is our favorite food, mare's milk our best drink. Houses
we have none. Our chief diversion is to inspect our flocks and
our herds of horses." ⁷

The attempt to reconcile this hereditary nomadism with the
demands of a semisedentary empire centered upon Signakhi
defeated Abu'l Khair. Yet his story is instructive. Abu'l Khair's
adventure is the adventure of a Jenghiz Khan who did not succeed. He had seemed chosen to unite the hordes and to found
a huge dominion (it was already influential enough to arbitrate
among the Timurids of Transoxiana); he had then watched his
nomad empire crumble away before the onslaught of other, more

savage nomads, though it was weakened chiefly by the defection of some of his own tribes, who resented his liking for the sedentary life. For one Jenghiz Khan who fulfills himself, how many Abu'l Khairs have gone to make up the history of the steppes! Yet where Abu'l Khair failed, his own descendants were to succeed.

MUHAMMAD SHAYBANI AND THE SHAYBANID KHANATE OF TRANSOXIANA

Shah Budaq, Abu'l Khair's son, died the same year as his father (1468). Yunus, the Jagataite khan of Mogholistan, who had come to help the Kirghiz-Kazakhs against the Uzbeks, surprised and beheaded him at Kara Sengir Tughai, between Tashkent and Turkestan.[8] Shah Budaq's son, the seventeen-year-old Muhammad Shaybani, began his career as a soldier of fortune.[9] Having lost everything, he entered the service of the Jagataite khan of western Mogholistan, Mahmud khan, who reigned in Tashkent. Mahmud, pleased with his services, gave him the city of Turkestan as his fief (between 1487 and 1493). Still with the help of Mahmud khan—whom the *Ta'rikh-i Rashidi* bitterly reproaches for having cherished a serpent in his bosom—Shaybani soon prospered enough to intervene in Transoxiana, where, as mentioned, the quarreling among the last Timurids left the country wide open to invasion. He lost no time, and in the summer of 1500 entered Bukhara, where local disputes prevented any resistance, and then, as has been mentioned, appeared before Samarkand. Here 'Ali, the reigning Timurid, was rash enough to come out and speak with him. Shaybani had him put to death, proclaimed the fall of the Timurid dynasty, and ascended the throne of Transoxiana (1500).

To his new realm Shaybani soon added Khwarizm, or the land of Khiva, a dependency of the Timurid king of Khurasan, Husain-i Baiqara. In 1505–6 he laid siege to Khiva, which was defended by a governor named Husain Sufi. The city was taken after a ten-month siege. Next it was the turn of Khurasan, or the kingdom of Herat, where Husain-i Baiqara had just died and had been replaced by the incapable Badi' az-Zeman, the last Timurid of Iran. Muhammad Shaybani began his conquest of Khurasan by besieging Balkh, which capitulated (1506–7). Herat itself, the last Timurid capital, surrendered after three days (May 27, 1507), and he treated the inhabitants well. This prince, whom Baber and the *Ta'rikh-i Rashidi* depict as a semibarbarian adventurer, appears to have been a very remarkable character, profoundly aware of the grandeur of his race and conscious of the importance of the Jenghiz-Khanite restoration personified in him, under which the brilliant Turko-Persian renaissance that had dawned in Samarkand and Herat under the Timurids continued to thrive. "Uzbek though he was," says Grenard, "Shaybani was a highly cultured man of letters, versed in the Arabic and Persian languages, a reasonably good poet in Turkish, and a liberal patron of poets and artists." [10]

The other Jenghiz-Khanite dynasty, that of the Jagataite khans of Mogholistan (Ili and Tashkent), then represented in Tashkent by Khan Mahmud (1487–1508), had favored the rise of Muhammad Shaybani. But Shaybani had not long been ruler of Transoxiana when he wearied of his subordinate position and attacked Tashkent. Khan Mahmud appealed for help to his brother Ahmed, who governed (1487–1503) Aksu and Uiguria. But in June, 1503, the two khans were defeated by Muhammad Shaybani at the battle of Akhsi in Fergana, northeast of Kokand and northwest of Andizhan, and were taken prisoner. He treated them with some courtesy and soon released them, in gratitude, he said, for their faults, to which he owed his good fortune; but he kept Tashkent and Sairam. Moreover, he demanded Khan Mahmud's daughter for his son, and so united for his posterity the rights of the two surviving Jenghiz-Khanite branches, Jöchi's line and Jagatai's. In 1508–9, when Mahmud had once more fallen into Muhammad Shaybani's power, Shaybani had him put to death near Khodzhent, observing that a statesman may show mercy once, but that only a fool errs twice.[11]

Muhammad Shaybani, master of western Turkestan, Transoxiana, Fergana, and Khurasan, had made the Uzbek Empire the chief power in Central Asia. He then clashed with Persia, which, after submitting for four and a half centuries (1055–1502) to many Turkic and Mongol overlords, had just recovered its independence. The national dynasty of the Safavids (1502–1736), which had ascended the throne after overthrowing the Turkoman horde of the White Sheep, now aimed at completing the reintegration of Iran by winning back Khurasan from the

Uzbeks. Safavids and Uzbeks were indeed opposed in every sphere, being respectively Iranians and Mongol-Turks, ardent Shi'ites and determined Sunnites. Racial war, as so often, took on the character of a war of religion. In his double role of champion of Sunnism and descendant of Jenghiz Khan, Shaybani commanded the Safavid shah Isma'il to abjure the Shi'ite "heresy" and to submit, failing which the Uzbeks would come to Azerbaijan to "convert him by the sword." And alluding to the origins of the Safavid dynasty (a family of Shi'ite sheiks), the Uzbek sovereign sent the shah of Persia a dervish's begging bowl, inviting him to resume the career of his ancestors and leave temporal power to the grandson of Jenghiz Khan. To this insolence Shah Isma'il is said to have replied that since he was a dervish he would come—with his army—on pilgrimage to the sanctuary of Imam Beza at Meshed (Mashhad) in the heart of Khurasan.

The shah of Persia kept his word. At the time, Muhammad Shaybani had been taken in the rear by the Kirghiz, who brought disaster to his son Muhammad Timur.[12] Taking advantage of this diversion, Shah Isma'il invaded Khurasan and, as he had promised, entered Meshed. Muhammad Shaybani, who had been awaiting him at Merv, was defeated and killed near that city on December 2, 1510.

This victory made a considerable impact in the East. That the restorer of Iranian independence should have killed the restorer of Turko-Mongol power—that the heir of the great Sassanid kings should have defeated and slain Jenghiz Khan's grandson—was a sign that the times had changed and that, after many centuries of invasions patiently endured, the sedentary was beginning to get even with the nomad and cultivation was winning against the steppe. Tradition has it that in token of this revenge the Persian sovereign had a drinking cup made of the Shaybanid khan's skull, and that in renewed defiance he sent the skin of that head, stuffed with straw, to the other Turkish potentate, the Ottoman Sultan Bajazet II.

The Shaybanid dynasty and the Uzbek realm seemed lost. Baber, the heir of the Timurids, the future emperor of India, who since his expulsion from Transoxiana had founded a small kingdom in Kabul, hastened back and with forces lent him by Shah Isma'il made a triumphal entry into Samarkand (October, 1511). After Samarkand, Bukhara opened its gates to him, while the Uzbeks withdrew to Tashkent. The Timurid restoration in Transoxiana, buttressed by the Iranian victory in Khurasan, seemed complete. But now unforeseen difficulties began to confront Baber. The Persians from whom he had had to ask help and accept suzerainty were Shi'ites. The populations of Bukhara and Samarkand, convinced Sunnites, rebuked him for treating with "heretics" and dissociated themselves from him, their sectarian passion being stronger than their loyalty to the Timurids. Encouraged by these religious disturbances, the Uzbeks reappeared. The Persian general Nejm Sani and Baber encountered them in a great battle at Ghajawan, north of Bukhara, and this time were defeated (December 12, 1512). Nejm was killed. Baber, giving up all idea of Transoxiana, retired to his kingdom of Kabul, whence, seven years later, he set forth to conquer India.

Bukhara, Samarkand, and all Transoxiana thus reverted to the Uzbeks. The Amu Darya marked the frontier between Safavid Iran and the Uzbek khanate, as it had once separated Sassanid Iran from the Hunnic hordes.

After its restoration, the Shaybanid family reigned over Transoxiana throughout the sixteenth century, from 1500 until 1599. Samarkand was the official capital of the khanate, though Bukhara was often the appanage of members of the royal family no less powerful than the khan himself, including the heir presumptive. Tashkent too had its local Shaybanids. This dynasty, Mongol in origin although completely Turkicized in language and culture, may be said to have fallen into almost as great a state of disintegration as the Timurids had done. Yet unlike them, it had been able to preserve a minimum of unity in face of a common foe.

Under Khan Köchkünji (1510–30), Muhammad Shaybani's uncle, the Uzbeks wrested from the Persians part of Khurasan, with Meshed and Asterabad (1525–28). Tahmasp, shah of Persia (1524–76), recovered this country by his victory over the Uzbeks of September 26, 1528, near Turbat-i-Jam, between Meshed and Herat. The Timurid Baber, who since 1526 had been emperor of India, took advantage of the Uzbeks' defeat by trying to recapture Transoxiana from them. His son Humayun, in alliance with Shah Tahmasp, occupied Hissar, north of the Amu Darya, but had to evacuate it when Tahmasp left that theater of opera-

tions for the West to fight the Ottomans (1529). Köchkünji, in
the year of his death (1529–30), had driven Persians and
Timurids south of the Amu Darya. Khan 'Ubaidallah (1533–39),
nephew of Muhammad Shaybani and Köchkünji, successfully
resisted Isma'il II, shah of Persia. 'Abd-Allah II, the most remarkable of the Shaybanids after Muhammad Shaybani, reunited
the family possessions which had been distributed among his
kinsmen.[13] It was thus that he became ruler of Bukhara in 1557,
of Samarkand in 1578, and of Tashkent in 1582. Having governed
in the name of his father Iskander (1560–83), he reigned in his
own right from 1583 to 1598. In the spring of 1582, to protect
Transoxiana from the incursions of the Kirghiz-Kazakhs, he led
a campaign into the steppes of the Little Horde as far as the
Ulu-Tau Mountains, between the Sary-Su and the Turgai. He
also made an expedition to Kashgaria, in the course of which
he devastated the area around Kashgar and Yarkand. Finally, he
seized Khurasan from Persia, including Herat, which succumbed
after a siege lasting nine months, and Meshed, the holy Shi'ite
city which young Shah 'Abbas failed to save and which the
Uzbeks, like good Sunnites, conscientiously sacked, massacring
part of its population. Similarly 'Abd-Allah II took Nishapur,
Sebzewar, Isfarain, and Tebes from Persia—in short, all the
strong points in Khurasan, from Herat to Asterabad. As for Balkh,
it had been made into a viceroyalty for 'Abd al-Mu'min, 'Abd-
Allah's son, as early as 1582.

'Abd-Allah II's good fortune deserted him in the last years of
his life. In 1597, Shah 'Abbas the Great, king of Persia, won a
resounding victory over the Uzbeks near Herat, and with this
Khurasan was freed. 'Abd-Allah's son al-Mu'min rebelled against
him and the Kirghiz took this opportunity to plunder the
Tashkent region. 'Abd-Allah died at the beginning of 1598, having beheld all his work in ruins. Al-Mu'min, who succeeded him,
was assassinated within six months. This was the end of the
Shaybanids.

The dynasty had reigned in Transoxiana for rather less than
a century, during which time it had succeeded in re-establishing
"Jenghiz-Khanite" dominion over Bukhara and Samarkand. Yet
each time it had fancied itself in possession of the Iranian territory of Khurasan (first under Muhammad Shaybani and then
under 'Abd-Allah II), it had been repulsed by the shahs of

Persia. At the moment when empires were crystallizing, Persia was destined to remain to the Persians, as was ethnically fitting, and Turkestan to the Turks.

THE KHANATE OF BUKHARA UNDER THE ASTRAKHANIDS AND MANGITS

The Uzbek khanate of Transoxiana now passed to another family, the Janids or Astrakhanids.

When in 1554 the Russians annexed the khanate of Astrakhan, a prince of the Jenghiz-Khanite dynasty of Astrakhan (house of Orda and Urus khan) named Yar Muhammad, and his son Jan, took refuge in Bukhara with the Shaybanid khan Iskander (1560–83), who gave his daughter to Jan in marriage. As the male Shaybanid line became extinct in 1599 with the death of 'Abd al-Mu'min, the throne of Bukhara passed in the regular manner to the "Astrakhanid" Baqi Muhammad, son of Jan and of the heiress of the Shaybans.

The Astrakhanid dynasty reigned over Transoxiana from 1599 to 1785, with Bukhara as its capital. It also held Fergana until about 1700, when an independent khanate was founded at Kokand, and Balkh, which was the appanage of the Astrakhanid heirs presumptive until the conquest of the city by Nadir-shah, king of Persia, in July, 1740. On September 22, 1740, Nadir-shah, who conquered the Uzbeks by means of artillery, appeared before Bukhara. The Astrakhanid khan Abu'l Faiz (who reigned from 1705 until 1747) was forced to accept Nadir-shah's suzerainty and to recognize the Amu Darya as the southern boundary of Bukharia.

Among the Mongol clans who had linked their fortunes with those of Muhammad Shaybani at the beginning of the sixteenth century was a Nogai or Mangit clan from the steppes between the mouths of the Volga and the Ural, the territory of a horde of that name. Under the Astrakhanid dynasty, this clan acquired increasing influence at Bukhara, where in the second half of the eighteenth century its leaders held the position of mayor of the palace. During the reign of the last Astrakhanid, Abu'l Ghazi (1758–85), the Mangit chief Ma'sum Shah Murad, who married the ruler's daughter, became the true sovereign and later ascended the throne (1785–1800). Ma'sum tried to encroach upon land south of the Oxus, near Merv and Balkh, at the expense of Timur-shah the Durrani, king of Afghanistan.[14] Nevertheless, Balkh was not annexed to the khanate of Bukhara until 1826, and in 1841 it was permanently reconquered by the Afghans. Merv, however, remained part of the khanate of Bukhara.

The Mangit dynasty reigned in Bukhara from 1785 to 1920. In 1866, it had to accept the status of a Russian protectorate. In 1920, the last descendant of Jenghiz Khan was overthrown by the Soviets.

THE KHANATE OF KHIVA

In 1505–6, the Uzbek conqueror Muhammad Shaybani had taken possession of Khwarizm, or land of Khiva, and of Transoxiana. After his death on the battlefield of Merv in December, 1510, when the victorious Persians occupied Transoxiana and Khwarizm (1511–12), the profoundly Sunnite population of Urgench and Khiva rose up against the Persian generals, who were Shi'ites, and drove them out. The chief of a collateral Shaybanid branch, Ilbars, who had headed the revolt, founded the independent khanate of Bukhara.[15]

The Shaybanid dynasty reigned over Khwarizm from 1512 to 1920. Besides its founder Ilbars (1512–25) may be mentioned Hajji Muhammad (1558–1602), during whose reign the khan of Bukhara 'Abd-Allah II achieved a temporary conquest of Khwarizm (1594, 1596). Under 'Arab Muhammad (1603–23), a column of a thousand Russians marching on Urgench was slaughtered to the last man. Around 1613, Khwarizm suffered an invasion by Kalmucks, who afterward left, laden with plunder. Halfway through 'Arab Muhammad's reign, Urgench ceased to be the capital, owing to the drying up of the left arm of the Amu Darya, and Khiva was substituted.

The most famous of the khans of Khiva was Abu'l Ghazi Bahadur (1643–65). He was one of the greatest historians of the Jagatai Turkic language and the author of *Shajare-i Turk,* a work most valuable for its history of Jenghiz Khan and the Jenghiz-Khanites, and particularly of the house of Jöchi, to which the writer belonged.[16] As khan he repulsed an invasion of Khoshot Kalmucks, who had come in to plunder the Kath region in 1648 and whose leader Kundelung Ubasha he surprised, beat, and wounded. He also beat back another incursion by Torghut Kalmucks who plundered the neighborhood of Hezarasp (1651–53).[17] In addition, he made war on the khan of Bukhara, 'Abd al-'Aziz, and in 1661 made a plundering expedition against that city.

Khan Ilbars II of Khiva, by killing some Persian ambassadors, drew upon himself the wrath of Nadir-shah, king of Persia. In October, 1740, Nadir marched on Khwarizm; compelled the fortress of Khanka, where Ilbars had taken refuge, to capitulate; and took Khiva (November). Less merciful here than at Bukhara, he executed Ilbars, who had outraged him in the person of his ambassadors. From 1740 until Nadir's death in 1747, the khans of Khiva remained in strict vassalage to Persia.

In 1873, the khan of Khiva, Sayyid Muhammad Rahim-khan, was forced to submit to a Russian protectorate. In 1920, the last Jenghiz-Khanite of Khiva, Sayyid 'Abd-Allah-khan, was deposed by the Soviets.

THE KHANATE OF KOKAND

Fergana had formed part of the khanate of Transoxiana at the time of the Shaybanids and under the first Astrakhanids. But during the latter period, this integration was only nominal, since Fergana had largely fallen into the hands of the Kirghiz-Kazakhs, to say nothing of the khojas established at Chadak, north of the Syr Darya. About 1710, a Shaybanid named Shah Rukh, a descendant of Abu'l Khair, overcame these khojas and succeeded in founding an independent Uzbek khanate in Fergana, with Kokand as its capital (ca. 1710–1876).[18]

In 1758, Irdana or Erdeni, khan of Kokand, was compelled to recognize the suzerainty of China, whose armies had reached his frontiers. He tried to form a coalition against them with Ahmed the Durrani, king of Afghanistan, but a demonstration by Durrani between Kokand and Tashkent in 1763 had no effect.

Between 1800 and 1809, 'Alim khan of Kokand doubled his territory by annexing Tashkent. Muhammad 'Umar, 'Alim's brother and successor (ca. 1809–22), annexed also the city of Turkestan (1814). Under Muhammad 'Ali, or Madali, 'Umar's son and successor (ca. 1822–40), the Kirghiz-Kazakhs of the Great Horde, in occupation of the region between the city of Turkestan and the southern shores of Lake Balkhash, recognized the suzerainty of the khanate of Kokand, which was now at the height of its power. But shortly before 1865 the khanate of Bukhara reconquered Tashkent, only to be deprived of it again, this time by the Russians, in June of the same year (1865).

In 1876, the khanate of Kokand was annexed by Russia.

THE SHAYBANIDS OF SIBERIA

In the fifteenth century, at Isker (Sibir) on the middle Irtysh, southeast of modern Tobolsk in western Siberia, a Turko-Mongol khanate had arisen whose khans were of "the issue of Taibugha-bäki" and not of Jenghiz-Khanite lineage. But the Jenghiz-Khanites of Shayban's house, who roamed south of the Ural Mountains and near the headwaters of the Tobol, soon occupied all the land east of that river. It was in the region of the Tura, a tributary of the Tobol, that Abu'l Khair, head of the Shaybanid house, had been proclaimed khan in 1428. About 1480, another Shaybanid prince of a junior branch, Ibak (d. 1493), seized from the khans of Sibir the "town" of Tyumen, near the confluence of the Tura and the Tobol. (This was the Ibak who in 1481 surprised and slew Ahmed, khan of the Golden Horde.) Kuchum, Ibak's grandson (ca. 1556–98), was at war with Yadigar, the khan of Sibir. Yadigar appealed in 1556 to the czar of Muscovy, Ivan the Terrible, but between 1563 and 1569 he was defeated and killed by Kuchum, who remained master of the khanate of Sibir. In order to consolidate his rule, Kuchum consented to recognize the czar's suzerainty, but once established in his khanate he disputed with Russia over the protectorate of Ostyak and attacked the blockhouse trading posts founded by the Russian Stroganov. At the same time he zealously strove to propagate the faith of Islam in Siberia.

Ivan the Terrible sent the Cossack chief Ermak against Siberia in 1579. Meanwhile, Kuchum entrusted his forces (Turko-Mongol warriors and Votiak and Vogul natives) to his nephew Makhmet-kul (Muhammad-quli), who set up a "fortified camp at the mouth of the Tobol, under the Chuvash mountain, to protect the approaches to Sibir." But in 1581 the Russians, "thanks to their arquebuses," captured this position and took possession of Sibir, forcing Kuchum to flee.

Nevertheless, old Kuchum continued his bush fighting, and in 1584 he surprised Ermak on an island of the Irtysh. The Cossack chief was drowned while retreating, his companions were killed, and Kuchum reoccupied Sibir.

The Russians had to reconquer the khanate yard by yard, and as they advanced they founded military colonies at Tyumen (1586), Tobolsk (1587), and Tomsk. Kuchum, defeated in a final battle on the Ob on August 20, 1598, took refuge with the Nogai, where he was assassinated (1600). His resistance had shed a last ray of glory on the history of the Jenghiz-Khanites in the North.[19]

14

The Last Jagataites

After an eclipse in Tamerlane's day, the khanate of Jagatai—
or, as Turkish and Persian historians call it, Mogholistan—enjoyed
an unlooked-for renaissance in the fifteenth century. It will be
remembered that this khanate comprised, on the one hand,
Mogholistan proper—that is, the Issyk Kul region round Tokmak
and Karakol, the Ili basin and its tributaries, the Tekes and the
Kunges, the Kara-Tal basin, and the basin of the Ebi Nor and
the Manas; on the other, it included Uiguristan, or former country
of the Uigur, that is, the region of Kucha, Kara Shahr, and
Turfan or Kara-khoja. To this may be added Kashgaria or Alti-
shahr, with the cities of Kashgar, Yarkand, and Khotan. Under
the suzerainty of the Jagataite khans, Kashgaria comprised the
patrimony of the Dughlat emirs. These, like the Jagataites, were
of Mongol stock, and were in fact as powerful as they throughout
this region.

Several of the Jagataite khans of the fifteenth century seem
to have had interesting personalities, as may be deduced from
fragmentary data in the *Ta'rikh-i Rashidi*. One of them, Vais-
khan (ca. 1418–28), is mentioned as having worked at the irrigation of the Turfan or Kara-khoja oasis.[1] As a good Muslim, he
waged war upon the Oirat or Kalmucks—the western Mongols
who were "pagan"—and was taken prisoner by their chief Esen-
(Ye-hsien in Chinese) taiji (or Taichi), the son of their khan
Toghon. The Oirat khans, although pure Mongols, were not

491

Jenghiz-Khanites, and the *Ta'rikh-i Rashidi* notes that Esen
treated Vais-khan with the greatest respect and released him at
once.[2] In a second defeat inflicted upon him by Esen, in the
Ili region,[3] Vais, whose horse had fallen, was saved by the devotion of his vassal Sayyid 'Ali, head of the Dughlat house and
lord of Kashgar, who gave him his own mount, and was himself
fortunate in making his escape.[4] At a third encounter with the
Oirat, near Turfan, Vais was once more taken prisoner, and this
time he was not set free until he allowed his sister to enter
Esen-taiji's family. As was seen earlier, in connection with Transoxiana, all the leaders of secondary hordes sought to ennoble
their posterity by marrying Jenghiz-Khanite princesses.

On the death of Khan Vais (1429), his two sons Yunus and
Esen-bugha (or Esen-buqa) II quarreled over the throne; or
rather, their respective supporters did so in their names, for
Yunus the elder was hardly more than thirteen years old. It was
the younger boy Esen-bugha II who won the contest, and Yunus
took refuge in Samarkand with the Timurid Olugh-beg.[5]

Notwithstanding his youth, Esen-bugha II reigned over all the
territories of Mogholistan (1429–62). The Dughlat emir Sayyid
'Ali (d. 1457–58), who had helped him to the throne, became
more influential than ever. At this time the Dughlats, under the
suzerainty of the Jagataite khan Aqsu, held Bai and Kucha, but
they had temporarily lost Kashgar, which had been seized from
them by the Timurids of Transoxiana and Khurasan, Shah Rukh
and his son Olugh-beg.[6] About 1433–34, Sayyid 'Ali succeeded
in recovering Kashgar from the agents of Olugh-beg.[7] The
Ta'rikh-i Rashidi praises his reconstructive administration in
Kashgar and the attention he paid to agriculture and the raising
of livestock.

Esen-bugha II was fighting Abu Sa'id, the Timurid king of
Transoxiana. In 1451 he led a plundering expedition against the
towns of Sairam, Turkestan, and Tashkent on the northern borders of the Timurid realm. Abu Sa'id pursued him as far as
Talas.[8] After another attack by Esen-bugha, this time in the
Andizhan region of Fergana, Abu Sa'id determined to split the
forces of the house of Jagatai. He summoned Yunus from exile
in Shiraz, and lent him troops with which to fight his younger
brother Esen-bugha. Thus supported, Yunus was recognized as
khan in the western part of Mogholistan, near the Ili, while

Esen-bugha remained lord of the eastern provinces, namely, Aksu, Yulduz, and Uiguristan (1456). A little later, Yunus tried to subjugate Kashgar. The ruler of Kashgar, the Dughlat emir Sayyid 'Ali, summoned Esen-bugha to his aid. Esen-bugha hastened from the Yulduz and joined forces with Sayyid 'Ali, and together they put Yunus to flight at Kona Shahr, northeast of Kashgar on the Aksu road.[9] Having lost his followers, Yunus sought reinforcements from Abu Sa'id in Transoxiana. In this way he was able to re-establish himself in the Ili and Issyk Kul region.

Esen-bugha, still ruler of Aksu, the Yulduz region, and Mogholistan, died in 1462. His son Dust Muhammad, a young man without experience (he was only seventeen), alienated the mullahs by his dissolute behavior and angered the powerful Dughlat family by a plundering raid on Kashgar. He died in 1469, in time to escape a general revolt. Yunus, his uncle, khan of the Ili and the Issyk Kul, at once took possession of Aksu, which was then regarded as the "capital" of Mogholistan. Dust Muhammad's young son Kebek II was rescued by supporters and taken to Kara Shahr (Jalish) and Turfan in Uiguria, where he was proclaimed khan. But four years later, these same adherents put the child to death and brought his head to Yunus. Although by this murder Yunus became sole lord of all Mogholistan, he expressed only horror at the assassins and ordered their execution (1472).[10]

YUNUS AND THE JAGATAITE REVENGE UPON THE HOUSE OF TAMERLANE

After his restoration at Aksu, Yunus was faced with only one serious threat: an invasion by the Oirat or Kalmucks, led by Amasanji-taiji, son of Esen-taiji. The Oirat attacked him near the Ili (the Ailah of the *Ta'rikh-i Rashidi*), defeated him, and forced him to withdraw to the neighborhood of the town of Turkestan.[11] But their action shows that this was no more than a nomad coup without political consequences. As soon as the Oirat had gone, Yunus returned from the Syr Darya to the Ili, from semisedentary to nomad country. This he had to do to please the tribes of Mogholistan, who expected their khan, as a good Jenghiz-Khanite, to forget his urban tastes and his Shirazi culture and lead the ancestral life in felt tents.[12] Meanwhile, Kashgar and Yarkand, the cities dependent on Mogholistan, were governed by the two sons of the Dughlat emir Sayyid 'Ali, Saniz-mirza first (1458–64) and then Muhammad Haidar I (1465–80). The *Ta'rikh-i Rashidi* asserts that Saniz, a violent but generous man, governed Kashgar so well that his times were afterward remembered as a Golden Age.[13] Muhammad Haidar, who followed him, at first governed Kashgar and Yarkand in peace under the suzerainty of Khan Yunus. But Abu Bakr, Saniz' son and Muhammad Haidar's nephew, did not long delay before disturbing that peace.[14] After taking possession of Yarkand, he seized the city of Khotan from other princes related to the Dughlat family. From that time forth, he acted as an independent sovereign. Muhammad Haidar begged Yunus' help against this rebellious nephew, but both he and Yunus were twice defeated by Abu Bakr before Yarkand (1479–80). After this double victory, Abu Bakr took Kashgar too from his uncle Muhammad Haidar, who was compelled to withdraw in 1480 to Aksu and Khan Yunus.[15]

Though Yunus was unable to get his own way in these quarrels between the Dughlat emirs of Kashgaria proper, the end of his reign was marked by considerable successes both in China and Transoxiana. The *Ming-shih* relates that in 1473 a sultan of Turfan named 'Ali (Ha-li) seized the Hami oasis in the Gobi Desert from a Khitan dynasty in vassalage to China. A Chinese column dispatched to Turfan failed to catch the aggressor, who, as soon as his pursuers turned back, reoccupied Hami. In 1476 this 'Ali or "Ha-li" sent an embassy with "tribute" to Peking. If the chronology of the *Ming-shih* is accurate, "Ha-li's" reign corresponds to that of Yunus.[16]

However this may be, Khan Yunus seized the occasion (p. 463) of the decline of the Timurid dynasty to intervene as arbitrator in Transoxianan affairs. The two Timurid princes, Ahmed king of Samarkand and 'Umar-shaikh king of Fergana, Sultan Abu Sa'id's sons, expended all their strength in fruitless rivalry for the possession of Tashkent, which 'Umar-shaikh had appropriated. More than once Yunus had to protect 'Umar against Ahmed, with the result that the principality of Fergana became his vassal state. Lastly he profited by his role of arbiter and disinterested mediator to win in 1484 the assent of both parties to his acquisition of contested Tashkent and Sairam.[17] Yunus then chose Tashkent for his residence and it was there that he died, in 1486.[18]

By settling in an ancient city like Tashkent, on the threshold of populous Transoxiana, Yunus-khan fulfilled his life's dream. Ever since his years of exile, when as a young man in Shiraz he had tasted the delights of Persian civilization, this cultured Jenghiz-Khanite had dreamed nostalgically of the sedentary way of life. From a sense of duty to his "Mongols," he had constrained himself for years to live as a nomad in the valley of the Ili and the Yulduz, on the slopes of the T'ien Shan.[19] But in this he was merely fulfilling his obligations as a king.[20] The portrait of him in the *Ta'rikh-i Rashidi*, based on personal impressions given to Muhammad Haidar by Nasir ad-Din 'Ubaidallah, stresses the visitor's surprise: "I expected to see a Mongol, and I beheld a man of the Persian type, with a full beard; he was elegant and with a refinement of speech and manner such as is rarely found even among Persians." [21] Therefore, as soon as he became ruler of Tashkent (he was then nearly eighty), he decided to live there. Some of the nomads of his following, alarmed at the idea of leading a sedentary existence in the Tadzhik fashion, departed and sped loose-reigned to their beloved steppes of the Yulduz and Uiguristan, taking with them Yunus' second son Ahmed, who seems to have shared their taste for the free life. The khan did not give chase, since the presence of Ahmed among them guaranteed their loyalty.[22]

After his father died, Ahmed reigned over that part of the khanate—Ili, Yulduz, and the land of Turfan—until his own death (1486–1503). Happy in his steppes, he fought successfully against the Oirat or Kalmucks, on the one hand, and the Kirghiz-Kazakhs, on the other. The *Ta'rikh-i Rashidi* observes that the Oirat gave him the respectful surname of *Alasha*, "the Killer." [23] Around 1499, he seized Kashgar and Yangi-Hissar from the Dughlat emir Abu Bakr. At home this energetic Jenghiz-Khanite, by means of a series of punitive expeditions and executions, succeeded in subduing the chiefs of rebel tribes.

The *Ming-shih* gives an account of Ahmed's enterprises—in Chinese, he was "A-ha-ma, sultan of Turfan"—in the Hami oasis. In 1482, Hami had been reconquered from the Jagatai khanate by Prince Ha-shen, a descendant of the local Khitan dynasty, who was supported by China. In 1488, Ahmed killed Ha-shen in an ambush and took possession of the country. The following year, Ha-shen's people recovered Hami. In 1493, Ahmed captured the lord of Hami and the Chinese resident and held them prisoner. The court of Peking retaliated by closing its frontiers to caravans from Turfan and by expelling from Kansu the traders from Uiguria. This, says the *Ming-shih,* gave rise to such resentment against Ahmed in Uigur and Jagatai country that he had to resign himself to leaving Hami to the local dynasty, i.e., under Chinese influence.

THE JAGATAITES THROWN BACK EAST OF THE T'IEN-SHAN RANGE; INFLUENCE OF THE TIMURID RENAISSANCE IN KASHGARIA; THE HISTORIAN HAIDAR-MIRZA

While Ahmed reigned from Aksu and Turfan over eastern Mogholistan and Uiguristan (1486–1503), his elder brother Mahmud had succeeded their father Yunus at Tashkent and in western Mogholistan (1487–1508). It was related earlier that the last Timurids of Samarkand tried to recover Tashkent from Mahmud in 1488, but were defeated by him near the city, on the Chirchik or Parak, and Tashkent remained the seat of the Mongol khan.[24] Unluckily, Mahmud committed a grave error in welcoming the celebrated Muhammad Shaybani, who at that time was a mere adventurer and came to place his sword at the khan's service. In recognition, Mahmud gave him as fief the city of Turkestan (between 1487 and 1493).[25] Aided by overly trusting Mahmud, Muhammad Shaybani seized Bukhara and Samarkand from the last Timurids and in 1500 made himself king of Transoxiana. Mahmud had cause to regret his generosity, for hardly had Muhammad Shaybani possessed himself of Transoxiana than he turned against him. Mahmud appealed for help to his brother Ahmed, who hastened to Tashkent from Uiguria, but Shaybani defeated them and took them both prisoner at the battle of Akhsi, northeast of Kokand, in Fergana. This time he treated them courteously, though not without deriding the naiveté of Mahmud, to whom he owed his success, and he released them without delay (1502–3), retaining Tashkent and Sairam. Shortly afterward, in the winter of 1503–4 Ahmed died of paralysis at Aksu. Mahmud was foolish enough to fall once more into Shaybani's hands, and this time was put to death near Khodzhent (1508–9).[26]

Mahmud's death marks the final ejection of the Jagataites from western Turkestan. Having been thrust back east of the T'ien Shan, they remained there for another hundred years. In Uiguristan, Turfan, Kara Shahr (Jalish), and Kucha, Ahmed's eldest son Mansur-khan had been recognized as khan on his father's death, and he was to reign over this region for forty years (1503–43). At first he met with difficulties. The Dughlat emir of Kashgar, Abu Bakr, entered Aksu, where he plundered the treasure of the Jagataites, after which he went on to destroy the cities of Kucha and Bai.[27] In 1514, Mansur's younger brother Sa'id-khan in his turn captured Kashgar (May–June, 1514), Yarkand, and Khotan from Abu Bakr and forced him to flee to Ladakh.[28] In this war against a rebel Dughlat, Sa'id was seconded by another Dughlat, who was loyal to the house of Jagatai: the historian Dughlat-mirza. Sa'id would thereupon reign over Kashgaria proper (1514–33),[29] while his elder brother Mansur would govern Mogholistan (Ili, Yulduz) and Uiguristan (1503–43). The cordial relations between these two brothers ensured peace in Central Asia. "Travelers could journey from Fergana to Hami and into China in perfect safety." [30]

The *Ta'rikh-i Rashidi* of Muhammad Haidar II (Haidar-mirza), the heir of the Dughlat family, bears witness to the relatively advanced culture of the descendants of Jagatai and of the house of Dughlat at that time. It has been noted that during his stay among the Jagataites, Khan Yunus (1456–86), who had indeed spent part of his youth in Shiraz, acquired the manners and elegance of a Persian. Similarly, Haidar-mirza (1499 or 1500–1551) exemplifies a prince of Mongol origin completely transformed by his milieu.[31] Did he know Mongolian? Nothing is less certain, as Elias points out, for to so sincere a Muslim as he was, his ancestral tongue must have seemed no more than a language of "pagans." In fact, he spoke Jagatai Turkish, as his family had long done. Yet it was in Persian that he wrote his history of the Mongols of Central Asia, known by the title of *Ta'rikh-i Rashidi*,[32] while his neighbor and friend the Timurid Baber, who like himself was the author of some immortal memoirs, remained faithful to the Jagatai Turkish dialect. The existence of such cultured men as these shows that, in the first half of the sixteenth century, eastern Turkestan—the former khanate of eastern Jagatai—where today culture has sunk to a deplorably low level, was a flourishing intellectual center. Though it lacked the glories of the old literary heart of Transoxiana—since neither Kashgar, Aksu, nor Turfan could rival Bukhara and Samarkand—the influence of Samarkand and Bukhara was strong enough even there to illuminate the whole country during the Turko-Persian renaissance, which must ever be associated with the Timurids. Haidar-mirza's close friendship with the great Baber, who before founding the empire of India was the last Timurid king of Fergana, shows how the khans of the house af Jagatai and all the Dughlat emirs modeled themselves upon the West. Between Baber's Iranized Samarkand and what is today Chinese Turkestan, relations were unbroken and exchanges constant. Thus, while Baber the Transoxianan wrote in Jagatai Turkish, Haidar-mirza, emir of Mogholistan, wrote in Persian. The Jagataite Sa'id-khan, Haidar-mirza's suzerain, spoke Persian as beautifully as he spoke Turkish.

It would be wrong, therefore, to think of the empire of the last khans of Jagatai in the sixteenth century as a country in decline. The existence of such cultivated individuals as Khan Yunus and Haidar-mirza is evidence to the contrary. This land, in which the Chinese have stifled national characteristics and qualities, which they have jealously closed—this land was then refreshed and enlivened by every cultural breeze from Irano-Turkic Islam. The career of Khan Yunus proves it. This pupil of the literati of Shiraz later reigned over Kucha and Turfan. Haidar-mirza, a prince of the Renaissance, fought with Baber in Transoxiana and helped the Jenghiz-Khanite Sa'id-khan to recover Kashgar and Yarkand before going on in 1541 to conquer Kashmir for himself. Despite the inveterate nomadism of the Yulduz and Uiguristan tribes, which gave such trouble to the last descendants of Jagatai, the final result of Jagataite domination was to link not only Kashgaria but the ancient Uigur country of Kucha, Kara Shahr, and Turfan with the Persian and Iranized Turkic civilization of Samarkand and Herat.

The Last Jagataites

The Jagatai khans tried to bring this Muslim Turko-Iranian culture of the Timurid renaissance to the Far East, to the very frontiers of Ming China. The *Ming-shih,* corroborated by the *Ta'rikh-i Rashidi,* shows Khan Mansur waging war on China, and the second of these sources represents this conflict as a Holy War against the "pagans."[33] The stake was still the Hami oasis. In 1513, the local prince of Hami, called in Chinese transcription Pa-ya-tsi, made submission to Mansur. In 1517, Mansur settled in Hami and from there launched raids into China proper, in the direction of Tunhwang, Suchow, and Kanchow in Kansu. Meanwhile, his brother Sa'id-khan, ruler of Kashgaria, carried the Holy War into the Tibetan province of Ladakh, where in 1531 the historian Haidar-mirza was in command of his troops.[34]

Mansur was succeeded in the khanate of Uiguristan or Turfan by his son Shah-khan, who reigned from 1545 until about 1570. According to the *Ming-shih* (the *Ta'rikh-i Rashidi* ends at this reign),[35] Shah-khan had to fight his own brother Muhammad (Ma-hei-ma), who seized part of the Hami country and obtained the aid of the Oirat or Kalmucks. At Shah-khan's death, about 1570, Muhammad became ruler of Turfan, but had to defend himself in his turn against a third brother named Sufi-sultan (Sofei Su-tan), who by means of an embassy attempted to win the support of China. After his day, the texts are silent on the subject of the Jagataite khanate of Turfan. It is known, however, that a sultan of Turfan whom the Chinese regarded as a genuine Jagataite sent an embassy to the court of Peking in 1647, and a second one in 1657.[36]

In the Jagataite khanate of Kashgaria, Sa'id-khan had been succeeded by his son 'Abd ar-Rashid (1533–65). The new ruler promptly quarreled with the powerful Dughlat family and had one of its leaders, Sayyid Muhammad-mirza, the uncle of the historian Haidar-mirza, put to death.[37] Haidar-mirza himself, who had served Sa'id-khan faithfully and conquered Ladakh for him, feared a similar fate and left for India, where in 1541 he became ruler of Kashmir. According to the *Zabdat at-Tavarikh,* Rashid's reign was spent in curbing the Kirghiz-Kazakhs of the Great Horde, who made incursions into the Ili and Issyk Kul region. The brave 'Abd al-Latif, Rashid's eldest son, was killed during a battle against Nazar the Kirghiz khan.[38] Notwithstanding all his efforts, Rashid was unable to prevent the Kirghiz-Kazakhs from seizing the greater part of Mogholistan proper—that is, the Ili and Kungei region—so that his possessions were reduced to Kashgaria alone. This emerges clearly in a somewhat embarrassed passage in Haidar-mirza.[39]

Rashid, who lived until 1565, was succeeded as khan of Kashgaria by one of his sons, 'Abd al-Karim, who was still reigning in 1593, when Ahmed Razi wrote.[40] It seems that at this time the "capital" of Kashgaria—the khan's usual headquarters—was Yarkand. Kashgar was the appanage of one of 'Abd al-Karim's brothers, named Muhammad. It was apparently this Muhammad who had succeeded 'Abd al-Karim at Yarkand when the Portuguese Jesuit Benedict de Goës passed through the country at the end of 1603. Aksu was then governed by Muhammad's nephew, and Jalish (Kara Shahr, or Goës' "Cialis") by his bastard. The sources tell nothing more of this dynasty. Elias believes that one member of it may have been a certain Isma'il-khan who lived in the third quarter of the seventeenth century.[41] But by that time the Jagataite khanate of Kashgaria must have been parceled out into the subkhanates of Yarkand, Kashgar, Aksu, and Khotan, and effective control would have passed into the hands of the khojas.

THE KHOJAS OF KASHGARIA

The khojas, as that term was understood in Transoxiana and Kashgaria, were devout Muslims who claimed descent from the prophet Muhammad or from the first four Arab caliphs. In the Bukhara and Kashgar regions, there were many such families. The *Ta'rikh-i Rashidi* tells how strongly these saintly persons influenced Khan Sa'id (1514–33). So devout was this khan that he wanted to become a dervish, and only the opportune arrival at Kashgar of the khoja Muhammad Yusuf from Samarkand prevented him. Muhammad Yusuf convinced him that it was possible to win salvation while still living in the world.[42] Khan Sa'id welcomed another khoja with no less veneration: one Hazrat Makhdumi Nura, who was highly reputed both as a miracle worker and as a teacher. The *Ta'rikh-i Rashidi* mentions his apostolate in Kashgaria around 1530 and his departure for India in 1536.[43] In 1533, according to local tradition, an eminent khoja from Samarkand, who had come to Kashgar to take part in negotiations between the khan and the Uzbeks, "settled in the country, and by two wives, one from Samarkand, the other from

Kashgar, had two sons. These sons handed down their mutual hatred to their children, and Kashgaria was torn between two factions, the Aqtaghlik ("people of the White Mountain"), who ruled in Kashgar, and the Qarataghlik ("people of the Black Mountain"), who ruled in Yarkand." [44]

Whatever may have been the true origin of this division, from the end of the sixteenth century and for three quarters of the seventeenth the two factions—divided by religious disputes as well as personal rivalries—shared effective power in Kashgaria. The Aqtaghlik found support among the Kirghiz-Kazakhs of the Ili, the Qarataghlik among the Kara-Kirghiz of the southern T'ien Shan. The temporal khanate of the Jagatai family came gradually under the control of these two groups of "Muslim clergy" until in about 1678 Isma'il, the last khan of Kashgar, took action against them. He drove out the leader of the Aqtaghlik party, the khoja Hazrat Apak or Hazrat Afak. Hazrat Apak sought help from the Jungars or western Mongols (Kalmucks), who entered Kashgar, took Isma'il prisoner, and appointed Hazrat Apak in his place. Jungar help also enabled Hazrat Apak to triumph over the rival faction, the Qarataghliks of Yarkand, and to make that city his capital. Kashgaria was thus reunited, but under a "Muslim theocracy" and as a protectorate of the new Mongol empire of the Jungars. [45]

15

The Last Empires of Mongolia from the Fifteenth to the Eighteenth Century

ANARCHY IN MONGOLIA AFTER 1370

The empire founded in China by the Mongol grand khan Kublai had been overthrown in 1368 by the Chinese revolt. Driven from Peking by the Chinese, Kublai's descendant Toghan Temür died at Yingchang or Kailu, on the Shara Muren, on May 23, 1370, bewailing the magnitude of the disaster. The Chinese dynasty of the Ming (1368–1644), having thrust the Jenghiz-Khanites out of its national territory, was not slow in pursuing them into Mongol country.

In Karakorum, Toghan Temür's son, Prince Ayurshiridhara, on learning of his father's death, assumed the title of grand khan and reigned there from 1370 to 1378 in the vain hope of one day recovering the throne of China. So far from achieving this, he had to face an attack by the Chinese, who penetrated far into Mongolia. In 1372, their best general Hsü Ta advanced toward Karakorum, but was halted on the Tula. At Ayurshiridhara's death, his son Toquz Temür succeeded him at Karakorum (1378–88), capital of a Mongol Empire that was now reduced to its original territory. In 1388, a Chinese army of 100,000 men again entered Mongolia and defated Toquz Temür's troops in a great battle south of the Bor Nor, between the Khalka and the Kerulen.

After this disaster, Toquz was assassinated by one of his kinsmen. As a result of this repeated loss of face, the house of Kublai fell into such discredit that most of the Mongol tribes reclaimed their autonomy. Ugechi or Ökächi, the principal tribal chief to rebel against the fallen Kublaids, was, according to Sanang Sechen, the prince of the Kergüd—i.e., in Mongolian, of the Kirghiz—a people dwelling at that time along the upper Yenisei as far as Lake Kosogol.[1] Ugechi repudiated the suzerainty of the Kublaid grand khan Elbek, defeated and killed him in 1399, and usurped the hegemony of the tribes.

Yung Lo, emperor of China, the third and most remarkable of the Ming sovereigns, was naturally delighted by this usurpation, which added to Mongol dissension and, by overthrowing the house of Kublai in Mongolia, relieved the Chinese of the nightmare of a Jenghiz-Khanite revenge. He therefore recognized Ugechi. According to the *Ming-shih,* however, Ugechi was then beaten by two chiefs of rebel tribes: Aruqtai (in Chinese, A-lu-t'ai), chief of the Asod, and Mahamu, chief of the Oirat.[2] Asod is the Mongol name of the Alans or As. These people, who were of Iranian race (more precisely Scytho-Sarmatian) and who originated in the Caucasus (Kuban and Terek), had in the thirteenth century contributed large contingents to the Mongol army of China. Mongol regiments made up of Alans had been cut to pieces by the Chinese at Chenchow in 1275 and other groups of Alans in the service of Kublai's house had sent a letter to the Pope from Peking in 1336.[3] The Asod of 1400 no doubt represented one of the Alan clans that had followed the Kublaids on their retreat from China to Mongolia, and who, becoming assimilated with the Mongols, had remained to share their fortunes. The Oirat or Oirad, it will be remembered, was a powerful tribe of forest Mongols, established during the Jenghiz-Khanite period on the western shore of Lake Baikal. From the seventeenth century onward, the Oirat seem to have consisted of four subtribes: the Choros, the Turbet (Dörböd, Dörböt), the Khoshot, and the Törghüt or Torghut. The royal family—at least at this time—belonged to the Choros clan.

To emphasize their complete independence of other Mongol pretenders, Aruqtai and Mahamu made a point of rendering homage directly to the court of Peking, a formal gesture designed both to proclaim their own sovereignty and to win the favor of the Ming. It appears that the Oirat took advantage of the situation to extend their hegemony over the whole of western Mongolia, from the western shore of Lake Baikal to the upper Irtysh, with the intention of expanding yet farther to the southwest, in the direction of the Ili (as the *Ta'rikh-i Rashidi* will soon show). But central and eastern Mongolia was to remain in a state of confusion, for, with Aruqtai and Mahamu, Ugechi's son Essekü is said by Sanang Sechen to have persisted in his claim to the supreme khanate until his death in 1425.

In 1403–4, however, a Jenghiz-Khanite restoration occurred in the person of a son of Elbek, whom the Mongol historian Sanang Sechen names Oljäi Temür and whom the *Ming-shih* refers to only by the Sanskrit Buddhist designation of Punyasri (in Chinese, Pen-ya-shö-li).[4] Aruqtai soon rallied to the side of this representative of legitimacy. The court of Peking was understandably perturbed by the reappearance in China of Kublai's family, and Emperor Yung Lo tried to exact a gesture of vassalage from Oljäi Temür. On being met with refusal, he entered Mongolia, advanced as far as the upper Onon and Jenghiz Khan's native plains, and routed Oljäi Temür's and Aruqtai's forces (1410–11). This defeat was fatal to Oljäi Temür, for it deprived him of prestige. The Oirat chief Mahamu attacked him, crushed him, and seized the hegemony (ca. 1412).

Up to this time, Mahamu had maintained good relations with Emperor Yung Lo, because for the Oirats or western Mongols it was natural to seek the support of the court of China against the Kublaids and other Mongol chiefs of the east. But as soon as he became powerful enough, and believed himself able to impose his hegemony upon all the tribes and princely families of Mongolia, the Oirat chief did not hesitate to break with the Ming ruler. Yung Lo marched against him across the Gobi, but Mahamu inflicted serious losses on the Chinese army and then slipped away out of reach beyond the Tula (1414, 1415). These nomads, who until of late had been slackened and softened by the ease of Chinese life, regained their age-old toughness with their return to their native steppes. Moreover, these were Oirat, that is, western tribes from the forest. Having come less into contact with the fruits of the Jenghiz-Khanite conquest than the nomads of the Orkhon and the Kerulen, they no doubt retained more of their native vigor. Nevertheless, Mahamu's prestige must have suffered temporarily by the Chinese invasion, because he too had failed to keep the Ming armies out of the Mongol plains.

According to the *Ming-shih,* Aruqtai then reappeared on the scene and reinstated Pen-ya-shö-li, that is, Oljäi Temür, as grand khan (ca. 1422). He devastated the borders of Kansu as far as Ningsia and then, when Yung Lo came hurrying to chastise him, retreated northward across the Gobi, eluding capture. Shortly afterward, the *Ming-shih* continues, he put Oljäi Temür to death and proclaimed himself grand khan. Emperor Yung Lo more than once campaigned against him (1424, 1425), but without success, despite a fortunate diversion, when the Oirat chief Toghon Temür, Mahamu's son and successor, rebelled against Aruqtai's hegemony and defeated him.

This is the account of the Chinese history *Ming-shih.* It is to be feared, however, that under the name of A-lu-tai the writer confuses two individuals whom the Mongol historian Sanang Sechen very clearly distinguishes: namely, the Asod chief Aruqtai, whose activity has just been followed as far as 1414 (up to this point, the two sources more or less agree), and another prince named Adai, who in Sanang Sechen's work appears as the leader of the Khorchins or Qorchins.[5] The Khorchins were a tribe of eastern Mongols established east of the Khingan, in the neighborhood of the River Nonni on the Manchurian border. Their chiefs were descendants of either Temuge Ochigin or Qasar, both brothers of Jenghiz Khan. According to Sanang Sechen, in 1425 the khanate was occupied—at any rate in the east—by the Khorchin chief Adai, supported by Aruqtai—clear proof that two men are here involved, and not one as the *Ming-shih* implies. Adai and his vassal Aruqtai together waged war against the Oirat and against China, while, by the usual swing of the pendulum, the Oirat were once more making advances to Emperor Yung Lo. During his last campaigns in Mongolia against Adai (1422–25), Yung Lo supported this Oirat dissidence against the legitimist khanate of the Borjigins.

THE FIRST OIRAT EMPIRE: TOGHON AND ESEN-TAIJI

The policy pursued by the great Ming emperor—to help the young and growing Oirat power in order to bring down the house of Kublai—triumphed only after his death. Between 1434 and 1438, the Oirat chief Toghan or Toghon, Mahamu's son and successor, killed Adai. So Sanang Sechen relates; the *Ming-shih* states that he killed A-lu-t'ai. In any event, he possessed himself of the hegemony of the Mongol tribes. Adzai, a Kublaid prince, Elbek's son and Oljäi Temür's brother, was then proclaimed grand khan by the legitimists (1434 or 1439). In fact, the empire of Mongolia had passed to the Oirat.

The court of China must certainly have congratulated itself upon this revolution, which brought low the still-dreaded Jenghiz-Khanite family and the eastern Mongols—"more dangerous because nearer"—to the advantage of the western Mongols, who, being more remote, seemed less to be feared. The Jenghiz-Khanite nightmare was being dispelled. The new lords of the steppe were a people without any famous past who in Jenghiz-Khanite history had played an obscure and unsung role. Just in this way had the Chinese of the twelfth century foolishly rejoiced to see the Khitan replaced by the Jürchids. But in fact the western Mongols—the Oirat (Oirad) or Confederates, as they called themselves, the Kalmucks, as their Turkic neighbors of Kashgaria termed them—had no other ambition than to carry on the Jenghiz-Khanite tradition and to restore to their own advantage the great Mongol Empire that the degenerate Kublaids had so foolishly allowed to slip through their fingers.[6]

Oirat expansion began in the southwest, at the expense of the Jagataites of "Mogholistan" or Jenghiz-Khanite khans who reigned over the Ili and the Yulduz and over the region of Kucha and Turfan. The Oirat chief Toghon attacked the Jagataite Khan Vais (who reigned between 1418 and 1428). In this conflict, the battlefield of which shifted according to Oirat incursions from the Ili basin to the province of Turfan, the Oirat had the upper hand throughout. Toghon's son Esen-taiji took Vais prisoner and, as the *Ta'rikh-i Rashidi* tells, treated him with great consideration because of his Jenghiz-Khanite blood. In another battle fought near Turfan, Vais was again captured by Esen. This time, in return for the release of his prisoner, Esen demanded that Vais's sister, Princess Makhtum khanim, should become a member of his family. It is clear that the Oirat house, which was not of Jenghiz-Khanite blood, set great store by such an alliance.

When Esen-taiji—the Ye-hsien of the Chinese historians—succeeded his father Toghon, the Oirat or Kalmuck realm was at-

taining the height of its power (1439–55). It now stretched from
Lake Balkhash to Lake Baikal, and from Baikal to the approaches
of the Great Wall. Karakorum, the former Mongol capital, was
one of its possessions. Esen also seized the Hami oasis and, in
1445, the Chinese province of Wu-liang-ha, which corresponds to
later Jehol. Five years later, he requested the hand of a Chinese
princess, just as earlier he had sought that of a Jagataite. The
court of Peking promised this, but failed to keep the promise.
Esen then ravaged the Chinese border near Tatung, north of
Shansi, and the Ming emperor Ying-tsung and his minister the
eunuch Wang Chan marched to meet him. The clash occurred at
T'u-mu, near Süanhwa in northwest Hopei (now Chahar). Esen
inflicted a disastrous defeat upon them, killed more than 100,000
of their men, and took Emperor Ying-tsung prisoner (1449). Yet,
having no aptitude for siege warfare, he was unable to reduce
either Tatung or Süanhwa, the fortified towns of the region, and
returned to Mongolia with his imperial prisoner.[7] Three months
later he came back, advanced as far as Peking, and camped on
the northwestern outskirts of the great city; but all his assaults
were repulsed and he soon ran short of forage. Reinforcements
for the Chinese arrived from Liaotung. As Esen had failed in his
main attack and was now threatened by superior forces after a
setback in an important action, he retreated hurriedly by way of
the Kiu-yung-kuan (Nankow) Pass. Soon afterward he decided to
release Emperor Ying-tsung (1450) and in 1453 he made peace
with China.

The *Ming-shih* further narrates that Esen had recognized as
grand khan a Jenghiz-Khanite figurehead named Toqtoa-buqa,
who had married his sister, and that he wanted the son of this
union to be recognized as the legitimate Jenghiz-khanite heir.
Toqtoa-buqa refused, and Esen killed him. He then (in 1453)
declared himself the vassal of China, a move which placed him
in the light of independent khan without the fiction of Jenghiz-
Khanite suzerainty. He in his turn was assassinated in 1455.

According to the *Ta'rikh-i Rashidi*, Esen was succeeded at the
head of the Oirat or Kalmuck realm by his son Amasanji. At some
ill-defined date between 1456 and 1468, Amasanji invaded the
Jagataite khanate of Mogholistan and defeated the reigning khan
Yunus near the Ili. Yunus was compelled to take flight to the
town of Turkestan. The same source tells that the Jagataite queen

Makhtum khanim, whom Esen had earlier introduced into the Oirat household, made trouble there. An ardent Muslim, she had brought up her sons Ibrahim Ong (Wang) and Ilyas Ong in her own faith. Later, these young men came into conflict with Amasanji, and, after some civil strife, Ibrahim and Ilyas are said to have taken refuge in China.[8]

Notwithstanding these domestic disturbances, the Oirat continued for a long time to alarm their neighbors—particularly in the southwest—by their periodic raids. In that direction lay the territory of the nomad Kirghiz-Kazakhs, very Islamized barbarian Turks whose tribes roved in the steppes of the lower Ili, the Chu, the Sary-Su, and the Turgai, and who under their khans Qasim (ca. 1509–18) and Mumash (ca. 1518–23) were the terror of Shaybanid Transoxiana.[9] It is true that Mumash's successor Tahir-khan (ca. 1523–30) irked these unruly nomads by his authoritarianism, and many clans, according to Haidar-mirza, broke away.[10] Nevertheless, the Kirghiz-Kazakh khanate was reconstituted under Khan Tawakkul, but in the course of the years 1552–55, Tawakkul was forced to flee before an invasion of Oirat who came down like a whirlwind from the Kobdo region to the Ili. Thus the Turkic nomads of the great Balkhash steppe, the terror of the sedentary peoples of Transoxiana, were themselves put to flight by the Mongol nomads of the Altai. It need hardly he said that their fear was shared by the civilized inhabitants of the great Transoxianan towns. Tawakkul had taken refuge in Tashkent with the local Shaybanid Nauruz Ahmed. To the request for help made by his guest, Nauruz replied: "Not even ten princes such as they could do anything against the Kalmucks" (that is, the Oirat).[11] About 1570, the Oirat still held sway from the upper Yenisei to the valley of the Ili.

In short, although after the death of their *taiji* Esen (1455) the Oirat suffered eclipse in the east, where they came face to face with the Jenghiz-Khanites of eastern Mongolia, in the west they continued to threaten the steppes between the Ili and the Caspian.

THE LAST JENGHIZ-KHANITE RESTORATION: DAYAN-KHAN
AND ALTAN-KHAN

The eclipse of the Oirat or western Mongols did not immediately benefit of Jenghiz-Khanites of eastern Mongolia. At the time, the latter were exterminating one another in exhausting family battles. Grand Khan Mandaghol, Jenghiz Khan's twenty-seventh successor, died in 1467 as the result of a war against his great-nephew and heir Bolkho *jinong*, and the latter in his turn was assassinated before he could be proclaimed khan (1470). Of the once so numerous Kublaid family there remained now only a five-year-old boy, Dayan, the son of Bolkho *jinong*, who was "deserted by everyone, even by his mother, who had remarried." [12] Mandaghol's young widow, khatun Mandughai, took the child under her protection and proclaimed him khan. She herself then assumed command of the loyal Mongols and inflicted a defeat on the Oirat. In 1481, she married young Dayan. In 1491–92, this heroic woman, whose exploits recall those of Oelun-eke, Jenghiz Khan's mother, "is again depicted at the head of an army which repulsed the Oirat." It is to her that tradition gives credit for having overthrown Oirat supremacy and restored the hegemony to the eastern Mongols.

Dayan's long reign (1470–1543), through the energy of the queen regent his future wife and later through his personal valor, marked the renaissance of Jenghiz-Khanite authority, if only in the regrouping of the eastern tribes according to the traditional division into left wing (*jun-ghar, jegün-ghar,* or *segon-ghar*) to the east and right wing (*barun-ghar, baraghun-ghar*) to the west. [13] (The whole formation was orientated toward the south.) "The first wing was under the direct command of the khagan, the second under a *jinong* chosen by the khagan from among his brothers or sons. The first consisted of Chahars (the sovereign's section), Khalkas, and Uriangkhans, while the second comprised the Ordos, Tümed, [14] and Jungshiyabo, also known as Kharachins or Karchins." [15] Dayan did not carry through this reorganization without some violence. Some of the Baraghon Tümed, or Tümed of the right (that is, the west), killed one of Dayan's sons whom he had appointed as their leader. "A bitter fight broke out between the two Mongol wings in consequence. Dayan, beaten at first, later triumphed, thanks to the support of the Khorchin, a tribe [from the Nonni basin] that owed obedience to the descendants of Qasar, Jenghiz Khan's brother. He pursued the rebels as far as the Koko Nor, where he received their submission. He then gave them as their *jinong* his third son Barsa-bolod (1512)." Dayan also had to smother a revolt of the Uriangkhans by disbanding their group and dividing them up among the five others.

Lastly, from 1497 to 1505, he led a series of successful raids against the Chinese frontiers, from Liaotung to Kansu.

After Dayan's death in 1543, his children and grandchildren shared out the tribes among themselves. The Chahar tribes went to Bodi-khan, head of the senior branch; he was Dayan's grandson and became grand khan. Bodi-khan settled in the Kalgan and Dolonnor country, which even today forms the center of the Chahar domain. The Mongol supreme khanate continued to be vested in the Chahar royal family from 1544 to 1634 under the khans Bodi (1544–48), Kudang (1548–57), Tümen Sasaktu (1577–93), Sechen (1593–1604), and Legdan (1604–34), this last khan being deposed by the Manchu emperors. Dayan's third son, *jinong* Barsa-bolod, and the latter's son *jinong* Gün Biliktü Mergen (d. 1550), who commanded the Ordos, set up their camp in the loop of the Yellow River (ca. 1528, 1530). Gün Biliktü's younger brother Altan-khan (the Yen-ta of the *Ming-shih*), the most notable of Dayan's grandsons and leader of the Tümed, settled in the northeastern part of the loop, centering at Köke-khoto (Kuku Hoto) or Kweihwacheng.[16] Lastly, Dayan's youngest son, Geresandza Ochigin, was given command of the Khalka tribes, which at this time, according to Courant, must have been concentrated round the River Khalka, the Bor Nor, and the lower Kerulen. From there the Khalkas, driving the Oirat or Kalmucks before them, spread westward to the Ubsa Nor.

These conquests, which thrust the Oirat back toward the Kobdo region, were won by the united Dayanid Mongols under the personal leadership of the king of the Tümed, Altan-khan, with the aid of his great-nephew Khutuktai Sechen khongtaiji, prince of the Ordos. The Oirat, beaten in several encounters, lost Karakorum, the seat and symbol of Mongol imperial sovereignty, in 1552. Two of their tribes, the Törghüt or Torghut and the Khoshot, having been repulsed and beaten by the Dayanids, and driven as far as the Urungu and the Black Irtysh, began their move toward the west.

Altan-khan's reign dates between 1543 and 1583, but even during the reign of his grandfather Dayan he had begun to distinguish himself in the field, particularly in bearing arms against Ming China. In 1529, he plundered the Tatung area in northern Shansi. In 1530, he devastated the district of Ningsia in Kansu, and then that of Süanhwa, northwest of Peking. In 1542, he killed the Chinese general Chang Shih-ch'ung, and is said to have taken 200,000 prisoners and 2,000,000 head of livestock. In thus invading Chinese territory almost every year, via Tatung or Süanhwa, he was reviving the old Jenghiz-Khanite tradition. In 1550, he advanced to the gates of Peking and set fire to the outskirts of the city. Before returning home, he went on to ravage the Paoting region. Nevertheless, this energetic Jenghiz-Khanite thought of other things besides war. Twice, in 1550 and 1574, he demanded that the Chinese should set up markets at the frontier posts for the barter of Mongol livestock and Chinese merchandise. In his expeditions he was actively supported by his great-nephew, the Ordos prince Khutuktai Sechen khongtaiji, who was born in 1540 and died in 1586, and who at various times harried the Chinese frontier between Ningsia and Yülin. Khutuktai's campaigns were recorded by his great-grandson, the Mongol historian Sanang Sechen.

PARTITION OF THE DAYANID EMPIRE: THE ORDOS AND KHALKA KHANATES

The great weakness of these Mongol nations was their custom of dividing up the family inheritance. The Dayanid empire was not unlike that of Jenghiz Khan in its constitution, although it achieved hardly any conquests abroad and its expansion was limited to Mongolia. After its founder's death, it became a sort of federal family state, of which the various leaders, all brothers or cousins, recognized the supremacy of the leader of one branch in the person of the Chahar chief. This partition resulted in more complete disintegration than Jenghiz Khan's successors had ever known. An example is the case of the founder of the Ordos realm, Gün Biliktü Mergen *jinong*, a powerful ruler. At his death in 1550, his tribes were meticulously shared out among his nine sons.[17] Noyandara, the eldest, received no more than the "banner" of the Dörben Qoriya, the present-day tribe of Wang.[18]

Federal ties were also slackened, together with the theoretical obedience due to the branch in which the supreme khanate was vested. Here again the process is similar to the one that had undermined the authority of Jenghiz Khan's immediate successors. From the middle of the thirteenth century, those princes whose appanages lay farthest from Karakorum were like independent sovereigns. Rubruck has pointed out that Batu the khan of Kipchak was to all intents and purposes the equal of the grand khan Mongka. Twenty years later, the grand khan Kublai could not even command the obedience of Qaidu, khan of the Imil. The same thing happened with Dayan's descendants. When the Khalka princes had driven the Oirat back to Kobdo and occupied the vast territory between the Kerulen and the Khangai Mountains, those who lay farthest from the Chahar country felt practically independent. One such was a great-grandson of the Khalka prince Geresandza, named Shului Ubasha khongtaiji, who around 1609 had occupied the heart of the former Oirat realm, in the region of the Kirgis Nor and the Ubsa Nor, whence he drove back the Oirat to the Black Irtysh and Tarbagatai (1620, 1623). He took the title of Altyn (or Altan)-khan and founded a khanate of that name which lasted until about 1690. Another Khalka prince, one of his cousins, Laikhor-khan, who was also a conqueror of the Oirat, settled east of Altyn-khan, and west of Uliassutai; his son Subati took the title of Dzasagtu-khan, and he too gave his name to the khanate. A third Khalka prince, Geresandza's grandson Tumengken, founded the khanate of Sain Noyan at the headwaters of the Orkhon, on the upper Ongkin and on the Selenga. Tumengken's brother Abatai was the progenitor of the Tushetu-khans, whose khanate, separated from Sain Noyan by the Orkhon, included the basin of the Tula, the region known as Urga (Ulan Bator). Family precedence decreed that the Sain Noyan house should be the vassal of the Tushetu khanate, from which it did not gain independence and equal status until 1724. Finally a great-grandson of Geresandza, also named Shului, who settled on the Kerulen, took the title of Sechen-khan and gave this name to the fifth Khalka khanate.[19]

Although they were all descendants of Geresandza, these five khans were not always very closely united. In 1662, Altyn-khan Lobdzang (ca. 1658–91) attacked his neighbor the Dzasagtu-khan, took him prisoner, and put him to death. As a result of this, Tushetu-khan formed a league with the other Mongol princes and so forced Altyn-khan to flee. Thanks to foreign support (the Oirat tribe of the Jungar and the court of Peking), Altyn was able temporarily to reinstate himself, but in 1682 he was surprised and captured by the new Dzasagtu-khan; in 1691, he disappeared and with him his khanate. This disappearance of the most westerly of the Khalka khanates, as will be seen, enabled the old Oirat or Kalmucks to take their revenge and recover the Altyn-khan territory, later known as the province of Kobdo.[20]

The Dayanid Mongol empire, or restoration, over a restricted area, of the Jenghiz-Khanite empire, foundered like its predecessor among family quarrels. Within a hundred years, the Chahar grand khans enjoyed no more than a purely nominal supremacy over the Ordos khans, and certainly no more, if as much, over the four surviving Khalka khans. The eastern Mongols thus relapsed into the same disorganized state that had prevailed before the days of Dayan.

CONVERSION OF THE EASTERN MONGOLS TO LAMAISM

At this time, the eastern Mongols were coming very strongly under the influence of the reformed Tibetan lamaism of the Yellow Church. Having been shamanists up to that time, or slightly tinged with the doctrines of the old Tibetan Red Church, the Mongols had escaped Buddhist influence, once so strongly felt by their ancestors in China during the Yüan period that their expulsion from that country had necessarily entailed a certain intellectual impoverishment. But the lamaist Yellow Church, established in Tibet at the beginning of the fifteenth century by Tsong-kha-pa, now aimed at the moral conquest of these peoples, in whom it saw potential defenders.

The Ordos set an example by adopting lamaism in 1566.[21] One of their chiefs, *jinong* Khutuktai Sechen khongtaiji,[22] of the Ushin Banner, had that year brought back from an expedition to Tibet a number of lamas, who began the work of conversion. Khutuktai Sechen in his turn converted in 1576 the powerful chief of the Tümed, his great-uncle Altan-khan, who was then at the zenith of his power.[23] The Ordos and the Tümed next resolved upon the ceremonial restoration among the Mongols of Tibetan Buddhism, in the form of the Yellow Church. There is no doubt, as will be seen, that the precedent of their ancestor Kublai and the lama Phags-pa encouraged them in this policy. Altan-khan and Khutuktai Sechen even invited the grand lama bSod-nams rgya-mts'o, head of the Yellow Church, to come from Tibet. They received him with great pomp on the banks of the Koko Nor, and with him held a Diet at which the Mongol Church was officially inaugurated (1577). Altan-khan recalled that he was the reincarnation of Kublai, while bSod-nams rgya-mts'o was that of Phags-pa. Altan conferred upon bSod-nams the title of Dalai Lama or Tale-Lama, which has been borne by his successors ever since. Thus the Yellow Church consecrated the Jenghiz-Khanite restoration achieved by Dayan and Altan, while in return the regenerated Mongols placed themselves at the service of that church.

On leaving for Tibet, bSod-nams rgya-mts'o left a "living Buddha," Dongkur Manjusri khutukhtu, who took up residence near Altan at Kuku Hoto. After Altan-khan's death (1583), bSod-nams rgya-mts'o returned in 1585 to the Tümed to officiate at his cremation.

The Chahar grand khan Tümen Sasaktu (1557–93) was converted in his turn and promulgated a new Mongol code based on Buddhist doctrines. His second successor, the grand khan Legdan (1604–34), also built temples and had the Buddhist compilation of the Kanjur translated from Tibetan into Mongolian. The Khalka people, as early as 1558, had begun to embrace the same beliefs, and in 1602 another "living Buddha," Maitreya khutukhtu, settled among them in the Urga region, where his reincarnations succeeded one another until 1920.[24]

In being converted with their people to Tibetan Buddhism, Altan-khan and the other Dayanids believed that they were following in Kublai's footsteps. But when Kublai was converted, the Mongol conquest of China had been almost complete. And although Altan-khan had more than once crossed the Great Wall and burned the suburbs of Peking, he had achieved no more than that, and the Mongol conquest had to be started again from the beginning. But the prevailing lamaism had an immediately slackening effect on the eastern Mongols. Ordos and Tümed, Chahar and Khalka, especially the former, soon lost their virile qualities under the pious influence of Tibetan clericalism. This Buddhist Church, which had already transformed the terrible Tibetans of the T'ang period into the dreamers and miracle workers of Tsong-kha-pa, brought the modern Mongols even lower, for, lacking any philosophical qualities, they derived nothing from their new religion but bigotry and clericalism. They who at the end of the fifteenth century had set forth to repeat the Jenghiz-Khanite epic now abruptly stopped and sank into pious inertia, with no other concern than to feed their lamas on the fat of the land. Their history, as recorded by the Ordos prince Sanang Sechen, shows that they had forgotten the Conqueror of the World and his glory and dreamed only of the conquest of souls.[25]

Having attained this degree of spiritual advancement and sanctity, the eastern Mongols were ripe to succumb to Kalmuck or Manchu conquest. As Courant has remarked, the only question was which of the two would bring them low.

CONQUEST OF CHINA BY THE MANCHUS

The Tungus people, as we saw, occupy a very large zone in northeast Asia: Manchuria (the Manchu, Dahur, Solon, Manegir, Birar, and Gold peoples), the Russian maritime province (the Oroch people), the east bank of the middle Yenisei and the basin of the two Tunguskas in Siberia (the Yenisei and Chapogir peoples), the Vitim region between the Lena and the Shilka (the Orochon people), and the lands round the Sea of Okhotsk, from the Amur to the approaches of Kamchatka (the Kile, Samagir, Olcha, Negda, Lalegir, Inkagir, Lamut, Uchur, and other peoples). Contrary to what was long believed, these peoples played no part in the ancient history of the Far East, nor during the first part of the Middle Ages until the twelfth century, except for the kingdom of Pohai, founded at the end of the seventh century by one of their tribes. This realm lasted until 926 and included the whole of Manchuria and the extreme north of Korea. Even then, the organization of Pohai was partly owing to Korean emigrants who civilized the Mal-kal Tungus. This state, with its capital at Hu-han-ch'eng south of Ninguta (Ningan) on the Hurka (Mutan), a tributary of the Sungari, represented the first civilized political entity of the Tungus race. As noted earlier, it was destroyed in 926 by the Khitan conqueror A-pao-ki, that is, by a Mongol people.

The Tungus first enter major history with the Jurchids, Jurchens, or Ju-chen, tribes of their own race established in the Ussuri basin in the mountainous forest region that extends across the northeast of later Manchukuo and then across the Russian maritime province. In the first years of the twelfth century, these Jurchids, under an energetic chief named A-ku-ta of the

Wan-yen clan (1113–23), conquered the Khitan realm of Manchuria, Chahar, and northern China (1122), seized from the
Sung Empire of China nearly all the Chinese provinces north
of the Yangtze (1126), and founded a first Tungus empire: the
Kin or Golden Empire, of which Peking was one of the capitals
and which endured from 1122 until its final destruction by the
Jenghiz-Khanite Mongols in 1234. Chinese annals note the valor
with which the last Jurchids disputed every foot of ground with
Jenghiz Khan and his son Ogödäi, and so staved off defeat for
nearly twenty-five years; they note too that the Mongol generals
were often filled with admiration by this hopeless heroism and
loyalty.[26]

After the fall of the Mongol Empire of China, at the beginning
of the Ming dynasty, the Jurchids—or Manchus, as they would
soon be called—dwelling between the Sungari and the Sea of
Japan had more or less recognized Chinese suzerainty. Like their
eleventh-century forebears, they were a group of forest clans
that lived by hunting and fishing, cut off from the mainstreams
of culture.[27] In 1599, the energetic chief Nurkhatsi, or Nurhachi
(in Chinese, Nu-ul-ha-ch'e), began reuniting the seven Jurchid
ayman or tribes into a single khanate and in 1606 founded the
historic Manchu realm. The first headquarters of the royal clan
was Odoli, by the headwaters of the Hurka, a tributary of the
Sungari near the later town of Ninguta; but even before that
time, Nurhachi had established himself farther south, at Chang-
chun, northeast of Mukden, where lay the tombs of four generations of his ancestors. Until then, the Manchu tribes had used
the ancient Jurchid writing, which they owed to the twelfth-
century Kin and which was derived from Chinese ideographs,
but these Sino-Jurchid characters were inadequate to render
Tungusic phonemes, and about 1599 Nurhachi's Manchus
adopted, with some modification, the Mongol alphabet which
stemmed from the old Uigur writing.

Nurhachi soon discovered the state of decadence into which
Ming China had fallen during the reign of Emperor Wan Li
(1573–1620), and in 1616 he proclaimed himself emperor. In
1621–22, he captured the frontier post then called Shenyang,
the Mukden of today, and here in 1625 he established his capital.
In 1622, he occupied Liaoyang. In 1624, he received the submission of the Mongol tribe of the Khorchin, who roamed east

of the Khingan Mountains and west of the Sungari elbow. By the time he died (September 30, 1626), he had made of Manchuria a well-knit realm with a good military organization.

Abakhai (1626–43), Nurhachi's son and successor, continued his father's work. While the Manchus were building up their unity, the Mongols were destroying theirs—or what was left of it. The khan of the Chahar, Legdan or Lingdan (1604–34), who bore the title of grand khan of all the eastern Mongols, had tried in vain to maintain his suzerainty over the tribes. The Ordos and Tümed rebelled against his hegemony. The Ordos chief Erinchin *jinong*, helped by the Kharachin and Abagha tribes, defeated him (1627). The Ordos and Tümed, rather than obey the Chahar khan—a chief of their own race—transferred their homage to the Manchu sovereign Abakhai. The Manchus attacked Legdan and forced him to flee into Tibet, where he died in 1634. The Chahar then submitted in their turn to Abakhai, who allowed the Legdan family to remain as their leaders. Erkekhongor, Legdan's chief son, acknowledged himself Abakhai's vassal in 1635. In that same year, Abakhai also received the homage of *jinong* Erinchin, the chief of the Ordos. In 1649, the Ordos were reorganized into six banners (*gushu*), each under the command of a prince (*jasak*) who descended from the Jenghiz-Khanite *jinong* Gün Biliktü Mergen.[28] Thus the whole of Inner Mongolia found itself enclosed within the Manchu Empire; thenceforth the Chahar, Tümed, and Ordos khans were bound to the Manchu dynasty by ties of loyalty and by a feudal oath of allegiance which was to endure until the fall of the dynasty in 1912.

Strictly speaking, Ming China did not succumb to Manchu attacks; it committed suicide. The Ming emperor Ch'ung-cheng (1628–44) was a literary scholar, and no more. Li Tzu-ch'eng, a bold adventurer, made himself ruler of Honan and Shansi (1640 and later) and at last, on April 3, 1644, took possession of Peking, while the luckless Ch'ung-cheng hanged himself to avoid falling into his hands. One last army remained to the Chinese Empire, the one fighting the Manchus in the Shanhaikwan area. The leader of this army, Wu San-kuei, wishing above all to chastise Li Tzu-ch'eng, came to an understanding with the Manchus and, supported by their troops, descended upon Peking. After a victory on the threshold of Yungping, he

drove the usurper from the capital. He then rendered thanks
to his Manchu auxiliaries and urged them courteously to withdraw. But the Manchus, once inside Peking, behaved as its lords.
Their khan Abakhai died on September 21, 1643, and they proclaimed his six-year-old son Shuen-chih emperor of China. Wu
San-kuei, their dupe and now of necessity their accomplice,
received from them a principality in Shensi before being invested with a larger and more remote viceroyalty in Szechwan
and in Yunnan. It was he, incidentally, who undertook to remove
Li Tzu-ch'eng, the only Chinese military leader capable of opposing the invasion (1644).

Thus the Manchus found themselves lords of northern China,
less by conquest than by trickery. It took them longer to achieve
the submission of southern China; yet they met with nothing
comparable to the resistance put up by the Sung against the
Jenghiz-Khanite Mongols, which had lasted half a century (1234–
79). A Ming prince had been proclaimed emperor in Nanking.
The Manchus took the town and the pretender drowned himself
(1645). Three other Mings, the princes of Lu, Tang, and Kwei,
endeavored to organize resistance farther south, the first at
Hangchow in Chekiang, the second at Fuchow in Fukien, and
the third in the Canton region. But the dissension between them
helped the invader. In 1646, the Manchus overcame the princes
of Lu and Tang and subjugated Chekiang and Fukien. The
prince of Kwei, Yung-li or Yung-ming, who had taken up residence at Kweilin in Kwangsi, and whose entourage was largely
Christian, put up a better fight. His general, also a Christian,
the valiant Chiu Shih-ssu, repulsed the first Manchu offensive
against Kweilin (1647–48). But the Manchus, helped by Chinese
adherents, wiped out the little loyalist army and took Canton,
while the last of the Ming rulers fled to Yunnan (1651).

Now masters of all China, the Manchus, like the Mongols
before them, and even more completely, adapted themselves
to their Chinese surroundings. Their leaders—Shuen-chih (1643–
61), the regents who at the latter's death governed on behalf
of his young son K'ang-hsi (1661–69), and above all K'ang-hsi
himself during his long reign (1669–1722), and then K'ang-
hsi's son Yung-cheng (1723–35), and Yung-cheng's son Ch'ien-
lung (1736–96)—all behaved as Sons of Heaven in the most au-

thentic Chinese tradition. No doubt they were better able to dedicate themselves to this role than Kublai and his grandsons. The Jenghiz-Khanite emperors of China in the thirteenth and fourteenth centuries had always remained Mongol grand khans even after becoming Sons of Heaven; while accepting the heritage of the nineteen Chinese dynasties, they remained the heirs of Jenghiz Khan and suzerains of the other khanates of Turkestan, Persia, and Russia, where their cousins of the houses of Jagatai, Hulägu, and Jöchi held sway. The Manchus, on the other hand—apart from their meager native Manchuria, which at that time was all forests and clearings —had no other interest than the Chinese Empire; that is why they became far more completely Sinicized, with far fewer mental reservations than the house of Kublai. And indeed they were never expelled from China as the Kublaids were; they became assimilated. When in 1912 the Chinese people overthrew their dynasty, the ancient Manchu conquerors had long been absorbed, drowned in the Chinese mass, despite the imperial decrees designed to preserve the purity of their race; and this not only on Chinese soil but in Manchuria itself, where the Tungus element had been so thoroughly assimilated or eliminated by settlers from Hopei or Shansi that ethnographical maps show the country as completely Chinese. The Tungus domain begins only at the Amur. As a result of this penetration, the Manchurian forests, cleared by Celestial immigrants from Mukden to Harbin and from Harbin to Hailung, have given way to plantations of rice and soya.

THE WESTERN MONGOLS IN THE SEVENTEENTH CENTURY

The eastern Mongols, or, more exactly, those of Inner Mongolia, had contributed to the triumph of the Manchu dynasty by rallying to its support in 1635, nine years before the capture of Peking. Afterward, when Manchu domination had been consolidated, some of the Mongols had second thoughts. In 1675 the khan of the Chahar, Burni, chief of the senior branch of Kublaids, tried to provoke a mass rising of eastern Mongols against the emperor K'ang-hsi, beginning with his neighbors the Tümed, but he was too late. Burni was defeated and taken prisoner by the imperial troops. This was the last upheaval in Inner Mongolia, and from then on its "Banners" were docile vassals.

The real danger threatening the Manchu Chinese Empire lay elsewhere. It was not the eastern Mongols, now in hopeless decline, who were to be feared, but those of the west, who, favored by that decline, were attempting to revive Jenghiz Khan's empire for themselves.

Attention has been called to the important part played in the fifteenth century by the western Mongols—the Oirat or Confederates, as they called themselves or, as the Turks named them, the Kalmucks.[29] After ruling all Mongolia from 1434 until about 1552, they had been vanquished by the eastern Mongols, in the person of the Tümed chief Altan-khan, and driven back into the Kobdo region. Even from there they had been expelled by Altyn-khan, one of the Khalka princes, and pushed further westward into Tarbagatai.

Moreover, since the death of their khan Esen-taiji about 1455, the Oirat union had disintegrated. The four confederate peoples who for so long had formed the khanate of western Mongolia had regained their independence. These four peoples, whose history will now be followed, were, on the evidence of Emperor Ch'ien-lung, the Choros or Tsoros; the Dörböd, Dörböt, or Turbet; the Törghüt or Torghut and the Khoshot; plus the Khoit, vassals of the Dörböt.[30] Choros, Dörböt, Torghut, and Khoshot, though politically dissociated, continued to be grouped under the general title of "Four Confederates," *Dörben Oirat.* They were also designated by the name of "people of the left wing" or, literally, of the "left hand," *jägün-ghar* or Jungar, whence the western term Dzungars. This name must originally have applied to the four tribes, as Ch'ien-lung testifies, although it was afterward restricted to the dominant tribe, the Choros.[31] Further, it is known that the princes of the Choros, the Dörböt, and the Khoit belonged to the same family. As for the Torghut (thus named from the Mongol word *torghaq,* plural *torgha'ut,* "guard, sentinel"), they owed obedience to a dynasty which even today boasts of its descent from the ancient Kerayit kings.[32] Finally, the reigning house of the Khoshot claimed descent from Qasar, Jenghiz Khan's brother. The dominant tribe was that of the Choros, known also by the name of Olöt, whence western writers have formed Eleuthes, a term which by a false etymology has sometimes been applied pejoratively to all four Oirat.[33]

In this period, the western Mongols demonstrated not only political unrest (yet to be discussed) but also a new intellectual activity. It was about 1648 that through Zaya Pandita's reform they perfected the ancient Uiguro-Mongol alphabet, introducing by means of diacritical signs seven new characters intended to facilitate the transcription of Mongol sounds.[34]

MOVEMENTS OF PEOPLES AMONG THE WESTERN MONGOLS:
THE KALMUCK MIGRATION

At the beginning of the seventeenth century, the pressure exerted by the Khalka of Altyn-khan on the four Oirat tribes, by crowding them one upon the other, gave rise to a great shifting of peoples. Altyn-khan, in driving the Choros back from the Kobdo region to the upper Yenisei, forced the Torghut in their turn to move farther west. It was then that the Torghut chief Khu Urluk, forsaking Dzungaria (1616), took the westward trail across the Kirghiz-Kazakh steppes, north of the Aral and the Caspian. The Kirghiz-Kazakhs of the Little Horde tried to stop him west of the Emba, and the Nogai horde near Astrakhan. He beat them both. Northward his sphere of influence extended as far as the upper Tobol, and he gave his daughter in marriage to Ishim-khan, the son of Kuchum, the last Shaybanid khan of Sibir (1620). Southward, in 1603, his bands plundered the khanate of Khiva in the course of invasions that were resumed during the reigns of ʿArab Muhammad I (1602–23) and Isfendiyar (1623–43), khans of Khiva. Southwestward, from 1632, the Torghut began to settle on the lower Volga. In 1639, Khu Urluk subjugated the Turkomans of the mountainous peninsula of Mangyshlak, east of the Caspian; this region ever afterward remained subject to his house. In 1643, he moved his people's encampments—about 50,000 tents—to the neighborhood of Astrakhan, but was killed in a battle with the local inhabitants.[35]

Despite this misadventure, the Torghut continued to occupy the steppes north of the Caspian, from the mouth of the Volga to the Mangyshlak Peninsula, whence they went on to plunder the towns of the Khiva khanate: Hezarasp, Kath, and Urgench. During the reign of Khan Puntsuk-Monchak (1667–70), Khu

Urluk's grandson, the Torghut deported three Turkmen tribes from the Mangyshlak to the Caucasus.[36] On the other hand, the Torghut had been able to win the friendship of Russia, and had more than once recognized its suzerainty (1656, 1662). Their khan Ayuka (1670–1724), Puntsuk's son, reinforced this policy. On February 26, 1673, he waited upon the governor of Muscovy in Astrakhan to acknowledge himself client of the czar and was given a magnificent reception. The Torghut were Buddhists, and Russian policy aimed at using them against the Muslim khanate of the Crimea and against the Bashkir of the Ural and the Nogai of Kuban, who were also Muslims. Broadly speaking, this is what happened. Nevertheless, certain quarrels took place between Russians and Kalmucks, as in 1682, the year when Ayuka, offended by a request to hand over hostages, rebelled and led a plundering expedition to Kazan, after which he re-entered the czar's clientele. In 1693, he led a successful campaign on behalf of the Russians against the Bashkir, and then against the Nogai. In 1722, Peter the Great, in recognition of his services, received him with great honor at Saratov.[37]

On the whole, the Torghut khanate prospered under the Russian protectorate. It extended from the Ural River to the Don, and from Tsaritsyn to the Caucasus, when in 1770 the clumsiness of certain Russian agents induced Khan Ubasha to withdraw his horde into Central Asia. The Torghut grand lama fixed the date of departure for January 5, 1771. More than 70,000 families were involved in this exodus. The Torghut people traversed the Ural and after countless hardships and perils arrived in Turgai. There they were harassed by the Kirghiz-Kazakhs of the Little Horde under their khan Nur 'Ali, and later by those of the Middle Horde under Ablai. Having at last arrived at Lake Balkhash, the unfortunate emigrants were subjected to further attacks, this time by the Kara-Kirghiz or Burut people. The survivors finally reached the Ili basin, where they were fed and settled by the Chinese authorities.[38]

THE KHOSHOT KHANATE OF TSAIDAM AND THE KOKO NOR, PROTECTOR OF THE TIBETAN CHURCH

While the Torghut went to carve an empire for themselves in the Aralo-Caspian steppe, another of the Oirat or Kalmuck peoples turned their eyes toward Tibet.

In the first quarter of the seventeenth century, as a result of Khalka pressure which had thrust back the Dörben Oirat toward the west, the Khoshot were encamped about Lake Zaisan and on the Irtysh, in what is today the Semipalatinsk region, as far as Yamishevsk or Peschanaia. About 1620, their chief Boibeghus Ba'atur was converted to the lamaism of the Tibetan Yellow Church. Such was his zeal that at his instigation the three other Kalmuck princes—Khara Kula, chief of the Choros; Dalai taiji, chief of the Dörböt; and Khu Urluk, chief of the Torghut—each sent one of his sons to study lamaism in Tibet. Boibeghus was succeeded by his two sons, Uchirtu-sechen, who reigned over the Zaisan area, and Ablai-taiji, who reigned over the Irtysh in Semipalatinsk. No less zealous a Buddhist than his father, he founded a lamaist monastery west of the Irtysh, between Semipalatinsk and Tara.

In 1636, a brother of Boibeghus, Gushi khan, went to seek his fortune near the Koko Nor and carved himself a domain round this lake and Tsaidam. He increased his possessions in Khamdo or eastern Tibet, which he subjugated both to his temporal power and to the spiritual authority of the Yellow Church. For Gushi khan, like all the Khoshot princes, was a devout lamaist. At this time, the Yellow Church was threatened by a grave danger. A Tibetan prince, the *de-srid* of gTsang, protector of the old Red clergy, took possession of Lhasa (between 1630 and 1636). The head of the Yellow Church, the Dalai Lama Nag-dbang bLo-bzang, appealed to Gushi khan, who came at once to the defense of the Yellow Church by forming a "holy league." This was joined by all the other Kalmuck princes: his nephews Uchirtu-sechen and Ablai-taiji of Zaisan and Semipalatinsk; Ba'atur-khongtaiji, chief of the Choros, who reigned over the Urungu, the Black Irtysh, and the Imil in Tarbagatai; and even Khu Urluk, the Torghut chief, then engaged in conquering the steppes north of the Aral and the Caspian. But it was Gushi khan who with his brother Kundelung Ubasha undertook to wage the Holy War. On his first expedition (ca. 1639?), he entered Tibet and defeated all the Dalai Lama's enemies, whether adherents of the Red clergy or sectaries of the ancient *bon-po* sorcery. In the course of a second campaign, he imprisoned the *de-srid* of gTsang (ca. 1642?), occupied Lhasa, and proclaimed the Dalai Lama Nag-dbang bLo-bzang sovereign of central Tibet (Dbus and Tsang). In token of the temporal sovereignty conferred upon him by the Khoshot prince, bLo-bzang built a residence for himself on the site of the palace of the former kings of Tibet, the Potala of Lhasa (1643–45). In return, Gushi khan, already lord of the Koko Nor, of Tsaidam, and of northern Tibet, was recognized by the pontiff, in Lhasa itself, as protector and temporal vicar of the Yellow Church. Until his death in 1656, he was indeed, as he was called by the court of Peking, "the khan of the Tibetans." [39]

The Khoshot realm of the Koko Nor and Tsaidam, with the Tibetan protectorate, passed on Gushi khan's death to his son Dayan khan (1656–70) and then to his grandson Dalai khan (1670–1700). Dalai khan's son Latsang khan (1700–1717) also proved to be a zealous protector of the Yellow Church; he took his function very seriously and summoned councils to elect "living Buddhas." It was thus that he had to intervene in Tibet in opposition to the all-powerful minister Sangs-rgyas rgya-msho, who, in the name of an infant Dalai Lama, ruled as the head of the Yellow Church. In 1705–6, Latsang khan entered Lhasa, put the redoubtable minister to death, deposed the wrongly chosen little Dalai Lama, and had him replaced by a more authentic one (1708–10). From Gushi khan to Latsang khan, the Khoshot rulers of the Koko Nor and Tsaidam stood in about the same relation to the Tibetan Holy See as Pepin and Charlemagne did to the Papacy.

But this exalted position, so important by reason of the Yellow Church's influence in the politics of Central Asia and the Far East, was bound to arouse jealousy. Another Kalmuck tribe, that of the Choros, which had become the most important in Dzungaria, aimed at securing this key position for itself. In June, 1717, the Choros chief Tsereng Dondub marched upon Tibet. For three months Latsang khan succeeded in holding the Choros north of the Tengri Nor (Nam Tso); then, outnumbered, was forced to retreat to Lhasa. From there he was driven out by Tsereng Dondub, who on December 2 took possession of the city. Latsang, who had defended the Potala to the last, was killed as he fled. [40] Thus ended the Khoshot protectorate of Tibet; yet the Khoshot people brought from the Irtysh by Gushi khan still form the basis of the population of the Tsaidam region, and three other groups of the same race survive west and northeast of the Koko Nor as well as in the district of Lutsang and Lakiashih (Aru-rarja) in Sokpa, southeast of the lake.

Those Khoshot who had remained on the Irtysh near Lake Zaisan under the command of the two brothers Uchirtu-sechen and Ablai suffered by the discord between the two chiefs. Ablai, vanquished, emigrated and fought the Torghut for possession of the steppes between the Ural and the Volga, capturing their chief Puntsuk-Monchak (ca. 1670). But the Torghut lost no time in retaliating, took Ablai prisoner, and dispersed his horde. Uchirtu-sechen, who had remained on Lake Zaisan, was attacked and put to death in 1677 by the Choros chief Galdan, who subjugated some of his people, while the rest went to join the Khoshot who had settled in Tsaidam and the Koko Nor.[41]

THE DZUNGAR KINGDOM UNDER THE CHOROS DYNASTY: BA'ATUR-KHONGTAIJI'S REIGN

Like the Torghut and Khoshot, the Oirat tribes—or Kalmuck or Dzungar tribes, since the three names designate the same group —i.e., the Choros and the Dörböt, had been driven from northwestern Mongolia and thrust even farther west by the Khalka. About 1620, after bitter fighting with the Khalka Altyn-khan in the Ubsa Nor region in the later province of Kobdo, the Choros had been forced to scatter. Some of them fled with a portion of the Dörböt northward into Siberia, into the mountainous region of the upper Ob, round Ulala, where the Soviets later formed an "Autonomous Republic of the Oirat," and even farther north, toward present-day Barnaoul, at the confluence of the Chumysh and the Ob. But the majority of the Choros, followed by their Dörböt allies, finally settled in the region of the Black Irtysh, the Urungu, the Imil, and the Ili, round Tarbagatai. A source of strength for the Choros—strength that enabled them to maintain their hegemony of the other Oirat—was that they remained in contact with their native Mongolia, while the Torghut emigrated north of the Caspian and the Khoshot moved to the Koko Nor. The Choros khans, with their Dörböt and Khoit clients, were thus enabled to rebuild the Oirat or—as it will be called henceforth—the Dzungar nation. The name Dzungar will designate the Choros and their confederates— Dörböt and Khoit—who owed obedience to the Choros khans.[42]

The first Choros chief who thus arrested the collapse of his people and settled them in Tarbagatai before setting forth for the reconquest of Mongolia was Khara Kula, whose death, according to Barthold, occurred in 1634.[43] His son Ba'atur-khongtaiji, who succeeded him (1634–53), continued his work.[44] Wishing to settle the Dzungar in Tarbagatai, he built a capital of stone at Kubak-sari, on the Imil, near modern Chuguchak. "Sometimes in his new capital," says Courant, "and sometimes in his encampments on the Ili or in the region [southwest] of Kobdo, he took pleasure in receiving with dignity and splendor the envoys of foreign princes and of the voivodes of Siberia; the nomad warrior was being transmuted into a lawgiving, farming, and trading prince."[45]

Ba'atur-khongtaiji led victorious expeditions against the Kirghiz-Kazakhs of the Great Horde, whose nomad territory extended from the town of Turkestan in the west to the Ili in the east. In the course of a first campaign against their khan Ishim, in 1635, he took Yehangir, the son of that khan, prisoner. The prisoner, however, escaped. In 1643, Ba'atur once more attacked Yehangir, who had now become sultan, and with the help of the Khoshot chiefs Uchirtu and Ablai again defeated him. Thus the Kirghiz, those nomad Turks who were so superficially Muslim and before whom the sedentary peoples of Bukharia trembled, were now raided by other and even more mobile hordes who were Mongol by race and Buddhist by religion. For Ba'atur-khongtaiji was a sincere Buddhist; it has already been noted how around 1638 he helped Gushi khan, king of the Khoshot of Tsaidam and the Koko Nor, in a Holy War which liberated the Tibetan Yellow Church from its oppressors.[46]

GALDAN'S REIGN (1676–97): FOUNDATION OF THE DZUNGAR EMPIRE

On Ba'atur-khongtaiji's death in 1653, according to Pozdneev, the Dzungar throne was occupied by one of his sons named Sengge (ca. 1553–1671). Sengge was killed about 1671 by two of his brothers, Sechen-khan and Tsotba Ba'atur. A fourth son of Ba'atur-khongtaiji, Galdan, who was born in 1645, had been sent to the Dalai Lama in Lhasa, where he took monastic orders. About 1676 he returned from Lhasa, having received canonical dispensation from the Dalai Lama, killed his brother Sechen-khan, expelled his other brother Tsotba Ba'atur, and obtained recognition as khan of the Choros and suzerain of the other Dzungar tribes.[47]

Galdan's triumph was due to the support of the khan of the Khoshot of Lake Zaisan, Uchirtu-sechen. Nevertheless, in 1677 he did not hesitate to turn upon the latter; he defeated him, killed him, annexed his territory and some of his horde, and drove the rest back toward Kansu.[48]

After this coup, Galdan found himself lord of a solidly established Dzungar realm extending from the Ili to the south of Kobdo, a realm in which the Dörböt, the remnants of the Khoshot, and the Khoits—in short, all the Oirat tribes that had not emigrated—rendered disciplined obedience to the royal house of the Choros. In the same way, Jenghiz Khan had unified all the thirteenth-century Mongols under the Borchigin clan. Now that he too had reliable clients at his disposal around his patrimony of Tarbagatai, Galdan embarked upon the conquest of Central Asia.

His first move was in Kashgaria. In this country, religious khoja families had increasingly undermined the authority of the Jagatai khans and slyly substituted or superimposed a sort of Muslim clericalism or Islamic theocracy within the ancient Jenghiz-Khanite khanate. Two khoja families—the Aqtaghlik and the Qarataghlik—had thus grasped effective power, the former in Kashgar, the latter in Yarkand. About 1677, the last khan, Isma'il, reacted by forcing the Aqtaghlik leader, Hazrat Apak, to flee Kashgar.[49] Hazrat Apak took refuge in Tibet, where he implored the help of the Dalai Lama. This démarche may seem strange when one considers the gulf separating the Buddhist theocracy from the Muslim. But in the sphere of politics, the two forms of clericalism were as one, irrespective of doctrine. The "Pope of Buddhism," who still thought of his former "altar boy" Galdan as submissive to his words, invited him to reinstate Muhammad's representative in Kashgar. Galdan obeyed all the more zealously in that such a mission made him the advocate of both the lamaist and Muslim "churches," in addition to the fact that it would enable him to establish a Dzungar protectorate over Kashgaria.

And so it came about. Galdan had little difficulty in occupying

Kashgaria. He took Khan Isma'il prisoner and sent him into captivity at Kuldja on the Ili (1678–80). Not content with re-installing the khoja Hazrat Apak as viceroy in Kashgar, he gave him Yarkand as well, at the expense of the other khoja family, the rival Qarataghliks. Thus Kashgaria became a Dzungar protectorate in which the khojas were no more than prefects of the Choros khan. This became evident when after Hazrat Apak's death the old quarrels between Aqtaghliks and Qarataghliks were revived. The Dzungars achieved general agreement by taking prisoner the chiefs of both clans, Ahmed-khoja the Aqtaghlik and Daniyal-khoja the Qarataghlik. Daniyal was then chosen to be viceroy of Kashgaria (1720), with his residence in Yarkand, but on condition that he make a humble act of vassalage before the Dzungar khongtaiji at Kuldja. Also, the Dzungar lords appropriated wide domains in Kashgaria.

After the conquest of Kashgaria—and apparently later than 1681—Galdan took possession of Turfan and Hami, where up to that time there had no doubt dwelt an eastern branch of Jagataites.

Galdan now aimed at reviving the Jenghiz-Khanite epic. He exhorted all Mongols to join in seizing the empire of the Far East from the Manchus—those upstarts whose Jurchid ancestors had once been overwhelmed by Jenghiz Khan. "Are we to become the slaves of those who were once at our command? The empire is the heritage of our forebears!" [50]

In order to unite the Mongol race, Galdan had now to draw the four Khalka khans within his clientele. In this he was helped by their quarrels, especially the rivalry between the Dzasagtu-khan and the Tushetu-khan. He sided with the former against the latter and soon had the most legitimate reason for intervening. The troops of Tsagun Dorji, the Tushetu-khan, commanded by his brother the *chept-sun dampa*, conquered Shara, the Dzasagtu-khan, who was drowned while trying to escape; they then invaded Dzungar territory and killed one of Galdan's brothers.[51]

Galdan reacted vigorously. At the beginning of 1688, he in his turn invaded the territory of the Tushetu-khan, annihilated his army on the Tämir, a tributary of the Orkhon, and allowed his men to plunder the Jenghiz-Khanite temples of Erdeni Dzu at Karakorum: a visible sign that the Dzungar were supplanting the eastern Mongols as leaders of the Mongol nations. Fleeing from Galdan, the Tushetu-khan and the other Khalka khans (including Tsewang Shab, brother and heir of the last Dzasagtu-khan, who had been killed by Tushetu) took refuge near Kuku Hoto, in Tümed country on the northwestern frontier of Shansi, which was under the protection of the Chinese Empire, and entreated the help of the Manchu emperor K'ang-hsi. Having subjugated the Orkhon and Tula country, Galdan went down the valley of the Kerulen as far as the approaches to Manchuria (spring of 1690). The entire Khalka country was conquered by the Dzungar people, whose empire thenceforth extended from the Ili to the Bor Nor. Galdan even ventured to advance upon Inner Mongolia along the Urga-Kalgan road.

Emperor K'ang-hsi could not allow this new Mongol Empire to arise at the very threshold of China. He marched to meet Galdan and halted him "at Ulan-put'ung between Kalgan and Urga, eighty leagues from Peking." [52] The artillery manufactured for K'ang-hsi by the Jesuits was too much for Galdan, and the new Jenghiz Khan, disconcerted, evacuated Khalka country (end of 1690). In May, 1691, K'ang-hsi summoned a Diet in Dolonnor at which the principal Khalka chiefs, headed by Tushetu-khan and Sechen-khan, acknowledged themselves vassals of the Sino-Manchu Empire and agreed to pay tribute, in return for which they were to receive a pension from the imperial treasury. They further acknowledged themselves bound to the empire by a bond of personal loyalty, which was to be strengthened from time to time by family alliances. It may be noted here that though this system was based on Chinese administrative experience in dealing with "barbarians," it was founded mainly on the nomad-to-nomad form of attachment of the Mongol khans to the Manchu grand khan. Thus when in 1912 the Manchu dynasty fell and was replaced by the Chinese Republic, the Mongol princes, deeming themselves released from their oath of loyalty, declared their independence.

In 1695, war between Galdan and the empire broke out again. Again Galdan crossed the Khalka country and penetrated as far as the Kerulen valley, intending to link up with the Khorchin of the River Nonni, whom he hoped to entice away from the imperial clientele. But the Khorchin warned the court of Peking of these intrigues, and in the spring of 1696 Emperor K'ang-hsi marched against Galdan with all his forces and from Kalgan spurred directly toward the Kerulen, turning upstream in pursuit of the enemy.[53] The Dzungar khan tried to elude him, but K'ang-hsi's chief officer, Fei-yang-ku, who commanded the vanguard, met him on the Tula and, thanks once more to the use of artillery and muskets, defeated him at Chao-modo south of Urga on June 12, 1696. Galdan's wife was killed and her suite captured, and her herds remained in the hands of the imperial troops. Having lost half his forces, the Dzungar leader fled westward, while K'ang-hsi returned to Peking in triumph. The Khalkas, saved by the imperial victory, repossessed themselves of their territory. In the following summer, K'ang-hsi was preparing to set forth on campaign again to thrust the Dzungars back into Tarbagatai, when he learned that on May 3, 1697, Galdan had died after a short illness.[54]

The chief benefit that Manchu China derived from this victory was the permanent establishment of a protectorate over the Khalkas. The four Khalka khans whom K'ang-hsi had saved from Dzungar domination could refuse him nothing. Imperial residents took up their abode among them and an imperial garrison was installed at Urga, in the heart of their territory. Apart from this, K'ang-hsi, who remained very Manchu in his outlook and understood the nomad psychology, was careful not to interfere with the national organization of the eastern Mongols. He respected "the old tribal, military, and administrative division of the country into *tsuglans* (Diets or leagues), *aymaqs* (tribes or army corps), *qosighuns* or *qoshuns* ('banners'), and *sumuns* ('arrows,' i.e., squadrons)." [55]

The same thing had happened among the Ordos. Father Mostaert notes: "The various tribes were organized in banners (Mongolian, *qosighun;* Ordos, *gushu*), on the pattern of the eight Manchu banners, and although the greater number continued to be governed by princes of the old reigning family, some, such as the Chahar and the Tümed of Kweihwacheng, lost these chiefs and came under the authority of a Manchu official. . . . Individuals belonging to the same banner were distributed among a certain number of *sumu* and these in turn among various *qariya,* the *sumu* being commanded by *janggins* and the *qariya* by *jalans*. This system resulted in some relaxation of the ties uniting the nobles (*tayiji*, from *taji*) and their subordinates (*albatu*) and in a narrowing of the gulf that once separated these same nobles from commoners (*qarachu*)."[56]

From the territorial point of view, K'ang-hsi gained control of the starting point of the eastern Turkestan caravan route by inducing the Muslim prince of Hami, 'Abd-Allah Tarkhan-beg, to recognize his suzerainty.

THE DZUNGAR EMPIRE UNDER TSEWANG RABDAN (1697–1727)

Emperor K'ang-hsi, content to have established a protectorate over the Khalka and reassured by Galdan's death, made no attempt to subjugate the Dzungar country of Tarbagatai. He allowed Galdan's nephew Tsewang Rabdan, the son of Sengge, to ascend the Choros throne. Moreover, Tsewang Rabdan, whom Galdan had once tried to put to death, had in the end rebelled against his uncle; therefore, the court of Peking believed that the Dzungar tribes were now to be governed by an ally of China. The fact was, as Courant has clearly shown, that Tsewang Rabdan needed to consolidate his position in Tarbagatai and on the Ili before adopting his uncle's anti-Chinese policy. The Ili region was of particular interest to the new khan; he seems to have chosen Kuldja for his capital and left the town of Imil to his brother Tsereng Dondub.[57]

In the Ili area, the Dzungar hegemony clashed with the Kirghiz-Kazakhs, the Muslim Turkic nomads who dominated the land from Lake Balkhash to the Ural River. Their three hordes, somewhat loosely united, still obeyed one and the same khan, Tyawka (d. 1718), who was known, says Barthold, as the legislator of his people, and under whom these eternal nomads acquired some small measure of organization and stability. Since about 1597–98, under their khan Tawakkul's reign, the Kirghiz-Kazakhs had seized the cities of Turkestan and Tashkent from the Uzbek or Shaybanid khanate of Bukhara. A hundred years later, Tyawka would be receiving embassies from Russia (1694) and the Kalmucks (1698) in Turkestan.[58] Being in so strong a position and able to take advantage of the disturbance caused among the Dzungar by their conflict with China, Tyawka had no hesitation in having a number of Dzungar envoys put to death, along with the five hundred men of their escort, in particularly odious circumstances.[59]

This slaying of a whole embassy at the end of the seventeenth century, in a corner of the steppe between the Ili and the Syr Darya, was apparently just one more battle between nomad hordes; yet underlying it was an ancient ethnic and religious conflict. Was the western empire of the steppes to belong to Turks or Mongols, Muslims or Buddhists? It was the latter who finally prevailed. Tsewang Rabdan attacked Tyawka and beat him (1698). Bulat or Pulad khan, chief of the Middle Horde, who in 1718 succeeded Tyawka, was even less fortunate. The Dzungar seized from the Kirghiz-Kazakhs the towns of Sairam, Tashkent, and Turkestan (1723). The three hordes, disrupted by defeat, separated. Some of the chiefs of the Great and Middle Hordes recognized Tsewang Rabdan's suzerainty; so did the Kara-Kirghiz or Burut of the Issyk Kul, and Tsewang Rabdan maintained Dzungar dominion over the khojas of Kashgar and Yarkand, as established by his predecessor Galdan. In the north, his brother Tsereng Dondub, whose own domain was on Lake Zaisan and the Imil, took arms against the Russians and for a time forced them to evacuate the strong point of Yamishevsk on the Yenisei (1716). In the spring of 1720, a Russian punitive expedition clashed with Tsewang Rabdan's son Galdan Tsereng near the Zaisan; Galdan Tsereng with 20,000 Dzungar fighters succeeded in halting the Russians, despite the inequality of weapons: bows against firearms. The basin of the Zaisan remained in Dzungar possession. The Russo-Dzungar frontier was finally fixed at the fort of Ust-Kamenogorsk, founded by the Russians in that year, 1720, on the Yenisei at the 50th parallel.[60]

Tsewang Rabdan had not waited to consolidate his empire in the west before adopting his uncle Galdan's policy against Manchu China in the east. The politico-religious unrest in the Tibetan Church gave him his opportunity. Since the death between 1680 and 1682 of the Dalai Lama Nag-dbang bLo-bzang, the lamaist church had been administered by the lay *de-srid* Sangs-rgyas rgya-msho, who ruled as he pleased, first in the name of the late lama, who was officially still alive, and later (1697) in the name of a young boy whom he appointed as the new Dalai Lama. Sangs-rgyas sided with the Dzungar party against China. Emperor K'ang-hsi incited against him the Khoshot khan of the Koko Nor, Latsang khan, who in 1705–6 entered Lhasa, put Sangs-rgyas to death, and deposed the young Dalai Lama.[61] After some rather complicated intrigues, Latsang khan and K'ang-hsi caused a new Dalai Lama to be nominated, with China's official sanction (1708–10).

Tsewang Rabdan observed these changes with a malevolent eye. The moral influence of the Tibetan Church was too strong in Mongolia for him to allow it to be put at the service of China. Around June, 1717, he sent into Tibet an army commanded by his brother Tsereng Dondub. From Khotan, by a march of unprecedented daring over the Kunlun range and the high desert plateaus, Tsereng Dondub advanced directly upon the district of Nagchu, where the Khoshot khan Latsang, the representative of the Chinese party, was enjoying the pleasures of the chase. Although taken by surprise, Latsang was able to hold the enemy in a defile between Nagchu and the Tengri Nor, no doubt at the pass of Shang-shung-la, until October, when he was forced to retreat to Lhasa, trailed closely by Tsereng Dondub's army. On December 2, 1717, the gates of Lhasa were treacherously opened to Tsereng Dondub, and for three days the Dzungar troops massacred all adherents, real or supposed, of the Chinese party. Latsang khan, who had tried to defend the Potala, was killed as he fled. The Potala itself, the holy of holies, was thrown open to pillage. Courant is surprised to find the Dzungar, those pious lamaists, ransacking the holy city of their religion in order to adorn the Kuldja lamaseries with their spoils; but was it not thus that the Venetians of medieval Christendom behaved in Alexandria and Constantinople? And did not the "war of relics" date from the very beginnings of Buddhism?

Meanwhile, Emperor K'ang-hsi was loath to leave the Dzungar in possession of Tibet, or to tolerate a Dzungar empire that extended from Lake Zaisan and Tashkent to Lhasa. In 1718, he ordered the viceroy of Szechwan to march against Tibet; but on his arrival in Nagchu, this dignitary was repulsed and killed by the Dzungar forces. In 1720, two other Chinese armies penetrated Tibet, one again by Szechwan and the other by Tsaidam. The second one defeated the Dzungar forces, who had aroused the hatred of the Tibetan population and were now (autumn of 1720) compelled to evacuate Tibet in haste. Tsereng Dondub brought less than half his army back to Dzungaria. A pro-Chinese Dalai Lama was enthroned and two Chinese high commissioners were

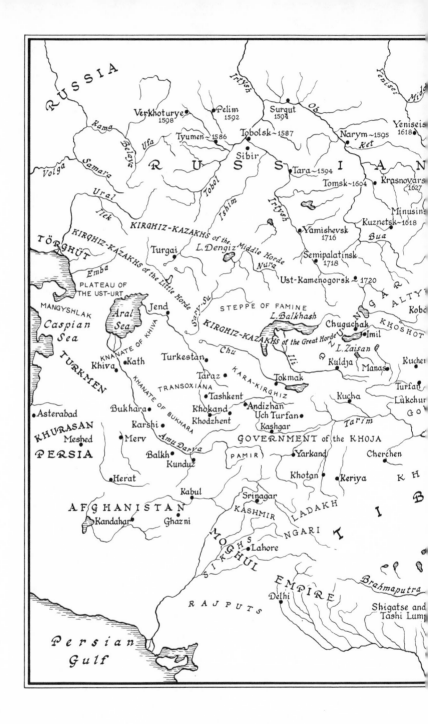

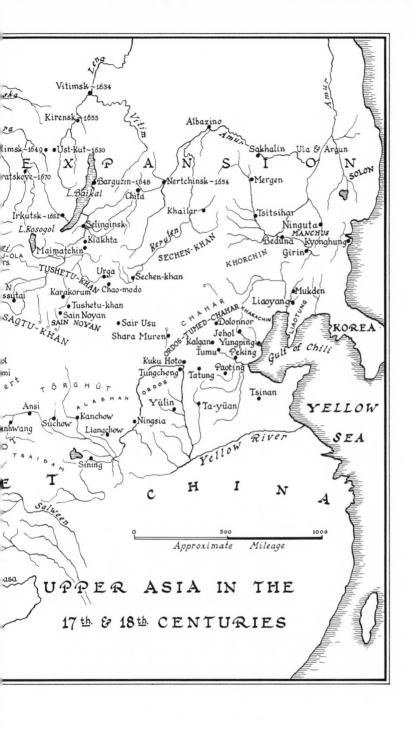

Vitimsk ~1634

Lena

Kirensk ~1655

Albazino

Amur

Sakhalin   Ula & Argun

imsk ~1649   Ust-Kut ~1630

Vitim

EXPANSION

SOLON

ratskoye~1670

Barguzin~1648   Nertchinsk ~1654   Mergen

L.Baikal   Chita

Khailar   Tsitsihar

Irkutsk~1652

Ninguta

L.Kosogol   Selinginsk

MANCHUS

i   Kiakhta

Beduna   Kyonghung

J-OLA   Maimatchin

Kerulen

Girin

TS.

TUSHETU-KHAN   Urga   Sechen-khan

SECHEN-KHAN

KHORCHIN

N   Karakorum   Chao-modo   Mukden

ssutai   Tushetu-khan

CHAHAR   Liaoyang

Sain Noyan   Sair Usu   Dolonnor   KHARACHIN

SAGTU-KHAN   SAIN NOYAN

ORDOS-TUMED-CHAHAR   LIAOTUNG

Shara Muren   Jehol   KOREA

Kalgan   Yungping

Tumu   Peking   Gulf of Chili

Kuku Hoto

Tungcheng   Tatung   Paoting

ORDOS

ol

mi   TÖRGHÜT

Yülin   Ta-yüan   Tsinan   YELLOW

ert   ALASHAN

Ansi

SEA

nhwang   Suchow   Kanchow   Ningsia

Liangchow   Yellow River

TSAIDAM

E   T   Sining

Salween

C   H   I   N   A

0   500   1000

Approximate   Mileage

asa   UPPER ASIA IN THE

17th & 18th CENTURIES

appointed to his service with the task of directing the policy of the Yellow Church.[62]

Tsewang Rabdan was no more fortunate in the Gobi, and his troops were unable to capture Hami from the Chinese garrison (1715). The imperial troops, taking the offensive in their turn, occupied Barkol in 1716. Then, moving both armies against Tsewang Rabdan in two columns, one departing from Barkol and the other operating farther to the north, they occupied Turfan and at the end of 1720 went on to beat the Dzungar at Urumchi. Though the Chinese did not retain Urumchi, they did establish a military colony at Turfan. It is interesting to note that their operations were made easier by the revolt of the Muslims of Turfan against Dzungar domination.[63]

It may be that Emperor K'ang-hsi, who had a taste for distant conquest, would have undertaken that of Dzungaria itself; but his death in December, 1722, and the accession of his son, the unwarlike Yung-cheng, led the court of China to make peace with Tsewang Rabdan in 1724. This peace, however, was no more than a truce. Tsewang Rabdan had resumed the offensive by occupying Turfan (whence the Muslim population fled to Tunhwang in Chinese territory),[64] when he himself died, at the end of 1727.

GALDAN TSERENG'S REIGN (1727–45)

Tsewang Rabdan was succeeded by his son Galdan Tsereng. From the beginning, the new Dzungar king showed such hostility to China that Emperor Yung-cheng reopened the war in 1731. From Barkol, a Chinese army marched on Urumchi and there scattered the enemy troop concentrations, but did not remain.[65] Farther north, another army advanced as far as Kobdo and even beyond, into the heart of Dzungar country,[66] but two months later it was defeated and almost entirely wiped out. Emperor Yung-cheng, discouraged, ordered the evacuation not only of Kobdo but also of Turfan.

Galdan Tsereng tried to exploit the Chinese disaster by sending his uncle Tsereng Dondub to invade the Khalka country. From liberated Kobdo, Tsereng Dondub pressed on to the Kerulen,[67] but the Khalka put up a determined resistance, fortifying the crossing points of the rivers Baidarik, Tula, and Ongkin—so the *Tung hua lu* tells—and the Dzungar were unable to remain there beyond the end of 1731. In the spring of 1732, the Dzungar groups who had left Urumchi to drive the imperial garrison out of Hami were no more successful. At the end of the summer, a small Dzungar army that was raiding Khalka country was taken by surprise and partially massacred by one of the Khalka princes near Karakorum.[68] The imperial forces now took the offensive in their turn. In 1733–34, they seized Uliassutai, in the heart of the Khangai, and advanced as far as the Black Irtysh. Even Kobdo was reoccupied.[69]

In 1735, notwithstanding these successes and, while apparently still occupying—perhaps temporarily—Uliassutai and Kobdo, Emperor Yung-cheng offered to make a pact with Galdan Tsereng by which China would keep the lands east of the Khangai Mountains (Khalka country) while the Dzungar should have the territory west and southwest of that range (Dzungaria and Kashgaria). A tacit truce was made on this basis, which in 1740, after Yung-cheng's death (1735), was ratified by his son and successor Ch'ien-lung. Peace was maintained until the death of the Dzungar Khan Galdan Tsereng at the end of 1745.[70]

DAWAJI AND AMURSANA: ANNEXATION OF DZUNGARIA BY THE MANCHU EMPIRE

Galdan Tsereng's death was followed by a troubled period in the Dzungar Empire. His son Tsewang Dorji Namgyal (ca. 1745–50), a dissipated and cruel young man, was blinded and imprisoned at Aksu by the nobles. A new khan, the lama Darja (1750–53), failed to command obedience. The Dörböt, Khoshot, and Khoit tribes, which for a century had been subject to the khongtaijis of the Choros, threatened to break free. Unity was gone and with it the Dzungar state. At last, in 1753, an energetic leader named Dawaji or Tawaji, Tsereng Dondub's grandson, supported by the Khoit prince Amursana, Galdan Tsereng's son-in-law, marched on Kuldja and put Darja to death.[71] Dawaji, proclaimed khan (1753–55), had now to contend with his former ally Amursana, who, established on the Ili, was conducting himself like an independent prince. Dawaji defeated him and drove him out.

Together with a number of Khoit, Dörböt, and Khoshot chiefs, Amursana took refuge on Chinese territory, where he offered his services to Emperor Ch'ien-lung (1754). Ch'ien-lung received him in solemn audience in Jehol, took him under his protection, and in the spring of 1755 sent him back to Dzungaria with a Chinese army commanded by the Manchu marshal Pan-ti. Pan-ti entered Kuldja without a fight. Dawaji had fled, but was found soon afterward at Aksu and handed over to the Chinese, who sent him to Peking. He was treated kindly by Emperor Ch'ien-lung, and died a natural death there in 1759.[72]

Meanwhile Marshal Pan-ti, now established in Kuldja as commissioner general, had been prompt in proclaiming the political dissolution of the Dzungar people and in nominating individual khans for each of the Choros, Dörböt, Khoshot, and Khoit tribes. Amursana, who had hoped to gather up at least a part of Dawaji's heritage, was bitterly disappointed. To curb his anger, Pan-ti forced him to leave for Peking. On the way, however, Amursana escaped, returned to Kuldja, and roused the Dzungar people against Chinese domination. Pan-ti, who had rashly reduced his military strength, found himself surrounded without hope of rescue and committed suicide (late summer and autumn, 1755).[73]

An energetic Manchu marshal named Chao Huei retrieved the situation. Besieged in Urumchi during the winter of 1756, he held out until the arrival of reinforcements from Barkol. In the spring of 1757, he penetrated as far as the Imil in Tarbagatai, while other Chinese columns were sent to reoccupy Kuldja. Amursana, hunted from all sides, took refuge with the Russians in Siberia (summer of 1757).[74]

This was the end of Dzungar independence. Dzungaria, broadly speaking—the Kobdo district, Tarbagatai, and the Ili or Kuldja province—was directly annexed to the Chinese Empire. Even the population was changed. The Dzungar people, in the form of Choros and Khoit elements (the Dörböt had suffered less of an ordeal), were almost exterminated. The Chinese repopulated the country with immigrants from every quarter: Kirghiz-Kazakhs, Taranchis or Muslims from Kashgaria, Dungans or Muslims from Kansu, Chahar and Khalka populations, Uriangqai or Soyot people of Tovinsk stock, and even Sipo and Solon settlers from Manchuria. In 1771, other settlers arrived, namely, the Torghut, who under their khan Ubasha had abandoned the lower Volga to return to their native country on the Ili. Emperor Ch'ien-lung received Ubasha at Peking, gave him a most flattering welcome, supplied his exhausted emigrants with food, and in the same year settled them south and east of Kuldja, in the Yulduz valley and on the upper Urungu,[75] where they helped to fill the gap left by the extermination of their Choros and Khoit brothers.

THE UNFULFILLED DESTINY OF THE WESTERN MONGOLS

The destruction of the Dzungar realm brings the history of the Mongols to a close. If the word is used in its restricted sense and the ancient peoples probably or certainly Mongol by race, such as the Juan-juan and the Khitan, are excluded, the history of the Mongols proper begins at the end of the twelfth century with Jenghiz Khan. The Mongols attained their zenith at once, for Jenghiz Khan needed only twenty years after his imperial election in which to unify the steppe world and begin operations in China and Iran (1206–27). In another fifty years, the remainder of Iran and China had been conquered; and except for India—a continent in itself, cut off by its barrier of mountains—the Mongol Empire had become the empire of the Asian continent. This dominion crumbled almost as rapidly as it had been built. By 1360, the Mongols had lost China and Iran, and virtually Transoxiana as well, and all they retained in Asia was Mongolia and Mogholistan, the latter then constituting the northern part of Chinese Turkestan.

Yet the Jenghiz-Khanite conquest and empire had been achieved by the eastern Mongols alone: those of the Onon, the Kerulen, and the Orkhon. The Mongols of the west, the Oirat or Kalmucks, who were associated with the Jenghiz-Khanite epic in the capacity of allies, never played any but a subordinate role. Consequently, after the disastrous humiliation, the unprecedented loss of face that Jenghiz Khan's expulsion from China represented in the eyes of his descendants, the western Mongols tried to snatch the empire of the steppes from the failing hands of the eastern tribes, and like Jenghiz Khan achieve the conquest of China. They came near to succeeding, for in 1449 they took the emperor of China prisoner. But as they never managed to capture Peking, their exploits led to nothing. Less than fifty years later, this first Oirat empire had so far collapsed as to allow a curious Jenghiz-Khanite restoration to take place in eastern Mongolia, with Dayan and with his grandson Altan-khan. This restoration was impressive enough at the time, and the Chinese could fancy that the days of Jenghiz Khan had come again. But Dayan was no more the Conqueror of the World than Altan was Kublai. The resurgence was scarcely felt beyond Kobdo in the northwest and the Great Wall in the southeast, and the last of its energies were diverted to spiritual aims, in the zeal of a total conversion of the Mongols to the Buddhism of the Tibetan Yellow Church. The waking Mongol spirit slumbered again amid the mumur of lamaist prayers. Manchu China was to have no trouble in domesticating these monkish warriors lost in devotion.

Once more, therefore, the chief role fell to the western Mongols, who in their bleak valleys of the Altai had remained tougher and more belligerent. At the beginning of the seventeenth century, they were caught up in a great surge of expansion. The Torghut, following the trail of Batu and the Golden Horde, moved to the lower Volga near Astrakhan in southern Russia. The Khoshot settled in Koko Nor and reigned as far as Lhasa in Tibet. The Choros or Jungar proper held sway from the frontiers of Muscovite Siberia to those of the Bukhara khanate, on the one hand, and of China, on the other, from Kobdo to Tashkent, from Kobdo to the Kerulen. Their "capitals," Kobdo and Kuldja, seemed destined to replace Karakorum. As a sign of the times, moreover, they had already plundered its Jenghiz-Khanite sanctuaries. By the political action of the first Galdan and then by the warfare of Tsewang Rabdan and Tsereng Dondub, they had become the rulers of Lhasa, where the spiritual power of the lamaist church was at their command. At Kashgar and Yarkand, the khojas, the Muslim "clergy," were similarly their tools. For more than a hundred years they remained the true masters of continental Asia. Their leaders, the khongtaijis Ba'atur, Galdan, Tsewang Rabdan, and Galdan Tsereng, reveal themselves as resourceful politicians, bold and far sighted, as well as stubborn fighters, adept at making the most of the wonderful mobility—the ubiquity—of their mounted archers, the arm that won Jenghiz Khan his victories. These too came near success. How might they have avoided failure? By appearing a few years earlier, before Manchu domination had brought a new vigor and military structure to old China. The China of the later Ming had become so decrepit that anyone—Mongol, Japanese, or Manchu—might have seized it. But as soon as the Manchu dynasty had seated itself firmly on the throne of the Sons of Heaven, China was inspired with new life for another hundred and fifty years. The first Manchu emperors, who were intelligent, active, and still free from age-old prejudice, made a serious effort to modernize the country—the pieces of artillery made for them by Jesuit fathers bear witness to this. Galdan and Tsewang Rabdan, those spiritual companions of Jenghiz Khan but contemporaries of Louis XIV, stragglers from an earlier age, broke themselves against Manchu cannon in the eastern Gobi and against Muscovite firearms on the Yenisei. The thirteenth century clashed with the eighteenth, and the match was unequal. The last Mongol Empire crumbled even as it arose because it was a historical anachronism.

ANNEXATION OF KASHGARIA BY THE MANCHU EMPIRE

Kashgaria, with Yarkand as its capital, formed before 1775 a sort of Muslim religious state under the control of the Qarataghlik khoja family and the very effective protectorate of the Dzungar khans. After the death of the Qarataghlik Daniyal-khoja, the Dzungar khan Galdan Tsereng (1727–45) distributed the dead chief's possessions among his four sons: Jagan took Yarkand, Yusuf took Kashgar, Ayyub was to rule at Aksu, and 'Abd-Allah was to have Khotan. At the time of the civil wars between Dzungar pretenders, Yusuf, a zealous Muslim, took the opportunity to deliver Kashgaria from "pagan" suzerainty (1753–54). In 1755, Amursana, while he was still in agreement with Marshal Pan-ti, planned to quell the revolt of the Qarataghliks by unleashing the Aqtaghliks, the other khoja family, who were their hereditary enemy. Since 1720, the Aqtaghliks had been held by the Dzungar rulers in semicaptivity at Kuldja. The Aqtaghlik chief Burhan ad-Din, known as the Great Khoja, and his brother Khojo Jan, the Little Khoja, accepted the proposal with enthusiasm. With a small army lent by Amursana and the Chinese, Burhan ad-Din first captured Uch Turfan from the Qarataghliks, then Kashgar, and finally Yarkand, that is to say, the whole of Kashgaria.

No sooner were they in possession of the country than Burhan ad-Din and Khojo Jan took advantage of the war that had just broken out between Amursana and the Chinese government to declare their independence from both the Dzungar and the Chinese. An imperial detachment was slaughtered (late spring of 1757). But those bright days were few. When the Chinese had annexed Dzungaria, they turned against the two khojas. In 1758 a Chinese army commanded by Marshal Chao Huei came down from the Ili to the Tarim. Khojo Jan, having been beaten near Kucha,[76] took cover in Yarkand, where he put up a vigorous resistance. Meanwhile, Burhan ad-Din shut himself up in Kashgar. After an eventful and fluctuating war of siege, in the course of which the besieging Chinese were themselves beleaguered, Chao Huei was enabled to resume the offensive at the beginning of 1759, thanks to reinforcements brought to him by Fu-te. Yarkand was the first to capitulate, though not before Khojo Jan had fled; then it was the turn of Kashgar, similarly abandoned by Burhan ad-Din (1759).[77]

Both khojas took refuge in Badakhshan, but, despite Muslim solidarity, the local bey yielded to Chinese threats.[78] He executed the two fugitives and sent Khojo Jan's head to the imperial general Fu-te. Chao Huei annexed Kashgaria to the Sino-Manchu Empire (where it formed the "New March," *Sin-kiang*) and showed tact in his handling of the Muslim inhabitants.

Ch'ien-lung's annexation of the Ili and Kashgaria marks the fulfillment of the aim pursued since the time of Pan Ch'ao by the Chinese Asian policy of eighteen centuries: the retaliation of the sedentary peoples against the nomads, of agriculture against the steppe.

Notes

Introduction

1. For the history of the Turko-Mongol empires regarded as a study of human geography, see Owen Lattimore, "The Geographical Factor in Mongol History," *GJ*, XCI (January, 1938).

2. It appears, nevertheless, as if the Yakut were immigrants to the north and that their origins should be sought in the region of Lake Baikal. Although in the region they now occupy they make exclusive use of reindeer, the skulls of horses figure in certain of their ceremonies, in memory of their sojourn on the borders of the Mongolian steppe. This phenomenon is the opposite to that revealed by the Pazyryk tombs. See *ibid.*, pp. 1, 8.

3. Pelliot states: "We have wisely given up speaking, at the present stage of our studies at least, of an Uralo-Altaic linguistic family comprising, in addition to the Finno-Ugrian and Samoyed tongues, the Turkic, Mongol, and Tungus languages." Paul Pelliot, "Les mots à H initiale, aujourd'hui amuie, dans le mongol des XIIIe et XIVe siècles," *JA* (1925), p. 193.

4. Poppe postulates a primitive Altaic language, from which primitive Turkic, Mongol, and Tungus may have derived, but adds: "The period of primitive Turkic could not have extended later than the first centuries B.C." N. Poppe and V. V. Barthold also affirm "that in general the Turkic languages are more highly evolved than those of the Mongol group. The Mongol language of no matter which region of the Mongol world is far more archaic than the most ancient of the known Turkic languages. Written Mongol is, from the phonetic point of view, at almost the same point of evolution as the primitive Altaic language." Cf. N. Poppe, in *Ungarische Jahrbücher*, VI, 98. On the subject of "community," see Jean Deny, "Langues turques, mongoles et tongouzes," in A. Meillet and M. Cohen, *Les langues du monde* (Paris, 1924), p. 185.

5. The substitution of horses for the reindeer of the Siberian forests, for which evidence is found in the disguising of sacrificial horses as reindeer in the Pazyryk tombs (Tannu-Tuva, Siberian Altai, ca. 100 B.C.), gives a vivid glimpse of the transition of a tribe from the life of forest hunters to that of nomad livestock breeders. Cf. Lattimore, "Geographical Factor," p. 8.

6. The mythical ancestor of the Turko-Mongols is the russet wolf with the white patch, Börte-cino, among the Mongols of the *Secret History*, and the gray wolf Kök-böri among the Turks of the *Oghuz-name:* "From a beam of light came a great dog-wolf with a gray coat and mane."

Chapter 1

1. Cf. Teilhard de Chardin, "Esquisse de la préhistoire chinoise," *Bulletin 9, Catholic University of Peking* (1934), and "Les fouilles préhistoriques de Péking," *Revue des questions scientifiques* (March,

1934), pp. 181–193; Tolmatchov, "Sur le paléolithique de la Mandchourie," *ESA*, IV (1929); M. C. Burkitt, "Some Reflexions on the Aurignacian Culture and Its Female Statuettes," *ESA*, IX (1934), 113; J. G. Andersson, "Der Weg über die Steppen," *BMFEA* (1929).

2. Cf. L. Bachhofer, "Der Zug nach dem Osten, einige Bemerkungen zur prähistorischen Keramik Chinas," *Sinica* (1935), pp. 101–128; Max Loehr, "Beiträge zur Chronologie der älteren chinesischen Bronzen," *OZ*, I (1936), 3–41; L. Bachhofer, "Zur Frühgeschichte Chinas," *Die Welt als Geschichte*, III (1937), 4.

3. A scheme of comparative chronology for Maikop was suggested by A. V. Schmidt: "Kurgane der Stanica Konstantinovskaia," *ESA*, IV (1929), 18. For the uncertainties of these various datings and the discrepancies between them, according to the system used, cf. A. M. Tallgren, "Caucasian Monuments," *ESA*, V (1930), 180, and "Zu der nordkaukasischen Bronzezeit," *ESA*, VI (1931), 144.

4. Thracian names persist in some of the legends about the Scythians recounted by Herodotus (E. Benveniste, statement to the Société Asiatique [April 7, 1938]) and even in the historical kingdom of the Cimmerian Bosporus in the Greco-Roman period (M. I. Rostovtzeff, *Iranians and Greeks in South Russia*, Oxford, 1922, p. 39).

5. Cf. A. M. Tallgren, "La Pontide préscythique après l'introduction des métaux," *ESA*, II (1926), 220.

6. Franz Hančar places the Transcaucasian culture groups of Ganja-Karabakh and of Lelvar and Talysh between the fourteenth and eight centuries B.C. These cultures, he notes, are all oriented on the contemporary cultures of Western Asia. This may be seen in the shape of the axes, in the belt plaques, and in ceramics ("Kaukasus-Luristan," *ESA*, IX [1934], 107).

7. Tallgren's conclusions on the Cimmerian culture, given in "La Pontide préscythique après l'introduction des métaux," *ESA*, II (1926), are summarized here. For the Cimmerian migration, see Hančar, "Kaukasus-Luristan," p. 47. In this article the author seeks to link the animal art of Koban, north of the Caucasus, and the Luristan bronzes with the Cimmerian and Scythian migrations of the seventh century. Another study of this subject by Hančar is "Probleme des Kaukasischen Tierstils," *Mitteilungen der Anthropologischen Gesellschaft in Wien*, LXV (1935), 276.

8. Cf. N. Makarenko, "La Civilisation des Scythes et Hallstatt," *ESA*, V (1930), 22.

9. Persian Achaemenid nomenclature distinguishes between (a) the *Saka Haumavarka*, corresponding to our Sakas in the strict sense, who must have inhabited Fergana and the neighborhood of Kashgar; (b) the *Saka Tigrakhauda* of the Aral region, on the lower Syr Darya;

and (c) the *Saka Taradrava*, that is "from overseas," in southern Russia, these being the historical Scythians.

10. Cf. W. Miller, "Die Sprache der Osseten," *Grundriss der iranischen Philologie*, I. In classifying the Scythian inscriptions of southern Russia, Miller finds an Iranian element varying according to area from 10 per cent to 60 per cent. Émile Benveniste too finds that according to Herodotus, IV, 5, the same social classes—warriors, priests, and farmers—existed among the Scythians as among the Avestic and Achaemenid Iranians (statement to the Société Asiatique, April 7, 1938).

11. Cf. E. H. Minns, *Scythians and Greeks* (Cambridge, 1913), pp. 48–49. Rostovtzeff, *Iranians and Greeks in South Russia*, Plates XXI, XXII. For breeds of horses on the Scytho-Hunnic steppe and their representation in art, see J. G. Andersson, "Hunting Magic in the Animal Style," *BMFEA*, No. 4 (1932), p. 259.

12. The stirrup question is of capital importance. For a long time this invention gave the northern nomads a tremendous advantage over the cavalry of sedentary peoples. The famous Greco-Scythian vase of Chertomlyk seems to show "a stirrup formed by a buckled strap issuing from the girth" (W. W. Arendt, "Sur l'apparition de l'étrier chez les Scythes," *ESA*, IX [1934], 208). Arendt adds that this is borne out by study of the materials of the Kozel tumulus, near Novo Alexandrovka in the Melitopol district, now in the Historical Museum of Moscow. Similarly, the use of the stirrup by the Hsiung-nu from the third century onward is said to have been demonstrated. Yet it hardly appears on the Chinese reliefs of the Han period. It is found on Oirotin saddles (Altai) of the first century B.C. In the West it was known neither by Greeks nor Romans, and it seems that only the Avars of the sixth century brought it into common use there.

13. For funerary rites among the Scythians, see Herodotus, IV, 71 (the custom of gashing arms, forehead, and nose in honor of the deceased, and the immolation and burial of servants and horses round the corpse). For those of the Hsiung-nu, or Huns of Mongolia, see *Ch'ien Han Shu*, summarized by Édouard Chavannes, in *Les mémoires historiques de Sse-ma Ts'ien* (5 vols., Paris, 1895–1905), I, lxv (immolation of victims on the chief's tomb, to the number of a hundred or a thousand women and servants). Lastly, for the T'u-chüeh or Turks of Mongolia in the sixth century, descendants of the Huns, see Stanislas Julien, "Documents sur les T'ou-kiue," *JA* (1864), p. 332: "They gash their faces with a knife, so that one may see blood flow with their tears."

14. According to Herodotus, IV, 13, the Scythian migration toward Europe was a repercussion of the surge from the east, or rather the

northeast; for the Scythians had been thrust back by the Issedones, and the Issedones by the Arimaspi. From Herodotus' description, the Issedones may have been Finno-Ugrians. Émile Benveniste seeks them, in the classical period, near the Urals, at the Ekaterinburg gap, for instance. The Arimaspi, who most probably lived farther to the east, near the Irtysh and the Yenisei, seem like the Scythians to have been Iranians, as is borne out by their name, which Benveniste derives from *Ariamaspa:* "friends of horses" (statement by Benveniste to the Société Asiatique, April 7, 1938). As for the Massagetae of the southeastern shores of the Aral Sea, Herodotus himself, I, 201, regards them as Scythians. Moreover, their name in Iranian is *Massyagata,* meaning "the fishers" (J. Marquart, "Skizzen zur geschichtlichen Völkerkunde des Mittelasien und Siberien," *FFH,* p. 292). Certain ancient authors such as Dio Cassius and Arrian see in the Massagetae the forebears of the Sarmatian race of Alans. Concerning the "agricultural Scythians," that is to say, no doubt the natives of the *Chernoziom* upon which nomad (or true) Scythians levied contributions, cf. Scherbakivski, "Zur Agathyrsenfrage," *ESA,* IX (1934), 208.

15. For subsequent Scythian history, principally in its relations with the Greek world, see Max Ebert, *Süd-Russland im Alterthum* (Leipzig, 1921).

16. Tallgren, "Sur l'origine des antiquités dites mordviennes," *ESA,* XI (1937), 123. Cf. K. Schefold, "Skytische Tierstil in Süd-Russland," *ESA, XII* (1938).

17. Emile Benveniste, statement to the Société Asiatique, April 7, 1938.

18. Tallgren, *ESA,* XI (1937), 128.

19. *Ibid.,* p. 127.

20. Cf. N. Makarenko, "La civilisation des Scythes et Hallstatt," *ESA,* V (1930), 22.

21. F. Hančar, "Gürtelschliessen aus dem Kaukasus," *ESA,* VII (1931), 146, and "Kaukasus-Luristan," *ESA,* IX (1934), 47.

22. Typical reproductions may be seen in M. I. Rostovtzeff, *Animal Style in South Russia and China* (Princeton, 1929), and *Le centre de l'Asie, la Russie, la Chine et le style animal* (Prague, 1929); G. I. Borovka, *Scythian Art* (New York, 1928).

23. J. G. Andersson, "Hunting Magic in the Animal Style," *BMFEA,* No. 4 (1932). See on pp. 259 *et seq.* of the same study, an essay on the classification of equine, cervid, and other animals of the steppe, and a comparison of these with the types shown on the Ordos bronzes. For the magical origin of ornamental motifs in steppe art, see also O. Janse, "Le cheval cornu et la boule magique," *Ipek,* I (1935), 66,

and Potapoff, "Conceptions totémiques des Altaïens," *RAA* (1937), p. 208.

24. Cf. Josef Zykan, "Der Tierzauber," *AA*, V (1935), 202.

25. Tallgren, "Sur l'origine des antiquités dites mordviennes," *ESA*, XI (1937), 133.

26. Nevertheless, Herodotus, IV, 116, mentions "Sauromatians" to the east of the mouth of the Don in the fifth century B.C., and speaks of them as being a mixture of Scythians and Amazons, speaking the Scythian language. Could these have constituted a vanguard that followed the Scythians well before the main body of the Sarmatians, who at this period were still leading a nomadic life north of the Caspian? (Cf. Max Ebert, *Süd-Russland im Alterthum*, pp. 339–340.) Yet Rostovtzeff points out that so essential a feature as matriarchy, which the Greeks affirm to have prevailed among the Sauromatians, is nowhere to be found among the Sarmatians. He believes that the two peoples have nothing in common (*Iranians and Greeks*, p. 113).

27. At that moment the Scythians must have found themselves trapped between the Sarmatians coming from Asia and the spreading Getae (the future Dacians) of Thraco-Phrygian stock, who carved themselves an empire in Hungary and Rumania.

28. Strabo, XI, 2.

29. For other characteristic bronzes, albeit discovered in what was doubtless a Finno-Ugrian rather than Sarmatian area, the reader is referred to the objects in the Ufa barrow, west of the southern Ural River, and those of the Ekaterinovka treasure between Ufa and Perm, all dated by Tallgren from between 300 and 100 B.C. (Tallgren, "Etudes sur la Russie orientale durant l'ancien âge du fer," *EAS*, VII [1932], 7). The "curled animal" plaques found at Gliadenovo, northeast of Perm, seem of equally Sarmatian inspiration, and Tallgren dates them from the beginning of this era. The large plaques in the treasure of Peter the Great, found in western Siberia, seem to constitute the transition from Scythian or "delayed Scythian" to Sarmatian. Nevertheless, they are of the Scythian period, being associated with coins of Nero and Galba. Cf. Joachim Werner, "Zur Stellung der Ordosbronzen," *ESA*, IX (1934), 260.

30. See the reproductions in Rostovtzeff, *Iranians and Greeks*, Plate XXV; Borovka, *Scythian Art*, pp. 46–48, figs. 7 and 8.

31. Cf. Tallgren, "Oglakty," *ESA*, XI (1937), 71.

32. Cf. Tallgren, *Collection Tovostine des antiquités de Minoussinsk* (Helsinki, 1917); J. Merhart, *Bronzezeit am Ienissei* (Vienna, 1926); Teplukhov, "Essai de classification des anciennes civilisations métalliques de la région de Minoussinsk," *Materialy po Etnographii* (Leningrad, 1929), IV.

33. These cup cauldrons, with their cylindrical body and straight, rectangular "ears," are to be found both in the Cernuschi Museum (Baye mission, in the Minusinsk region) and in the museums of Budapest. Cf. Zoltán Takács, "Francis Hopp Memorial Exhibition," *The Art of Greater Asia* (Budapest, 1933), pp. 17 and 68.

34. For the immolation of horses around the body of the chief in Scythian tombs, see Herodotus, IV, 72; and for reindeer, see *Acad. Cult. Matér.* (February, 1931).

35. For the group comprising Pazyryk, Shibe, Katanda, etc., cf. M. P. Griaznov, in *American Journal of Archaeology* (1933), p. 32; S. V. Kiseleff, "Fouilles de 1934 dans l'Altai," trans. in *RAA*, X, 4 (1937), 206; Laure Morgenstern, "L'exposition de l'art iranien à Léningrad et les découvertes de Pasyryk," *ibid.*, p. 199, and *Esthétiques d'Orient et d'Occident* (Paris, 1937). Joachim Werner in *ESA*, IX (1934), 265. For the Pazyryk mascarons, see A. Salmony, "Chinesische Schmuckform in Eurasien," *ibid.*, p. 329. For coins of the Bosporus, 3rd century B.C., found in Dzungaria, see *ibid.*, p. 249.

36. Griaznov, in *American Journal of Archaeology* (1933), p. 32; Tallgren, "Oglakty," *ESA*, XI (1937), 69.

37. The races may then have become mingled. Gardizi relates that in his day the Kirghiz still had white skin and red hair. Moreover, these Kirghiz of the Yenisei were not originally a Turkic-speaking people (W. V. Radloff, *Die alttürkischen Inschriften der Mongolei* [St. Petersburg, 1895–99], p. 425).

38. There may be grounds for relating to Sarmatian art—or at least to the late-antiquity forms derived from it—some part of the very curious rock paintings discovered in Siberia and even in Mongolia (on Mount Oglakty (Kizilkaya or Qyzyl-qaya ["Red Rocks"]), at Sulak near Minusinsk, at Morosova in Uriangkhai on the upper Yenisei, and lastly at Durbelji and at Ilkhe-Alyk on the Orkhon). The frescoes of Uriangkhai (Tannu-Ola) show remarkably realistic sketches of deer and bears, with a lineal movement evoking the best Greco-Scythian work (Buluk, Kedrala, Tsaghan-gol). On the other hand, certain rock drawings of Sulak near Minusinsk, representing horsemen wearing what looks like a conical helmet and carrying bow and long lance, are not at all unlike the Romano-Sarmatian frescoes of Kerch in the Crimea. It is true that at Sulak "runic" inscriptions have been found, which leads some people to date these paintings as late as the seventh century A.D. Cf. Tallgren, "Inner Asiatic and Siberian Rock Pictures," *ESA*, VIII (1933), 175–197. Elsewhere Fettich has shown the relationship between the last Minusinsk culture of the seventh century A.D. and the proto-Hungarian art of the Levedian epoch. Cf. Nandor

Fettich, "Die Reiternomadenkultur von Minussinsk," *Metallkunst der Landnehmenden Ungarn, AU* (1937), p. 202.

39. "Can the names Hsiung-nu, Hans, and Huna have no connection with one another? *A priori* this is not very likely" (Pelliot, "A propos des Comans," *JA* (1920), p. 141).

40. The official promoter of this dress reform was, according to Ssu-ma Ch'ien, the king of Chao, Wu-ling, in 307. See Chavannes, trans., *MHST*, V, 73.

41. Cf. *MHST*, I, lxv. Kurakichi Shiratori explains the word *shan-yü* by a Chinese estymology meaning "boundless immensity" (K. Shiratori, "A Study on the Titles of Khagan and Khatun," *MTB*, I, 11, and "On the Territory of the Hsiung-nu," *MTB*, V, 71.

42. Albert Herrmann, "Die Gobi im Zeitalter der Hunnenherrschaft," *Geografiska Annaler* (1935), p. 131.

43. *MHST.*

44. Shiratori notes that the Hsiung-nu wore the queue, and that from them the custom spread to the succeeding Turko-Mongol hordes, the Toba, Juan-juan, T'u-chüeh, Khitan, and Mongols. Cf. "The Queue among the Peoples of North Asia," *MTB*, IV (1929).

45. *Ch'ien Han Shu* in *MHST*, I, lxv and lxx.

46. Stanislas Julien, "Documents sur les T'ou-kiue," *JA* (1864), p. 332.

47. Herodotus, IV, 62, 64.

48. *Ch'ien Han Shu* in *MHST*, I, lxv.

49. *Ibid.*, p. lxiii. Cf. J. J. M. de Groot, *Die Hunnen der vorchristlichen Zeiten*, pp. 2 *et seq.*

50. After their great raid in the seventh century, the Scythians ceased to enjoy as great a reputation for plundering as did the Hsiung-nu, no doubt because their country was richer and because this nomad cavalry of the Black Sea borders lived on the "agricultural Scythians" who cultivated the Black Land of the Ukraine.

51. Shiratori, "Sur l'origine des Hiong-nou," *JA*, I (1923), 71. But the same author, by other linguistic arguments, has also maintained the Turkic nature of the Hsiung-nu; see "Über die Sprachen der Hsiung-nu und der Tung-hu Stämme," *BAIS*, XVII (1902), 2.

52. T. J. Arne, "Die Funde von Luan-p'ing und Hsuan-hua," *BMFEA*, V (1933), 166.

53. S. Umehara, *Shina kodo seikwa*, Yamanaka ed. (1935), III.

54. Karlgren, "New Studies on Chinese Bronzes," *BMFEA*, IX (1937), 97.

55. Cf. O. Janse, "Le style du Houai et ses affinités," *RAA*, VIII (1934), 159. For a survey of what has been established from a chrono-

logical point of view, see Joachim Werner, "Zur Stellung der Ordos-bronzen," *ESA*, IX (1934), 259, and Herbert Kühn, "Sur Chronologie der Sino-Siberischen Bronzen," *Ipek* (1934).

56. Other finds of the same order, closely linked with the Ordos style, have been made by Talko-Hryncewicz near Tultu on the lower Chita, and near Bichurskoye, on the Khilok, in the Selenga basin. Cf. Werner in *ESA*, IX (1934), 261.

57. G. I. Borovka, *et al.*, *Comptes rendus des expéditions pour l'exploration du nord de la Mongolie* (Leningrad, 1925); K. V. Trever, *Excavations in Northern Mongolia, 1924–1925* (Leningrad, 1932). Cf. Werner in *ESA*, IX (1934), 264.

58. Cf. Andersson, "Hunting Magic in the Animal Style," *BMFEA*, No. 4, p. 308; Tallgren, "Inner Asiatic and Siberian Rock Pictures," *ESA*, VIII (1933), 175.

59. Cf. *Guide to the Exhibitions of the Museum of Far Eastern Antiquities* (Stockholm, September 10, 1933), p. 40.

60. Cf. Solange Lemaître, "Les agrafes chinoises," *RAA*, XI (1938).

61. Arne, "Västsibirisk kultur för 1000 år sedan," in *Etudes archéologiques dédiées au Prince Héritier Gustave Adolphe* (Stockholm, 1932), pp. 351–367.

62. Pelliot, "Sceaux-amulettes de bronze avec croix et colombes," *RAA*, VII (1931).

63. Alfred Salmony, *Sino-Siberian Art in the Collection of C. T. Loo* (Paris, 1933), pp. 93–94. Two publications on Ordos art are those of V. Griessmayer, *Sammlung Baron von der Heydt, Ordos Bronzen . . .* (Vienna, 1936), and "Entwicklungfragen der Ordos-Kunst," *AA*, VII (1937), 122.

64. For this period, see J. J. M. de Groot, *Die Hunnen der vorchristlichen Zeiten*, and O. Franke, "Wiedergabe fremder Völkernamen durch die Chinesen," *OZ* (1920–21). Cf. G. Haloun, "Seit wann kannten die Chinensen die Tocharer oder Indogermanen überhaupt," *AM* (1926).

65. Cf. *MHST*, I, lxx.

66. In the current Chinese word Yüeh-chih, Gustav Haloun seeks an ancient pronunciation Z*gudja*, identical with the name of the Scythians (*Ashkuzai* in Assyrian). Cf. Haloun, "Zur Ue-tsi Frage," *ZDMG*, Vol. 91, 2 (1937), 316. See also in the same article the suggested location of the primitive Yüeh-chih on the map of northern and western Kansu (p. 258).

67. Ptolemy, VI, 16. Ninth-century Sogdian texts still designate the countries of Beshbaligh, Turfan, Kara Shahr, and so on as "the Four Tughri" (W. B. Henning, "Argi and the Tokharians," *BSAS* [1938], p. 560).

68. Strabo, XI, 8, 2, and *Ch'ien Han Shu*, trans. Toru Haneda, *Bulletin de la maison franco-japonaise*, IV, I (Tokyo, 1933), 7–8.

69. A lucid exposition of the Tokharian question, with a review of various hypotheses and a bibliography, may be found in Sigmund Feist, "Der gegenwärtige Stand des Tocharerproblems," in *FFH*, pp. 74–84. For later modifications of views, see René Grousset, "L'Orientalisme et les études historiques," *Revue historique, Bulletin critique*, CLXXXI, fasc. 1 (January–March, 1937). This article relates to H. W. Bailey, "Ttaugara," *BSAS*, VIII, 4 (1936), and Pelliot, "À propos du tokharien," *TP*. See also W. W. Tarn, *The Greeks in Bactria and India* (Cambridge, 1938).

70. The same custom is recorded by Herodotus, IV, 65, in connection with the Scythians.

71. Cf. *MHST*, I, lxx.

72. Pelliot, in *JA*, I (1934), 37.

73. It seems indeed that the Wu-sun were also immigrants into the Ili region and, like the Yüeh-chih themselves, were driven by the Hsiung-nu from the northwestern borders of China, notably from the Sobo Nor and Sogok Nor region north of Süchow, as is suggested in the *Atlas of China* of Albert Herrmann, Map 17; or slightly farther south, from Kanchow, as Shiratori believes; or again, as is possible, farther west, from Kwachow near Tunhwang. Cf. Kurakichi Shiratori, "On the Territory of the Hsiung-nu Prince Hsiu-t'u Wang and His Metal Statues for Heaven-Worship," *MTB*, I, 5 (1930), 16–20. The question has been raised as to whether the Yüeh-chih migration may have caused the backward surge of the Sarmatians, who went on to capture southern Russia from the Scythians. The chronology hardly supports this theory. Cf. Rostovtzeff, *Recueil Kondakov* (Prague, 1926), p. 239; N. Fettich, in *AU* (1937), p. 142.

74. Jarl Charpentier, "Die ethnographische Stellung der Tocharer," *ZDMG*, Vol. 71 (1917).

75. As the word *Asioi* bears a relation to the Turko-Mongol name for Alans (root *As*, plural *Asod* in Mongolian), Charpentier concludes that the Wu-sun are the ancestors of the Alans, a Sarmatian (that is northern Iranian) people. "Die ethnographische Stellung der Tocharer," *ZDMG*, Vol. 71 (1917), 357–361.

76. Bailey, *BSAS*, VIII, 4 (1936), 916; Tarn, *The Greeks in Bactria and India*, p. 290.

77. Toru Haneda, "À propos des Ta Yue-tche et des Kouei-chouang," *Bulletin de la maison franco-japonaise*, IV, I (Tokyo, 1933), 13.

78. Cf. O. Franke, "Das alte Ta-hia der Chinesen, ein Beitrag zur Tocharer Frage," *FFH*, p. 117.

79. Haneda's trans., in "À propos des Ta Yue-tche," p. 8.

80. Trans. Chavannes, in "Les pays d'Occident d'après le Heu-Han chou," *TP* (1906), p. 230.

81. Tarn, *The Greeks in Bactria and India*, p. 283, merely notes that the Saka conquest of Bactria in Strabo, XI, 8, 4, relates to the seventh century and not to the second. Cf. J. Przyluski, "Nouveaux aspects de l'histoire des Scythes," *Revue de l'Université de Bruxelles* (February–April, 1937), p. 3.

82. "From this moment," notes the *Hou Han Shu*, "the Yüeh-chih became exceedingly powerful. All the various kingdoms call them Kuei-shuang [Kuchan], but the Han call them Yüeh-chih, retaining their ancient name." (Trans. Chavannes in *TP* [1907], p. 192.)

83. Correction by Pelliot, *Tokharien et Koutchéen*, *JA*, I (1934), 30.

84. New chronology proposed by R. Ghirshman, "Fouilles à Begram," *JA* (1943–44), pp. 70–71; also, L. de La Vallée-Poussin, *L'Inde aux temps des Mauryas et des Barbares* (Paris, 1930), p. 343. There are great numbers of linguistic comparisons and ethnical hypotheses in Sten Konow, "Beitrag zur Kenntniss der Indoskythen," *FFH*, p. 220. But note the skepticism of La Vallée-Poussin and of the critical essay by H. W. Bailey, "Ttaugara," *BSAS*, VIII, 4 (1936), especially (p. 912) disputing the name of *Arshi*, identified with *Asioi* and applied to the Tokharians. See also Henning, "Argi and the Tokharians," *BSAS* (1938), p. 545.

85. Cf. Albert Herrmann, "Die Gobi im Zeitalter der Hunnenherrschaft," *Geografiska Annaler* (1935), p. 130.

86. For the wars of Wu-ti, see *MHST*, I, lxii–lxxxviii, and Avant, *History of Former Han*, 1938.

87. In 161 B.C., Kiun-ch'en had succeeded his father, the famous *shan-yü* Lao-shang.

88. Cf. *MHST*, I, lxxi–lxxii.

89. *Ibid.*, I, lxvii–lxviii; Kurakichi Shiratori, "On the Territory of the Hsiung-nu Prince Hsiu-t'u Wang and His Metal Statues for Heaven-Worship," *MTB*, I, 5, pp. 7–21.

90. *MHST*, I, lxviii. Cf. Albert Herrmann, *Atlas of China*, Map 17, 2; J. Lartigue, *Mission archéologique en Chine 1914 et 1917*, Paris, 1923–24, I, Pl. 1, and *L'art funéraire à l'époque Han* (Paris, 1935), p. 33; Zoltán Takács, *The Monument of Ho Ch'uping* (Budapest, Mahler ed., 1937).

91. *MHST*, I, lxxxvii.

92. *Ibid.*, pp. lxxiv–lxxv.

93. *Ibid.*, pp. lxxv–lxxvii. As has been well established by Perceval Yetts, the Chinese campaign in Fergana was no mere parade or display. China had great difficulty in dealing with the redoubtable Hsiung-nu horsemen, those terrible mounted archers who, astride

their little Mongolian horses (*Equus przhevalskii*), made periodic raids upon her borders. The Chinese, inferior riders mounted on the same breed of horse, were at a disadvantage. Fergana, like neighboring Sogdiana, possessed a superior war horse, the great horse of Transoxiana; perhaps the same as that known to the Greeks in Media as the Nisaean horse. The Chinese had the idea of acquiring remounts for part of their cavalry from this large foreign breed, which, they thought, must surpass the shaggy pony of the Huns. Hence the expedition to Fergana, by which they meant to ensure military superiority over the nomads. (Indeed, in reliefs of the second Han period, at Siao-t'ang-shan for example, one may see the big horse of Transoxiana beside the little Przhevalski animal.) The query has been raised as to whether Fergana did not still belong to the last of the Greco-Bactrians, as the Chinese name of that country, "Ta-yüan," has been thought to relate to the Indo-Iranian name for the Greeks, *Yavana:* that is, Ionians. See the fine article by Perceval Yetts, *The Horse: A Factor in Early Chinese History,* ESA, IX (1934), 231.

94. *MHST,* I, lxxv–lxxviii.

95. *Ch'ien Han Shu, ibid.,* p. xxxviii.

96. Cf. Kozlov *et al., Comptes rendus des expéditions pour l'exploration du nord de la Mongolie* (Leningrad, 1925).

97. It should be remembered that Greek coins from Panticapaeum (Kerch), of the third century B.C., were found in 1918 on the Borotala, in Dzungaria. Cf. J. Werner, in *ESA,* VIII (1933), 249.

98. Chinese monographs on these various kingdoms during the late Han period have been translated from the *Hou Han Shu* by Chavannes in "Les pays d'Occident," *TP* (1907), pp. 168–221.

99. E. Sieg and W. Siegling, *Tocharische Grammatik* (Göttingen, 1931), and observations by Sylvain Lévi, *Fragments des textes koutchéens* (Paris, 1933). For the relative positions of Kuchean and other dialects among the other Indo-European languages, see H. Pedersen, "Le groupement des dialectes indo-européens," in *Kgl. danske Vid. sel. hist. fil. meddelelser,* XI, 3 (1925).

100. Cf. Albert Herrmann, "Die alten Seidenstrassen zwischen China und Syrien," *Quell. u. Vorsch. z. alten Gesch. u. Geog.* (1910); "Die Seidenstrassen von China nach dem Römischen Reich," *Mitt. der Geogr. Ges.* (1915), p. 472; and "Die altesten chinesischen Karten von Zentral- und Westasien," *FFH,* p. 185.

101. "Biographie de Keng Ping," trans. from the *Hou Han Shu* by Chavannes, *TP* (1907), p. 222.

102. Biography of Pan Ch'ao, Pan Yung, and Liang K'in, trans. from the *Hou Han Shu* by Chavannes under the title of "Trois généraux chinois de la dynastie des Han," *TP* (1906), p. 218.

103. *Hou Han Shu,* trans. Chavannes, *TP* (1907), p. 156.

104. *Hou Han Shu,* "Biographie de Keng Ping," trans. Chavannes, *TP* (1907), pp. 222–223.

105. *Ibid.,* p. 226.

106. *Hou Han Shu,* "Biographie de Pan Tch'ao," *TP* (1907), pp. 218–220.

107. *Ibid.,* p. 197.

108. *Ibid.,* pp. 203–204.

109. This name is of course the Chinese transcription of an unknown Khotan name.

110. *Hou Han Shu, TP* (1907), p. 222.

111. *TP* (1906), pp. 226–229.

112. *Ibid.,* pp. 223–224.

113. *TP* (1907), p. 230.

114. *TP* (1906), pp. 224–227.

115. *Ibid.,* pp. 230–231.

116. *Ibid.,* pp. 231–232.

117. *Ibid.,* p. 233.

118. *Ibid.,* pp. 235–236.

119. *TP* (1907), p. 178.

120. *TP* (1906), pp. 256–257.

121. *Ibid.,* pp. 246–254.

122. Cf. Peter Boodberg, "Two Notes on the History of the Chinese Frontier," *HJAS,* 3–4 (November, 1936), 286.

123. Under heading 155 the *Hou Han Shu* speaks of the setting up of a Chinese garrison at K'iu-tsu, or Kucha. Peter Boodberg believes that this refers not to the Kucha on the River Muzart in Central Asia, but to one more recently founded by Kuchean deportees or emigrants in the northeastern part of Shensi, probably north of Yülin. *HJAS,* 3–4 (November, 1936), 286.

124. Reproductions in Sir Mark Aurel Stein's *Ancient Khotan* (Oxford, 1907), II, Pls. XIV *et seq.,* XLIX, and LXXI; *Serindia* (Oxford, 1921), IV, Pls. XL–XLII and Figs. 134, 136 *et seq.,* pp. 517, 520 *et seq.; On Ancient Central-Asian Tracks* (London, 1933), Pls. 54, 57. See also F. H. Andrews, "Central Asian Wall-Paintings," *Indian Arts and Letters,* VIII, 1 (1934).

125. Translated from the *Tripitaka* by Sylvain Lévi in "Le 'Tokharien B,' langue de Koutcha," *JA,* II (1913), 335.

126. Cf. E. Herzfeld, "Kushano-Sassanian Coins," *Memoirs of the Archaeological Survey of India,* No. 38 (1930); J. Hackin, "Répartitions des monnaies anciennes en Afghanistan," *JA* (April–June, 1935), p. 287.

127. Cf. A. Godard, Y. Godard, and J. Hackin, *Les antiquités bouddhiques de Bamiyan* (Paris, 1928); J. Hackin and J. Carl, *Nou-*

velles recherches archéologiques à Bâmiyân (Paris, 1933); J. Hackin and J. Carl, *Recherches archéologiques au col de Khair Khaneh* (Paris, 1936).

128. Hackin, "L'art indien et l'art iranien en Asie Centrale," in *Histoire des arts,* ed. L. Réau, IV, 253, and "Buddhist Art in Central Asia," in *Studies in Chinese Art and Some Indian Influences* (London, 1938), p. 12.

129. See *RAA,* XII (1938).

130. A. von Le Coq, *Bilderatlas zur Kunst- und Kulturgeschichte Mittel-Asiens* (Berlin, 1925), Figs. 32, 33, 50; M. I. Rostovtzeff, *Iranians and Greeks in South Russia* (Oxford, 1922), Pl. 29.

131. I think it possible that the influence of the Kucha frescoes may have penetrated very far to the north, into Siberia. It should be noted that the type of figure shown in the "Kizil knights" may be seen in the rock frescoes of Sulak, in the valley of the Kara-yus (Pisannaya gora) near Minusinsk; here are found horsemen in armor, with conical helmets and long lances, fairly similar to those of the "War of Relics" at Kizil (Von Le Coq, *Bilderatlas,* p. 54, Fig. 50). Tallgren considers that the "flying gallops" of the Sulak horsemen, which suggest the Sassanian and T'ang flying gallops, may date from the seventh century A.D. Even the coarse, anthropomorphic designs of the steles in the Semipalatinsk region, north of Lake Balkhash on the upper Irtysh (Kamennaya baba) recall, with their large turned-over coat collars, the influence of the Sassanizing center of Kucha. Cf. Tallgren, "Inner Asiatic and Siberian Rock Pictures," *ESA,* VIII, 193.

132. Sir Mark Aurel Stein's great publications, *Ancient Khotan* (1907), *Ruins of Desert Cathay* (London, 1912), *Serindia* (1921), *Innermost Asia* (Oxford, 1928), are summarized in the equally well-illustrated book by the same scholar, *On Ancient Central-Asian Tracks* (1933). The same is true of Von Le Coq's great albums, *Buddhistische spätantike in Mittelasien* (Berlin, 1922–33, 7 vols.), of which a résumé may be found in his two succeeding volumes: *Bilderatlas* and *Buried Treasures of Chinese Turkestan* (London, 1928). Also E. Waldschmidt, *Gandhara, Kutscha, Turfan* (Leipzig, 1925), and Hackin, "Recherches archéologiques en Asie Centrale," *RAA* (1936 and 1938, 1).

133. R. and K. Torii, "Études archéologiques et ethnologiques, populations primitives de la Mongolie orientale," *Journal of the College of Science, Imperial University of Japan,* Tokyo, XXXVI, 9 and 19. According to the Torii, the Hsien-pi had remained at a very backward stage, and used aeneolithic and bronze tools. Iron was not introduced among them until the end of the second century A.D. by Chinese refugees (pp. 70 and 96). Pelliot considers that the Chinese tran-

scription Hsien-pi must refer to an original Särbi, Sirbi, or Sirvi ("Tokharien et Koutchéen," *JA*, I [1934], 35).

134. *San Kouo tche,* summarized by Peter Boodberg in "Two Notes on the History of the Chinese Frontier," *HJAS*, 3–4 (November, 1936), 292.

135. For this period, which is as confused as the fifth century in the West, see *Chih Louh Kouoh Kiang Yuh Tchi,* in *Histoire géographique des seize royaumes,* pp. 304–407, trans. Des Michels. Peter Boodberg has attempted to sort out and reconstruct the genealogy and chronology of the Hsiung-nu *shan-yüs* of the third and fourth centuries in *HJAS,* 3–4 (November, 1936), 298.

136. The pronounciation of the modern Chinese word Toba must in old Chinese have been T'ak-b'uat. Pelliot, in *TP* (1912), p. 732.

137. For the origin of the Toba, see Pelliot, in *TP* (1915), p. 689; *JA* (1925), pp. 254–255, note 4; *TP* (1925–26), pp. 79 and 93. See also Boodberg, "The Language of the T'o-pa Wei," *HJAS*, 2 (July, 1936), 167–185, wherein the suggested explanation is also given, by Turkic roots, of the few Toba words which have come down to us in Chinese transcription.

138. L. Wieger, *Textes historiques,* II, 943.

139. The domains of the Mu-jung or kings of Yen, thus cut in two by the sudden expansion of the Toba kingdom of Wei, benefited two branches of the family: (1) The Yen kingdom of the north, Pei-Yen, in modern Jehol, extending from and northeastward of Yungping, with Lungcheng as its center, near the Chaoyang of the present day and on the frontiers of present-day Jehol and one-time Manchukuo. This kingdom lasted until 436. (2) The Yen kingdom of the south, Nan-Yen in Shantung, with its center at Kuangku, near Tsingchow (Yitu); this kingdom lasted from 398 to 410.

140. Cf. Marquart, *Historische Glossen,* p. 196, and *Êrânšchar,* Berlin, 1910, pp. 53 *et seq.;* Chavannes, *Documents sur les T'ou-kiue occidentaux* (St. Petersburg, 1903), pp. 221, 229; Pelliot, "À propos des Comans," *JA* (1920), p. 144; *TP* (1915), p. 688, and (1920), p. 328. K. Shiratori, "Khan and Khagan," *Proceedings of the Japanese Academy* (June, 1926).

141. With the exception of the Nan-Yen kingdom of Shantung, a fragment of the Mu-jung states which in 410 had been annexed by the southern Chinese empire.

142. Pelliot, in *TP* (1912), p. 792.

143. Cf. P. Demiéville, "L'inscription de Yun-kang," *BEFEO,* 3–4 (1925), 449.

144. So called for convenience. Actually, although in French (or English) the two characters representing Hung (father and son)

have a similar pronunciation, in Chinese writing they are quite different.

145. In Byzantine and Syriac geography, Loyang is sometimes referred to as Taugast, from the name of the Tabgatch or Toba.

146. Cf. Chavannes, "Le voyage de Song Yun dans l'Udyâna et le Gandhâra," *BEFEO* (1903), p. 379.

147. Cf. Tallgren, *Collection Tovostine* (Helsinki, 1917). The principal sites where examples of Minusinsk art of this period have been discovered are the villages of Anash, Ayoshka, Oiskaya, Byskar, Gorodcheskaya, Lugovskoye, Malyi-Terek, Protoshilovo, the banks of the River Askys, the village of Tyutshta on the right bank of the River Kazyr, and various points in the Abakan steppe. Weapons of the same style have been found in Russian eastern Mongolia, south of Lake Baikal; at Bichura, near Verkhneudinsk; at Selenginsk; and at Troitsk. Cf. N. Fettich, "Die Reiternomadenkultur von Minussinsk," in *Metallkunst der Landnehmenden Ungarn, AU* (1937), p. 202.

148. *Ibid.*, p. 205.

149. Marquart, "Über das Volkstum der Komanen," in *Osttürkische Dialektstudien* (Berlin, 1914), and Pelliot, "À propos des Comans," *JA* (1920), p. 140.

150. Chavannes, *Documents sur les T'ou-kiue occidentaux,* p. 223. Cf. Albert Herrmann, "Die Hephtaliten und ihre Beziehungen zu China," *AM*, II, 3–4 (1925), 564–580.

151. T. Noeldeke, *Etudes historiques sur la Perse ancienne,* pp. 161, 163; Marquart, *Êrânschar,* p. 57; A. Christensen, *L'Iran sous les Sassanides* (Paris, 1936), p. 284.

152. F. W. K. Müller, *Soghdische Texte,* I, 108.

153. Marquart, *Êrânschar,* pp. 60–63; Christensen, *L'Iran,* p. 289.

154. Localized by Christensen (in agreement with Marquart), *L'Iran,* end map.

155. Marquart, *Êrânschahr,* pp. 55–57; Christensen, *L'Iran,* pp. 287–288.

156. Pelliot, "Tokharien et Koutchéen," *JA*, I (1934), 42; Chavannes, in *TP* (1907), p. 188.

157. The sources, which are somewhat obscure, are discussed by La Vallée Poussin, *Dynasties et histoire de l'Inde,* pp. 52–54.

158. Tabari, *Annals,* trans. H. Zotenberg, Paris, 1867–74, II, 131.

159. Sung Yün, trans. Chavannes, *BEFEO* (1903), pp. 402, 417.

160. Cf. A. Foucher, *Art gréco-bouddhique du Gandhâra* (Paris, 1905–51), II, 589.

161. On Ephthalite numismatics, see Junker, "Die hephtalitischen Münzinschriften," *Sitz. der preuss. Akad. der Wissenschaften* (Berlin, 1930), p. 641; Morgan, *Num. Or.* (1936), pp. 446–457.

162. The texts are discussed in La Vallée Poussin, *Dynasties et histoire de l'Inde*, pp. 62–66.

163. Northwest of Delhi. The kingdom of Thaneswar or Thanesar must certainly have owed its rise to the role of frontier march which it played to protect the world of the Ganges against Hun invasions.

164. Turkology might provide some evidence of this early split between the Huns of Asia and those of Europe. According to N. Poppe, the present-day Chuvashes who occupy the region between Samara and Kazan on the Volga are the descendants of the western Huns. The Chuvash language has characteristics peculiar to itself and distinct from those of all other Turkic tongues. The separation from the other Turkic languages is thought by Poppe and Barthold to have occurred about the beginning of the Christian era. Cf. N. Poppe in *AM*, I, 775, and *Ungarische Jahrbücher*, VII, 151; and Barthold, "Türks," *EI*, p. 948.

165. For the Alans, who are of particular interest because they will be found again, under the name of Asod, in Jenghiz-Khanite Mongol history, cf. Tomaschek, "Alani," in *Real Encyclopädie* by Pauly-Wissowa; Barthold, "Allan," *EI*, p. 315; and V. F. Minorsky, "The Alan," in *Hudud al-Alam*, p. 444. Max Ebert writes: "Toward the end of the second century B.C., the Alans were still leading a nomadic life in the Aralo-Caspian steppe. From there they moved toward the Don. At the time of Strabo, they camped between the Caspian and the Don, whence they made plundering raids on Parthian Azerbaijan." *Süd-Russland im Alterthum*, p. 375. Cf. Marquart, *Osteuropäische und Ostasiatische Streifzüge* (Leipzig, 1903), pp. 164 *et seq.*

166. Cf. L. Franchet, "Une colonie scytho-alaine en Orléanais au Ve siècle. Les bronzes caucasiens du Vendômois," *RS* (February 8 and 22, 1930).

167. Ammianus Marcellinus, XXXI, 2. Sidonius Apollinaris adds: "Armed with a huge bow and long arrows, the Hun never misses his mark. Woe to him at whom he aims, for his arrows bring death!"

168. A Turkish historian, Dr. Reşit Saffet (Kara Şemsi), professor at the University of Istanbul, has outlined an interesting panegyric of Attila, *Contribution à une histoire sincère d'Attila* (Paris and Istanbul, 1934). For Hunnic art in Central Asia and in Hungary, see A. Alföldi, "Funde aus der Hunnenzeit und ihre ethnische Sonderung," *AU* (1932), and Zoltán Takács, "Congruencies Between the Arts of the Eurasiatic Migration Periods," *AA*, V, parts 2, 3, and 4 (1935), 177, in which Takács completes his previous works, "Chinesische Kunst bei den Hunnen," *OZ* (1916), pp. 174–186; "Chinesisch-hunnische Kunstformen," *Bulletin de l'Institut Archéo-*

logique Bulgare (1925), pp. 194–229; "Sino-Hunnica," read at the School of Oriental Studies, *Alexis Petrovics Anniversary Volume* (1934); "L'art des grandes migrations en Hongrie et en Extrême-Orient," *RAA* (1931), p. 32. For the art of eastern Russia at the same period, see Schmidt, "Katchka, Beiträge zur Erforschungen der Kulturen Ostrusslands in der Zeit der Völkerwanderung," *ESA*, I (1927), 18. For a general survey of the Sarmatian, Hunnic, and Avar problem of Hungary, see Fettich, *Metallkunst, AU* (1937; plus a volume of plates).

Chapter 2

1. Cf. Pelliot, "L'Origine de T'ou-kiue, nom chinois des Turcs," *TP* (1915), p. 687; Thomsen, in *ZDMG*, Vol. 78 (1924), 122; F. W. K. Müller, *Uigurica*, II, 67, 97; Marquart, *Untersuchungen zur Geschichte von Eran*, II (1905), 252; Barthold, "Türks," *EI*, p. 948.

2. The ancestor of the T'u-chüeh was suckled by a she-wolf. When grown-up, he mated with her and had ten sons, who were born in their mother's cave (Julien, "Documents sur les T'ou-kiue," p. 326). "At the top of their flagstaffs the T'u-chüeh place a she-wolf's head in gold. The bodyguards of their kings are called wolves. Being born of a she-wolf, they do not want to forget their ancient origin" (p. 331).

3. Cf. Chavannes, *Documents sur les T'ou-kiue occidentaux*, p. 221 (from the *Pei-Shih*, the *Chou Shu*, and the *Liang Shu*).

4. This is confirmed by the Byzantine historian Theophylactus Simocattes, who says that the remnants of the Avars took refuge in the Taugast country, that is to say, among the descendants of the Tabgatch or Toba. Quoted in Chavannes, *Documents*, p. 246.

5. "Chaganus magnus, despota septium gentium et dominus septem mondi climatum" (Theophylactus Simocattes, VII, 7). It has been pointed out that the titles of khagan and khan were Juan-juan—and therefore, it seems, Mongol—titles. So far as is known, the T'u-chüeh were the first Turkic people to use them.

6. Stanislas Julien translated the principal Chinese texts (*Sui Shu, T'ang Shu*, etc.) relating to the T'u-chüeh, notably those of the east, "Documents sur les T'ou-kiue," *JA* (1864). Chavannes continued this work, translating those parts which concern the western T'u-chüeh (*Documents sur les T'ou-kiue occidentaux*, St. Petersburg, 1903) and "Notes additionelles sur les T'ou-kiue occidentaux," *TP* (1904), pp. 1–110.

7. The title of *yabgu* or *yabghu* seems to have been passed on to the Turkic peoples by the ancient Kuchan or Indo-Scythian people.

The Kuchan ruler Kadphises I inscribed it on his coins. Cf. Foucher, *L'art gréco-bouddhique du Gandhâra,* II, 299; Marquart, *Êrânšchar,* p. 204; W. Bang, in *Ungarische Jahrbücher,* VI, 102.

8. For the affinities of the belt ornaments of Kochkar, south of Lake Balkhash, to the Avar bronzes of Hungary, cf. Fettich, *Metallkunst, AU* (1937), pp. 211, 274.

9. The Turks who, at the time of this first contact, found northern China occupied by the Tabgatch, or Toba, continued to call the country by the name of that people; and it is by this same name, Hellenized to Taugast, that Byzantine writers such as Theophylactus Simocattes came to know it. Cf. Thomsen, "Inscriptions de l'Orkhon," in *Mémoires de la Société finno-ougrienne* (Helsinki, 1896), V, 26.

10. For the variants of his name, cf. Marquart, *Historische Glossen zu den alttürkischen Inschriften,* p. 185, and (by the same author) *Êrânšchar,* p. 216. The story of Istämi has been compiled from Chinese, Byzantine, and Arabian sources by Chavannes, *Documents,* pp. 226 *et seq.*

11. For the culture and beliefs of the T'u-chüeh, see Thomsen, "Alttürkische Inschriften aus der Mongolei," in *ZDMG,* n.s., Vol. 3, Part 2 (1924), p. 131.

12. It should be recalled that the Byzantine (Menander and Theophylactus) and Chinese sources are the subject of a comparative study by Chavannes in his *Documents,* pp. 233–252.

13. Indeed, the Armenian historian Sebeos tells that in 597–598 the Persians, led by the Armenian general Sempad Bagratuni, made a counterattack on Turkic territory as far as Balkh. Cf. Marquart, *Êrânšchar,* pp. 65–66; Chavannes, *Documents,* p. 251; Hsüan-tsang, *Histoire de la vie,* trans. Stanislas Julien (Paris, 1851), pp. 61–66.

14. Thomsen, "Inscriptions de l'Orkhon," *Mémoires de la Société finno-ougrienne,* V, 97–98.

15. Thomsen, "Alttürkischen Inschriften aus der Mongolei," *ZDMG* (1924), p. 130.

16. Tängri denotes both sky and god. Pelliot, "Le mont Yu-tou-kin (Ütükän) chez les anciens Turcs," *TP,* 4–5 (1929), 215–216.

17. And no doubt also àn earth goddess, personified in the goddess of Mount Ötükän and identical with Ätügän or Itügän, goddess of the earth among the Mongols of the thirteenth century. Pelliot, "Le mont Yu-tou-kin (Ütükän) chez les anciens Turcs," *TP,* 4–5 (1929), 212–219.

18. The example of Tonyuquq shows that this Chinese accusation is often ill-founded.

19. Julien, "Documents," *JA* (1864), p. 331.

20. Thomsen, "Inscriptions de l'Orkhon," pp. 98–99.

21. From 575 to 585, the khan T'o-po gave hospitality to Jnanagupta, the Gandharan missionary, who had been driven from China, and was converted by him to Buddhism. Cf. Chavannes, "Jinagupta," *TP* (1905), pp. 334, 346.

22. Cf. Chavannes' reconstituted biography of Tardu in *Documents*, p. 48, notes 1 and 241.

23. The Chinese form of the Turkic original Ishpara? Cf. Pelliot, "Sur quelques mots d'Asie Centrale," *JA* (1913), p. 211.

24. It was about this time, in 598, that Tardu sent an embassy to Emperor Maurice in Constantinople with a letter in which he explicitly styles himself supreme khagan, "Great Chief of the Seven Races and Master of the Seven Climates" (Theophylactus in Chavannes' *Documents*, p. 246).

25. Cf. the *Sui Shu*, trans. Chavannes, in *Documents sur les T'ou-kiue occidentaux*, pp. 15–20; F. Jäger, "Leben und Werke des P'ei-kiu, chinesische Kolonialgeschichte," *OZ* (October, 1921).

26. Cf. Pelliot, "Note sur les T'ou-yu-houen et les Sou-p'i," *TP* (1920), p. 323.

27. The Chinese account of this episode, written with a fine epic sweep, has been translated by Julien in "Documents sur les T'ou-kiue," *JA* (1864), pp. 213–219.

28. Chinese sources (the *T'ang Shu*) trans. in Stanislas Julien, "Documents sur les T'ou-kiue," *JA* (1864).

29. *T'ang Shu*, trans. Chavannes, in "Documents," p. 95.

30. Cf. Thomsen, "Inscriptions de l'Orkhon," p. 99. Chinese sources already translated in A. Gaubil, "Histoire de la dynastie des Tang," in *Mémoires concernant les Chinois*, XV, 441.

31. *T'ang Shu*, trans. Chavannes, in *Documents*, pp. 24–25, 52–53.

32. Hsüan-tsang, *Vie*, trans. Julien, p. 55.

33. Chavannes, *Documents*, p. 192.

34. *T'ang Shu*, trans. Chavannes, in *Documents*, pp. 25–26, 53.

35. *Ibid.*, pp. 27–32, 56–58.

36. Cf. Pelliot, "Tokharien et Koutchéen," *JA*, I (1934), 52. Without plunging into linguistics, we may give random instances of the Indo-European character of much of the Kuchean and allied vocabularies: *st* and *nessi* = to be; *ste* = he is; *pâtar, mâter* = father, mother; *pracer* (*frater*) = brother; *se* = son; *tkacer* = daughter; *okso* = ox; *yakwe* (*equus*) = horse; *ñem* = name; *knân* = to know; *klautke, kaklau* = circle; *sâlyi* = salt; *malkwer* = milk; *wek* = voice; *ek* = eye; *trai* = three; *okt* = eight; *ikam* = twenty; *kante* = hundred; *meñe* = moon; *pest* = after.

37. Pelliot, "Le Cha-tcheou Tou tou fou t'ou king et la colonie sogdienne du Lob-nor," *JA*, I (1916), 120.

38. Hackin, notably in "L'art indien et l'art iranien en Asia Centrale," 253, and "Buddhist Art in Central Asia," p. 12.

39. Cf. Hackin, "Recherches archéologiques en Asie Centrale," *RAA* (1936).

40. Cf. Pelliot, "Note sur les anciens noms de Koutcha, d'Aqsu et d'Utch-Turfan," *TP* (1923), p. 127, and "Tokharien et Koutchéen," *JA* (1934), pp. 86–87; H. Lüders, "Weitere Beiträge zur Geschichte und Geographie von Osttürkistan," *Sitz. der preuss. Akad. der Wissenschaften* (Berlin, 1930), p. 17. In the so-called "Tokharian A" texts, Sieg believed he recognized the name *ârçi* as denoting the Tokharian people, and to this the names of the *Asioi, Wu-sun, Alans,* etc., were already beginning to be related. But Bailey proved that this was a case of mistaken interpretation, *ârçi* being merely the "Tokharization" of a Prakrit word *ârça,* representing the Sanskrit word *ârya.* Cf. Bailey, "Ttaugara," *BSAS,* VIII, 4 (1936), 912.

41. The capital of the kingdom of Turfan under the T'ang was not situated on the modern site bearing that name, but farther east, at Idigutschai, which is the old Kara-khoja and which therefore does not entirely correspond to the Kara-khoja of today. Cf. Pelliot, "Kaotch'ang, Qotcho, Houo-tcheou et Qara-khodja," *JA,* I (1912), 579. The Chinese sources of information (*T'ang Shu*) on Turfan have been translated by Chavannes in *Documents,* pp. 101–110, and summarized by Sylvain Lévi in *Fragments des textes koutchéens* (Paris, 1933), p. 15.

42. For the "Tokharian" and Sogdian name (Arg and Ak?) of Kara Shahr, to be found in the Sanskrit transcription Agni, cf. Pelliot, "À propos du tokharien," *TP,* p. 265, and Henning, "Argi and the Tokharians," *BSAS* (1938), p. 564. Chinese sources of information on Kara Shahr have been translated by Chavannes, *Documents,* pp. 110–114, and summarized by Lévi, *Fragments,* pp. 8–15. Confirmation of the Sanskrit name Agni for Kara Shahr is to be found in Lüders, "Weitere Beiträge," p. 20.

43. Chinese sources (*T'ang Shu*) relating to the history of Kucha have been translated by Chavannes, *Documents,* pp. 114–121, and summarized by Sylvain Lévi, "Le 'Tokharien B,' langue de Koutcha," *JA,* II (1913).

44. Hsüan-tsang, *Vie* (trans. Julien), p. 48.

45. The Kuchean for "flower" is *pyapyo* (Lévi, *Fragments des textes koutchéens,* p. 140).

46. Chinese sources (*T'ang Shu*) in Chavannes, *Documents,* pp. 121–128. Cf. Sten Konow, "Khotan Studies," *JRAS* (1914), p. 339; Lévi, "Les rois Fou-tou de Khotan," *ibid.,* p. 1020; F. W. Thomas, "The Language of Ancient Khotan," *AM,* II, 2 (1925), 251.

47. *T'ang Shu,* trans. Chavannes, in *Documents,* p. 121.

48. *Ibid.,* pp. 174–178.

49. *Ibid.,* pp. 32–38, 59–66.

50. The Tibetan documents brought from Tunhwang by Pelliot (Bibliothèque Nationale, Pelliot Fund) and studied by J. Bacot have proved that Tibet's general conversion to Buddhism—hitherto attributed to the Tibetan kings of the seventh century—occurred later (Bacot, communication to the Société Asiatique, 1937).

51. Thomsen, "Inscriptions de l'Orkhon," p. 100.

52. The Quriqan are supposed to have lived on the western shore of Lake Baikal.

53. Thomsen, "Inscriptions de l'Orkhon," pp. 101–102.

54. "The seat of government of the empire was the forest of Ötükän," reads Mo-ki-lien's inscription (*ibid.,* p. 116). The location was suggested by Thomsen in *ZDMG,* Vol. 78 (1924), 123.

55. Radloff, *Die alttürkischen Inschriften der Mongolei,* II. (Radloff, "Die Inschrift des Tonjukuk;" F. Hirth, "Nachworte zur Inschrift des Tonjukuk;" V. V. Barthold, "Die alttürkischen Inschriften und die arabischen Quellen.")

56. Cf. Radloff, *Alttürkischen Inschriften,* II, 31.

57. Hirth's identification, "Nachworte," pp. 56–58.

58. *T'ang Shu* in Chavannes, *Documents,* p. 119.

59. The form Türgish is found in Uigur; see, for example, A. von Gabain, "Die uigurische Uebersetzung der Biographie Hüen-tsangs," *Sitz. der preuss. Akad. der Wissenschaften* (Berlin, 1935), p. 24.

60. *T'ang Shu* in Chavannes, *Documents,* pp. 43, 79 (where two residences of the Türgish khan are mentioned: a "great encampment" in the Tokmak valley and a "small encampment" at Kungyueh, north of the Ili. Cf. Chavannes' remarks, *ibid.,* p. 283).

61. Pelliot, "Neuf notes sur des questions d'Asie Centrale," *TP,* 4–5 (1929), 206–207.

62. Cf. Stanislas Julien, "Documents sur les T'ou-kiue," *JA* (1864), pp. 413–458. On Mo-ch'o and Bäk-chor, see Pelliot, *TP* (1914), p. 450.

63. Julien, "Documents," p. 420.

64. Thomsen, "Inscriptions de l'Orkhon," p. 109.

65. *Ibid.,* p. 105.

66. *Ibid.,* p. 109.

67. Marquart, *Chronologie der alttürkischen Inschriften* (Leipzig, 1898), pp. 17 and 53; Chavannes, *Documents,* p. 283. For So-ko—in Turkic Saqal, according to Pelliot—see *T'ang Shu, ibid.,* pp. 43–44, 79–81.

68. Thomsen, "Inscriptions de l'Orkhon," pp. 110, 111.

69. Cf. Pelliot, "La fille de Mo-tch'o qaghan et ses rapports avec Kül-tegin," *TP* (1912), p. 301.

70. Mo-ki-lien had been nominated earlier by his uncle Mo-ch'o, khan of the Syr Tardush, a Turkic tribe of the Kobdo region.

71. The Thirty Tatars (Otuz Tatar) were slightly farther away. Cf. Thomsen, "Inscriptions de l'Orkhon," p. 140.

72. The Uigur, or the Töläch of old, probably roamed about the Tarbagatai region, southwest of the Altai range of the Mongols, and the Qarluq doubtless grazed near the eastern extremity of Lake Balkhash. The Uigur chiefs, like those of the Qarluq, bore the title of *eltäbir*. Cf. *ibid.*, pp. 127, 128.

73. *Ibid.*, pp. 112, 125–126.

74. *Mémoires concernant les Chinois*, XVI, 11. Cf. J. Marquart, "Skizzen zur geschichtlichen Völkerkunde des Mittelasien und Siberien," *FFH*, p. 291.

75. Thomsen, "Inscriptions de l'Orkhon," pp. 117–118.

76. On the death of Mo-ki-lien, Hsüan-tsung was to give high praise to the peaceful sentiments and sincere friendship which this khagan had shown toward the empire. Cf. Pelliot, "L'inscription chinoise de Bilgä qaghan," *TP*, 4–5 (1929), 238.

77. Cf. Pelliot, "Les funérailles de Kül-tegin," *TP*, 4–5 (1929), p. 246.

78. Pelliot, "L'inscription chinoise de Bilgä qaghan," *TP*, 4–5 (1929), 229–246.

79. A question much disputed among Turkologists is whether or not the Uigur should be identified with the Oghuz. This well-known controversy is based upon the following points:

The case for identifying Uigur with Oghuz is supported by Thomsen ("Inscriptions de l'Orkhon," p. 147) and by Marquart (*Chronologie der alttürkischen Inschriften*, p. 23, and *Osteurspäische und Ostasiatische Streifzuge*, p. 91). Barthold has opposed this theory ("Toghuzghuz," *EI*, p. 848, and "Vorlesungen," p. 53). No less debatable is the exact localization of the Toquz Oghuz or Nine Oghuz mentioned in eighth-century T'u-chüeh inscriptions and in Uigur inscriptions of the ninth century. Barthold ("Türks," *EI*, p. 948) places them very hypothetically north of Ötükän (the Khangai Mountains?); other experts, followed by Albert Herrmann (*Atlas of China*, pp. 35, 39), place them on the middle Kerulen. Those who claim that Uigur and Toquz Oghuz were identical advance the following arguments: (1) In the Orgötü inscription, the Uigur khagan Mo-yen-cho calls his people "On Uigur Toquz Oghuz" (although this may denote a confederation of two separate elements). (2) In the *Oghuz-name*, Oghuz-Khan, the eponymous hero of the Oghuz, says, "I am the khagan of the Uigur" (quoted by Pelliot,

"Sur la légende d'Oghouz-khan en écriture ouigoure," *TP*, 4–5 [1930], 351). But Pelliot is of the opinion that the *Oghuz-name* "was composed in the Uigur tongue of Turfan about 1300"; thus the passage cited may represent no more than a local stylistic addition, made at a later date. (3) Mas'udi, Gardizi, and Yaqut tell us that the Toquz Oghuz were at one time Manichaeans, which would seem to identify them with the Uigur, who became Manichaeans between 763 and 840. The question turns on whether there may have been some confusion in the minds of these three writers between Uigur and Oghuz, owing to the similarity in names. The contrary argument, sustained by Barthold, is that the Toquz Oghuz should be identified not with the Uigur but with the old T'u-chüeh; in effect, the T'u-chüeh khagan Mo-ki-lien, in the Kosho-Tsaidam inscription, calls the Toquz Oghuz "my own people." Nevertheless, those same Orkhon inscriptions show the Toquz Oghuz to have been at least partially autonomous, since they mention the campaigns led by Mo-ki-lien and Kul-tegin to quell their revolts. It is therefore obvious that we cannot be sure that Uigur and Toquz Oghuz were identical. We do not even know whether the Toquz Oghuz of Mongolia mentioned in the Orkhon inscriptions in the eighth and ninth centuries were identical with the Toquz Ghuz and the Ghuzz, mentioned, for example, in the Persian geography *Hudud al-Alam* in the tenth century. At the time, indeed, according to this text, Turks known as Toquz Ghuz lived south of Lake Balkhash, in modern Semirechye, the region of the Ili, Charin, Tekes, and Muzart (Minorsky, *Hudud al-Alam*, pp. 263–279, and map, p. 279); and other Turks called Ghuzz inhabited the region occupied today by the Kirghiz-Kazakh, west of Lake Balkhash and north of the Aral Sea, in the steppes of Sary-Su, Turgai, and Emba (*ibid.*, p. 311, and map, p. 307). It seems that the Ghuzz of the Kirghiz steppe must have been a branch of the Toquz Ghuz of Semirechye, as it is certain that it was from the Ghuzz that the Uzes (*Ouzoi*) of southern Russia emerged in the eleventh century, as well as the Seljuk Turks of Persia also in the eleventh, and the Turkomans of today. But there our certainty ends.

80. *T'ang Shu*, trans. Chavannes, *Documents*, pp. 44–46; *T'ang Shu*, pp. 81, 83. As Marquart has shown, Baga-tarkhan is the Koûrçoûl of Tabari (koûrçoûl = kul-chur). Marquart, *Chronologie der alt-türkischen Inschriften*, p. 38, n. 1; Barthold, "Die alttürkischen Inschriften und die arabischen Quellen," p. 27.

81. *Tse tche t'ong kien* in Chavannes, *Documents*, p. 286, n. 1.

82. *Ibid.*

83. *T'ang Shu, ibid.*, p. 45, n. 1, and p. 143.

84. *Ibid.*, p. 286, n. 1.

85. *Ibid.*, pp. 127, 207.

86. For this period, see the critical essay on Muslim sources in Barthold, *Turkestan down to the Mongol Invasion* (London, 1928), pp. 184–196.

87. *Ibid.*, pp. 184–185, according to Tabari and Baladhuri.

88. Cf. Marquart's opinion in *Chronologie der alttürkischen Inschriften*, p. 8. This is, however, opposed by Barthold in "Die alttürkischen Inschriften und die arabischen Quellen," p. 10, where he expresses his belief that the khagan's nephew was not necessarily Kul-tegin.

89. For the alleged Arab conquest of Kashgar, see H. A. R. Gibb, "The Arab Conquests in Central Asia," *BSAS*, II (1923). An establishment of the facts according to Arab sources (Tabari, Baladhuri) is given by Barthold in *Turkestan*, pp. 185–188. The Chinese sources (*T'ang Shu, Tch'e fou yuan kouei*) are translated by Chavannes in *Documents*, pp. 203, 294.

90. Fergana = Ningyüan in the geographic nomenclature of the T'ang.

91. *Tse tche t'ong kien* in Chavannes, *Documents*, p. 148.

92. *T'ang Shu, ibid.*, pp. 136, 138.

93. In 719 the viceroy of Tokharistan named Tesh (Ti-shö) sent to the Chinese court a Manichaean versed in astronomy (Chavannes and Pelliot, "Un traité manichéen retrouvé en Chine." *JA*, I [1913], 153). For the Chinese patents conferred upon the *yabghu* of Tokharistan, see *T'ang Shu* and *Tse tche t'ong kien* in Chavannes, *Documents*, pp. 157, 206.

94. Barthold, *Turkestan*, pp. 189–192 (according to Tabari), and Chavannes, *Documents*, pp. 203–207.

95. *T'ang Shu* in Chavannes, *Documents*, pp. 132, 166; *Tch'e fou yuan kouei, ibid.*, pp. 209, 213.

96. *T'ang Shu, ibid.*, pp. 151 and 214 (pp. 151–152, biography of Kao Sien-chih according to the *T'ang Shu*), and Chavannes' reconstruction, p. 296.

97. *Ibid.*, pp. 142, 297; Barthold, *Turkestan*, pp. 195–196.

98. Cf. Barthold, "Türks," *EI*, pp. 948–949.

99. The king of Khotan, Wei-chö Cheng (of the Wei-chö dynasty), also brought a contingent of troops to aid the T'ang against the rebels.

100. From this Chinese transcription Mo-yen-cho, Schlegel has postulated a Turkic name Moyun-chor; whereas, as Pelliot notes, the equivalent would more probably be Bayan-chor (Pelliot, "À propos des Comans," *JA* [1920], p. 153). The Uigur title of this prince is *Tängrida qut bulmysh il ytmish bilgä qaghan*. In the Orgötü valley, between the Orkhon and the Selenga, his tomb has been found, and on it an inscription still in ancient or "runic" Turkic. Cf. Ramstedt, *Zwei*

Uigurischen Runeninschriften in der Nord-Mongolei (Helsinki, 1913), XXX, and Chavannes, in *TP* (1913), p. 789.

101. In a Manichaean fragment and in the Karabalgasun inscription of approximately 820, this khagan is referred to by a series of qualificatives: "*Ulug ilig* [great king], *tängrida qut bulmysh* [by Heaven having obtained majesty], *ärdämin il tutmysh* [through merit holding in his hand the kingdom], *alp* [heroic], *qutlugh* [majestic], *külüg* [glorious], *bilgä* [wise]" (F. W. K. Müller, *Uigurica*, II, 95).

102. Cf. Chavannes and Pelliot, "Un traité manichéen retrouvé en Chine," *JA*, I (1913), 190, 195–196.

103. *Ibid.*, p. 276. At this time China stood in great need of an Uigur alliance against the Tibetans. About 787, the Tibetans had seized the Kucha oasis from the last of the T'ang garrisons, but they were afterward driven out by the Uigur. In 791 they attacked the Chinese outpost of Lingwu, near Ningsia in Kansu, and once more it was thanks to the Uigur that they were repulsed. From 783 until 849, and again until 860, they stubbornly held the Sining and Linchow region in southwest Kansu.

104. Cf. Radloff, *Atlas der Alterthümer der Mongolei* (St. Petersburg, 1892–99), Pls. XXXI–XXXV; Radloff, *Antiquités de l'Orkhon* (Helsinki, 1892), pp. 50–60; F. W. K. Müller, *Sitz. der preuss. Akad. der Wissenschaften* (Berlin, 1909), p. 276.

105. We may note that the Manichaean prohibition against consuming milk and butter, difficult to observe in this land of cattle raising and kumiss (fermented mare's milk), must, together with the admonition to eat vegetables, have turned the Uigur from their pastoral life to one based on agriculture (cf. Chavannes and Pelliot, "Traité manichéen," p. 268).

106. The evidence provided by the Sogdian inscription of Karabalgasun, Beshbaligh, Turfan, Kara Shahr, etc., shows that "the Four Tughri" were subjugated by the Uigur about 800. Henning, "Argi and the Tokharians," *BSAS* (1938), p. 550.

107. Cf. A. von Le Coq, *Buddhistische spätantike in Mittelasien*, II, *Manichäische Miniaturen* (Berlin, 1923), and *Chotscho* (Berlin, 1913), Pls. 1–6.

108. Von Le Coq, *Chotscho*, Pls. 30–32, and *Buddhistische spätantike*, III, Pl. 17; also E. Waldschmidt, *Gandhara, Kutscha, Turfan*, Pls. 16–21.

109. Waldschmidt, *Gandhara, Kutscha, Turfan*, Fig. 18.

110. A Uigur prince of Turfan, of the tenth century, Bughra Sali Tutuq, is represented on one of the Bezeklik frescoes.

111. Cf. von Le Coq, *Kurze Einführung in die uigurische Schriftkunde* (Berlin, 1919), pp. 93–109.

112. See, for instance, Annemarie von Gabain, "Die uigurische Uebersetzung der Biographie Hüen-tsangs," *Sitz. der preuss. Akad. der Wissenschaften* (Berlin, 1935).

113. One of the last Uigur khagans, Wu-kiai (Ugä?), more adventurer than ruler, attempted to maintain his position in the Gobi by waging war both on Kirghiz and Chinese. He was killed in some obscure action in the Altai in 847.

114. See Barthold, "Beshbalik," *EI,* p. 746.

115. The Uigur kings of Kanchow pretended to the title of khagan (Chavannes and Pelliot, "Traité manichéen," p. 179).

116. This appears to be corroborated by the mention of Uigur "celestial khagans" of Kanchow on a number of Buddhic panels of the Caves of the Thousand Buddhas at Tunhwang. Chavannes and Pelliot, "Traité manichéen," p. 303.

117. Barthold, "Türks," *EI,* p. 952. The Basmil, who in the seventh century preceded the Uigur in the region of Kucheng, the former Beshbaligh, had in addition to Turkic their own particular language.

118. We may mention, for instance, the Uigur translation of the *Life of Hsüan-tsang,* dating from the second quarter of the tenth century and recently translated by Miss von Gabain in "Die uigurische Uebersetzung."

119. Barthold, "Toghuzghuz," *EI,* p. 848, and "Türks," *ibid.,* p. 949. Yet the Chinese sources quoted by Chavannes, while stressing the close kinship of Sha-t'o and Ch'u-yueh, mention as a distinction that in the seventh century the former roamed east of Lake Bar Kol and the latter to the west.

120. Barthold, "Toghuzghuz," and Türks," p. 948. Cf. Minorsky, *Hudud al-Alam,* p. 266. The *T'ang Shu,* trans. by Chavannes (*Documents,* p. 96), tells that the Sha-t'o were of western T'u-chüeh stock, deriving in particular from the Ch'u-yueh, a Turkic tribe which in the seventh and eighth centuries roamed seasonally between Kucheng and Lake Bar Kol.

121. For the Khitan, see G. von Gabelentz, *Geschichte der grossen Liao,* trans. from the *Liao-shih* (St. Petersburg, 1877); E. Bretschneider, *Mediaeval Researches* (London, 1888), I, 209; Chavannes, "Voyageurs chinois chez les Khitan et les Joutchen," *JA,* I (1897), 377; J. Mullie, "Les anciennes villes de l'empire des Grands Leao au royaume mongol de Barin," *TP* (1922), p. 105. In Mongol, the singular is Kitan, the plural Kitat.

122. Pelliot, "À propos des Comans," *JA* (1920), pp. 146–147. Let us note that Rashid ad-Din states explicitly that "the Khitan language conforms very closely to that of the Mongols." See also Willy Baruch, "The Writing and Language of the Si-Hia and K'i-tan," in A. Salmony,

Sino-Siberian Art in the Collection of C. T. Loo (Paris, 1933), p. 24, and W. Kotwicz, *Les Khitai et leur écriture* (Lwow, 1925), p. 248. Father Mostaert thought that Khitan was a Mongol plural of Khitai (Mostaert, "Ordosica," *Bulletin 9, Catholic University of Peking* (1934), p. 40.

123. Cf. Chavannes, "Voyageurs chinois," *JA,* I (1897), 382; Bretschneider, *Mediaeval Researches,* I, 265.

124. The cultural influence of the Uigur over the Khitan was apparently considerable. One of the two Khitan scripts seems to have been derived from Uigur writing, the other from Chinese characters. Marquart, *Guwaini's Bericht über die Bekehrung der Uiguren,* pp. 500–501; Chavannes and Pelliot, "Traité manichéen," p. 377.

125. Known as "of the Shu-lü clan"; in Chinese transcription, "Shu-lü shih."

126. Wieger, *Textes historiques,* II, 1537–1538.

127. Cf. Mullie, "Les anciennes villes de l'empire des Grands Leao," *TP* (1922), p. 105. From 1044, Tatung also ranked as a western capital, *hsi-ching.*

128. "Kikow lies thirty *li* southwest of Chochow. By the end of the T'ang dynasty, a 'barrier' (*kuan*) had been set up there. According to the commentator Hu San-sheng, the barrier was north of the river Kiu-ma which rises in the region northwest of Siling and runs slightly to the south of Yichow" (note by des Rotours).

129. The identification of Shenchow, M. des Rotours writes to us, has been utterly confused, first by Mailla and then by Cordier. Mailla (VIII, 147) tells us that the Khitan camped north of Tanyüan. Des Rotours says that this is Mailla's misreading of Shenyüan, another name for Shenchow under the Sung. Cordier muddles the point still further by making Shenchow a different town from Mailla's Tanyüan: "The Khitan camped north of Tanyüan or Taichow—now Kaichow—and besieged Chenchow" (*Histoire générale de la Chine,* Paris, 1777–85, II, 87). In fact, only one single town is in question, the one known during the Sung period as Shenchow, Shenyüan, or Chenchow; as Kaichow during the seventeenth, eighteenth, and nineteenth centuries; and as Puyanghsien under the Chinese Republic, as M. des Rotours has been good enough to establish for me in correcting Mailla's and Cordier's errors.

130. Cf. Chavannes, "Voyageurs chinois," p. 414; Bretschneider, *Mediaeval Researches,* I, 209; Herrmann, *Atlas of China,* pp. 43, 44.

131. Cf. Marquart, *Osttürkische Dialektstudien,* p. 54; Barthold, "Qara-Khitai," *EI,* p. 782, and *Turkestan down to the Mongol Invasion,* p. 279.

132. Cf. Pelliot, "Les documents chinois trouves par la mission Kozlov," *JA* (May–June, 1914), p. 503, and *TP* (1925), pp. 6, 399; Ivanov, "Les monuments de l'écriture tangout," *JA*, I (1920), 107; Willy Baruch, "The Writing and Language of the Si-Hia and K'i-tan," *Sino-Siberian Art*. On Hsi-Hsia art, see A. Bernhardi, "Buddhist. Bilder der Glanzzeit der Tanguten," *OZ* (October, 1917).

133. Barthold, "Kara Khitâi," *EI*, p. 782.

134. Pelliot and L. Ker, "Le tombeau de l'empereur Tao-tsong des Leao (1055–1101) et les premières inscriptions connues en écriture k'i-tan," *TP* (October, 1923), p. 292; W. Kotwicz, "Les Khitai et leur écriture," *Rocznik Orjentalistyczny* (1925), p. 248.

135. Pelliot considers the form Djürtchät (Jurchid) to be the original one. Cf. *TP* (1930), pp. 297 and 336: "Joutchen [Ju-chen] is in fact a corrupt form of Djürtchät."

136. Cf. Chavannes, "Voyageurs chinois chez les Khitan et les Joutchen," *JA*, I (1897), 378; Wieger, *Textes historiques*, II, 1621.

137. The name Wan-yen borne by the royal family may be no more than a Tungusic transcription of the Chinese word *wang*, meaning king or prince. Pelliot, "Sur quelques mots d'Asie Centrale," *JA* (1913), p. 467.

138. Pelliot, *TP* (May–July, 1922), p. 223; C. J. de Harlez, *Histoire de l'empire kin ou empire d'or, traduit de l'Aisin Gurun* (1887).

139. One detail of this war concerns the history of Christendom. In the course of their invasion, the Kin took prisoner certain members of the Öngüt tribe, which later settled in the area of Toqto in northern Shansi, but of which various clans had emigrated in the direction of Lintao in southern Kansu. The Kin deported them into southern Manchuria. These Öngüt were Nestorians, and a vision seen by the king Wu-k'i-mai and explained by one of their icons won them their freedom and resettlement by the Kin at Tsingchow, north of the Yellow River. Pelliot, "Chrétiens d'Asie Centrale et d'Extrême-Orient," *TP* (1914), p. 630.

140. Cf. Barthold, *Turkestan*, p. 381; Pelliot, in *JA* (1920), p. 146.

141. Pelliot, "Chaman," *JA* (March–April, 1913), p. 468; W. Grube, "Note préliminaire sur la langue et l'écriture des Jou-tchen," *TP* (1894), p. 334.

Chapter 3

1. Mirkhond, *Histoire des Samanides* (Paris, 1845), trans. C. F. Defrémery, p. 113.

2. Tabari in Barthold, *Turkestan*, p. 210.

3. This date is discussed in *ibid.,* p. 225.

4. *Ibid.,* p. 224, according to Narshakhi, Tabari, and Mas'udi. This last source states that the Nestorians compulsorily converted by the Samanids were Qarluq Turks.

5. *Ibid.,* p. 243.

6. *Ibid.,* pp. 249–251.

7. Cf. Pelliot, "Notes sur le Turkestan," *TP* (1930), p. 16.

8. Barthold, *Turkestan,* pp. 261, 262.

9. *Ibid.,* p. 268. The date is given by Gardizi.

10. At about the same time, Kashgar is supposed to have been occupied by the Yaghma, another Turkic tribe and a clan of the Toquz Oghuz (first quarter of the tenth century?). For the name of this clan, see Pelliot, in *JA* (1920), p. 135, and *TP* (1930), p. 17; also Minorsky, *Hudud al-Alam,* p. 277. The history of the Karakhanids, hitherto extremely confused, has been clarified by Barthold, who has collated all the Oriental material in his *Turkestan down to the Mongol Invasion* [London, 1928], pp. 254 *et seq.*).

11. Cf. *ibid.,* pp. 258–259.

12. Pelliot suggests the reading Ilig rather than Barthold's Ilek, Ilig being the Uigur word for king. "Notes sur le Turkestan," *TP* (1930), p. 16.

13. Dated by Gardizi in Barthold, *Turkestan,* p. 273. Mahmud's victory over the Karakhanids is attributed to his use of Indian elephants.

14. Communication to the Académie des Inscriptions, 1937.

15. Barthold, *Turkestan,* pp. 285–286, according to Gardizi.

16. For the title of Tamgatch-khan, that is to say, "king of northern China" (Tabgatch), cf. Barthold, *Turkestan,* p. 304. Concerning the Muslim piety of this ruler, see *ibid.,* p. 311 (according to Ibn al-Athir). He was a quite interesting example of a non-nomadic Turk and an able administrator.

17. Minorsky, *Hudud al-Alam,* p. 311 and map, p. 307.

18. Barthold, "Kipčak," *EI,* p. 1082.

19. Cf. Barthold, "Ghuzz," *EI,* p. 178, and "Turkmenes," *ibid.,* p. 943. J. Deny, *Grammaire de la langue turque* (Paris, 1921), p. 326, accounts for the name "Turkmen," adopted by the Ghuzz, by its "augmentative" suffix *män* (or *men*), which in the Turkic language has a sense of intensification. Turkmen would thus signify something like "Turk of pure blood," "thoroughbred Turk."

20. The traditional spelling in Arabo-Persian history became Seljûq (or Saljûq). But originally the correct spelling was Seljuk. Cf. Barthold, *Turkestan,* p. 257.

21. *Ibid.,* p. 257.

22. For the history of the Seljuks, see Ibn al-Athir, *Kâmil fi't Ta'rikh,* partial trans. in *Recueil des historiens des Croisades. Historiens Orientaux* (Paris, 1872–1906, 5 vols.); M. T. Houtsma, *Recueil des textes relatifs à l'histoire des Seljoucides* (Leiden, 1886–1902, 4 vols.); "Histoire des Seljoucides et des Ismaéliens (Târikh-i guzida)," trans. Defrémery, *JA* (1848); Houtsma, "Tughril I," *EI,* p. 872, and "Malik-shâh," *ibid.,* p. 225; Barthold, *Turkestan,* pp. 302 *et seq.*

23. Cf. Claude Cahen, "La campagne de Mantzikert d'après les sources musulmanes," *Byzantion,* IX, 2 (1934), 613.

24. Barthold, *Turkestan,* p. 309.

25. Cf. J. Laurent, *Byzance et les Turcs seldjoucides* (Paris, 1913), pp. 96–98.

26. Barthold, "Ghuzz," *EI,* p. 178.

27. Bibliography in Zettersteen, "Sulaimân," *EI,* p. 559, and Houtsma, "Tutush," *ibid.,* p. 1034; René Grousset, *Histoire des Croisades* (Paris, 1934–36), I, xiv.

28. Cf. Ibn al-Qalanisi, *Damascus Chronicle,* trans. Gibb (1932). I have told the story—a fairly short one—of the Seljuks of Aleppo and Damascus in Vol. I of my *Histoire des Croisades,* to which I refer the reader.

29. "The plateaus of Lycaonia are cold, bare lands where great numbers of onagers graze, but they are almost entirely devoid of drinking water. This lack of water does not prevent livestock from thriving wonderfully throughout the country. The fleece of the flocks, it is true, is somewhat coarse. Here also are salt lakes" (Strabo, XII, 6, 1, Tardieu ed., p. 533).

30. For the effect on Turkish history of the personalities of the first three Seljuks, cf. Barthold, *Turkestan,* p. 305.

31. Cf. Ibn al-Athir, in *Historiens Orientaux,* I.

32. Bibliography in Zettersteen, "Kizil Arslan," *EI,* p. 1113; cf. Houtsma, "Tughril II," *ibid.,* p. 871.

33. Cf. Barthold, *Turkestan,* p. 319.

34. Arslan-khan was deposed in consequence of the intrigues of the Sunnite Muslim "clergy," who were assuming ever greater importance in the affairs of Bukhara and Samarkand. This "clericalism" was to increase in Transoxiana under the shahs of Khwarizm and, after the Jenghiz-Khanite storm, under the Timurids and Uzbeks. *Ibid.,* p. 320.

35. Barthold, *Turkestan,* pp. 326–327, refutes (with Juvaini) Ibn al-Athir, who accuses Atsiz, shah of Khwarizm, of having enlisted the aid of the Kara-Khitai against Sanjar. The victorious Kara-Khitai were just as active in pillaging Khwarizmian territory. The accusation

originated from the fact that Sanjar's defeat proved greatly to Atsiz' advantage.

36. According to Juvaini, Sanjar died on May 8, 1157; cf. *ibid.*, p. 332.

37. The Seljuks even exported Iranian culture to Asia Minor. Those of Konya adopted Persian as their official language, and it remained the court language there, as has been noted, until about 1275 (J. H. Kramers, "Karamân-oghlu," *EI*, p. 793.

38. It was in 1123 that, according to the *Liao-shih*, Ye-lü Ta-shih fled from Peking in the direction of Beshbaligh. Cf. Pelliot, in *JA* (April–June, 1920), p. 174. The name Ta-shih may represent the Chinese title *t'ai-tsu*, prince, or *t'ai-shih*, great teacher. Pelliot, "Notes sur le Turkestan," *TP* (1930), p. 45.

39. Concerning this name, see Bretschneider, *Mediaeval Researches*, I, 18, and Pelliot, "Notes sur le Turkestan," p. 18.

40. For these events, see Juvaini, *Ta'rikh-i Jahan-gusha*, trans. in d'Ohsson, *Histoire des Mongols*, I, 441, and in Bretschneider, *Mediaeval Researches*, I, 225.

41. Cf. Pelliot, "Notes sur le Turkestan," p. 49.

42. Barthold, *Zur Geschichte des Christentums in Mittelasien bis zur Mongolischen Eroberungen* (Tübingen, 1901), p. 58.

43. Rukn ad-Din Mahmud had had to flee with the defeated Seljuk army, but another Karakhanid, Tamgatch-khan Ibrahim, became lord of Samarkand under Kara-Khitai suzerainty (d. 1156). After him, Chagri-khan Jalal ad-Din reigned in this city; he too was a Karakhanid and a vassal of the Kara-Khitai (1156–63). His place was taken by his son Qilich Tamgatch-khan Mas'ud (1163–78).

44. Cf. Barthold, *Turkestan*, pp. 332–333, according to Ibn al-Athir and Juvaini.

45. Cf. Barthold, "Kara Khitâi," *EI*, p. 782, summarizing his history of Semirechye (in Russian, 1898), II, 102 *et seq.*

46. Defrémery has translated the *Histoire des sultans du Kharezm* by Mirkhond (Paris, 1842). The collected Oriental sources, with critical comments, are listed in Barthold's *Turkestan down to the Mongol Invasion*, pp. 322 *et seq.*

47. Barthold, *Turkestan*, pp. 337–340, according to Ibn al-Athir, Juvaini, and Mirkhond.

48. Dated by Ibn al-Athir (*ibid.*, p. 347).

49. The occupation of Herat by the Ghorids in 1175–76 made them the natural enemies of the shah of Khwarizm (*ibid.*, p. 338).

50. Cf. *ibid.*, pp. 350–351.

51. Dated by Juvaini (*ibid.*, p. 353).

52. Juvaini gives two different versions of these events. They are narrated and discussed, *ibid.*, pp. 355–360, with complementary details supplied by Ibn al-Athir.

53. *Ibid.*, pp. 365–366 (according to Juvaini and Ibn al-Athir).

54. Concerning the breach between Muhammad and the caliph, see the review of the sources (Ibn al-Athir, Nasawi, and Juvaini), *ibid.*, pp. 373–375.

Chapter 4

1. See the discussion of Marquart's theories (*Osttürkische Dialektstudien* [1914]) by Pelliot, "À propos des Comans," *JA* (1920), p. 141.

2. Herrmann, *Atlas of China*, p. 32.

3. Minorsky, *Hudud al-Alam*, p. 448.

4. *Atlas of China*, p. 30.

5. The Juan-juan are said to be the Kermikhions of Byzantine historians.

6. See Pelliot, in *BEFEO* (1903), p. 99; Chavannes, *Documents sur les T'ou-kiue occidentaux*, pp. 229–233; Pelliot, "À propos des Comans," p. 141.

7. Theophylactus, I, 8.

8. "Principem suum chagana, honoris causa, nominarunt," writes Theophylactus. And Gregory of Tours: "Vocabatur gaganus; omnes enim reges gentis illius hoc appellantur nomine."

9. Gregory of Tours, IV, 23.

10. Pelliot, "L'origine de T'ou-kiue," *TP* (1915), p. 689.

11. It is interesting to note, with Nandor Fettich, that the art of Lombard Italy was to respond to the influence of the culture of Martinovka (near Kiev), an influence which was felt from the Po to the Kama, the Crimea, and the northern Caucasus. For the goldsmiths' work of Martinovka, see Fettich, *Metallkunst der Landnehmenden Ungarn*, *AU* (1937), pp. 282 *et seq.*

12. *Exc. leg.*, p. 162.

13. I wonder whether this "formicarum instar" may be related to the term describing swarming insects: a term applied by the Chinese to the Juan-juan, and from which these derive their name.

14. Chavannes, *Documents*, p. 241.

15. The finds of Sadovets prove that the northern part of Bulgaria came under Bayan's zone of influence. Fettich, *Metallkunst*, p. 290.

16. And not, as Amédée Thierry has it, in 616. Cf. Howorth, "The Avars," *JRAS* (1889), p. 779.

17. This title is found in the ancient T'u-chüeh inscriptions. Cf. W. Radloff, *Die alttürkischen Inschriften der Mongolei*, pp. 197, 257.

18. On the question of the Onoghundur, see J. Moravcsik, "Zur Geschichte der Onoguren," *Ungarische Jahrbücher,* X, Books 1–2 (1930), 53, and Minorsky, *Hudud al-Alam,* p. 467.

19. Cf. F. Fettich, "Über die Erforschung der Völkerwanderungs-kunst in Ungarn," *Ipek;* N. Fettich, "Das Kunstgewerbe der Avarenzeit in Ungarn," *AU* (1926), "Der zweite Schatz von Szilagy-somlio," *AU* (1932), and *Metallkunst der Landnehmenden Ungarn, AU* (1937), esp. pp. 148 and 205; A. Marosi and N. Fettich, "Trouvailles avares de Dunapentele," *AU* (1936); D. von Bartha, "Die avarische Doppelschalmei von Janoshida," *AU* (1934); Tibor Horvath, "Die avarischen Gräberfelder von Üllo und Kisköprös," *AU* (1935); Andreas Alföldi, "Zur historischen Bestimmung der Avaren-funde," *ESA,* IX (1934), 285. For the art of Finno-Ugrian popula-tions remaining in Russia, cf. Tallgren, "Les provinces culturelles finnoises de l'âge récent du fer dans la Russie du Nord (900–1200)," *ESA,* III (1928).

20. J.-J. Mikkola, "Die Chronologie der türkischen Donaubulgaren," *Journal de la Société finno-ougrienne,* XXX (1918), fasc. 33; Barthold, "Bulghâr," *EI,* p. 805 (with bibliography); Minorsky, *Hudud al-Alam,* p. 467; A. Lombard, *Constantin V* (Paris, 1902), p. 41; A. Rambaud, *Constantin Porphyrogénète* (Paris, 1870), p. 315; N. Mavrodinov, *L'industrie d'art des Protobulgares.*

21. See J. Deny, "Langues turques, mongoles et tongouzes," in *Les langues du monde* (1924), p. 185, and Pelliot, "Les mots à H initiale," *JA* (1925), p. 193. The researches of Guillaume de Hévésy tend to link the Finno-Ugrian languages (notably Ostyak and Vogul) with the Munda languages of pre-Aryan India. We should remember that, anthropologically speaking, the Turko-Mongols are brachycephalic, whereas the Finnish peoples are dolichocephalic. Deniker, *Races et peuples* (1926 ed.), pp. 435, 459.

22. The Bashkirs of the Urals were, according to Professor J. Németh, a tribe of Hungarian origin which later adopted the Turkic ways of life. Cf. J. Németh, "Magna Ungaria," in H. von Mžik, *Beiträge* (Leipzig, 1929), pp. 92 *et seq.*

23. Cf. Minorsky, in *Revue de Hongrie* (1937), and *Hudud al-Alam,* pp. 317–324.

24. Rambaud, *Constantin Porphyrogénète,* p. 352. For Hungarian origins, see B. Munkácsi, "Die Urheimat der Ungarn," in *Keleti Szemle,* VI (1905); J. Németh, "Magna Ungaria"; Gyula Németh, "La préhistoire hongroise," *Nouvelle Revue de Hongrie* (June, 1932), p. 460; A. Zakharov and W. Arendt, "Studia Levedica, Archaeolo-gischer Beitrag zur Geschichte der Altungarn im IX Jahrhundert," *AU;* Nandor Fettich, "Der Handel in Russland und das Ungartum

von Levedien," in *Metallkunst der Landnehmenden Ungarn, AU* (1937), pp. 62–202. For the art of ancient Levedia, *ibid.*, pp. 280–293 ("Kulturkunst der Pseudoschnallen").

25. Barthold, "Türks," *EI*, pp. 949–951, believes that the Khazar language and the old language of the Bulgars belonged to the ancient western Turkic group, of which the only modern representative is Chuvash. A bibliography on the Khazars is to be found in Barthold, "Khazar," *EI*, p. 990, and in Minorsky, *Hudud al-Alam*, p. 450. The political constitution of the Khazars, as expounded by Constantine Porphyrogenitus, consisted of a sovereign, the *khaganos*, and a sort of mayor of the palace, the *pekh*, called also *bek* by Ishthakri (cf. Minorsky, *Hudud al-Alam*, p. 451). For the Khazars and Byzantium, cf. L. Drapeyron, *L'empereur Héraclius* (Paris, 1869), p. 215; Lombard, *Constantin V*, p. 31; Rambaud, *Constantin Porphyrogénète*, p. 394; Chavannes, *Documents*, pp. 252–253.

26. In Russian, Sarkel was known by the name of Bela Vezha (Belaya Vezha), "White Tower," quite similar to al-Baida, applied by the Arabs to Itil. Cf. Naftula Fajner, *Annali del Istituto superiore orientale di Napoli*, III (1936), 51; Minorsky, *Hudud al-Alam*, p. 453.

27. Marquart, *Osteuropäische und Ostasiatische Streifzüge* (Leipzig, 1903), p. 5. For the tradition of the khagan Bulan's conversion to Judaism, about 740, after a debate between Christian, Muslim, and Jewish priests, cf. Naftula Fajner, "Sull'origine dei Chefsuri," *Annali del Istituto superiore orientale di Napoli*, XIV (1936), 13.

28. According to Marquart, Samandar—which is thought to be identical with the Tarqu of other sources—should be sought southwest of Petrovsk, between the Terek and Derbent (*Osteuropäische . . . Streifzüge*, p. 16).

29. Cf. Pelliot, "À propos des Comans," *JA* (1920), p. 133; J. Németh, "Zur Kenntniss der Petschenegen," *Körösi Csoma-Archiv*, pp. 219–225.

30. Byzantine sources in F. Chalandon, *Essai sur le règne d'Alexis Ier Comnène* (Paris, 1900), pp. 2–5, 108–134.

31. Cf. Barthold, "Ghuzz," *EI*, p. 178.

32. Cf. Minorsky, *Hudud al-Alam*, p. 316.

33. Barthold, "Kipčak," *EI*, p. 1082; Rasovsky, *Polovtsi* (Prague, 1935); Marquart, "Über das Volkstum der Komanen," in *Osttürkische Dialektstudien* (Berlin, 1914), pp. 25–238; Pelliot, "À propos des Comans," *JA* (1920), p. 125.

34. Barthold, "Kimäk," *EI*, p. 1068; Minorsky, *Hudud al-Alam*, p. 305.

35. Marquart, "Über das Volkstum der Komanen," p. 136; Pelliot, "À propos des Comans," p. 149.

36. For the sack of the city of Kiev by the Kipchaks, Cumans, or Polovtsy in 1204, see Bruce Boswell, "The Kipchak Turks," *Slavonic Review*, VI (1927), 70 *et seq.*; C. A. Macartney, "The Pechenegs," *ibid.*, VIII (1929), 342.

Chapter 5

1. Pelliot, *La Haute Asie* (Paris, 1931), p. 28.

2. Translation by Denison Ross, in *History of the Moghuls of Central Asia* (London, 1895), p. 290.

3. Or rather Kereit, as Mostaert suggests in "Ordosica," *Bulletin No. 9, Catholic University of Peking* (1934), p. 52. The transcription of the *Secret History* renders it as Kereyid (*ibid.*, p. 33). The modern form is K'erit.

4. Pelliot, "Chrétiens d'Asie Centrale et d'Extrême-Orient," *TP* (1914), p. 629.

5. Pelliot, *La Haute Asie*, p. 25.

6. But Pelliot wonders whether the word Kerayit may not have been interpolated here by Bar Hebraeus.

7. Bar Hebraeus, *Chron. eccles.*, III, 280–282.

8. For the Christian names of Kerayit kings, see Pelliot, "Chrétiens d'Asie Centrale," p. 627.

9. We do not know the site of Qara'un Qabchal, where, according to the *Secret History* (trans. E. Haenisch, p. 48), Togrul was nearly captured by Gur-khan; nor the site of Qurban Telesut, where, thanks to Yesugei's help, Togrul defeated Gur-khan. Cf. d'Ohsson, *Histoire des Mongols*, I, 73.

10. The question has been raised whether these Märkit might be the Mukri, mentioned by Byzantine writers of the sixth century (cf. Pelliot, "À propos des Comans," *JA* [1920], p. 145). Others relate the Mukri to the Mo-ho of Chinese historiography, that is to say, with the Tungus of the Amur during the seventh and eighth centuries.

11. This is the region of the hypothetical location of the eighth-century confederation of the Three Quriqan, mentioned in the Kosho-Tsaidam inscriptions (cf. Thomsen, "Inscriptions de l'Orkhon," p. 98).

12. Cf. Thomsen, "Inscriptions de l'Orkhon," p. 140. For the false linguistic relation between Tatar and Ta-t'an, see Pelliot, "À propos des Comans," p. 145.

13. The name of the Mongols seems to appear first during the T'ang period: "From the T'ang period, Chinese texts reveal to us among the She-wei tribes [of the lower Kerulen and the northern Khingan range], who were almost certainly Mongolian-speaking, a

Mong-wu or Mong-wa tribe, in which for the first time we seem to detect the name of the Mongols." *Ibid.,* p. 146.

14. *Ibid.,* pp. 146–147.

15. B. Y. Vladimirtsov, *The Life of Chingis-khan* (London, 1930), I. Elsewhere, Vladimirtsov translates *ulus* by nation, reserving to the word *irgen* the sense of tribe, and to *ulus-irgen* that of state. Vladimirtsov, *Obschestvennyi stroy Mongolov: Mongolskii kochevoy feodalizm* (Leningrad, 1934), pp. 59, 98.

16. Taiyichi'ut, or Tayich'iut in the translation of the *Secret History* by Haenisch, p. 10. Cf. Pelliot, in *TP* (1930), p. 54. The list of Nirun and Dürlükin tribes according to Rashid ad-Din is given in detail (Persian transcriptions) in F. von Erdmann, *Temudschin* (Leipzig, 1862), pp. 168, 194–230.

17. Rashid ad-Din, according to d'Ohsson, *Histoire des Mongols,* I, 426. The spelling in the *Secret History* (p. 8) is Onggirat. Pelliot notes that the Jajirat and the Qongirat are mentioned, along with the Märkit, in the Chinese history of the Khitan, as of 1123–24 ("À propos des Comans," p. 146).

18. D'Ohsson, *Histoire des Mongols,* I, 29.

19. B. Y. Vladimirtsov, *The Life of Chingis-khan,* p. 3. For the feudal character of Mongol society in the thirteenth century, see Vladimirtsov, *Obschestvennyi stroy Mongolov,* which Madame Olav Jansé had the kindness to translate for me.

20. For this theory, see Pelliot, "Notes sur le Turkestan," *TP* (1930), p. 50.

21. Pelliot, "Sur quelques mots d'Asie Centrale, III, Chaman," *JA* (1913), p. 466.

22. "There are also the Orengay (Uriangqai) who wear small, well-polished bones tied to their feet, with which they speed so swiftly over the ice and snow that they catch animals in flight" (Rubruck, Chap. XXXIX).

23. Vladimirtsov, *Obschestvennyi stroy Mongolov,* pp. 34, 41 and 39, 128.

24. *Ibid.,* p. 41.

25. Cf. Owen Lattimore, "The Geographical Factor in Mongol History," *GJ,* XCI (January, 1938), 9.

26. *Ibid.,* pp. 14–15.

27. The numerous words relating to civilization or to command which have passed from Turkic to Mongolian attest to the relative cultural superiority of the Turks over the Mongols. Cf. Vladimirtsov, *Zapiski vost. otd. imp. russk. arkheol. ob.,* XX (1911). The Turks' supremacy in the intellectual sphere is evident above all in the

comparative evolution of the two languages. "In general," writes Barthold in summarizing Poppe, "the Turkic languages are more highly evolved than the Mongol ones. Mongolian, from whatever region in the world, is far more archaic than the most ancient of the known Turkic languages. Written Mongolian remains, from the phonetic point of view, at almost the same degree of evolution as primitive Altaic (Turko-Mongolian)."

28. *Manghol un Niuca Tobca'an* (*Secret History of the Mongols*), ed. Haenisch (1937), p. 6.

29. Pelliot, "Notes sur le Turkestan," *TP* (1930), p. 24.

30. Barthold, *Turkestan*, p. 381. In the *Secret History*, Qabul's sons are given as Oquin-barqaq, Bartan-ba'atur, Qutuqtu-munggur, Qutula-khagan, Qada'an, and Tödöyän-ochigin (based upon Haenisch's transcription, p. 6).

31. D'Ohsson, *Histoire des Mongols*, I, 33.

32. Deli'ün boldaq in Haenisch's translation of the *Secret History*, p. 8. Tradition puts Jenghiz Khan's birth at about 1155, the date given by Persian historians, while the official history of the Yüan dynasty gives 1162. But in a communication made to the Société Asiatique on December 9, 1938, Pelliot revealed that new researches into Chinese sources had led him to accept 1167 as the date of the Conqueror's birth. At his death in 1227, therefore, he would have been barely sixty years old. In the same paper, Pelliot recalled that in Mongolian the interpretation of the name Temujin by "smith" is phonetically correct.

33. Barthold, *Turkestan*, p. 459, and "Cinghiz-Khân," *EI*, p. 877.

34. Oelun-eke: mother Oelun. For the name Oelun, cf. Pelliot, "Mots à H initiale dans le mongol," *JA* (1925), p. 230. In the *Secret History*, it is Hö-lun.

35. Jöchi-Qasar. We purposely refer to him by the name Qasar only so as to avoid confusion with Jenghiz Khan's eldest son, who was also called Jöchi.

36. Spelling of the *Secret History*, corresponding here (in English transliteration) to Targhutai Kiriltuq (pp. 12 and 35).

37. Börtä-üjin, Princess Börtä (Börte).

38. The original of this name appears to be Toktagha. Pelliot, in *JA* (1920), p. 164.

39. Translation of the curious passage in the *Secret History* by Pelliot, *La Haute Asie*, p. 26.

40. Qorqonah Djoubour in Haenisch's translation of the *Secret History*, p. 22.

41. Vladimirtsov, *Life of Chingis-khan*, p. 33, and Barthold, "Cinghiz-Khân," p. 878.

42. The reading *jourki, jourkin,* or *yourkin* (*jurki, jurkin, yurkin*) is that of the *Secret History,* p. 28. It had been rightly admitted by Hammer (*Geschichte der Goldenen Horde,* p. 61), who was blamed for this by Erdmann, *Temudschin,* p. 386. But Erdmann's reading, *bourkin,* derives from a false writing.

43. Afterward, not finding Temujin as amenable as he had expected, Altan repented of this act, rebelled against the man whom no doubt he considered an upstart, and allied himself with Temujin's enemies. But it was then too late.

44. Tchinggiz (in our transliteration, Chinggis), Pelliot remarks, might be a palatalized form of the Turkic word *tengiz* (in Uigur) or *dengiz* (in Osmanli), which means sea, like *dalai* in Mongolian. "It may be the same formation as the Mongolo-Tibetan word *dalai lama:* ocean lama. We know by the letter from the Vatican that the grand khan Güyük, Jenghiz Khan's second successor, termed himself oceanic khan (*dalai qaan* in Mongolian, *talui qaan* in Turkic). Further etymologies have been sought in the Mongol *chingga:* strong, powerful." Cf. Pelliot, "Les Mongols et la Papauté," *Revue de l'Orient chrétien,* Nos. 1–2 (1922–23), p. 25. Rashid ad-Din's opinion on the word *Jinkiz,* strong, is carried over in Erdmann, *Temudschin,* p. 601. Lastly, Vladimirtsov imagines that Tchinggiz (Chinggis) could be the name of a spirit of light worshiped by the shamans (*Chingis-khan,* pp. 37–38).

45. Vladimirtsov, *Chingis-khan,* p. 32.

46. *Ibid.,* pp. 36–37.

47. Rather than Muquli. The *Secret History* gives Mouqali.

48. D'Ohsson (*Histoire des Mongols,* I, 54) believes that the Wang-khan's arrival, as an exhausted fugitive, at Jenghiz Khan's door may be dated in the spring of 1196.

49. The *Secret History,* pp. 36, 48, gives Erke-qara, Erge-qara.

50. *Yüan Shih,* trans. F. E. A. Krause, *Cingis Han* (Heidelberg, 1922), p. 15.

51. The *Secret History,* p. 36, gives Djaqa-gambou (Jaga-gambu). On this doubtless Tibeto-Tangut title, cf. Pelliot, "Notes sur le Turkestan," *TP* (1930), pp. 50–51.

52. Cf. d'Ohsson, *Histoire des Mongols,* I, 53, 74.

53. The *Secret History* locates these operations around Bayidarah-belchir, a site which Howorth ("The Kireis and Prester John," *JRAS* [1889], p. 400) seeks near the River Baidarik. This watercourse runs down from the Khangai range in a north-to-south direction to join the little Lake Bunchagan. The Kökse'u Sabrah or Sabraq of the *Secret History* (p. 49) becomes, with d'Ohsson (*Histoire des Mongols,* I, 75), Geugussu Sairac.

54. *Yüan Shih,* trans. Krause, *Cingis Han,* p. 17; *Secret History,* p. 40; translation from the same *Secret History* in Howorth, "Kireis," pp. 400–401.

55. D'Ohsson, *Histoire des Mongols,* I, 60: "Targhutai perished at the hand of Chilaocan, son of the Selduz Sheburgan Shire." D'Ohsson's Sheburgan Shire is the So'orqan-shira or Sorqan-shira of the *Secret History* (pp. 34 and 72). Another Tayichi'ut chief, Qudu'udar, was killed at the same time as Targhutai. A third chief of the same tribe, Aquchu or A'uchu, was able to escape.

56. D'Ohsson, *Histoire des Mongols,* I, 75–76.

57. The *Secret History* relates that the Wang-khan inflicted the cangue on the three accomplices of Jagambu: Elqutur, Qulbar, and Arin-taize. See Howorth, "Kireis," p. 396.

58. Howorth, "Kireis," p. 395, seeks the Köyitän of the *Secret History* near the northern part of the Dalai Nor (Hulun Nor) between Kerulen and Argun.

59. His former name was Djirqo'adai (Jirqo'adai), according to the *Secret History,* p. 35.

60. Sübötäi, born about 1176, died in 1248. "Spelt Sübügätäi in Mongolian, Sübü'ätäi in the Mongol text of the *Yüan-ch'ao-pi-shih,* pronounced Sübötäi or Sübütäi," according to Pelliot, in *JA* (1920), p. 163. His biography has been translated by A. Rémusat, *Nouveaux mélanges asiatiques* (Paris, 1829), II, 97. The name of the Dürlükin-Mongol tribe of the Urianqut, to which Sübötäi belonged, reappears in the seventeenth century in a Turkic people, the Uriangqai, who lived by breeding reindeer and by hunting on the upper Yenisei (M. Courant, *L'Asie Centrale aux XVIIe et XVIIIe siècles,* p. 78).

61. Trans. Krause, *Cingis Han,* p. 19. It was the Wang-khan who, as we saw, forced Toqto'a to flee to Barghu or Barquchin. For the word Bargut, cf. A. Mostaert, "Ordosica," *Bulletin 9, Catholic University of Peking* (1934), p. 37.

62. Transcription of the *Secret History,* pp. 41, 42.

63. *Yüan Shih,* p. 20. For the name of Nilqa or Ilqa, see Pelliot, "À propos des Comans," *JA* (1920), p. 176, and "Notes sur le Turkestan," *TP* (1930), pp. 22–24. For the title *tsiang-kiun = sängün,* see Pelliot, in *JA* (1925), p. 261. (Other borrowings of Chinese titles by Turko-Mongol languages are *Tu-tu,* which in Turkic became *tutuq; t'ai-tsu,* imperial prince, which in Mongolian became *Taiji.*)

64. *Yüan Shih,* p. 20.

65. He conferred upon them the title of *tarkhan,* with the privilege of maintaining a bodyguard of quiver bearers (quiver = *qorchin*). Cf. Pelliot, in *TP* (1930), p. 32.

66. *Yüan Shih*, p. 21; d'Ohsson, *Histoire des Mongols*, I, 70. A translation of the passage in the *Secret History* is in Howorth, "Kireis," p. 405; Haenisch's transcription is in *Manghol un Niuca Tobca'an*, p. 44.

67. Vladimirtsov's translation, *Chingis-khan*, p. 51, and in Howorth, "Kireis," p. 407.

68. Jenghiz Khan, says the *Secret History*, withdrew along the River Ulquui-silugeljit (the modern Olkhui, which runs from the Khingan Mountains into a little lake of the eastern Gobi) and then along the Khalka (cf. Howorth, "Kireis," p. 408; Haenisch's transcription, p. 46).

69. Or more accurately, according to the *Secret History*, from the vicinity of a River Tungge or Tungeli, which Howorth believes to be a tributary of the Onon ("Kireis," p. 408) and which may be that of the Khalka.

70. Cf. d'Ohsson, *Histoire des Mongols*, I, 73, and Howorth, "Kireis," p. 409. The *Secret History* and the *Yüan-ch'ao-pi-shih*, on the one hand, and the *Sheng-wu-ts'in-cheng-lu* and Rashid ad-Din, on the other, give conflicting versions of "The Complaint of Jenghiz Khan." In reality, these two groups of sources are here complementary, as d'Ohsson perceived.

71. Translation of the *Secret History* in Howorth, "Kireis," p. 410.

72. Cf. F. Grenard, *Gengis-khan*, p. 46.

73. The Baljuna is the river Pan-chu-ni of the *Yüan Shih* (trans. Krause, *Cingis Han*, p. 23). But the *Secret History* says that it is a lake or pond: "Baljuna na'ur, that is to say, Baljuna Nor" p. 51).

74. *Secret History*, p. 52; *Yüan Shih*, trans. Krause (*Cingis Han*, p. 24).

75. Albert Herrmann, *Atlas of China*, p. 49, F. 2; Howorth, "Kireis," p. 417, places the Jerqabchiqai defile and the heights of Jeje'er Undur on the lower Kerulen.

76. *Secret History*, trans. Pelliot, *JA* (1920), p. 176.

77. Restoration of the text by Pelliot, *JA* (April–June, 1920), pp. 183–184.

78. Later, after a dream, Jenghiz Khan handed over Ibaqa-bäki to one of his most valiant lieutenants, Jurchedäi of the Uru'ud clan.

79. For the name Toqto'a, cf. Pelliot, in *JA* (April–June, 1920), p. 164, and *TP* (1930), p. 24.

80. The sending of envoys (Yüqunan to the Öngüt, Torbitashi to Jenghiz Khan) is mentioned both in the *Secret History* (p. 55) and in Rashid ad-Din (*Temudschin*, pp. 299–300). For the genealogy of Alaqush-tigin-quri, cf. Pelliot, "Chrétiens d'Asie Centrale et d'Extrême-Orient," *TP* (1914), p. 631. Alaqush-tigin-quri is mentioned in the *Secret History* (p. 55). Öngüt Nestorianism is attested from the

beginning of the twelfth century (cf. Pelliot, "Chrétiens d'Asie Centrale," p. 630).

81. The *Secret History*, summarized by Barthold, *Turkestan*, pp. 383–384.

82. Albert Herrmann, *Atlas of China*, p. 49, E. 2.

83. Vladimirtsov's translation, *The Life of Chingis-khan*, p. 60. The *Yüan Shih*, always more laconic, tells merely that Jamuqa, alarmed by the power of the Mongol army, forsook the *Tayang* and fled with his Jajirat followers before the battle began (Krause, *Cingis Han*, p. 26); this flight is confirmed by Rashid ad-Din (*Temudschin*, p. 302).

84. *"Tayang un eke Gurbesu,"* the *Secret History* has it (pp. 54 and 60). Rashid ad-Din, in d'Ohsson, *Histoire des Mongols*, I, 89, makes her the *Tayang's* favorite wife.

85. Goutchouloug (Guchulug) in the transcription of the *Secret History* (p. 61).

86. If we are to believe the *Yüan Shih* (Krause, *Cingis Han*, p. 26), Küchlüg and Toqto'a had gone to find Buyiruq, the *Tayang's* brother, who earlier had been driven as far as the upper Yenisei by Jenghiz Khan. We saw how, unlike Rashid ad-Din and the *Yüan Shih*, the *Secret History* states that Buyiruq died soon after his defeat by the Mongols, on his flight to the Urungu (Howorth, "Kireis," p. 398). But the *Secret History* is very ill-informed where the more remote campaigns are concerned.

87. Cf. Grenard, *Gengis-khan*, p. 57.

88. Barthold, *Turkestan*, p. 361. The same date is given in the *Yüan Shih* (trans. Krause, *Cingis Han*, p. 29).

89. Sübötäi's last campaign, in which he was aided by Toquchar, Jenghiz Khan's son-in-law, directed against the last of the Märkit bands, is stated by the *Sheng-wu-ts'in-cheng-lu* to have taken place in 1217. Rashid ad-Din gives an almost identical date, whereas the *Secret History* sets the battle in 1206. But this latter source, although vital for the internal history of Mongolia, is unreliable when dealing with more distant military actions (cf. Pelliot, in *JA* [1920], pp. 163–164). The defeat of the Märkit people by Sübötäi is said to have occurred on the River Chäm or Jäm, which Barthold believes to have been in western Uiguria, and Bretschneider near the upper Irtysh. Cf. Barthold, *Turkestan*, p. 362.

90. It is from the Chinese transcription alone that we know the name "T'a-t'a-t'ung-a." Pelliot rejects Barthold's suggested derivation of this form from "Tashatun" (Barthold, *Turkestan*, p. 387); Pelliot, "Notes sur le Turkestan," *TP* (1930), p. 33.

91. Pelliot contends that for this word the form *quriltai* (*qouriltaï* in French) is preferable to the *qurultai* (*qouroultaï* in French) of

Barthold and Vladimirtsov ("Notes sur le Turkestan," *TP* [1930], p. 52, and "Sur la légende d'Utuz-khan," *ibid.*, p. 347).

92. Khagan was the old Juan-juan—therefore Mongol—title, afterward adopted by the kings of the T'u-chüeh Turks, destroyers of and successors to the Juan-juan empire in the second half of the sixth century. The Jenghiz-Khanite Mongol form of the word is *qahan* in the *Secret History* (Haenisch's transcription) and *qaan* in other texts (*qân* in modern Ordos, according to Mostaert, "Ordosica," *Bulletin 9, Catholic University of Peking* [1934], p. 73). Pelliot writes: "I doubt whether Jenghiz Khan ever bore the title of khagan. His true title seems to me to have been Chingis-qan or Chinggiz-qan." Pelliot, "Notes sur le Turkestan," p. 25, and "Les Mongols et la Papauté," *Revue de l'Orient chrétien* (1922–23), p. 19.

93. The Jenghiz-Khanite Mongols sometimes called themselves Blue Mongols (*Kökä Mongol*). Cf. Sanang Sechen (trans. Schmidt), p. 70. Even the old T'u-chüeh gave themselves the name of Blue Turks (*Kök Türk*) in the Kosho-Tsaidam inscriptions. Cf. Thomsen, "Inscriptions de l'Orkhon," p. 98. The epithet "blue" is derived from the sky, the Tängri, of which the T'u-chüeh khagans and later the Jenghiz-Khanite grand khans proclaimed themselves the representatives and agents, the envoys on earth (*jayagatu* or *jaya'atu* in Jenghiz-Khanite Mongolian). We know from other sources that the Mongols were improperly termed Tatars or Tartars, and that they protested about this to western travelers of the thirteenth century. Rubruck notes: "The Mongols do not wish to be called Tartars, because the Tartars were a different people, as I shall show from what I have learned" (Rubruck, Chap. XVIII).

94. E. Haenisch translates *Täb-tängri* (*Teb-tenggeri* in his transcription of the *Secret History*) as "ganz göttlich, Übergott, Erzgott," that is, very divine, supreme god, archgod (*Manghol un Niuca Tobca'an*, p. 119). The *Secret History* has the spelling Kököchu.

95. As confidential adviser to Yesugei and Oelun-eke, Munglik, on Yesugei's death, was charged with the task of seeking out the young Temujin among the Qongirat and bringing him home. In this he succeeded, but shortly afterward Munglik forsook Temujin, then aged thirteen, and removed the last of the clan's herds. However, after Jenghiz Khan's first successes, Munglik returned to him. It was he who warned Jenghiz Khan to beware of a rendezvous with the Kerayit Wang-khan because of an ambush prepared by the *Sängün*. Meanwhile, Munglik may have married the widowed Oelun-eke.

96. Pelliot, "Les Mongols et la Papauté," p. 22.

97. Cf. Pelliot, "Notes sur le Turkestan," p. 32.

98. Vladimirtsov's translation, *Life of Chingis-khan*, p. 63; Grenard, *Gengis-khan*, p. 63. Not long before, in 1204, Qasar had distinguished himself when commanding the center of the Mongol army in the decisive battle against the Naiman *Tayang*.

99. Barthold, *Turkestan*, p. 391.

100. In this connection, Jenghiz Khan revived the spirit if not the letter of the old protocols of the T'u-chüeh khagans of the seventh and eighth centuries as they appear in the Kosho-Tsaidam inscriptions: "I who resemble Heaven and am appointed by Heaven, Bilghä khagan of the Turks"—*Tängritäg Tängri jaratmysh Türk Bilghä qaghan* (Thomsen, "Inscriptions de l'Orkhon," p. 122).

101. Rashid ad-Din, in d'Ohsson, *Histoire des Mongols*, I, p. 123; Vladimirtsov, *Life of Chingis-khan*, p. 92.

102. "In the august edicts of the emperor Jenghiz Khan, it is said: Concerning the *ho-shang* (Buddhist monks), *ye-li-k'o-wen* (Nestorian monks), *hsien-sheng* (Taoist monks), and *ta-chih-man* (Muslim religious leaders), let them be subject neither to land tax, nor trade tax, nor any kind of requisition, but let them invoke Heaven and request happiness for the emperor" (edict of the emperor Kublai, 1275, in Chavannes, "Inscriptions et pièces de chancellerie chinoises de l'époque mongole," *TP* (1908), pp. 377–378).

103. Pelliot, "Notes sur le Turkestan," *TP* (1930), p. 34.

104. For the *tamgha* (Turkic word, Mongol transcription *tamagha*), cf. *ibid.*, p. 35.

105. Like Pierre de La Garde d'Hozier's seventeenth-century *Généalogie des principales familles de France*. Pelliot, "Notes sur le Turkestan," pp. 38, 40 *et seq.*, amending Barthold and Vladimirtsov.

106. *Jasaq* or *jasa* in Mongolian, *yasaq* or *yasa* in Turkic: "to regulate, fix." Cf. Pelliot, in *JA* (April–May, 1913), p. 458, and (April–June, 1925), p. 256.

107. This is how Joinville (ed. Wailly, *Histoire de Saint Louis* [Paris, 1874], p. 263) summarizes what he knows of the *yasaq* from Franciscan missions: "The ordinances which he [Jenghiz Khan] gave them were designed to keep the peace among the people; and they were such that no one stole the possessions of another, nor struck him, unless he desired to lose his fist, and that no one lay with the wife or daughter of another, unless he desired to lose fist or life. He gave them many other good ordinances to secure peace."

108. "In the *Hua yi yi yu* vocabulary of 1389, *noyan* is the equivalent of *kuei*, noble. The modern pronunciation is *nogon*, but it appears to have been heard approximately as *noin* by foreigners in the Middle Ages." The plural is *noyad* or *noyat*. Pelliot, in *Revue de l'Orient chrétien* (1924), pp. 306 (110).

109. The *tarkhan* or *darqan* was in principle *vir immunis*, exempt

from taxation (Mostaert, "Ordosica," p. 38). For the *nökur*, see Ralph Fox, *Genghis-khan*, p. 109.

110. For these terms, see Pelliot, "Notes sur le Turkestan," pp. 28 *et seq.*, amending Barthold, *Turkestan*, p. 383, and Chavannes, in *TP* (1904), pp. 429–432.

111. Barthold, *Turkestan*, p. 384. We have seen that the group of 10,000 men was called *tumen;* that of 100,000 was the *tuq* (from *tuq*, flag).

112. Literally, "left hand."

113. Literally, "right hand."

114. Barthold, "Cinghiz-Khân," *EI*, p. 881, gives 129,000 men as the total strength of the Mongol army. The above enumeration, borrowed from Rashid ad-Din, may be found in d'Ohsson, *Histoire des Mongols*, II, 3–5. Erdmann, *Temudschin*, p. 455, deduces different figures from the same Persian sources: bodyguard, 1,000 men; center, 101,000; right wing, 47,000; left wing, 52,000; imperial princes' guard, 29,000; 230,000 men in all.

115. Grenard, *Gengis-khan*, p. 76. Piano Carpini, under the date 1246, describes this armament very minutely, especially the hooked pike for spearing and unseating the horseman.

116. *Ibid.* Fermented mare's milk or kumiss (*qumiz*) was the favorite drink of the Mongols. Cf. Pelliot, in *JA* (1920), p. 170.

117. Cf. G. Altunian, *Die Mongolen und ihre Eroberungen in kaukasischen und kleinasiatischen Ländern im XIII Jahrhundert* (Berlin, 1911), p. 74.

118. *Yüan Shih*, trans. Krause, *Cingis Han*, p. 28.

119. Cf. Pelliot, "Chrétiens d'Asie Centrale et d'Extrême-Orient," *TP* (1914), p. 630.

120. "Alaghai-bäki, a woman of energy, showed herself capable of ruling her tribe after her husband's death." *Ibid.*, p. 631.

121. It may be recalled that the Mongols designated the Kin emperor by the name of Altan-khan. *Altan* in Mongolian has the same meaning as the Chinese word *kin*. The Altan-khan is thus the king of *gold*.

122. The source of this acount of Jenghiz Khan's campaign is the *Yüan Shih*, which, while terse, is topographically very precise.

123. *Yüan Shih*, p. 32.

124. *Yüan Shih*, p. 33. But it makes no mention of massacre. In the *Secret History* (trans. Haenisch, p. 86), Peking is designated in Mongolian as Jungdu, a name derived from the Chinese Chung-tu.

125. "I thought," says Shigi-qutuqu to Jenghiz Khan, "that everything in the city [of Peking] belonged to you after the conquest, and that none but you had the right to dispose of it." On the basis of Persian sources, the attitudes of Shigi-qutuqu on the one hand and of

Unggur and Arqai on the other are described, from Persian sources, in Erdmann, *Temudschin*, p. 329. Cf. *Secret History*, p. 86.

126. For an account of atrocities perpetrated in China by Jenghiz Khan's army, notably in Peking, and for a description of heaps of corpses rotting on the ground, of fields covered with human bones, and of the epidemics born of this carnage, see the Muslim evidence of the *Tabaqat-i-Nasiri*, provided by the Khwarizmian ambassador and eyewitness Beha ad-Din Razi (Barthold, *Turkestan*, pp. 393–394). The *Yüan Shih*, for which the Mongol conqueror became retrospectively—and very posthumously—an emperor of China, tends to draw a discreet veil over these facts.

127. Of the Salji'ut tribe; see Erdmann, *Temudschin*, p. 328.

128. Sixty-two thousand men in all, as Barthold estimates ("Cinghiz-Khân," *EI*, p. 882).

129. *Yüan Shih*, pp. 35–38.

130. But here again, the Mongols did not effect a permanent occupation of Taming, for Muqali was compelled to capture it again in 1220 (*Yüan Shih*, p. 36).

131. It was thus Ming-an, a Kin officer gone over to the Mongols, who, with a corps of Jurchids who had similarly transferred their allegiance, fought beside Samuqa for the conquest of Peking. Cf. Erdmann, *Temudschin*, p. 328.

132. In the Jenghiz-Khanite period, the Uigur kings bore the title of *iduq-qut* or *idiqut*, "sacred majesty," which had been used in the eighth century by the leaders of the Basmil Turks, who were established in this same region of Beshbaligh (the Dzimsa of today), near Kucheng. Cf. Barthold, "Türks," *EI*, p. 949.

133. According to Juvaini (Barthold, *Turkestan*, p. 362).

134. Al'altun in the *Secret History*.

135. Cf. Barthold, *Turkestan*, p. 362, n. 4.

136. *Ibid.*, p. 356, according to Juvaini.

137. Juvaini, who is the principal original source, gives two versions of these events. See Barthold's discussion, *Turkestan*, pp. 358, 362, 367.

138. This khan was called Arslan-khan Abu'l Muzaffar Yusuf (d. 1205). His son, the last Karakhanid, was Arslan-khan Abu'l Fath Muhammad (d. 1211). Cf. Barthold, *Turkestan*, pp. 363, 366 (according to Juvaini and Jamal Qarshi).

139. *Ibid.*, p. 368.

140. About 1211, according to Jamal Qarshi. Juvaini corresponds to 1217–18. Cf. Barthold, *Turkestan*, pp. 401 and 368.

141. Here again, Juvaini and Jemal Qarshi give different versions. Barthold, *Turkestan*, p. 401.

142. Cf. Barthold, *Turkestan*, p. 402 (according to Juvaini and

Rashid ad-Din, with a critique by Abu'l Ghazi, trans. Desmaisons, *Histoire des Mongols et des Tatares* [St. Petersburg, 1871–74, 2 vols.], p. 102).

143. Pelliot, "Notes sur le Turkestan," p. 55.

144. In the Mongolian of the *Secret History*, the Khwarizmians are called Sartes: Sarta'ut, Sartaghol (trans. Haenisch, p. 87).

145. Even in Transoxiana, Muhammad had incurred the hostility of the Muslim "clergy" by executing, in 1216, the sheikh Majd ad-Din Baghdadi of the order of Sufi Kubrawi. Regarding the history of the Mongol invasion of the Muslim world, a critique of the Arabo-Persian sources will be found in Barthold's *Turkestan down to the Mongol Invasion*, pp. 38–58. It should be recalled that the three chief original sources are Nasawi, who in 1223 was secretary to Jalal ad-Din, the shah of Khwarizm, whose life he wrote in Arabic in 1241; Juzjani, who in 1227 fled from Afghanistan to India to escape Mongol domination, and there, about 1260, wrote, in Persian, the *Tabaqat-i-Nasiri*; and Juvaini, the son of a Persian in Mongol service, who from his youth had himself been a Mongol official. In 1249–51 and again in 1251–53, he made the journey to Mongolia; in 1262, the Mongols appointed him governor (*malik*) of Baghdad. Around 1260 he wrote Jenghiz Khan's history ("History of the Conqueror of the World," *Ta'rikh-i Jahangusha*). Juvaini died in 1283. Lastly there was Rashid ad-Din (1247–1318). At this time he was partly dependent on Juvaini for his material.

146. For these names, see Pelliot, "Notes sur le Turkestan," *TP* (1930), pp. 52–53.

147. Nasawi attributes the slaying of the caravaneers to Inalchiq's greed. Juzjani believes that he had the tacit approval of Muhammad. Ibn al-Athir lays the blame for the crime on Muhammad himself. Juvaini reports that Inalchiq had been offended by the lack of respect shown him by one of the caravaneers (Barthold, *Turkestan*, p. 398).

148. *Ibid.*, pp. 409–410.

149. *Ibid.*, p. 413.

150. Two notable figures at the siege of Urgench were Bo'orchu, who commanded a detachment of Jenghiz Khan's personal guard, and Tulun-cherbi, captain of a thousand on the right wing. Both warriors are celebrated in Mongol epic. In the course of this difficult siege, Jöchi showed himself to be a very poor leader. His wrangles with Jagatai, who upbraided him fiercely for his indecision, compelled Jenghiz Khan to subordinate both of them to their brother Ogödäi. For this siege, based on the accounts in Arab and Persian sources (Nasawi, Juvaini, Rashid ad-Din, etc.), see Barthold, *Turkestan*, pp. 433, 437.

151. Cf. Barthold, *Turkestan*, pp. 420–426, after review of the data from Nasawi, Juzjani, and Juvaini.

152. Here again I follow the chronology suggested by Barthold, *Turkestan*, pp. 427–455, where one may find the critical exposition of data furnished by Nasawi, Juzjani, and Juvaini.

153. According to Juvaini and Rashid ad-Din. It is strange that neither Juzjani nor Nasawi mention this siege, but describe Jenghiz Khan as going directly from Thaleqan to Ghazni. Cf. Barthold, *Turkestan*, p. 444.

154. In Turkic, the name is Mängüberti: "Given by God."

155. H. G. Raverty wonders whether this is indeed the Perwan in the valley of the Pandshir, and suggests another Perwan situated near the sources of the Lugar, a tributary of Kabul River (Raverty, translation of the *Tabaqat-i-Nasiri* [Calcutta, 1881–97, 2 vols.], pp. 288, 1021).

156. Nasawi, trans. Houdas, *Histoire du sultan Djelal eddin Mankobirti* (Paris, 1891), pp. 138–141.

157. Cf. Barthold, *Turkestan*, pp. 446–449, taken chiefly from Nasawi and Juvaini.

158. For the journey of K'iou Ch'ang-ch'uen, alias K'iou Ch'u-ki, see Bretschneider, *Mediaeval Researches*, I, 35–108; Arthur Waley, *Travels of an Alchemist* (London, 1931); Pelliot, in *TP* (1930), p. 56. Ch'ang-ch'uen brought back from his stay with Jenghiz Khan an edict protecting Taoist monasteries. In 1228 his companion, the monk Li Chih-ch'ang, wrote an account of this journey. Cf. Chavannes, "Inscriptions et pièces de chancellerie chinoises," *TP* (1908), p. 298.

159. Minorsky ("Raiy," *EI*, p. 1184) wonders whether Ibn al-Athir exaggerates in stating that the whole population of Rai was massacred by the Mongols in 1220. Ibn al-Athir adds indeed that there was a second massacre, of survivors, in 1224. Minorsky observes: "Juvaini says merely that the Mongol generals killed a great number of people in Khwar-i Rai [in the countryside inhabited by Shi'ites?], but that in Bai they were met by the [Shafi'ite?] cadi, who made submission to them, after which the invaders departed. Rashid ad-Din admits that Jebe's and Sübötäi's Mongols killed and plundered in Rai, but he seems to make a distinction between Rai and Qum, of which the inhabitants [Shi'ites] were massacred to the last man."

160. See the account of the invasion of "Sabada Bahadur" by the Armenian chronicler Kirakos, trans. E. Dulaurier, in *JA*, I (1858), 197–200, and in M. F. Brosset, *Histoire de la Géorgie* (St. Petersburg, 1849–57, 2 vols. in 3), I, 492.

161. R. Grousset, *Histoire des Croisades*, III, 230 *et seq.*

162. For the touching welcome they extended in 1253 to the Franciscan Rubruck, see *Voyage de Rubrouck*, Chap. XIII.

163. At this period the Kipchaks were becoming converts to Christianity. One of their chiefs killed by the Mongols in 1223, Yuri Konchakovich, had a Christian name. Pelliot, "À propos des Comans," *JA* (1920), p. 149.

164. Bretschneider, *Mediaeval Researches*, I, 297.

165. Cf. Erdmann, *Temudschin*, pp. 434 *et seq.*

166. Hammer, *Geschichte der Goldenen Horde*, p. 87. Politically, Soldaia (Sudak) was a dependency of the Greek empire of Trebizond (G. I. Bratianu, *Recherches sur le commerce génois dans la Mer Noire au XIIIe siècle* [Paris, 1929], p. 203).

167. *Yüan Shih*, trans. Krause, *Cingis Han*, p. 40.

168. Date given in the *Yüan Shih*.

169. D'Ohsson, *Histoire des Mongols*, II, 12–13. The funereal immolation of attendants and horses had been preserved unchanged in the steppes from the Scythians of Herodotus to Jenghiz Khan (Herodotus, IV, 71–72).

170. Jenghiz Khan was not only illiterate; he did not even speak Turkic, a language known to many Mongols (Juzjani, in Barthold, *Turkestan*, p. 461, and d'Ohsson, *Histoire des Mongols*, II, 95).

171. Rashid ad-Din, in d'Ohsson, *Histoire des Mongols*, I, 404.

172. *Ibid.*, I, 416.

173. Chavannes, "Inscriptions et pièces de chancellerie chinoises de l'époque mongole," *TP* (1908), p. 300.

174. An example of this is the case of Kökchü, the faithless groom of the Kerayit *Sängün*, in 1203 (*Secret History*, trans. Pelliot, *JA* [1920], pp. 179–180).

175. *History of the Yüan*, trans. A. C. Moule, *Christians in China Before the Year 1550* (New York, 1930), p. 235.

176. Mailla, IX, 78–126.

177. Jenghiz Khan charged him to teach them Mongolian in Uigur writing. See Pelliot, "Les systèmes d'écriture en usage chez les anciens Mongols," *AM* (1925), p. 287, and *TP* (1930), p. 34.

178. Cf. Barthold, "Caghatâi-khân," *EI*, p. 832.

179. A. Rémusat, *Nouveaux mélanges asiatiques*, I, 64.

180. Rémusat, "Vie de Yeliu Thsoutsai," in *Nouveaux mélanges asiatiques*, II, p. 64; cf. Bretschneider, *Mediaeval Researches*, I, p. 9. Ye-lü Ch'u-ts'ai 1190–1244) entered Mongol service in 1214 or 1215.

181. Cf. Deveria, "Notes d'épigraphie mongole-chinoise," *JA*, II (1896), p. 122.

182. Marco Polo, ed. J. P. G. Pauthier, *Le livre de M. Polo* (Paris, 1865, and Peking, 1924–28), I, 183; Joinville, ed. Wailly, p. 263.

183. Abu'l Ghazi Bahadur khan, *Histoire des Mongols et des Tatares*, trans. Desmaisons, p. 104. See also in the Georgian chronicle what is said of "the excellent laws of Jenghiz Khan, the impartiality of the Mongols where justice is concerned" (Brosset, *Histoire de la Géorgie*, I, 486). Also observe the impression of majesty, order, and "divine right" produced by the memory of Jenghiz Khan on the Armenian "Hayton" (Hethum) (*Recueil des historiens des Croisades. Documents arméniens* [Paris, 1869–1906, 2 vols.], II, 148–150). The same impression of stern justice and perfect order appears in Piano Carpini (Part IV).

184. Note his concern, before the Khwarizmian war, to establish permanent trade relations with the Khwarizmian empire. It was indeed the attack on a "Mongol" commercial caravan which brought about the breach with Sultan Muhammad (Barthold, *Turkestan*, p. 396).

Chapter 6

1. Cf. Barthold, "Cinghiz-Khân," *EI*, p. 882.

2. For this name, see Pelliot, "Sur quelques mots d'Asie Centrale," *JA* (1913), p. 459. (Possible etymology is *jochin*, host.)

3. Cf. Barthold, "Bâtû-khân," *EI*, p. 699.

4. Or Chaghatai. From the Mongolian *chaghan*, white? Cf. Barthold, "Caghatâi-khân," *EI*, p. 831. Here we keep to the form Jagatai (Djaghatai in the classical French spelling of the "Turkic-Jaghatai" language).

5. Or Ogädäi. From the Mongolian *ögädä*, on high?

6. For this name, see Pelliot, "Sur quelques mots d'Asie Centrale," p. 460. (Possible etymology: *toli*, mirror.) Cf. Rashid ad-Din, in Erdmann, *Temudschin*, p. 641.

7. According to some sources, the date of Ogödäi's accession was September 13, 1229. Tolui died three years after Ogödäi's election, on October 9, 1232, when only forty. He had ably performed his function as regent.

8. The Chinese name of this city is Holin, the normal transcription of (Kara)korum. For the date of its foundation, see Pelliot, "Note sur Karakorum," *JA*, I (1925), 372, and Barthold, "Karakorum," *EI*, p. 785. A plan of the ruins of Karakorum may be found in Radloff, *Atlas der Alterthümer der Mongolei*, Pl. XXXVI.

9. Juvaini and Rashid ad-Din, in d'Ohsson, *Histoire des Mongols*, II, 63; Marco Polo, Chap. 97.

Notes: Chapter 6, pp. 257–260 593

10. Mailla, IX, 132. Yet the rough Mongol may have been more clearsighted than his Chinese adviser, at least where the interests of the Mongol people were concerned. Ogödäi wanted to send Muslim contingents to China and contingents from the Far East to the western areas. Ye-lü Ch'u-ts'ai dissuaded him, on the ground that the marches would be too fatiguing. As a result, fifty years later, the Mongols of the Far East had become Chinese, while those of the (Mongol) West had become Turks or Persians (cf. Mailla, IX, 212).

11. Pelliot, "Chrétiens d'Asie Centrale et d'Extrême-Orient," *TP* (1914), p. 628. Pelliot notes that two of Chinqai's sons bore the Christian names Yao-shu-mu (Yoshmut) and K'uo-li-ki-ssu (George).

12. The name of Nin-kia-su given in Chinese histories comes from *Nangkiyas* or *Nang-kiyas*, the name by which the Mongols designated the Chinese (*nikasa* in Manchu). Pelliot believes that the Mongols took the term from the Jurchids or Kin, who themselves referred to the Sung as Nan-kia, "people of the south" in Chinese. Cf. Pelliot, "Nankias," in *JA*, I (1913), 460–466, and *TP* (1930), p. 17.

13. Mongol tradition ascribes to the dying Jenghiz Khan the strategical plan for dealing finally with the Kin.

14. The narrative from the *Yüan Shih* is summarized by Mailla, IX, 133–155. The passage from Rashid ad-Din is translated in d'Ohsson, *Histoire des Mongols*, II, 613. Tolui was accompanied on this campaign by two of his father's old generals, Shigi-qutuqu and Tuqulqu-cherbi, brother of the great Bo'orchu. Cf. *ibid.*, II, 614, and Erdmann, *Temudschin*, pp. 207, 462.

15. Mailla, IX, 156–207. Among the heroic deaths at the fall of the Kin, Pelliot mentions that of the Nestorian Ma K'ing-siang in 1234.

16. A curious example of this Chinese irredentism among the Sung will be found in the *Instruction d'un futur empereur de Chine en 1193*, trans. Chavannes (*Mémoires concernant l'Asie Orientale*, I [1913], 28–29).

17. We must not confuse Godan, Ogödäi's second son, with Qada'an, his sixth. Pelliot, "Les Mongols et la Papauté," *Revue de l'Orient chrétien* (1931–32), p. 63 (203).

18. Pelliot, "Chrétiens d'Asie Centrale et d'Extrême-Orient," *TP* (1914), p. 631.

19. H. B. Hulbert, *The History of Korea* (Seoul, 1901–03), pp. 189, 195; Demiéville, *BEFEO*, 1–2 (1924), 195.

20. Sources: Nasawi, trans. Houdas, *Histoire du sultan Djelal eddin Mankobirti;* d'Ohsson, *Histoire des Mongols*, IV, 64 *et seq.*, according to Nasawi, Juvaini, Nowairi, and Ibn al-Athir; Juzjani, trans. Raverty; B. Spuler, "Quellenkritik zur Mongolengeschichte Irans," *ZDMG* (1938), p. 219.

21. Cf. Minorsky, "Tiflis," *EI*, p. 795.

22. Cf. Grousset, *Histoire des Croisades*, III, 366.

23. For details regarding this general, see Pelliot, "Les Mongols et la Papauté," p. 51.

24. The Arran (afterward the Karabakh) is, generally speaking, the plain between the eastern courses of the Aras and the Kura; the Mugan is the plain south and east of the lower course of the Kura, from its confluence with the Aras to the Caspian.

25. Ibn al-Athir, in d'Ohsson, *Histoire des Mongols*, III, 70.

26. Cf. G. Altunian, *Die Mongolen und ihre Eroberungen*, pp. 35 *et seq.*

27. Pelliot, "Les Mongols et la Papauté," p. 246 (51).

28. On Rabban-ata (Lie-pien-a-ta in Chinese), see *ibid.*, pp. 236 (41) *et seq.* The Armenian chronicler Kirakos of Ganja eulogizes Rabban-ata in the most glowing terms: "He built churches in the cities of the Tadzhiks [i.e., Muslims], where until then men had been forbidden so much as to pronounce the name of Christ, as for example in Tabriz and Nakhichevan, where the inhabitants had shown particular hostility toward Christians. He built churches, raised crosses, and commanded the celebration of Christian ceremonies with Gospel, crosses, candles, and chants. He punished his opponents with death. All Tatar troops did him honor. His people, under the protection of his *tamgha*, passed freely everywhere. Even Tatar generals offered him gifts . . ." (*ibid.*, p. 244 [49]).

29. For Baiju, cf. *ibid.*, pp. 303 (109) *et seq.*

30. D'Ohsson, *Histoire des Mongols*, III, 83 (according to Nowairi, Bar Hebraeus, and Maqrizi). Cf. "Kaikhusraw II," *EI*, pp. 679–680; Altunian, *Die Mongolen und ihre Eroberungen*, p. 38.

31. Cf. Grousset, *Histoire des Croisades*, III, 526.

32. According to a text of the *Yüan Shih* (trans. Pelliot), Batu was sent to Europe in 1234, and it was not until 1235 that Mongka received the order to join him there.

33. "The ruins of Bolgar correspond to the modern village of Bolgarskoye [Bolgary], or Uspenskoye, in the district of Spassk, 155 kilometers south of Kazan and 7 kilometers from the left bank of the Volga" (Minorsky, *Hudud al-Alam*, p. 461).

34. Pelliot, "À propos des Comans," *JA* (1920), pp. 166–167.

35. Cf. *ibid.*, p. 169; Minorsky, *Hudud al-Alam*, p. 446.

36. Cf. G. Strakosch-Grassmann, *Der Einfall der Mongolen in Mitteleuropa in den Jahren 1241–1242* (Innsbruck, 1893); Altunian, *Die Mongolen und ihre Eroberungen* (Berlin, 1911); H. Morel, "Les campagnes mongoles," *Revue Militaire française* (June–July, 1922).

37. D'Ohsson believes that Qada'an's army did not join in the

troop concentration or in the battle of the Sajo. L. Cahun, on the other hand, maintains that it had time enough to take part in it. In fact, the information furnished by Persian historians is quite confused. Juvaini and especially Rashid ad-Din, whose data concerning the geography of the West were inadequate, often muddled their facts, and events unfortunately do not appear in the clear light desired by Cahun. His historical account was influenced by his novel *La Tueuse,* which, as such, is amazingly vivid.

38. A plan of the battlefield of Mohi is in Spruner-Menke, *Hand-Atlas für die Geschichte des Mittelalters und der neuren Zeit* (Gotha, 1850), Map 73.

39. Cahun (*Introduction à l'histoire de l'Asie* [Paris, 1896], p. 376) attempted to reverse the sense of certain statements in the *Carmen miserabile* in order to prove that there was an incipient entente between Magyars and Mongols. In fact, it is d'Ohsson, as always, who seems to strike the right note (*Histoire des Mongols*, II, 146–155).

40. For this princess, see Pelliot, "Les Mongols et la Papauté," *Revue de l'Orient chrétien* (1931–1932), p. 53 (193 of the separate reprint).

41. A Qudu, Toqto'a-bäki's son.

42. He escaped Törägänä's enmity by flight. Her son Güyük's accession in 1246 was to restore him to his former position.

43. Jagatai, who had caused the regency to be entrusted to her, died the following year (1242).

44. Cf. Barthold, "Bâtû-khân," *EI*, p. 700.

45. Cf. "Chronique de Kirakos," *JA*, I (1858), 452; *Recueil des historiens des Croisades. Documents arméniens*, I, 605.

46. Törägänä died two or three months after the election of her son.

47. D'Ohsson, *Histoire des Mongols*, II, 199.

48. Pelliot, "Chrétiens d'Asie Centrale et d'Extrême Orient," *TP* (1914), p. 628.

49. Pelliot, "Chrétiens d'Asie Centrale," p. 628, and "Les Mongols et la Papauté," *Revue de l'Orient chrétien* (1922–23), p. 247 (51). Yet of course Güyük, however favorably disposed toward Nestorianism, in no way departed from the universal "superstitious tolerance" of his own people with regard to other Mongol religions. It is known that his younger brother Godan, who held an appanage in Kansu (he died in Lanchow in 1251), protected the lamas of the famous Tibetan monastery of Sas-Kya. Cf. Pelliot, "Les systèmes d'écriture chez les anciens Mongols," *AM* (1925), p. 285.

50. Persian text, Turkic preface, and Mongol seal. Cf. Pelliot, "Les Mongols et la Papauté," p. 21 (18).

51. Cf. *Recueil des historiens des Croisades. Documents arméniens,* I, 605, 651; Nangis, "Vie de saint Louis," *Recueil des historiens de la France,* XX, 361–363; Grousset, *Histoire des Croisades,* III, 526–527.

52. The administrative responsibilities of Baiju and Eljigidäi are ill-defined, but, as Pelliot points out, it seems likely that the powers with which Güyük invested Eljigidäi were superior to those of Baiju.

53. Juvaini and Rashid ad-Din in d'Ohsson, *Histoire des Mongols,* II, 206; "Chronique de Kirakos," *JA,* I (1858), 451; Brosset, *Histoire de la Géorgie,* Add. I, 298.

54. Barthold, "Bâtû-khân," *EI,* p. 700; Pelliot, "Les Mongols et la Papauté," pp. 58 (196) and 61 (199).

55. Bar Hebraeus is mistaken in stating that Güyük's death took place on July 22, 1249.

56. D'Ohsson (*Histoire des Mongols,* II, 246) is mistaken in saying that Oghul Qaimish was the daughter of the former Oirat king Qutuqu-bäki. (The correction is made by Pelliot, "Les Mongols et la Papauté," p. 61 [199].)

57. For this name (possibly Solomon), cf. Pelliot, "Les Mongols et la Papauté," pp. 63–64 (203–204).

58. Cf. *ibid.,* p. 196 (199).

59. Sorghaqtani was the daughter of Jagambu, the *Wang-khan's* brother. She died in February, 1252, shortly after her son Mongka's accession.

60. D'Ohsson, *Histoire des Mongols,* II, 204.

61. *Mongka* in Mongolian, *mängü* or *mangu* in Turkic, means "eternal." Cf. Pelliot, "Sur quelques mots d'Asie Centrale," *JA* (1913), p. 451.

62. Pelliot's reconstruction, in "Les Mongols et la Papauté," p. 62 (200).

63. D'Ohsson, *Histoire des Mongols,* II, 249 *et seq.* (according to Juvaini and Rashid ad-Din).

64. Pelliot, "Les Mongols et la Papauté," p. 63 (201).

65. *Ibid.,* pp. 66 (204) and 79 (217).

66. D'Ohsson, *Histoire des Mongols,* II, 266 (according to Juvaini and Rashid ad-Din).

67. According to Rubruck (Chap. XXV), the frontier dividing the two dominions was in the Ala-Tau area, north of the Issyk Kul. The same traveler states that Mongka and Batu constituted a true dyarchy; but, as Mongka himself said to Rubruck, "The head has two eyes in it, and although they are two, they both look the same way." Nevertheless, Mongka, with his authoritarian temperament and economic sense, had no difficulty in refusing even Batu's demands

for money (d'Ohsson, *Histoire des Mongols,* II, 320–321, on the basis of the *Yüan Shih*).

68. Cf. Pelliot, "Chrétiens d'Asie Centrale," p. 629.

69. Cf. Chavannes, "Inscriptions et pièces de chancellerie chinoises," *TP* (1904), pp. 364, 374; (1908), pp. 356, 362.

70. Cf. Bazin, "Recherches sur les ordres religieux chinois," *JA,* II (1856), 138, and Chavannes, "Inscriptions et pièces de chancellerie chinoises," *TP* (1904), pp. 367, 383.

71. Grousset, *Histoire des Croisades,* III, 522.

72. Pelliot thinks that Rubruck left Palestine for Constantinople at the beginning of 1253 and not in 1252, as Rockhill has it. "Les Mongols et la Papauté," p. 77 (221).

73. For the different sorts of kumiss, see Pelliot, in *JA* (1920), p. 170.

74. Despite Rubruck, whose prejudice against Nestorianism may have misled him somewhat, Sartaq's Nestorianism is corroborated by the Armenian chronicler Kirakos (*JA,* I [1858], 459). Rubruck's comments on the profound ignorance of the Nestorian clergy are confirmed by the Polo family, to whom the great Kublai Khan made the same remark when requesting that Catholic scholars be sent to him to enlighten his court as to true Christian thought (Marco Polo, *Il Milione,* ed. Benedetto, pp. 70–71).

75. Minorsky, *Hudud al-Alam,* p. 276.

76. "Ah! The jewel is indeed in the lotus!"

77. According to Rubruck (Chap. XXXVI), these Nestorian feasts ended as carousals. After the ceremony mentioned above, Mongka's wife became extremely drunk: "We were brought beer made of rice to drink, and light red wine resembling the wine of La Rochelle, with kumiss. The lady, taking a full goblet, knelt down and asked a blessing. As the priests chanted, she drank. . . . The day passed thus until the evening. At last the lady, as drunk as the rest, returned home in her cart accompanied by the priests, who chanted, or rather howled, incessantly."

78. The name of *Tuinan* or *Tuin,* by which Rubruck and other western missionaries designated Buddhist monks, must come from the Chinese *tao-jen,* "men of the road," or "of the way," referring to the *sramana.*

79. Compare the formula of the monk Hethum or "Hayton": "Changius Can, empereor par le comandement de Deu [*sic*]" (*Recueil des historiens des Croisades. Documents arméniens,* II, 148–150).

80. Grousset, *Histoire des Croisades,* III, 527, 636.

81. *Yarligh* in Turkic, *jarliq* in Mongolian: imperial edict. Cf. Pelliot, in *TP* (1930), p. 292.

82. Hayton, *Documents arméniens*, II, 164–166; cf. "Chronique de Kirakos," *JA* (1833), p. 279, and I (1858), 463–473; Grousset, *Histoire des Croisades*, III, 527–529. Incidentally, it may be appropriate to correct certain unintentionally tendentious statements made by Armenian historians. Mongka's designs against the caliphate were purely political. He was in no way hostile to Islam as such. On the contrary, as Juvaini testifies, he listened to Muslim prayers with the same reverence as to Christian or other kinds. Thus it was that at the feasts of *bairam* in 1252 the great judge Jamal ad-Din Mahmud of Khodzhent came to recite a prayer in his *ordu*. "Mongka caused him to repeat it a number of times, and loaded the Muslims with presents."

83. Cf. Bretschneider, *Mediaeval Researches*, I, 168.

84. I have purposely used the form Kublai for the prince of this name, after using that of Qubilai for Jenghiz Khan's lieutenant, not because these words are of different origin, but in order to avoid confusion in the mind of the reader.

85. D'Ohsson states that the Mongols took possession of Chengtu in the year of Ogödäi's death (December, 1241). In 1252, the *T'ung-chien-k'ang-mu* shows the Mongols plundering Chengtu afresh, proof that there had been no effective occupation of it by the Mongols.

86. Cf. Herrmann, *Atlas of China*, Map 52.

87. Cf. Pelliot, "Les Mongols et la Papauté," p. 77 (201). In Persian, Uriankqadai.

88. Cf. Chavannes, "Inscriptions et pièces de chancellerie chinoises d'époque mongole," *TP* (1905), pp. 1–7; *Nan-chao ye-shih*, trans. C. Sainson (Paris, 1904), p. 109.

89. The government of Yunnan—alongside that of the old dynasty—was entrusted to Jenghiz-Khanite princes, among whom were Ugechi, Kublai's son, Tughlugh, and Esen Temür, this last being Ugechi's son. For the Mongols' policy in Yunnan and the way in which they succeeded in winning the co-operation of the one-time kings of Tali as loyal auxiliaries, cf. Chavannes, "Inscriptions," pp. 7, 31, and *Nan-chao ye-shih*, pp. 110–112.

90. Cf. Chavannes, "Inscriptions," pp. 6, 29.

Chapter 7

1. *Qubilai* in the Mongolian of the *Secret History*. The Chinese transcription is *Hu-pi-lie*. Persian transcriptions are *Qubilay* or *Qublay*. We have adhered to the classic transcription Kublai (Khubilai), which conforms to Mongol spelling and at the same time recalls the Chinese transcription.

2. Among the Jenghiz-Khanites present at Kublai's election, hardly anyone is mentioned by name except Qada'an, Ogödäi's son, and Togachar, the son of Temuge Ochigin. Kublai's most energetic partisans included the Öngüt princes Kün-buqa, and Ai-buqa (both Nestorians), who in 1260 defeated Qara-buqa, Ariq-bögä's general. Cf. A. C. Moule, *Christians in China* (New York, 1930), p. 236.

3. Mailla, IX, 275–282.

4. Pelliot, "Chrétiens d'Asie Centrale et d'Extrême-Orient," *TP* (1914), p. 629.

5. Bayan, in Mongolian, means rich, favored by fortune. This general belonged to the Ba'arin tribe. The Chinese transcription is Po-yen.

6. Marco Polo credits his father and uncle with the construction of these machines (ed. Pauthier, II, 470–476; ed. Moule-Pelliot [London, 1938], p. 318).

7. At the time of the siege of Chenchow by the Mongols, a body of Christian Alans (of the Greek rite) who were serving in the Mongol army were overrun and massacred more or less treacherously in a renewed offensive by the Chinese (June, 1275). Bayan, enraged by this, avenged the Alans at the time of the final conquest of the city in December, 1275, by robbing the population and allocating the revenues of Chenchow to the victims' families. Cf. Marco Polo, ed. Benedetto, p. 141; Pelliot, "Chrétiens d'Asie Centrale," p. 641; Moule, *Christians in China*, p. 140.

8. Marco Polo, ed. Pauthier, II, 460; ed. Moule-Pelliot, p. 313. Cf. Moule, "Hang-chou to Shang-tou," *TP* (1915), p. 393.

9. Cf. Bretschneider, *Recherches . . . sur Pékin* (Paris, 1879), Maps III, V, pp. 52, 84. This name of *khan-baligh*, city of the khan, like that of *ordu-baligh*, city of the court, was often bestowed by Turko-Mongol peoples on their royal residences. In the Uigur translation of the life of the pilgrim Hsüan-tsang, Changan or Sian, the capital of the Chinese T'ang emperors, was also called *Qan-baliq*. A. von Gabain, "Die uigurische Uebersetzung der Biographie Hüen-tsangs," *Sitz. der preuss. Akad. der Wissenschaften* (Berlin, 1935), p. 30.

10. Cf. Demiéville, in *BEFEO*, 1–2 (1924), 195. The king Ko-tjong's policy of resistance to the Mongols was inspired by his minister Ch'eu Ou, last representative of a family of hereditary mayors of the palace who had wielded power since 1196.

11. Courant writes: "Korea was from that time forward no more than a Mongol province ruled by native kings. These, being married to Mongol women, sons of Mongol mothers, and counseled by Mongol residents, could be summoned to Peking and exiled or deposed at the khan's pleasure. They spoke the language and wore the clothes of the Yüan, and had nothing Korean about them any more."

12. Cf. J. Murdoch and I. Yamagata, *History of Japan* (London, 1925–26, 3 vols.), I, 491–592; also N. Yamada, *Ghenkō, the Mongol Invasion of Japan* (London, 1916; with bibliography of Japanese works and sources, p. 269). Passages from the *Taiheiki* are translated in W. G. Aston, *A History of Japanese Literature* (New York, 1925), p. 70. For Japanese paintings of this war, see Shizuya Fujikake, "On the Scroll Painting of the Mongol Invasion," *Kokka* (1921), Nos. 371–379.

13. Cf. Georges Maspero, "Histoire du Champa," *TP* (1911), p. 462, and separate volume (1928), pp. 174–187; Pelliot, *BEFEO*, II (1902), 140.

14. Cf. Huber, "La fin de la dynastie de Pagan," *BEFEO* (1909), pp. 633–680; Harvey, *History of Burmah* (1925), pp. 64–69.

15. This narrative, the *Chen-la Fung t'u ki*, has been translated and studied by Pelliot. (Cheu Ta-kuan, "Mémoire sur les coutumes du Cambodge," trans. Pelliot, *BEFEO* [1902], p. 123.)

16. Cf. Pelliot, "Deux itinéraires de Chine en Inde," *BEFEO* (1904); G. Cœdès, "Les origines de la dynastie de Sukhodaya," *JA*, I (1920), 242. The kingdoms of Chiangmai (Xiengmai) and Sukhotai were known respectively in Chinese by the names of Pape and Hsien.

17. Cf. Mailla, IX, 452; N. J. Krom, *Hindoe-javaansche Geschiedenis* (The Hague, 1926), pp. 352–359. At the time of the Mongol invasion of Java, the raja of Malayu, in Sumatra, being alarmed, also acknowledged himself a tributary for a short time. G. Ferrand, *L'empire sumatranais de Çrivijaya*, p. 231.

18. Qaidu was the son of Qashi, a younger brother of Güyük.

19. In Chinese, No-mu-han.

20. In Chinese, Hsi-li-ki.

21. Rashid ad-Din (d'Ohsson, *Histoire des Mongols*, II, 456) traces Nayan's descent from Temuge, while the *Yüan Shih* traces it from Belgutai.

22. Cf. d'Ohsson, *Histoire des Mongols*, II, 456, and Erdmann, *Temudschin*, p. 569.

23. Marco Polo, ed. Moule-Pelliot, p. 200; ed. Benedetto, pp. 69–70. Cf. Pelliot, "Chrétiens d'Asie Centrale et d'Extrême-Orient," *TP* (1914), p. 635.

24. In Chinese, Kan-ma-la. He was the son of prince Chinkim (Rashid ad-Din's transcription) or Chen-kin (transcription of the *Yüan Shih*), himself Kublai's second son.

25. Cf. Rashid ad-Din, in d'Ohsson, *Histoire des Mongols*, II, 513; and *Yüan Shih*, trans. Moule, in *Christians in China*, pp. 237–238.

26. Cf. Barthold, "Hulägu," *EI*, II, 353.

27. Ed. Pauthier, I, 236; ed. Moule-Pelliot, I, 192.

28. Marco Polo, ed. Pauthier, p. 481; ed. Moule-Pelliot, I, 322.

29. Marco Polo, ed. Pauthier, p. 345; ed. Moule-Pelliot, I, 250.

30. Marco Polo, ed. Pauthier, p. 346; ed. Moule-Pelliot, I, 251.

31. The Sayyid Ajall, Shams ad-Din 'Umar (Chinese transcription, Sai-tien-ch'e Shen-ssu-ting Wu-ma-eul), was born about 1210 and died in 1279. From 1274 to 1279 he was administrator of Yunnan. His sons Nasir ad-Din (d. 1292) and Husain succeeded him in the administration of the same province, which this dynasty of Muslim officials helped to Islamize. The Sayyid Ajall himself caused the two first mosques in Yunnan to be built. See A. J. A. Vissière and Lepage, "Documents sur le Seyyid Edjell," in Vissière, *Mission d'Ollone, Recherches sur les musulmans chinois* (Paris, 1911), pp. 20–203, and Vissière, "Le Seyyid Edjell," *Revue du monde musulman*, IV, No. 2 (February, 1908); Bretschneider, *Mediaeval Researches*, I, 271; Chavannes, "Inscriptions et pièces de chancellerie chinoises," *TP* (1905), p. 19.

32. Ahmed Fenaketi (Chinese transcription, A-ha-ma) was in power from 1270 until his assassination in 1282. Sanga (Chinese transcription, Sang-ko) was appointed to the finance ministry from about 1288 to 1291. Cf. Marco Polo, ed. Moule-Pelliot, pp. 214, 238.

33. Marco Polo, *Il Milione*, ed. Benedetto, p. 70.

34. D'Ohsson, *Histoire des Mongols*, II, 491, after Rashid ad-Din.

35. Sanang Sechen, trans. Schmidt, *Geschichte der Ostmongolen*, pp. 113, 115.

36. Cf. Chavannes, "Inscriptions et pièces de chancellerie chinoises," *TP* (1908), p. 382.

37. Cf. G. Huth, *Geschichte des Buddhismus in der Mongolei* (Strassburg, 1892–96, 2 vols.), II, 139; Sanang Sechen, trans. Schmidt, *Geschichte der Ostmongolen*, p. 115.

38. Pelliot, "Les 'Kouo-che' ou 'maîtres du royaume' dans le bouddhisme chinois," *TP* (1911), p. 671.

39. It was in the Uigur writing that the oldest known monument in the Mongol language was inscribed. This is the stone known as Jenghiz Khan's in the Asiatic Museum of Leningrad, the inscription on which dates from about 1225. Pelliot says, "It can only have been in Uigur writing that the epic chronicle *Monghol-un ni'utcha tobtchi'an* (or *Manghol un Niuca Tobca'an*) was recorded. This *Secret History of the Mongols* has come down to us in Chinese translation and transcription" (Pelliot, in *AM* [1925], p. 288). Also in Uigur writing were the great Mongol inscription of 1362, found by Pelliot in Kansu in 1908, and the two letters of the khans of Persia, Arghun and Oljaitu, to Philip the Fair, preserved in the French Archives Nationales. Another example is the Mongol inscription on the seal

of Güyük's letter to Innocent IV in 1246. Cf. Pelliot, "Les Mongols et la Papauté," *Revue de l'Orient chrétien* (1922–23), pp. 3–30.

40. Cf. Pelliot, "Les systèmes d'écriture chez les anciens Mongols," *AM* (1925), p. 284, and "Les mots à H initiale, aujourd'hui amuie, dans le mongol des XIIIe et XIV siècles," *JA* (1925), p. 193.

41. D'Ohsson, *Histoire des Mongols*, II, 532, after Rashid ad-Din.

42. Sanang Sechen, trans. Schmidt, *Geschichte der Ostmongolen*, p. 398; d'Ohsson, *Histoire des Mongols*, II, 533.

43. Mailla, IX, 539. See the remarks by Quatremère in his edition of Rashid ad-Din (Paris, 1836), p. 189.

44. In China the Mongol regime had in the same way favored magical sects and secret societies formerly proscribed by the national dynasties. "Dissident sects, persecuted to a greater or lesser extent by the Sung, had helped the new dynasty. In return, they had been granted not only freedom of worship but also official recognition and a hierarchy. Thus it is that at the end of the thirteenth century and at the beginning of the fourteenth, both in the *History of the Yüan* and in the collection of edicts entitled *Yüan tien chang*, there is frequent mention of the religious tribunals of the 'White Cloud' and 'White Lotus' and of the sect of the 'Dhuta.' There are also references to many Taoist sects and to all sorts of foreign religions: Nestorian and Catholic Christianity, Islam, and Judaism." Chavannes and Pelliot, "Un traité manichéen retrouvé en Chine," *JA* (1913), p. 364.

45. Marco Polo, ed. Benedetto, p. 70.

46. The edicts of Ogödäi, Mongka, and Kublai carried tax exemption and various privileges in respect of *ho-shang* and *t'o-yin* (Buddhist monks), *hsien-sheng* (Taoist monks), *ye-li-k'o* or *ärkägün* (Nestorian priests), and *ta-chih-man* (*danishmend*, or Muslim doctors). See Deveria, "Notes d'épigraphie mongole-chinoise [edict of Buyantu-khan]," *JA*, II (1896), 396; Chavannes, "Inscriptions et pièces de chancellerie," *TP* (1904), p. 388; Pelliot, "Chrétiens d'Asie Centrale et d'Extrême-Orient," *TP* (1914), p. 637. A clan of Ordos Mongols bears to this day the name Erqüt or Erküt, a modern form of the medieval word *ärkägüd*. Father Mostaert, who has studied the Erküt people, has found that they are neither shamanists nor Buddhists, but that they revere the cross—in the form of the swastika—and, unknown to themselves, betray confused memories of Christianity. From this he concludes that they are doubtless the descendants of the Nestorians of the Öngüt country at the Jenghiz-Khanite period (Mostaert, "Ordosica," *Bulletin 9, Catholic University of Peking* [1934]).

47. Pelliot, "Chrétiens d'Asie Centrale," p. 634.

48. *Ibid.*, p. 630.

49. Alaqush-tigin(or tekin)-quri. See the *Secret History*, trans. Haenisch, p. 55.

50. See A. C. Moule, *Christians in China Before the Year 1550* (New York, 1930), p. 235.

51. Pelliot, "Chrétiens d'Asie Centrale," p. 631; Moule, *Christians in China*, p. 236.

52. Marco Polo, ed. Benedetto, pp. 60, 61; d'Ohsson, *Histoire des Mongols*, II, 513; Moule, *Christians in China*, p. 237.

53. Moule, *Christians in China*, p. 99.

54. *Ibid.*, p. 208.

55. *Ibid.*, p. 100.

56. Marco Polo, ed. Benedetto, pp. 58, 60; ed. Moule-Pelliot, I, 181.

57. Marco Polo, ed. Benedetto, p. 141; Pelliot, "Chrétiens d'Asie Centrale," p. 637; Moule, *Christians in China*, p. 145.

58. One of the Nestorian churches in Yangchow mentioned by Odorico da Pordenone had been founded at the end of the thirteenth century by a rich merchant named Abraham. Pelliot has found an edict of 1317 relating to this church ("Chrétiens d'Asie Centrale," p. 638).

59. *Ibid.*, p. 631; Moule, *Christians in China*, pp. 94–127.

60. *Duwa* became *Oqo* in the Syriac bibliography!

61. Moule, *Christians in China*, p. 101.

62. Pelliot, "Chrétiens d'Asie Centrale," *TP* (1914), p. 640, and (1927), p. 159, and "Les Mongols et la Papauté," *Revue de l'Orient chrétien*, 3–4 (1924), 248 (52). For information on the *ch'eng-hsiang* Bolod, see Pelliot, in *TP* (1927), p. 159.

63. C. de La Roncière and Dorez, *Bibliographie de l'École des Chartes*, LVI (1895), 29; Pelliot, in *TP* (1914), p. 641. Pelliot has found in the *Yüan Shih* the names of several of the Alan chiefs of Peking who sent this embassy: Fu-ting, Hsiang-shan, and Jayan-buqa, which in the letter to Benedict XII became Fodim Jovens, Chyansam (Shyansam), and Chemboga (Shemboga).

64. Pelliot, "Les traditions manichéennes au Fou-kien," *TP* (1923), p. 193. The so-called Christians noted by Marco Polo at Fuchow (*Fugiu*) must, Pelliot thinks, have been Manichaeans. Cf. Benedetto's edition, p. 158; Moule, *Christians in China*, p. 143; Pelliot, in *Journal des Savants* (January, 1929), p. 42.

65. At *Carachoço* Marco Polo mentions the presence of a Nestorian community (*Il Milione*, ed. Benedetto, p. 46; ed. Moule-Pelliot, II, xx), and at *Chingintalas*, in the region north of Beshbaligh, some asbestos mines.

66. Marco Polo, ed. Moule-Pelliot, I, 79; ed. Benedetto, pp. 70–71.

67. Pelliot has established that when Marco Polo speaks of Mosul and Baghdad, it is from hearsay only. H. Yule (Yule-Cordier edition [London, 1903], I, 19) is mistaken in attributing to him a journey between Mosul, Baghdad, and Basra. The most likely itinerary is that indicated by P. M. Sykes, *Persia*, p. 262.

68. Ed. Yule-Cordier, I, 129; ed. Moule-Pelliot, I, 128.

69. Stein, *Serindia*, Chap. IX, pp. 318 *et seq.* The identification of Pem with Keriya is Pelliot's.

70. Cf. Marco Polo, ed. Benedetto, p. 48; ed. Moule-Pelliot, I, 158 (*Succiu*); Pelliot, "Kao-tch'ang, Qotcho," *JA*, I (1912), 591.

71. Ed. Pauthier, I, 203; ed. Benedetto, p. 48; ed. Moule-Pelliot, p. 159.

72. Cf. Benedetto, p. 52; Moule-Pelliot, p. 178.

73. Cf. Benedetto, p. 58; Moule-Pelliot, p. 181.

74. "In Marco Polo's day, Persian must have served as a sort of *lingua franca* for Central and East Asia," Pelliot, in *JA*, II (1913), 185.

75. Ed. Benedetto, p. 137; cf. Pelliot, in *TP* (1927), pp. 164–168.

76. Marco Polo also mentions a Nestorian community in *Quengianfu* (ed. Benedetto, pp. 107–108; ed. Moule-Pelliot, p. 264).

77. Cf. Benedetto, p. 115; Moule-Pelliot, p. 277. On *Caragian*, see Pelliot, "Trois itinéraires," *BEFEO* (1904), p. 158.

78. Cf. Huber, "La fin de la dynastie de Pagan," *BEFEO* (1909), pp. 633–680.

79. *Cacianfu* is rightly identified with Hokien. A. J. H. Charignon, however (*Le livre de Marco Polo* [Peking, 1924–28, 3 vols.], III, 2), equates it with Chengting! Cf. Benedetto, p. 128.

80. Marco Polo calls the Yellow River the *Caramoran*, from its Mongol name Kara Muren: Black River.

81. Cf. G. Maspero, in *TP* (1911), p. 476.

82. Burqan, the Mongol name for the Buddha.

83. Ed. Pauthier, p. 588; ed. Moule-Pelliot, p. 407.

84. Ed. Pauthier, p. 325; ed. Moule-Pelliot, p. 239. Cf. note in Yule-Cordier edition, I, 426–430. See also Ibn-Batuta, ed. Defrémery (Paris, 1853–79, 4 vols.), IV, 259–260.

85. Cf. Heyd, trans. Furcy Raynaud, *Histoire du commerce du Levant au moyen-âge* (Leipzig, 1923), II, 670, 693.

86. The name *Quinsai*, or, according to various manuscripts, *Khansa, Khinsa, Khingsai, Khanzai, Cansay, Campsay*, comes from *king-tsai*: "temporary residence" (Pelliot). Cf. Moule, "Marco Polo's Description of Quinsay," *TP* (1937), p. 105.

87. "The port of Zayton is one of the largest in the world. I am wrong; it is the largest of all ports" (Ibn-Batuta, ed. Defrémery, IV, 269). Near Zayton was *Tingiu*, that is, Tö-hua, also in Fukien, of which

Marco Polo praises the ceramics (ed. Moule-Pelliot, p. 352; cf. Heyd, *Histoire du commerce du Levant*, II, 247).

88. Ed. Pauthier, p. 561; ed. Moule-Pelliot, p. 368; Heyd, *Histoire du commerce du Levant*, II, 644; and G. Ferrand, *Relations de voyages et textes géographiques arabes, persans et turcs* (Paris, 1913–14, 2 vols.), I, 31.

89. A work compiled in Florence between 1335 and 1343. Cf. Heyd, *Histoire du commerce du Levant*, I, xviii.

90. Heyd, *Histoire du commerce du Levant*, II, 218.

91. Pelliot, "Chrétiens d'Asie Centrale et d'Extrême-Orient," *TP* (1914), p. 633.

92. Moule, *Christians in China*, p. 191.

93. The date 1318 given in Andrew of Perugia's letter as that of his arrival in Peking is certainly erroneous, and Moule suggests that it should be corrected to read 1313 (*Christians in China*, pp. 191–192).

94. Odorico da Pordenone, ed. Cordier (Paris, 1891), p. 99.

95. Cf. H. Hosten, "St. Thomas and St. Thomé, Mylapore," *Journal of the Asiatic Society of Bengal* (1924), p. 153.

96. For the importance of *Sincalan* (especially for the export of Chinese ceramics to India and the Yemen), see also Ibn-Batuta, trans. Defrémery, IV, 272.

97. Cf. Moule, *Christians in China*, p. 241, and "The Ten Thousand Bridges of Quinsai," *New China Review* (1922), p. 32.

98. Marco Polo had already noted a Nestorian church in Hangchow (ed. Benedetto, p. 152).

99. Odorico da Pordenone, ed. Cordier, p. 375. Note also in this connection what Marco Polo says of the part taken by Kublai in the great Christian festivals (ed. Benedetto, pp. 69, 70).

100. Ed. Benedetto, pp. 60–61.

101. Odorico, ed. Cordier, p. 450. Cf. B. Laufer, "Was Odoric of Pordenone ever in Tibet?" *TP* (1914), p. 405.

102. The letter from the Alans of Peking to Pope Benedict XII, dated July 11, 1336, states that Montecorvino had died eight years earlier (Moule, *Christians in China*, p. 198).

103. *Ibid.*, p. 197.

104. Pelliot, "Chrétiens d'Asie Centrale," *TP* (1914), p. 642.

105. See Marignolli's "chronicle" in Moule, *Christians in China*, p. 254.

106. This viceroyalty, given by Kublai to his third son Mangala and later transmitted to Ananda, Mangala's son, comprised also Shensi and had as its capital Sian, or Changan.

107. Cf. L. Ligeti, "Les noms mongols de Wen-tsong des Yuan," *TP* (1930), p. 57.

108. Courant, *L'Asie Centrale aux XVIIe et XVIIIe siècles*, p. 5.

Chapter 8

1. Or Chaghatai. In the *Secret History,* the name is given as Cha'adai. Here, with Pelliot (*TP* [1930], p. 304) and Barthold (*Turkestan*), we use the form Jagatai (Djaghatai) customary in the West.

2. Wassaf, in d'Ohsson, *Histoire des Mongols,* III, 436.

3. Rashid ad-Din, *ibid.,* II, 101–102.

4. Rashid ad-Din, *ibid.,* II, 93, 100.

5. Cf. Barthold, "Caghatâi-khân," *EI,* p. 832.

6. *Ibid.*

7. Juvaini, in d'Ohsson, *Histoire des Mongols,* II, 102–107.

8. *Mongka* in Mongolian is the same word as *Mangu* in Turkic. I use the two forms deliberately so as to avoid confusion between the Jagataite in question and the grand khan who deposed him in 1252.

9. D'Ohsson, *Histoire des Mongols,* II, 204; Barthold, "Caghatâi-khân," *EI,* pp. 833–834.

10. D'Ohsson, *Histoire des Mongols,* II, 271.

11. Barthold, "Caghatâi-khân," *EI,* pp. 833–834.

12. Muhammad Qazvini points out that Juvaini's spelling is Ksmain (unvocalized; *Ta'rikh-i Jahan-gusha,* p. 34), or Kshmain (*ibid.,* Bérézine ed., I, 165).

13. Saindi in Juvaini, I, 34, and in Rashid ad-Din, Bérézine ed., I, 165 (communication from Muhammad Qazvini).

14. This prince, reports Muhammad Qazvini, is mentioned in Juvaini by the unvocalized form of the name: Uknj or Oukndj (Juvaini, I, 38).

15. D'Ohsson, *Histoire des Mongols,* II, 271–273, according to Rashid ad-Din.

16. D'Ohsson, *Histoire des Mongols,* II, 352–354. In this exposition of the history of the khanate of Jagatai, I am compelled to repeat some facts already briefly stated, from the point of view of Kublai's history, in Chap. 7.

17. Barthold, "Caghâtai-khân," *EI,* p. 833, and "Berke," *ibid.,* p. 726.

18. The usual form of this name, *Boraq* or *Borraq,* is an Islamization. Pelliot, recalling Marco Polo's *Barac* and the *Pa-la* of the *Yüan Shih,* emphasizes that the Mongol name was Baraq ("Sur la légende d'Ughuz-khan," *TP* [1930], p. 339). For the reign of this prince, see d'Ohsson, *Histoire des Mongols,* II, 359–360, and Barthold, "Burâk," *EI,* p. 814.

19. It was on the Talas that Qaidu usually lived after his victory over the Jagataites (cf. Pelliot, in *TP* [1930], p. 272), and it was there

that he was visited by Rabban Sauma and Mar Yahballaha on their way from Peking to Iran.

20. D'Ohsson, *Histoire des Mongols*, III, 435 (according to Wassaf and Rashid ad-Din). The Büri mentioned here should not be confused with the Büri who had had Batu executed in 1252. Nikpai must have reference to Nägübäi (Pelliot, in *JA*, II [1927], 266).

21. D'Ohsson, II, 450–451, and III, 427–453; Barthold, "Burâk," *EI*, p. 814.

22. Rashid ad-Din and Wassaf, d'Ohsson, *Histoire des Mongols*, II, 451, who give the date of Nikpai Oghul's death as 1272.

23. *Ibid.*, III, 457–458, according to Wassaf.

24. Cf. Barthold, "Caghatâi-khân," *EI*, p. 833.

25. D'Ohsson, *Histoire des Mongols*, II, 451–452, and Cordier, II, 310–311. In 1274, Qaidu had driven Kublai's representatives from Kashgar, Yarkand, and even from Khotan. In 1276, Kublai reoccupied Khotan and also—temporarily—Yarkand and Kashgar.

26. D'Ohsson, *Histoire des Mongols*, II, 512–515.

27. *Ibid.*, II, 516–517; Mailla, IX, 479.

28. "Transoxiana," Wassaf notes, "prospered under the rule of Qaidu, a just and humane ruler." See d'Ohsson, *Histoire des Mongols*, III, 458.

29. *Ibid.*, II, 511, and III, 431; Barthold, "Burâk-khân," *EI*, p. 814.

30. Moule, *Christians in China*, p. 101.

31. D'Ohsson, *Histoire des Mongols*, II, 518.

32. *Ibid.*, II, 519, and III, 557–558; Barthold, "Caghatâi-khân," *EI*, p. 833.

33. D'Ohsson, *Histoire des Mongols*, II, 520.

34. *Ibid.*, II, 520–521, and IV, 558–559, according to Wassaf.

35. *Ibid.*, IV, 560.

36. *Ibid.*, IV, 561.

37. Hafiz-i Abru, trans. K. Bayani (Paris, 1936–38, 2 vols.), pp. 37–41.

38. *Ibid.*, pp. 43–46; d'Ohsson, *Histoire des Mongols*, IV, 563–565.

39. Hafiz-i Abru, pp. 67–74, 80–88; d'Ohsson, *Histoire des Mongols*, IV, 567–568, 618–629, 642–644.

40. Barthold, "Caghatâi-khân," *EI*, p. 834.

41. D'Ohsson, *Histoire des Mongols*, IV, 562.

42. Tombstones inscribed in Syriac and Turkic from Pishpek (Semirechye), dating from 1264 to 1338, in the Guimet Museum (Nau, *Expansion nestorienne*, p. 300).

43. Barthold, "Caghatâi-khân," *EI*, p. 834.

44. Moule, *Christians in China*, pp. 255–256.

45. *Ibid.*, p. 255.

46. In 1362, one last missionary, James of Florence, titular archbishop of Zayton (i.e., Chüanchow in the modern Chinese province of Fukien), died a martyr's death in Central Asia, apparently in the khanate of Jagatai, though possibly in Persia (*ibid.*, pp. 197, 255).

47. *Zafer-name*, trans. Pétis de la Croix, I, 2.

48. Hejira 747, the Year of the Pig (*Zafer-name*, I, 4).

49. *Zafer-name*, I, 4–5.

50. *Zafer-name*, I, 6–18.

51. Hejira 759, the Year of the Dog (*Zafer-name*, I, 19).

52. *Zafer-name*, I, 21–22.

53. Cf. Barthold, "Dûghlât," *EI*, p. 1112.

54. *Ta'rikh-i Rashidi*, trans. Denison Ross, pp. 7–8.

55. *Ibid.*, pp. 6–9.

56. *Ibid.*, pp. 10–15.

57. *Ibid.*, p. 15.

58. *Zafer-name*, trans. Pétis de la Croix, pp. 29–32.

59. *Ibid.*, pp. 37–38.

60. *Ta'rikh-i Rashidi*, trans. Ross, p. 18.

61. *Zafer-name*, trans. Pétis de la Croix, pp. 41–45; *Ta'rikh-i Rashidi*, trans. Ross, pp. 20–22.

Chapter 9

1. On Chormaghan, see Pelliot, "Les Mongols et la Papauté," *Revue de l'Orient chrétien* (1924), p. 247 (51).

2. *Ibid.*, p. 244 (49).

3. On Baiju, see *ibid.*, pp. 303 *et seq.* (109 *et seq.*).

4. This summer headquarters of the Mongols is called Sisian or "Sitiens" in Armenian and Latin sources. It seems that it should be placed in the Haband district, between the Siuni and the Artsakh, "in the mountains just to the east of Lake Gokcha." Pelliot, "Mongols et la Papauté," p. 302 (106).

5. On Eljigidäi (Äldjigidäi), see Pelliot, "Mongols et la Papauté" (1931–32), p. 33 (171).

6. On Aibeg and Särgis, see *ibid.* (1924), p. 327 (131).

7. *Ibid.* (1931–32), pp. 172 (174) and 193 (195); Grousset, *Histoire des Croisades*, III, 520.

8. Pelliot, "Mongols et la Papauté," pp. 175 (177) *et seq.*; Grousset, *Histoire des Croisades*, III, 521.

9. His son Arghasun or Harqasun had plotted against Mongka and had already been put to death in Mongolia.

10. Pelliot, "Mongols et la Papauté" (1931–32), p. 65 (203).

11. Bibliography (Georgian and Armenian sources, and Juvaini) in Minorsky, "Tiflis," *EI*, p. 796.

12. Cf. "Kaikâ'ûs II," *EI*, pp. 677–678.

13. Cf. d'Ohsson, *Histoire des Mongols*, III, 103–107 (according to Juvaini).

14. Beha ad-Din Muhammad, Juvaini's father, had been taken prisoner at Tus by the Mongol chief Kül-Bulat. He was treated kindly by his captor and entered Mongol service as *sahib-divan* of Khurasan. He remained a Mongol official until his death at Ispahan in 1253. Cf. Barthold, "Djuwainî," *EI*, p. 1100.

15. D'Ohsson, *Histoire des Mongols*, III, 116–117 (according to Juvaini).

16. *Ibid.*, III, 120 (according to Juvaini).

17. Juvaini, who served with his father as a government official under the orders of Arghun Agha, could not refrain from protesting violently against the ascendancy of Uigur scholars over the Arabo-Persians: "In the revolution that has just shaken the world, colleges have been destroyed and learned men slain, especially in Khurasan, which was the source of enlightenment and the meeting place of doctors. All men of letters in the country have perished by the sword. The creatures from nowhere who have replaced them care for nothing but the Uigur language and writing." See *ibid.*, I, xxv.

18. Juvaini and Rashid ad-Din, *ibid.*, III, 121–128.

19. *Ibid.*, III, 129–131.

20. *Ibid.*, III, 131; Minorsky, "Kutlugh-khân," *EI*, p. 1238; T. W. Haig, "Salghurides," *EI*, p. 109.

21. Hulägu comes from the Mongolian root *hülä-* or *ülä-*, meaning "in excess." In Persian, the name is Hulaku. Pelliot, "Les mots à H initial, aujourd'hui amui, en mongol des XIIIe et XIVe siècles," *JA* (1925), p. 236.

22. Rashid ad-Din, trans. Quatremère, p. 145; d'Ohsson, *Histoire des Mongols*, III, 139.

23. Cf. Rashid ad-Din, trans. Quatremère, pp. 217, 219; d'Ohsson, *Histoire des Mongols*, III, 197.

24. Cf. Abu'l Fida, *Recueil des historiens des Croisades. Historiens Orientaux*, I, 136; Rashid ad-Din, trans. Quatremère, p. 247; d'Ohsson, *Histoire des Mongols*, III, 212 (according to Wassaf); Grousset, *Histoire des Croisades*, III, 568.

25. Rashid ad-Din, trans. Quatremère, p. 231.

26. Rashid ad-Din, in d'Ohsson, *Histoire des Mongols*, III, 217.

27. Cf. Grousset, *Histoire des Croisades*, III, 571.

28. Abu'l Fida, *Historiens des Croisades*, I, 136.

29. Rashid ad-Din, trans. Quatremère, p. 299; cf. Kirakos, trans. Dulaurier, *JA*, I (1858), p. 489.

30. Cf. Kirakos, *JA* (1858), p. 491.

31. Abu'l Fida, *Historiens des Croisades*, p. 137.

32. Kirakos, *JA*, I (1858), p. 493.

33. Vartan, *JA*, II (1860), 291.

34. D'Ohsson, *Histoire des Mongols*, III, 270. See the account by the monk Hayton in *Recueil des historiens des Croisades. Documents arméniens*, II, 169–170; see also Grousset, *Histoire des Croisades*, III, 574–575.

35. Kirakos, *JA*, I (1858), p. 492.

36. Grousset, *Histoire des Croisades*, III, 575–576.

37. Daughter of Jagambu or Jaqambu, the *Wang-khan's* brother.

38. Rashid ad-Din, trans. Quatremère, p. 145.

39. *Ibid.*, pp. 94–95.

40. Vartan, *JA*, II (1860), 290, 309; *Historiens des Croisades. Documents arméniens*, I, 433.

41. Vartan, *JA*, II (1860), 300–301.

42. *Ibid.*, p. 302; corroborated by Rashid ad-Din, trans. Quatremère, p. 393.

43. Barthold, "Hûlâgû," *EI*, p. 353.

44. Rashid ad-Din, trans. Quatremère, p. 225; Kirakos, *JA*, I (1858), 484; d'Ohsson, *Histoire des Mongols*, III, 262.

45. Grousset, *Histoire des Croisades*, III, 549.

46. *Ibid.*, p. 515.

47. *Ibid.*, p. 579.

48. *Ibid.*, pp. 577–578.

49. Vartan, *JA*, II (1860), 294.

50. Kirakos, *JA*, I (1858), 496; Rashid ad-Din, trans. Quatremère, pp. 330–331, 350–375.

51. Hayton, *Recueil des historiens des Croisades. Documents arméniens*, II, 170; Vartan, *JA*, II (1860), 293.

52. "Gestes des Chiprois," *Documents arméniens*, p. 751; Grousset, *Croisades*, III, 581.

53. Bar Hebraeus, in d'Ohsson, *Histoire des Mongols*, III, 316.

54. *Ibid.*, III, 308–309; Grousset, *Croisades*, III, 581–582.

55. Abu'l Fida, *Historiens des Croisades*, I, 140.

56. *Ibid.*; Bar Hebraeus, *Chronicon Syriacum*, p. 533; Hayton, *Documents arméniens*, II, 171; Grousset, *Croisades*, III, 583.

57. Abu'l Fida, *Historiens des Croisades*, p. 141; "Gestes des Chiprois," *Recueil des historiens des Croisades. Documents arméniens*, II, 751; Grousset, *Croisades*, III, 586.

58. Abu'l Fida, *Historiens des Croisades*, p. 143.

59. *Ibid.;* "Gestes des Chiprois," *Documents arméniens,* II, 751; d'Ohsson, *Histoire des Mongols,* III, 325; Grousset, *Croisades,* III, 589.

60. D'Ohsson, *Histoire des Mongols,* III, 377; Barthold, "Berke," *EI,* pp. 725–726.

61. Kirakos, *JA,* I (1858), 498; Hayton, *Documents arméniens,* II, 173.

62. *Ibid.,* p. 174.

63. Delaborde, "Lettres des chrétiens de Terre Sainte, 1260," *Revue de l'Orient latin,* II (1894), 214; Grousset, *Croisades,* III, 584.

64. Hayton, *Documents arméniens,* p. 174; "Gestes des Chiprois," p. 752; Grousset, *Croisades,* III, 594.

65. Rashid ad-Din, trans. Quatremère, p. 347.

66. "Gestes des Chiprois," p. 753; "Manuscrit de Rothelin," *Historiens des Croisades,* p. 637; Grousset, *Croisades,* III, 601–603.

67. Kirakos, *JA,* I (1858), 498.

68. Rashid ad-Din, trans. Defrémery, pp. 351–353.

69. *Ibid.,* p. 393; cf. Vartan, *JA,* II (1860), 302.

70. Cf. Barthold, "Berke," *EI,* p. 726; Hayton, *Documents arméniens,* II, 176.

71. Rashid ad-Din, trans. Quatremère, p. 399; d'Ohsson, *Histoire des Mongols,* III, 380–381.

72. D'Ohsson, *Histoire des Mongols,* III, 362, 370–374 (according to Rashid ad-Din and Bar Hebraeus).

73. *Ibid.,* III, 397–404 (according to Rashid ad-Din and Mirkhond); cf. T. W. Haig, "Salghurides," *EI,* p. 109.

74. Cf. Rashid ad-Din, trans. Quatremère, p. 403; Minorsky, "Kutlugh-khân," *EI,* p. 1238.

75. D'Ohsson, *Histoire des Mongols,* IV, 148.

76. *Ibid.,* IV, 281.

77. Barthold, "Djuwainî," *EI,* p. 1100.

78. According to d'Ohsson, *Histoire des Mongols,* III, 407–408.

79. Mar Denha, patriarch from 1266 to 1281, had succeeded Makikha.

80. W. Budge, *The Monks of Kublai-khan,* pp. 139–140.

81. "Vie de Mar Yahballaha," trans. J. B. Chabot, *Revue de l'Orient latin* (1893), pp. 593–594.

82. Having left China ca. 1275, they arrived in Mesopotamia ca. 1278.

83. Budge, *Monks of Kublai-khan,* p. 148.

84. "Vie de Mar Yahballaha," pp. 607–608.

85. *Ibid.,* pp. 609–610.

86. D'Ohsson, *Histoire des Mongols,* III, 418–419.

87. *Ibid.,* III, 432–449 (according to Rashid ad-Din).

88. *Ibid.*, III, 441–442; IV, 179–183.

89. Abu'l Fida, *Historiens des Croisades*, I, 155; Hayton, *Documents arméniens*, p. 180; d'Ohsson, *Histoire des Mongols*, III, 481–488; Grousset, *Croisades*, III, 694.

90. Cf. Hayton, *Documents arméniens*, pp. 180–181.

91. Cf. Abu'l Fida, *Historiens des Croisades*, I, 158–159; Hayton, *Documents arméniens*, pp. 183–184; Bar Hebraeus, *Chronicon Syriacum*, pp. 592–593; d'Ohsson, *Histoire des Mongols*, III, 524; R. Röhricht, "Les batailles de Homs," *Archives de l'Orient latin*, I, 638; Grousset, *Croisades*, III, 699.

92. "Täghüdär" in Mongolian.

93. Hayton, *Documents arméniens*, p. 185.

94. "Vie de Mar Yahballaha," pp. 75–77.

95. Cf. d'Ohsson, *Histoire des Mongols*, IV, 31–38, 49–57 (according to Wassaf).

96. Chabot, "Relations du roi Argoun avec l'Occident," *Revue de l'Orient latin* (1894), p. 571; Moule, *Christians in China*, p. 106; Grousset, *Croisades*, III, 711.

97. *Revue de l'Orient latin* (1894), pp. 82–83.

98. *Ibid.*, p. 89.

99. *Ibid.*, p. 91. Cf. Grousset, *Croisades*, III, 715–716.

100. Chabot, *Revue de l'Orient latin* (1894), p. 104.

101. *Ibid.*, pp. 106–111; Grousset, *Croisades*, III, 717–718.

102. Chabot, *Revue de l'Orient latin* (1894), pp. 113–121.

103. *Ibid.*, p. 112; Grousset, *Croisades*, III, 720.

104. Chabot, "Relations du roi Argoun," pp. 576–591.

105. Chabot, *Revue de l'Orient latin*, pp. 121–122. Rabban Sauma lived another four years, and died at Baghdad on January 10, 1294.

106. Chabot, "Relations du roi Argoun," pp. 604, 611, 612; Moule, *Christians in China*, pp. 117–118; Grousset, *Croisades*, III, 724.

107. Chabot, "Relations du roi Argoun," pp. 617, 618.

108. D'Ohsson, *Histoire des Mongols*, IV, 42–49.

109. *Ibid.*, p. 42. Cf. Barthold, "Mangû Timur," *EI*, p. 260, emending his other article (*ibid.*, p. 436) on "Arghûn."

110. D'Ohsson, *Histoire des Mongols*, IV, 101–106; Barthold, "Gaikhâtû," *EI*, p. 135. Gaikhatu had gained information about the *chao* from the *ch'eng-hsiang* Bolod, Kublai's envoy at the court of Persia.

111. Chabot, *Revue de l'Orient latin* (1894), pp. 127–128.

112. *Ibid.*, p. 133.

113. Bar Hebraeus, *Chronicon Syriacum*, p. 609; cf. d'Ohsson, *Histoire des Mongols*, IV, 141.

114. D'Ohsson, *Histoire des Mongols*, IV, 132.

115. Rashid ad-Din, *ibid.*, IV, 359–360.

116. *Ibid.*, IV, 281–282.

117. Rashid ad-Din, no fanatic, testifies to the religious sincerity of Ghazan, who long before his accession had apparently announced his intention of forsaking the cult of Buddhist "idols" for Islam. *Ibid.*, IV, 148.

118. "Vie de Mar Yahballaha," pp. 134–142, 239–250.

119. D'Ohsson, *Histoire des Mongols*, IV, 174–190 (according to Rashid ad-Din and Mirkhond).

120. Barthold, "Ghâzân," *EI*, p. 158.

121. Rashid ad-Din, in d'Ohsson, *Histoire des Mongols*, IV, 367.

122. Rashid ad-Din, *ibid.*, IV, 417–418.

123. E. Berthels, "Rashîd al-Dîn Tabîb," *EI*, p. 1202.

124. "Vie de Mar Yahballaha," pp. 251–265.

125. "Öljäitü" in Mongolian.

126. J. H. Kramers, "Olčaitu Khudâbanda," *EI*, p. 1042.

127. "Vie de Mar Yahballaha," pp. 266–300.

128. Hafiz-i Abru, trans. Bayani, p. 4.

129. Berthels, "Rashîd ad-Dîn Tabîb," *EI*, p. 1202. For the building of Sultaniyeh, cf. Hafiz-i Abru, trans. Bayani, pp. 5–7.

130. D'Ohsson, *Histoire des Mongols*, IV, 587–597.

131. *Ibid.*, IV, 532 (according to Nowairi and Maqrizi).

132. Hafiz-i Abru (trans. Bayani, p. 35) claims that the besieged townsfolk made submission.

133. D'Ohsson, *Histoire des Mongols*, IV, 576; J. H. Kramers, "Karamân-oghlu," *EI*, p. 794.

134. G. Pachymeres, II, 433–444; d'Ohsson, *Histoire des Mongols*, IV, 536.

135. J. H. Kramers, " 'Othmân I," *EI*, p. 1075.

136. Hafiz-i Abru, trans. Bayani, pp. 17–29; d'Ohsson, *Histoire des Mongols*, IV, 497, 527.

137. D'Ohsson, IV, 568–571; Hafiz-i Abru, trans. Bayani, pp. 37, 43, 67.

138. D'Ohsson, *Histoire des Mongols*, IV, 562–564.

139. *Ibid.*, IV, 565, 567–568, 612–629, 642–644; Hafiz-i Abru, trans. Bayani, p. 86.

140. Hafiz-i Abru, trans. Bayani, pp. 71, 80–86; d'Ohsson, *Histoire des Mongols*, IV, 620–629.

141. Hafiz-i Abru, trans. Bayani, p. 56; d'Ohsson, *Histoire des Mongols*, IV, 609–612.

142. For the etymology of this word, see Barthold, "Cüpän," *EI*, p. 904.

143. For the eventful causes of this breach, cf. Hafiz-i Abru, trans. Bayani, p. 91.

144. *Ibid.*, pp. 100–105.

145. *Ibid.*, p. 107.

146. "Timurtash distinguished himself as governor of Rum [in Seljuk Anatolia] by conquests extending to the very shores of the Mediterranean, where no Mongol troops had ever appeared before, and where he fought Greeks and rebel Turks in turn." D'Ohsson, *Histoire des Mongols,* IV, 686.

147. Hafiz-i Abru, trans. Bayani, pp. 111–119.

148. Hafiz-i Abru, trans. Bayani, p. 120; d'Ohsson, *Histoire des Mongols,* IV, 723–742.

149. Son of Timurtash, the former viceroy of Anatolia, himself the son of Chopan. Cf. Hafiz-i Abru, trans. Bayani, p. 124; d'Ohsson, *Histoire des Mongols,* IV, 726–734.

150. D'Ohsson, IV, 735; Hafiz-i Abru, trans. Bayani, pp. 127–140.

151. D'Ohsson, *Histoire des Mongols,* IV, 741–742; Hafiz-i Abru, trans. Bayani, pp. 153–156.

152. D'Ohsson, *Histoire des Mongols,* IV, 742, 745; Hafiz-i Abru, trans. Bayani, p. 153.

153. D'Ohsson, *Histoire des Mongols,* IV, 713–714; T. W. Haig, "Kart," *EI,* p. 822; *Zafer-name,* trans. Pétis de la Croix, I, 6.

154. Cf. V. F. Büchner, "Serbedârs," *EI,* p. 240.

155. Cf. Minorsky, "Tugha Tìmûr," *EI,* p. 863; Hafiz-i Abru, trans. Bayani, p. 122.

156. D'Ohsson, *Histoire des Mongols,* IV, 743–747; Zettersteen, "Muzaffarides," *EI,* p. 852.

157. Cf. Huart, "Kara-koyûn-lu," *EI,* p. 785.

158. "Artena," *EI,* p. 469; Huart, "Burhân al-Dîn," *ibid.,* p. 817.

159. Huart, "Ak-koyûn-lu," *EI,* p. 228.

160. J. H. Kramers, "Karamân-oghlu," *EI,* p. 792.

Chapter 10

1. Rubruck, Chap. XV.

2. Rashid ad-Din, in Erdmann, *Temudschin,* p. 453.

3. Barthold, "Bâtû-khân," *EI,* p. 698; Barthold, "Sarâi," *EI,* p. 163.

4. Rubruck, Chap. XXI.

5. Cf. Rashid ad-Din in d'Ohsson, *Histoire des Mongols,* II, 335–336.

6. See *Zafer-name,* trans. Pétis de la Croix, p. 278.

7. The Shaybanids subjugated the Siberian khanate of Tyumen or Sibir around 1480, and it remained in their possession until the Russian conquest of 1598 (see page 490). When the chief of the

White Horde, Khan Toqtamish, had conquered the Golden Horde in 1380, the greater part of the White Horde went with him into Europe. Orda's old fief north of the lower Syr Darya, being thus emptied of its inhabitants, was gradually reoccupied by the Shaybanid horde. The Shaybanid Abu'l Khair, who began his reign in 1428 in the Tura area of western Siberia, was to rule from Lake Balkhash to the Ural, his center being at Signakhi on the Syr Darya. His grandson, the famous Muhammad Shaybani, became the founder in 1500 of the Uzbek Empire at Bukhara and Samarkand, which will be discussed later.

8. Piano Carpini observed that Orda was in effect the dean of the senior Jenghiz-Khanite branch: "Ordu, the senior captain and duke of the Tatars" (Chap. V).

9. Rubruck, Chaps. XXV and XLVI.

10. Barthold, "Bâtû-khân," *EI*, p. 699.

11. Piano Carpini, Chap. III.

12. This subservience to the Mongol suzerains was not without its dangers, even for the most favored among the Russian princes. Piano Carpini (Chap. XIII) relates that when Yaroslav went to pay court in Mongolia (he was present at the election of the grand khan Güyük in 1246), the empress mother Törägänä served food to him "with her own hand," after which, on returning to his own quarters, he fell ill and died a week later, his body covered with suspicious-looking spots.

13. I need hardly say that I speak here of Ottoman Turkey and not of Kemalist Turkey, where the exact opposite was true.

14. Cf. R. P. Batton, *Wilhelm von Rubruk*, pp. 37–45, 62, *passim*.

15. This is not to say that in Islamic, Russian, and other cultures one will not find elements of a Golden Horde "civilization." In this connection, see Balodis, "Neuere Forschungen über die Kultur der Goldenen Horde," *Zeitschrift für Slavische Philologie*, IV (1927). But we must be clear as to the relative value of that culture.

16. Rubruck, Chap. XIX.

17. For the name Sartaq (the "Sart," the "Sarta'ul"), see Pelliot, "Les Mongols et la Papauté," *Revue de l'Orient chrétien* (1931–32), p. 78 (217).

18. Note especially Kirakos, *JA*, I (1858), 459.

19. Barthold, "Berke," *EI*, pp. 725–726; Juvaini, in d'Ohsson, *Histoire des Mongols*, II, 336.

20. So deep a mark did Berke leave on Kipchak (literally the *Desht-i Kipchak* or "steppe of Kipchak") that down to the fifteenth century the country was sometimes referred to as Berke's Steppe:

Desht-i Berke. Such is the practice in Ibn 'Arabshah (*Life of Tamerlane,* trans. Sanders [London, 1936], p. 73).

21. *Ibid.,* pp. 77–78.

22. Rashid ad-Din, trans. Quatremère, p. 393; Grousset, *Histoire des Croisades,* III, 612.

23. Wassaf, in d'Ohsson, *Histoire des Mongols,* III, 379.

24. Rashid ad-Din, trans. Quatremère, p. 399; Maqrizi, p. 211; d'Ohsson, *Histoire des Mongols,* III, 380–381.

25. Wassaf, in d'Ohsson, *Histoire des Mongols,* III, 381.

26. Conrad Chapman, *Michel Paléologue* (Paris, 1926), p. 79 (according to Pachymeres); G. I. Bratianu, *Recherches sur le commerce génois dans la Mer Noire,* pp. 233–234.

27. G. I. Bratianu, p. 205.

28. Chapman, *Paléologue,* p. 80; G. I. Bratianu, *Recherches sur Vicina et Cetatea Alba,* p. 39.

29. M. Canard, "Le traité de 1281 entre Michel Paléologue et le sultan Qalâ'un," *Byzantion* (1935), pp. 669–680; Grousset, *Histoire des Croisades,* III, 613, 625.

30. Barthold, "Sarâi," *EI,* p. 163.

31. Ibn 'Arabshah, trans. Sanders, pp. 76–79; cf. Heyd, *Histoire du commerce du Levant,* II, 227–229.

32. Ibn 'Arabshah, trans. Sanders, p. 78.

33. Barthold, "Mangû Timur," *EI,* p. 261.

34. Cf. Bratianu, *Recherches sur le commerce génois,* p. 259.

35. Cf. Bratianu, *Recherches sur Vicina,* pp. 38–39.

36. G. Golubovitch, *Bibliotheca Bio-bibliografica della Terra Santa e dell'Oriente francescano,* II, 444. Eulogy of Nogai in Marco Polo, ed. Moule-Pelliot, p. 488.

37. Various explanations will be found in Cheshire, "The Great Tartar Invasion of Europe," *Slavonic Review,* V (1926), 101, and in Bruce Boswell, "The Kipchak Turks," *ibid.,* VI (1927), 82.

38. Chapman, *Paléologue,* pp. 136–137; Bratianu, *Recherches sur le commerce génois,* p. 234.

39. G. Cahen, "Les Mongols dans les Balkans," *Rev. historique* (1924), p. 55; Bratianu, *Recherches sur Vicina,* p. 109. On Nogai, see Veselovskii's monograph in *Mémoires de l'Académie des sciences de l'U.R.S.S.,* XIII (1922), in Russian. Note that a daughter of Nogai's married the Russian prince Fedor of Ryazan.

40. In December, 1299, Nogai was before Sudak and marched from there to the Dnieper to fight his last battle.

41. Nowairi and Rashid ad-Din, in d'Ohsson, *Histoire des Mongols,* IV, 755, 758.

42. Cf. Bratianu, *Recherches sur Vicina,* pp. 39–40, 72.

43. Rashid ad-Din, in d'Ohsson, *Histoire des Mongols,* IV, 515.

44. Heyd, *Histoire du commerce du Levant,* II, 163; Bratianu, *Recherches sur le commerce génois,* p. 219; Hammer, *Geschichte der Goldenen Horde,* p. 254.

45. Heyd, *Histoire du commerce du Levant,* II, 170; Bratianu, *Recherches sur le commerce génois,* pp. 282–283.

46. D'Ohsson, *Histoire des Mongols,* IV, 573–575.

47. His sister Konchaka had married the Russian grand prince George (1318).

48. In the same way, at the petition of Peter, Metropolitan of Moscow, Özbeg had bestowed great privileges on the Russian Church (1313).

49. Moule, *Christians in China,* p. 255.

50. Heyd, *Commerce du Levant,* II, 170; Bratianu, *Recherches sur le commerce génois,* p. 283.

51. Heyd, *Commerce du Levant,* II, 181–183; Bratianu, *Recherches sur le commerce génois,* p. 286.

52. Heyd, *Commerce du Levant,* II, 187 *et seq.*

53. This siege was to start the spread of the Black Death to the West.

54. Heyd, *Commerce du Levant,* II, 197 *et seq.*

55. In an edict of 1320, Özbeg forbade the ringing of bells at Sudak (*ibid.,* II, 204).

56. D'Ohsson, *Histoire des Mongols,* IV, 741–742.

57. First on the Don, then at Sarai. Hammer, *Geschichte der Goldenen Horde,* pp. 318–326.

58. Heyd, *Commerce du Levant,* II, 205.

59. Barthold, "Toktamish," *EI,* p. 850.

60. *Zafer-name,* trans. Pétis de la Croix, I (II, Chaps. XX–XXI), 278.

61. Or Qutlugh-bugha.

Chapter 11

1. *Zafer-name,* in Denison Ross's translation of the *Ta'rikh-i Rashidi,* p. 15.

2. *Zafer-name,* trans. Pétis de la Croix, I, 28.

3. *Ibid.,* pp. 36–38.

4. *Ta'rikh-i Rashidi,* trans. Denison Ross, p. 18.

5. As he later executed Bayan Selduz.

6. *Ta'rikh-i Rashidi,* trans. Denison Ross, p. 22.

7. *Zafer-name,* trans. Pétis de la Croix, I, 45, 54.

8. *Ibid.,* pp. 68, 74; *Ta'rikh-i Rashidi,* trans. Denison Ross, pp. 27–29.

9. *Zafer-name*, trans. Pétis de la Croix, p. 75.

10. *Ibid.*, pp. 76–78; *Ta'rikh-i Rashidi*, trans. Denison Ross, pp. 29–31.

11. *Zafer-name*, trans. Pétis de la Croix, pp. 80–92; *Ta'rikh-i Rashidi*, trans. Denison Ross, pp. 31–37.

12. Nevertheless, Husain usually lived at Sali-Sarai, on the north bank of the Amu Darya, north of Kunduz.

13. *Zafer-name*, trans. Pétis de la Croix, I, 97.

14. *Ibid.*, I, 127–132.

15. *Ibid.*, I, 148–156.

16. *Ibid.*, I, 157–160.

17. *Ibid.*, I, 160–175.

18. *Ibid.*, I, 175.

19. *Ibid.*, I, 180–194.

20. Ibn 'Arabshah's furious vilifications of Tamerlane (trans. J. H. Sanders, 1936) are less telling than the pious excuses of Sharif ad-Din. Here the defense is more damning than the charge.

21. *Ta'rikh-i Rashidi*, trans. Denison Ross, p. 83.

22. *Zafer-name*, I, 186 and 193 (cf. *ibid.*, p. 181); *Ta'rikh-i Rashidi*, trans. Denison Ross, pp. 72, 83.

23. *Zafer-name*, II, 19–20; IV, 40.

24. *Ta'rikh-i Rashidi*, p. 83.

25. Ibn 'Arabshah, trans. Sanders, p. 299.

26. Barthold, "Khwârizm," *EI*, p. 962.

27. *Zafer-name*, I, 226.

28. Spring of 773 (1372), the Year of the Mouse; *Zafer-name*, I, 229.

29. *Ibid.*, I, 239.

30. *Ibid.*, I, 242.

31. Ramadan 774 (February 24–March 25, 1373), the Year of the Ox; *Zafer-name*, I, 243.

32. Spring of the year 777 (June 2, 1375–May 20, 1376), the Year of the Crocodile; *Zafer-name*, I, 260; *Ta'rikh-i Rashidi*, trans. Ross, p. 44.

33. The war began in Shawal 780 (January 21–February 18, 1379), the Year of the Sheep; *Zafer-name*, I, 299.

34. *Ibid.*, I, 301–302.

35. *Ibid.*, I, 305–306.

36. Barthold, "Dûghlât," *EI*, p. 1112.

37. *Ta'rikh-i Rashidi*, p. 38.

38. *Ibid.*, pp. 38–39.

39. *Ibid.*, pp. 39, 51.

40. *Ibid.*, p. 40.

41. This expedition started in Shaban 776 (January 5–February 2, 1375); *ibid.*, p. 41; *Zafer-name*, trans. Pétis, I, 251.

42. *Ta'rikh-i Rashidi*, p. 41.

43. *Ibid.*, p. 42; *Zafer-name*, I, 255.

44. *Ta'rikh-i Rashidi*, pp. 46–47; *Zafer-name*, I, 264–269.

45. *Ta'rikh-i Rashidi*, p. 50; *Zafer-name*, pp. 275–276.

46. Hejira 785 (March 6, 1383–February 23, 1384), the Year of the Mouse; *Zafer-name*, trans. Pétis, I, 361.

47. This campaign opened in Hejira 791 (December 31, 1388–December 19, 1389); *Zafer-name*, II, 35.

48. *Ibid.*, II, 43.

49. *Ibid.*, II, 45, 51. Cf. Chavannes, *Documents sur les T'ou-kiue occidentaux*, No. 5, p. 270.

50. *Zafer-name*, II, 46.

51. *Ta'rikh-i Rashidi*, p. 52.

52. *Zafer-name*, II, 50–53.

53. *Ibid.*, II, 53.

54. *Ibid.*, II, 54–55.

55. *Ibid.*, II, 66–70 (beginning of the year Hejira 792, starting on December 20, 1389, the Year of the Horse). Cf. Minorsky, *Hudud al-Alam*, pp. 195–196.

56. *Ta'rikh-i Rashidi*, p. 56.

57. *Ibid.*, p. 52.

58. *Ibid.*, p. 52; *Zafer-name*, II, 421.

59. This is the order given in the *Ta'rikh-i Rashidi*. The *Zafer-name* and Mirkhond know only of Muhammad-khan and Naksh-i Jahan (N. Elias and Denison Ross, *History of the Moghuls of Central Asia* [London, 1895], pp. 41–42).

60. *Zafer-name*, III, 213–220. Narrated under the heading of Hejira 802 (September 3, 1399–August 21, 1400), the Year of the Hare, when the news of this campaign reached Tamerlane, then in Persia.

61. *Zafer-name*, I, 317; Mu'in ad-Din, "Histoire de Hérat," trans. Barbier de Meynard, *JA* (1861), pp. 515–516.

62. Muharram 783 (March 28–April 26, 1381), the Year of the Dog; *Zafer-name*, I, 326.

63. End of 784 (1382–83); *Zafer-name*, I, 359.

64. *Ibid.*, I, 361.

65. Minorsky, "Tugha Tîmûr," *EI*, p. 863.

66. D'Ohsson, *Histoire des Mongols*, IV, 739–740.

67. *Zafer-name*, I, 329–330.

68. *Ibid.*, I, 330.

69. *Ibid.*, I, 331.

70. *Ibid.,* I, 338–346.

71. *Ibid.,* I, 353.

72. *Ibid.,* I, 377; Ibn 'Arabshah, trans. Sanders, pp. 25–27.

73. The taking of Zaranj was in Shawwal 785 (November 27–December 25, 1383), the Year of the Mouse.

74. *Zafer-name,* I, 379.

75. In 1936, the Hackin expedition explored the ruins of Sar-Otar or Tar-Ussar (Zahidan) in Seistan, amid once-cultivated land which had been submerged by sand dunes after the Timurid destruction of 1384.

76. Shawwal 786 (November 16–December 14, 1384).

77. *Zafer-name,* I, 388–395.

78. Barthold, "Ahmed Djalâir," *EI,* p. 200; cf. Ibn 'Arabshah, pp. 63–64.

79. Hejira 787 (February 12, 1385–February 1, 1386), the Year of the Panther; *Zafer-name,* I, 399–400; cf. Ibn 'Arabshah, p. 54.

80. *Zafer-name,* I, 407; Ibn 'Arabshah, p. 55.

81. *Zafer-name,* I, 408–411; Ibn 'Arabshah, pp. 57–58.

82. *Zafer-name,* I, 414; cf. Minorsky, "Tiflis," *EI,* p. 796.

83. *Zafer-name,* I, 425–429 (beginning of 789, the Year of the Hare, starting January 22, 1387).

84. *Ibid.,* I, 432.

85. Ibn 'Arabshah, pp. 27–30.

86. Cf. Zettersteen, "Muzaffarides," *EI,* p. 853; Ibn 'Arabshah, p. 36.

87. *Zafer-name,* I, 442–447.

88. *Ibid.,* I, 449–454; II, 173–183; Ibn 'Arabshah, pp. 43–46.

89. *Zafer-name,* I, 454–462 (Tamerlane's entry into Shiraz, Zu'lkadah 1, 789, or November 13, 1387).

90. *Zafer-name,* II, 143–154.

91. *Ibid.,* II, 183–198; Ibn 'Arabshah, pp. 36–42.

92. Ibn 'Arabshah, pp. 48–49; *Zafer-name,* II, 201–207.

93. Ibn 'Arabshah, p. 64; *Zafer-name,* II, 221–238 (Tamerlane's arrival before Baghdad: end of Shawwal 795, August 10–September 7, 1393).

94. Rabia I, 796 (January 4–February 2, 1394), the Year of the Hen; *Zafer-name,* II, 270.

95. Rabia II, 796 (February 3–March 3, 1394); *ibid.,* p. 275.

96. Cf. Minorsky, "Tiflis," *EI,* p. 796. In Hejira 798 (October 16, 1395–October 4, 1396).

97. Minorsky, "Tiflis."

98. *Zafer-name,* III, 363–371 (final assault on Baghdad: Zu'lkadah 27, 803, or July 9, 1401); Ibn 'Arabshah, pp. 165–169.

99. *Zafer-name,* IV, 93–97; Barthold, "Ahmed Djalâir," *EI,* p. 201.

100. I apologize for reverting here—and in greater detail—to facts already summarized in connection with Mongol Russia. Owing to the complexity of the subject, it is impossible to avoid these apparent repetitions. Without them, this account would be unintelligible.

101. Cf. Barthold, "Toktamish," *EI,* p. 850.

102. *Zafer-name,* I, 276–286 (end of the Year of the Dragon, beginning of 1377).

103. To be distinguished from the other Qaratal (Kara-Tal), or the southern tributary of Lake Balkhash east of the Ili, which was not in White Horde territory at all but in the Jagataite khanate of the Ili, that is, in Mogholistan.

104. *Zafer-name,* I, 292–294. Barthold's chronology, in "Toktamish," *EI,* p. 850.

105. *Zafer-name,* I, 402–404; E. G. Browne, *History of Persian Literature under Tartar Dominion* (Cambridge, 1920), III, 321; Minorsky, "Tabriz," *EI,* p. 616.

106. *Zafer-name,* I, 423–429 (erroneously dated in Pétis as the year of the Hejira 787, February 12, 1385–February 1, 1386, the Year of the Crocodile).

107. *Ibid.,* I, 463–465.

108. *Ibid.,* I, 465–469.

109. *Ibid.,* II, 22–26 (before Safar 791, January 30–February 27, 1389).

110. *Ibid.,* II, 27–31 (ca. Rabia I, 791, February 28–March 29, 1389).

111. Tamerlane left Tashkent on Safar 12, 793, that is, on January 19, 1391 (*Zafer-name,* II, 73).

112. *Ibid.,* II, 81, under the heading of the end of Jumada I, 793 (ending May 5, 1391).

113. *Ibid.,* II, 82.

114. *Ibid.*

115. *Ibid.,* II, 83 (first day of Jumada II, 793–May 6, 1391).

116. "Tamerlane mounted his horse in ceremonial dress. On his head he wore the golden crown enriched with rubies and he held in his hand a war club of gold in the shape of an ox head." *Zafer-name,* II, 85. The detailed description of this review, squadron by squadron, is amazingly colorful and one of the finest epic passages that I know.

117. *Zafer-name,* II, 93.

118. In the *Zafer-name,* II, 96–97, Tamerlane arrives first at the "Semmur" and only afterward at the Yaik (date of the Yaik arrival is Rajab 1, 793, June 4, 1391).

119. Barthold, "Toktamish," *EI,* p. 851.

120. *Zafer-name*, II, 110–120 (under the date Rajab 15, 793, or June 18, 1391).

121. *Ibid.*, II, 127.

122. Timur Qutlugh (or Qutluq) was the son of Timur-malik, himself the son of Urus, former khan of the White Horde.

123. *Zafer-name*, II, 124.

124. The episode of Idiqu (here Idakou, or Idaku) is narrated at length in Ibn 'Arabshah (pp. 82–84). The author, who pursues Tamerlane with savage hatred, delights to see him tricked by Idiqu. But whereas Sharif ad-Din (II, 124) places Idiqu's "escape" after Tamerlane's first "Russian campaign," Ibn 'Arabshah seems to date it after the second one; or rather, he confuses the two expeditions.

125. *Zafer-name*, II, 331–332.

126. 23rd of Jumada II, 797, or April 15, 1395 (*Zafer-name*, II, 446).

127. Barthold, "Toktamish," *EI*, p. 851.

128. Heyd, *Histoire du commerce du Levant*, II, 375.

129. *Zafer-name*, II, 368.

130. *Ibid.*, II, 379–382; Ibn 'Arabshah, p. 82; Heyd, *Histoire du commerce du Levant*, II, 229; Barthold, "Sarâi," *EI*, p. 163.

131. Prince Koirijak, said to be Urus' son (White Horde), whom Tamerlane nominally appointed khan of the Golden Horde in 1395 after the victory, never succeeded in gaining control. *Zafer-name*, II, 355.

132. Ibn 'Arabshah, pp. 84–87.

133. *Zafer-name*, III, 11; also *Malfuzat-i Timuri*, in Ishwari Prasad, *L'Inde du VIIe au XVIe siècle*, p. 342.

134. Cf. Ibn 'Arabshah, p. 95.

135. According to Prasad, *L'Inde*, p. 346; justifying essay in *Zafer-name*, III, 89–90.

136. *Zafer-name*, III, 100.

137. *Malfuzat-i Timuri*, in Prasad, *L'Inde*, p. 349; *Zafer-name*, III, 110–113.

138. *Zafer-name*, III, 106.

139. On the first day of Jumada I, Hejira 801, or January 9, 1399; *Zafer-name*, III, 118.

140. *Zafer-name*, III, 152.

141. Grousset, *Histoire des Croisades*, III, 603–607; G. Wiet, *Histoire de la nation égyptienne*, IV, 410.

142. Wiet, *Histoire*, IV, 526; *Zafer-name*, III, 294–298; Ibn 'Arabshah, p. 124.

143. Ibn 'Arabshah, pp. 128–130.

144. Wiet, *Histoire*, IV, 529. The *Zafer-name*, III, 325, specifies the 19th day of Jumada I, 803, or January 5, 1401.

145. Wiet, *Histoire*, IV, 530; cf. Ibn 'Arabshah, pp. 143, 296.
146. *Zafer-name*, III, 343–344.
147. Ibn 'Arabshah, p. 162.
148. Ibn 'Arabshah was born in 1392. Cf. J. Pedersen, "Ibn 'Arabshâh," *EI*, pp. 384–385.
149. Cf. J. von Hammer-Purgstall, *Histoire de l'empire ottoman* (Paris, 1835–43, 18 vols.), I, 292–356; N. Iorga, *Geschichte des osmanischen Reiches* (Gotha, 1908–13), I, 266–323.
150. 'Ala ad-Din, emir of Karaman, was defeated and taken prisoner at Akcay in 1390–91 by the Ottoman vizier Timurtash, who hanged him without trial. Cf. F. Babinger, "Tîmûrtâsh," *EI*, p. 823; J. H. Kramers, "Karaman-oghlû," *ibid.*, p. 795.
151. Cf. Ibn 'Arabshah, pp. 170–171; *Zafer-name*, III, 255–256.
152. *Zafer-name*, III, 259, 397, and 408; cf. Ibn 'Arabshah, p. 178.
153. *Zafer-name*, III, 261, 262. Cf. Ibn 'Arabshah, pp. 171–173; Hammer-Purgstall, *Histoire de l'empire ottoman*, II, 79–82.
154. Tamerlane entered the Ottoman Empire on Muharram 1, 803, or August 22, 1400. *Zafer-name*, III, 264.
155. *Ibid.*, III, 375–376; cf. Ibn 'Arabshah, p. 189.
156. *Zafer-name*, IV, 11–15; Ibn 'Arabshah, p. 182.
157. Monstrelet, I, 84.
158. Western sources on the battle of Ankara are Sanudo (L. A. Muratori, XXII, 791), the Religieux de St. Denis (III, 46–51), Monstrelet (ed. L. C. Douët d'Arcq, I, 84), J. Schiltberger (p. 73), and Juvenal des Ursins (II, 423). They are enumerated and used by J. M. Delaville-le-Roulx, *La France en Orient au XIVe siècle* (Paris, 1886), p. 393.
159. Ibn 'Arabshah, p. 188; *Zafer-name*, IV, 16–20, 32, 35.
160. *Zafer-name*, IV, 49, under the 6th day of Jumada I, 805, or December 2, 1402. Ibn 'Arabshah, p. 192, says that Smyrna was taken on the 2nd of Jumada II, or December 28, 1402. For western sources, see Delaville-le-Roulx, *La France en Orient au XIVe siècle*, p. 395.
161. *Zafer-name*, IV, 51, 53.
162. *Ibid.*, IV, 56, 58.
163. *Ibid.*, IV, 38–39.
164. *Ibid.*, IV, 33.
165. *Ibid.*, IV, 60.
166. Cf. *Zafer-name*, IV, 301; Ibn 'Arabshah, p. 239.
167. Hejira 777 (June 2, 1375–May 20, 1376). *Ta'rikh-i Rashidi*, trans. Denison Ross, p. 48.
168. To be distinguished from his cousin and namesake, the heir to the throne.
169. *Zafer-name*, IV, 281, 284; Ibn 'Arabshah, p. 243.

170. Ibn 'Arabshah, pp. 259, 268. The date of Pir Muhammad ibn-Jahangir's defeat by Khalil's army is the beginning of Ramadan 808, which starts February 20, 1406.

171. *Zafer-name,* IV, 191.

172. For the reign of Shah Rukh, see 'Abd ar-Razzaq Samarqandi, *Matla' es-sa'dein,* trans. Quatremère, *JA,* II (1836), 193–233, 338–364; and L. Bouvat, *Empire mongol* (Paris, 1927), pp. 96 *et seq.*

173. E. G. Browne, *History of Persian Literature.*

174. *Matla' es-sa'dein,* trans. Quatremère; pp. 193 *et seq.*

175. See Khondemir, in Bouvat, *Empire mongol,* pp. 110–111.

176. Ibn 'Arabshah, p. 280.

177. See Khondemir, in Bouvat, *Empire mongol,* pp. 114 *et seq.*

178. Shah Rukh sent another embassy in 1421. Cf. *Matla' es-sa'dein,* p. 387.

179. *Matla' es-sa'dein,* in Elias and Denison Ross, *History of the Moghuls of Central Asia,* p. 43, and Barthold, "Dûghlât," *EI,* p. 1113.

180. The same *Matla' es-sa'dein* tells elsewhere that Khudaidad's son Sayyid Ahmed had been driven from Kashgar in 1416 by the Timurids, and that it was Sayyid Ahmed's son Sayid 'Ali (d. 1458) who recaptured the two cities from them. It is hard to reconcile these statements.

181. Barthold and Beveridge, "Abû Sa'îd," *EI,* p. 107; Bouvat, *Empire mongol,* p. 136.

182. Cf. Barthold, "Abu'l-Khair," *EI,* p. 98.

183. *Ta'rikh-i Rashidi,* p. 79.

184. Mu'in ad-Din, "Chronique de Hérat," trans. Barbier de Meynard, *JA,* XX (1862), 304–309.

185. *Ta'rikh-i Rashidi,* pp. 81–82, 83–88.

186. Mu'in ad-Din, "Chronique de Hérat," pp. 317–319; Huart, "Karakoyûn-lu," *EI,* p. 785.

187. Cf. Minorsky, "Uzun Hasan," *EI,* p. 1123.

188. *Ta'rikh-i Rashidi,* pp. 95–97.

189. *Ibid.,* pp. 112–113.

190. Khondemir, trans. Ferté in *Vie du sultan Hosein Baykara* (1898); A. S. Beveridge, "Husain Mîrzâ," *EI,* p. 364; *Bâbur-name,* ed. Beveridge (Leiden, 1905; cf. Bouvat, *Empire mongol,* p. 162).

191. Cf. E. Belin, "Notice sur Mîr 'Alî Chîr Néwaï," *JA,* XVII (1861), 175, 281; (1866), 523; Bouvat, "Débat sur les deux langues," *JA* (1902), p. 367.

Chapter 12

1. Timur Qutlugh was the son of Timur-malik and grandson of Urus, the famous khan of the White Horde and Tamerlane's adversary.

2. Ibn 'Arabshah's "Rashadibeg." *Life of Tamerlane,* trans. Sanders (1936), p. 86.

3. Cf. Barthold, "Mangit," *EI,* p. 259.

4. Ibn 'Arabshah, pp. 86–87. Idiqu is the Yedigei of Russian sources.

5. Khan of the Crimea from 1469 to 1475 and 1478 to 1515.

6. Barthold, "Girây," *EI,* p. 181.

7. Cf. Heyd, *Histoire du commerce du Levant,* II, 399.

8. Cf. Howorth, *History of the Mongols,* II, 365–429; Barthold, "Kazân," *EI,* p. 887, and "Kasimov," *EI,* p. 848.

9. Cf. Howorth, *History of the Mongols,* II, 349–362.

10. In Russia as in China, it was artillery that quelled the last Mongol reactions. See page 529, on the cannonade of Khan Galdan's Jungar bands by the emperor K'ang-hsi. The immemorial tactical superiority of the nomads, which was due to the extraordinary mobility and ubiquity of the mounted archer, yielded before the artificial superiority conferred at a stroke upon sedentary civilizations by the use of artillery.

Chapter 13

1. Cf. Barthold, "Shaibânides," *EI,* p. 283.

2. *Zafer-name,* II, 70–93.

3. Cf. Barthold, "Abu'l-Khair," *EI,* p. 98; Howorth, *History of the Mongols,* II, 687; *Ta'rikh-i Rashidi,* trans. Denison Ross, p. 82.

4. Cf. Barthold, "Kazak," *EI,* p. 886; Barthold, "Kirgiz," *EI,* p. 1084; *Ta'rikh-i Rashidi,* pp. 272–273.

5. Among the Kirghiz themselves, the three "hordes" are called *jüz* or "hundreds." They are known respectively as *Ulu-jüz,* Great Hundred (Great Horde); *Kishi-jüz,* Little Hundred; and *Orta-jüz,* Middle or Medium Hundred. This division into three hordes was not completed until the end of the seventeenth century. Barthold notes: "The khan Tyawka, who was known as the legislator of his people, and who received a Russian embassy in 1694 and a Kalmuck embassy in 1696, still ruled over the three hordes and had a representative in each" ("Kirgiz," p. 1085).

6. Cf. N. Elias and Denison Ross, *History of the Moghuls of Central Asia,* p. 272.

7. *Ibid.,* pp. 274, 276. Qasim had his winter quarters in the valley of the Kara-Tal, south of Lake Balkhash and east of the Ili.

8. *Ta'rikh-i Rashidi,* pp. 92–93.

9. Cf. Bouvat, "Shaibânî-khân," *EI,* p. 281, and *Empire mongol,* p. 191; Howorth, *History of the Mongols,* II, 652–739; A. Vambéry, II, 35–98; Abu'l Ghazi Bahadur khan, *Histoire des Mongols et des Tatares,* trans. Desmaisons.

10. Grenard, *Baber* (Paris, 1930), p. 75; cf. Vambéry, II, 64.

11. *Ta'rikh-i Rashidi*, p. 120.

12. This was indeed the time of the great expansion of the Kirghiz-Kazakhs. Their khan Qasim, who died in 1518, was particularly powerful. Cf. Barthold, "Kirgiz," *EI*, p. 1085.

13. Cf. Barthold, in *EI*, p. 25, emending Vambéry, II, 191.

14. Timur-shah, second king of Afghanistan of the Durrani dynasty (1772–93), son and successor of the celebrated Ahmed the Durrani.

15. Abu'l Ghazi, trans. Desmaisons, pp. 194–220; cf. Barthold, "Khwârizm," *EI*, p. 963.

16. Cf. Abu'l Ghazi, trans. Desmaisons, pp. 338–358; Bouvat, *Empire mongol*, p. 347.

17. Cf. Courant, *L'Asie Centrale aux XVIIe et XVIIIe siècles*, pp. 36–37.

18. Cf. Barthold, "Farghâna," *EI*, p. 70, and "Khokand," *EI*, p. 1020; Nalivkine trans. Dozon, *Histoire du khanat de Khokand* (Paris, 1889).

19. Cf. Howorth, *History of the Mongols*, II, 982; Barthold, "Kučum khân," *EI*, p. 1156; Courant, *L'Asie Centrale aux XVIIe et XVIIIe siècles*, pp. 38 *et seq.*; Abu'l Ghazi, trans. Desmaisons, p. 177; 'Abd al-Karim Bukhari, trans. C. Schefer, *Histoire de l'Asie Centrale* (Paris, 1876, 2 vols.), p. 303.

Chapter 14

1. *Ta'rikh-i Rashidi*, p. 67.

2. *Ibid.*, p. 65. The author places the battle in which Esen took Vais prisoner at a site called Ming-lak.

3. The *Ta'rikh-i Rashidi* (p. 65) places this second battle "at Kabaka, on the borders of Mogholistan, not far from the River Ailah," identified with the Ili: the Ila of the *Hudud al-Alam* (ed. Minorsky, p. 71).

4. *Ta'rikh-i Rashidi*, pp. 65–66. Sayyid 'Ali was the son of Sayyid Ahmed-mirza and grandson of the celebrated Khudaidad (*ibid.*, p. 61).

5. For the affectionate welcome given by Olugh-beg and Shah Rukh to Yunus, despite the stupidities of the latter's adherents, see *ibid.*, pp. 74, 84.

6. *Ibid.*, p. 75.

7. *Ibid.*, p. 76.

8. *Ibid.*, pp. 79–80.

9. *Ibid.*, p. 86.

10. *Ibid.*, p. 95.

11. Events occurring prior to 1468 (*Ta'rikh-i Rashidi*, pp. 91–92).

12. *Ibid.*, p. 95.

13. *Ibid.,* pp. 87–88.

14. *Ibid.,* pp. 99–107.

15. *Ibid.,* pp. 106–107.

16. The "Ha-li" of the *Ming-shih* is given as Khan Ahmed's father and predecessor. But Yunus was the father of Ahmed, who succeeded him in Uiguristan. It appears therefore that the *Ming-shih* and the *Ta'rikh-i Rashidi* identify the same person by different names.

17. *Ta'rikh-i Rashidi,* pp. 112–113, where Muhammad Haidar II cites Mirkhond. Cf. Vambéry, II, 19–20.

18. *Ta'rikh-i Rashidi,* pp. 112–114.

19. *Ibid.,* p. 95.

20. *Ibid.,* pp. 112–113.

21. *Ibid.,* p. 97.

22. *Ibid.,* pp. 112–113, 120.

23. *Ibid.,* p. 122.

24. *Ta'rikh-i Rashidi,* pp. 115–116.

25. *Ibid.,* p. 118.

26. *Ibid.,* pp. 120, 122–123.

27. *Ibid.,* pp. 123–124, 126.

28. *Ibid.,* pp. 133, 325, 327.

29. He conquered Kashgar in May–June, 1514, and died on July 9, 1533.

30. *Ta'rikh-i Rashidi,* p. 134.

31. Haidar-mirza was doubly Mongol in origin. Through his mother he was a Jenghiz-Khanite, a grandson of Khan Yunus.

32. The book was written between 1541 and 1547. Cf. Barthold, "Haidar-mîrzâ," *EI,* p. 233.

33. *Ta'rikh-i Rashidi,* p. 127.

34. Elias and Denison Ross, *History of the Moghuls of Central Asia,* pp. 13–14.

35. "He reigns today in Turfan and Jalish [Kara Shahr]" wrote Haidar-mirza in 1545 (p. 129).

36. *Mémoires concernant les Chinois,* XIV, 19.

37. *Ta'rikh-i Rashidi,* pp. 143, 450.

38. *Zabdat at-Tavarikh,* in Elias and Denison Ross, *History of the Moghuls of Central Asia,* p. 121.

39. Pp. 377, 379.

40. *Heft Iqlim,* in Quatremère, *Notes et extraits,* XIV, 474.

41. Elias and Ross, *History of the Moghuls of Central Asia,* p. 123.

42. *Ta'rikh-i Rashidi,* p. 371.

43. *Ibid.,* p. 395.

44. Courant, *L'Asie Centrale aux XVIIe et XVIIIe siècles,* p. 50.

45. See Martin Hartmann, "Ein Heiligenstaat im Islam," *Islam. Orient.*, I, 195. Generally speaking, the Jenghiz-Khanites disappeared from Kashgaria under different circumstances from those of China, yet the underlying causes may not have been dissimilar. In China, in the first half of the fourteenth century, Kublai's descendants had allowed Buddhism to acquire a somewhat excessive influence, and this aroused the hostility of the Chinese literati. In Kashgaria, the descendants of Jagatai had become so steeped in Muslim pietism as to allow themselves to be elbowed out by the "holy families" of Islam. Later, as will be seen, in the seventeenth century Tibetan lamaism had a no less emasculating effect upon the Ordos, Chahar, and even the Khalka Mongols. All these former barbarians, when converted, took to Muslim or Buddhist pietism with touching fervor, but in that conversion they may have lost some "virtue," or at least their warlike qualities. Without denying the moral beauty of Buddhism or of the Muslim mystique, we must recognize the fact that in Mongolia lamaism dulled the Mongol spirit just as Islam denationalized the last Mongols of Kashgaria and led them into a bigotry that paved the way for their abdication in favor of the astute khojas.

Chapter 15

1. Courant (*L'Asie Centrale*, p. 11) identifies Ugechi as a prince not of the Kergüd but of the Törgüd or Torghut, which were one of the four Oirat tribes. For all this, see Sanang Sechen, pp. 143–155.

2. I am of Pelliot's opinion that the Aruqtai of the Mongol historian Sanang Sechen corresponds phonetically to the A-lu-t'ai of the *Ming-shih*. It is true that the *Ming-shih* shows A-lu-t'ai playing a major part in events at a time when Sanang Sechen mentions his Aruqtai as being held prisoner. Howorth (*History of the Mongols*, I, 353) takes this as his grounds for identifying the A-lu-t'ai of the Chinese not with the Asod chief Aruqtai but with the Khorchin chief Adai. Such an identification appears phonetically untenable. There seems in any case to be some confusion in this part of the *Ming-shih*. The same discrepancy is to be found between Sanang Sechen and the *Ming-shih* in connection with the Oirat chief Mahamu. Sanang Sechen says that the Oirat chief in power during the first years of the fifteenth century was called Batula, and that he was succeeded (ca. 1415, 1418) by his son Bakhamu "surnamed Toghon." Yet according to the *Ming-shih*, the person corresponding to Batula was called Mahamu and his son's name was Toghon.

3. Pelliot, in *TP* (1914), p. 641; Moule, *Christians in China*, pp. 260, 264.

4. Sanang Sechen's Oljäi Temür and the Pen-ya-shö-li of the *Ming-shih* do seem to represent one and the same person, although the chronological data of the two sources (and these are equally confused) do not exactly correspond in detail.

5. The Khorchins, in the Jenghiz-Khanite military vocabulary, were the bodyguard, the "quiver bearers." Pelliot, in *JA* (1920), p. 171, and *TP* (1930), p. 32; Mostaert, in "Ordosica," p. 41.

6. Yet according to Sanang Sechen (trans. Schmidt, p. 151), the Oirat chief Toghon was done to death in 1439 in a mysterious and miraculous way by the shade of Jenghiz Khan, who was angered by the boldness of the usurper in robbing his descendants.

7. Sanang Sechen testifies that the captive was well-treated: "Esen entrusted the emperor to the care of the *chingsang* Alima, bidding him to tend to the captive among the Six Thousand Uchiyeds, in a country where the climate is mild in winter." As soon as he was released, the emperor expressed his gratitude to the Uchiyeds by loading them with presents.

8. *Ta'rikh-i Rashidi*, p. 91. The passage is obscure or corrupt.

9. Cf. *Ta'rikh-i Rashidi*, p. 272.

10. *Ibid.*, p. 273.

11. Barthold, "Kalmucks," *EI*, p. 743.

12. Courant, *L'Asie Centrale*, p. 6.

13. *Bara'un-ghar, je'un-ghar,* in the *Secret History*. Cf. Mostaert, "Ordosica," pp. 49–50.

14. Tümet or Tümed signifies the Ten Thousand.

15. Courant, *L'Asie Centrale*, pp. 7–9. Most of these tribes exist today: the Chahars north of the Great Wall, north of Shansi; the Khalkas in Outer Mongolia, from the Ubsa Nor to the Bor Nor; the Uriangkhans were abolished by Dayan himself; the Ordos still inhabit the "Ordos" (loop of the Yellow River); the Tümed lie northeast of the loop; and the Kharachin remain in southern Jehol, north of Hopei.

16. The "capital," that is, Altan's walled camp at Kweihwacheng, then bore the name of Baishing. Cf. Mostaert, "Ordosica," p. 37.

17. Noyandara *jinong*, Bayisangghur, Oyidarma, Nomtarni, Buyang-ghulai, Banjara, Badma Sambhava, Amurdara, and Oghlaqan (Mostaert, "Ordosica," p. 28).

18. *Ibid.*, p. 51.

19. Courant, *L'Asie Centrale*, pp. 27 *et seq.*, according to the *Tung hua lu*.

20. *Ibid.*, p. 31, according to the *Tung hua lu*.

21. It seems that in the Ordos country there were still survivals of the Nestorianism of the Öngüt period. This was true of the clan of

the Erkegüd, whose name denoted "Christian" in Jenghiz-Khanite Mongolian (*ärkägün*). Cf. Mostaert, "Ordosica."

22. Born in 1540, died in 1586. He was the great-grandfather of the historian Sanang Sechen.

23. Cf. Mostaert, "Notes sur le Khutuktai Setsen Khung Taidzi," in "Ordosica," p. 56.

24. G. Huth, *Geschichte des Buddhismus in der Mongolei*, II, 200 *et seq.*, 221, 326; G. Schulemann, *Geschichte des Dalailamas* (Heidelberg, 1911), pp. 110 *et seq.*, 121 *et seq.*; Courant, *L'Asie Centrale*, p. 13.

25. Sanang Sechen, of the princely (Jenghiz-Khanite and Dayanid) family of the Ordos of the Ushin Banner, received in 1634 from Erinchin *jinong*, head of the senior Ordos branch (Banner of Wang), the title of Erke Sechen Khongtaiji. He completed his history of the eastern Mongols in 1662. The date of his death is unknown.

26. Cf. Mailla, IX, 133–156.

27. For the old Manchu clans, see E. Haenisch, "Beiträge zur altmandschurischen Geschlechterkunde," *FFH*, pp. 171–184.

28. Mostaert, "Ordosica," pp. 26, 39.

29. For the origin of this word, see Barthold, "Kalmucks," *EI*, p. 743.

30. Courant, *L'Asie Centrale*, p. 6.

31. Cf. Pelliot, in *JA*, II (1914), 187, drawing attention to certain confusions by Courant.

32. Pelliot, "Notes sur le Turkestan," *TP* (1930), p. 30.

33. Cf. Pelliot, in *JA*, II (1914), 187, and J. Deny, "Langues mongoles," in *Les langues du monde*, p. 223. At times Courant identifies the Olöt not with the Choros but with the Khoshot.

34. Deny, "Langues mongoles," p. 231.

35. Courant, *L'Asie Centrale*, p. 40.

36. Barthold, "Mangishlak," *EI*, p. 259.

37. Courant, *L'Asie Centrale*, pp. 44–45.

38. *Ibid.*, pp. 134–136.

39. Huth, *Geschichte des Buddhismus*, II, 248, 265 (according to the *Jigs-med-nam-mka*), *Tung hua lu*, in Courant, *L'Asie Centrale*, pp. 23–25; Schulemann, *Geschichte des Dalailamas*, p. 133; W. Rockhill, "The Dalai-Lamas of Lhasa," *TP* (1910), p. 7.

40. Cf. Huth, *Geschichte des Buddhismus*, II, 269; Schulemann, *Geschichte des Dalailamas*, pp. 161–170; Rockhill, "The Dalai-Lamas of Lhasa," *TP* (1910), p. 20; Courant, *L'Asie Centrale*, p. 10. Some vivid pages are in Mailla, XI, 216.

41. Courant, *L'Asie Centrale*, p. 37.

42. The Mongol *dz* became *z* in Kalmuck, so that the pronunciation of the word *Dzungar* became Zungar, whence the spelling "Soungar"

used by Courant. Cf. Deny, "Langues mongoles," in *Langues du monde,* p. 224.

43. Cf. *Tung hua lu,* in Courant, *L'Asie Centrale,* p. 49.

44. Khongtaiji, from the Chinese *huang t'ai-tsu,* prince imperial. Cf. Pelliot, "Notes sur le Turkestan," *TP* (1930), p. 44.

45. Courant, *L'Asie Centrale,* p. 46.

46. *Ibid.,* p. 47.

47. The events that took place between Ba'atur-khongtaiji's death and Galdan's accession are somewhat obscure. There are contradictory versions in the *Tung hua lu,* the *Sheng wu ki,* Mailla, and the *Mémoires concernant les Chinois.* Reconstitution by Pozdneev, in Courant, *L'Asie Centrale,* p. 48, n. 1.

48. *Ibid.,* p. 49, according to the *Tung hua lu.*

49. Cf. M. Hartmann, *Chinesisch-Turkestan* (Halle, 1908), pp. 17, 45; Barthold, "Kashgar," *EI,* II, 835; Courant, *L'Asie Centrale,* p. 50; *Sheng wu ki,* trans. Lepage, in *Mission d'Ollone, Recherches sur les musulmans chinois,* p. 330.

50. *Tung hua lu,* in Courant, *L'Asie Centrale,* p. 54.

51. *Ibid.,* pp. 33–34, 55.

52. *Ibid.,* p. 57. Date of the battle: 29th day, 7th moon of 1690 (September 2).

53. K'ang-hsi was accompanied on this campaign by Père Gerbillon, to whom we owe the picturesque details given by Mailla, XI, 95 *et seq.*

54. *Tung hua lu,* in Courant, *L'Asie Centrale,* pp. 56–63.

55. Deny, "Langues mongoles," in *Langues du monde,* p. 221.

56. Mostaert, "Les noms des clans chez les Mongols Ordos," in "Ordosica," pp. 21 *et seq.*

57. Cf. Courant, *L'Asie Centrale,* pp. 64, 67.

58. Barthold, "Kirgiz," *EI,* p. 1085; Courant, *L'Asie Centrale,* p. 65.

59. Courant, *L'Asie Centrale,* p. 66, according to the *Tung hua lu.*

60. *Ibid.,* p. 68.

61. Cf. Huth, *Geschichte des Buddhismus,* II, 269; Schulemann, *Geschichte des Dalailamas,* pp. 161–170; Rockhill, "The Dalai-Lamas of Lhasa," *TP* (1910), pp. 20–36; Mailla, XI, 216.

62. Cf. Courant, *L'Asie Centrale,* p. 77 (according to the *Tung hua lu*); Schulemann, *Geschichte des Dalailamas,* p. 171; Rockhill, "The Dalai-Lamas of Lhasa," *TP* (1910), pp. 38–43; E. Haenisch, "Bruchstücke aus der Geschichte Chinas, I, Die Eroberung von Tibet, aus dem 'Feldzug gegen die Dzungaren,'" *TP* (1911), p. 197.

63. Courant, *L'Asie Centrale,* p. 79, according to the *Tung hua lu.*

64. Courant, *ibid.,* p. 84, thinks this would have been about 1724.

65. Seventh moon (August), 1731.

66. Fifth moon (June), summer of 1731.

67. Tenth moon (November), 1731.

68. Eighth moon, 5th day (September 23), 1732.

69. According to the *Tung hua lu*, in Courant, *L'Asie Centrale*, p. 86.

70. *Tung hua lu, ibid.*, pp. 87–89.

71. Darja's execution and Dawaji's accession, 1753, before the 5th moon (starting June 2). Courant, *L'Asie Centrale*, p. 99, according to the *Tung hua lu.*

72. *Tung hua lu, ibid.*, pp. 99–103.

73. Pan-ti's suicide, 29th day of the 8th moon of 1755 (October 4), according to the *Tung hua lu, ibid.*, pp. 105–106.

74. Information from the *Tung hua lu* about this struggle, which took the form of guerrilla and counterguerrilla warfare, accompanied by merciless repressive measures by the Chinese (*ibid.*, pp. 106–114).

75. *Tung hua lu, ibid.*, p. 137. Cf. Albert Herrmann, *Atlas of China*, Map 67.

76. Fifth and 6th moons (June–July), 1758.

77. Capture of Kashgar by the Chinese, 6th moon (August), 1759. For all these events, the best source is the *Tung hua lu*, in Courant, *L'Asie Centrale*, pp. 115–120.

78. Cf. 'Abd al-Karim Bukhari, trans. Schefer, *Histoire de l'Asie Centrale*, pp. 285, 286.

Index

Aachen, see Aix-la-Chapelle
Abagha, 517
Abakan, 558n
Abakhai, 517, 518
Abaqa, 296, 304, 305, 333, 334–335,
  366–372 passim, 398
Abares, Abaroi, see Avars
Abatai, 512
'Abbas (the Great), 485
Abbasids (Baghdad caliphate), xxx,
  141, 147, 150, 151, 158, 169, 189,
  237–238, 245, 261, 269, 282, 312,
  349, 353, 354–356, 357, 359, 398
Abbaswali, 421
'Abd al-'Aziz, 488
'Abd al-Karim, 500
'Abd-Allah (d. 1452), 460
'Abd-Allah (fl. 1750), 541
'Abd-Allah II (1557–98), 485, 487
'Abdallah ibn-Qazghan (Mirza 'Ab-
  dallah), 343, 345, 409
'Abd-Allah Tarkhan-beg, 531
'Abd al-Latif (d. 1450), 460
'Abd al-Latif (fl. 1540), 499
'Abd al-Malik I, 143
'Abd al-Malik II, 144
'Abd al-Mu'min, 485, 486
'Abd ar-Rahman, 268, 271–272
'Abd ar-Rashid, 499–500
'Abd ar-Razzaq, 390
'Abd ar-Razzaq Samarqandi, Matla'
  es-sa'dein, 459, 624n
Abeskun, 240
'Abish-khatun, 366
Ablai (Ablai-taiji), 522, 523, 525,
  526
Abraham, Mar, see Mar Abraham
Abramovka, 4
Abu 'Ali, 143–144

Abu Bakr (1231–60), 353, 354, 359
Abu Bakr (fl. 1298), 335
Abu Bakr (fl. 1403), 435, 451, 456,
  458
Abu Bakr (fl. 1460–1514), 494, 495,
  497
Abu'l Faiz, 486
Abu'l Fath Muhammad, 588n
Abu'l Ghazi, 486
Abu'l Ghazi Bahadur, Shajare-i Turk,
  214, 252, 406, 487–488
Abu'l Khair, 460, 479, 480–481, 489,
  615n
Abu'l Muzaffar Yusuf, 588n
Abu Sa'id (1317–34), 387, 389, 396
Abu Sa'id (d. 1469), 460–462, 463,
  464, 479
Achaemenids, 9, 12, 13, 15, 28,
  545n–546n
A-chu, 286–287
Acre, 305, 349, 360, 363, 364, 373
Adai, 505, 506
Adaj, 254, 392
Adana, 370
Adrianople, 157, 174, 184
Adriatic, 267
Adzai, 506
Aëneolithic period, 5
Aetius, 76
Afghanistan, 346, 409, 411, 412,
  414, 419, 429, 456, 457, 487; see
  also Ghaznavids; Ghorids; Kerts
Agni, see Kara Shahr
A-ha-ma, see Ahmed (1486/87–
  1503); Ahmed Fenaketi
Ahmed (fl. 1089), 147, 153
Ahmed (fl. 1282), see Tekuder
Ahmed (fl. ca. 1387), 431, 432, 433
Ahmed (fl. 1460–81), 470–471, 489

633

Emba, 148, 181, 394, 521
Emnedzar, 78
Engels, *see* Pokrovsk
Enos, 184
Ephesus, 452
Ephtha (Ye-ta), 67
Ephthalites (Hayathelites; Ye-tai;
  White Huns; Huna), 65, 67–72,
  80, 82, 172, 173, 193, 217, 417;
  see also Avars
"Equius," 277
Eran, 71
Erbil, *see* Arbela
Ercis (Arjish), 262
Erdeni, *see* Irdana
Erdeni Dzu, 528
Eregli, *see* Heraclea Pontica
Erginul, Ergiuul, *see* Liangchow
Eric (of Friuli), 175
Erinchin, 517
Erkegüd, 630n
Erke-khongor, 517
Erkene-qun, 193
Erke-qara, 204, 206, 581n
Erküt, *see* Erqüt
Ermak, 489, 490
Ermanarich, 73
Ermenak, 385
Ernac, 78
Erqüt (Erküt), 602n
Erzerum, 263, 430, 449, 450
Erzincan, 261, 263, 281, 382, 430,
  449, 450, 462
Esen (Esen-taiji; Ye-hsien Taichi),
  491, 492, 506, 507, 508, 520
Esen-buqa (Esen-bugha), 315, 338–
  339, 340, 386
Esen-buqa II (Esen-bugha), 460–
  461, 480, 492–493
Esen Temür (Yesen Temür; Essan-
  temur), 308
Eskisehir, 385
Essantemur, *see* Esen Temür
Essekü, 504
Esztergom, *see* Gran
Eternal Heaven, *see* Tängri
Etsin Gol, 36, 212
Etzina, *see* Karakhoto
Eukratides, 29
Euphrates, 295, 361, 365, 371, 385,
  446
Euphrosyne, 400

Eurasia, Sea of, xxi
Eutychios, 84

Fadl Allah Rashid ad-Din Tabib, *see*
  Rashid ad-Din
Fakhr ad-Din Kert, 380, 385–386
Fancheng, 287
Fang Kuo-chen, 323, 324
Faraj, 447
Fars, 151, 158, 169, 260, 261, 353,
  354, 359, 366, 382, 390, 426, 431,
  433, 456, 457, 459, 461
Fatimids, 154
Fedor (of Ryazan), 616n
Fedulovo, 16
Fei-yang-ku, 530
Fenek, 176
Fengsiang, 257
Fengyang, *see* Chungli
Fengyüanfu, *see* Changan
Feodosiya, *see* Caffa
Fergana (Ta-yüan), xxii, 8, 28, 29,
  36, 40, 43, 48, 116, 117, 142, 144,
  234, 344, 423, 426, 438, 463, 464,
  482, 486, 488, 492, 494, 496, 497,
  498, 554n
Fettich, Nandor, 67, 176
"Fighting States," *see* "Warring
  States"
Finance, *see* Crimea, Genoese and
  Venetian bankers; Currency; Tax-
  ation
Finno-Ugrian languages, xxv
Finno-Ugrians, 10–11, 14, 15, 73,
  177, 178
Firdausi, 243
Five Hordes, 56
Flor des estoires d'Orient, see Hayton
Fokuru, 8
Four Confederates, *see* Oirat
Four Garrisons, *see* Kara Shahr;
  Kashgar; Khotan; Kucha
"Four Tughri," 551n, 568n
Francesco da Podio, 319
Francis (of Alexandria), 342
Franks, 56, 60, 62, 173, 174, 175,
  178, 359–360, 364, 371, 449; *see
  also* Syria
Friuli, 174
Fu An (Chih Tao), 453, 459
Fu Chien, 59, 300

674